The Death Penalty in America

The Death Penalty in America

THIRD EDITION

Edited by
HUGO ADAM BEDAU

New York   Oxford
OXFORD UNIVERSITY PRESS

Library of Congress Cataloging in Publication Data
Main entry under title:
The death penalty in America.
   Bibliography: p.   Includes index.
   1. Capital punishment—United States.
I. Bedau, Hugo Adam.
KF9227.D42   1982   364.6′6′0973   81-9565
ISBN 0-19-502986-0   AACR2
ISBN 0-19-502987-9 (pbk.)

Printing (last digit): 9 8 7 6 5 4

Printed in the United States of America

Preface

Nearly twenty years ago, in the preface to the first edition of this book, I noted that, "Unfortunately much of the information necessary for a thorough study of capital punishment in the United States has never been published or else it is inaccessible except to the scholar with a major research library at his disposal. In preparing this volume, I have been able to examine most of the published and unpublished legal, criminological, penological, and psychological literature touching the subject. The book has been designed to allow the partisans and authorities on both sides of disputed questions to speak for themselves. The result, I hope, has been to bring under one cover a selection of the best recent writing on capital punishment, and, through the footnotes, index, and bibliography, a guide to its farthest reaches." These remarks bear repeating because they express the goal of this new edition as well as of its predecessors. However, much has changed over the past two decades that affects a project such as this, and anyone familiar with the earlier editions will find several contrasts in this one.

Production costs in book publishing have soared in recent years, so much so that no one would be willing to publish the multi-volume encyclopedia that would result if I had tried to match in all respects for the 1980s what the first edition of this book provided for the 1960s. This volume is smaller than its predecessor, contains fewer excerpts, and many of the sources reprinted here have been abbreviated rather than reproduced entire. Some issues discussed in the previous editions (e.g., case histories of the successful rehabilitation of convicted murderers, and of the struggle between the political forces for and against abolition in particular jurisdictions) are wholly omitted. Other issues that have loomed in importance only in recent years—notably, the conditions of life for the several hundred prisoners on the "death rows" of America—have also had to be neglected. On the other side of the ledger, however, this volume contains some material unlike any included in the previous editions. Bulking very large here where there was nothing before are excerpts from the major death penalty cases decided by the United States Supreme Court; yet only a fraction of what the Court has written since 1972 on this subject could be reprinted. The result has been to crowd out many scholarly essays in which research on important topics is contained. No one will be wholly comfortable with the many compromises of this sort that I have had to strike.

Second, the book has been reorganized to make more prominent right from the start the empirical investigations and research data on all the major controversial issues, rather than to polarize the readers by introducing them immediately (as the earlier editions did) to the arguments for and against the death penalty. Under this new format, the reader will be presented first with the incontrovertible data drawn largely from government sources and opinion polls; then progressively more evaluative studies of controversies over deterrence and the administration of criminal justice will be reviewed; this is followed by an examination of how the Supreme Court has viewed the constitutionality of the death penalty; and only after all this are the forthright partisans on both sides allowed to plead their case. This strategy should help the reader to evaluate for himself the claims and hypotheses advanced by advocates on each side. Insofar as these claims are testible, they can be tested on the basis of the evidence already presented in the book. Of course, it is open to any reader to study the materials in the book in any order that seems useful, including reading the book backwards, by starting with one or the other of the two final chapters, then turning to the views of the Supreme Court, and in this way confronting the evidence assembled by the social scientists, statisticians, and other investigators. But my own advice, especially for those who do not come to this book with firm convictions for or against capital punishment, is to postpone until the end any attempt to cast up the balance sheet on the merits of the abolitionist or the retentionist positions, and instead bend every effort in trying to get a firm grasp on all the relevant facts to the extent that the bulk of the book enables one to do that.

Third, as with the first edition of this book, I have not been able to fill out the design of the volume without supplying more summary and evaluation from my own hand than ideally would be needed. A remark from the preface to the first edition will serve as explanation and apology here as it did there. "The essays I have written for this volume are a result of the inherent difficulties in carrying out the conception of a book such as this. A desire for the earliest possible publication prevented commissioning articles on several subjects. Yet in a few cases, these topics were so fundamental that they could not be omitted. Where nothing about such questions was available or where the existing literature was either too out-of-date or too inaccurate, I felt I owed the reader a brief essay even if I had to write it myself. No one is more conscious than I am of the inadequacies of the results." This caveat applies to Chapter One, §2 of Chapter Two, §5 of Chapter Four, and §4 of Chapter Five. I was spared the need to write another such essay by being able to publish here for the first time the discussion of the death penalty as a deterrent to murder within prison (Chapter Four, §4) written specially for this volume by Dr. Wendy Phillips Wolfson. One possible fruit of this volume may be to stimulate other social scientists and legal scholars into undertaking research in the years ahead on the many other relevant issues about which, today, little is known and virtually nothing published.

Finally, any reader who is familiar with the previous editions of this book may be surprised that under these covers he or she will find an entirely new book. Only the title and fragments of paragraphs in the introductory chapter remain the same. So much has changed in the years between this edition and the revised edition published in 1967 that only a completely new book could meet the need. Not that everything published in earlier editions has been superceded by more recent research, or in other ways made irrelevant; far from it. The reader who wants a thorough familiarity with the death penalty in America during this century will need to have access to the earlier editions of this book, as they contain indispensable information not—or only inconveniently—available elsewhere. Rather, this book contains so much new material because so much has been published by other investigators, whose interest in the subject has grown concurrently with the rebirth of capital punishment in the mid-1970s, after what at first looked like its abolition by the Supreme Court in its 1972 ruling in *Furman* v. *Georgia*. I hasten to add that there are other books by other authors that have appeared during the past decade (notably, by Bowers, Gettinger, Mackey, and Sellin, as well as one that I co-edited and another that I wrote; see the references at the end of this book) and that provide information not excerpted or duplicated in this volume. There are also at least two more books on capital punishment in America now under preparation by others. So there is, in short, much to be read and studied if one wants to digest and master all aspects of the death penalty controversy. The present volume is no more than a partial compendium of current knowledge, interpretation, and dispute.

Since the publication of the first edition of this volume, I have written many essays and published the results of empirical research in a way that leaves no doubt about my own position on the death penalty. In what I have written here, I have tried to walk a narrow line between misrepresenting my own abolitionist convictions and allowing them to interfere with the presentation and evaluation of evidence and the view of others. Again, it seems appropriate to quote from the preface to the first edition. "Although my own opposition to the death penalty will be evident throughout, I have tried to keep my convictions from distorting my account of the views of those who disagree with me, especially in those cases where their writings have been reprinted here. If the reader, to his annoyance, finds that I have succeeded badly in maintaining the necessary editorial neutrality, I can only assure him that the idea of this book was not conceived in dispassionate scholarly curiosity, and that there are any number of passages in articles reprinted here, including some by my fellow abolitionists, with which I heartily disagree though I managed to curb my desire to single them out for comment."

A word about the references listed at the end of this volume. In the bibliography are listed all and only writings (published and unpublished) that are mentioned in the material that I have written for this book. No attempt has been made to include every source cited by every author whose writing is reprinted. I have, however, tried to prepare introductions to each chapter that not only will give a context to the selections that follow, but will also be a guide to the wealth of literature on the same or related topics. To do that I have had to cite a large fraction of the research and writing on capital punishment in America that has come to my attention and was written since 1970. So, although a few energetic and obsessive readers may want to trace out the citations in the footnotes of all the writings reprinted here, lest a single scrap of information elude them, the truth is that most of what is needed for an informed and up-to-date grasp of the whole topic will be found summarized or noted in my introductions and cited in the references.

Concord, Mass.   H. A. B.
January 1981

Acknowledgments

Many persons have assisted me during the past two years in preparing this new edition, and it is a pleasure to acknowledge their help. John C. Boger and Carol Palmer, NAACP Legal Defense and Educational Fund, Inc.; Sarah Dike, editor, *Crime & Delinquency;* Eric Prokosch, Amnesty International (International Secretariat); Henry Schwarzschild, director, Capital Punishment Project, American Civil Liberties Union; and Dr. Jan Stepan, assistant librarian at Harvard Law School, have each given me much-needed help. Many scholars have sent me reprints and preprints of their work, and it has materially assisted me in mine. The Institute of Criminology, Cambridge University, granted me a visiting fellowship during 1980, and its library and study provided an ideal setting in which to do the preliminary work for this edition. Without the cooperation of the many authors and publishers whose work is reprinted here, the book would have been impossible to produce. (Specific acknowledgments in each case appear as a footnote to the reprinted excerpt or essay.) My daughter, Lauren Bedau, gave help at an important juncture, just as she did in preparing the first edition of this book. I am grateful to our departmental secretary at Tufts, Barbara Keesey, for typing much of the manuscript. Finally, months of encouragement, hard work, and editorial skill were provided by Constance Putnam. Without her help the book would have taken much longer to finish and the result would have been distinctly inferior.

Contents

Contents   xiii

The Death Penalty in America

1

Background and Developments

In the more than three centuries since the earliest recorded lawful execution on these shores—1622, Daniel Frank, Colony of Virginia, for the crime of theft—there have been an estimated 18,000 to 20,000 persons lawfully put to death (Espy 1980:192), 7,000 of them since 1900 alone (Bowers 1974:40). Probably an equal number has been sentenced to death but spared for one reason or another (resentencing, retrial, hospitalization as insane, executive clemency, natural death). In the past century, lynching—capital punishment "in the streets"—has claimed about half as many victims as have judicially authorized executions. At a time when there are over 900 persons under death sentence in thirty states, and seven other states as well as the federal government have one or more death penalty statutes in force, only an optimist would describe capital punishment as vestigial.

Massive and familiar as its presence has been in American society, the practice of capital punishment has undergone major developments during the past century; in order to understand and evaluate its current status one needs to examine the several distinguishable strands in this history. Each strand also constitutes a theme in the struggle between those who would retain the death penalty, whether on Biblical, retributive, or utilitarian grounds, and those who would abolish it. Indeed, the history of the death penalty in the United States for the past two centuries is inseparable from the history of this struggle. Almost every aspect of reduction in the use of penal execution is a result of efforts by those who would do away with it completely; every important change in its continued administration short of abolition represents a compromise between the two contending forces. The end of public executions and of mandatory capital sentencing, introduction of the concept of degrees of murder, development of appellate review in capital cases, decline in annual executions, reduction in the variety of capital statutes,

3

experiments with complete abolition, even the search for more humane ways to inflict death as a punishment—the history of each of these shows the struggle between abolitionists and retentionists, as well as larger social forces shaping the pattern and institutions of criminal justice. Although our preoccupation in this volume is with the current situation and the immediately preceding decade, an adequate account of recent developments must include something of America's history from the earliest days.

Inventing Degrees of Murder. From time immemorial, death has been regarded as the supremely suitable punishment for murderers. The Bible bluntly tells us, "Whoso sheddeth man's blood, by man shall his blood be shed" (Genesis 9:6). But what is the crime of murder, as distinct from the fact of homicide? Sir William Blackstone, writing authoritatively for the Anglo-American tradition as of the end of the eighteenth century, declared:

> all homicide is malicious, and ... amounts to murder unless where *justified* by the command or permission of the law; *excused* on account of accident or self-preservation; or *alleviated* into manslaughter, by being either the involuntary consequence of some act not statutorily lawful, or (if voluntary) occasioned by some sudden and sufficiently violent provocation. (Blackstone 1769:IV, 201)

The effect of this definition, which became a standard interpretation of the law of murder in England as well as in this country, was to make into "murder," and thus punishable by death, all homicide not involuntary, provoked, justified, or excused.

With the intention of giving the trial jury an opportunity to exclude from the punishment of death all murderers whose crime was not of the gravest nature, William Bradford, the Attorney General in Pennsylvania, proposed in 1793 the following now-classic division of murder into "degrees":

> all murder, which shall be perpetrated by means of poison, or by lying in wait, or by any other kinds of wilful, deliberate and premeditated killing, or which shall be committed in the perpetration or attempt to perpetrate arson, rape, robbery, or burglary, shall be deemed murder of the first degree; and all other kinds of murder shall be deemed murder in the second degree; and the jury, before whom any person indicted for murder shall be tried, shall, if they find such person guilty thereof, ascertain in their verdict, whether it be murder of the first or second degree. . . . (Keedy 1949:772f.)

Bradford added the stipulation, "That no crime whatsoever hereafter committed (except murder of the first degree) shall be punished with death in the State of Pennsylvania." The legislature adopted these proposals in 1794, thus abolishing the death penalty for all except first-degree murder. With certain minor modifications, the distinction of degrees of murder with the death penalty limited to murder in the first degree was quickly adopted in Virginia (1796), somewhat later in Ohio (1815), and during the next generation in most other states; today all but a few states use it.

The idea that murder can be distinguished into crimes of different degrees has not always been hailed as an improvement over the common-law notion of murder. It is arguable whether the common-law concept of "malice" is really clarified by the equally shadowy notions of willfulness, deliberateness, and premeditation. But it was an effective compromise of the policy that murderers should be punished with death; the jury was left to decide in each case whether the accused, though guilty, had committed homicide with sufficient conscious calculation to deserve the maximum punishment.

Is the concept of degrees of murder, even so, an intelligible one? Benjamin Cardozo, first a justice on New York's highest appellate court and later a Justice of the United States Supreme Court, did not think so. A century after New York had adopted the doctrine, Cardozo protested:

> I think the distinction is much too vague to be continued in our law.... The statute is framed along the lines of a defective and unreal psychology.... The present distinction is so obscure that no jury hearing it for the first time can fairly be expected to assimilate and understand it. I am not at all sure that I understand it myself after trying to apply it for many years and after diligent study of what has been written in the books. Upon the basis of this fine distinction with ifs mystifying psychology, scores of men have gone to their deaths. (Cardozo 1931:99ff.)

One of the main objections to the doctrine of degrees of murder is that—if taken literally—it can have the opposite of the intended effect. For example, a mean, impulsive, and violently brutal person who kills suddenly and without a weapon or in the course of another felony (and thus kills in absence of willfulness, deliberation, or premeditation) may be an even greater menace to society than another person, e.g., a lonely and frightened wife who plots the death of her violent husband. Indeed, in such a case, a jury might wish to mete out light, or even no, punishment.[1] But it could do so only by flouting the letter of the law, since the wife's crime is clearly first-degree murder.

After weighing the merits of the doctrine of degrees of murder for more than a century, the English concluded that it is a clumsy tool for demarking the class of murderers meriting execution. In 1953, the Report of the Royal Commission on Capital Punishment trenchantly observed:

> There are strong reasons for believing that it must inevitably be found impracticable to define a class of murderers in which alone the infliction of the death penalty is appropriate. The crux of the matter is that any legal definition must be expressed in terms of objective characteristics of the offense, whereas the choice of the appropriate penalty must be based on a much wider range of considerations, which cannot be defined but are essentially a matter for the exercise of discretion. (1953:173)

---

1. For a discussion of this matter in connection with recent cases, though not involving capital sentencing, see Bedau 1978.

Besides the difficulties surrounding the distinction of degrees of murder, another equally disastrous tendency originated in the same 1794 Pennsylvania statute and has spread throughout American criminal law. Under the common law of England, as we have seen, all homicides not excusable or justifiable were considered to be murder and were punishable by death. In the sxiteenth century, manslaughter was made noncapital on the ground that such homicide lacked the required *mens rea*, or criminal intent, to deserve such severe punishment (Kaye 1967). According to the Pennsylvania statute, however, first-degree murder included not only willful, deliberate, and premeditated homicide, but also all homicides "in the perpetration or attempt to perpetrate any arson, rape, robbery, or burglary." This notion that a killing in the course of a felony is on a par with willful, deliberate, and premeditated killing seems a complete throwback to the primitive theory that a person is to be punished not only for the criminal harm he does intentionally (e.g., robbing a store) but for whatever harm results from his action (e.g., the death, however unintended, of the storekeeper). The most remarkable feature of the concept of felony murder is the way it has grown in several states to encompass homicides done in the course of *any* felony, thereby allowing a felon to be punished as a first-degree murderer for a homicide committed by a co-felon or even by a *police officer*, as well as for a homicide committed nearby an hour later and in another place (Fletcher 1978:317)![2] Considerable experience with this doctrine has shown both that it has thoroughly defeated any hope its originators may have had to mitigate the severity and inequity of capital punishment, and that it makes such bad law that the American Law Institute years ago advocated abandoning the entire doctrine.[3]

Reducing the Variety of Capital Statutes. The greatest single influence on American criminal law initially was, of course, the English law of the sixteenth and seventeenth centuries with which the colonists were already familiar. By the end of the fifteenth century, English law recognized eight major capital crimes: treason (including attempts and conspiracies), petty treason (killing of a husband by his wife), murder (killing a person with "malice"), larceny, robbery, burglary, rape, and arson (Plucknett 1956:424ff.). Under the Tudors and Stuarts, many more crimes entered this category; by 1688 there were almost fifty. During the reign of George II, nearly three dozen more were added, and under George III the total was increased by another sixty (Radzinowicz 1948).

In the American colonies there was no uniform criminal law, and the direct influence of England's "Bloody Code" was uneven. The range of variation in the capital laws adopted in the American jurisdictions during the seventeenth and eighteenth centuries was considerable, as the penal codes of Massachusetts, South Jersey, Pennsylvania, and North Carolina illustrate.

2. See also Morris 1956, Note 1957, and Comment 1978.
3. See the American Law Institute's Model Penal Code §210.2(1)(b), as well as ALI Proceedings, 36th Annual Meeting (1959), pp. 123–133.

The first execution in Massachusetts was in 1630, though the earliest capital statutes in the Bay Colony do not appear until 1641. This early codification lists a dozen capital crimes: idolatry, witchcraft, blasphemy, murder (homicide involving "premeditated malice, hatred or cruelty, not in a man's necessary and just defense, nor by mere casualty against his will"), manslaughter, poisoning, bestiality, sodomy, adultery, man-stealing, false witness in a capital trial, and rebellion (including attempts and conspiracies). Each of these crimes has accompanied in the statute with a text from the Old Testament as its authority. In later decades, this theocratic criminal code gave way in all but a few respects to the purely secular needs. Before 1700, rape, arson, and treason, as well as the third offense of theft of goods valued at over forty shillings, were made capital, despite the absence of any Biblical justification. By 1780, the Commonwealth of Massachusetts recognized seven capital crimes, and they bore only slight resemblance to the dozen capital laws of the Bay Colony: murder, sodomy, burglary, buggery, arson, rape, and treason (Powers 1966).

Far milder than the earliest Massachusetts laws were those adopted in South Jersey and Pennsylvania by the original Quaker colonists. The Royal charter for South Jersey in 1646 did not prescribe the death penalty for any crime, and there was no execution in this colony until 1691.[4] In Pennsylvania, William Penn's Great Act of 1682 specifically confined the death penalty to the crimes of treason and murder. These ambitious efforts to reduce the number of capital crimes were defeated early in the eighteenth century when the colonies were required to adopt, at the direction of the Crown, a harsher penal code. By the time of the War of Independence, many of the colonies had roughly comparable capital statutes. Murder, treason, piracy, arson, rape, robbery, burglary, sodomy, and from time to time counterfeiting, horse-theft, and slave rebellion were usually all punishable by death. Benefit of clergy[5] was never widely permitted, and hanging was the usual method of inflicting the death penalty.

4. This case is of unusual interest, as it involved the attempt to detect the murderer by means of "the right of bier," the superstition that if a murderer is brought near his victim's corpse, it will bleed ("blood will out") and thus identify him: *Rex et Regina* v. *Lutherland* (Sickler 1948).
5. Benefit of clergy arose from the struggle between church and state in England, and originally provided that priests, monks and other clerics were to be remanded from secular to ecclesiastical jurisdiction for trial on indictment of felony. In later centuries, this privilege was applied in secular criminal courts to more and more persons and for an ever larger number of felonies. Eventually, any person convicted of a capital crime was spared a death sentence if the crime was a first felony offense and if it was clergyable, provided only the criminal could recite the "Neck verse" (the opening lines of Psalm 51); thus benefit of clergy became the device whereby first offenders were given a lesser punishment.
   The phrase "without benefit of clergy," by which legislatures in England and in America modified traditional capital statutes during the nineteenth century, meant not that a condemned man must go to his grave without the consolations of a spiritual advisor during his last moments, but that his conviction for a capital crime was not subject to a reduction in sentence on the ground that it was a first offense. In general see Dalzell 1955.

Some states, however, preserved a severer code. As late as 1837, North Carolina required death for all the following crimes: murder; rape; statutory rape; arson; castration; burglary; highway robbery; stealing bank notes; slave-stealing; "the crime against nature" (buggery, sodomy, bestiality); duelling, if death ensues; burning a public building; assault with intent to kill; breaking out of jail if under a capital indictment; concealing a slave with intent to free him; taking a free Negro or mulatto out of the state with intent to sell him into slavery; the second offense of forgery, mayhem, inciting slaves to insurrection, or circulating seditious literature among slaves; and being an accessory to murder, robbery, burglary, arson, or mayhem. Highway robbery and bigamy, both subject to capital punishment were also clergyable.[6] This harsh code persisted so long in North Carolina partly because the state had no penitentiary and thus no suitable alternative to the death penalty.

In more recent years, there has been a striking contrast between the large variety of crimes subject to a statutory death penalty (whether mandatory or discretionary), and the small number for which persons were actually executed. Data reported in Chapter Two show that the 3,862 lawful executions between 1930 and 1980 were carried out as the punishment for only eight crimes: murder, rape, armed robbery, kidnapping, sabotage, espionage, burglary, and aggravated assault by a life-term prisoner. Contrast this with the wealth of capital statutes in force as recently as the early 1960s (see Table 1–1). Several categories of capital felonies in this list conceal some surprises; they include such crimes as using a machine gun or shotgun (whether or not it is fired) in the course of committing any crime (Virginia) and exploding dynamite near any boat with persons aboard, whether or not they are injured (Alabama). Even more revealing is the category of "Other," which includes assault with intent to rob (Kentucky), forcing a woman to marry (Arkansas), boarding a train with intent to commit a felony (Wyoming), "foeticide" (Georgia), and the most sanctimonious of them all, desecration of a grave (Georgia). It can be argued that these and some other capital statutes are surely mere legislative eccentricities, that no one would be prosecuted under them, no jury would convict, and no court would sentence to death. This might be true, but since we have no adequate history of capital punishment in any of these jurisdictions, we cannot be sure. In any case, as recently as twenty years ago, the penal codes in this nation presented to the world a remarkable variety of several dozen different offenses punishable by death.

This embarrassing (or, if one prefers, amusing) spectacle is at an end, but not owing to rational reform of the penal code by the legislatures. It is largely the product of a series of Supreme Court rulings against the death penalty

6. *Revised Statues of North Carolina*, chapter 34 (1837). Virginia laws of a slightly earlier date punished Negro slaves with death for any of seventy crimes, though for whites only five crimes were capital. See Spear 1844:227–31. For South Carolina, see McAninch 1981.

Table 1-1. Capital Crimes in the United States by Jurisdictions, 1965

Type of offense	Number of jurisdictions[a]
Capitally punishable homicide	44
Murder	40
Other homicide	20
Kidnapping	34
Treason	21
Rape	19
Carnal knowledge	15
Robbery	10
Perjury in a capital case	10
Bombing	7
Assault by a life-term prisoner	5
Burglary	4
Arson	4
Train wrecking	2
Train robbery	2
Espionage	2
Other	17
Total	44

[a] Fifty-five jurisdictions: fifty states, District of Columbia, Puerto Rico, Virgin Islands, Federal civil and military.

during the 1970s, in which the Court nullified all nonmandatory death penalties in 1972 (*Furman* v. *Georgia*), and then in 1976 all mandatory penalties as well where no victim is killed, or in which life is not endangered (see below, Chapter Six). These decisions had the salutary effect of forcing each state legislature to start from a clean slate and think through exactly which crimes (if any) it wanted punishable by death. At present, therefore, as the next chapter will show, the capital laws of the nation present a far more circumspect picture than they did until very recently.

Giving the Jury Sentencing Discretion. Traditionally, under English law, death penalties were mandatory; once the defendant was found guilty of a capital offense, the court had no alternative but a death sentence. Thus the jury could avoid a death penalty in a capital case only by acquitting the defendant or by a finding of guilt on a lesser offense (e.g., manslaughter rather than murder). Remission of the death sentence in favor of transportation to the colonies, or some lesser punishment, of course, remained a prerogative of the Crown. But as long as the death penalty was a mandatory punishment, there was always the possibility of acquitting a clearly guilty defendant in order to avoid a death sentence, especially in rare cases where the defendant was unusually pitiable or his conduct was thought to be morally excusable. This threat of "jury nullification," as it has come to be called, on the one side, and the undemocratic character of unbridled executive power to pardon, on the other, encouraged the American colonies to reject the traditional mandatory death penalty in favor of some alternative. What eventually developed was the characteristically American practice that divided murder into degrees and gave the court some sentencing discretion in capital cases.

The history of the criminal law in Massachusetts, for example, shows that from the earliest days, "any capital offender had a very good chance of escaping the hangman's noose, unless he were found guilty of murder, witchcraft or piracy—and even in such cases an execution was not inevitable" (Powers 1966:275). The first of the Bay Colony's capital statutes to authorize an alternative penalty to the death sentence was for the crime of rape. Under a law enacted in 1642, rape was punishable by death or by some "other grievous punishment," at the discretion of the court. A severe whipping and the humiliation of standing on the gallows with a rope around one's neck quickly became the most common punishment for the convicted rapist (unless he was a Negro or an Indian, in which case his punishment was likely to be sale into slavery). This heritage of sentencing discretion did not carry over into the post–Revolutionary period, however. Already by 1780 Massachusetts's seven capital felonies (including rape) were subject to a mandatory death penalty, and it was not until 1951 that the mandatory death penalty for murder was repealed in favor of the discretionary death penalty (Powers 1966).

Elsewhere in the nation, discretionary capital laws slowly replaced mandatory death penalties, and while the history of this development has yet to be written, its broad outline is clear.[7] In Maryland, where the jury already had the power to fix degrees of murder, the death penalty became optional in 1809 for treason, rape, and arson, but not for homicide. Tennessee (1838) and Alabama (1841) were the first to authorize a discretionary death sentence for murder, and Louisiana (1846) appears to have been the first jurisdiction to make all its capital crimes optionally punishable by life imprisonment. Between 1860 and 1900, twenty states and the federal government followed suit; by 1926, the practice had been adopted in thirty-three jurisdictions. Between 1949 and 1963, seven more—North Carolina, Connecticut, Massachusetts, Hawaii, Vermont, District of Columbia, and New York, in that order—introduced this procedure for the punishment of murder.[8]

It is perhaps not surprising that many of those states that were the first to accept the doctrine of degrees of murder were among the last to add the

---

7. A fuller record is available in Bowers 1974:8, Table 1–2.
8. For an instructive debate focussed on the mandatory death penalty, see *Congressional Record*, 14 March, 1962, pp. 3771–801.

doctrine of jury discretion for this crime. Ohio did not accept it until 1898, for example, and New Jersey not until 1916, nor Pennslyvania until 1925.

Abolitionists used to maintain that if the death penalty were abolished, convictions would increase (Shipley 1909). In a parallel fashion, it was argued that the shift from mandatory to discretionary death penalties would discourage jury nullification in capital cases (Mackey 1974a). Whether this was ever so is not certain; most of the existing studies have not sufficiently controlled all the variables. The only adequate research covers fairly recent years, and was confined to studying three of the last jurisdictions to make the shift in question (Massachusetts, New York, and District of Columbia); no evidence was found of any significant effect of this sort (Wolfgang and Riedel 1979). This research did show, however, that the mandatory death penalty was a more powerful weapon than the discretionary death penalty in the pretrial process of "plea bargaining," because the certainty of a death sentence upon conviction was a more effective inducement to the defendant to avoid trial and plead guilty to a lesser crime (usually second-degree murder). But the extensive plea bargaining characteristic of our criminal justice system at present was wholly unknown in 1850 or 1900, and the expectation of enhancing (or diminishing) the effectiveness of capital punishment for this prosecutorial purpose is not likely to have played any role in the shift from mandatory to discretionary death penalties in most jurisdictions.

No doubt the development of jury sentencing-discretion in capital cases was seen in part in some jurisdictions as an effective compromise with forces that might otherwise continue to press for complete abolition (as seems to have been true in New Jersey; see Bedau 1964b:28ff.), or as a feature of the reintroduction of the death penalty after its abolition (as in Oregon; see Bedau 1965:21ff.). In other jurisdictions, however, a very different motivation prevailed. In the postbellum South, research has shown that where the number of capital statutes increased dramatically, as they did in Virginia, they tended to be enacted in a discretionary rather than a mandatory form. With black Americans newly freed from slavery, but disqualified from testifying against whites, excluded by law from serving on juries, and lacking in trained counsel of their own race, the dominant white class could comfortably "place their trust in the judgment of white judges and white juries" to administer these discretionary death penalty statutes in the desired manner (Note 1972:106).[9]

Not only in the Old South did the exercise of discretion in capital cases prove an irresistible door through which arbitrary and discriminatory results could enter (see Chapter Five). By the 1960s this abuse was so systematic and

9. See also Partington 1965. Since Knowlton's article (1953), which pioneered research on jury discretion in capital cases, surprisingly little has been published on the history and operation of such statutes.

widespread throughout the nation that such statutes became vulnerable to constitutional objection, as the Supreme Court acknowledged in *Furman*. The ruling in this case brought to an end the familiar "unguided discretion" exercised by trail courts in capital sentencing. From the vantage point of history, one might have thought that the legislative response to the mandate of *Furman* would be anything but an attempt to turn back the clock and reintroduce mandatory death penalties. Not so. Within two years after *Furman*, legislatures in fourteen states (most of them outside the Deep South, viz., California, Idaho, Indiana, Kentucky, Montana, New Hampshire, Nevada, New Mexico, New York, Oklahoma, Rhode Island, and Wyoming, as well as Louisiana and Mississippi) enacted new mandatory death penalties for various forms of criminal homicide, while in two states (Delaware and North Carolina) the state supreme courts simply nullified the jury-discretion feature of the capital statutes then in force, thereby returning them to the older mandatory form.[10] For reasons to be examined in Chapter Six, these statutes were judged unconstitutional in *Woodson* v. *North Carolina* (1976) and related cases. So the historic trend against mandatory death penalties, which seemed so firm until the backsliding during 1972–76, was restored, and future death penalties will have to be enacted and enforced in a manner that avoids both "unguided discretion" and no discretion whatever.

Ending Public Executions. Well into the nineteenth century, in both England and America, executions were conducted in public and were usually arranged so hundreds, even thousands, could watch the ritual that began with the arrival of the condemned person in the custody of the sheriff and ended with the corpse being carted off to ignominious burial in some potter's field. Many such execution scenes were described by eye-witnesses during the eighteenth and nineteenth centuries.[11] William Thackeray witnessed a hanging in London in 1840, and his reaction ("I feel myself ashamed and degraded at the brutal curiosity which took me to that brutal sight" [Thackeray 1840:156]) must have been shared by most intelligent and socially concerned contemporaries. The chief argument for public executions (as well as for cruel methods of inflicting the death penalty) has been that it is the best way to maximize the deterrent effect.[12] However, if Thackeray's reaction is to be trusted, the truth lies in precisely the opposite direction; the spectacle is brutalizing to all who witness it (see Chapter Five), whether or not they also feel shame as Thackeray did. Moreover, terror and hatred of the criminal about to meet his doom may give way either to pity or even grudging respect if he takes his

10. For thorough discussion of these statutes, see Browning 1974:652ff., and Note 1974.
11. See Cooper 1974 and Lofland 1977. There is no study of the history of public executions in the United States comparable to Cooper's fine monograph.
12. This was a factor in John Stuart Mill's opposition to private executions and the abolition of the death penalty; see Mill 1868. See also Hardman 1977.

punishment "like a man." As the New York Legislative Commission on Capital Punishment observed a century ago,

> the very boldness with which he [the condemned man] marched from the cell to the scaffold is extolled as an act of heroism and as evidence of courage and valor. "He was game to the last" has been many a ruffian's eulogy. (1888:93)

Public executions in this country have been under attack at least since 1787, when Dr. Benjamin Rush delivered an address in Benjamin Franklin's house on "The Effects of Public Punishments Upon Criminals and Upon Society." In response to his arguments and the support they aroused, the Walnut Street Jail was built in Philadelphia three years later. From this primitive beginning sprang the whole penitentiary system, and a realistic alternative to hangings at last was available. But nothing was done about public executions until New York, in 1830, imposed some control on the county sheriffs, requiring them (at their discretion!) to hold executions away from public view. In 1835 New York increased the stringency of this law and prohibited executions in public. Within the next few years, several other states followed suit, and this reform, though a mere sop to abolitionists, was under way.

The reform was by no means universal or throughgoing, however. Pennsylvania and New Jersey, for instance, stipulated only that executions should take place within the walls or buildings of the county jail. Since in most cases the gallows was erected out of doors in the jail yard, it was usually a simple matter for any interested spectator to find a convenient vantage point from which to watch the entire proceeding. Not until nearly the end of the last century were such abuses prohibited. Even so, public executions continued in some states until fairly recently. The last such events in the United States were the hanging of a black man, Rainey Bethea, for rape in Owensboro, Kentucky, on 14 August 1936, and of a white man, Roscoe Jackson, in Galena, Missouri, on 21 May 1937. A news-service photograph taken moments after the "drop" in Owensboro shows some 20,000 people packed around the gallows, with the dead man dangling at the end of his rope. Several spectators are atop a nearby utility pole, and others are leaning out of windows a block away. The platform is jammed with official witnesses.[13] Nine months later, in Galena, some 500 persons, mostly men, watched Jackson meet his end. Those who could afford the price of admission were allowed to enter the forty-foot-square stockade that surrounded the gallows in front of the country court house; for the throng outside, the view was hampered by the twenty-foot-high walls. Many of those present took away a souvenir piece of the rope used in the hanging.[14]

13. The photograph is reproduced in Teeters 1960:117.
14. See *Springfield* (Mo.) *Daily Leader and Press*, 21 May 1937, p. 1; also Espy 1980:192.

Even today, most states allow considerable discretion to the warden in charge of an execution as to how many persons shall qualify as official guests and witnesses. Wardens and executioners have often told how the announcement (required by law) of an execution brings a flood of requests for permission to attend. Such requests, they say, are never granted. But if the condemned man is enough of a celebrity, the mass news media will send their representatives, and these, plus the officials directly and indirectly involved, often swell the total to several dozen, as in the execution of Julius and Ethel Rosenberg at Sing Sing in 1953 and of Caryl Chessman at San Quentin in 1960.

The relative privacy of executions nowadays (fewer than three dozen witnessed Florida's 1979 execution; and photographs of the condemned man dying are almost invariably strictly prohibited) means that the average American literally does not know what is being done when the government, in his name and presumably on his behalf, executes a criminal. In recent years, it has been suggested that executions should be televised for public viewing. Not until 1977, however, did the suggestion take a serious turn. In that year, a Dallas newsman went to court, arguing that the city's public television station had a right to cover an impending electrocution as long as the prison regulations allowed the print media to do so. The Circuit Court of Appeals, reversing a lower federal court, ruled that neither the "free press" clause (First Amendment) nor the "equal protection" clause (Fourteenth Amendment) required Texas to admit television cameras to an execution.[15] The controversy was dropped as moot, in part because the execution itself was indefinitely postponed.

Whether public executions in the 1980s, via television or in other ways, would play into the hands of abolitionists or of retentionists is arguable. More than one abolitionist has wistfully recalled the days when all executions were holiday occasions, confident that if this were to happen today, the whole practice of killing criminals would be rapidly outlawed.[16] The adage "Out of sight, out of mind" goes some distance toward explaining why the opponents of the death penalty today are rarely as evangelical as were the reformers of a century ago.

Humanizing the Methods of Execution. The variety of ways in which men have put one another to death under the law is appalling. History records such exotic practices as flaying and impaling, boiling in oil, crucifixion, pulling asunder, breaking on the wheel, burying alive, and sawing in half. Fortunately, these are virtually unknown in the Anglo-American tradition. Yet as late as the eighteenth century in both England and America criminals were occasionally pressed to death, drawn and quartered, and burned at the stake.[17]

15. *Garrett* v. *Estelle*, 556 F.2d 1274 (1977).
16. See Duffy 1962:21.
17. On burning at the stake in New York in colonial times, see Riddell 1929.

It is curious that any of these barbarous and inhumane methods of execution survived so long, for the English Bill of Rights (1689) proscribed "cruel and unusual punishments." This phrase worked its way through several of the early American state constitutions and into the federal Bill of Rights (Eighth Amendment) of 1789. Prior to the 1970s, Supreme Court opinions interpreting this clause were few; but they agreed in declaring that the intent of the framers of the Constitution was to rule out the painful and torturous aggravations attendant on execution (see Granucci 1969). These practices had all but disappeared by 1789, never having taken firm root here; but their implied exclusion by Jefferson, Madison, and the other authors of the Bill of Rights was a service to the interests of a free and humane people. Except when executing spies, traitors, and deserters, who could be shot under federal law, the sole acceptable mode of execution in the United States for a century after the adoption of the Eighth Amendment was hanging.[18]

In the late 1880s, in order to challenge the growing success of the Westinghouse Company, then pressing for nationwide electrification with alternating current, the advocates of the Edison Company's direct current staged public demonstrations to show how dangerous their competitor's product really was: If it could kill animals—and awed spectators saw that, indeed, it could—it could kill human beings as well.[19] In no time at all, this somber warning was turned completely around. In 1888, the New York legislature approved the dismantling of its gallows and the construction of an "electric chair," on the theory that in all respects, scientific and humane, executing a condemned man by electrocution was superior to executing him by hanging (see N.Y. Report 1888:52–92). On 6 August 1890, after his lawyer had unsuccessfully argued the unconstitutionality of this "cruel and unusual" method of execution, William Kemmler became the first criminal to be put to death by electricity. Although eyewitness reports allege that the execution was little short of torture for Kemmler (the apparatus was makeshift and the executioner clumsy), the fad had started. Authorities on electricity, such as Thomas Edison and Nikola Tesla, continued to debate whether electrocution was so horrible that it should never have been invented. The late Robert G. Elliott, electrocutioner of 387 men and women, assured the public that the condemned person loses consciousness immediately with the first jolt of current (Elliott 1940). The matter continued to generate scientific interest until fairly recently.[20] Despite the record of bungled executions,[21] the unavoidable

18. The use of the firing squad in Utah, upheld by the Supreme Court in 1878 and now the sole lawful method of execution there, is owing to the Mormon interpretation of the Biblical doctrine of "blood atonement," and not to any scientific or humane claims in favor of death by shooting. See, for a full discussion, M. Gardner 1979a and 1979b.
19. For a full and fascinating discussion, see T. Hughes 1965.
20. See Bernstein 1975 and sources cited therein.
21. Several were cited by the defense in the remarkable case of *Louisiana ex rel. Francis* v. *Resweber*, 329 U.S. 459 (1947); some are mentioned in Prettyman 1961:105ff.

absence of first-hand testimony, the disfiguring effects, and the odor of burning flesh that accompany every electrocution, the electric chair remains the only lawful mode of electrocution in most American jurisdictions.[22]

Not satisfied with shooting, hanging, or electrocution, the Nevada legislature enacted a "Humane Death Bill" in 1921, to provide that a condemned person should be executed in his cell, while asleep and without any warning, with a dose of lethal gas. Governor Emmet Boyle, an avowed opponent of capital punishment, signed the bill, confident that it would be declared unconstitutional as a "cruel and unusual punishment." Nothing much was done one way or the other until a convicted tong-war murderer, Gee Jon, was sentenced to death. When the Nevada Supreme Court upheld the constitutionality of lethal gas, a chamber was hurriedly constructed after practical obstacles were discovered in the original plan for holding the execution in the prisoner's cell. On 8 February 1924, Jon became the first person to be legally executed with a lethal dose of cyanide gas. Within the next two years, Arizona, Colorado, Wyoming, North Carolina, and California also installed the gas chamber.[23]

It is doubtful whether any serious scientific inquiry has ever substantiated the superiority claimed on behalf of electrocution or gassing over hanging. According to a 1953 Gallup Poll, the American public strongly favored electrocution over lethal gas, while hanging and shooting had very few supporters (12 percent registered no opinion, or recommended "drugs" or "any of them, but let the prisoner choose"). Also during 1953, though few Americans knew it, the British Royal Commission on Capital Punishment stated:

> we cannot recommend that either electrocution or the gas chamber should replace hanging as the method of judicial execution in this country. In the attributes we have called "humanity" [rapidity with which unconsciousness is induced] and "certainty" [simplicity of the apparatus] the advantage lies, on balance, with hanging; and though in one aspect of what we have called "decency" [decorum with which executions can be conducted, and absence of mutilation to the body of the condemned man] the other methods are preferable, we cannot regard this as enough to turn the scale. (1953:256)

In this country, voices have occasionally been heard, protesting the risks, indignities, and mutilations incidental to hangings, shootings, electrocutions,

22. For a review of the constitutional challenges to hanging, electrocution, and lethal gas, see Berkson 1975:21–31. No doubt the most bizarre recent proposal is that the automobile airbag safety device should be adopted as a "humane alternative" to the electric chair, and gas chamber. "By inflating an airbag directly under a subject's head, . . . 'a force of 12,000 pounds can be instantly brought to bear which will snap the neck of the person to be executed far more effectively than the hangman's noose and with an action so instantaneous as to preclude any pain.'" *Los Angles Times*, 30 March 1978, p. 5. The device has been patented by a former Ford Motor Company engineer; it has not, to my knowledge, been proposed for adoption to any legislature.
23. For further discussion, see Berkson 1975:29ff.

and gassings. "Contemporary methods of execution," it has been said, "are unnecessarily cruel"; they are "archaic, inefficient, degrading for everyone involved." Novelties, such as allowing the condemned man to choose the method of his execution, or even to administer it to himself, or to become the subject of medical experiments until he dies of a fatal one, have even been suggested.[24] But during the 1950s, when executions were still fairly frequent (about three every two weeks), these objections and suggestions alike went unheeded. Retentionists usually had no curiosity about the regrettable details of actual executions, and abolitionists, being totally out of sympathy with the whole business, had no interest in finding a more humane way to do what they disapproved of on principle.

The resumption of executions in 1977, inaugurated with blazing rifles as Gary Gilmore was killed by a Utah firing squad, prompted interest in a new mode of inflicting the death penalty: lethal injection. To retentionists it may appear to be an expedient reform, and even some abolitionists might favor it if executions *must* be held. In May 1977, Oklahoma became the first American jurisdiction to authorize carrying out the death sentence by "continuous, intravenous administration of a lethal quantity of an ultrashort-acting barbiturate in combination with a chemical paralytic agent." The legislature's reasoning was partly economic; the old electric chair, last used in 1966, would require costly repairs, and a gas chamber would involve a capital investment of over $200,000. Lethal injection, on the other hand, was estimated to run no more than $10 or $15 "per event" (Malone 1979). The legislatures of Texas, Idaho, and New Mexico were quick to enact similar legislation. A side issue that may favor this mode of execution arises from the condemned man's alleged "right" to donate his bodily organs for medical transplants. Where Gary Gilmore hoped to give the corneas of his eyes, a person executed by lethal injection might be able to donate a good deal more, as some death row convicts have insisted they want to do.[25]

In Florida, however, a lethal-injection bill was defeated in 1979, largely because professional anesthesiologists and other physicians were strongly opposed to it on scientific and humane grounds (as were their predecessors in New York in the 1880s when such a method was proposed during the electrocution controversy). Unless great skill is used, they argued, the barbiturate could wear off; the dying prisoner would wake up only to realize that he was slowly suffocating. At the least, electrocution, hanging, and the gas chamber avoid this unsettling possibility. Whether opposition of the medical profession could prove decisive either to the actual employment of this method (it still awaits its first use) or adoption by other state legislatures, is unclear. At its annual meeting in 1980, the American Medical Association

24. See, respectively, Farrer 1958:567, R. King 1961:669, and Kevorkian 1959.
25. For discussion, see Bedau & Zeik 1979.

passed a resolution to urge physicians not to participate in execution by lethal injection. Even if physicians comply with this resolution, it may prove to be of little significance; none of the new statutes requires that the toxic substance be injected by a licensed physician. Some doctors would condemn outright the use of lethal injection to cause death, on the ground that to administer death even in conformity with a valid statute and a death warrant is to violate the Hippocratic Oath and international medical principles, and to engage in "a corruption and exploitation of the healing profession's role in society." Accordingly, they have urged that the medical profession "should formally condemn all forms of medical participation in this method of capital punishment" (Curran & Casscells 1980). Humane and effective or not, relative to other lawful methods of execution, lethal injection is undeniably attractive to a society that wants to keep the death penalty but does not want its executions to repel those who must authorize, administer, and witness them, lest it thereby turn those officials (as it has so often their predecessors) into fervent abolitionists.

Expanding the Role of Appellate Courts. Early Massachusetts law provided that if a defendant had been found guilty of a capital crime by no more than a bare majority of the trial court, he had a right of appeal for review of his trail to the General Court (Powers 1966:58). This is a striking illustration of the principle, recognized in several of the Supreme Court's anti-death penalty decisions of the 1970s, that "death is different." Yet a closer inspection of the historical record shows that this principle has not always been acknowledged. Far more typically the appellate courts, state or federal, have given no more scrupulous review to capital cases under their jurisdiction than they have to other criminal cases. The modern successor to the early Massachusetts provision for special review in capital cases are those statutes that authorize "automatic" appeal to the state supreme court of every capital conviction. Such statutes effectively remove all obstacles to review, including the problem faced by the indigent defendant whose court-appointed trial attorney waves him goodbye soon after the sentencing. "Automatic" appeal seems like an obvious and proper protection for the capital defendants if, indeed, "death is different." Yet no jurisdiction had enacted such a statute until California did in 1935,[26] and even now not all states have followed this lead. Gilmore was executed in Utah in 1977 without review in the Utah supreme court of his trial, conviction, or sentence. The truth is that one of the more painful phases of the history of the death penalty in this country is the tardy development of appellate review in capital cases (quite apart from the unpro-

26. Calif. Penal Code §1239(b). For a study of the operation of this California statute between 1942 and 1956, see Note 1958:103-7. No history has been written concerning the adoption and function of "automatic" appeal statutes.

ductive character of that review in most of the cases where it has been granted), something easily forgotten under the influence of the past decade, when the federal judiciary has regularly proved to be the one branch of government most hesitant to see the death penalties imposed and executed.

The character of the problem can be sketched by noting three of the several obstacles to appellate review that the death row defendant traditionally faces. First, the appellate courts have always deferred to trial courts on *questions of fact*; higher courts have refused (except in extreme instances) to second-guess trail courts on their evaluations of testimony, circumstantial evidence, and other factual considerations on which the judgment to convict the defendant is professedly based. What appellate courts will do under certain circumstances is second-guess trial judges on questions of applicable law. From the standpoint of the administration of justice, this distinction in grounds for review is a reasonable self-restraint by the higher courts, lest otherwise every conviction leading to a severe punishment be tried a second time in the higher court. Second, the judiciary has always deferred to the legislature on *the kind of punishments* that may be attached to a given type of offense. Not even the death penalty for a relatively trivial offense has been an exception to this deference. This, too, is a reasonable self-restraint, given the division of powers among the branches of government. However, the two factors together meant that a death row defendant had almost no way to get an appellate court to review the justice of his sentence as such; instead, he could attack only the fairness of the procedures that got him his conviction in the first place. Until very recently (see Chapter Six), a successful attack in appellate court by a death row defendant merely meant getting a new trial, not a reduced sentence as such. Finally, the federal-state relationship created by our constitution has been understood by the *federal* judiciary to require it to step very cautiously before intervening in *state*-court criminal matters. This has meant both that a state death row defendant must first "exhaust" his state remedies before he could turn to the federal courts for review of his rights under the federal constitution, and that the federal courts would exercise very limited jurisdiction even then with respect to the scope of matters they would review.[27]

The combined impact of these and other restrictions on the availability of appellate review of death sentences can be traced through the actual record of appeals filed in state and federal courts by persons sentenced to death and

27. The states themselves, of course, have constitutional protections (in some cases, antedating those of the federal constitution) that might be thought to serve as a basis for appellate litigation to nullify certain capital sentences and statutes. In only two states, however, California and Massachusetts, has the state supreme court interpreted the state constitutional provisions as inconsistent with the death penalty. See *People* v. *Anderson*, 100 Cal. Rptr. 152 (1972), *Commonwealth* v. *O'Neal*, 369 Mass. 242 (1975), and *District Attorney for Suffolk District* v. *James Watson et al.*, 411 N.E.2d 1274 (1980).

executed.[28] Scholars have yet to give us research for more than a few capital jurisdictions on this matter,[29] but what we do know presents a consistently grim picture. Consider by way of illustration the stories for New Jersey and Oregon since the beginning of this century.

Between 1907 and 1948, in New Jersey about three fourths of all death sentences were appealed on some ground or other to some court or other. Not surprisingly, most of these appeals came in the more recent years. During the first half of this period (1907–25), only slightly more than half of the cases show any appeal. No one sought relief in the federal courts until 1936; until 1946, only 2 out of nearly 200 death row prisoners had sought relief in both state and federal courts. And not until after 1946 did every death row convict seek relief in the state courts. It was 1964 before New Jersey law authorized a writ of error to be issued, with a stay of execution, to any death row convict upon his appeal. Since the initiative in seeking the writ still lay with the convict, the review of his conviction by the New Jersey supreme court was no means "automatic" (Bedau 1964b:35–40).

In Oregon, appeal of death penalty cases was not even possible in some cases, because no trial record had been prepared to serve as the basis of the appeal (a version of this problem, by the way, was a crucial issue in controversy in the Chessman case in California during the 1950s, and it tainted the execution of Gilmore in Utah in 1977).[30] By contrast, in 1955 "automatic" appeal of all death sentence convictions was authorized by statute, as was provision for appellate counsel for the indigent death row defendant. Appeal initiatives by defendants had been taken in the Oregon courts anyway in most capital cases up to that point—in all but 8 out of 40 between 1903 and 1914, and in all but 6 out of 31 between 1920 and 1944 (there was no death penalty in Oregon between 1914 and 1920). Relief was also sought in federal courts as early as 1913; this case was exceptional, however, and no relief was

28. One of the many valuable aspects of the Teeters-Zibulka record of executions (reprinted and extended in Bowers 1974:200–401) is that, through its records of appeals taken by the executed, it allows just such a review. However, the data are incomplete, they do not indicate any details about the type of result of review, and they provide no information about the persons under death sentences who did obtain appellate review and who were never executed.

29. See especially Partington 1965 and Note 1972 (both on Virginia) and Note 1958 (on California).

30. In the Chessman case, the problem arose because the court reporter died before he could transcribe his notes, and no one else could with certainty decipher them correctly. See Machlin & Woodfield 1961. In the Gilmore case, the trial record had not been fully transcribed, and the Utah supreme court (as well as the United States Supreme Court) refused to delay execution on this ground in the absence of any demand by Gilmore to do so. See Bessie Gilmore, Application for Stay of Execution, filed 2 December 1976 with the U.S. Supreme Court. The Oregon case cited in the text occurred in 1909; see Bedau 1965:23.

granted. As in New Jersey, federal appeals were infrequent until the 1940s. And as late as 1953, an execution took place without any stay, reprieve, or appeal in any court (Bedau 1965:23–27).

In that same year, Supreme Court Justice Robert H. Jackson remarked that "[when] the penalty is death . . . judges are tempted to strain the evidence and even, in close cases, the law to give a doubtfully condemned man another chance" (*Stein* v. *New York*, 1953).[31] Yet, as we have seen, for most of our history in most of our appellate courts this claim rings hollow. Without doubt, the most important part of the recent story of capital punishment in the United States concerns the revolution in the willingness of the federal courts (and of some state courts, notably in California and Massachusetts) to review on constitutional grounds the death sentence itself. The courts have indeed concluded that "death is different," but it is a conclusion they have reached only quite recently.

Experimenting with Total Abolition. As early as the 1830s, legislatures in several states (notably Maine, Massachusetts, Ohio, New Jersey, New York, and Pennsylvania) were besieged each year with petitions from their constituents on behalf of total abolition. Special legislative committees were formed to receive these messages, hold hearings, and submit recommendations. Anti-gallows societies came into being in every state along the eastern seaboard, and in 1845 an American Society for the Abolition of Capital Punishment was organized. With the forces arrayed against slavery and saloons, the anti-gallows societies were among the most prominent groups struggling for social reform in America.[32]

The high-water mark was reached in 1846, when the Territory of Michigan voted to abolish hanging and to replace it with life imprisonment for all crimes except treason. This law took effect on 1 March 1847, and Michigan thus became the first English-speaking jurisdiction in the world to abolish the death penalty. In 1852, Rhode Island abolished the gallows for all crimes, including treason; the next year Wisconsin did likewise, and Iowa and Maine followed in the 1870s.

Not until the Progressive Era and the First World War did the abolition movement score any further major successes. Then, within a decade, nine states—Kansas (1907), Minnesota (1911), Washington (1913), Oregon (1914), South Dakota (1915), North Dakota (1915), Tennessee (1915), Arizona (1916), and Missouri (1917)—abolished the death penalty completely or with reservations confined to rare and exceptional crimes. Most of these states, how-

---

31. See in general Prettyman 1961.
32. For colonial as well as modern developments toward abolition, see the useful sketch provided in Mackey 1976:xi–liii.

ever, promptly restored it; only two (Minnesota and North Dakota) resisted the trend as the nation struggled in the wake of an unprecedented "crime wave" during the Roaring Twenties and the Great Depression.

The first signs of renewed vigor in the abolition movement did not appear until a generation later, in the aftermath of the 1953 report in England of the Royal Commission on Capital Punishment. As England (and later Canada) debated whether to abolish or merely narrow the scope of the death penalty, the Delaware legislature voted in 1958 to end hanging. In short order, abolition groups were again active and moderately well organized in nearly two dozen death penalty states in this country. Public hearings on abolition bills were again echoing in legislative chambers, reminiscent of the 1840s and 1910s. Except for Delaware, however, abolitionists were able to obtain no more than a few legislative committee reports in their favor. Then in November 1964, all capital penalties in Oregon were voted out in a public referendum by a large majority, and the log-jam was broken. Within six months, New York and three other states followed suit. After the victory four years later in New Mexico, the legislative campaign to abolish the death penalty ground to a halt. By 1969, other forces were at work—the Vietnam war, a rapidly increasing rate of violent crime, urban unrest, loss of confidence in "liberal" reforms—that discouraged further legislative repeal of the death penalty. Meanwhile, and largely unnoticed, the struggle had shifted from the state legislatures into the federal appellate courts, a transformation that culminated in the sudden end of virtually all death penalties in the nation as of July 1972, when the Supreme Court announced its long-awaited decision in *Furman* v. *Georgia*. As events were quickly to prove, the nation's legislatures were not ready for abolition, especially when it was thrust on them from Washington. By the first anniversary of *Furman*, twenty states had already re-enacted the death penalty, and by the second, more than 100 persons were under sentence of death in seventeen states.

The checkered pattern of state experimentation with total abolition between 1846 and 1970 is summarized in Table 1–2.

As this table shows, over the past century and a half no fewer than twenty-two states have experimented with abolition, and these experiments have gone on in every region of the nation except the South. One naturally wonders what has been the experience in those few jurisdictions (Michigan, Wisconsin, Minnesota, Rhode Island, North Dakota) that have long relied on imprisonment rather than death as the penalty for even the gravest crimes. One is also more than curious to know what accounts for the reintroduction of the death penalty in several states (Washington, Iowa, Delaware, Missouri, Arizona, Colorado) no more than a few years after it had been abolished. Surprising though it may be, and except for one or two instances, the full story has never been told. (However ardent abolitionists may be, they have conspicuously failed to recruit many state and local historians into their

Table 1-2. Partial Abolition, Abolition, Year of Restoration, and Year of Re-abolition of Death Penalty, by State, 1846–1970

	Year of partial abolition	Year of complete abolition	Year of restoration	Year of reabolition
New Mexico	1969[a]	—	—	—
New York	1965[b]	—	—	—
Vermont	1965[c]	—	—	—
West Virginia	—	1965	—	—
Iowa	—	1872	1878	1965
Oregon	—	1914	1920	1964
Michigan	1847[d]	1963	—	—
Delaware	—	1958	1961	—
Alaska	—	1957	—	—
Hawaii	—	1957	—	—
South Dakota	—	1915	1939	—
Kansas	—	1907	1935	—
Missouri	—	1917	1919	—
Tennessee	1915[e]	—	1919	—
Washington	—	1913	1919	—
Arizona	1916[f]	—	1918	—
North Dakota	1915[g]	—	—	—
Minnesota	—	1911	—	—
Colorado	—	1897	1901	—
Maine	—	1876	1883	1887
Wisconsin	—	1853	—	—
Rhode Island	1852[h]	—	—	—

[a] Death penalty retained for the crime of killing a police officer or prison or jail guard while in the performance of his duties, and in cases where the jury recommends the death penalty and the defendant commits a second capital felony after time for due deliberation following commission of 1st capital felony.

[b] Death penalty retained for persons found guilty of killing a peace officer who is acting in line of duty, and for prisoners under a life sentence who murder a guard or inmate while in confinement or while escaping from confinement.

[c] Death penalty retained for persons convicted of 1st-degree murder who commit a second "unrelated" murder, and for the 1st-degree murder of any law enforcement officer or prison employee who is in the performance of the duties of his office.

[d] Death penalty retained for treason. Partial abolition was voted in 1846, but was not put into effect until 1847.

[e] Death penalty retained for rape.

[f] Death penalty retained for treason.

[g] Death penalty retained for treason, and for 1st-degree murder committed by a prisoner who is serving a life sentence for 1st-degree murder.

[h] Death penalty retained for persons convicted of committing murder while serving a life sentence for any offense.

Source: National Prisoner Statistics, Capital Punishment 1930–1970, p. 50.

ranks.) The lack of any punishment for treason, and anxiety over the likelihood of a wave of violent crime (Oregon, 1920; see Dann 1952); anger at the
murder of a white woman by a black man and another unsolved murder of
a white woman (Delaware, 1961; see Cobin 1964 and Samuelson 1969); an
hysterical reaction to a shoot-out between armed robbers and police, in
which two law officers were killed (Missouri, 1919; see Guillot 1952); fear of
crimes perpetrated by returning soldiers after the Great War (Washington,
1919; see Hayner & Cranor 1952); three lynchings by whites of blacks within
two years of abolition (Colorado, 1901; see Cutler 1907)—this is about the
extent of the information at our disposal to explain the reintroduction of the
death penalty in states that had only recently abolished it. It is not a very
impressive set of partial explanations, because all these factors (with the possible exception of the lynchings in Colorado) were present or equally likely
in states that never abolished the death penalty and states that had and did
not restore it. As for longtime abolitionist states such as Michigan and
Rhode Island, historians seem to have ignored their experience, too. All we
have for both groups of states are general statistics tending to show that (a)
these states experienced no remarkable rise in homicides during abolition by
comparison with their death penalty neighbors; (b) homicide in prison or
after release by convicted murderers, who might have been sentenced to
death and executed were it not for the abolition of the death penalty, was no
greater a problem than in states that retained the death penalty and used it;
and (c) the lives of law-enforcement officers were not at greater risk in abolition states than in death penalty states (see Sellin 1959 and 1980). All this
no doubt helps present a picture of plausibility for abolition as settled policy,
but it leaves any number of relevant (political, sociological, practical) questions unanswered.

In any case, most of the nation's population has never had the opportunity
to be persuaded in favor of abolition either by experiencing it directly or by
being told the full story of how crime and punishment, social vindictiveness,
and fear of violence are managed without recourse to the threat of executions.

Reducing the Number of Executions. Even though outright abolition of the
death penalty for all crimes has been achieved, as we have seen, in few American jurisdictions, abolitionists have taken some consolation from the steady
decline in the annual volume of executions. This decline is immediately
evident from the data presented in Table 1–3, which records all executions
annually since 1930. The de facto moratorium on executions, created in 1967
by the litigational efforts of the NAACP Legal Defense and Educational
Fund, Inc. (LDF), lasted through 1976; it accounts for the complete absence
of any executions for nearly a ten-year period. A closer inspection of the data
shows that the critical period of decline begins much earlier, in the 1940s,

Table 1-3. Prisoners Executed Under Civil Authority in the United States, 1930–1980

	All offenses		All offenses
All years	3,862	1955	76
1980	—	1954	81
		1953	62
1979	2	1952	83
1978	—	1951	105
1977	1	1950	82
1976	—		
1975	—	1949	119
1974	—	1948	119
1973	—	1947	153
1972	—	1946	131
1971	—	1945	117
1970	—	1944	120
		1943	131
1969	—	1942	147
1968	—	1941	123
1967	2	1940	124
1966	1		
1965	7	1939	160
1964	15	1938	190
1963	21	1937	147
1962	47	1936	195
1961	42	1935	199
1960	56	1934	168
		1933	160
1959	49	1932	140
1958	49	1931	153
1957	65	1930	155
1956	65		

Source: National Prisoners Statistics, Capital Punishment 1978, Table 1, p. 16 (for all years except 1980).

especially in the immediate postwar years. After a record high of 199 executions (1935), equivalent to three or four every week, executions steadily became less frequent. It was a decade or more before one could identify this trend and two decades before it was evident to perceptive observers that social forces of several sorts (growing doubts about the morality of capital punishment, consciousness among high officials that most of western Europe had abandoned the death penalty, abatement of the "crime wave" of the 1930s, mounting scientific evidence that undermined belief in the deterrent efficacy of executions and strengthened belief in its racially discriminatory use, increased willingness in appellate courts to delay executions in order to consider constitutional issues) were converging to bring about this decline.

If one studies annual execution data by state and region (see Table 2-3-1), it will be evident that by the 1940s the death penalty had already become predominantly a regional—Southern—phenomenon. Apparently "whatever emerging climate of unwillingness to execute there may have been, it was not a national phenomenon but a historical development at the regional level during the war years" (Bowers 1974:28). States outside the South led the way in reducing executions (the last one in Massachusetts was in 1947). But by the late 1950s executions had begun to decline in much of the South as well. The campaign launched by the LDF in the mid-1960s thus to some extent masked, by being superimposed upon, a trend that was already underway but at different rates and starting in different years throughout most of the nation during the previous two decades.[33]

With the de facto moratorium on executions now at an end, with hundreds under death sentence in many states, and with one execution in 1977, two more in 1979, and another early in 1981, there are grounds for speculation whether the historic downward trend in executions set in motion more than a generation ago will reverse itself in the remaining years of this century. Talk of a "bloodbath," of dozens of executions month after month as a possible result of the 1976 Supreme Court rulings upholding the constitutionality of certain death penalty statutes that now serve as models for any state legislature wishing to reintroduce capital punishment, has been heard in several quarters. That bloodbath has yet to wash over us, but an ominous portent is on the horizon. It was recently announced that a National Council of Capital State Prosecuting Attorneys had met to "find ways to remove legal roadblocks" that have been developed to prevent the execution of all but a few death row prisoners. Nearly "100 prosecutors from 23 . . . states with capital punishment laws reviewed tactics, arguments and source materials to counter death penalty appeals."[34] This is yet another new development in the struggle over the death penalty, only this one brings the nation a step closer to resuming executions, and at what could prove to be an unprecedented rate.

Conclusion. It would be premature to attempt an estimate of either the merits or the probability of complete abolition of the death penalty in this country.

33. What has not been studied by sociologists is whether there has been a comparable decline in death sentences, a question far more difficult to answer because prior to 1930 there were no national data on the annual number of death sentences. It would appear that more persons were sentenced to death during the decade of the 1970s than during the decade of the 1960s, though not necessarily more per capita, nor more in proportion to the annual murder rate, nor more in proportion to the arrest rate for murder. Whether, if so, this is because of or despite the belief by trial courts that these sentences would not be carried out, is not known. In any case, the significance of the declining rate of executions since the 1940s will remain uncertain until some parallel measurements on the rate of death sentencing have also been made.

34. *Boston Globe*, 24 August 1980, p. 78.

Table 1-4. Status of the Death Penalty in Europe, Canada, and Mexico

	Year of most recent execution[a]	Death penalty provisions
Albania	1973	Many offenses
Austria	———	Abolished
Belgium	———	Death sentences automatically commuted
Bulgaria	1977	Many offenses
Canada	———	Several military offenses
Czechoslovakia	1977	Many offenses
Cyprus	1962	Many offenses
Denmark	———	Abolished
Finland	———	Abolished
France	1977	Abolished
German Democratic Republic	1976	Many offenses
Germany, Federal Republic of	———	Abolished
Greece	1972	Many offenses
Hungary	1977	Many offenses
Iceland	———	Abolished
Ireland, Republic of	1954	Murder, treason, and various military offenses
Italy	———	During wartime only
Luxembourg	———	Death sentences automatically commuted
Mexico	NI	Abolished in 26 of 32 jurisdictions; retained in 6 for several offenses
Netherlands	———	During wartime only
Norway	———	During wartime only
Poland	1977	Many offenses
Portugal	———	Abolished
Rumania	NI	Many offenses
Spain	1975	Military offenses only
Sweden	———	Abolished
Switzerland	———	During wartime only
Turkey	NI	Many offenses
USSR	1976	Many offenses
United Kingdom	1964	Treason and piracy
Yugoslavia	1975	Many offenses

[a] Executions prior to 1950 and subsequent to 1977 are not indicated, although news releases from the London headquarters of Amnesty International report executions during 1978–80 in some of these countries.
NI—No information

Source: Amnesty International, *The Death Penalty* (1979), pp. 104–42, 152, 160.

Supporters of abolition in the past have been noticeably sanguine in their predictions. Sixty years ago, Raymond Bye, one of the sociologists to pioneer in the study of this subject, remarked, "There is reason to believe that in the course of the present century the use of the death penalty will finally pass away" (Bye 1919:245). Thirty years ago, another sociologist said "the over-all, international trend is toward the progressive abolition of capital punishment" (Hartung 1952:19). It is true, at least in regard to the nations of Europe and our immediate neighbors on this continent to the north and south, that executions and death sentences are increasingly rare and are prohibited by law in many countries under the ordinary criminal law (see Table 1-4). Yet as these lines are being written, Angola announced that it had executed 16 persons for carrying out a bombing campaign against the government, China reported that 198 persons had been executed during the fiscal year ending in June 1980 for crimes ranging from murder to gold speculation, and South Africa shows no inclination to dismantle the scaffolds on which 132 persons were executed in 1978 alone. Sporadic executions for various offenses have been carried out recently in Pakistan, Singapore, Taiwan, and Saudi Arabia, as well as in other countries of Asia, Africa, and Latin America. The executions in Iran under the "Islamic Revolutionary Tribunals" are too numerous and too well known to require more than mention.[35]

In the United States, as the next chapter will show, the death penalty is used so sparingly that it plays virtually no role in law enforcement and crime control. It may call up "strong emotions deeply rooted in the nature of man," but "the significance of availability or nonavailability of the death penalty as a sanction could hardly be *under*estimated" (Morris & Hawkins 1977:81). Of all the persons today in state and federal prisons, only about one in four thousand is under sentence of death. At one time flanked by a wide variety of accepted brutal practices (judicial torture and punitive flogging in particular), it now stands alone—an anachronism, a vestigial survivor of an era when the possibilities of incarcerative or rehabilitative penology were hardly imagined, and equal respect for all persons convicted of crimes was a requirement unknown to our constitutional law. Although killing persons in the name of the law for racial, political, and military crimes remains a familiar social phenomenon elsewhere in the modern world, the infrequency with which ordinary peacetime criminal offenses against persons and property are punished with death outside the United States focusses attention on the persistence of this ancient practice in our own land. It is for the rest of this book to describe in detail the surroundings and the consequences of the practice and to weigh the results as they bear on the justification of capital punishment in the present and for the future.

35. Executions throughout the world have been reported on a monthly basis by the London office of Amnesty International since late 1979; see also the AI Report 1979. For a recent and brief overview of the death penalty internationally, see López-Rey 1980.

2

The Laws, the Crimes,
and the Executions

INTRODUCTION

In order to evaluate what is presently at issue in the capital punishment controversy, one needs at a minimum to understand three categories of basic
legal and social facts. One needs to know, first, which *laws* if violated in a
given jurisdiction are punishable by death, as well as the lawful method of
carrying out a death sentence. Second, one needs information on the nature
and volume of the *crimes* that are or are likely to be punished by death. For
various reasons, this effectively reduces to questions about crimes of criminal
homicide, murder in its various forms. Finally, data are needed on the *executions* that have actually been carried out, their number and jurisdictions,
the racial and other characteristics of those recently executed, and the number and jurisdiction of those currently under sentence of death. The materials
assembled in this chapter supply reasonably complete and current answers to
all these questions.

The first section, "Offenses Punishable by Death," consists of three tables.
Table 2-1-1 presents a digest of the legal status of the death penalty in the
fifty-five jurisdictions of the United States competent to impose such a penalty, viz., the fifty states, the federal government (civil, military, and territorial), the District of Columbia, and the Commonwealth of Puerto Rico.[1]
Included also for each jurisdiction is the mode of execution currently authorized by law. This table shows that the death penalty today is virtually confined to the crime of murder. There are a few exceptions, but in light of

1. For similar compilations reporting data for earlier years, see *Congressional Record*, 1 March
   1962:3019–23; Bedau 1964a:39–52; Finkel 1967; and *House Hearings* 1972:261–4. For a
   detailed survey of the procedures authorized by current death penalty laws, see Gillers
   1980:101–19.

recent rulings by the Supreme Court (see below, Chapter Six), any attempt to enforce these capital statutes for nonhomicidal crimes is unlikely to succeed. However, as Table 2-1-2 shows, murder is given many different statutory definitions. At least thirteen distinguishable elements are cited in current stat-utes,with the result that what is capitally punishable murder in one jurisdiction may not be in a neighboring jurisdiction (compare, for example, the differences in the way murder is defined in Connecticut and New York, California and Nevada, North and South Carolina, and in Montana, Utah, and Wyoming). Moreover, as Tables 2-1-3 and 2-1-4 show, further variations are introduced by the statutes governing what capital trial juries must take into account in determining whether a convicted murderer should be sentenced to death or to life imprisonment. These factors divide into two groups, those that "aggravate" the crime (and thus tend to justify the death sentence) versus those that "mitigate" the crime (and thus tend in the opposite direction). Omitted is any attempt to catalogue the ways in which these factors are to be weighed and combined; the laws vary considerably on this point, too. All these divergences show that there is no settled agreement in the United States today over precisely what factors should count strongly against a murderer as a warrant for his death nor why some rather than other factors should play this decisive role.

The information supplied in these selections must be read and used with caution. All aspects of the laws governing the death penalty are under vir-tually continual litigation, so that each year in one or another capital juris-diction the appellate courts compel some change in the legal structure gov-erning the death penalty. This in turn prompts legislatures to enact statutory revisions in conformity with the mandate of the courts. Consequently, only a dedicated research team can hope to keep abreast of the actual status at every given moment of all the laws in the nation pertinent to the lawful employment of the death penalty. The materials reprinted in this chapter are at best useful guidelines to the end.

The second section, "Volume and Rate of Capital Crimes," although it presents a considerable array of data concerning criminal homicide, barely scratches the surface of the wealth of information available. The chief pur-pose of the materials gathered in this section is to show the salient features of murder as all investigators tend to see it: Along with other crimes of violence, murder has been growing in both volume and rate during the past two decades (Klebba 1975), even if not at the explosive rate that some other crimes have shown during the same period; murder is a crime committed largely by young men against other men; murder is committed by nonwhites disproportionately to their fraction of the total population; during the 1970s murder became one of the leading causes of death, especially in the cities. One might well echo the cry of dismay uttered by an earlier observer, "The land is full of bloody crimes and the city is full of violence." There is some consolation to be drawn from the realization that this despairing comment came not from the editorial page of a recent metropolitan newspaper but from the Bible.[2]

To shed further light on the current facts about murder, data concerning other crimes and other causes of death are also reported. Particular attention is paid to the volume, rate, and circumstances of killings of law-enforcement officers (a crime for which the death penalty is often invoked) and to the apparent growth of firearms as the preferred weapon for criminal homicide (see Tables 2-2-12 and 2-2-6, respectively).

Naively, one might expect that combining the laws concerning capital punishment with the volume and locale of such offenses as are punishable by death would give an equation with a product equal to the number of persons executed, or at least the persons sentenced to death. The reality is not quite so simple. The tables gathered into §3, "The Death Sentence and Executions," show that only a few of all those who commit murder are eventually executed (and Chapter Five explains how these few are selected). Calculations published elsewhere indicate that earlier in this century, the murder/execution ratio was estimated at 70:1 (Bye 1919:58) and 85:1 (Lawes 1924:36). For the 1960s, with 96,220 murders reported by the FBI and only 191 executions, the ratio fell to 504:1. There is no need to compute it for the 1970s, as there were over 180,000 murders reported and only three executions. If we shift from the murder/execution ratio to the murder/death-sentence ratio, the spread is not so great—but it is still quite large. During the 1960s, with 1043 persons received under death sentence, the ratio is 92:1. During the 1970s the ratio becomes 117:1.[3] However one wishes to calculate it, therefore, the gap between the annual volume of murder committed in this nation and the annual volume of persons sentenced to death and executed is enormous, and it continues to widen.

The data selected to portray the recent history and current status of the death sentence and executions are drawn (with one exception) from those published by the Department of Justice in its annual series on capital punishment. Four tabulations have been selected for reproduction here from among the many now available from this source. Table 2-3-1 records the aggregate number of executions in each jurisdiction since 1930, the initial year for which such data were collected and tabulated. Tables 2-3-2 and 2-3-3 report the race, sex, and offense of each person executed since 1930, and the year and jurisdiction in which the execution took place. Table 2-3-4 reports the number of persons who arrived on death row in each year since 1968, the number of jurisdictions that sent them there, and shows how that total has risen to the present record-breaking numbers. Table 2-3-5 presents a profile

2. Ezekial 7:23, quoted in Archer et al. 1978:73.
3. All calculations reported here for the 1960s and 1970s are based on the latest revised figures as published in *Uniform Crime Reports* and *National Prisoner Statistics*.

of those currently under sentence of death: their race, sex, and jurisdiction.[4] More discursive (narrative, biographical) accounts of these men and women who are being "warehoused for death" are readily available in several other sources; none is reprinted here.[5]

On the basis of these data we can make several generalizations, some of which were mentioned in Chapter One. 1. The execution rate has dropped precipitously from a high in the mid-1930s to zero during the de facto moratorium on executions (July 1967 through December 1977). 2. Although many women commit murder, almost no women—only 32 since 1930 (and most of them nonwhite)—have been executed. 3. The death penalty is used with greatest frequency in the Sun Belt, from Virginia south to Florida and west to California.[6] 4. More than half of all persons executed are black, and the vast majority (89%) of those executed for rape have been black. (Whether such facts demonstrate or merely suggest the effect of racism is examined in greater detail in Chapter Five.) 5. The number of persons sentenced to death did not abate during the 1967–77 moratorium on executions.

§1.   Offenses Punishable by Death

Table 2-1-1. Capital Laws and Mode of Execution, State, Federal, and Territorial, 1980

Jurisdiction	Mode of execution[a]	Death penalty not authorized as of 12/31/80	Offenses for which death penalty is authorized[b]
Alabama	E		Murder
Alaska	———	✓	
Arizona	LG		1st-degree murder
Arkansas	E		Aggravated murder

4. A new serial, *Death Penalty Reporter,* to be issued monthly, has been published since September 1980 by the National College for Criminal Defense, College of Law, University of Houston. The issue for November 1980 contained the names and other information about the 675 persons then known to be under death sentence. Updates on death row prisoners have been announced at quarterly intervals.

5. See especially Jackson & Christian 1980 (on Texas's death row), Johnson 1980 (on Alabama's death row), Lewis 1979 (on Florida's death row), and C. Davis 1980 (on Georgia's death row). For more general accounts see Gettinger 1979 and Magee 1980.

6. Whether the death penalty is increasingly a regional phenomenon, and is to be seen as one more manifestation of a larger regional pattern of social violence, has been argued by Glaser & Zeigler 1974; Bailey 1976b; and Glaser 1976.

Table 2-1-1. Capital Laws and Mode of Execution, State, Federal, and Territorial, 1980 (*Continued*)

Jurisdiction	Mode of execution[a]	Death penalty not authorized as of 12/31/80	Offenses for which death penalty is authorized[b]
California	LG		1st-degree murder; treason; assault by life prisoner resulting in death; hindering preparing for war causing death; omitting to note defects in articles of war resulting in death; perjury resulting in the death penalty; train wrecking resulting in death
Colorado	LG		1st-degree murder; 1st-degree kidnaping; treason; certain drug offenses
Connecticut	E		Murder
Delaware	H		1st-degree murder
District of Columbia	——	✓	
Florida	E		Murder; sexual battery[c]
Georgia	E		Murder; treason; aircraft hijacking
Hawaii	——	✓	
Idaho	LI		1st-degree murder; treason; aircraft hijacking
Illinois	E		Murder
Indiana	E		Murder Class A felony
Iowa	——	✓	
Kansas	——	✓	
Kentucky	E		
Louisiana	E		1st-degree murder; kidnaping when victim is killed
Maine	——	✓	
Maryland	LG		1st-degree murder
Massachusetts	——	✓	
Michigan	——	✓	
Minnesota	——	✓	
Mississippi	LG		Murder; treason; aircraft piracy; capital rape[d]
Missouri	LG		Murder
Montana	H		Deliberate homicide; aggravated kidnaping[e]
Nebraska	E		1st-degree murder
Nevada	LG		1st-degree murder
New Hampshire	H		Murder
New Jersey	——	✓	
New Mexico	LI		1st-degree murder
New York	E		Murder by life prisoner
North Carolina	LG		1st-degree murder
North Dakota	——	✓	
Ohio	——	✓	
Oklahoma	LI		Murder

Table 2-1-1. Capital Laws and Mode of Execution, State, Federal, and Territorial, 1980 (*Continued*)

Jurisdiction	Mode of execution[a]	Death penalty not authorized as of 12/31/80	Offenses for which death penalty is authorized[b]
Oregon[f]	LG		Murder
Pennsylvania	E		1st-degree murder
Puerto Rico	———	✓	
Rhode Island	———	✓	Murder while in prison
South Carolina	E		Murder
South Dakota	E		
Tennessee	E		1st-degree murder
Texas	LI		Murder
Utah	FS		Murder
Vermont	E		Murder[g]
Virginia	E		Aggravated murder
Washington	H		Aggravated 1st-degree murder
West Virginia	———	✓	
Wisconsin	———	✓	
Wyoming	LG		1st-degree murder
Federal	[h]		
Civil			Aircraft piracy resulting in death[i]
Military	H		Murder; rape; espionage; aiding the enemy; mutiny; sedition; desertion; misbehavior before the enemy; assaulting or willfully disobeying a superior officer; improper use of a countersign; misbehavior of a sentinel

[a] LG = lethal gas, E = electrocution, H = hanging, FS = firing squad, LI = lethal injection

[b] Although varying somewhat from jurisdiction to jurisdiction, the types of homicide most commonly specified in these statutes are murder perpetrated during the course of another felony; murder of a peace officer, corrections employee, or fireman engaged in the performance of official duties; murder by an inmate serving a life sentence; and murder for hire. Different statutory terminology may be used by different states to designate substantively identical crimes; thus in some states, but not necessarily all, such terms as "murder," "1st-degree murder," "murder Class A felony," etc., may denote the same offense.

[c] The sexual battery of a female child age 11 or under by a male age 18 or older.

[d] The rape of a female child under the age of 12 by a person age 18 or older.

[e] Kidnapping that results in the death of the victim.

[f] In early 1981, the 1978 Oregon statute was invalidated; see *State* v. *Quinn,* 623 P.2d 630 (Oregon Supreme Ct., 1981).

[g] This statue was last revised in 1971 and has not been brought into conformity with *Furman* (1972) and *Gregg* (1976); it is therefore currently unenforceable.

[h] For those sentenced to death under Federal (civil) law, the method of execution is determined by the law of the state in which the punishment is to be carried out.

[i] Title 18, U.S. Code, contains approximately 15 capital offenses; however, "the death penalty cannot constitutionally be imposed under [these] provisions. . . ." Report of the Committee on the Judiciary ... to Accompany H.R. 6915, 25 September 1980, p. 434, citing *United States* v. *Weedell,* 567 F.2d 767 (8th Cir. 1977).

Source: National Prisoner Statistics, Capital Punishment 1979, pp. 3, 9–13, revised and updated through 31 December 1980 from various sources, including "Death Row USA," released from the NAACP Legal Defense and Educational Fund, Inc., 20 December 1980 and 20 April 1981. Data used by permission of the NAACP Legal Defense Fund, Inc.

Table 2-1-2. The Statutory Elements of Homicide, by State, 1974

Specified definitional elements of homicide

	First degree	With premeditation	During specified felonies	During escape from custody	Of a guard, police, fireman, official	By use of explosives	Of multiple victims	When offender under life or death sentence	For pecuniary gain	By convicted murderer	Of kidnapped victim	During sale of narcotics	Of a witness against defendant
Arizona	✓												
Arkansas	a	✓	✓		✓		✓	✓					
California	✓b												
Colorado	✓							✓		✓	✓	✓	✓
Connecticut	c				✓								
Delaware	✓d	✓	✓	✓	✓	✓							
Florida	✓												
Georgia	✓												
Idaho	✓	✓			✓						✓		
Illinois	✓												
Indiana	✓												
Kentucky	c												
Louisiana	✓		✓		✓		✓	✓	✓	✓			
Mississippi	e		✓		✓	✓		✓	✓				
Montana	f		✓j		✓						✓		
Nebraska	✓								✓				
Nevada	g				✓	✓	✓	✓h	✓				
New Hampshire	i		✓		✓								
New Mexico	✓	✓	✓										
New York	✓				✓i			✓					
North Carolina	✓	✓	✓										
Ohio	k												
Oklahoma	✓		✓		✓	✓	✓	✓	✓				✓
Pennsylvania	✓												
Rhode Island	l							✓m					
South Carolina	c	✓	✓		✓		✓		✓	✓			
Tennessee	✓	✓	✓		✓				✓				
Texas	n		✓	✓	✓				✓				
Utah	✓		✓	✓					✓	✓			
Wyoming	✓												

a "Unlawful killing" under specified circumstances
b Also some cases of "deadly assault" by a life-term prisoner, where victim dies within a year and a day as proximate result of the assault
c "Murder" under specified conditions
d Also suicide caused by force or duress by offender
e "Capital murder" ("killing of a human being without the authority of law" under specified circumstances)
f "Deliberate homicide" ("criminal homicide" under specified circumstances)
g "Capital murder" ("murder" under specified circumstances)
h Offender under life sentence without possibility of parole
i "Capital murder" ("knowingly causing death" under specified circumstances)
j Offender must be over 18
k "Aggravated murder"
l "Murder" only by a prison inmate
m Any prisoner, regardless of sentence, in adult correctional institution or state reformatory for women
n "Capital murder" ("killing" under specified circumstances)

Source: Appendix A, Brief for Petitioner in *Fowler* v. *North Carolina*, U.S. Supreme Court, October term 1974.

35

Table 2-1-3. Statutory "Aggravating" Circumstances Pertinent to Imposing a Death Sentence, by State, 1974

	Offender characteristics			Offense characteristics							Victim characteristics				
	Prior conviction	Offender hired, paid, etc.	Offender imprisoned	Prevention of arrest	Use of explosives	Knowingly create risk to others	Heinous method	Premeditated	During course of specified felonies	Hinder government function	Multiple victims	Kidnapped victim	Witness victim	Police, guard, or fireman	Official
Arizona	✓[a]	✓		✓		✓	✓								
Arkansas	✓[a,b]	✓	✓[c]										✓		
California	✓[d]	✓				✓	✓	✓	✓	✓	✓	✓		✓	
Colorado	✓[f]	✓	✓[c]		✓	✓	✓	✓[c]	✓					✓	
Connecticut	✓[a,b]	✓				✓	✓		✓						
Florida	✓[a,f]	✓	✓[c]	✓		✓	✓		✓						
Georgia	✓[a,f]	✓		✓					✓	✓				✓	
Illinois									✓		✓			✓	✓

Indiana	√[d]			√[g]					√	√	√
Kentucky	√[d]	√		√[c]			√	√	√	√	√
Montana	√[b,d]	√			√	√	√	√		√	√
Nebraska	√[d,b]	√		√[i]	√	√	√	√		√	√
Ohio	√[a]	√		√[g]		√	√	√	√		√
Pennsylvania	√[d,k]						√	√		√	√
Texas											
Wyoming	√	√		√[k]	√		√	√		√	√

[a] Prior conviction for which death or life sentence is imposable.
[b] Prior conviction for felony involving force or threat of force.
[c] Under any sentence of imprisonment.
[d] Prior conviction for murder.
[e] By lying in wait or from ambush.
[f] Prior conviction on two felonies involving serious bodily injury.
[g] Under sentence for life.
[h] Or attempted murder.
[i] By "prisoner in detention."
[j] The Texas provisions are significantly different from other States in one respect. Following a conviction for "capital murder" ("killing" under specified circumstances) the jury, at a separate hearing, must determine three specified issues. Apart from the fairly normal issues of "reasonableness" and "provocation," the jury must set forth findings as to "whether there is a probability that the defendant would commit criminal acts of violence that would constitute a continuing threat to society."
[k] During some felony-murder with prior convictions for same crime.

Source: Appendix A, Brief for Petitioner, Fowler v. North Carolina, U.S. Supreme Court, October term 1974.

Table 2-1-4. Statutory "Mitigating" Circumstances Pertinent to Imposing a Death Sentence, by State, 1974

	Diminished capacity	Duress	Minor role in the offense	Mental disturbance	Age of offender	No prior criminal record	Risk not reasonably foreseeable	Victim participation or consent
Arizona	✓	✓	✓	✓			✓	
Arkansas	✓[a]	✓	✓	✓	✓			
Colorado	✓	✓	✓		✓		✓	
Connecticut	✓	✓	✓		✓		✓	
Florida	✓	✓	✓	✓	✓	✓		✓
Nebraska	✓	✓		✓	✓	✓		✓
Ohio	✓			✓	✓			✓
Pennsylvania		✓[b]			✓			✓
Texas			✓	✓	✓	✓	✓	
Utah	✓	✓	✓	✓	✓			

[a] Mental disease, defect, intoxification, or drug abuse.
[b] Provocation not amounting to a defense at law.

Source: Appendix A, Brief for Petitioner in *Fowler v. North Carolina*, U.S. Supreme Court, October term 1974.

§2.   Volume and Rate of Murder

Our knowledge about murder comes from many sources, but for most purposes it can be divided into two types.[1] The first is information of an aggregate sort, in which all offenses in one or more jurisdictions are tallied and then analyzed for certain salient characteristics, such as the age, race, and sex of offender and victim. The pioneering example of this kind of research is *Patterns in Criminal Homicide* (1958) by the sociologist Marvin E. Wolfgang. Wolfgang's data were derived from the 588 cases of criminal homicide in Philadelphia committed during the five-year period 1948–52. A more recent study in the same genre is Henry P. Lundsgaarde's *Murder in Space City* (1977), on homicide in Houston. Secondly, there is clinical information, case studies based on interviews that attempt to reveal the murderer's motives, his state of mind before, during, and after the crime, and other factors of a psychosocial character. A classic study of this type is by the psychiatrist Manfred S. Guttmacher, *The Mind of the Murderer* (1960); more recently there is *The Murdering Mind* (1973) by David Abrahamsen, also a psychiatrist. All the information contained in the discursive and tabular material reprinted below is of the first type. The bulk of this material is supplied from one source, the *Uniform Crime Reports* (UCR) published annually by the FBI, and is limited to aggregate national (rather than regional, state, or local) data for selected recent years.

This basic source for all information on crimes in the United States consists of "crimes known to the police." Reports of these crimes are supplied by local police forces to the FBI, which in turn publishes them in the UCR. Our focus here is on the category of crime this source describes as "murder and non-negligent manslaughter" (hereinafter "murder"). Major portions of the FBI's most recent report on this crime (1979) are reprinted below.

We can regard the 21,456 murders reported there as the total of *capitally punishable homicides* that were committed in 1979, but only if our purposes are rather crude. For one thing, this number is an estimate, not an actual count of all criminal homicides. In 1978, for example, crimes were reported for areas incorporating an estimated 98 percent of the total national population (*UCR* 1978:4). Furthermore, even in the areas covered by reports, such as all the major cities, some murders were surely undetected and the victims of these crimes wrongly classified as death by suicide, accident, or natural

---

1. For data derived from representative studies of each type, see Wolfgang 1967. A more comprehensive recent volume, with citation to over 700 publications, is Kutash et al. 1978. A popular recent account is Godwin 1978.

causes, and thus never reported to the police or FBI as murder.[2] Finally, and of most importance, many of these murders are never treated as capital crimes. For example, either the prosecutor indicts the accused for voluntary manslaughter, or the jury brings in a conviction of second-degree murder; there are a number of ways to dispose of "capital" cases within the criminal justice system without trying to get the murderer sentenced to death (see below, Chapter Five). All these considerations are lost in the aggregate total of 21,456 reported murders. Consequently, we can speak with rigor of "capital cases" or of "homicides that deserve the death penalty" only if we are able to take these subtleties into account. How this is to be done is far from clear, and no attempt will be made to do it here.[3]

In order to provide a perspective from which to judge the current volume and rate of murder, information is provided in Tables 2-2-1 and 2-2-2 for other crimes during the past two decades.[4] These tables show that, although murder has indeed increased, other crimes have increased (with few exceptions) at an even greater rate in every year where the comparison is reported.

Another source of data on the volume of criminal homicide is provided by the vital statistics collected by local boards of health and published nationally by the Public Health Service. These data show that homicide is now one of the ten leading causes of death for men (Table 2-2-3), that homicide is much less frequent than suicide, and that both homicide and suicide rates vary considerably from jurisdiction to jurisdiction (Table 2-2-4). Some have argued that murder is increasingly an urban phenomenon, that the larger the city the higher the murder rate, and—worst of all—that under the homicide patterns prevailing in the early 1970s, three out of every hundred men born in those years in the fifty largest American cities would ultimately be murdered. This risk, however, does not fall on all young men equally; blacks are at risk several times greater than whites (Barnett et al. 1975).[5]

The central demographic factors in murder are reported in Table 2-2-5. They show that intraracial murder dominates interracial murder to a marked

2. For an example of such errors, see *The New York Times,* 17 September 1974, p. 60. John O. Sullivan, manager of the NIJ Forensic Science Program in Washington, D.C., was recently reported as of the opinion that "As many as 50 percent of all homicides in this country go undetected because of poor and inconsistent investigative procedures at the scene of the crime." *Boston Sunday Globe,* 8 February 1981, p. 24. Errors of this magnitude, of course, would make traditional crime statistics worthless.

3. The best recent discussion of this problem is in Sellin 1980:121–37.

4. For some years, it appears the *UCR* give discrepant totals; for example, for 1976 the total for murder appears as 18,780 (Table 2-2-1) and as 16,605 (Table 2-2-7). This discrepancy is explained by variations in the reports received by the FBI, which make some of the reported murders unusable for certain tabular comparisons.

5. See also the follow-up study, Barnett et al. 1979. For an attempt to explain some of the basic features of urban homicide, relying mainly on data for countries other than the U.S., see Archer et al. 1978.

extent. The vast majority of whites who are killed are killed by other whites, as are blacks by blacks, a pattern noted decades ago in the important study of homicide in North Carolina by Garfinkel (1949). The remaining seven tables fall into two groups, four that provide some further information about the offender and the offense, and three that give information about the victims. Table 2-2-6 shows that for many years guns have been the major weapon used to commit murder, and that this weapon has been increasingly used during recent years (except for fractional declines in the late 1970s). Research published elsewhere strongly suggests that the great increase in the homicide rate in the cities is attributable to "a greater number of firearm killings in general and handgun murders in particular" (Fisher 1976:397). Whether this high rate could be reduced by effective state or federal firearms control (registration, controlled production and sale, or even outright confiscation) is a highly controversial matter; in any case, national firearms control seems a political impossibility. Table 2-2-7 shows that of all murders, around 20 percent are known by the police to be felony-murder (homicide committed by the offender during the commission of another felony, usually burglary, robbery, or rape), and that another 6 percent or so are estimated to have this origin. The trend in this type of murder during the early and mid-1970s was on the increase; more recent data suggest a return to earlier patterns.[6] Table 2-2-8 shows (assuming that arrested offenders are representative of all offenders) that men are murderers about four times as frequently as women; and that blacks commit more murders than whites, and thus disproportionately more, given that the national population ratio of the races for the years in question was about nine whites for every black. Table 2-2-9 shows that most murders are committed by persons in their late teens or early twenties. Table 2-2-10, on the age, sex, and race distribution for the victims of murder in the most recent year available, shows that male victims exceed female victims by a ratio of three to one, and that most of the victims, no matter what race or sex, are in their twenties. Table 2-2-11 shows that the sex ratio among victims has held steady for more than a decade, whereas the race ratio has shifted slightly in recent years from predominantly black to white.

The final selection, "Homicide of Law Enforcement Officers," is an excerpt from the most recent issue of *UCR* concerning the killing of police officers, a crime for which the death penalty is often proposed and reportedly favored by a large majority of the public (see Chapter Three). The data reported here show that for the decade 1970–79, killings of law enforcement officers amounted to a tiny fraction (0.006%) of all murders reported for those years, and that nearly 1 in 7 of these killers were themselves killed by

6. See the discussion on "stranger/stranger" homicide in New York City in *The New York Times*, 23 March 1975, p. 1, and 13 June 1976, p. 1.

the police and never taken into custody. Whether the readiness of the police to use lethal force during arrest is a function of their doubts about society's willingness to mete out a death sentence to convicted felons is a matter for speculation.[7]

One issue not addressed directly in the data below, but of considerable relevance to the death penalty controversy, is whether there is any striking pattern to the homicide rate in abolition jurisdictions as a group by contrast to death penalty jurisdictions. Even if the death penalty is a uniquely effective deterrent, the rate of homicide in a given abolition jurisdiction might be considerably lower, year after year, than in a typical death penalty jurisdiction, owing to the causal role in the homicide rate played by factors other than the severity of the penalty (e.g., the certainty of arrest, the unemployment rate, the population distribution). However, the reader can easily see by examining Table 2-2-4 below and Table 1-1 in Chapter One that the traditional abolition states as a group have a much lower homicide rate than do those states that have never abolished the death penalty, a phenomenon noted long ago and stable through most of this century (see Schuessler 1952:57–58). Conversely, those states that have executed most frequently have among the highest homicide rates in the nation. Whether such facts can be fitted into the deterrence hypothesis is discussed in Chapter Five.

Murder and Nonnegligent Manslaughter*

Definition. Murder and nonnegligent manslaughter, as defined in the Uniform Crime Reporting Program, is the willful (nonnegligent) killing of one human being by another.

The classification of this offense, as in all other Crime Index offenses, is based solely on police investigation as opposed to the determination of a court, medical examiner, coroner, jury, or other judicial body. Not included in the count for this offense classification are deaths caused by negligence, suicide, or accident; justifiable homicides, which are the killings of felons by law enforcement officers in the line of duty or by private citizens; and attempts to murder or assaults to murder, which are scored as aggravated assaults.

Volume. In the United States during 1979, there were an estimated 21,456 murders representing approximately 2 percent of the total violent crimes.

A geographic breakdown of murder by region revealed that 42 percent of the murders occurred in the southern states, which account for the largest regional population. Twenty-one percent were reported by the north central

---

7. For discussions of justifiable homicide by the police, see Robin 1963, Sherman & Langworthy 1979, and Sherman 1980.

From: FBI Uniform Crime Reports 1979, pp. 7–12 (with omissions).

states; 20 percent by the western states; and 17 percent by the northeastern states.

December had a higher frequency of murder offenses in 1979 than any other month of the year.

Trend. Nationally, the number of murders increased 10 percent from 1978 to 1979, and all four geographic regions registered upswings. The southern states reported a rise of 11 percent; the northeastern and western states, increases of 10 percent each; and the north central states, a 7 percent upturn.

Also experiencing increases in the number of murders in 1979, the suburban areas and large core cities of 250,000 or more people recorded 7 and 14 percent upswings, respectively. In the rural areas, the volume of murders was down 2 percent. [. . .]

Rate. In 1979, there was an average of 10 murder victims for every 100,000 inhabitants in the nation.

The number of murder victims in relation to population was highest in the southern states with 13 murders per 100,000 inhabitants, a 9-percent rate increase over the previous year. The western states' rate was 10 per 100,000, a 7-percent rise over the 1978 rate. Both the north central and northeastern states experienced rates of 8 per 100,000 population; however, the northeast's rate represented a 10-percent increase, and the north central region's rate a rise of 7 percent.

Collectively, the SMSAs reported a murder rate of 11 victims per 100,000 inhabitants; the rural areas recorded a rate of 7 per 100,000 inhabitants; and cities outside metropolitan areas (other cities) reported a murder rate of 6 per 100,000 inhabitants.

Nature. To allow for a more detailed analysis of murder, the Uniform Crime Reporting Program collects supplemental information on this offense. Data are collected monthly on the age, sex, and race of murder victims and offenders; the types of weapons used in murders; the circumstances surrounding the offenses; and the relationships between victims and offenders.

As in recent years, murder victims were male in approximately 3 of every 4 instances in 1979. On the average, 54 of every 100 victims were white, 43 were black, and the remainder were of other races.

During 1979, 16,955 offenders were identified in connection with the murders of 15,040 victims. Most of the victims (14,024) were slain in single victim situations. Of these, 12,429 were killed by single offenders and the remainder by more than one offender. Concerning homicides involving multiple victims, 815 persons were killed by 357 offenders in incidents involving one assailant and multiple victims, and 201 victims were slain by 207 offenders in multiple victim/multiple offender situations.

In 1979, firearms predominated as the weapons most often used in the commission of murders throughout the nation. The accompanying chart [omitted here] illustrates the breakdown of murder offenses in the United States by type of weapon used. In both the north central and southern regions, firearms were used in 65 percent of the murders; in the western states, they were employed in 58 percent; and in the northeastern states, they were used in 53 percent. Nationwide, 63 percent of the murders were committed through the use of firearms. Handguns were the weapons used in 50 percent of all murders.

A comparative study for the past 5 years showed a decrease in the use of firearms to commit murder. In 1975, firearms were used in 66 percent of all murders, while 63 percent of all murders in 1979 were perpetrated with these weapons. [. . .]

Of weapons other than firearms employed in murder offenses reported in 1979, cutting or stabbing instruments were used in 19 percent. The most widespread use of such weapons occurred in the northeastern states, where 25 percent of the murders were committed with a knife or cutting instrument. In the western states these types of weapons were employed in 22 percent of the murders, while the southern and north central states had the least incidence of use of such weapons, 19 and 16 percent, respectively. Nationwide, other weapons such as blunt objects, poisons, explosives, etc., were used in 12 percent of the murders. In the remaining 6 percent, personal weapons, such as hands, fists, and feet, were used.

That murder is largely a societal problem beyond the control of the law enforcement community is emphasized by the relationship of the murder victim to the offender. Fifty-two percent of the murder victims in 1979 were acquainted with their assailants, and 1 of every 5 victims was related to the offender.

The greatest percentage of murders in 1979 (43 percent) resulted from arguments. Seventeen percent occurred as a result of felonious activity, and 5 percent were suspected to be the result of some felonious act.

Clearances. The clearance rate for murder in 1979 was higher than for any other Crime Index offense. City and suburban law enforcement agencies were successful in clearing 73 percent of the murders during the year, while those in rural areas cleared 83 percent. In 1979, persons under 18 years of age accounted for 5 percent of the willful killings cleared by law enforcement in cities and rural areas; 7 percent of those cleared in suburban areas involved only persons in that age group.

Persons Arrested. Arrests of youthful offenders under 18 years of age for murder decreased 12 percent during the period 1975-1979, and adult arrests for that offense fell 9 percent in the same period. In 1979, 44 percent of all persons arrested for murder were under age 25, and 9 percent were under 18. The 18- to 22-year age group, accounting for 25 percent of the total 1979 murder arrests, showed the heaviest involvement in this offense. Whites made up 49 percent of the total arrestees for murder in 1979, blacks comprised 48 percent, and the remaining 3 percent were of other races.

Homicide of Law Enforcement Officers*

In 1979, 106 local, county, state, and federal law enforcement officers were feloniously killed as compared to 93 in 1978. During the 10-year period, 1970–79, 1143 officers were slain. It should be noted that the collection of statistics regarding officers killed in the line of duty was expanded in 1971 to include United States' territories (Puerto Rico, the Virgin Islands, and Guam). Also, the gathering of data on slain federal officers was begun in 1972. Therefore, 10-year data on officers killed include figures for United States' territories since 1971 and federal officers since 1972.

	Number of victim officers
1970	100
1971	129
1972	116
1973	134
1974	132
1975	129
1976	111
1977	93
1978	93
1979	106
Total	1143

[. . .] During the year, 19 officers were slain by persons engaged in the commission of a robbery or during the pursuit of robbery suspects, and 7 lost their lives at the scene of burglaries or while pursuing burglary suspects. Twenty-one officers were killed while attempting arrests for crimes other than robbery or burglary.

Ambush situations accounted for 11 officers' deaths in 1979. Seventeen officers were slain responding to disturbance calls (family quarrels, man-with-gun calls, bar fights, etc.) and 15 were killed while enforcing traffic laws. Nine officers lost their lives while investigating suspicious persons or circum-

*From: FBI Uniform Crime Reports 1979, pp. 309–13 (with omissions).

stances, 4 while handling mentally deranged persons, and 3 while engaged in the handling, transporting, or custody of prisoners.

Seventy-one of the officers slain in 1979 were on patrol duty, and of those, 68 were assigned to vehicles and 3 were on foot patrol. The perils inherent in patrol duties are substantiated by the fact that, in recent years, officers assigned in this capacity have consistently been the most frequent victims of the police killer. The patrol officer is often placed in dangerous situations and must react to circumstances as they occur without the benefit of detailed information or planning. He is repeatedly in contact with suspicious or dangerous individuals, each of whom could constitute a threat to his personal safety. [. . .]

During 1979, there were 17 offenders justifiably killed either at the scene of the police killing or in ensuing confrontations. Five of these assailants were killed and an additional 11 were wounded by the victim officers themselves. Four of the offenders committed suicide.

For the years 1968–77, the most recent 10-year period for which complete disposition data are available, 1536 known persons were involved in the killings of 1094 law enforcement officers. Of these known offenders, 1280 were arrested and charged with the killings of the officers. The available court disposition data regarding the offenders found guilty of the officers' murders disclosed that 107 were sentenced to death, 407 were sentenced to life imprisonment, and 265 received prison terms ranging from 1 to 2001 years. Four offenders received probation; 5 received suspended sentences. The sentences of 14 offenders who were found guilty are unknown.

Table 2-2-1. Volume and Rate (per 100,000 inhabitants) of Offenses Known to Police, by Offense, 1960–79

	Population	Total Crime Index		Property Crime[a]		Violent Crime[b]		Murder and Nonnegligent Manslaughter	
		Volume	Rate	Volume	Rate	Volume	Rate	Volume	Rate
1960	179,323,175	3,384,200	1,887.2	3,095,700	1,726.3	288,460	160.9	9,110	5.1
1961	182,992,000	3,488,000	1,906.1	3,198,600	1,747.9	289,390	158.1	8,740	4.8
1962	185,771,000	3,752,200	2,019.8	3,450,700	1,857.5	301,510	162.3	8,530	4.6
1963	188,483,000	4,109,500	2,180.3	3,792,500	2,012.1	316,970	168.2	8,640	4.6
1964	191,141,000	4,564,600	2,388.1	4,200,400	2,197.5	364,220	190.6	9,360	4.9
1965	193,526,000	4,739,400	2,449.0	4,352,000	2,248.8	387,390	200.2	9,960	5.1
1966	195,576,000	5,223,500	2,670.8	4,793,300	2,450.9	430,180	220.0	11,040	5.6
1967	197,457,000	5,903,400	2,989.7	5,403,500	2,736.5	499,930	253.2	12,240	6.2
1968	199,399,000	6,720,200	3,370.2	6,125,200	3,071.8	595,010	298.4	13,800	6.9
1969	201,385,000	7,410,900	3,680.0	6,749,000	3,351.3	661,870	328.7	14,760	7.3
1970	203,235,298	8,098,000	3,984.5	7,359,200	3,621.0	738,820	363.5	16,000	7.9
1971	206,212,000	8,588,200	4,164.7	7,771,700	3,768.8	816,500	396.0	17,780	8.6
1972	208,230,000	8,248,800	3,961.4	7,413,900	3,560.4	834,900	401.0	18,670	9.0
1973	209,851,000	8,718,100	4,154.4	7,842,200	3,737.0	875,910	417.4	19,640	9.4
1974	211,392,000	10,253,400	4,850.4	9,278,700	4,389.3	974,720	461.1	20,710	9.8
1975	213,124,000	11,256,600	5,281.7	10,230,300	4,800.2	1,026,280	481.5	20,510	9.6
1976	214,659,000	11,304,800	5,266.4	10,318,200	4,806.8	986,580	459.6	18,780	8.8
1977	216,332,000	10,935,800	5,055.1	9,926,300	4,588.4	1,009,500	466.6	19,120	8.8
1978	218,059,000	11,141,300	5,109.3	10,079,500	4,622.4	1,061,830	486.9	19,560	9.0
1979	220,099,000	12,152,730	5,521.5	10,974,191	4,986.0	1,178,539	535.5	21,456	9.7

[a] Includes burglary, larceny-theft, and motor vehicle theft.
[b] Includes murder, forcible rape, robbery, and aggravated assault.

Source: FBI Uniform Crime Reports 1975, p. 49; 1978, p. 39; 1979, p. 40.

Table 2-2. National Crime, Rate, and Percent Change, by Offense, 1970–79

Crime index offenses	Estimated crime 1979		Percent change over 1978		Percent change over 1975		Percent change over 1970	
	Number	Rate per 100,000 inhabitants	Number	Rate per 100,000 inhabitants	Number	Rate per 100,000 inhabitants	Number	Rate per 100,000 inhabitants
Total[a]	12,152,700	5,521.5	+9.1	+8.1	+8.0	+4.5	+50.1	+38.6
Violent	1,178,540	535.5	+11.0	+10.0	+14.8	+11.2	+59.5	+47.3
Property	10,974,200	4,986.0	+8.9	+7.9	+7.3	+3.9	+49.1	+37.7
Murder	21,460	9.7	+9.7	+7.8	+4.6	+1.0	+34.1	+22.8
Forcible rape	75,990	34.5	+13.2	+12.0	+35.5	+31.2	+100.0	+84.5
Robbery	466,880	212.1	+12.0	+10.9	+.4	−2.8	+33.4	+23.2
Aggravated assault	614,210	279.1	+10.1	+9.1	+26.7	+22.7	+83.4	+69.4
Burglary	3,299,500	1,499.1	+6.3	+5.3	+1.5	−1.8	+49.6	+38.2
Larceny—theft	6,577,500	2,988.4	+9.9	+8.9	+10.0	+6.5	+55.7	+43.7
Motor vehicle theft	1,097,200	498.5	+10.6	+9.6	+9.7	+6.2	+18.2	+9.1

[a] Due to rounding, offenses may not add to Crime Index totals.

Source: FBI Uniform Crime Reports 1979, p. 37.

48

Table 2-2-3. Deaths and Death Rates for the 10 Leading Causes of Death, by Sex, 1976

Rank	Causes of death ... [according to] Eighth Revision International Classification of Diseases, Adapted, 1965	Number	Rate per 100,000 population
	Male		
	All causes	1,051,983	1,007.0
1	Diseases of heart	400,601	383.5
2	Malignant neoplasms, including neoplasms of lymphatic and hematopoietic tissues	205,406	196.6
3	Cerebrovascular diseases	80,597	77.1
4	Accidents	70,277	67.3
5	Influenza and pneumonia	32,513	31.1
6	Cirrhosis of liver	20,668	19.8
7	Suicide	19,493	18.7
8	Bronchitis, emphysema, and asthma	17,784	17.0
9	Homicide	15,142	14.5
10	Certain causes of mortality in early infancy	14,198	13.6
	Female		
	All causes	857,457	778.3
1	Diseases of heart	323,277	293.4
2	Malignant neoplasms, including neoplasms of lymphatic and hematopoietic tissues	171,906	156.0
3	Cerebrovascular diseases	108,026	98.0
4	Accidents	30,484	27.7
5	Influenza and pneumonia	29,353	26.6
6	Diabetes mellitus	20,483	18.6
7	Arteriosclerosis	17,553	15.9
8	Cirrhosis of liver	10,785	9.8
9	Certain causes of mortality in early infancy	10,611	9.6
10	Suicide	7,339	6.7

Source: U.S. Dept. HEW Publ. No. (PHS) 79-1222, 1978, p. 32.

Table 2-2-4. Deaths from Murder and Suicide, by State, 1978

	Murder		Suicide	
	Total	Rate per 100,000	Total	Rate per 100,000
Alabama	499	13.3	392	10.5
Alaska	52	12.9	61	14.8
Arizona	221	9.4	459	19.3
Arkansas	199	9.1	228	10.5
California	2,611	11.7	3,627	16.3
Colorado	196	7.3	481	17.8
Connecticut	129	4.2	320	10.3
Delaware	39	6.7	85	14.6
District of Columbia	295	9.7	70	10.4
Florida	949	11.0	1,533	17.7
Georgia	731	14.4	688	13.6
Hawaii	60	6.7	106	11.8
Idaho	47	5.4	118	13.4
Illinois	1,108	9.9	1,121	10.0
Indiana	334	6.2	642	11.9
Iowa	74	2.6	344	11.8
Kansas	133	5.7	253	10.8
Kentucky	316	9.0	436	12.5
Louisiana	625	15.8	471	11.8
Maine	30	2.7	152	13.9
Maryland	338	8.2	453	10.9
Massachusetts	216	3.7	511	8.9
Michigan	972	10.6	1,132	12.3
Minnesota	81	2.0	410	10.2
Mississippi	302	12.6	231	9.6
Missouri	505	10.4	590	12.2
Montana	38	4.8	121	15.5
Nebraska	47	3.0	145	9.2
Nevada	102	15.5	165	24.8
New Hampshire	12	1.4	130	15.0
New Jersey	398	5.4	524	7.2
New Mexico	124	10.2	208	17.1
New York	1,820	10.3	1,703	9.6
North Carolina	600	10.8	654	11.7
North Dakota	8	1.2	64	9.8

Table 2-2-4. Deaths from Murder and Suicide, by State, 1978 (*Continued*)

	Murder		Suicide	
	Total	Rate per 100,000	Total	Rate per 100,000
Ohio	741	6.9	1,356	12.6
Oklahoma	244	8.5	384	13.5
Oregon	123	5.0	381	15.5
Pennsylvania	725	6.2	1,398	11.9
Puerto Rico	484	14.4	NA	
Rhode Island	37	4.0	107	11.5
South Carolina	336	11.5	327	11.3
South Dakota	13	1.9	81	11.7
Tennessee	411	9.4	392	10.5
Texas	1,853	14.2	1,660	12.7
Utah	49	3.7	169	12.8
Vermont	16	3.3	72	14.8
Virginia	452	8.8	731	14.1
Washington	175	4.6	537	14.2
West Virginia	127	6.8	261	14.0
Wisconsin	118	2.5	583	12.4
Wyoming	30	7.1	75	17.6
Total	19,555	9.0	27,294	12.5

NA = Not available

Source: FBI Uniform Crime Reports 1978, pp. 46–57, 83; Monthly Vital Statistics Report, vol. 29, No. 6, supp. (2), 1978, p. 39.

Table 2-2-5. Murder and Nonnegligent Manslaughter by Race and Sex of Offender and Victim, 1978

			Offender				
			White		Black		
			M	F	M	F	Total
Victim	White	M	3211	594	397	29	4231
		F	1343	97	139	3	1582
	Black	M	158	20	3352	1090	4620
		F	15	5	1000	156	1176
	Total		4727	716	4888	1278	11,609

Source: FBI Uniform Crime Reports 1978, p. 10.

Table 2-2-6. Murder and Nonnegligent Manslaughter Known to Police, by Type of Weapon Used, 1964–79

				Type of weapon used (in percent)			
	Gun[a]	Cutting or stabbing	Blunt object (club, hammer, etc.)	Personal weapons (hands, fists, feet, etc.)	Other	Unknown or not stated	Total[b]
1964	55	24	5	10	3	2	100
1965	57	23	6	10	3	1	100
1966	59	22	5	9	2	1	100
1967	63	20	5	9	2	1	100
1968	65	18	6	8	2	1	100
1969	65	19	4	8	3	1	100
1970	66	18	4	8	3	1	100
1971	66	19	4	8	2	1	100
1972	66	19	4	8	2	1	100
1973	66	17	5	8	1	2	100
1974	68	18	5	8	1	1	100
1975	66	18	5	9	2	2	100
1976	64	18	5	6	4	3	100
1977	63	19	5	6	5	3	100
1978	64	19	5	6	4	3	100
1979	63	19	5	6	4	3	100

[a] In 1978, 77% of the guns used were handguns, 13% shotguns, and 10% rifles.
[b] Because of rounding, percentages may not add to total.

Source: FBI Uniform Crime Reports 1964, p. 104; 1965, p. 106; 1966, p. 107; 1967, p. 112; 1968, p. 108; 1969, p. 106; 1970, p. 118; 1971, p. 114; 1972, p. 118; 1973, p. 8; 1974, p. 18; 1975, p. 18; 1976, p. 10; 1977, p. 10; 1978, p. 13 (with corrections for earlier years); 1979, p. 11.

Table 2-2-7. Murder and Nonnegligent Manslaughter by Type of Crime, 1966–78

	Total murder and nonnegligent manslaughter[a]	Percent known felony-type	Percent suspected felony-type
1978	18,714	16.7	5.6
1977	18,033	16.7	5.9
1976	16,605	17.7	7.0
1975	20,510	23.0	9.4
1974	20,710	22.2	5.6
1973	19,640	21.6	7.4
1972	18,670	22.1	5.3
1971	17,780	20.4	7.1
1970	16,000	20.4	8.4
1969	14,640	19.3	7.2
1968	13,690	17.4	7.5
1967	12,130	15.6	5.9
1966	10,950	14.8	7.0

[a] The totals for 1976–78 in this column are significantly less than the totals reported elsewhere in Uniform Crime Reports for these years.

Source: FBI Uniform Crime Reports 1972, p. 9, for 1966–69; 1975, p. 19, for 1970–75; 1978, p. 13, for 1976–78.

Table 2-2-8. Sex and Race of Arrestees for Murder and Nonnegligent Manslaughter, Biennially, 1968–78

	Sex		Race		
	Male	Female	White	Black	Other
1978	16,103	2652	8703	9243	752
1976	12,011	2102	5792	6886	197
1974	12,616	2202	4897	7122	445
1972	12,727	2322	5145	8347	314
1970	10,857	1979	4503	7097	336
1968	8,722	1672	3536	5699	223

Note: Totals for sex and for race do not agree because the number of reporting jurisdictions for each factor differ.

Source: FBI Uniform Crime Reports 1968, pp. 118, 120–22; 1970, pp. 124, 131–33; 1972, pp. 130, 131–33; 1974, pp. 189, 191–93; 1976, pp. 184, 185; 1978, pp. 197, 198.

Table 2-2-9. Age of Arrestees for Murder and Nonnegligent Manslaughter, Biennially, 1970–78

Age	1978	1976	1974	1972	1970
12 & under	46	42	41	45	43
13 to 14	198	148	165	176	144
15 to 16	821	613	659	732	669
17 to 18	1,601	1,191	1,228	1,374	1,167
19 to 20	1,853	1,410	1,451	1,382	1,217
21 to 22	1,858	1,338	1,367	1,545	1,226
23 to 24	1,759	1,261	1,314	1,324	1,109
25 to 29	3,445	2,652	2,556	2,550	2,031
30 to 34	2,237	1,648	1,553	1,804	1,368
35 to 39	1,575	1,123	1,061	1,197	1,081
40 to 44	1,095	761	760	953	898
45 to 49	786	652	610	698	677
50 to 54	602	455	413	496	471
55 to 59	360	339	236	294	326
60 to 64	224	199	181	191	179
65 and over	285	263	214	278	224
Total	18,755	14,113	13,818	15,049	12,836

Source: FBI Uniform Crime Reports 1970, pp. 126–27; 1972, pp. 126–27; 1974, pp. 186–87; 1976, pp. 181–82; 1978, pp. 194–95.

Table 2-2-10. Age of Murder Victims, by Sex and Race, 1979

	Number	Percent	Sex		Race					
			Male	Female	White	Negro	Indian	Chinese	Japanese	All others
Total	20,591	100.0ª	15,777	4,814	11,154	8,934	140	43	23	297
Percent			77.6	23.4	54.2	43.4	.7	.2	.1	1.4
Infant (under 1)	163	.8	94	69	87	70	1	1	—	4
1 to 4	336	1.6	171	165	194	130	2	3	2	5
5 to 9	178	.9	103	75	109	61	2	—	—	6
10 to 14	203	1.0	121	82	124	77	1	—	—	1
15 to 19	1,866	9.1	1,387	479	1,098	728	17	1	3	19
20 to 24	3,465	16.8	2,665	800	1,842	1,545	22	7	4	45
25 to 29	3,337	16.2	2,645	692	1,645	1,620	21	4	3	44
30 to 34	2,525	12.3	2,063	462	1,253	1,217	16	8	1	30
35 to 39	1,824	8.9	1,453	371	925	857	9	3	3	27
40 to 44	1,404	6.8	1,115	289	740	631	16	2	1	14
45 to 49	1,232	6.0	956	276	699	505	12	4		12
50 to 54	1,044	5.1	844	200	578	442	7	2	2	13
55 to 59	805	3.9	654	151	453	333	5	2	3	9
60 to 64	603	2.9	453	150	364	229	3	2	1	4
65 to 69	470	2.3	331	139	308	154	1	2	—	5
70 to 74	316	1.5	194	122	221	85	1	2	—	7
75 and over	443	2.2	225	218	322	119	—	—	—	2
Unknown	377	1.8	303	74	192	131	4	—	—	50

ª Because of rounding, percentages may not add to total.

Source: FBI Uniform Crime Reports 1979, p. 10.

54

Table 2-2-11. Victims of Criminal Homicide, by Race and Sex, 1964–78

| | Race of victim (in percent) | | | Sex of victim (in percent) | | | |
	White	Black	All others (including race unknown)	Male	Female	Total[a]	Total number of murders
1964	45	54	1	74	26	100	7,990
1965	45	54	1	74	26	100	8,773
1966	45	54	1	74	26	100	9,552
1967	45	54	1	75	25	100	11,114
1968	45	54	1	78	22	100	12,503
1969	44	55	2	78	22	100	13,575
1970	44	55	1	78	22	100	13,649
1971	44	55	2	79	21	100	16,183
1972	45	53	2	78	22	100	15,832
1973	47	52	1	77	23	100	17,123
1974	48	50	2	78	23	100	18,632
1975	51	47	2	76	24	100	18,642
1976	51	47	2	76	24	100	16,605
1977	54	46	2	75	25	100	17,646
1978	55	45	2	76	24	100	18,312
1979	54	43	2	78	23	100	20,591

[a] Because of rounding, percentages may not add to total.

Source: FBI Uniform Crime Reports 1964, p. 104; 1965, p. 106; 1966, p. 107; 1967, p. 112; 1968, p. 108; 1969, p. 106; 1970, p. 118; 1971, p. 114; 1972, p. 118; 1973, p. 8; 1974, p. 17; 1975, p. 17; 1976, p. 11; 1977, p. 12; 1978, p. 9; 1979, p. 10.

Table 2-2-12. Disposition of Persons Identified in the Killing of Law Enforcement Officers, 1968–77

	Total	Percent distribution
Known persons	1536	100
Fugitives	16	1
Justifiably killed	196	13
Committed suicide	44	3
Arrested and charged	1280	83
Arrested and charged	1280	100
Guilty of murder	802	63
Guilty of lesser offense related to murder	102	8
Guilty of crime other than murder	105	8
Acquitted or otherwise dismissed	160	13
Committed to mental institution	41	3
Case pending	56	4
Died in custody	14	1

Source: FBI Uniform Crime Reports 1979, p. 313.

§3. The Death Sentence and Executions

Table 2-3-1. Prisoners Executed Under Civil Authority in the United States—Regions and States: 1930-80

	Total	1980	1979	1978	1977	1976	1975	1970–1974	1965–1969	1960–1964	1955–1959	1950–1954	1945–1949	1940–1944	1935–1939	1930–1934
Total	3862	—	2	—	1	—	—	—	10	181	304	413	639	645	891	776
Federal	33	—	—	—	—	—	—	—	—	1	3	6	6	7	9	1
State	3829	—	2	—	1	—	—	—	10	180	301	407	633	638	882	775
Northeast	608	—	—	—	—	—	—	—	—	17	51	56	74	110	145	155
Maine	—	—	—	—	—	—	—	—	—	—	—	—	—	—	—	—
New Hampshire	1	—	—	—	—	—	—	—	—	—	—	—	—	—	1	—
Vermont	4	—	—	—	—	—	—	—	—	—	—	2	1	—	—	1
Massachusetts	27	—	—	—	—	—	—	—	—	—	—	—	3	6	11	7
Rhode Island	—	—	—	—	—	—	—	—	—	—	—	—	—	—	—	—
Connecticut	21	—	—	—	—	—	—	—	—	1	5	—	5	5	3	2
New York	329	—	—	—	—	—	—	—	—	10	25	27	36	78	73	80
New Jersey	74	—	—	—	—	—	—	—	—	3	9	8	8	6	16	24
Pennsylvania	152	—	—	—	—	—	—	—	—	3	12	19	21	15	41	41
North Central	403	—	—	—	—	—	—	—	5	16	16	42	64	42	113	105
Ohio	172	—	—	—	—	—	—	—	—	7	12	20	36	15	39	43
Indiana	41	—	—	—	—	—	—	—	—	1	—	2	5	2	20	11
Illinois	90	—	—	—	—	—	—	—	—	2	1	8	5	13	27	34
Michigan	—	—	—	—	—	—	—	—	—	—	—	—	—	—	—	—
Wisconsin	—	—	—	—	—	—	—	—	—	—	—	—	—	—	—	—
Minnesota	—	—	—	—	—	—	—	—	—	—	—	—	—	—	—	—
Iowa	18	—	—	—	—	—	—	—	—	2	—	1	4	3	7	1
Missouri	62	—	—	—	—	—	—	—	1	3	2	5	9	6	20	16
North Dakota	—	—	—	—	—	—	—	—	—	—	—	—	—	—	—	—
South Dakota	1	—	—	—	—	—	—	—	—	—	—	—	1	—	—	—
Nebraska	4	—	—	—	—	—	—	—	—	1	—	1	2	—	—	—
Kansas	15	—	—	—	—	—	—	—	4	—	1	5	2	3	—	—

	Total								
South	2307	1	2	102	183	244	419	413	524	419
Delaware	12	—	—	—	—	—	2	2	6	2
Maryland	68	—	—	1	4	2	19	26	10	6
District of Columbia	40	—	—	—	1	3	13	3	5	15
Virginia	92	—	—	6	8	15	22	13	20	8
West Virginia	40	—	—	—	4	5	9	2	10	10
North Carolina	263	—	—	1	5	14	62	50	80	51
South Carolina	162	—	—	8	10	16	29	32	30	37
Georgia	366	—	—	14	34	51	72	58	73	64
Florida	171	—	1	12	27	22	27	38	29	15
Kentucky	103	—	—	1	8	8	15	19	34	18
Tennessee	93	—	—	1	7	1	18	19	31	16
Alabama	135	—	1	4	6	14	21	29	41	19
Mississippi	154	—	—	10	21	15	26	34	22	26
Arkansas	118	—	—	9	7	11	18	20	33	20
Louisiana	133	—	—	1	13	14	23	24	19	39
Oklahoma	60	1	—	5	3	4	7	6	9	25
Texas	297	—	—	29	25	49	36	38	72	48
West	511	2	2	45	51	66	76	73	100	96
Montana	6	—	—	—	—	—	—	1	4	1
Idaho	3	—	—	—	1	2	—	—	—	—
Wyoming	7	—	—	1	—	—	—	2	1	3
Colorado	47	1	—	5	2	1	7	6	9	16
New Mexico	8	—	—	1	1	2	2	—	—	2
Arizona	38	—	—	4	6	2	3	6	10	7
Utah	14	—	1	1	4	2	1	3	2	—
Nevada	30	—	1	2	—	9	5	5	3	5
Washington	47	—	—	2	2	4	7	9	13	10
Oregon	19	—	—	—	—	5	6	6	1	1
California	292	1	—	29	35	39	45	35	57	51
Alaska[a]	—	—	—	—	—	—	—	—	—	—
Hawaii[a]	—	—	—	—	—	—	—	—	—	—

[a] As states, Alaska and Hawaii are included beginning 1 January 1960.

Source: National Prisoner Statistics, Capital Punishment 1979, p. 17.

Table 2-3-2. Prisoners Executed Under Civil Authority, by Race and Offense: 1930–80

	All races						White					
	All offenses	Murder	Rape	Armed robbery	Kidnaping	Other[a]	All offenses	Murder	Rape	Armed robbery	Kidnaping	Other
Total	3862	3337	455	25	20	25	1754	1667	48	6	20	13
Federal	33	15	2	2	6	8	28	10	2	2	6	8
State	3829	3322	453	23	14	17	1726	1657	46	4	14	5
Northeast	602	606	—	—	2	—	424	422	—	—	2	—
Maine	—	—	—	—	—	—	—	—	—	—	—	—
New Hampshire	1	1	—	—	—	—	1	1	—	—	—	—
Vermont	4	4	—	—	—	—	4	4	—	—	—	—
Massachusetts	27	27	—	—	—	—	25	25	—	—	—	—
Rhode Island	—	—	—	—	—	—	—	—	—	—	—	—
Connecticut	21	21	—	—	—	—	18	18	—	—	—	—
New York	329	327	—	—	2	—	234	232	—	—	2	—
New Jersey	74	74	—	—	—	—	47	47	—	—	—	—
Pennsylvania	152	152	—	—	—	—	95	95	—	—	—	—
North Central	403	393	10	—	—	—	257	254	3	—	—	—
Ohio	172	172	—	—	—	—	104	104	—	—	—	—
Indiana	41	41	—	—	—	—	31	31	—	—	—	—
Illinois	90	90	—	—	—	—	59	59	—	—	—	—
Michigan	—	—	—	—	—	—	—	—	—	—	—	—
Wisconsin	—	—	—	—	—	—	—	—	—	—	—	—
Minnesota	—	—	—	—	—	—	—	—	—	—	—	—
Iowa	18	18	—	—	—	—	18	18	—	—	—	—
Missouri	62	52	10	—	—	—	29	26	3	—	—	—
North Dakota	—	—	—	—	—	—	—	—	—	—	—	—
South Dakota	1	1	—	—	—	—	1	1	—	—	—	—
Nebraksa	4	4	—	—	—	—	3	3	—	—	—	—
Kansas	15	15	—	—	—	—	12	12	—	—	—	—

| | Black | | | | | | All other races | | | | | |
	All offenses	Murder	Rape	Armed robbery	Kidnaping	Other	All offenses	Murder	Rape	Armed robbery	Kidnaping	Other
Total	2066	1630	405	19	—	12	42	40	2	—	—	—
Federal	3	3	—	—	—	—	2	2	—	—	—	—
State	2063	1627	405	19	—	12	40	38	2	—	—	—
Northeast	177	177	—	—	—	—	7	7	—	—	—	—
Maine	—	—	—	—	—	—	—	—	—	—	—	—
New Hampshire	—	—	—	—	—	—	—	—	—	—	—	—
Vermont	—	—	—	—	—	—	—	—	—	—	—	—
Massachusetts	2	2	—	—	—	—	—	—	—	—	—	—
Rhode Island	—	—	—	—	—	—	—	—	—	—	—	—
Connecticut	3	3	—	—	—	—	—	—	—	—	—	—
New York	90	90	—	—	—	—	5	5	—	—	—	—
New Jersey	25	25	—	—	—	—	2	2	—	—	—	—
Pennsylvania	57	57	—	—	—	—	—	—	—	—	—	—
North Central	144	137	7	—	—	—	2	2	—	—	—	—
Ohio	67	67	—	—	—	—	1	1	—	—	—	—
Indiana	10	10	—	—	—	—	—	—	—	—	—	—
Illinois	31	31	—	—	—	—	—	—	—	—	—	—
Michigan	—	—	—	—	—	—	—	—	—	—	—	—
Wisconsin	—	—	—	—	—	—	—	—	—	—	—	—
Minnesota	—	—	—	—	—	—	—	—	—	—	—	—
Iowa	—	—	—	—	—	—	—	—	—	—	—	—
Missouri	33	26	7	—	—	—	—	—	—	—	—	—
North Dakota	—	—	—	—	—	—	—	—	—	—	—	—
South Dakota	—	—	—	—	—	—	—	—	—	—	—	—
Nebraska	—	—	—	—	—	—	1	1	—	—	—	—
Kansas	3	3	—	—	—	—	—	—	—	—	—	—

Table 2-3-2. Prisoners Executed Under Civil Authority,
by Race and Offense: 1930–80 (*Continued*)

	All races						White					
	All offenses	Murder	Rape	Armed robbery	Kidnaping	Other[a]	All offenses	Murder	Rape	Armed robbery	Kidnaping	Other
South	2307	1825	443	23	5	11	638	586	43	4	5	—
Delaware	12	8	4	—	—	—	5	4	1	—	—	—
Maryland	68	44	24	—	—	—	13	7	6	—	—	—
District of Columbia	40	37	3	—	—	—	3	3	—	—	—	—
Virginia	92	71	21	—	—	—	17	17	—	—	—	—
West Virginia	40	36	1	—	3	—	31	28	—	—	3	—
North Carolina	263	207	47	—	—	9	59	55	4	—	—	—
South Carolina	162	120	42	—	—	—	35	30	5	—	—	—
Georgia	366	299	61	6	—	—	68	65	3	—	—	—
Florida	171	134	36	—	1	—	58	56	1	—	1	—
Kentucky	103	88	10	5	—	—	51	47	1	3	—	—
Tennessee	93	66	27	—	—	—	27	22	5	—	—	—
Alabama	135	106	22	5	—	2	28	26	2	—	—	—
Mississippi	154	130	21	3	—	—	30	30	—	—	—	—
Arkansas	118	99	19	—	—	—	27	25	2	—	—	—
Louisiana	133	116	17	—	—	—	30	30	—	—	—	—
Oklahoma	60	54	4	1	1	—	42	40	—	1	1	—
Texas	297	210	84	3	—	—	114	101	13	—	—	—
West	511	498	—	—	7	6	407	395	—	—	7	5
Montana	6	6	—	—	—	—	4	4	—	—	—	—
Idaho	3	3	—	—	—	—	3	3	—	—	—	—
Wyoming	7	7	—	—	—	—	6	6	—	—	—	—
Colorado	47	47	—	—	—	—	41	41	—	—	—	—
New Mexico	8	8	—	—	—	—	6	6	—	—	—	—
Arizona	38	38	—	—	—	—	28	28	—	—	—	—
Utah	14	14	—	—	—	—	14	14	—	—	—	—
Nevada	30	30	—	—	—	—	28	28	—	—	—	—
Washington	47	46	—	—	1	—	40	39	—	—	1	—
Oregon	19	19	—	—	—	—	16	16	—	—	—	—
California	292	280	—	—	6	6	221	210	—	—	6	5
Alaska[b]	—	—	—	—	—	—	—	—	—	—	—	—
Hawaii[b]	—	—	—	—	—	—	—	—	—	—	—	—

[a] In this category, the 8 Federal executions were for sabotage (6) and espionage (2). The 9 executions in North Carolina and the 2 in Alabama were for burglary. In California, the 6 executions were for aggravated assault committed by prisoners under life sentence.

[b] As states, Alaska and Hawaii are included beginning 1 January 1980.

Source: National Prisoner Statistics, Capital Punishment 1979, p. 18.

	Black						All other races					
	All offenses	Murder	Rape	Armed robbery	Kidnaping	Other	All offenses	Murder	Rape	Armed robbery	Kidnaping	Other
South	1659	1231	398	19	—	11	10	8	2	—	—	—
Delaware	7	4	3	—	—	—	—	—	—	—	—	—
Maryland	55	37	18	—	—	—	—	—	—	—	—	—
District of Columbia	37	34	3	—	—	—	—	—	—	—	—	—
Virginia	75	54	21	—	—	—	—	—	—	—	—	—
West Virginia	9	8	1	—	—	—	—	—	—	—	—	—
North Carolina	199	149	41	—	—	9	5	3	2	—	—	—
South Carolina	127	90	37	—	—	—	—	—	—	—	—	—
Georgia	298	234	58	6	—	—	—	—	—	—	—	—
Florida	113	78	35	—	—	—	—	—	—	—	—	—
Kentucky	52	41	9	2	—	—	—	—	—	—	—	—
Tennessee	66	44	22	—	—	—	—	—	—	—	—	—
Alabama	107	80	20	5	—	2	—	—	—	—	—	—
Mississippi	124	100	21	3	—	—	—	—	—	—	—	—
Arkansas	90	73	17	—	—	—	1	1	—	—	—	—
Louisiana	103	86	17	—	—	—	—	—	—	—	—	—
Oklahoma	15	11	4	—	—	—	3	3	—	—	—	—
Texas	182	108	71	3	—	—	1	1	—	—	—	—
West	83	82	—	—	—	1	21	21	—	—	—	—
Montana	2	2	—	—	—	—	—	—	—	—	—	—
Idaho	—	—	—	—	—	—	—	—	—	—	—	—
Wyoming	1	1	—	—	—	—	—	—	—	—	—	—
Colorado	5	5	—	—	—	—	1	1	—	—	—	—
New Mexico	2	2	—	—	—	—	—	—	—	—	—	—
Arizona	10	10	—	—	—	—	—	—	—	—	—	—
Utah	—	—	—	—	—	—	—	—	—	—	—	—
Nevada	2	2	—	—	—	—	—	—	—	—	—	—
Washington	5	5	—	—	—	—	2	2	—	—	—	—
Oregon	3	3	—	—	—	—	—	—	—	—	—	—
California	53	52	—	—	—	1	18	18	—	—	—	—
Alaska[b]	—	—	—	—	—	—	—	—	—	—	—	—
Hawaii[b]	—	—	—	—	—	—	—	—	—	—	—	—

Table 2-3-3. Women Executed Under Civil Authority in the United States, by Year, Offense, Race and State: 1930–80

	Total	Offense		Race		State in which executed
		Murder	Other[a]	White	Black	
All years	32	30	2	20	12	
1962	1	1	—	1	—	California
1957	1	1	—	1	—	Alabama
1955	1	1	—	1	—	California
1954	2	2	—	1	1	Ohio
1953	3	1	2	3	—	Alabama, Federal (Missouri and New York)
1951	1	1	—	1	—	New York
1947	2	2	—	1	1	California, South Carolina
1946	1	1	—	—	1	Pennsylvania
1945	1	1	—	—	1	Georgia
1944	3	3	—	—	3	Mississippi, New York, North Carolina
1943	3	3	—	1	2	South Carolina, Mississippi, North Carolina
1942	1	1	—	1	—	Louisiana
1941	1	1	—	1	—	California
1938	2	2	—	2	—	Illinois, Ohio
1937	1	1	—	—	1	Mississippi
1936	1	1	—	1	—	New York
1935	3	3	—	2	1	Delaware
1934	1	1	—	1	—	New York
1931	1	1	—	1	—	Pennsylvania
1930	2	2	—	1	1	Arizona, Alabama

Note: There have been no executions of women since 1962.

[a] Includes one kidnaping and one espionage case (both Federal).

Source: National Prisoner Statistics, Capital Punishment 1979, p. 19.

Table 2-3-4. Prisoners on Death Row by Year, Race, and Sex, 1968–80

	Received under death sentence			Number of sentencing jurisdictions during year	Number of jurisdictions with death row prisoners at year end	Total under death sentence at year end		
	Total	White	Non-white			White	Non-white	Total[a]
1968	138	69	69	25	36	243	274	517
1969	143	66	77	24	33	263	310	575
1970	133	66	67	26	32	293	338	631
1971	113	54	59	24	33	306	336	642
1972	83	32	51	19	28	167	167	334
1973	42	15	27	7	19	64	70	134
1974	165	77	88	18	23	109	133	242
1975	320	143	177	27	30	215	269	484
1976	249	141	103	30	24	222	194	416(7)
1977	150	69	64	20	24	222	188	410(4)
1978	183	109	74	23	25	261	184	445(5)
1979	159	98	61	25	25	344	223	567(7)
1980	187	NI	NI	25	33	390	328	718(9)

[a] Figures in parentheses indicate number of females included in total.
NI = No information available.

Sources: For 1968 through 1975, National Prisoner Statistics, Capital Punishment 1977, pp. 18, 22; for 1976, *ibid.,* 1976, pp. 20–21; for 1977 and 1978, *ibid.,* 1978, pp. 25, 28; for 1979, *ibid.,* 1979, p. 20; for 1980, Bureau of Justice Statistics Bulletin, Capital Punishment 1980, p. 2, and NAACP Legal Defense and Educational Fund, "Death Row U.S.A.," release of 20 December 1980, by permission of the NAACP Legal Defense Fund, Inc.

Table 2-3-5. Prisoners Under Sentence of Death, by Jurisdiction, Race and Sex, 1980

	Total[a]	Black	Native American	Hispanic	White	Asian	Unknown
Alabama	30	19	—	—	11	—	—
Arizona	32	3	—	3	26	—	—
Arkansas	14	6	—	1	7	—	—
California	44	14	2	6	20	2	—
Delaware	3	1	—	—	2	—	—
Florida	150(1)	55	—	3	91 [b](1)	—	1
Georgia	91(3)	48(2)	—	—	43 (1)	—	—
Idaho	1	—	—	—	1	—	—
Illinois	31	17	—	4	10	—	—
Indiana	5	3	—	—	2	—	—
Kentucky	5(1)	—	—	—	5 (1)	—	—
Louisiana	21	10	—	—	11	—	—
Maryland	1	1	—	—	—	—	—
Mississippi	13	9	—	—	4	—	—
Missouri	8	5	—	—	3	—	—
Montana	3	1	—	—	2	—	—
Nebraska	10	2	—	—	8	—	—
Nevada	10	1	—	—	9	—	—
New Mexico	1	—	—	—	1	—	—
N. Carolina	14(1)	6	—	—	8 (1)	—	—
Oklahoma	30(1)	6	—	—	24 (1)	—	—
Oregon	3	—	—	—	3	—	—
Pennsylvania	10	6	—	—	4	—	—
S. Carolina	13	6	—	—	7	—	—
Tennessee	14	5	1	—	8	—	—
Texas	137(2)	54	—	15	68 (2)	—	—
Utah	4	2	—	—	2	—	—
Virginia	13	9	—	—	4	—	—
Washington	5	—	—	—	5	—	—
Wyoming	1	—	—	—	1	—	—
U.S. Military	1	1	—	—	—	—	—
Total	718(9)	290(2)	3	32	390(7)	2	1

[a] Figures in parentheses indicate number of females included in total.
[b] Includes one male convicted of sexual battery.

Source: NAACP Legal Defense and Educational Fund, Inc., "Death Row U.S.A.," release of 20 December 1980. By permission of the NAACP Legal Defense Fund, Inc.

3

American Attitudes
Toward the Death Penalty

INTRODUCTION

Since the late 1960s, according to every available measure, the American public has professed support for capital punishment by a majority of more than
two to one. This is a return to the degree of support that prevailed a half
century ago during the Great Depression, an era typified by the wild forays
of the Ma Barker Gang in the Midwest and the ruthless "contract" slayings
carried out in New York by Murder, Inc. This level of support contrasts
sharply with the mid-1960s, the high point of abolition sentiment, when the
pros and cons were about equally divided.[1] Such a remarkable shift in public
attitude poses several different problems, some for social scientists and edu-
cators, and others for those in government: What explains public attitudes
toward the death penalty? What attitudinal and demographic factors corre-
late with support for (or opposition to) the death penalty? How stable are
attitudes for or against execution (under what conditions will they shift, by
how much and how quickly)? How much does the public really know about
capital punishment? Is the public opinion that favors (or opposes) the death
penalty adequately informed opinion? How should democratically elected
legislatures and governors regard the evidence of public support for (or
opposition to) the death penalty in their deliberations over statutory changes
in the laws affecting execution, or in the exercise of executive clemency?

1. The American Institute of Public Opinion reported in July 1966 that to the question "Are you
   in favor of the death penalty for persons convicted of murder?" the sample surveyed
   responded as follows: For—42 percent; Against—47 percent; No opinion—11 percent. See
   Erskine 1970:291. In March 1981, the latest Gallup Poll reported that "66 percent favor the
   death penalty for persons convicted of murder . . . 53 percent of the public [oppose] the death
   penalty for rape, 49 percent for treason and 68 percent for airplane hijacking." *Boston Sunday
   Globe,* 1 March 1981, p. 13.

Should appellate courts, staffed by judges appointed for life, take public opinion into account when they interpret the constitution—especially the prohibition against "cruel and unusual punishment"? These and other questions are discussed below in §1, where all the available survey research through 1972 is reviewed. The authors, social psychologists Phoebe C. Ellsworth (Yale University) and Neil Vidmar (University of Western Ontario), write out of the experience of undertaking their own research on public attitudes toward the death penalty.[2]

Several developments in the years since Vidmar and Ellsworth published their report call for comment. According to the Harris Survey of February 1977, public attitudes professing support for mandatory death penalties have increased significantly over what they were in 1973, despite the Supreme Court's ruling in 1976 against mandatory capital penalties for murder, in *Woodson* v. *North Carolina* (see below, Chapter Six). This is not the only instance where the public has seemed to support capital punishment under conditions rejected on constitutional grounds by the Supreme Court, as a recent study in Boston showed. Whereas the offender's race by itself should not (and in this research, did not seem to) have any significant impact on the choice of sentence (prison versus death) for murder, as soon as the factor of nonwhite race was joined with a factor of mental deficiency and abnormality to produce the "subnormal black defendant," the combination of these factors (which should have been as irrelevant as race by itself) did significantly influence the respondents to favor the harsher penalty (Hamilton & Rotkin 1979). Second, the so-called "Marshall hypothesis" has been tested and confirmed. Justice Thurgood Marshall, writing in *Furman,* argued that the public that supports the death penalty is relatively uninformed about the effects and circumstances of this penalty as it is actually used in our society. Marshall also claimed that as this ignorance is remedied, attitudes favoring the death penalty will weaken and change, so that only persons of a strongly retributivist outlook will continue to support capital punishment. Both parts of this hypothesis seem to be true (Sarat & Vidmar 1976; Chandler & Andrus 1979).[3]

From these results, as well as from other evidence, researchers have been able to show that the attitudes of some persons favoring (or opposing) the death penalty are fairly deeply embedded in their values, convictions, and "personality structure." Are these attitudes rational or not? Opponents of the

2. See Vidmar 1974; Sarat & Vidmar 1976; Ellsworth & Ross 1976; Ellsworth & Ross 1980; Vidmar & Dittenhoffer 1981. See also the discussion of Ellsworth's research in *Psychology Today,* January 1979, p. 13.

3. Ellsworth & Ross (1980) argue that even those who strongly favor a mandatory death penalty turn out to be reluctant to impose a death sentence, and hence a guilty verdict, in particular (hypothetical) cases. They conclude that "People's willingness to endorse a mandatory death penalty in the abstract is no indication of their willingness to put such a policy into practice" (p. 23).

death penalty have tried on occasion to show that the staunch defenders of executions display a psychological profile of the "authoritarian personality"—conservative, dogmatic, law-and-order fanatics. Ellsworth and Vidmar are not persuaded (see below §1), and subsequent research tends to justify their caution. Data from a Virginia sample of several thousand respondents indicate that "the public is willing to impose the death penalty because they believe that it is morally just and that it serves a useful purpose." The attitude of sheer "retributiveness" by itself explains very little in the public's support of the extreme sanction (C. Thomas 1977:1023f; cf. C. Thomas & Foster 1975 and C. Thomas & Mason 1980). Another recent analysis explains the currently high level of public approval for the death penalty as a rational response to the widespread reports of "relatively large increases in the official crime rate" that became part of the national consciousness beginning with the 1968 elections, when "law and order" and "crime in the streets" became important political issues (Rankin 1979:207; also T. Smith 1975).[4]

In §2 below, eleven tables report recent survey research data from national samples on a variety of topics involving the death penalty. Table 3-2-1, published by the National Opinion Research Center (NORC), breaks down national public opinion on the death penalty by reference to nine variables, including sex, race, and age.[5] Table 3-2-2, published by the Gallup organization, covers much the same ground as does the NORC survey; the results of the two surveys also largely coincide and so tend to confirm each other. All but one of the remaining nine tables are from Harris Surveys. They explore attitudes toward mandatory capital punishment (Table 3-2-3), the type of crime for which the death penalty might be imposed (Table 3-2-4), and the role of deterrence and other reasons in support of the death penalty (Tables 3-2-6 through 3-2-9). The two concluding tables touch on special topics. After the Supreme Court in 1976 ratified the death penalty statutes of Florida, Georgia, and Texas, proposals were aired in various state legislatures to permit public viewing of executions on television (recall Chapter One). The Harris Survey of January 1977 (Table 3-2-10) reported that the public overwhelmingly rejected this idea. At the same time, public controversy over the execution of Gilmore in Utah included heated discussion of whether a capital offender had the "right" to be executed (see Bedau 1977a:121–25) and whether a convicted murderer should be allowed to "choose" a life or a

4. Ellsworth & Ross (1980:27–28, 40) also confirm the high levels of public ignorance of even the most general facts about the death penalty. They did not test, however, whether new "information" can change significant numbers of retentionists into abolitionists, or vice versa. Most of their respondents alleged that their convictions were impervious to such new "information." This would be consistent with the findings reported earlier by Lord et al. 1979.

5. NORC reports the following data from its most recent surveys in answer to the question surveyed in Table 3-2-1: (1978) Favor the death penalty—66%; Oppose—28%; Don't know— 6%. (1980) Favor the death penalty—67%; Oppose—27%; don't know—6%. (Personal communication from NORC to the author.)

death sentence. The Harris Survey (Table 3-2-11) showed that the public opposed this option, too.

One question that has proved more difficult to answer than all others is *what* the present high levels of public support for the death penalty really support. Is it only the *legal threat* of the death penalty, coupled with the judicial ritual of trying, convicting, and occasionally sentencing a murderer to death, rather than *actual executions?*[6] There seems little doubt that the public is in favor of having the death penalty "on the books," given the unbroken record during the past decade of public referenda enacting death penalties: Illinois (1970), California (1972), Washington (1975), and Oregon (1978). Each of these referenda carried by a wide margin; the one in Oregon reversed an earlier referendum (1964) abolishing the death penalty (see Bedau 1980c). Yet since 1967 *over two thousand* death sentences have been vacated on constitutional grounds alone! There has been a surprising absence of public clamor over the failure to execute these death sentences, just as in earlier years there was little or no evidence of widespread satisfaction when a death sentence, with or without delay, was finally carried out. One might hazard the hypothesis that the average person seems convinced the death penalty is an important legal threat, abstractly desirable as part of society's permanent bulwark against crime, but that he or she is relatively indifferent to whether a given convict is executed on a given date as scheduled, or is indeed ever executed. To put it another way, there is no evidence that the two-to-one majority in favor of the death penalty for murder is also a two-to-one majority in favor of executing right now the hundreds of persons currently under death sentence. Thus the significance of the data reported in §2 below remains in some doubt.

§1.   Research on Attitudes Toward Capital Punishment*

NEIL VIDMAR and PHOEBE C. ELLSWORTH

Our literature review is divided into seven substantive areas: 1. general levels of support for the death penalty, 2. the types of crime and circumstances for

6. Ellsworth & Ross (1980) report that two thirds of their respondents would support the death penalty even if it were proven to be no better a deterrent than life imprisonment, and half professed they would support it even if it caused as many murders as it prevented!

*Excerpted from Neil Vidmar and Phoebe Ellsworth, "Public Opinion and the Death Penalty," *Stanford Law Review*, 26 (June 1974), pp. 1245–70, where this material was first published. Footnotes have been renumbered and cross-references adjusted accordingly. Copyright 1974 by the Board of Trusteees of the Leland Stanford Junior University.

which the death penalty is favored, 3. levels of support among various sub-populations, 4. reasons for favoring capital punishment, 5. social-psychological and other attitudinal correlates of death penalty attitudes, 6. knowledge and attitudes about capital punishment, and 7. various levels of attitudes toward the death penalty.

1. Erskine has listed all of the available nationwide and statewide polls on the death penalty from 1936 to 1969.[1] The overwhelming majority of the polls have asked only general questions about the death penalty for murder. Basically, the data contained in her article indicate that until 1966 public support for the death penalty declined at a fairly consistent rate. According to the Gallup polls, support fell from 62 percent in favor of capital punishment in 1936 to 42 percent in 1966. After 1966, however, the trend reversed and Erskine's review indicates that by 1969 the Gallup poll showed that 51 percent of the American public supported the death penalty. Nationwide polls conducted subsequent to 1969 show that this upward trend in support has continued, with the most recent poll showing 59 percent of the people supporting capital punishment.

Given the constraints imposed by *Furman,* however, the data from these polls are no longer very relevant, if at all relevant, to judicial and legislative decision-making. With the 1973 Harris Poll as an exception, the survey questions dealt only with capital punishment for murder, were broadly phrased, and did not ask about the circumstances under which capital punishment should be imposed.

2. Most of the polls have asked only about the death penalty for murder or measured general sentiment for it. There are, however, some data, mostly very recent, that provide information concerning attitudes about the kinds of persons who should or should not be executed, the specific circumstances under which people should be given the death penalty and, most important, the issue of mandatory capital punishment.

A February 1965 Gallup survey showed that 45 percent of the respondents supported capital punishment for murder, but only 23 percent favored it for persons under 21 years of age.[2] A 1953 Gallup poll indicated that while 68 percent of respondents favored capital punishment, only 65 percent favored it for women.[3] Despite the studies showing rather conclusively that blacks are more likely to receive capital punishment than whites[4] and other studies

---

1. Erskine, *The Polls: Capital Punishment,* 34 Pub. Opinion Q. 290 (1970).
2. Erskine, *supra* note 1, at 297.
3. *Id.* at 298. Snortum & Ashear, *Prejudice, Punitiveness, and Personality,* 36 J. Personality Assessment 291 (1972), also found a tendency toward leniency for females, but their report does not allow us to separate preferences for the death penalty from preferences for prison sentences.
4. See, e.g., Wolfgang & Reidel, *Race, Judicial Discretion, and the Death Penalty,* 407 *The Annals,* May 1973, at 119.

showing that people who favor capital punishment are somewhat more prejudiced, no study in the literature we reviewed has attempted a direct assessment of whether capital punishment is favored more for blacks or other
minority groups than for whites.

One survey asked general questions that give information about the types
of crime for which people feel the death penalty is appropriate. The 1970
Gallup poll asked respondents what the penalty should be for persons convicted of specified crimes.[5] Six percent felt that someone convicted of putting
a bomb in a public building should be executed, 4 percent favored the death
penalty for hijacking an airplane, and 2 percent favored it for someone starting a serious riot. The same poll also showed that 4 percent favored death
for a person who sells heroin, and 2 percent favored it for a person who sells
marijuana. The Gallup survey, however, posed the questions without reference to a mandatory death penalty and without allowing respondents who
chose lesser penalties to indicate whether they would favor the death penalty
only under some circumstances.

In the wake of the *Furman* decision two polls have asked about mandatory
death penalties and about the specific kinds of crime for which respondents
would favor a mandatory death penalty. A May 1973 poll in Minnesota asked
whether the "death penalty should or should not be made automatic" for
four types of crimes. Forty-nine percent favored "automatic" capital punishment for "murder of a law enforcement officer," 59 percent favored it "when
a kidnapper or hijacker kills a person," 58 percent favored it in the case of
"assassination of federal officials," and 39 percent favored it for "crime
against the federal government such as treason, sabotage and espionage."[6]

Although these data tend to show considerable support for mandatory
death sentences, this poll suffers from a shortcoming of polling technique
that belies its reliability; it did not offer the respondents a clear definition of
"automatic" nor did it offer a range of alternative responses sufficient to
gauge their attitudes with any specificity. For example, they were not given
the option of saying that they preferred each case to be decided on its own
merits, considering all of the circumstances before the death penalty is
administered. Had the respondents understood "automatic" to mean that no
exceptions regardless of circumstances were to be made, and had the poll
brought to their attention certain extenuating circumstances, it is possible
that the level of support for the "automatic" death penalty would have been
substantially lower.

5. 3 G. Gallup, The Gallup Poll: Public Opinion 1935–71, at 2246–47 (1972).
6. The Minnesota Poll, Minneapolis, Minn., May 27, 1973. The specific wording of the question
   was, "The death penalty is not permitted for any crime now. Do you think the death penalty
   should or should not be made automatic for the following crimes . . . ?"

This possiblity is reinforced by the June 1973 Harris survey that undertook the most comprehensive survey of public attitudes toward the death penalty that we found in our literature search.[7] The survey found that in response to the question, "Do you believe in capital punishment (the death penalty) or are you opposed to it?" 59 percent of the respondents gave support to capital punishment. However, in another series of questions, respondents were given a list of crimes and asked whether they felt that all persons convicted of the crime should get the death penalty, that no one should get the death penalty, or that it "should depend on the circumstances of the case and the character of the person." [. . .] It is clear that no more than 41 percent of the respondents favored a mandatory death sentence for any single type of the listed crimes. The other respondents were either opposed to capital punishment or felt it should be used in a discretionary way.[8] In contrast to the Minnesota survey, then, the Harris survey might lead to the tentative conclusion that there is not strong support for mandatory capital punishment; the persons opposed to the death penalty and the persons who wanted it administered in a way that depends on the circumstances of the case outnumbered those persons who supported mandatory capital punishment by a sustantial majority.

More detailed research into specific attitudes about capital punishment is needed. In particular we need to know if the public understands what mandatory capital punishment means, whether there is support for it in the context of options that are available under *Furman,* and whether support for the death penalty diminishes as we move from general endorsement to the realities of applying it in specific circumstances. For example, do people understand that a mandatory death statute really means no exceptions are to be made for a certain class of criminals convicted of certain crimes and that all mitigating factors would be automatically ruled invalid in any appeal for leniency? Would they favor a mandatory death penalty under such circumstances? Would they favor the death penalty when faced with the choice of a mandatory death penalty (or some other form of nondiscretionary death

---

7. The Harris Survey, Louis Harris and Associates, Inc., New York, N.Y., June 11 and 14, 1973 (Copyright, The Chicago Tribune, 1973). (Some of the data from the Harris Survey are reported in 1 *Current Opinion,* Aug. 1973, at 80–81. Other data reported in this article were not contained in the public releases and are reported with permission of Louis Harris Associates, Inc.)

8. It is noteworthy that 8% and 9% of the respondents supported mandatory capital punishment for the crimes of mugging and bank robbery respectively. Thus, of those persons who endorsed an automatic death penalty for killing a policeman, murder, skyjacking, or rape, more than one fourth of them indicated they would apply it in circumstances where it clearly must be considered an excessive punishment for the crime committed. One is tempted to ask whether these persons have socio-legal attitudes that are out of step with contemporary values concerning criminal justice, *Id.*

statute) or no death penalty at all? Only when the answers to these questions
are known will we be able to draw reasonable conclusions about support for
post-*Furman* death penalty statutes.

3. The assessment of support for the death penalty in different segments of
the population is important for at least two reasons. First, knowing the characteristics of certain subpopulations may give insight into the dynamics
behind death penalty attitudes and thus yield information bearing on standards of morality. Second, both legislative and judicial decisionmakers sometimes rely on the opinions of groups such as policemen, psychiatrists, or ministers who are presumed to be "expert" or "informed" with regard to
questions about the deterrent efficacy of the death penalty or its morality.

Examination of the polls reported by Erskine, as well as other polls
reviewed in this article, indicates that the demographic correlates of death
penalty attitudes are rather consistent across the polls. Note again, however,
that most of the data are based on attitudes for the crime of murder with no
consideration for post-*Furman* restrictions. Generally, people who support
the death penalty tend to be older, less educated, male, more wealthy, white,
and from urban areas. A greater percentage of white collar workers, manual
laborers, and farmers favor capital punishment than do professionals and
businesspersons. Among Catholics there is more support for the death penalty than among Protestants, and Republicans tend to favor capital punishment more than Democrats and independents. While these demographic correlates are at best gross indicators that may be confounded with other
variables and do not account for much variability in attitudes, they strongly
suggest the need for more sophisticated research which can better examine
people's understanding and underlying attitudes about the death penalty.

There are also a few studies, generally unsophisticated, and now somewhat
out of date, that show differential support for capital punishment among
occupational groups. A clear majority of policemen tend to support the death
penalty,[9] as do most sheriffs, district attorneys, and prison guards.[10] On the
other hand most psychiatrists, clergymen, and prisoners tend to oppose it.[11]
More research should be devoted to the study of the attitudes of certain
"expert" occupational groups in the population. For example, surveys of the
attitudes of wardens and other prison officials who have had direct experience with administering the death penalty, and are therefore well-informed
about certain aspects of its use, would yield useful information for judging

9. Campion, *Attitudes of State Police Toward the Death Penalty,* in The Death Penalty in
    America (H. Bedau ed. 1967), at 252. *See also* M. Reidel, Correlates of Capital Punishment,
    Jan. 1966, at 6–8 (unpublished thesis in Bowling Green State University Library).
10. See H. Bedau, *supra* note 9, at 233.
11. Id.: Roche, *A Psychiatrist Looks at the Death Penalty,* 38 *Prison J.* 46–47 (1958).

whether capital punishment is cruel.[12] Ministers and clergymen are often considered moral leaders of the community and thus new and more comprehensive studies of their attitudes might also yield useful information about whether the death penalty is offensive to evolving standards of decency.[13]

4. An examination of the justifications people give for their attitudes toward the death penalty can provide several important kinds of information. First, a knowledge of people's expressed reasons for supporting or opposing the death penalty can provide theoretical insights into the meaning of the overall percentages of support and opposition. Second, such an examination allows us to assess whether support for capital punishment is directed toward legislatively and judicially acceptable goals. Third, the analysis of people's justifications for favoring the death penalty provides some insight into whether support for it is founded on misinformation or lack of thought.

While a few polls have asked the public about the bases for their support or opposition, potentially important response alternatives have always been omitted and the questions asked have often been ambiguous. In most cases the respondent's initial justification has been accepted without further probing to determine whether his answers are sincere and complete. Nevertheless, some of the data raise important questions and merit further examination.

Belief in deterrent effectiveness is probably the most frequently assessed rationale for support of capital punishment. A 1960 Minnesota poll asked, "If all states did away with the death sentence, do you think the crime rate in the United States would go up, down, or wouldn't it make any difference?" Eighteen percent thought it would go up, 5 percent thought it would go down, 73 percent thought it would make no difference, and 4 percent had no opinion.[14] A February 1972 poll in Texas asked, "Do you think we would have fewer murders committed in Texas if those given the death penalty were actually executed?" Fifty-two percent of the sample said yes and 36 percent said no, with 12 percent saying they did not know.[15] Of those persons in the 1973 Iowa poll who thought the death penalty should be restored, 44 percent felt it was a deterrent to crime while 23 percent indicated that things were too lenient now.[16] The Iowa Poll also asked those who opposed restoration

12. Ehrmann, For Whom the Chair Waits. Fed. Probation Q., Mar. 1962, at 14, suggests that prison officials and others who have witnessed executions are generally against capital punishment, presumably because it is an abhorrent experience. See also Rubin, The Supreme Court, Cruel and Unusual Punishment, and the Death Penalty, 15 Crime & Delinquency 121, 127–29 (1969).

13. See also Note, Furman v. Georgia—Death Knell for Capital Punishment, 47 St. John's L. Rev. 107, 120–21 (1972).

14. See Erskine, supra note 1, at 305.

15. 1 Current Opinion, Sept. 1972, at 11.

16. 1 Current Opinion, Aug. 1973, at 78. Seven percent said it would relieve the tax burden and 30% gave the ambiguous answer that it should be used only for severe crimes.

of the death penalty why they were against it. Thirty-four percent merely indicated that they were "personally opposed" to it, 25 percent felt that the government should not decide life or death, 17 percent said it was not a deterrent to crime, 9 percent said prison was worse than death, and 5 percent said innocent persons sometimes die.[17]

The most detailed and comprehensive inquiry into various common justifications for support of the death penalty was made in the 1973 Harris Survey. One question in that survey asked respondents whether they felt the death penalty was more effective as a deterrent than was a sentence of life imprisonment. Fifty-six percent of those interviewed indicated they felt it was more effective, while 32 percent felt that it was not. Among the proponents of capital punishment, 76 percent felt that it was more effective than a life sentence, but only 29 percent of capital punishment opponents felt that it was more effective. While this finding suggests the possibility that belief in the deterrent efficacy of capital punishment may be at least partially responsible for public support, there is one caveat that must be considered; expressed belief in deterrent efficacy may be seen by proponents as the most socially acceptable justification for favoring the death penalty and thus may be used as a cover for other, less acceptable reasons.[18]

Additional questions on the Harris survey lend strong support to the hypothesis that for many respondents a belief in deterrence is not the more fundamental reason for favoring capital punishment. In one question respondents were asked, "[s]uppose it could be proved to your satisfaction that the death penalty was not more effective than long prison sentences in keeping other people from committing crimes such as murder, would you be in favor of the death penalty or would you be opposed to it?" Fifty-four percent of those who favored capital punishment said they would favor capital punishment even if it had no deterrent effect. This finding is very similar to that found in a sample of English-speaking Canadian adults.[19]

---

17. Id.
18. The literature in social psychology is replete with examples showing that in interviews or other testing situations people will give answers that they think are compatible with the views of the interviewer or what they assume to be the generally accepted views of society, even if these answers conflict with their own personal opinion. Thus, even if a person really favors the death penalty for revenge, he is less likely to indicate his true feelings if he thinks this might make him look bad in the eyes of the interviewer or other persons who might see his answers. Sometimes more extensive questioning or indirect questions can reveal his true feelings. For a more extended discussion of this problem, see E. Webb et al., Unobtrusive Measures 1–22 (1966); Cannel & Kahn, *Interviewing*, in 2 The Handbook of Social Psychology 526 (G. Lindzey & E. Aronson eds. 1968); Scott, *Attitude Measurement*, in id. at 234–36.
19. See Neil Vidmar, *Retributive and Utilitarian Motives and Other Correlates of Canadian Attitudes toward the Death Penalty*, 15 The Canadian Psychologist, 337–56 (1974). Fifty-

The Harris Survey also gave respondents a list of reasons for supporting capital punishment and asked them to indicate the extent to which each reason reflected their own viewpoint. While a majority of the respondents indicated that they felt capital punishment is an effective deterrent or endorsed other reasons relating to deterrence,[20] about 40 percent of the sample endorsed the reason of Biblical retribution, and 41 percent endorsed the reason of giving someone perceived to be an animal his just desert.

Thus, these different ways of assessing reasons why people favor the death penalty yielded data that suggest that retribution may be an important motive in capital punishment attitudes. Taken by themselves, the data do not allow us to compare precisely the relative importance of retributive versus deterrence reasons for favoring the death penalty. However, additional data on the correlates of death penalty attitudes, as well as more general observations that large segments of the population are more concerned with punishing criminals than rehabilitating them,[21] lend credence to the retribution hypothesis.

5. A number of studies have shown that attitudes about the death penalty are related to other social and legal attitudes and to personality variables. These findings can provide insight into the perceptions, attitudes, and motives of survey respondents and thus give us a better understanding of their attitudes about capital punishment.

In a study of 839 respondents in Volusia County, Florida, Thomas and Foster adminstered a number of multi-item scales measuring support for capital punishment, perception of crime rates, fear of victimization, perception of the effectiveness of punishment as a deterrent to crime, and willingness to employ punishment as a reaction to crime.[22] All of the scales were postively

---

five percent of Canadian adults who favored capital punishment indicated they would favor the death penalty regardless of its deterrent value. While these findings might only be reflecting the fact that people support the death penalty as a symbol of law and order, Vidmar also found that persons who supported the death penalty were also more likely to score high on measures of retributiveness. It has been noted previously that Canadian attitudes on the death penalty closely parallel attitudes of Americans. See Bedau, *supra* note 9, at 240.

20. These reasons and the percentage of the sample endorsing each of them are as follows: "Crime is getting out of hand in this country and we need capital punishment to show that we really mean business about wiping out crime," 58%. "We need capital punishment to help protect the police," 54%. "We've had capital punishment all these years and we would be taking a chance getting rid of it—a new crime wave might spread across the country," 49%. The Harris Survey, *supra* note 7.

21. See F. Alexander & H. Staub, The Criminal, The Judge, and the Public 209–23 (1931); H. Weihofen, The Urge to Punish 130–70 (1956); Frankel, *Lawlessness in Sentencing*, 41 *U. Cin. L. Rev.* 1, 1–6 (1972).

22. Charles Thomas & Samuel Foster, A Sociological Perspective on Public Support for Capital Punishment, Apr. 18, 1974 (paper delivered to the Southern Sociological Society, Atlanta, Ga.).

and highly correlated with one another. The authors interpreted their findings as supportive of a complex sociological mode which assumes that support for the death penalty is a utilitarian response to rising crime rates. They argued that perception of an increasing rate of criminal behavior results in fears of victimization and willingness to employ punishment. Finally, perception of increasing crime rates, fear of victimization, and increased perceptions of the effectiveness of punishment all contribute to increased willingness to use punishment, including capital punishment, as a means of resolving the crime problem.

The [1973] Harris survey studied people's attitudes about corporal punishment for criminals. Specifically, respondents were asked, "Would you favor or oppose restoring the penalty of whipping for certain crimes?" Twenty-four percent of the supporters of capital punishment favored whipping, while only 14 percent of the opponents favored it.[23]

In a complex psychometric study, Comrey and Newmeyer examined the responses of 212 Los Angeles adults on a battery of psychological scales, including attitudes toward capital punishment.[24] Attitudes favorable toward capital punishment were positively related to factors of general conservatism, nationalism, religiousness, and racial intolerance.

The national survey by Rokeach found that persons who favored capital punishment differed from persons who opposed capital punishment on 11 of Rokeach's 36 terminal and instrumental values.[25] Those favoring capital punishment cared more for the terminal values of a sense of accomplishment, family security, and national security and the instrumental values of being ambitious, logical, and responsible. They cared less for the terminal values of a world of peace, equality, and true friendship, and the instrumental values of being forgiving and loving.[26]

23. Id. N. Vidmar, *supra* note 19, in his Canadian study found that 33% of those persons who supported capital punishment favored whipping, while only 15% of the opponents favored it.

24. Comrey & Newmeyer, *Measurements of Radicalism-Conservatism*, 67 J. Soc. Psychol. 357 (1965).

25. M. Rokeach, The Nature of Human Values 28 (1973); Rokeach & Vidmar, *Testimony Concerning Possible Jury Bias in a Black Panther Murder Trial*, 3 J. App. Soc. Psychol. 19, 23 (1973). Terminal values are those concerned with desirable end-states of human existence and instrumental values as desirable modes of conduct. Values serve adjustive, ego-defensive, knowledge, and self-actualizing functions for the individual. Both terminal and instrumental values can be "separately organized into relatively enduring hierarchical organizations along a continuum of importance." M. Rokeach, *supra*, at 3–25.

26. Rokeach & Vidmar, *supra* note 25, at 23–24. Differences in these values have been shown to be related to many differences in attitudes and behaviors, see generally Rokeach, *supra* note 25, but in particular, relatively lower regard among whites for the values of equality has been found to be associated with, among other things, prejudice toward blacks (espe-

Blumenthal, Kahn, Andrews, and Head conducted a nationwide survey of American males between the ages of 16 and 64 during the summer of 1969.[27] The study was a major inquiry into attitudes and values regarding the use of violence to achieve social goals. The authors identified attitudes toward two types of violence: violence to maintain social control (e.g., police violence to control ghetto riots, hoodlum gangs, and student disturbances) and violence used to effect social change (e.g., protests in which people are hurt or property is destroyed). Sizeable percentages of the population endorsed one or the other of these two types of violence,[28] and the single best predictor of endorsement of either type of violence was belief in what the authors called "retributive justice." Retributive justice was measured by an index consisting of five intercorrelated items, the major item being belief in capital punishment. Those persons who believed in retributive justice were most likely to endorse violence as a means of achieving social ends, whether it be social control or social change.[29]

Additional research relating support for the death penalty to other attitude and personality variables has been stimulated by *Witherspoon v. Illinois*,[30] in which a partially successful challenge was made to the use of a "death-qual-

---

cially regarding civil rights for blacks) and poor people. Id. at 97–105, 123–28. While a conclusion that people who favor capital punishment are more likely to be prejudiced against blacks and poor people requires two steps of inference (i.e., people who favor the death penalty have lower regard for equality; people who have lower regard for equality are prejudiced against blacks and poor people), such a conclusion is consistent with other findings reported in this section.

27. See M. Blumenthal et al., Justifying Violence (1972).

28. Id. at 19–40. Among other findings, 76–80% of the sample felt that clubs should be used in dealing with ghetto riots, hoodlum mobs, and student disturbances. Forty-eight of sixty-four percent indicated the police should shoot (but not to kill) "always" or "sometimes" in such situations, and 19–32% felt the police should shoot to kill. Id. at 39. Approximately 20% of the sample indicated that protests involving some property damage or personal injury were necessary to bring about sufficiently rapid social change, and 10% felt extensive property damage and some deaths were necessary to achieve such a goal. Id. at 39–40.

29. Id. at 216–17, 230–31, and 240–41.

30. 391 U.S. 510 (1968). Witherspoon was convicted in a capital murder trial but he challenged the fairness of the "death-qualified" jury, arguing that such juries were conviction prone. The Court set aside Witherspoon's death sentence due to jury bias on the punishment issue but did not find that the existing data on proneness toward conviction compelled holding that the jury was biased on the question of guilt. Research in the post-*Witherspoon* era has attempted to provide additional scientific evidence on this problem. See Oberer, *Does Disqualification of Jurors for Scruples Against Capital Punishment Constitute Denial of Fair Trial on the Issue of Guilt?* 39 Tex. L. Rev. 545 (1961); White, *The Constitutional Invalidity of Convictions Imposed By Death-Qualified Juries,* 58 Cornell L. Rev. 1176 (1973), for

ified" jury (i.e., a jury from which persons not in favor of the death penalty are excluded) in a capital case. Subsequent to *Witherspoon,* a number of studies have examined whether persons favoring the death penalty are different from persons opposed to it in terms of attitudes, values and personality dispositions. Zeisel used data from both Gallup polls and California polls to compare supporters and opponents of capital punishment on five social attitudes.[31] He found that people who favored the death penalty were less likely to favor open housing legislation or to approve of gun registration laws, and more likely to indicate they would move if Negroes moved into their neighborhoods, to approve of the John Birch Society, and to favor restrictive abortion laws. Research by Crosson,[32] Jurow,[33] Rokeach and McLellan,[34] and Snortum and Ashear[35] has shown that persons who favor the death penalty are more likely than opponents to score high on various psychological mea-

---

detailed discussions of the rationale linking psychological concepts to the legal issue of the death-qualified jury. Jurow, *New Data on the Effect of a Death Qualified Jury on the Guilt Determination Process,* 84 Harv. L. Rev. 567 (1971), has reviewed the scientific evidence bearing on the problem. Some of the research has shown a direct link between expressed attitudes favorable to the death penalty and tendency to convict, while other research has attempted to investigate the underlying attitudinal and personality dispositions associated with death penalty attitudes so as to provide psychological understanding of proneness toward conviction. Although intended for a different purpose, these latter research findings are also useful in the context of the present article and are discussed in the text accompanying notes 31–36, *infra.*

31. H. Zeisel, Some Data on Juror Attitudes Toward Capital Punishment 19–24 (1968).
32. R. Crosson, An Investigation into Certain Personality Variables Among Capital Trial Jurors, Jan. 1966 (unpublished thesis in Western Rerserve University Library).
33. Jurow, *supra* note 30, at 585–88.
34. Rokeach & McLellan, *Dogmatism and the Death Penalty: A Reinterpretation of the Duquesne Poll Data,* 8 Duquesne U.L. Rev. 125 (1970).
35. Snortum & Ashear, *supra* note 3, at 293.
36. In the psychological literature the concepts of authoritarianism, dogmatism, and conservatism are broad theoretical concepts used to describe the functional relationships between an individual's beliefs about the world, relationships to authority systems, and personality functioning. Some theorists have tended to view these concepts in terms of clinical personality syndromes. Others have argued that high scores on such measures are due, at least in part, to restricted breadth of perspective resulting from lack of cultural and environmental experience, which in turn causes intolerance toward different persons or different values. Still others have suggested that commonly used measures of these variables evoke response biases or measure the respondent's sophistication, awareness of social norms, and tendency to make stereotyped responses to social stimuli. See generally T. Adorno et al., The Authoritarian Personality (1950); J. Kirscht & R. Dillehay, Dimensions of Authoritarianism (1967); M. Rokeach, The Open and Closed Mind (1960).

A large body of psychological literature has shown that people who score relatively high on the various measures of authoritarianism, dogmatism, and conservatism are more likely to endorse extreme or intolerant positions and to show prejudice against minority groups sures of authoritarianism, dogmatism and conservatism in legal, social, and political views.[36]

Taken together, the studies reported in this section suggest that in comparison to people opposed to capital punishment, persons who favor capital punishment are more likely to be persons threatened by rising crime rates and to hold attitudes favoring general social and political conservatism.[37] They support the more direct poll results that suggest that at least for some people the death penalty may be favored more for retribution than deterrence. They also point out that persons who say they favor the death penalty are more likely to be willing to endorse attitude statements supporting such things as discrimination against minority groups, restrictions on civil liberties, and violence for achieving social goals than are persons who say they

---

and low status groups than persons who score relatively low. See Adorno, *supra;* Kirscht & Dillehay, *supra;* Rokeach, *supra;* McCloskey, *Conservatism and Personality,* 52 *Amer. Pol. Sci. Rev.* 27 (1958). Recent research in settings examining attitudes toward criminal behavior has shown that people scoring higher on authoritarianism are more likely to exhibit bias or prejudice than people scoring lower on authoritarianism. See, e.g., H. Mitchell & D. Byrne, Minimizing the Influence of Irrelevance Factors in the Courtroom: The Defendant's Character, Judge's Instructions, and Authoritarianism, May 5, 1972 (paper presented at the Midwestern Psychological Association Meetings, Cleveland, Ohio); Boehm, *Mr. Prejudice, Miss Sympathy, and the Authoritarian Personality: An Application of Psychological Measuring Techniques to the Problem of Jury Bias,* 1968 *Wis. L. Rev.* 734; Mitchell & Byrne, *The Defendant's Dilemma: Effects of Jurors Attitudes and Authoritarianism on Judicial Decisions,* 25 *Per. Soc. Psych.* 123 (1973). Persons scoring higher on authoritarianism are also more likely to punish for retributive reasons, as opposed to deterrence or other utilitarian reasons, than less authoritarian persons. N. Vidmar & L. Crinklaw, Retribution and Utility as Motives in Sanctioning Behavior, May 10, 1973 (paper presented at Midwestern Psychological Association Meetings, Chicago, Ill.); Sherwood, *Authoritarianism, Moral Realism, and President Kennedy's Death,* 5 *Brit. J. Soc. & Clin. Psychol.* 264 (1966).

We strongly caution against interpreting the psychological concepts of authoritarianism and dogmatism in laymen's terms or drawing the conclusion that all or even most people who favor capital punishment are extremists. (See W. Hays, Statistics 323–33 (1963), for a discussion of the fact that although a statistically significant finding indicates that two variables are associated with each other in a way that is unlikely to be attributable to chance, it does not necessarily tell us the strength of the association, i.e., the extent to which knowing how a responent scored on one variable will tell us how he scored on the other variable.) At the same time, however, we do note that there is a statistically significant association between death penalty attitudes and the psychological concept of the authoritarianism-dogmatism-conservatism syndrome, that there is an association between the syndrome and prejudice and retributiveness, and that literature reviewed in this article has shown a more direct association between death penalty attitudes and prejudice and retributiveness.

37. H. Zeisel, *supra* note 31; Comrey & Newmeyer, *supra* note 24; and Jurow, *supra* note 30, at 585–88, 591–96, have drawn similar conclusions regarding an association between pro-death penalty attitudes and sociopolitical conservatism.

are against the death penalty.[38] Whether these findings reflect true differences
in underlying values and attitudes, a lack of knowledge on the part of respondents, stereotyped, careless, or thoughtless replies in interview situations, or
a combination of these factors, they are a further admonishment to consider
more than mere levels of general support for capital punishment as reflected
in public opinion polls.

6. Information on the public's factual knowledge about the death penalty
is critical for assessing whether support for capital punishment is based on
"informed" opinion. In *Furman*, Justice Marshall set forth two empirically
testable assertions which put the issue into focus. The first assertion was that
the public is ill-informed about capital punishment.[39] The second assertion
was that if the public was informed of its purposes and liabilities, the majority of people would be against capital punishment.[40] No systematic survey
has investigated either of the hypotheses that follow from Marshall's assertions. There are, however, some informal studies that bear on them, and
there are general social science studies that yield indirect evidence, as well.

Psychiatrist Louis H. Gold conducted informal interviews with approximately 50 persons, asking them what they felt and how much they knew
about the issue of capital punishment.[41] From these interviews Gold concluded that " . . . the average American appears to have only a limited concept of the issue, has done very little reading on the subject, and has not taken
much time to think it through in an objective manner. More folks accept the

---

38. Other social science research has shown that substantial segments of the population are
    willing to endorse extreme political positions. For example, studies have shown that many
    people indicate willingness to reject some of the fundamental guarantees in the Bill of
    Rights. McCloskey, *Consensus and Ideology in American Politics,* 58 *Amer. Pol. Sci. Rev.*
    361 (1964); Protho & Grigg, *Fundamental Principles of Democracy: Bases of Agreement
    and Disagreement,* 22 *J. of Politics* 276 (1960). It may be that such findings are at least par-
    tially artifactual and not really valid indicators of public opinion. See e.g., notes 18 & 36
    supra. However, if that is so, we must also consider the possibility that most public opinion
    polls, including those showing general levels of support for the death penalty, are also not
    valid.
39. 408 U.S. 238, 362 (1972) (Marshall, J., concurring): "It has often been noted that American
    citizens know almost nothing about capital punishment."
40. Id. at 363: "Thus, I believe that the great mass of citizens would conclude on the basis of
    [existing empirical evidence] that the death penalty is immoral . . ."
41. See Gold, *A Psychiatric Review of Capital Punishment,* 6 *J. Forensic Sci.* 465 (1961). Gold
    did not describe the characteristics of his subject population, but presumably it was infor-
    mally chosen. Gold only reported that some of his subjects were friends, relatives, or profes-
    sional colleagues, that the various interviews took place in three states, and that his subjects
    included a school principal, a surgeon, and a grocery clerk. Id. at 466–68. The author also
    asserted that religious and political persuasion, social status, and economic status were not
    related to opinions on the death penalty. Id. at 466.

idea in a traditional sense without an intelligent appraisal of its significance."[42]

Gold's conclusion is not surprising in the light of general findings about public opinion. A number of studies have shown that substantial segments of the public are ill-informed or completely ignorant about some of the most elementary and important political and social questions.[43] Furthermore, it has been found that survey respondents will often endorse positions of advocate actions even though they lack knowledge about the subject, have no commitment to what they are endorsing, or both.[44] Other findings suggest that public opinion is often directly shaped by actions and statements of politicians or other public figures.[45] Thus, from this broader social science perspective it seems quite plausible that people are ill-informed about the death penalty, and that their support for it is based, at least in part, on tradition, uncritical acceptance of assumptions about its deterrent effect, or the endorsement of political leaders, e.g., President Nixon or California's Governor Reagan. However, with specific reference to the death penalty, the evidence from these studies is far for conclusive.

There are two ways to examine Justice Marshall's assertion that people who are informed about the death penalty will be opposed to it. The first way is to test the amount of knowledge people have about the death penalty and then determine whether people who are better informed are more likely to be against the death penalty. No study to date has attempted such an examination;[46] when one does, it should be conducted in the context of all

---

42. Id. at 466. See also id. at 467. Gold also concluded that there was a strong "affective" component in the reasons expressed when respondents were asked to explain their position on the issue and that this may account for "the rigid stand taken by some who were in favor of the death sentence." Id. at 470. Gold attempted to explain this affective reaction: "Murder is imagined as a horrible deed of such great and thunderous violence that man instinctively recoils from this concept because it is too painful to bear. His immediate reaction is obviously emotionally conditioned and it is this type of affective imprint which does not lead itself readily to rational and logical confrontation by words of wisdom or statements of fact." Id. at 475–76.

43. See L. Bogart, Silent Politics 100 (1972); C. Roll & A. Cantril, Polls: Their Use and Misuse in Politics; S. Stouffer, Communism, Conformity and Civil Liberties 233 (1955); Subcommittee on Intergovernmental Relations, U.S. Senate Committee on Government Operations, Confidence and Concern: Citizens View American Government 72–78 (1973).

44. See L. Bogart, *supra* note 43, at 100–101, 129–39.

45. See id. at 45–54; C. Roll & A. Cantril, *supra* note 43, at 145; S. Stouffer, *supra* note 43, at 233.

46. There are the findings that people opposed to the death penalty are better educated. See text accompanying note 10 *supra*. General education, however, does not tell us about specific knowledge about the death penalty, and, moreover, educational status is confounded with other variables, such as socioeconomic status, which could influence death penalty attitudes.

accumulated research knowledge about the death penalty. However, although such a study would provide useful information, an inherent difficulty with that type of analysis is that if Gold's conclusion is correct and the majority of the American people have generally low levels of information about capital punishment, any relationship between information and death penalty attitudes would not be very meaningful.[47]

The most direct and appropriate way of testing the empirical validity of Justice Marshall's second assertion is to create an experimental situation where a randomly selected group of people is exposed to all relevant arguments that relate to all of the utilitarian, humanistic, and moral issues about the death penalty. The post-exposure death penalty attitudes of the people in this experimental control group could then be compared to people not receiving the treatment.[48] Although economic cost and other problems of feasibility would necessarily require the research to be limited to a relatively small sample of people, the extremely important advantage of the study would accrue from the fact that we could be certain that the people were fully knowledgeable about the issues. Thus, there would be no question about whether their attitudes were based in "informed" opinion.[49] Such research would give the best possible information on whether the death penalty is inconsistent with contemporary standards of decency.

47. Such a relationship would only be a relative one between poorly informed persons and even more poorly informed persons. .

48. Smith, *Attitude Changes During a Course in Criminology,* 48 *School and Soc'y* 698 (1938), in fact conducted such a study. The capital punishment attitudes of college students enrolled in a criminology course were assessed during the first week of the semester. The students were then exposed to lectures, discussion, reading, and field trips to penal institutions, and capital punishment attitudes were assessed again at the end of the course. Id. at 698–99. Smith found no statistically significant attitude change between the pre-test and the post-test. Id. at 699. However, while the study is illustrative of the kind of research that needs to be done, it is inappropriate to draw any conclusions from it. First, there was a major methodological flaw in the study. Pre-test scores show that almost all of the students were initially unfavorable toward capital punishment, id. at 699–700, and, therefore, there was a "ceiling" on the possible amount of change against capital punishment. In fact, death penalty attitudes became slightly more favorable at the end of the semester, but because of the initial distribution of scores, this shift was probably an artifact of "statistical regression." See D. Campbell & J. Stanley, Experimental and Quasi-Experimental Designs for Research 5, 10–12 (1963). Second, most of the empirical research on capital punishment has been conducted since 1938, and, therefore, the empirical information base relevant to drawing conclusions about the issue has changed. Finally, public values and morality have probably changed in the 3½ decades since 1938.

49. The study sample might be randomly drawn from jury lists, and the people assigned to a number of 6–12-person "study groups" which would meet in a number of sessions over a period of days or weeks. The people could also be questioned about their comprehension of the issues and motives for their attitudes.

Despite their critical importance in assessing the validity of public attitudes toward the death penalty, the general extent of public knowledge about capital punishment and the relationship of the knowledge to capital punishment attitudes are the two most under-researched topics in the literature. Studies in this area are possible and deserve top research priority.

7. Responses to generally phrased questions asking about support for, or opposition to, the death penalty do not reveal whether the view is embraced solely in an abstract manner without regard to how the person would feel or behave in more concrete situations. A person who says he favors the death penalty may be unwilling to see it carried out when faced with an actual execution or threat of execution. Similarly, a person stating that he is generally opposed to the death penalty may favor it in specific cases. In brief, there may be varying levels of attitudes toward the death penalty.

There is some evidence which bears on this hypothesis. Jurow asked subjects about their general attitudes toward capital punishment and then asked how they would express these feelings when serving as jurors under circumstances where they could recommend the death penalty.[50] On the general question he found that 35 percent of his subjects were opposed to capital punishment, 20 percent indicated neutral feelings, and 45 percent were in favor of it. However, when he asked respondents about how they would behave on a jury when a defendant had been convicted of a very serious crime and the jury's options were death, life imprisonment, or some lesser penalty, many of the persons favoring capital punishment changed to the neutral category: 29 percent indicated they would probably not vote for the death penalty, 63 percent expressed neutral attitudes, and only 8 percent indicated they would probably vote for the death penalty. Thus, some of the people initially opposed to the death penalty indicated they were at least willing to consider it as a member of a jury, and many of the people initially favoring the death penalty became more neutral when confronted with a more specific situation. Jurow concluded that "there is an important difference between how people generally feel about capital punishment and how they claim they will express those feelings when serving as a juror."[51]

The 1973 Harris survey also indicates that respondents' self-predicated behavior as jurors is different than what might be inferred from their general abstract levels of support or opposition. Respondents were asked to assume that they were being considered as possible jurors in a trial where the defendant, if found guilty, would automatically be sentenced to death. Although 59 percent of them had previously expressed approval of the death penalty for certain crimes (with 31 percent opposed and 10 percent not sure) only 39

50. Jurrow, *supra* note 30, at 577, 599.
51. Id. at 591.

percent felt they could always vote guilty if guilt were proven for a crime that mandated the death sentence, another 33 percent could not say whether they would vote guilty even if guilt were proven, 16 percent said they would never vote guilty, and 12 percent were not sure. Thus, the basic findings are similar to those of Jurow. Although many people endorsed capital punishment at the general level, the degree of support for it dropped considerably when they were asked a more precise question about how they would behave if serving on a jury. Moreover, it also appears that although 31 percent of the people initially expressed opposition to capital punishment, some of them indicated willingness to vote guilty even though the death penalty would be given.

We should also note that the rather sharp difference in support for capital punishment at the general level and support for it in more specific circumstances is consistent with a hypothesis that some people may favor the *idea* of capital punishment either without realizing or without accepting its implications. There is also a great deal of general social science literature which has documented major discrepencies between attitudes expressed in the abstract and attitudes and behaviors expressed in specific circumstances[52] as well as evidence that people sometimes express views on public policy that they know are unrealistic or that they do not actually want to see carried out.[53]

Until more research is completed, we cannot determine whether the discrepancy between the percentages of support on general questions about the death penalty and the percentages of support on questions about specific circumstances are due to an emotional attachment to the death penalty as a symbol of law and order without any real desire to see executions carried out, to inconsistencies between general attitudes and specific attitudes, to frivolous or uninformed responses to survey questions, to a desire for "discretionary" and limited use of the death penalty, or to some combination of these factors. Whichever is the case, the problem of determining the various levels of support for capital punishment on both the general and specific levels, and why any discrepancies exist, needs serious consideration and much additional empirical investigation. The answers would help to ascertain whether people who favor the death penalty are actually willing to see it carried out.[54][. . .]

---

52. See e.g., McCloskey, *supra* note 38, at 373–79; Prothro & Grigg, *supra* note 38, at 291; Wicker, *Attitudes Versus Actions: The Relationship of Verbal and Overt Behavior Responses to Attitude Objects*, 25 J. Social Issues 41 (1969)
53. See L. Bogart, *supra* note 43, at 135–36.
54. Conversely, we should also determine whether people who say they are generally opposed to the death penalty are opposed in all cases.

§2 Recent Survey Research Data on the Death Penalty

Table 3-2-1. Attitudes Toward Capital Punishment for Persons Convicted of Murder, by Demographic Characteristics, United States, 1972–1977 (in percent)

Question: "Do you favor or oppose the death penalty for persons convicted of murder?"

	1972[b]			1973[b]			1974			1975			1976			1977		
	Favor	Oppose	Don't know	Favor	Oppose	Don't know	Favor	Oppose	Don't know	Favor	Oppose	Don't know	Favor	Oppose	Don't know	Favor	Oppose	Don't know
National	53	39	8	60	35	5	63	32	5	60	33	7	66	30	5	67	26	6
Sex																		
Men	61	34	5	68	29	4	68	29	3	67	27	6	73	24	3	75	22	3
Women	45	44	11	54	40	6	59	35	7	54	38	8	60	34	6	61	30	9
Race																		
White	58	35	7	64	32	5	66	29	5	63	30	6	68	28	5	70	24	6
Nonwhite	29	62	10	36	57	8	38	54	8	33	57	10	44	51	4	46	47	8
Education																		
College	54	40	6	57	39	4	58	38	4	58	37	4	63	33	3	66	29	6
High school	53	38	8	61	34	5	66	28	6	60	33	7	68	27	4	69	24	7
Grade school	51	40	9	63	30	7	64	30	6	62	28	11	61	30	8	65	29	6
Occupation																		
Professional and business	53	40	7	60	34	5	58	35	7	60	34	6	63	33	5	63	29	8
White collar	51	39	10	56	39	5	69	27	4	60	34	6	66	27	7	64	26	9
Farmers	60	34	6	69	29	3	76	24	0	60	23	17	70	20	10	74	20	6
Manual	53	40	8	61	34	5	64	32	4	60	33	7	68	29	3	71	25	4
Income																		
$15,000 and over	NA	NA	NA	NA	NA	NA	69	27	4	62	33	5	74	23	3	71	24	5
$10,000 to $14,999	NA	NA	NA	NA	NA	NA	66	30	4	67	28	5	68	26	5	67	27	5
$7,000 to $9,999	NA	NA	NA	NA	NA	NA	60	34	6	61	32	7	61	35	4	70	22	7
$5,000 to $6,999	NA	NA	NA	NA	NA	NA	60	33	6	58	35	6	54	40	6	65	28	7
$3,000 to $4,999	NA	NA	NA	NA	NA	NA	58	39	3	54	35	11	59	36	5	56	37	7
Under $3,000	NA	NA	NA	NA	NA	NA	54	40	6	42	47	11	51	43	6	58	35	7

Table 3-2-1. Attitudes Toward Capital Punishment for Persons Convicted of Murder, by Demographic Characteristics, United States, 1972–1977 (in percent) (*Continued*)

Question: "Do you favor or oppose the death penalty for persons convicted of murder?"

	1972[b]			1973[b]			1974			1975			1976			1977		
	Favor	Oppose	Don't know	Favor	Oppose	Don't know	Favor	Oppose	Don't know	Favor	Oppose	Don't know	Favor	Oppose	Don't know	Favor	Oppose	Don't know
Age																		
18 to 20 years	40	56	5	47	50	3	55	43	2	53	42	5	55	42	3	69	30	2
21 to 29 years	46	48	6	48	48	4	58	39	3	53	40	7	58	38	4	63	31	6
30 to 49 years	56	37	7	63	32	5	65	31	4	62	33	5	69	27	4	66	27	7
50 years and older	56	34	10	66	28	6	66	27	8	64	28	8	68	26	6	70	23	7
Region																		
East	64	30	6	61	35	3	66	29	4	66	30	4	70	26	4	64	31	6
Midwest	62	32	6	59	35	6	61	34	5	59	34	7	68	28	4	69	24	7
South	40	51	9	59	36	4	61	33	6	56	35	10	60	33	7	63	29	8
West	49	42	9	63	32	5	67	28	5	61	34	5	62	34	4	75	22	2
Religion																		
Protestant	50	42	9	62	33	5	63	32	5	59	33	8	65	30	5	67	26	7
Catholic	60	34	6	64	32	4	71	25	4	67	30	3	69	27	4	70	25	5
Jewish	65	26	9	62	33	5	39	52	9	61	39	0	74	26	0	66	26	9
None	47	49	4	36	58	7	43	50	7	50	42	7	55	41	4	64	34	2
Politics																		
Republican	63	31	6	71	25	4	73	22	5	67	26	7	73	23	4	74	21	6
Democrat	50	40	10	55	40	5	59	36	5	57	36	6	65	30	5	67	27	6
Independent	50	44	6	59	36	5	62	33	5	59	34	7	62	34	4	64	29	7

[a] Percents may not add to 100 because of rounding.
[b] The question in 1972 and 1973 was: "Are you in favor of the death penalty for persons convicted of murder?"
NA = Not available.

Source: National Opinion Research Center.

Table 3-2-2. Attitudes Toward Capital Punishment for Persons Convicted of Murder, by Demographic Characteristics, United States, Selected Years, 1969–76 (in percent)

Question: "Are you in favor of the death penalty for persons convicted of murder?"

	1969: February			1971: November			1972: March			1972: November			1976: March		
	Yes	No	No opinion	Yes	No	No opinion	Yes	No	No opinion	Yes	No	No opinion	Yes	No	No opinion
National	51	40	9	49	40	11	50	41	9	57	32	11	65	28	7
Sex															
Male	60	34	6	56	36	8	55	39	6	64	26	10	69	25	6
Female	44	45	11	43	44	13	45	43	12	50	37	13	63	30	7
Race															
White	54	38	8	51	38	11	53	39	8	60	29	11	70	24	6
Nonwhite	NA	NA	NA	30	58	12	24	64	12	32	52	16	38	51	11
Education															
College	52	43	5	50	45	5	48	47	5	57	36	7	62	33	5
High school	52	38	10	50	39	11	51	39	10	60	29	11	69	24	7
Grade school	48	42	10	45	39	16	50	40	10	49	34	17	62	30	8
Community size															
1,000,000 and over	55	37	8	55	35	10	58	35	7	54	34	12	68	25	7
500,000 to 999,999	54	39	7	46	43	11	46	44	10	59	31	10	65	30	5
50,000 to 499,999	57	36	7	43	47	10	45	45	10	59	28	13	64	30	6
2,500 to 49,999	47	44	9	48	42	10	48	43	9	52	38	10	64	28	8
Under 2,500, rural	46	42	12	51	37	12	51	40	9	58	32	10	67	26	7
Region															
East	51	39	10	49	38	13	55	34	11	NA	NA	NA	65	28	7
Midwest	51	43	6	48	43	9	42	49	9	NA	NA	NA	70	22	8
South	46	45	9	47	42	11	46	46	8	NA	NA	NA	59	35	6
West	63	28	9	54	38	8	59	33	8	NA	NA	NA	70	25	5

Table 3-2-2. Attitudes Toward Capital Punishment for Persons Convicted of Murder, by Demographic Characteristics, United States, Selected Years, 1969–76 (in percent) (*Continued*)

Question: "Are you in favor of the death penalty for persons convicted of murder?"

	1969: February			1971: November			1972: March			1972: November			1976: March		
	Yes	No	No opinion	Yes	No	No opinion	Yes	No	No opinion	Yes	No	No opinion	Yes	No	No opinion
Religion															
Protestant	51	40	9	50	38	12	49	42	9	57	32	11	65	28	7
Catholic	54	37	9	50	42	8	52	38	10	60	29	11	70	24	6
Politics															
Republican	55	36	9	53	37	10	59	29	12	62	29	9	75	18	7
Democrat	50	40	10	44	44	12	49	44	7	51	37	12	62	31	7
Independent	50	43	7	11	45	14	44	48	8	59	30	11	66	29	5

NA = Not available.

Source: The Gallup Poll, Princeton, N.J. George H. Gallup, *The Gallup Opinion Index,* Report No. 45, p. 15; Report No. 78, p. 19; Report No. 82, p. 14; Report No. 123, p. 27; Report No. 132, p. 24.

Table 3-2-3. Attitudes Toward Mandatory Use of Capital Punishment for Selected Crimes, United States, 1973 and 1977 (in percent)

Question: "Do you feel that all persons convicted of (READ LIST) should get the death penalty, that no one convicted of (SAME CRIME) should get the death penalty, or do you feel that whether or not someone convicted of (SAME CRIME) gets the death penalty should depend on the circumstances of the case and the character of the person?"

	All	No one	Depends	Not sure
Killing a policeman or prison guard				
1977	49	14	33	4
1973	41	17	38	4
First-degree murder				
1977	40	13	44	3
1973	28	16	53	3
Skyjacking				
1977	22	29	44	5
1973	27	27	41	5
Rape				
1977	20	27	48	5
1973	19	27	50	4
Mugging				
1977	8	44	43	5
1973	9	41	43	7

Source: Harris, Louis. *The Harris Survey.* New York: Chicago Tribune, N.Y. News Syndicate, February 7, 1977. Reprinted by permission.

Table 3-2-4. Percent of Respondents Favoring Capital Punishment for Selected Offenses, by Political Philosophy, United States, 1977

	Total	Liberal	Moderate	Conservative
Murder	87	89	87	87
Rape	24	22	23	24
Kidnapping	6	4	7	6
Killing policemen	5	5	5	5
Child rape/abuse	5	7	5	3
Other	5	4	5	3

Source: CBS News, "CBS News/New York Times Poll—Part II," New York, 1977. (Mimeographed.) P. 6, Table 18a.

Table 3-2-5. Percent of Persons Who Would Vote "Guilty" as Jurors even if that
Verdict Would Demand the Death Penalty for the Defendant, 1973

Question: "Suppose you were being considered as a possible juror for a trial where if the person
were convicted of the crime he would automatically get the death penalty. If the job of the jury
were just to decide whether or not the person was guilty, which statement on this card best
describes how you would feel in advance of trial?"

If guilt were proven, I could always vote guilty even though the defendant would automatically receive the death penalty.	39
I could not say in all cases, even if guilt were proven, that I would vote guilty knowing the defendant would automatically receive the death penalty.	33
I could never vote guilty, even if guilt were proven, knowing the defendant would automatically receive the death penalty.	16
Not sure	12

Source: Harris, Louis. *The Harris Survey.* New York: Chicago Tribune, N.Y. News Syndicate, June 14, 1973.
Reprinted by permission.

Table 3-2-6. Attitudes Toward Capital
Punishment of Murderers as a Deterrent
to Murder, United States, 1977

Question: "Do you feel that executing people
who commit murder deters others from committing murder or do you think such executions don't have much effect?"

	Percent
Deters others	59
Not much effect	34
Not sure	7

Source: Harris, Louis. *The Harris Survey.* New
York: Chicago Tribune, N.Y. News Syndicate,
February 7, 1977. Reprinted by permission.

Table 3-2-7. Attitudes Toward Capital Punishment if Proven Not More Effective Than Long Prison Sentences as a Deterrent to Murder, United States, 1973 and 1977 (in percent)

Question: "Suppose that it could be proven to your satisfaction that the death penalty was NOT more effective than long prison sentences in keeping other people from committing crimes such as murder, would you be in favor of the death penalty or opposed to it?"

	Favor	Oppose	Not sure
Total 1973	35	48	17
Total 1977	46	40	14
Age			
18 to 29 years	42	47	11
30 to 49 years	45	40	15
50 and older	51	34	15
Race			
Black	25	51	24
White	49	39	12
Political philosophy			
Conservative	55	32	13
Middle of the road	45	41	14
Liberal	38	50	12

Source: Harris, Louis. *The Harris Survey.* New York: Chicago Tribune, N.Y. News Syndicate, February 7, 1977. Reprinted by permission.

Table 3-2-8. Percent Favoring the Death Penalty Compared with Life Sentence as a Deterrent, 1973

Question: "Do you feel that the death penalty is more effective (a better deterrent) or not more effective than (READ LIST) in keeping other people from committing such crimes as murder?"

	More effective	Not more effective	Not sure
Compared with			
Life sentence with possible parole	56	32	12
Life sentence without parole	57	29	14

Source: Harris, Louis. *The Harris Survey.* New York: Chicago Tribune, N.Y. News Syndicate, 11 June 1973. Reprinted by permission.

Table 3-2-9. Percent Agreeing with Various Statements About Capital Punishment, 1973

Question: "Now I'd like to read you some statements other people have made about why they support capital punishment. For each one would you tell me if it represents your own view completely, fairly well, only slightly, or not at all?"

	Reflects own view	Does not	Not sure
Capital punishment is more effective than other penalties in keeping people from committing crimes.	61	33	6
A government which cannot execute criminals is going to become weak and lose the respect of the people.	49	42	9
The Bible is right when it preaches "an eye for an eye and a tooth for a tooth."	40	49	11
Someone who has committed a terrible crime such as murder is an animal and deserves to be executed.	41	51	8

Source: Harris, Louis. *The Harris Survey.* New York: Chicago Tribune, N.Y. News Syndicate, 11 June 1973. Reprinted by permission.

Table 3-2-10. Attitudes Toward Televising Criminal Executions, United States, 1976

Question: "If they go back to executing people convicted of murder, would you favor or oppose putting such executions on television?"

	Percent
Favor	11
Oppose	86
Not sure	3

Source: Harris, Louis. *The Harris Survey.* New York: Chicago Tribune, N.Y. News Syndicate, 13 January 1977. Reprinted by permission.

Table 3-2-11. Attitudes Toward Legislation Allowing a Convicted Murderer To Choose Life Imprisonment or Execution, United States, 1976

Question: "Would you favor or oppose a law that allowed a person convicted of murder to choose either his own execution or to remain in jail for life?"

	Percent
Favor	39
Oppose	53
Not sure	8

Source: Harris, Louis. *The Harris Survey.* New York: Chicago Tribune, N.Y. News Syndicate, 13 January 1977. Reprinted by permission.

4

Deterrence: Problems, Doctrines, and Evidence

INTRODUCTION

No issues raised by the controversy over the death penalty have been more hotly contested than those that focus on its efficacy as a deterrent. Nowhere in the argument regarding the desirability of death as a method of punishment is it more crucial to understand exactly what is in dispute, the available evidence, and what lessons can be extracted in light of this evidence. The issues can be grouped conveniently, though unevenly, into three main categories: conceptual, empirical, and moral.

The central conceptual question is the easiest both to identify and to answer: What is deterrence?

Consider five hypothetical cases. 1. Smith is executed for murder and therefore cannot commit any further crimes. 2. Jones, learning of Smith's execution and afraid that the same would happen to him if he were to commit murder, calculates that the risk is too great and decides for that reason to commit no murders. 3. Brown, contemplating the murder of Black, proceeds to kill him but without giving any prior thought to what the penalty is; he has planned the crime carefully and expects not to get caught. 4. Box has strong moral convictions against the deliberate and unprovoked use of violence and it never occurs to him to try to "eliminate" his rival, Cox, even though he has long harbored a strong dislike of Cox. 5. Cox, who thoroughly hates Box, would like to murder him; after Smith is executed he decides not to do so. Question: On the evidence given, in which if any of these cases do we have deterrence of a murder by the death penalty?

Answer: At best, only in 2. This is the only case in which the explanation for the person's not committing a murder is solely or primarily his fear of being punished by death for the crime. (The crucial unanswered question regarding cases such as 2, of course, is whether the same deterrent result might have been obtained by threatening Jones with a sanction less severe than death.) In case 1 deterrence clearly failed, though the execution of Smith does incapacitate him from committing any further crimes. (Deterrence as in 2 is constantly confused in the popular mind and public debate with incapacitation as in 1.) In case 3 deterrence has also failed; again, the crucial unanswered question here is whether all, or most, or only a few of the murders that actually occur can be understood on this or some similar model, and whether increasing the sanctions against Brown might produce an effective deterrent. Cases such as 4 and 5 raise interesting questions, and why neither is a clear case of deterrence is explained in §1 below, in the essay by the sociologist Jack P. Gibbs, in which he draws upon the analyses in his important treatise *Crime, Punishment and Deterrence* (1975).[1]

Gibbs's discussion shows both that we are easily confused over the concept of deterrence (mainly because it is not only through its deterrent effect that a punishment can reduce or prevent crime), and that it is important to remove these confusions before attempting to interpret empirical research on the alleged deterrent efficacy of a given penalty. On Gibbs's view, virtually *all* of the empirical research so far published on the deterrent effect of the death penalty is inconclusive. Such persuasiveness as it has depends on our making tacit assumptions about several crucial factors, the chief of which is the degree and extent to which persons *perceive* themselves as likely to suffer a given penalty for a given offense, based on what they *perceive* as the effect of this or similar punishments on others. As Gibbs rightly argues, the theory of deterrence thus has to be part of a more general theory in which human behavior is seen as a function or effect of perceived causes in the social environment; the problem is that this more general theory is far from being formulated or developed in a way that makes it usable in current research on deterrence.

Traditionally, the two main empirical questions raised by thinking about the death penalty as a deterrent—Is it a deterrent at all, ever, to anyone? Is it a more effective deterrent than long-term imprisonment?—have not been answered with any explicit attempt to take the perception factor into account.[2] For our purposes it is convenient to divide all deterrence research on the death penalty into two groups of studies, both of which ignore this factor. The first and earlier group of studies was largely conducted or inspired by the criminologist Thorsten Sellin.[3] The second group of studies

1. See also Gibbs 1978a and 1978b for his most recent arguments.
2. Thus, whereas both Graves 1956 and Savitz 1958 attempted to study the deterrent effect of actual executions (in California and in Philadelphia, respectively), only Savitz tried to incorporate a perception factor into the research. He did it by measuring the amount of newspaper publicity devoted to each execution. For a recent study like Savitz's, on South Carolina, see King 1978; on England, see Phillips 1980.
3. See Sellin 1959, in part reprinted in Bedau 1964a and in Sellin 1967, and revised and updated in Sellin 1980.

was inaugurated by the economist Isaac Ehrlich in his pioneering paper, "The Deterrent Effect of Capital Punishment: A Question of Life and Death," first circulated in 1973 and published in 1975. The differences between these two groups of studies are a lesson in changing methods of empirical research, and a fascinating topic for both the history and the philosophy of social science. Here, however, we must content ourselves with noting the central findings of each.

Sellin's research, and similar research of others, seemed to lead to one or the other of two negative conclusions, depending on the assumptions and caution with which the researcher interpreted his own findings: Regardless of whether any punishment, including the death penalty, is a very significant deterrent, either (a) the evidence showed that the (threat of the) death penalty was not a better deterrent than (the threat of) long-term imprisonment, or (b) there was no evidence that either penalty (or the threat thereof) was a better deterrent than the other. These conclusions were a basic theme in the argument presented to the Supreme Court in 1971 to support a finding by the Court that the death penalty was a "cruel and unusual punishment": If there was no evidence that executing a person gave society more protection against murder than imprisonment did, then the finality and presumptively greater severity of death must be unnecessarily severe and hence "cruel and unusual" (see Chapter Six). The ink was hardly dry in the Court's judgment in *Furman* v. *Georgia* (1972) when reports announced that an entirely new line of research, using methods of inquiry characteristic of mathematical studies of economic behavior (econometrics), had shown that in the United States between 1933 and 1969, "each execution prevent[ed] between eight and twenty murders" (Tullock 1974:108). Ehrlich's novel results were given unusual publicity when they were incorporated into the brief filed *amicus curiae* in 1974 by the Solicitor General in the death penalty case, then pending, of *Fowler* v. *North Carolina*.[4] From that time to the present, Ehrlich's results have been under constant review by other investigators using essentially his methods and identical or comparable data. The next two selections in this chapter give the reader an introduction to this controversy.

The first is by Hans Zeisel, co-author with Harry Kalven of *The American Jury* (1967) and a sociologist with wide experience in the use of statistical methods to assess the effectiveness of the criminal justice system. His essay

---

4. Ehrlich's results were also cited in *The New York Times*, 24 April 1978, p. 22, in a paid advertisement by the "Citizens' Crusade Against Crime." In the period immediately after *Furman* but before the first publicity of Ehrlich's results appeared, the Nixon administration and others who favored reintroduction of the death penalty cited two alleged "studies" of deterrence that supposedly confirmed the special efficacy of the death penalty. One was a so-called American Bar Association study of 1960; there is no such "study," and whether it was excusable negligence that explains the many references to it is not clear. For a full discussion see Bedau 1973b. The other was a memorandum prepared by the Los Angeles Police Department in 1971, but never made public. The Solicitor General's brief in *Fowler* wisely chose to ignore these two "studies" in preference to exclusive reliance on Ehrlich.

(reprinted without omissions), in §2, is unusually accessible to the technically untrained reader, and provides a clear account of the contrast between the methodologically elementary work of Sellin and the sophisticated research of Ehrlich and other econometricians. Zeisel is not the only sociologist who has examined Ehrlich's research against the background of Sellin's and remained unconvinced.[5] The selection following Zeisel's essay, in §3, is typical of the kind of technical discussion to be found in the new deterrence research. It is a paper commissioned during 1976 by the Panel on Research on Deterrent and Incapacitative Effects of the Committee on Research on Law Enforcement and Criminal Justice from the Assembly of Behavioral and Social Sciences of the National Research Council. Its principal author, Laurence R. Klein, is the 1980 Nobel Laureate in Economics and a professor at the Wharton School of the University of Pennsylvania; at time of this research he was President of the American Economic Association. His coauthors are Brian Forst, an economist with the Institute for Law and Social Science in Washington, D.C., and Victor Filatov, on the staff of the Wharton School. On the strength of this paper, the Panel (a group of nine distinguished social scientists) concluded that "the available studies provide no useful evidence on the deterrent effect of capital punishment" (Blumstein, Cohen, & Nagin 1978:9). Presumably, "no useful evidence" means both no evidence that the death penalty is a deterrent, or a more (or less) effective deterrent than imprisonment, and no evidence that it is not. This judgment was a severe rebuff to the scientific respectability of the line of research pioneered by Ehrlich, and he replied vigorously (Ehrlich & Mark 1977) as he had done to previously published criticisms of his results and methods.[6] Who has the better of the argument is not easy to say, and the debate is far from concluded.[7]

What, then, is the present state of our knowledge of the deterrent effect of the death penalty, especially as compared with the deterrent effect of long-term imprisonment? As almost every month brings the publication of new findings, one can hazard generalizations only at great risk. It may be helpful,

5. See Baldus & Cole 1975, Gibbs 1977, and Glaser 1977. As for Sellin himself, he has been content to report the findings of Zeisel 1977 and of Klein et al. 1978, reprinted here (§§2 and 3); see Sellin 1980:176f.
6. See Ehrlich 1975b, replying to the criticism of Bowers & Pierce 1975; also Ehrlich 1977a and Ehrlich & Gibbons 1977, replying to Passell & Taylor 1976. For other critical discussions of Ehrlich's results, or of the defense of conclusions contrary to Ehrlich's while based on Ehrlich-type methods and data, see especially Passell 1975; Forst 1977; Boyes & McPheters 1977; Barnett 1978; Hoenack et al. 1978; and Hoenack & Weiler 1980. Friedman 1979 provides an unusually lucid and patient discussion of the problems in establishing a causal connection by means of multiple-regression correlations.
7. Mention should also be made of the less well known research by the economist John Yunker, of the Center for Business and Economic Research, Western Illinois University. Yunker claimed to have shown that "one execution will deter 156 murders" (1976:65). This finding has been criticized by Sesnowitz & McKee 1977 and Fox 1977, but defended by Yunker 1977.

therefore, to look first at the results from two independent lines of current research. By far the most sustained research effort directly in point is being conducted by William C. Bailey, a sociologist at Cleveland State University. Using standard multiple-regression techniques and testing for several variables, Bailey has studied the possible deterrent effects on first-degree murder (rather than either of the usual broader categories of "homicide" or "murder and nonnegligent manslaughter") of executions versus imprisonment (Bailey 1974 and 1977a); of the role of celerity in the use of the death penalty (Bailey 1980a); of actual executions in each of six states—California, New York, North Carolina, Ohio, Oregon, and Utah (Bailey 1979a; Bailey & Peterson 1980; Bailey 1979d, 1979b, 1979c, 1978, respectively); of executions under mandatory versus discretionary capital statutes (Bailey & Lott 1977); and of executions on assaults against the police (Bailey 1980b). He also looked for a deterrent effect of executions on rape (Bailey 1977b). In *every* case, either no deterrent effect was found or the degree of effect lacked statistical significance. Meanwhile, Arnold Barnett of the Sloan School of Management at M.I.T. has for several years been studying the causes of and fluctuations in the rate of urban homicide. He also undertook to review the work of Forst (1977) and of Ehrlich (1977b), which came too late to be evaluated by the National Research Council's investigation of deterrence (see §3, below). Barnett concluded that his examination of these studies provided "new evidence" in support of the Panel's sceptical conclusion, quoted in the paragraph above. He argued that these newer studies (Bailey's work was not under review) were subject to systematic errors several times the magnitude of the deterrent effect, if any, and so all were "insufficiently sensitive to answer delicate questions about the impact of executions at a time when executions were rare," i.e., during the 1950s and 1960s (Barnett 1979:20).

Whether the continuing work of these and other investigators will result in models and techniques that will command general assent, or whether data sources as yet unused will be discovered and prove more revealing than those so far employed, remains to be seen. If one must draw the balance sheet at the present moment, it appears that despite the introduction of econometric techniques, the negative judgment on the deterrent superiority of the death penalty over long-term imprisonment reached a generation ago by Sellin and other criminologists has not been seriously undermined or contradicted. So far, only two independent investigators have thought their methods and the available data showed that executions provide a measurable deterrent effect; all other investigators (more than a dozen) have refused to agree.[8]

8. For research on deterrence prior to 1967, see Bedau 1967b: 258–332 and Bedau 1971. Other recent research worthy of examination includes: Kleck 1979 (on the role of gun ownership in increasing the rate of criminal homicide); Black & Orsagh 1978; Beyleveld 1979 (a conceptual analysis of deterrence); Beyleveld 1980 (a comprehensive bibliography and digest of results on deterrence); Sarat 1977 (the role of deterrence in judging the death penalty as unconstitutionally "cruel and unusual"); Bechdolt 1977 (on the rate of unemployment as a

Historically, there has always been an alternative to the doctrine of the death penalty's unique deterrent effect, viz., the view that the death penalty "brutalizes" any society that uses it. This is the doctrine of "counterdeterrence," as it is also called, a shocking inversion of common sense, at least for anyone imbued with the idea that the threat of severe punishment *must* yield greater compliance. Two centuries ago, Cesare Beccaria (1738–94), in his short but highly influential treatise *On Crimes and Punishments* (1764), asserted: "The death penalty cannot be useful, because of the example of barbarity it gives men." Implicit in such a view is the hypothesis that the use of execution by government under color of law encourages people—consciously or subconsciously—to imitate the same extreme methods, and that we are to understand lawless acts of murder (and especially of lynching) as products of this imitation and example. Clinical studies by some psychiatrists attest to the "executioner syndrome," whereby someone takes it upon himself to put another person to death as an imagined social service, as well as to the suicidal murderer—the person who is afraid to take his own life and so murders another in the hopes that the state will snuff out his life.[9] Such cases, where they are not disregarded altogether as sheer fabrications or preposterous interpretations of the clinical evidence, are usually dismissed as extremely rare and as mere examples of warped and unbalanced minds at work, and so not relevant to (and surely infinitesimal in numbers by comparison with) the sobering deterrent effect of executions. Yet as long ago as 1853, the London correspondent for New York's *Daily Tribune* was struck by the apparent increase in England both in reported suicides and in reported homicides following a public execution. The correspondent was no less an acute social observer and theorist than Karl Marx.[10] Meanwhile, a few years earlier, a much closer analysis of the same phenomenon had already been made by an American lawyer and critic of the death penalty, Robert Rantoul.[11] The observations and speculations of Rantoul and Marx have not gone wholly ignored by sociologists; in at least three studies in the past fifty years attempts have been made to measure the inflating effect of executions upon homicide rates.[12] But these studies are vulnerable to basic objections, and this plus the way the brutalization hypothesis runs counter to intuition in the first place has left the matter largely unsettled. In 1977, however, the first reports

significant cause in the fluctuation of homicide rates); Glaser 1979 (an argument that the death penalty reduces certainty of conviction); and Hardmann 1977 (a satirical discussion of how the deterrent effect could be augmented, e.g., by gory public executions).

9. See West 1975, Solomon 1975, and Diamond 1975.

10. The news item is reprinted in Louis Feuer, ed., *Marx and Engels: Basic Writings in Politics and Philosophy,* New York, Doubleday Anchor, 1959, pp. 485ff.

11. See Mackey 1976:52, and the passages cited in Bowers & Pierce 1980a:460.

12. Dann 1935, Graves 1956, and Savitz 1958. A fourth study, Kringel 1974, was never completed; see Bedau & Pierce 1976:xxii.

were made public of a scientifically more adequate investigation into the brutalization hypothesis by William J. Bowers and Glenn L. Pierce at the Center of Applied Social Research, Northeastern University. According to their analysis, based on a study of all the executions (692) in New York between 1906 and 1963, and all the homicides that occurred during that same period, each execution "adds roughly three more to the number of homicides in the next nine months of the year after the execution" (1980a:481). It is far too early for abolitionists to trumpet such findings—the very opposite of those Ehrlich reached—because future work by other investigators could make them evaporate just as Ehrlich's equally stunning and memorable findings have. They are important, however, because they are the first fruits of a line of investigation that may in time prove to be the new orthodoxy.[13]

The dispute over the death penalty as a specially effective deterrent is not confined to the general problem of criminal homicide, so far discussed. It arises with particular force in at least four narrower contexts: homicide in prison committed by incarcerated murderers; homicide by murderers after parole or release; the murder of law-enforcement officers; and "special crimes," such as kidnapping for ransom in the 1930s and terrorism in the 1970s. On most of these questions sociologists and other investigators have very incomplete data and unsophisticated analyses to offer us. It is also true that the death penalty in these cases is often defended not only on grounds of deterrence or incapacitation. The murderer who kills again while serving a prison term or while on parole, or the murderer of a police officer, or the terrorist—each is a prime candidate for a retributive use of the death penalty. Nevertheless, there is a strong component of deterrent and preventive thinking in many appeals for the death penalty for such crimes. Several Supreme Court Justices have even suggested that the death penalty may be uniquely appropriate because "other sanctions may not be adequate" in precisely such cases.[14] For these reasons, something further must be said about each in the present context.

Research on the special protection allegedly afforded to police officers by the death penalty has been conducted by several investigators, and none has found any evidence of a special deterrent effect on police assault or killings in death penalty jurisdictions as opposed to abolition jurisdictions (see Sellin 1955 and 1980; Campion 1955; Cardarelli 1968). In the best and most recent of these studies, the results were "straightforward" and "negative." There was "no evidence that either the statutory provision for capital punishment, or its actual level of use, provided an effective deterrent to police killings" (Bailey 1980b:20).

13. See also the research reported in King 1978 (and note 2, *supra*). For a general discussion see Glaser & Zeigler 1974 and Glaser 1979.
14. *Gregg* v. *Georgia*, 428 U.S. 153 (1976), at 186. The remark appeared in the plurality opinion written by Justice Stewart and joined by Justices Powell and Stevens. See Chapter Six, §2.

Recidivism among capital murderers is a more troubling and less closely examined phenomenon. Whatever may be the ideal alternative to the death penalty,[15] for the immediate future it is bound to be some form of long-term confinement. In recent years, the typical convicted murderer served a prison term averaging 80 months, nearly seven years.[16] The vast majority of those not sentenced to death and executed are eventually released, though many of them will have spent far longer than seven years behind bars. What is their "safety record"? The question divides into two parts, having to do with recidivism while in prison and recidivism after release. Killings in prison by persons convicted of murder, as well as murder by released murderers, are not unknown, and they understandably inflame the public and provide perhaps the most durable argument for a wider (albeit selective) use of the death penalty. In the essay in §5 (published here for the first time), Wendy Phillips Wolfson reviews the evidence on prison homicide and the deterrent efficacy of the death penalty in controlling it. My essay in §6, revised from testimony presented in a 1978 Congressional hearing on the federal death penalty, shows a partial record in selected states and nationally for released murderers. Both Wolfson and I argue that there is no evidence that the death penalty is any better a deterrent than imprisonment for the two sorts of murderers under investigation, and that if advantage is to be taken of the incontestably superior power of capital punishment to incapacitate, the social cost in the needless execution of thousands who could safely be incarcerated and eventually released would be staggering.

Even if the superior deterrent efficacy of the death penalty seems doubtful where criminal homicide is involved, it still manages to claim adherents whenever a particular kind of crime strikes terror into large segments of society, or where a particularly loathsome type of criminal violence rises to command the headlines. During the 1930s kidnapping seized the public imagination in this country as never before (or since), particularly after the death of the Lindbergh infant in 1932. State and federal legislatures were perceived as having enacted death penalty statutes designed to curb kidnapping, kidnapping for ransom, felony murder kidnapping, and related offenses (Alix 1978). The apparent decline in such crimes during the following decades has often been attributed to the singular deterrent powers of the death

15. Some years ago I argued against (a) life imprisonment without possibility of commutation, parole or release; against (b) a minimum of twenty years in prison before any eligibility for parole consideration (the alternative recommended by Lewis E. Lawes, a leading abolitionist of the 1920s and 1930s); and for (c) a minimum of ten years imprisonment (Bedau 1964a:228–231). A prison term longer than that recommended in (c) above is not necessary on grounds of deterrence or retribution; but there is little reason to think that this would be approved by the public today as a reasonable alternative to the death penalty (see Chapter Three).

16. Hindelang et al. 1975:485, Table 6.53, reporting data on persons released during 1965–70 after imprisonment for willful homicide.

penalty, although there is no evidence to support such an inference (Bedau 1964a:57f. and Alix 1978:190f.). In the 1950s and early 1960s, blasting aircraft out of the sky by planting bombs aboard threatened public confidence in air travel; the Kennedy and King assassinations (1963 and 1969) were even more troubling. Congress acted swiftly to impose the death penalty under the federal criminal code for both types of crimes. In the 1970s, throughout the world, the crime of the hour was terrorism in its many forms: aircraft hijacking, hostage-taking in foreign embassies, extortion, and especially indiscriminate bombings in public places. Much as with kidnapping a half century ago, terrorism has provoked renewed cries for the death penalty on deterrent (as well as retributive) grounds. The Antihijacking Act of 1974 easily passed in Congress and was promptly signed by President Gerald Ford. Many would agree with Congressman Paul G. Rogers who, in the course of arguing for legislation he had filed to require the death penalty for anyone convicted of bombing public facilities, said that "the death penalty can act as an effective deterrent to these crimes of premeditation. We must require that the planner of a bombing take into account that if his bomb kills anyone he will be punished by death,"[17] a sentiment echoed on the Supreme Court by those Justices who conjectured that the death penalty might be a uniquely effective deterrent for certain "calculated murders," and as an example cited "the use of bombs or other means of indiscriminate killing" typical of terrorist attacks (*Gregg* v. *Georgia*, 1976). Yet serious students of domestic and international terrorism are virtually unanimous in not recommending the death penalty as a weapon in the fight against such crimes; it "confers not only martyrdom but glamour and glamour is the best of all recruiters amongst the minute field from which the terrorist—and their supporters—are drawn" (Clutterbuck 1975:139). In this country, the major study of the problem, *Disorders and Terrorism* (1976), by the Task Force on Disorders and Terrorism of the National Advisory Committee on Criminal Justice Standards and Goals, completely ignored the death penalty in its more than six hundred pages of analysis and recommendations. Reprinted here, in §7, are excerpts from the only essay in which anyone has discussed the subject in a comprehensive manner. The author, Dr. Thomas Perry Thornton, was at the time a member of the State Department's policy planning council.

However the central empirical questions about deterrence are answered, they become relevant to the death penalty controversy only to the degree that one accepts what might be called "the morality of deterrence" (Andenaes

---

17. Quoted in Bell 1978:150–51. See also Congressman Rogers's remarks in *Congressional Record*, 20 January 1976, H110–H111, as well as the remarks on behalf of S.2511 (mandatory death penalty for terrorist bombing-murders) in *Congressional Record*, 28 January 1976, S646–S647. It is also worth noting that between 1961 and 1972, 75 aircraft hijackers were taken into custody, but the Department of Justice did not seek the death penalty for any; see A. Evans 1973.

1970). On this assumption it is morally permissible (or compelling) to take into account the deterrent effect of a penalty in the course of deciding whether to authorize it by law, or, having authorized it, whether to use it. That this assumption is not necessary is proved by the dominance in other societies and at other times of primarily expiatory and retributive attitudes toward the justification of punishment. That it is undesirable from the moral point of view has been argued by many philosophers and moralists who reject utilitarianism, notably by Immanuel Kant (1724–1804) and those who followed his lead. The validity of this assumption, however, takes us well beyond the death penalty, since it pertains as well to *any* mode of punishment and the penalty schedule that might be adopted for *any* crime. Accordingly, no attempt can be made here to deal with this problem, and certainly not at the length it deserves.[18] Yet it has an important bearing on the death penalty debate because of the way abolitionists and retentionists can be divided by reference to how they view the morality of deterrence.

There are, first, those who favor or oppose capital punishment primarily on deterrent grounds; they agree in accepting the morality of deterrence, but disagree over the correct answers to empirical questions about the deterrent efficacy of executions versus imprisonment. Persons who reason in this way will find the information summarized and reprinted in this chapter relevant but vexatious, because it does not strongly favor either side and thus cannot resolve their fundamental dispute over whether to favor or oppose the death penalty on what is for them the only rational ground for such a decision. In contrast, there are those who favor or oppose the death penalty mainly on nondeterrent grounds; they reject or are unsure about the morality of deterrence and would not change their views on the merits of using or abolishing the death penalty even if convincing evidence were brought forward to show that it is not, or that it is, an effective deterrent. Instead, their attitudes are shaped primarily by evidence on other issues, for example, religious teachings or whether the death penalty is adequately and properly retributive or whether it can be administered without significant risk of error and without racial or class bias (see Chapter Five). We have already seen (in Chapter Three) that actual attitudes on the death penalty do not vary simply as a function of whether persons (profess to) believe that it is a (uniquely) effective deterrent. Now we can see that the entire controversy over its deterrent efficacy presupposes the morality of deterrence, a presupposition that empirical studies by themselves cannot validate.

All but extreme Kantians will grant that the deterrent efficacy of punishments should play *some* role in deciding on rational grounds whether they are morally appropriate. The difficulty comes when one must specify how much weight is to be given to this factor in relation to other relevant factors.

18. See, however, von Hirsch 1976, Richards 1977, Cederblom & Blizek 1977, and Gross 1979.

Without a full-scale theory of just punishment, in terms of which alone a final answer might be given to the problem, and without more empirical knowledge of the deterrent, preventive, and incapacitative effects of (the threat of) punishment on specific populations at given times, it is possible for reasonable people to disagree on the weight they find it rational to assign to deterrent efficacy. One assumption that might gain general acceptance under these circumstances is this: The more severe, irreversible, and beyond compensation a punishment is, the more evidence is needed of its deterrent, preventive, and incapacitative efficacy before it can justifiably be used in preference to a less severe penalty. If this principle is accepted, then in light of the evidence reviewed and reprinted here, it will not be easy to defend the death penalty as a morally permissible form of punishment in our society.[19]

§1. Preventive Effects of Capital Punishment other than Deterrence*

JACK P. GIBBS

Philosophers write as though deterrence or retribution is the only possible justification of legal punishment[1] while social scientists commonly create the impression that punishment prevents crimes, if at all, only through deterrence.[2] Opinions of those scholars notwithstanding, there are many possible mechanisms by which legal punishment may prevent crimes other than through deterrence. No real effort is made here to marshal research evidence of those nondeterrent mechanisms; indeed, the evidence is largely limited to general observations, some of which border on sheer conjecture. Yet, viewed the other way, there is certainly nothing remotely approaching conclusive evidence that legal punishments prevent crimes only through deterrence; and Supreme Court Justices seem to be fully aware of the possibility of nondeter-

---

19. See especially the discussions by Conway 1974 and Schedler 1976. Elsewhere I have considered some of the relevant issues in greater detail; see Bedau 1977b and 1980a.

1. See Ezorsky, *Philosophical Perspectives on Punishment* (1972).

2. See Tullock, "Does Punishment Deter Crime?" 36 Pub. Int. 103–111 (Summer 1974); Yunker, "Is the Death Penalty a Deterrent to Homicide?" 5 J. Behavioral Econ. 45–79 (Summer 1976).

rent preventive effects, even though they do not employ distinctive labels to identify those effects.[3] More serious, none of the Justices recognize more than two kinds of possible nondeterrent preventive effects, and, for understandable reasons, they do not pretend to base their arguments about those effects on systematic empirical evidence.

The nondeterrent prevention of crime is not the only important subject that has gone largely ignored in research on and debates over capital punishment. Perhaps even more important, social scientists, and economists in particular, commonly ignore the point that the deterrence doctrine is a far cry from a systematic theory; consequently, the relevance of what purports to be evidence is inherently debatable. Surely, the principles of economics in themselves scarcely constitute a theory of deterrence, nor can they be readily translated into such a theory.[4] To illustrate, contemplate two questions. First, what assumptions about the public's knowledge of statutory penalties and perceptions of the certainty of their application are necessary for a defensible statement of the deterrence doctrine? And, second, how can such assumptions be deduced from the principles of economics? In reporting their deterrence research or stating "deterrence models," economists do not confront such questions, let alone answer them; and it is surely significant that econometric research on deterrence has never treated the perceived certainty of punishment as an empirical variable.[5] For that matter, there are nine properties of punishment that could be relevant in stating the deterrence doctrine as a theory,[6] but each deterrence investigation has been limited to one or two

3. Opinions of the Justices clearly suggest that they see the primary purpose of capital punishment as being deterrence and/or retribution; nonetheless, they seem to be more sensitive to other kinds of possible preventive effects than do scholars in the humanities or social sciences, even those with an interest in legal punishments. See *Furman* v. *Georgia*, 408 U.S. 238 (1973).

4. See, e.g., Tullock, note 2 *supra*, at 104. "Most economists who give serious thought to the problem of crime immediately come to the conclusion that punishment will indeed deter crime. The reason is perfectly simple: demand curves slope downward. If you increase the cost of something, less will be consumed. Thus, if you increase the cost of committing a crime, there will be fewer crimes."

5. The deterrence doctrine is a *perceptual* theory, if a theory at all. It asserts that the threat of legal punishment deters crime only to the extent that the threat is perceived by potential perpetrators of crimes as certain, swift, and severe. The policy implications cannot be exaggerated. Legislators further deterrence by manipulating the objective properties of punishment (e.g., statutory terms of imprisonment) only to the extent there is a close empirical relation between those objective properties and perceived properties (i.e., legal punishment as perceived by the public); and legislators scarcely control that relation. The "perceptual" character of the deterrence doctrine is no less important in contemplating evidential problems in attempts to test the doctrine. In particular, all of the numerous critics of Ehrlich's research appear oblivious to the point that Ehrlich employed no measure of the perceived certainty of executions; indeed, his assumptions about perceptual properties of punishment are at best obscure. See Ehrlich, "The Deterrent Effect of Capital Punishment: A Question of Life and Death," 65 Am. Econ. Rev. 397–417 (1975).

6. See Gibbs, *Crime, Punishment, and Deterrence* (1975).

properties, virtually always the presumptive severity of statutory penalties, the presumptive severity of actual legal punishments, and/or the objective certainty of punishment.[7] The range of properties of legal punishments could be just as important as nondeterrent preventive effects, and the same can be said for distinctions regarding types of deterrence, such as absolute, restrictive, and specific.[8] Unfortunately, however, space limitations make it necessary to restrict this paper to general observations about possible nondeterrent preventive effects of capital punishment.

"Deterrence" is here defined in a legal context as an instance where an individual refrains from a criminal act or somehow limits its commission because of fear that otherwise someone will be legally punished. Space limitations preclude clarifying the definition beyond three brief considerations: 1. The term "fear" implies some perception of risk, however realistic or accurate; 2. the definition does not preclude distinguishing types of deterrence; and 3. the definition admits vicarious deterrence, which stems from fear that someone other than the perpetrator of a crime will be punished.

With few exceptions,[9] writers on deterrence have been indifferent to its definition. Yet, the majority of the definitions in the literature do emphasize the fear of punishment, and, hence, the present definition is conventional. However, because some critics will attempt to deny or belittle the distinctions drawn here between deterrence and other possible preventive effects to legal punishments, there is an issue to confront. Such critics can do so only by rejecting any definition of deterrence that emphasizes the fear of punishment. Even though no definition is demonstrably right or wrong, a definition of deterrence that encompasses all preventive effects of legal punishment would be unconventional and make the term "deterrence" superfluous. Moreover, as argued here, and elsewhere at greater length,[10] the distinction between deterrence and other preventive effects of punishment is crucial in debating penal policy.

7. As a reaction against the older tradition of an exclusive concern with statutory penalties, especially in early studies of capital punishment, contemporary deterrence investigators have abandoned that concern and focused on the objective certainty and presumptive severity of actual legal punishments (admissions to prison, length of prison sentences served, and executions). Yet, legislators and jurists are concerned with statutory penalties, and they scarcely have control over other facets of punishment (e.g., objective certainty). Hence, the empirical question with the most direct bearing on penal policy in the debate over capital punishment is of this form: Given such-and-such change in the statutory death penalty, what will happen to the capital crime rate? Of all of the numerous critics of Ehrlich's research (see note 5 *supra*), only Baldus and Cole emphasize the point that Ehrlich's findings have less policy implications than those of earlier investigators. See Baldus & Cole, "A Comparison of the Work of Thorsten Sellin and Isaac Ehrlich on the Deterrent Effect of Capital Punishment," 85 Yale L.J. 170–86 (1975). See also Sellin, *Capital Punishment* (1967).

8. Note 6 *supra*.

9. See Bedau, *The Death Penalty in America: An Anthology* (1968).

10. Note 6 *supra*.

Some legal punishments are such that individuals subjected to them are *incapacitated;* meaning that the individuals' opportunities for committing subsequent offenses are reduced by the very nature of the punishment. The death penalty is a unique punishment in that it incapacitates absolutely and permanently. But, in recent years, retentionists and revivalists have sought to justify capital punishment primarily by alleging that it deters, while its incapacitative function is seldom emphasized. Indeed, it seems that jurists, Supreme Court Justices in particular, are more sensitive to the notion of incapacitation than are social scientists or even advocates of capital punishment. Still, no one is likely to deny the distinction between deterrence and incapacitation, or fail to recognize that the consequences of incapacitation could be readily misconstrued as evidence of deterrence. Hence, not surprisingly, incapacitation is the only nondeterrent preventive mechanism that has been the subject of systematic research. Yet, attempts to estimate incapacitating effects are riddled with conjectures and admissions to the use of dubious data.[11] Accordingly, there is no justifiable basis for arguing that the findings of Ehrlich and Yunker are evidence that executions prevent murders *through deterrence.*[12]

Of course, one may grant the distinction between deterrence and incapacitation, but deny its importance. That denial cannot be supported by systematic evidence at present, but the reasons for questioning the incapacitating function of capital punishment could be strategic in debates over the death penalty.

If the dramatic quality of executions and the attendant widespread publicity prompts individuals to overestimate the certainty of capital punishment, then the death penalty could deter, even though rarely inflicted. Hence, whereas the deterrence doctrine provides a possible justification for the death penalty even if its application is most uncertain, incapacitation is a defensible rationale only if the death penalty is applied frequently.[13]

11. See Ehrlich, note 5 *supra;* Clarke, "Getting 'Em Out of Circulation: Does Incarceration of Juvenile Offenders Reduce Crime?" 65 J. Crim. L. 528–35 (1975); Greenberg, "The Incapacitative Effect of Imprisonment: Some Estimates," 9 Law & Soc. Rev. 541–8l (1975).
12. See Ehrlich, note 5 *supra;* Yunker, note 2 *supra.*
13. Justice Marshall in *Furman* v. *Georgia,* note 3 *supra,* at 355, explicitly recognizes incapacitation (as do some other U.S. Supreme Court Justices), but emphasizes that it prevents repetition of offenses only to the extent that the application of the death penalty is certain. However, he makes the same argument about deterrence and seems to conclude that the death penalty is now (or was) so uncertain that it cannot deter. That conclusion ignores Bentham's argument that the deterrent impact of a legal punishment is contingent on its severity and celerity as well as its certainty. Of course, the severity of the death penalty may not be such that it somehow "compensates" for negligible certainty; but the more immediate consideration is that no one has been able to demonstrate the exact nature of the alleged mutual contingency of certainty and severity (e.g., whether their impact is additive or interactive and if interactive exactly how). That consideration is only one of several reasons for rejecting the presumption that the deterrence doctrine is a systematic theory; rather, it is little more than a conglomeration of vague ideas.

One glaring defect of death penalty studies is that investigators have not been able to compute capital crime rates, but not even those rates would reveal the incapacitating effects of executions, because the capital crime rate, like any conventional crime rate, is merely the ratio of the number of offenses to population.[14] By contrast, a special kind of rate, the repetitive, is needed to estimate incapacitating effects. The repetitive rate is the average number of times that members of a population have committed a designated kind of crime, with members who have never committed it excluded from the numerator and offenses committed after punishment of the alleged perpetrator excluded from the denominator. For very complicated reasons, such as selectivity in apprehension, not even repetitive crime rates would be an incontrovertible basis for inferring the number of crimes prevented through incapacitation, but the rates are essential for defensible estimates. Generally speaking, an incapacitating punishment prevents offenses only to the extent that the type of crime in question is characterized by a high repetitive rate.

Although the findings of the few relevant studies indicate that the repetitive criminal homicide rate is much lower than the Jack-the-Ripper stereotype of the murderer suggests, those findings are questionable because the studies were limited to statistics on the arrest or conviction histories of individuals who have been charged with or incarcerated for some kind of homicide.[15] Such statistics yield dubious estimates of the frequency with which individuals repeat capital crimes, if only because they exclude individuals who are never arrested, and they are *not* limited to first-degree murder.

Even if a truly defensible repetitive capital crime rate could be computed and even if that rate should prove to be very low, the remote possibility that a capital offender may repeat the offense makes the incapacitating effect of the death penalty a central consideration. Hence, it is surprising that in seeking to justify capital punishment, the retentionists and revivalists have not emphasized incapacitation more than they have, especially in seeking to refute the claim that imprisonment prevents capital crimes just as effectively as does the death penalty. Their argument could be that murderers may repeat their offense in prison. They may refrain from emphasizing that argument because it would suggest a limitation of capital punishment to offenses committed by prisoners, but that limitation could be a constructive step. It would establish a basis for compromise in debates over policy and justify a

---

14. Bailey may well be the first investigator to compute capital murder rates from numerous American jurisdictions and he himself admits that the data employed are far from satisfactory and extremely laborious to gather. See Bailey, "Murder and Capital Punishment: Some Further Evidence," in Bedau & Pierce (eds.), *Capital Punishment in the United States* 314–35 (1976).

15. See Waldo, "The Criminality Level of Incarcerated Murderers and Non-Murders," 61 J. Crim. L. Crim. & Police Sci. 60–70 (1970). Justice Marshall in *Furman* v. *Georgia*, note 3 *supra*, at 352, grasps the significance of these findings, but he does not emphasize the shortcomings of the data.

focus of capital punishment research on prisons, which is more feasible than investigations of the general population.

All research on the death penalty has been limited to marginal deterrence, that is, the efficacy of the death penalty relative to that of imprisonment. In that connection, abolitionists can argue that imprisonment deters more than does capital punishment because the objective certainty of imprisonment seems much greater. True, as already suggested, retentionists or revivalists can argue that the absolute and permanent incapacitation realized through the death penalty is an additional and compelling consideration. But another argument—that the incapacitating effects are less costly in monetary terms than those of imprisonment—is crass and no longer convincing. As long as provisions are made for appeals and supposed humanitarian delays, the death penalty is inexpensive only insofar as no attempt is made to apply it. Yet even if severe statutory penalties deter, they do not incapacitate unless actually applied. In light of such considerations, it is surely difficult to see how the distinction between deterrence and incapacitation could be regarded as insignificant, either as posing evidential problems in deterrence research or as giving rise to issues in debates over penal policy.

There is no conventional label for still another nondeterrent preventive mechanism, but the notion itself has a long history. Some eighty years ago, Emile Durkheim argued forcibly that the major function of legal punishment is not deterrence, but, rather maintenance of the moral condemnation of crime. One must look to a brief statement by Sir James Stephen for a simple exemplification of Durkheim's argument: "The fact that men are hanged for murder is one great reason why murder is considered so dreadful a crime."[16]

The phenomenon described by Durkheim and Stephen is here designated as *normative validation*. Defined explicitly, "normative validation" occurs when an individual's condemnation of some type of criminal act is maintained as a consequence of prescribed legal punishments or their application to other individuals. Given that definition, it is difficult to deny a distinction between normative validation and deterrence. Observe that fear of a risk of legal punishment is necessary for deterrence, but not for normative validation; and, no less important, it would be extremely dubious to argue that individuals refrain from acts only out of fear of punishment. To the contrary, the *primary* determinant of the incidence of any act may well be not the fear of punishment, but rather the extent to which the act is disapproved on moral, religious, or ethical grounds. Even so, legal punishments may play a role in the process by which the condemnation of a particular kind of act is maintained. Indeed, an individual is not likely to persist in the condemnation of some type of act if he or she observes that the act is committed openly and frequently with impunity.

16. See Zimring & Hawkins, *Deterrence: The Legal Threat in Crime Control* 80 (1973).

Despite the foregoing, some social scientists may deny the distinction between normative validation and deterrence, especially if they have identified their research findings as evidence of deterrence without even recognizing normative validation. A reluctance to recognize normative validation would be understandable because validation effects and deterrent effects cannot be distinguished readily. To illustrate, an inverse relation between the crime rate and the presumptive severity of statutory penalties could not be readily attributed to incapacitation, but the relation might reflect normative validation rather than deterrence. The evidential problem stems from recognition that the very conditions that supposedly maximize deterrence—severe, swift, and certain punishment—could also maximize normative validation.

Rather than deny the distinction between normative validation and deterrence, some critics may question the significance of the distinction, either by suggesting that normative validation is a rare phenomenon or by arguing that its preventive effects are negligible. And, in truth, there is a basis for doubting the importance of normative validation. Only a few studies bear even indirectly on the phenomenon itself, and the findings do not suggest that knowledge of the law has an appreciable impact on moral judgments.[17] Yet, the findings of those studies cannot be taken as conclusive, if only because neither the certainty nor the severity of legal punishments were treated as variables. Evidence of normative validation is suggested more by several studies of children's conceptions of law. The findings clearly suggest that punishment looms large in those conceptions. However, it must be recognized that the findings do not demonstrate the extent to which children's morality is shaped by their perceptions of legal punishment.[18] Moreover, whatever the extent of normative validation, the magnitude of its preventive effect on the incidence of crime is another matter; and there has been no research on that question.

While there is a real need for research on capital punishment and normative validation, no amount of research along that line will answer the central question for penal policy: How much normative validation is realized through capital punishment relative to that realized through lengthy prison sentences? Although they do not use the term normative validation, Justices Brennan and Marshall clearly recognize the notion, and they seem to answer

17. Appearance to the contrary, theories or findings about the determinants of attitudes toward legal punishments (see Bedau & Pierce, note 14 *supra*) have no direct bearing on the present argument about normative validation. Specifically, executions of convicted rapists may maintain an individual's condemnation of rape, even though he or she is opposed to the death penalty. See also Berkowitz & Walker, "Laws and Moral Judgement," 30 Sociometry 410–22 (1967).

18. See Tapp & Kohlberg, "Developing Senses of Law and Legal Justice," 27 J. Social Issues 65–91 (1971).

the central question this way[19]: Imprisonment validates norms as much as, if not more than, capital punishment. That answer reflects the emphasis of the two Justices on the infrequent application of the death penalty. No one would question the relevance of that emphasis, but it could be that Justices Brennan and Marshall have not given sufficient weight to the awesome severity and dramatic quality of executions. There is now some research evidence (although based on a very small and select sample) that the public perceives execution as more severe than life imprisonment.[20] However, it could be argued that the perceptual difference does not assure a substantial contrast in the amount of normative validation realized through the two kinds of punishment, especially since the objective certainty of imprisonment is much greater than that of capital punishment.

Although there are nine possible kinds of nondeterrent preventive effects of legal punishments, the importance of most of them is surely questionable. Arguments to that end are strategic if only because there are some definite limits as to what researchers can accomplish in estimating the relative weight of different kinds of preventive effects.

Insofar as criminal behavior is learned through association with convicted felons, the character of legal punishments may determine the incidence of criminality independently of deterrence. Specifically, if a punishment is such that those subjected to it can no longer interact with former associates, then those associates are "insulated" from an influence that could be conducive to criminality. Imprisonment and banishment create some *normative insulation,* but, obviously, *absolute* normative insulation is realized through an execution.

Granted that absolute normative insulation is realized through executions, skepticism about the impact of that insulation on the capital crime rate is surely justified. A brief commentary on first-degree murder must suffice as an illustration. No one, so it seems, has estimated the proportion of murderers whose parents, siblings, or friends were also murderers, yet general observations suggest that the proportion is negligible. Stating the matter more generally, there is simply no systematic evidence that the death penalty could prevent an appreciable number of capital crimes through normative insulation. True, frequent executions might well prevent an appreciable number of noncapital offenses through normative insulation, but who today is prepared

19. See *Furman* v. *Georgia,* note 3 *supra,* at 303; and *Gregg* v. *Georgia,* 96 S. Ct. 2971 (1976). Parties to the debate over capital punishment, including jurists, should commence using the term "infrequent application" with greater care. It can be construed as referring either to the absolute number of executions or to the proportion of capital crimes in which the death penalty was applied. If the latter meaning is intended, it would be more appropriate to speak of the "objective certainty of execution," with the understanding that unless qualified otherwise (e.g., certainty given arrest) the term refers to certainty given *commission* of a capital crime.

20. Hamilton & Rotkin, "Interpreting the Eighth Amendment: Perceived Seriousness of Crime and Severity of Punishment," in Bedau & Pierce (eds.), note 14 *supra,* at 502–24.

to argue that some individuals should be put to death so that others will not commit, say, shoplifting? In any case, where the existence of the death penalty may deter without frequent executions, normative insulation is realized only through actual executions. Hence, since all evidence indicates that the objective certainty of capital punishment is negligible by any reasonable standard, there is every reason to assume that it prevents very little crime through normative insulation.

Even if individuals commonly commit crimes solely out of ignorance of the law and even if the publicized punishment of criminals furthers dissemination of legal knowledge, it is surely difficult to believe that executions prevent an appreciable number of capital offenses through *enculturation.* That is the case because it seems that the vast majority of the risk population knows that rape and murder are crimes and subject to some kind of legal punishment. More specifically, it seems unlikely that executions truly advance the public's knowledge of criminal law. True, executions may possibly correct underestimations of the range of capital offenses and thereby further deterrence, but the preventive function of enculturation has nothing to do with deterrence. Rather, for some individuals, knowledge of a criminal law is a sufficient condition for conformity to it, that is, without regard to fear of punishment. Stating the matter another way, individuals who respect the law are informed, but not deterred, by punishments.

The foregoing argument in no sense questions the distinction between enculturation and deterrence. The distinction itself is not in doubt; rather, the significance of enculturation is debatable, because there is reason to believe that the preventive effects of legal punishment through enculturation are negligible, especially in the case of capital punishment. Moreover, even if the preventive effect of enculturation were substantial, the argument is a thin reed for advocating capital punishment. A truly grotesque morality would be required to argue that human beings should be put to death for the sake of educating the public, especially since there are all manner of alternative means to that end—imprisonment in particular.

Some individuals fear the extralegal consequences of legal punishment as much as if not more than the legal punishment itself. Such extralegal consequences are here designated as *stigmatization.* A precise definition of the term cannot be formulated, but illustrations are easily provided—ostracism, loss of employment, divorce, and disinheritance. Such a termination of a social relation may occur, of course, even when someone is only suspected of a crime. However, social relations are particularly likely to be terminated as a consequence of legal guilt and punishment, because punishment is commonly viewed as the ultimate criterion of guilt. Hence, the supposition is that numerous individuals refrain from criminal acts because they fear stigmatizing consequences over and beyond the immediate and direct pain of a legal punishment.

Stigmatization is the most complex nondeterrent preventive effect of legal punishments. Since fear of a painful consequence is the essential feature of both mechanisms, it may seem that there is no real difference between prevention through deterrence and prevention through stigmatization. However, in the case of stigmatization, the prospective perpetrator refrains from a criminal act out of a fear of the risk of something distinct from, and actually beyond, the legal punishment itself. Yet the assumption is not that everyone fears the extralegal consequences of criminal sanctions or that such fear is substantial for some individuals in all social conditions. The fear is especially likely to be negligible where members of a caste or social class are exploited and controlled coercively. In such a case, the members are prone to view criminal law as imposed on them and hence devoid of moral significance.[21] For that matter, if the theory of secondary deviance is valid, stigmatization may offset specific deterrence and actually generate more crimes than it prevents.[22] However, such possibilities make the notion all the more important; it facilitates explanation of what seems to be indisputable—that the relation between the character of legal punishment and the crime rate is neither close nor constant.

Since stigmatization probably has no impact on the crime rate in some conditions or may generate more crimes than it prevents, there is some justification for ignoring it in conducting deterrence research. Moreover, should advocates of the death penalty emphasize its preventive effects through stigmatization, their opponents can counter with a plausible argument—that life imprisonment stigmatizes as much as if not more than execution.

An old-fashioned word—"habit"—is appropriate in describing another possible consequence of punishment. The idea is that a particular behavior pattern may be established by the threat of punishment. Of course, those subject to the threat are initially fully aware of it and conform to the behavior pattern consciously. Eventually, however, the behavior is conditioned without any immediate awareness of a threat of punishment. When conformity to a law takes on such an uncritical, unreflective quality, it is *habituation* rather than deterrence.

Whatever the justification for distinguishing between habituation and deterrence, habituation is hardly relevant in contemplating the preventive effects of the death penalty. The threat of punishment cannot establish a habit unless the behavior is such that individuals engage in it frequently. Eating, driving, and various forms of entertainment qualify, but capital crimes scarcely have anything to do with everyday behavior.

Classical versions of the retributive doctrine explicitly reject a utilitarian justification of legal punishment. Yet a legal punishment may be something

---

21. See Balbus, *The Dialetics of Legal Repression: Black Rebels Before the American Criminal Courts* (1973).
22. See Grove, *The Labeling of Deviance: Evaluating a Perspective* (1975).

more than pure retribution; it can also be a substitute for private vengeance and, as such, prevent crimes. If legal punishments are truly substitutes for private vengeance, and if the public comes to perceive the statutory penalty for a particular type of crime as highly improbable or extremely lenient, then increasingly the victims of that crime or their surrogates will seek private vengeance. However, what an otherwise law-abiding citizen construes as justified revenge, the police may regard as battery, extortion, murder, or kidnapping. So, viewed that way, the *retribution* realized through legal punishments may prevent vengeful crimes.[23]

While the death penalty is likely to satisfy a citizen's demand for vengeance, the public evidently perceives life imprisonment as a very severe punishment. Surely, there is no evidence that private vengeance of crimes is more common in jurisdictions where the death penalty has been abolished. For that matter, movie and television scripts notwithstanding, despite a decline in the certainty and presumptive severity of legal punishments in general, only rarely do Americans seek private vengeance for crimes, especially in cases where a legal punishment has been imposed. It may well be that once the certainty of legal punishment is perceived by the citizens as virtually nil, then there will be an upsurge of private vengeance of crimes. In that connection, since juries are evidently more reluctant to convict in a capital trial, then imprisonment may prevent more crime through its retributive function than does the death penalty.

The severity of the death penalty is so awesome that its other qualities receive less attention in contemporary debates than in Bentham's day. In particular, at least two kinds of nondeterrent preventive effects of legal punishments are clearly irrelevant in contemplating the death penalty, and it is perhaps significant that neither kind is even tacitly recognized in the recent decisions by the Supreme Court about capital punishment.

Legal punishments can be such that their imposition makes the behavior of potential recidivists more subject to the scrutiny of the public and/or officials; and, insofar as potential recidivists are aware of being subject to *surveillance*, they are likely to refrain from criminal acts as a consequence.

---

23. Unlike normative insulation, enculturation, habituation, and stigmatization, this possible consequence of capital punishment was expressly or tacitly recognized in recent opinions of U.S. Supreme Court Justices. Justice Stewart in *Furman* v. *Georgia*, note 3 *supra*, at 308, places particular emphasis on the phenomenon in question, but he does not literally use the term "prevention of crime" in alluding to the retributive function of legal punishments. The point is important primarily because Justice Marshall in *Gregg* v. *Georgia*, note 19 *supra*, at 2971, rejects "retribution for its own sake," thereby suggesting that the retributive doctrine is acceptable only insofar as it has a utilitarian character (e.g., that legal punishments prevent vengeful crimes). However, as previously suggested, Justice Stewart at least tacitly recognizes a utilitarian character of retribution, while some statements by the other Justices about retribution do not suggest that recognition. So, whether a *purely* retributive punishment is "constitutionally permissible" remains an open question.

Since they refrain out of fear of being punished again, the effect in question may appear to be specific deterrence. However, consider probation and parole, the only legal punishments in Anglo-American jurisdictions other than imprisonment that have real surveillance potential. If the suspicion of surveillance leads a probationer or parolee to refrain from a criminal act, he or she refrains not out of fear of being placed on probation or parole again, but, rather, out of the fear that probation or parole will be revoked and a more severe punishment applied.

Advocates of capital punishment surely view its absolute incapacitating effect as the "final solution," and that view is likely to persist until abolitionists offer something other than incarceration as an alternative. Granted that the possibility appears remote, communication technology may change to the point that surveillance becomes still another way to check recidivism. If so, surveillance will become the control issue in debates over penal policy, and arguments over it have already commenced.[24]

The idea of *reformation* is so alien to contemporary America that parties to the debates over penal policy commonly confuse it with rehabilitation. A distinction can be drawn if one is willing to believe that being punished in itself can alter an individual's values and sense of obligation to the point that he or she refrains from recidivism. Like specific deterrence, reformation commences with punishment for a criminal act, but the two differ in that reformation does not require continuation of the threat of punishment.

Opponents of the death penalty are particularly likely to question the idea that any legal punishment reforms, just as they question the reality of specific deterrence. However, advocates of capital punishment may share that very skepticism, and they see in the absolute incapacitative effect of executions something that is beyond conjecture. Those advocates evidently suffer from gloomy doubts about the perfectability of *homo sapiens,* individually if not collectively, and it may well be that those doubts alone sustain the death penalty.

Since there is virtually no systematic evidence of the nondeterrent preventive effects just described, critics may allege that this paper provides advocates of the death penalty with an unwarranted argument. However, most of those nondeterrent kinds of effects have been expressly or tacitly recognized by others;[25] and there are reasons for explicitly introducing the subject into the scholarly literature on capital punishment—one reason being that jurists and legislators at least tacitly recognize the possibility of nondeterrent preventive effects. For that matter, it is difficult to imagine anyone attempting research on nondeterrent preventive effects of capital punishment without initial

24. See Shapiro, "The Use of Behavior Control Technologies: A Response," 7 Issues in Crim. 55–93 (1972).
25. See Zimring & Hawkins, *Deterrence: The Legal Threat in Crime Control* (1973). See also Andenaes, *Punishment and Deterrence* (1974).

arguments as to the potential significance of the research. No less important, courts in Anglo-American jurisdictions clearly appreciate the role of argumentation; and if empirical questions cannot be introduced without systematic evidence to answer them, that requirement would virtually terminate the debate over capital punishment.

As for the allegation that this paper will aid the advocates of capital punishment, such is not the intention. Moreover, only two kinds of nondeterrent preventive effects of capital punishment are recognized here as possibly important, those two being incapacitation and normative validation; and even recognition of incapacitation is qualified by the argument that the impact of that effect on the capital crime rate may well be negligible. The impact of normative validation on the rate could be substantial, but, even so, there is no truly compelling evidence that life imprisonment validates criminal laws less than does capital punishment.

Debates over legal punishments and crime prevention should not be limited to arguments about deterrence. There are nine possible mechanisms or ways by which crimes could be prevented other than through deterrence, and some of these mechanisms have been emphasized by parties to the debate over capital punishment. Hence, the debate gives rise to empirical questions that can never be answered if research is limited to the subject of deterrence. As for the objection that the different kinds of preventive effects are irrelevant in contemplating penal policy, that objection ignores some very important distinctions concerning the properties of legal punishments. Thus, to illustrate, what seems to be a very severe statutory penalty may prevent some crimes through deterrence, normative validation, or both, but statutory severity cannot prevent crimes through either incapacitation or normative insulation, for those mechanisms operate only in the case of actual punishments.

Such distinctions have yet to be taken seriously in research on capital punishment, and the situation may appear to be one of those rare and refreshing cases where a call for more research is *not* needed. The different preventive mechanisms become relevant in assessing research evidence only if the evidence indicates that the punishment in question prevents crimes through one mechanism or another. The remarkable feature of research on capital punishment is that the findings hardly constitute systematic evidence of *any kind* of preventive effect, and that is particularly so, given widespread criticism of Ehrlich's study.[26] That feature of the research is all the more remarkable if viewed this way: Given all of the various ways that capital punishment could prevent crimes, there is no systematic evidence that it prevents crimes in any way more than does imprisonment. Such a summary will strike advocates of capital punishment as all too paradoxical, but it is not so in the light of this

26. See note 5 *supra*.

paper's central theme. In all studies of capital punishment the investigators have wittingly or unwittingly compared that penalty with imprisonment, and there is every reason to suppose that the two penalties have the same kind of preventive effects. Indeed, given the much greater objective certainty of imprisonment, its preventive effects, whatever the kind, may well exceed those of the death penalty.

Appearances to the contrary, the foregoing argument does not amount to an assertion that additional research on capital punishment would be a wasted effort. Yet a continuation of traditional lines of work, including the econometric approach, would be a wasted effort. Specifically, it may be that the findings have been negative largely because the investigators failed to consider all of the different possible ways by which capital punishment could prevent crimes, and manifestations of all such possible effects, if any, will not be detected until investigators cease limiting their research to one property of that punishment. There are nine possible relevant properties of punishment and it is ludicrous to presume that all of them are taken into account by such grotesque expressions as "let C equal the cost of committing a crime." The possible preventive effects of capital punishment will be assessed properly only when the research design is such that each property of punishment is treated as a distinct empirical variable, and one that is represented numerically.

§2.   The Deterrent Effect
of the Death Penalty:
Facts v. Faith*

HANS ZEISEL

I. Once again in the 1975 Term, the Justices of the Supreme Court found themselves unable to express a unified position on the validity of the death penalty. The problem is a complex one because of murky precedents, disputed facts, and strong emotional commitments. It is proposed here to address just one of the issues raised in the cases, the question of the data supporting or controverting the deterrent effect of the death penalty.

*From Hans Zeisel, "The Deterrent Effect of the Death Penalty: Facts v. Faith," in Philip B. Kurland, ed., *The Supreme Court Review 1976*, pp. 317–43. © 1977 by the University of Chicago, all rights reserved. Tables and figures have been renumbered and cross-references adjusted accordingly.

In one of the opinions in *Gregg* v. *Georgia*[1]—there was no opinion for the Court—Mr. Justice Stewart, speaking for himself and Justices Powell and Stevens, stated: "Statistical attempts to evaluate the worth of the death penalty as a deterrent to crimes by potential offenders have occasioned a great deal of debate. The results simply have been inconclusive."[2] The Justice went on to cite with approval the position of Professor Charles L. Black, that no conclusive evidence would ever be available on the question of deterrence:

> after all possible inquiry, including the probing of all possible methods of inquiry, we do not know, and for systematic and easily visible reasons cannot know, what the truth about this "deterrent" effect may be. . . .
> . . . A "scientific"—that is to say, a soundly based—conclusion is simply impossible, and no methodological path out of this tangle suggests itself.[3]

It is the purpose of this paper to show that both the Court's and Professor Black's views are wrong; that the evidence we have is quite sufficient if we ask the right question; and that the request for more proof is but the expression of an unwillingness to abandon an ancient prejudice.

II. All studies that explore the possible deterrent effect of capital punishment are efforts to simulate the conditions of what is conceded to be an impossible controlled experiment. In such an experiment the population would be divided by some lottery process (randomly) into two groups. The members of one group, if convicted of a capital crime, would receive the death penalty; the members of the other group, if convicted of a capital crime, would receive a sentence of life in prison.

The random selection would assure that other conditions that could possibly affect the capital crime rate remain the same—within the calculable limits of the sampling error—in both groups, so that the "death penalty–life sentence" difference remains the only relevant difference between them.

Figure 4-2-1 shows the basic analytical structure of such an experiment. This hypothetical graph, denoting the constellation that would confirm the existence of a deterrent effect, begins with two populations of would-be murderers $(X + Y + Z)$, equal in every respect except that the one lives under threat of the death penalty, the other does not. (X) is the number of would-be murderers in both groups deterred, even by the threat of prison; it can be read from the first bar and projected to the second. At the bottom end of each bar (Z) is the proportion of would-be murderers whom even the threat of the death penalty would not deter. It can be read from the second bar and projected to the first. The crucial test is whether a group (Y) can be found which would be deterred by the death penalty but would not be deterred if

1. 96 S. Ct. 2909 (1976).
2. Id. at 2930.
3. Id. at 2931, quoting Black, Capital Punishment: The Inevitability of Caprice and Mistake 25–26 (1974).

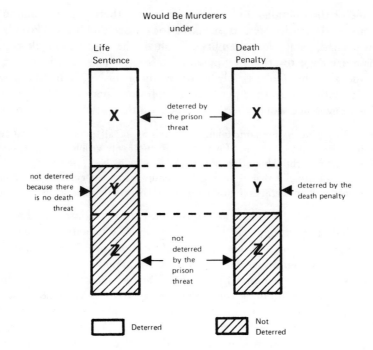

Figure 4-2-1. Experimental Paradigm Showing a Deterrent Effect of the Death Penalty Over the Life Sentence

there were only the life sentence. The statistical test that would establish the existence of group (Y) would reveal a significantly lower level of murders[4] under threat of the death penalty.

In principle, it should be possible to identify individual members in each of the three groups. As a practical matter one can identify only the murderers who have not been deterred.[5] Efforts have been made to identify members of the (Y) group. The Los Angeles Police Department, for instance, filed a report with the California legislature in 1960 to the effect that a number of apprehended robbers had told the police that while on their job they had used either toy guns or empty guns or simply simulated guns "rather than take a chance on killing someone and getting the gas chamber."[6] Quite apart from

4. The paradigm is limited to murder. See also, however, Bailey, *Rape and the Death Penalty: A Neglected Area of Deterrence Research,* in Bedau & Pierce, eds. Capital Punishment in the United States 336 (1976).
5. The task of tracing the effect of an experimental treatment through case histories of the persons who had been affected by it is less difficult if the treatment aims at a positive effect, not a negative, deterrent one. See Zeisel, Say It with Figures ch. 11 (1965 ed.).
6. Report of the California Senate on the Death Penalty 16–17 (1960).

this being hearsay evidence reported by a very interested party, this is poor evidence, if any, on the issue. The unresolved and probably unresolvable difficulty is whether these robbers would not have minded "killing someone," if the risk had been no more than life in prison.

Figure 4-2-2 represents the paradigm diagram for proving the deterrent effect of increasing executions. Proof of deterrence would be established if groups (Y_1) and (Y_2) were found to exist.

III. Such diagrammed evidence would be cogent if derived from a controlled experiment. How morally and legally impossible such an experiment is can easily be seen if its details are sketched out. In one conceivable version a state would have to decree that citizens convicted of a capital crime and born on odd-numbered days of the month would be subject to the death penalty; citizens born on even-numbered days would face life in prison. A significantly lower number of capital crimes committed by persons born on uneven days would confirm the deterrent effect. The date of birth here is a

Figure 4-2-2. Experimental Paradigm Showing a Deterrent Effect of Increasing the Rate of Executions

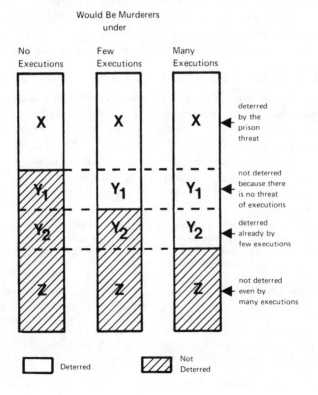

device of randomly dividing the population into halves by a criterion that we will assume cannot be manipulated.[7]

The equally impossible experiment that would test the effect of differenial frequencies of execution would require at least three randomly selected groups. In the first group everybody convicted of a capital crime would be executed. In the second, only every other such convict (again selected by lot) would be executed. In the third, nobody would be executed.

The data available to us for study of the deterrent effect of the death penalty are all naturally grown; none derive from a controlled experiment. Yet they are all analyzed as if they had come from a controlled experiment. The structure of analysis is the same. What is missing is the prior randomization which insures comparability in all other respects. The analysis of naturally grown data must try to reproduce comparability by other means. Since none of these means is ever perfect, none of the studies based on naturally grown data ever completely simulates the impossible experiment.

It is this impossibility of the experiment and the unavoidable imperfection of nonexperimental data that account for despair of ever discovering "the truth about this 'deterrent' effect."[8] The despair is unwarranted. Even in the so-called natural sciences proofs that are incomplete have nevertheless, for good reasons, been accepted by the scientific community.

Let us see then what proofs have been afforded by the many studies that have been done. They are stated here, not in their historical sequence, but in terms of the varying degree with which they approximate the ideal of the controlled experiment.

IV. The first approximation to the impossible experiment is the simple comparison of the capital crime rates in jurisdictions with and without capital punishment. The comparison could take two forms. Historically the first and most obvious comparison was made of the capital crime rate in one state before and after the abolition of the death penalty. If it showed no increase, it gave ground for the belief that the withdrawal of the death penalty had no ill effect.[9] The second form of simple comparison was between states that have the death penalty and states that do not have it.[10]

---

7. Worried, expectant mothers, of course, could demand Caesarian delivery on an even-numbered date. Such intervention, however, would affect the purity of the experiment only if these mothers were also farsighted, i.e., if their artificial birthdates would comprise a higher rate of future murderers than the normal deliveries.

8. Note 3 *supra*.

9. The first comprehensive data on before-and-after comparison were presented by Thorsten Sellin to the Royal Commission on Capital Punishment. *The Deterrent Value of Capital Punishment,* Report of the Royal Commission on Capital Punishment App. 6 (Cmd. 8932 1953). Sellin's memorandum is published in the Minues of the Evidence, 647. *Cf.* also Koestler, Reflections on Hanging App. (1956); United Nations, Capital Punishment, Report (1960); Samuelson, *Why Was Capital Punishment Restored in Delaware?* 60 J. Crim. L.C. & P.S. 148 (1969).

10. Sellin, *Homicides in Retentionist and Abolitionist States,* in Sellin, ed., Capital Punishment

Table 4-2-1. Homicide Death Rates in Contiguous States with[D] and without Capital Punishment, 1940–1955 (average annual rate per 100,000 population)

Midwest		New England	
Michigan	3.5	Maine	1.5
Indiana (D)	3.5	New Hampshire (D)	0.9
Ohio (D)	3.5	Vermont (D)	1.0
Minnesota	1.4	Rhode Island	1.3
Wisconsin	1.2	Massachusetts (D)	1.2
Iowa (D)	1.4	Connecticut (D)	1.7
N. Dakota	1.0		
S. Dakota (D)	1.5		
Nebraska (D)	1.8		

These early comparisons failed to show higher capital crime rates when there was no death penalty. But to take this as proof that the death penalty had no deterrent effect involved important assumptions. The before and after comparison implies that none of the other conditions that could have affected the capital crime rate had changed between the two periods. The state-by-state comparison implies that the states were identical with respect to the other conditions.

The first improvement on the simplistic structure of these comparisons was to put the before-and-after comparison side by side with developments in states which during that period had not changed their death penalty rule. Similarly, the comparison between states was improved by limiting it to contiguous states, for which the assumption of comparability seems more justified.

Table 4-2-1 provides an example of contiguous states comparison.[11] Only in one of the five groups is the homicide crime rate in the no-death-penalty state (Maine) higher than in the other two states. In all others it is either the same or lower. This is neither evidence of a deterrent effect of the death penalty nor clear evidence of its absence. Even contiguous states are not strictly comparable. Over a span of sixteen years, the period covered by this table, the conditions favoring crime in those states may develop in different directions.

---

135 (1967); Reckless, *The Use of the Death Penalty—a Factual Statement,* 15 Crime & Delinq. 43 (1969); Zimring & Hawkins, Deterrence 265 (1973); Baldus & Cole, *A Comparison of the Work of Thorsten Sellin and Isaac Ehrlich on the Deterrent Effect of Capital Punishment,* 85 Yale L.J. 170, 171 (1976).

11. Zimring & Hawkins, note 10 *supra,* at 265.

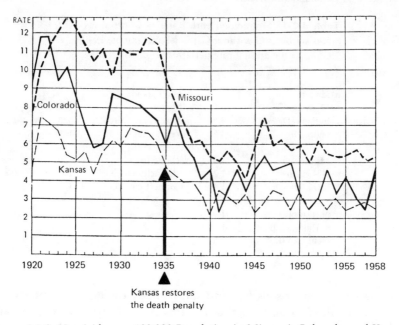

Figure 4-2-3. Homicides per 100,000 Population in Missouri, Colorado, and Kansas, 1920–1958

The state-by-state analysis becomes more convincing if averages for a long time period are replaced by the annual figures from which these averages were computes. In Figure 4-2-3, the homicide rate in Kansas is compared with that of its neighbor states, Missouri and Colorado. Kansas was an abolitionist state until 1935.[12]

Figure 4-2-3 allows several observations. First, that annual rates exhibit considerable random fluctuations. It suggests that changes from one year to the next are unlikely to be significant. Figure 4-2-3 also shows that looking only at one state may lead to false conclusions. The Kansas homicide rate, except for the first two years, shows a sharp decline after 1935 and some early observers jumped to the conclusion that it was the restoration of the death penalty that did it. A glance at the homicide rates of Colorado and Missouri warns against this conclusion. The development of the Kansas rate does not noticeably differ from those of the two neighboring states, which had the death penalty throughout the entire span of years.

V. Comparing the development of the capital crime rate in contiguous states with and without the death penalty has been challenged on the ground that contiguity is not a sufficiently solid guaranty of likeness. Three responses to this challenge have been forthcoming. One was to show that the contig-

12. From Sellin, note 10 *supra*, at 137.

uous states were in fact alike with respect to a great variety of factors that could, if they had differed from state to state, independently affect the capital crime rate. Table 4-2-2 is an example of such efforts.[13]

Michigan, the state without a death penalty, had no higher homicide rate than neighboring Indiana, even though it had a lower probability of apprehension and conviction, a higher unemployment rate, a larger proportion of blacks in the population, greater population density—all factors which should tend to increase the capital crime rate. On the other hand, it had a higher per capita police expenditure. Ohio had a lower homicide rate and a higher apprehension rate. On most of the remaining characteristics Ohio was in an intermediary position.

The second analytical device for improving comparability was to replace the comparison of entire states by comparing more homogeneous subsections of these states, such as communities of comparable size or counties of comparable income levels.[14] The third, most sophisticated response to the problem of comparability was to apply to it a tool called regression analysis. This is an instrument designed mainly to resolve problems such as this which call for separating the effect of one particular variable from the possible effect of a multitude of others.

Before discussing regression analysis in more detail, I turn to two additional efforts to sharpen the analytic approach aimed at detecting the existence of a deterrent effect for the death penalty.

Table 4-2-2. Demographic Profile of Contiguous States Compared in Group 1 of Table 4-2-1 (1960 data)

	Michigan	Indiana	Ohio
Status of death penalty	. . .	D	D
Homicide rate	4.3	4.3	3.2
Probability of apprehension	.75	.83	.85
Probability of conviction	.25	.55	.33
Labor force participation	54.9%	55.3%	54.9%
Unemployment rate	6.9%	4.2%	5.5%
Population aged 15–24	12.9%	13.4%	12.9%
Real per capita income	$1292	$1176	$1278
Nonwhite population	10.4%	6.2%	9.8%
Civilian population (000's)	7811	4653	9690
Per capita government expenditures[a]	$363	$289	$338
Per capita police expenditures[a]	$11.3	$7.6	$9.0

[a]State and local.

13. From Baldus & Cole, note 10 *supra*, at 178.
14. Cf. e.g., Sutherland, *Murder and the Death Penalty*, 15 J. Crim. L.C. & P.S. 520 (1925); Campion, *Does the Death Penalty Protect the State Police?* in Bedau, ed., The Death Penalty in America 361 (1967); Vold, *Can the Death Penalty Prevent Crime?* 12 Prison J. 4 (1932).

VI. If the death penalty deters murder, the rate of willful homicides should show the effect. There are, however, grades of willfulness and some types of homicide will have a higher likelihood of resulting in the death penalty. These types of homicide should provide a more sensitive index for detecting deterrent effect, if one exists, than the overall homicide rate.[15]

The difficulty of developing such an index, of course, is the lack of adequate data. With one exception, namely, the killing of a police officer, records are not generally separated according to the type of homicide committed. An effort has been made to obtain counts of first degree murders from the country's prisons.[16] But these numbers are affected by regionally differing apprehension and conviction rates, and indirectly also by differential standards of plea bargaining and jury nullification. Suffice it to note that this effort too failed to detect a deterrent effect of the death penalty.

Killing a policeman is a genuine "high death penalty risk" category and it is well recorded and counted. Again it was Thorsten Sellin who investigated them; Table 4-2-3 summarizes his findings.[17] Even this measure, rightly thought to be more sensitive than the general homicide rate, failed to reveal any difference between the threat of the death penalty and that of life imprisonment.

VII. A sentence is likely to deter by the differential degree of fear it engenders in the would-be perpetrator. It has been argued, therefore, that the dichotomy of jurisdictions with and without capital punishment is but a crude approximation to the reality of the threat. What matters was not the death penalty on the books but the reality of executions.

One response to this consideration was to transform the death penalty–life sentence dichotomy into the gradations provided by the number of executions carried out during any one year. I will return to this approach later. The other response was to try to find out whether publicized executions had a short-range depressing effect on the homicide rate.

Leonard Savitz recorded the homicide rates during the eight weeks before and after well-publicized executions in Philadelphia.[18] He found no depressing effect of these executions, although he used one of the potentially more sensitive measures of deterrence, the frequency of felony murders, rather than the overall homicide rate.[19]

A similar effort with California data showed an effect, albeit an ambiguous one. William Graves compared homicide rates during execution weeks with

15. Zimring & Hawkins, *Deterrence and Marginal Groups*, J. Res. in Crime & Delinq. 100 (July 1968).
16. Bailey, *Murder and Capital Punishment: Some Further Evidence*, in Bedau & Pierce, note 4 *supra*, at 314.
17. Sellin, *The Death Penalty and Police Safety*, in Sellin, note 10 *supra*, at 138, 144, 145.
18. Savitz, *A Study in Capital Punishment*, 49 J. Crim. L.C. & P.S. 338 (1958).
19. A count of felony murders (for the non-lawyer: a homicide committed in the course of another felony such as robbery) can be made only with great difficulty and only in places, such as Philadelphia, where detailed police records are kept.

Table 4-2-3. Rate of Municipal Police Killings, 1920–1954 (per 10 years and 100,000 population)

No Capital Punishment		Capital Punishment	
Maine	.00	Vermont	.00
Rhode Island	.17	New Hampshire	.14
		Massachusetts	.22
		Connecticut	.14
Michigan[a]	.36	Ohio	.61
		Indiana	.64
		Illinois	.31
Minnesota	.42	Iowa	.56
Wisconsin	.53		
N. Dakota	.53	S. Dakota	.00
		Montana	1.58
		New York	.25
Detroit, Mich.	.85	Chicago, Ill.[b]	1.54

[a] Without Detroit.
[b] 1928–1944.

non-execution weeks.[20] He had the weeks begin on Tuesday in order to keep Fridays, the execution day in California, at the midpoint. The comparison (Figure 4-2-4a) suggested a depressing effect during the days preceding the execution and an increase in homicides on the days following it. Graves was puzzled; others considered the data as proof of a counter-deterrent effect. Conceivably the data could be rearranged, as in Figure 4-2-4b, with the week beginning on Friday, the execution day. The results would then suggest a reduction of homicides during the first three days following executions compensated by an increase during the rest of the week. In any event, Grave's data show, at best, a delaying rather than a deterrent effect, and the failure of the more sensitive Philadelphia data to show any effect casts doubt on the strength of the California result.

VIII. Isaac Ehrlich was the first to introduce regression analysis to efforts designed to determine whether the death penalty had a deterrent effect beyond the threat of life imprisonment.[21] This was a new, powerful way of

20. Graves, *The Deterrent Effect of Capital Punishment in California,* in Bedau, The Death Penalty in America 322 (1967). (The rearrangement in Figure 4-2-4b is not precise because the curves for Tuesdays through Thursdays will change under the redefinition.)
21. Ehrlich, *The Deterrent Effect of Capital Punishment: A Question of Life and Death,* Working Paper No. 18, National Bureau of Economic Research (1973). The paper was subsequently published under the same title in an abbreviated form in 65 Am. Econ. Rev. 397 (1975).

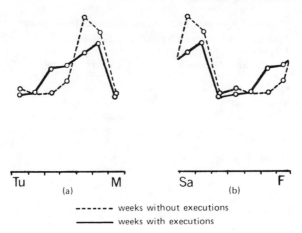

------- weeks without executions
———— weeks with executions

Figure 4-2-4. Homicides During Weeks With and Without Executions

coping with the task of isolating the death penalty effect, if it should exist, uncontaminated by other influences on the capital crime rate. Ehrlich's paper was catapulted into the center of legal attention even before it was published, when the Solicitor General of the United States cited it with lavish praise in his Amicus Curiae Brief in *Fowler* v. *North Carolina*,[22] and delivered copies of the study to the Court. The Solicitor General called it "important empirical support for the a priori logical belief that use of the death penalty decreases the number of murders."[23]

In view of the evidence available up to that time, Ehrlich's claim was indeed formidable, both in substance and precision: "[A]n additional execution per year . . . may have resulted in . . . 7 or 8 fewer murders."[24] The basic data from which he derived this conclusion were the executions and the homicide rates as recorded in the United States during the years 1933 to 1969, the former generally decreasing, the latter, especially during the sixties, sharply increasing.[25] Figure 4-2-5 presents the crucial divergence between 1960 and 1969. Ehrlich considered simultaneously other variables that could affect the capital crime rate through calculations I shall discuss presently.[26]

22. 96 S. Ct. 3212 (1976).
23. Reply Brief, p. 36.
24. Ehrlich, note 20, *supra*, 65 Am. Econ. Rev. at 414.
25. Data on murders from *The Deterrent Effect of Capital Punishment: A Question of Life and Death,* Sources and Data, May 1975, Memorandum by I. Ehrlich. Data on executions from: National Prisoner Statistics, U.S. Bureau of Prisons.
26. Ehrlich's analysis included the following variables: the arrest rate in murder cases; the conviction rate of arrested murder suspects; the rate of labor force participation; the unemployment rate; the fraction of the population in the age group 14 to 24; and per capita income.

IX. Regression analysis proceeds essentially in the following manner. Suppose one knew for certain that, aside from the possible deterrent effect of executing murderers, there was but one other factor that influenced the capital crime rate: the proportion of men between the ages of 17 and 24 in the total population. The analysis would then begin by relating the capital crime rate in the various states to the proportion of young men in those states, as in Figure 4-2-6.

The points in this graph may represent either different jurisdictions at one point of time, or different points of time in the same jurisdiction, or both. The straight line (the regression line) represents the best estimate of the relationship between the proportion of young men in the population and the capital crime rate. The vertical distance of each point from the regression line represents the residual part of the variations in the capital crime rate, the part that remains unexplained after the effect of the "proportion of young men" has been eliminated. One then proceeds to test whether these residuals are related to the frequency of executions, by plotting them against the number of executions in the respective states as in Figure 4-2-7. If no relationship exists, a horizontal regression line will indicate that executions have no deterrent effect (a): No matter how executions vary, the capital crime rate remains the same. If a relationship exists (b), the downward slope of the regression line would indicate that as the frequency of executions increases, capital crime decreases. That graph, one will note in passing, is in appearance

Figure 4-2-5. United States Homicide Rates and Number of Executions, 1960–1969

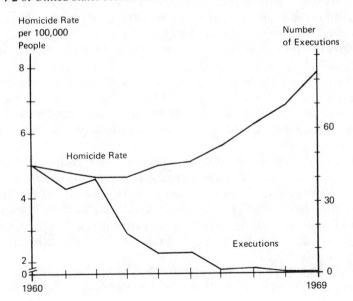

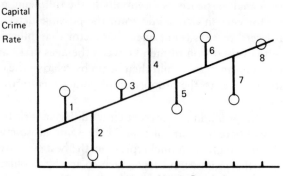

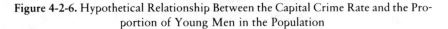

Figure 4-2-6. Hypothetical Relationship Between the Capital Crime Rate and the Proportion of Young Men in the Population

indistinguishable from the finding of a controlled experiment, if one could be made.

The complete apparatus of regression analysis is more complicated, primarily by encompassing several control variables, not just one, as in our example. Many more problems must be resolved along the way. One requirement is to include all variables that affect the outcome. If one is omitted its effect could be erroneously attributed to one of the included variables. This danger of spurious correlation is particularly great if the analysis is concerned with so-called time series data, such as corresponding constellations of executions and capital crime over a series of consecutive years.

Another requirement is that the analysis account for feedback effects. Estimates of deterrent effects of punishment, for example, may be distorted if they fail to separate the simple statistical association between crime and punishment into its potential two components: the effect of punishment on crime, and the possible reverse effect of crime on punishment. For example, an increase in crime may overload the law enforcement system and thereby increase the defendant's chances of a lower sentence in the plea bargaining process.

All these and other technical refinements of the regression analysis have but one goal: to isolate, through a process of mathematical purification, the effect of any one variable upon the other, under conditions that exclude the interference from other variables. Regression analysis, thus, is but another effort to simulate with the help of nonexperimental data the experimental conditions outlined in Figure 4-2-2 of this paper.[27] These examples suggest

27. A more elaborate effort by me to explain regression analysis to the non-statistician is in preparation and will be published in the *American Bar Foundation Research Journal.*

the sophistication of this analytic instrument, but its sophistication is matched by a corresponding measure of delicacy. Applied to nonexperimental data, regression analysis is not a naturally robust instrument. Its results can be drastically affected by minor changes in the analytic pattern, for which the investigator has, as a rule, many options.

X. Ehrlich's study, because it ran counter to all the hitherto available evidence except that of Graves, and because it was introduced into a litigation of historic import, received extraordinary attention from the scholarly community.

First, Peter Passell and John Taylor attempted to replicate Ehrlich's finding and found it to hold up only under an unusually restrictive set of circumstances.[28] They found, for example, that the appearance of deterrence is produced only when the regression equation is in logarithmic form; in the more conventional linear regression framework, the deterrent effect disappeared.[29] They found also that no such effect emerged when data for the years after 1962 were omitted from the analysis and only the years 1933–61 were considered.[30]

An effort to duplicate Ehrlich's findings from Canadian experience also failed.[31] Kenneth Avio of the University of Victoria, after analyzing the thirty-five-year span, concluded that "the evidence would appear to indicate that Canadian offenders over the period 1926–60 did not behave in a manner consistent with an effective deterrent effect of capital punishment."[32]

Figure 4-2-7. Two Hypothetical Relationships between the Frequency of Execution and the Residual Crime Rate

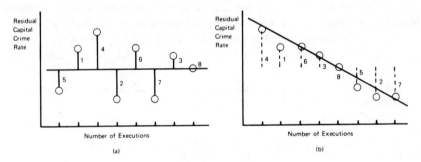

28. Passell & Taylor, *The Deterrent Effect of Capital Punishment: Another View*, March 1975 (unpublished Columbia University Discussion Paper 74-7509), reprinted in Reply Brief for Petitioner, *Fowler* v. *North Carolina*, App. E. at 4e-6e.
29. Id. at 6–8.
30. Id. at 5, 6.
31. Kenneth L. Avio, *Capital Punishment in Canada: A Time-Series Analysis of the Deterrent Hypothesis* (mimeo, 1976).
32. Id. at 22.

During 1975, the *Yale Law Journal* published a series of articles reviewing the evidence on the deterrent effect of capital punishment. Included in this series was a second attempt to replicate Ehrlich's result by William Bowers and Glenn Pierce.[33] In replicating Ehrlich's work, they confirmed the Passell-Taylor finding that Ehrlich's results were extremely sensitive to whether the logarithmic specification was used and whether the data for the latter part of the 1960s were included.[34] Bowers and Pierce also raised questions about Ehrlich's use of the FBI homicide data in preference to vital statistics data.[35]

Ehrlich defended his work in this series in the *Yale Law Journal* by addressing some of the criticisms raised against his study.[36] He refuted some, but not the crucial ones. In his article he referred to a second study he made of the problem, basing it this time on a comparison by states for the years 1940 and 1950. Ehrlich claimed that the new test bolstered the original claim. But he described these findings as "tentative and inconclusive."[37] In the meantime, Passell made a state-by-state comparison for 1950 and 1960 but did not find what Ehrlich allegedly had found. Passell concluded: "We know of no reasonable way of interpreting the cross-section [i.e., state-by-state] data that would lend support to the deterrence hypothesis."[38]

A particularly extensive review of Ehrlich's time series analysis was made by a team led by Lawrence Klein, president of the American Economic Association.[39] The authors found serious methodological problems with Ehrlich's analysis. They raised questions about his failure to consider the feedback effect of crime on the economic variables in his model,[40] although he did consider other feedback effects in his analysis. They found some of Ehrlich's technical manipulations to be superfluous and tending to obscure the accuracy of his estimates.[41] They, too, raised questions about variables omitted from the analysis, and the effects of these omissions on the findings. [42]

Like Passell-Taylor and Bowers-Pierce, Klein and his collaborators replicated Ehrlich's results, using Ehrlich's own data, which by that time he had

33. Bowers & Pierce, *The Illusion of Deterrence in Isaac Ehrlich's Research on Capital Punishment,* 85 Yale L.J. 187 (1975).
34. Id. at 197–205.
35. Id. at 187–89.
36. Ehrlich, *Deterrence: Evidence and Inference,* 85 Yale L.J. 209 (1975).
37. Id. at 209.
38. Passell, *The Deterrent Effect of the Death Penalty: A Statistical Test,* 28 Stan. L. Rev. 61, 80 (1975).
39. Klein, Forst & Filatov, *The Deterrent Effect of Capital Punishment: An Assessment of the Estimates,* Paper commissioned by the Panel on Research on Deterrence, National Academy of Sciences (June 1976).
40. Id. at 18, 19–24.
41. Id. at 14.
42. Id. at 14–17.

made available.[43] As in previous replications, Ehrlich's results were found to be quite sensitive to the mathematical specification of the model and the inclusion of data at the recent end of the time series.

By this time, Ehrlich's model had been demonstrated to be peculiar enough. Klein went on to reveal further difficulties. One was that Ehrlich's deterrence finding disappeared after the introduction of a variable reflecting the factors that caused other crimes to increase during the latter part of the period of analysis.[44] The inclusion of such a variable would seem obligatory not only to substitute for the factors that had obviously been omitted but also to account for interactions between the crime rate and the demographic characteristics of the population.

Klein also found Ehrlich's results to be affected by an unusual construction of the execution rate variable, the central determinant of the analysis. Ehrlich constructed this variable by using three other variables that appear elsewhere in his regression model: the estimated homicide arrest rate, the estimated homicide conviction rate, and the estimated number of homicides. Klein showed that with this construction of the execution rate a very small error in the estimates of any of these three variables produced unusually strong spurious appearances of a deterrent effect.[45] He went on to show that the combined effect of such slight errors in all three variables was likely to be considerable, and that in view of all these considerations, Ehrlich's estimates of the deterrent effect were so weak that they "could be regarded as evidence . . . [of] a counterdeterrent effect of capital punishment."[46] In view of these serious problems with Ehrlich's analysis, Klein concluded: "[W]e see too many plausible explanations for his finding a deterrent effect other than the theory that capital punishment deters murder." And further: "Ehrlich's results cannot be used at this time to pass judgment on the use of the death penalty."[47]

The final blow came from a study by Brian Forst, one of Klein's collaborators on the earlier study. Since it had been firmly established that the Ehrlich phenomenon, if it existed, emerged from developments during the sixties, Forst concentrated on that decade.[48] He found a rigorous way of investigating whether the ending of executions and the sharp increase in homicides during this period was casual or coincidental. The power of Forst's study derives from his having analyzed changes *both* over time and

43. Id. at 24, 25.
44. Id. at 28–30.
45. Id. at 17–19.
46. Id. at 18.
47. Id. at 33.
48. Forst, *The Deterrent Effect of Capital Punishment: A Cross-State Analysis of the 1960s* (September 1976, mimeograph).

across jurisdictions. The aggregate United States time series data Ehrlich used were unable to capture important regional differences. Moreover, they did not vary as much as cross-state observations; hence they did not provide as rich an opportunity to infer the effect of changes in executions on homicides.

Forst's analysis is superior to Ehrlich's in four major respects: 1. It focuses exclusively on a period of substantial variation in the factors of central interest. 2. Its results are shown to be insensitive to alternative assumptions about the mathematical form of the relationship between homicides and executions. The results were also invariant to several alternative methods of constructing the execution rate, to alternative assumptions about the nature of the relationships between homicides, and other offenses, executions, convictions and sentences, and to alternative technical assumptions. 3. By not requiring conversion of the data to logarithms, Forst's model does not require that false values be used when the true values of the execution are zero. 4. It incorporates more control variables.

Forst's study led to a conclusion that went beyond that of Klein: "The findings give no support to the hypothesis that capital punishment deters homicide."[49] "Our finding that capital punishment . . . does not deter homicide is remarkably robust with respect to a wide range of alternative constructions."[50]

XI. Forst saw that Ehrlich, by using aggregate data for the United States as a whole, was forced to disregard the differences between states that had capital punishment and executions, and states that had either abolished the death penalty or at least had ceased to carry it out. Ehrlich's model thus could not evaluate the natural experiment which legislative history had built into the data. If Ehrlich's thesis—that it was the reduction of executions during the sixties that made the capital crime rate grow—were correct, then no such growth should obtain in the states in which there could be no reduction in executions because there had been none to begin with. Yet as Figure 4-2-8 shows, the growth of the capital crime rate during the crucial sixties was as large in the states without executions as in states with executions.

XII. The evidence on whether the threat of the death penalty has a deterrent effect beyond the threat of the life sentence, its normal subsubstitute, is overwhelmingly on one side. None of the efforts to sharpen the measurement yardstick by replacing the overall homicide rate through more sensitive measures succeeded in discovering a deterrent effect. Nor did any effort to sharpen the analytical instruments of analysis help. Even regression analysis, the most sophisticated of these instruments, after careful application by the scholarly community failed to detect a deterrent effect. This then is the proper summary of the evidence on the deterrent effect of the death penalty:

49. Id. at 27.
50. Id. at 29.

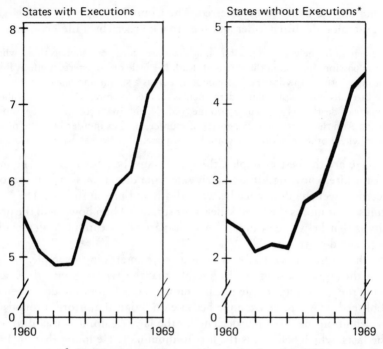

States with Executions States without Executions*

* Abolition states and 6 states with no executions since 1948

Figure 4-2-8. Homicide Rate 1960–1969 in States With and Without Executions

If there is one, it can only be minute, since not one of the many research approaches—from the simplest to the most sophisticated—was able to find it.[51] The proper question, therefore, is whether an effect that is at best so small that nobody has been able to detect it, justifies the awesome moral costs of the death penalty.

I can only speculate why the question concerning the deterrent effect of the death penalty has always been posed in its unanswerable form: whether or not it has such an effect. I suspect that at the root of the resistance to the evidence is the very ancient and deeply held belief that the death penalty is the ultimate deterrent.

The Solicitor General has called it a "logical a priori" belief. The logic probably runs as follows: If punishment has any deterrent effect (and surely it often has) then the most severe punishment should deter more than all others. Confronted with the failure to detect such an effect, those who share the belief have narrowed the claim. Only certain types of capital crime, they

---

51. The one exception pointing in the other direction, the dubious California finding that executions appear to postpone some homicides for a few days, is of small import. An effort to duplicate the finding in Philadelphia failed. See text *supra,* at notes 18 and 20.

say, not all, are likely to be deterred. The Court in *Gregg* v. *Georgia* gave two examples, the hired killer and the "free murder" by a life prisoner:[52]

> We may nevertheless assume safely that there are murderers, such as those who act in passion, for whom the threat of death has little or no deterrent effect. But for many others, the death penalty undoubtedly is a significant deterrent. There are carefully contemplated murders, such as murder for hire, where the possible penalty of death may well enter into the cold calculus that precedes the decision to act. And there are some categories of murder, such as murder by a life prisoner, where other sanctions may not be adequate.

If these are the best examples, the others must be poor indeed. The murderer for hire, knowing himself fairly safe from detection, is not likely to be concerned over the difference between death and prison for life. The "cold calculus" that moves the hired killer must surely tell him how small the probability is that he will be caught.[53] A good part of his careful contemplation goes to avoiding traces.

The life prisoner who kills is even a more interesting example. At first glance, the argument seems so irrefutable, that this type of homicide is occasionally the last capital crime on the statute books before the death penalty is abolished. It is a prize example because on "logical a priori" grounds his is by definition the "free murder" under the law. Again, it is useful to look at the facts, which Sellin was the first to illuminate. He found that, in 1965, the year for which he collected the data, sixteen prison homicides had been committed by men convicted of murder. Since not all murderers in prison are there with a life sentence, the true number of these "free murders" is likely to be even smaller.[54] In fact, of course, the "free murder" is probably altogether a figment because most life prisoners have some hope of being released before the end of their natural life, a hope that would be destroyed by a second murder. A prison, moreover, has ways of its own of punishing such a double murderer.

It is only fair, however, to take these examples of the Court for what they are, efforts to bolster with reasons the unwillingness to abandon the ancient sentiment. In that sentiment, the belief in deterrence plays but a small part.

52. 96 S. Ct. at 2931. Further examples are afforded in a footnote: "Other types of calculated murders, apparently occurring with increasing frequency, include the use of bombs or other means of indiscriminate killings, the extortion murder of hostages or kidnap victims, and the execution-style killing of witnesses to a crime." Id. at n.33.

53. An interview comes to mind with a former warden of the Cook County Jail who did not believe in the death penalty. The interviewer asked him, "You mean, you would even hesitate to execute a hired killer?" The warden's answer as I remember it was: "I shall cross that bridge when I come to it. In my many years here in the Cook County Jail, I have yet to meet the first hired killer. They are never caught, although Chicago would be a good place to catch them."

54. Sellin, *Prison Homicides,* in Sellin, note 10 *supra,* at 154, 157; see also Buffin, *Prison Killings and Death Penalty Legislation,* 53 Prison J. (1974).

It is the belief in retributive justice that makes the death penalty attractive, especially when clothed in a functional rationalization. The belief has ancient roots, even if the rationale is modern. The Court in *Gregg* approvingly cites *Furman* v. *Georgia*:[55]

> The instinct for retribution is part of the nature of man, and channeling that instinct in the administration of criminal justice serves an important purpose. . . . When people begin to believe that organized society is unwilling or unable to impose upon criminal offenders the punishment they "deserve," then there are sown the seeds of anarchy.

The depth of this feeling was revealed in a strange interchange during oral argument between Mr. Justice Powell and Professor Anthony Amsterdam, counsel for the petitioners:[56]

Mr. Justice Powell:
    Let me put a case to you. You've heard about Buchenwald, one of the camps in Germany in which thousands of Jewish citizens were exterminated. . . . If we had had jurisdiction over the commandant of Buchenwald, would you have thought capital punishment was an appropriate response to what that man or woman was responsible for?
Mr. Amsterdam:
    . . . We all have an instinctive reaction that says, "Kill him." . . . But I think the answer to the question that your Honor is raising, . . . [to] be consistent with the 8th Amendment to the Constitution . . . my answer would be, "No."

Mr. Justice Powell asked the same question again, this time about a man who might destroy New York City with a hydrogen bomb. Amsterdam's answer, of course, was again no.

Significantly, both examples went to the issue of retribution, not deterrence. It is hard to think of any crime that would be less deterred by the difference between the death penalty and life imprisonment, for instance, in Spandau prison. The sentiment in favor of the death penalty does not stem from the belief in its deterrence and perhaps we overestimate altogether the importance of that issue.

Nowhere was the worldwide decline of the death penalty significantly connected with arguments about its effectiveness or the lack thereof. In some countries abolition became simply the logical end-point of a gradual decline in executions, probably accompanied by a parallel change in moral sentiments.

In other countries, abolition was clearly an expression of moral sentiment. The first de jure abolition of executions in czarist Russia goes back to A.D. 1020. Capital punishment reappeared in the fourteenth century but was again

55. 96 S. Ct. at 2930, quoting 408 U.S. 238, 308 (1972).
56. The colloquy occurred during argument in *Woodson & Waxton* v. *North Carolina;* transcribed record No. 75-5491, at 20.

abolished when Elizabeth ascended the throne in 1742. On both occasions, the issue was one of morality not expediency.[57] In Germany, the 1947 Constitution abolished the death penalty as a deliberate act of repudiation of the Hitler era, when the death penalty, legally or illegally imposed, claimed millions of lives. In Great Britain, after a century of controversy, the abolitionists won when a man, protected by all the vaunted safeguards of British justice, was executed for a crime that he had not committed.

Ceylon abolished the death penalty when it acquired its independence, as an act of Buddhist faith. In Austria, the movement toward abolition reflected primarily moral sentiments. The parliament of the first Austrian republic unanimously abolished capital punishment as a renunciation of the monarchical past. In 1933, a semi-fascist chancellor restored the death penalty primarily as a political threat to the underground opposition. The second republic again abolished the death penalty, first in ordinary criminal cases and then also for cases triable under martial law, last used against the socialist political opposition in the civil war of 1934.

Abolition of the death penalty thus has reflected in the main a change in cultural sentiments, if not of the people, so at least of its legislators or its government. In the United States too capital punishment will end only when our cultural sentiments change. The people, a majority of whom now favor the death penalty, will be the last to change. The legislators will probably change before them; and our Supreme Court Justices conceivably may change even earlier.

Sentiment for the death penalty in the United States has grown during the last decade, stimulated by the unprecedented rise in violent crime during the second half of the sixties. In such times the demand for the death penalty grows because it is so easy to believe it will make law enforcement more effective. It is interesting to analyze the growth of this popular sentiment. In Figure 4-2-9, four Gallup polls on the death penalty spanning sixteen years are analyzed. Sentiment for the death penalty did not rise until 1967, and then only among the white population. Black sentiment for the death penalty, always far below the corresponding figures for whites, remained unchanged. In the South, sentiment for the death penalty among whites and blacks has traditionally been below the average for the country. For the blacks, this is still true; their proportion favoring the death penalty has been declining, reaching in 1976 a new low of 24 percent. Among the whites, sentiment in the South has caught up with that of the country as a whole, at 70 percent.

The petitioners in *Gregg* all came from the South. In the last analysis the

57. "Do not kill anyone, either guilty or not. ... Do not destroy a Christian soul, even in case death is well deserved." Testament of the Grand Prince of Kiev, A.D. 1125. Elizabeth purportedly promised God that if she were selected she would take no life. Adams, *Capital Punishment in Imperial and Soviet Criminal Law*, 18 Am. J. Comp. L. 575, 576 (1970).

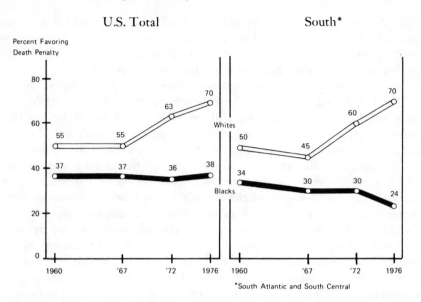

Figure 4-2-9. Proportion of Whites and Blacks Favoring the Death Penalty, 1960–1976

Court held that it had no power to override legislation that was grounded in a belief that even some of the Justices must have shared.

Still, one must not give up hope. The realization that the deterrent effect, if it exists at all,[58] can be only minute, should force us to look once more at the balance sheet, and weigh against the, at best, minimal benefit, the awesome costs of the death penalty: The inhumanity of the act, the ever present danger of error, the ultimate impossibility to make a fair decision as to who is to die and who is to live.

For the committed who believe that there should be more search for the elusive deterrent effect, a new opportunity has arisen. By the grace of the Court we are in the midst of a new natural experiment. After a number of

---

58. Two of the best studies—those of Forst and Passell—showed even a counterdeterrent balance for the death penalty. In both studies it was statistically insignificant. The possibility of a counterdeterrent effect does not come as a total surprise. It has theoretical support of long standing. There is the suicide-through-murder theory advanced first by Staub & Alexander, The Criminal, The Judge, and The Public—A Psychological Analysis (1931); see also H. von Weber, *Selbstmord als Mordmotiv,* Monatsschrift für Kriminalbiologie und Strafrechtsreform 161 (1937). Then there is concern over the generally brutalizing effect of the death penalty which just adds one more killing in cold blood. Also, as long as some states still consider crimes other than murder (e.g., rape) to be capital offenses, the old argument that killing the victim-witness may somehow "improve" the criminal's situation is still valid. Cf. Bedau, *supra* note 20, at 264 n.7. Consider also the case of Gary Gilmore, the Utah convict who succeeded in his objective to be the first person executed in the post-*Furman* period. See N.Y. Times, 18 Jan. 1977, p. 1.

years during which, through *Furman,* the death penalty was held in abeyance throughout the land, some of our states will resume executions. There is thus another opportunity to see whether the capital crime rate in these states will decline compared to the states that still have no executions.

In the end one must remain skeptical as to the power of evidence to change ancient beliefs and sentiments. The greater hope lies in the expectation that with better times our sentiments will reach the "standards of decency that mark the progress of a maturing society."[59] Justices Brennan and Marshall thought—wrongly it appears—that we had already sufficiently matured.

The conclusion that the personal sentiments of the judges play a decisive role is strengthened by reading the decision of the Massachusetts Supreme Judicial Court in *Commonwealth* v. *O'Neal,*[60] which held a mandatory death sentence upon a conviction for rape-murder to be unconstitutional. That court had before it on the deterrence issue the very same evidence that was before the United States Supreme Court in *Gregg.* Yet the majority of the Massachusetts court accepted the evidence as proof of the inability of the death sentence to deter. The lack of proof of deterrent effect deprived the government of a "compelling state interest" to justify the death penalty.

Why did the Supreme Court and the Massachusetts court arrive at a different decision? The decisive factor was the simple fact that in the United States Supreme Court only two of the nine Justices felt that "the standard of decency" required abolition while on the Massachusetts court five out of seven felt that way.

§3. The Deterrent Effect of Capital Punishment: An Assessment of the Evidence*

LAWRENCE R. KLEIN, BRIAN FORST, and VICTOR FILATOV

While the very thought of death as a legal penalty may be repugnant to many people, it generally seems to be tolerated under circumstances in which a sufficiently large number of innocent lives are spared. There has been little

59. Chief Justice Warren, writing for the Court, in *Trop* v. *Dulles,* 356 U.S. 86, 101 (1958).
60. 339 N.E.2d 676 (Mass. 1975).
*From Lawrence R. Klein, Brian Forst, and Victor Filatov, "The Deterrent Effect of Capital Punishment: An Assessment of the Estimates." Reproduced from *Deterrence and Incapacitation: Estimating the Effects of Criminal Sanctions on Crime Rates,* Alfred Blumstein, Jacqueline Cohen, and Daniel Nagin, eds., 1978, with the permission of the National Academy of Sciences, Washington, D.C. Pp. 336–60.

or no objection, for example, to the killing of persons caught in the act of hijacking airplanes. This is not precisely the same as the execution of a convicted murderer, but it may suggest nonetheless that most people might prefer capital punishment if it were known that executions deterred a sufficiently large number of homicides.

Of course, no one can reasonably claim to know exactly how many homicides would, in fact, be prevented as the result of an execution. The existence of data on executions and homicide does, however, provide an opportunity to estimate the average number of homicides that were deterred (or encouraged) by an execution. Such estimates have indeed been made.

Estimates of this sort ordinarily go no further than graduate seminars and scholarly journals. Estimates of the deterrent effect of capital punishment, however, have been introduced as evidence before the United States Supreme Court.[1] Hence, the empirical aspect of the issue has quite literally become a matter of life or death—certainly for death row inmates and quite possibly for potential victims.

It is the primary purpose of this paper to review the prominent analyses that have been done in this area of inquiry. These studies are by no means in agreement. We then address the major methodological issues raised by these studies, with emphasis on a time-series analysis by Isaac Ehrlich that has become a subject of particular controversy. We conclude with an assessment of the suitability of presenting available estimates as a basis for judicial or legislative decisions about capital punishment.

I. Theories about the deterrent value of punishment are two centuries old at the very least. A much earlier belief in the deterrence theory may be suggested by the especially public nature of executions and lesser punishments in imperial Rome, medieval Europe, and elsewhere. Cesare Beccaria, who argued against capital punishment in the eighteenth century in *Dei Deletti e dele Pene*, was nonetheless among the first to reason: "It is better to prevent crimes, than to punish them." Jeremy Bentham argued later in the same century in *The Rationale of Punishment* that punishments should be designed to discourage greater "evil," under the premise that each person behaves according to a "felicific calculus."

A. *The Work of Thorsten Sellin.* A paucity of data and limited computational capabilities prevented empirical tests of the deterrence theory of punishment until the 1950s. The first important statistical investigation of the deterrent effect of punishment, by Thorsten Sellin (1959), focused on the death penalty. Sellin's study is significant also because it provided no support for the deterrence hypothesis.

---

1. *Fowler* v. *North Carolina*, Case No. 73-7031. U.S. Supreme Court term beginning in October 1974; also five cases (Nos. 74-6257, 75-5394, 75-5491, 75-5706, and 75-5844) in the 1975 term.

Sellin's method consisted primarily of comparing homicide rates over time between contiguous states, some with statutes permitting executions, others with laws abolishing capital punishment. He attempted to control for other factors by matching states that were as nearly alike as possible except for the legal status of capital punishment. Sellin concluded:

> Within each group of states having similar social and economic conditions and populations, it is impossible to distinguish the abolition state from the others. . . . The inevitable conclusion is that executions have no discernable effect on homicide death rates. (p. 34)

Sellin's study has been both praised and criticized for its simplicity. Baldus and Cole (1975) regard it as a study that provides a more reliable basis for drawing inferences about the deterrent effect of capital punishment than a more recent study that was "statistically more sophisticated" (p. 173). The Solicitor General of the United States (Bork et al. 1974), on the other hand, has faulted Sellin's work for its failure "to hold constant factors other than the death penalty that might influence the rate of murders" (p. 37).

Sellin's analysis has been criticized also by Peck (1976) for its essentially subjective selection of states under comparison and its failure to separate the deterrent effect of executions on homicides from the reverse effect of changes in homicides on the demand for executions.

B. The Work of Isaac Ehrlich. Perhaps the strongest attempt at refutation of Sellin's work has come from Isaac Ehrlich, who writes that "the statistical methods used by Sellin and others to infer the nonexistence of the deterrent effect of capital punishment do not provide an acceptable test of such an effect and consequently do not warrant such inferences" (1975a, p. 398). Ehrlich has criticized Sellin's analysis along several lines, including those by the Solicitor General and Peck cited above (Ehrlich 1975a, pp. 411, 415; 1975b, pp. 221–24). Ehrlich adds that Sellin's analysis is flawed by its having ignored the extent of use of capital punishment in those states where it had not been abolished—he criticizes Sellin for drawing strong conclusions from the similarity of homicide rates in retentionist states and adjacent abolitionist states when, in fact, many of Sellin's retentionist states rarely used capital punishment (1975b, pp. 222–23).[2]

Ehrlich also formulated an elaborate theory, following that of Gary Becker. This theory "emphasizes the interaction between offense and defense—the supply of and the (negative) social demand for murder" (1975a, p. 398). A fundamental element of this analysis is that it "rests on the pre-

---

2. This criticism may be too strong, since the perception of the risk of execution in a retentionist state that only rarely uses capital punishment may greatly exceed that in an abolitionist state, even though the relative frequencies of execution are similar in the two states—identically zero in one and nearly zero in the other.

sumption that offenders respond to incentives" (p. 415). Ehrlich's theory leads eventually to his asserting that the deterrent effect of executions "must be identified empirically through appropriate simultaneous equation estimation techniques" (p. 406).

His first empirical test of this theory is based on a regression analysis of aggregate United States data for the individual years 1932–70.[3] This analysis is extraordinary at least insofar as it employs a vast array of manipulations: to create values of missing data, to test alternative time-lag structures, to reduce bias or efficiency loss associated with autoregressive disturbances, to avoid undefined values of the independent variable of central interest, and to test alternative systems of simultaneity.[4] An end product of this exercise is the statement (Ehrlich 1975a, p. 398):

> In fact, the empirical analysis suggests that on the average the tradeoff between the execution of an offender and the lives of potential victims it might have saved was of the order of magnitude of 1 for 8 for the period 1933–67 in the United States.

Ehrlich arrives at this conclusion by way of his "murder supply function:"

$$\frac{Q}{N} = kP_a^{\alpha_1}P_{c/a}^{\alpha_2}P_{e/c}^{\alpha_3}U^{\beta_1}L^{\beta_2}Y_p^{\beta_3}A^{\beta_4}\exp{(v_1)} \tag{1}$$

where Q/N is the homicide rate, k is a constant, P_a is the probability of apprehension, $P_{c/a}$ is the conditional probability of conviction of murder given apprehension, $P_{e/c}$ is the probability of execution given conviction, U is the unemployment rate of the civilian labor force, L is the labor force participation rate of the adult civilian population, Y_p is an estimate of real per capita income, A is the proportion of the residential population in the age-group 14–24, and v_1 is the disturbance term (pp. 406, 408). He finds data for the construction of each variable in equation 1 toward the estimation of α_3, the elasticity of the murder rate with respect to the conditional probability of execution.

3. A second empirical test reported by Ehrlich (1975b, p. 217) but not yet published is based on two cross-sectional analyses of the United States—one using 1940 state data and the other using 1950 data.

4. Specifically, values of missing data were produced via auxiliary regressions (Ehrlich 1975a, pp. 409, 412), using both linear and geometric interpolation techniques; alternative time lags were produced under linear and nonlinear distributed lag regressions (p. 408); the coefficient of serial correlation was estimated by way of the Cochrane-Orcutt iterative procedure (p. 410), with associated parameters estimated via Ray Fair's nonlinear three-round estimation procedure (p. 406); the arbitrarily selected number 1 was used to replace the observed value 0 in three instances in which Ehrlich took the logarithm of the probability of execution variable (p. 409); and the conditional probability of execution variable was treated alternatively as predetermined and endogenous (pp. 408, 410). The parameters of primary interest result from his regressing modified first differences of murder rates, in natural logarithms, on corresponding modified first differences of selected variables (p. 410).

C. Assessments of Ehrlich's Analysis. Ehrlich's study received considerable attention once it was introduced to the Supreme Court, by the Solicitor General of the United States, as evidence in support of capital punishment (Bork et al. 1974, pp. 35–38). It is surely accurate to state that Ehrlich's analysis has become controversial and has been attacked on several different fronts.

Passell and Taylor (1975) were among the first to criticize Ehrlich's regression estimates. They attempted to replicate his findings and were unable to do so up to rounding errors, although they have come close in most cases. They discovered nonetheless that their own estimates of the effect of changes in the execution rate on the homicide rate were quite sensitive to whether the regression equation was log linear or linear

$$\frac{Q}{N} = b_o + b_1 \cdot P_a + b_2 \cdot P_{c/a} + b_3 \cdot P_{e/c} + \cdots \qquad (2)$$

as in equation 1. In particular, they obtained a significant negative relationship between Q/N and $P_{e/c}$ (i.e., the appearance of a deterrent effect of executions on homicides) under Ehrlich's multiplicative form and a positive insignificant relationship under an additive model (pp. 6–8). They reported also that the finding of a deterrent effect did not hold up when the years after 1962 were excluded from the analysis (pp. 5, 21, 22).

A second attempt to replicate Ehrlich's work was reported by Bowers and Pierce (1975). Like Passell and Taylor, they obtained a much stronger appearance of a deterrent effect under the log-linear form than under the linear form (pp. 199–205). Also like Passell and Taylor, they obtained results consistent with the deterrence hypothesis only when data from the latter half of the 1960s were included in the analysis (pp. 197–202). Nor were Bowers and Pierce able to replicate Ehrlich's findings precisely. In addition, Bowers and Pierce faulted Ehrlich for his choice of data sources (pp. 187–89), specifically with respect to his use of FBI rather than Vital Statistics data.

D. Cross-sectional Analyses. Sellin's study of selected pairs of states and Ehrlich's time-series analysis of aggregate United States data represent two fundamentally different empirical approaches to the testing of the hypothesis that capital punishment deters homicide. Regional effects are explicitly accounted for in Sellin's work and ignored in the time-series analysis. Ehrlich's time-series study, on the other hand, attempts to isolate a pure deterrent effect of capital punishment by controlling explicitly for the effects of other variables, including alternative sanction variables; by accounting for simultaneity among the offensive and defensive aspects of homicide; and by measuring the magnitude of the execution rate, under several alternative constructions. The advantages cited here of each of these studies appear at the same time to be weaknesses of the other.

A recent study by Peter Passell (1975) has attempted to overcome these weaknesses by applying econometric techniques to cross-state data. This general approach provides the potential for a more thoroughly controlled estimate of the effect of changes in executions on homicides not only by way of the existence of large inter-regional variation in several of the included variables, the incorporation of a regional dummy variable, and a corresponding reduction in aggregation bias, but also by way of the opportunity to include a term-of-imprisonment variable, which is not available in time-series. We shall say more about this potentially important substitute sanction for capital punishment in a following section on omitted variables.

Passell tested the deterrence hypothesis using a model similar to those put forward by Becker and Ehrlich.[5] He reported separate results based on 1950 data for 41 states and 1960 data for 44 states (Passell, p. 66), using both ordinary least squares (OLS) and two-stage least squares (2SLS) estimation techniques (pp. 69–77), for both the linear and log-linear models (pp. 69–73), and using alternative constructions of the execution rate variable (pp. 77–78). Passell found five variables to be related systematically to the homicide offense rate: the homicide conviction rate, the average term of incarceration for convicted murderers, poverty, age, and racial migration. He summarized his findings for the execution rate variable as follows: "Students of capital punishment must look elsewhere for evidence confirming deterrence. We know of no reasonable way of interpreting the cross-section data that would lend support to the deterrence hypothesis" (p. 80).[6]

These cross-section results provide a useful complement to the aggregate national time-series analysis. By analogy with econometric analysis in more conventional economic settings, this is a common procedure. We often look at given problems from the point of view of cross-section analysis in econometrics. In the present context, state-to-state variation in homicide rates and execution rates are suggested with a similar or possibly amplified set of other variables, and it is necessary to think through the parametric specification as well as the classification of variables into endogenous and exogenous categories.

5. See Becker 1975, pp. 176–79; Ehrlich 1973, pp. 524–43; Ehrlich 1975a, pp. 398–406; and Passell 1975, pp. 64–66.
6. We find no serious problems with the Passell paper. The analysis appears fairly straightforward, with generally adequate robustness tests. It does not address the potential problem of heteroscedasticity, a not uncommon problem in cross-sectional analyses, and reports only unweighted regression results. This could have distorted the estimated standard errors of the regression coefficients, but ought not to have altered the positive sign for the execution rate variable. We have not attempted to check Passell's calculations, and so cannot attest to their accuracy. Isaac Ehrlich has also analyzed cross-state data and reports having found once again that capital punishment deters murder (1975b, p. 217). We do not explore the differences between Passell's cross-state results and Ehrlich's, prior to the publication of Ehrlich's paper. One cannot help but be puzzled, however, that two apparently similar approaches would yield such strikingly different findings.

Sellin's analysis (1959) is, in effect, a cross-section analysis, but it is not a parametric regression analysis, and it is not multivariate to the degree needed for comparison with the time-series results. Sellin's findings, however, together with Passell's, prompt us to contrast the cross-section and time-series cases.

The failure of these cross-section studies to find a significant negative deterrent effect is similar to discrepancies that have arisen in econometric investigations of consumer spending. In national time-series samples, there is evidence of significant positive association, at the margin, between an index of consumer attitudes and spending on durable goods; but in cross-section samples, with family-to-family variation, this same effect cannot readily be found. This lack of correspondence between the time-series and cross-section findings has always cast some doubt on the validity of the former. It has also been the case that significant time-series effects have not always carried over from sample to extrapolation. There have been serious enough reversals in appraisals of the macro-economy through methods based on time-series that we may be led by analogy to mistrust the policy extrapolation of Ehrlich's time-series results in the absence of cross section as well as other confirmations of his findings.

II. The deterrence problem examined in Ehrlich's time-series analysis is not strictly an econometric problem, and the methods used are not strictly econometric. There are various analogies to econometrics, but references to the methods of econometrics should not be used in support of the findings, and it should be remarked that the analogy to econometric method is not fully implemented—that being a strong reservation about some of the conclusions that are drawn.

Ehrlich's problem is one of generalized regression. The use of nonexperimental data and the attempt to deal with simultaneity give some superficial resemblances to econometrics. Ehrlich (1975a, p. 399) lays out a model of rational behavior for:

> analysis of the incentive to commit murder and other crimes against the person by explicitly incorporating into the model the uncertainties associated with the prospective punishments for crime.

His theoretical model is much like that used to derive specifications for demand and supply functions in the economic analysis of consumption and production. In that respect, we find his theory strongly contrived, i.e., set up in an essentially imitative way vis à vis the design of economic theory that is used to generate specifications of econometric models. We have doubts about the insight that this approach is likely to bring to an understanding of criminal behavior. There is much to be said for an investigation that links together economic, criminological, and other sociological aspects of behavior, but this is not to suggest that the analysis start from some rational utility analysis of criminal behavior that is designed to look like the standard model of rational utility analysis of economic behavior.

A much more fruitful approach would seem to be the methodology used in the smoking-cancer link studies. These do not attempt to lock the analysis into a utility calculus or some other limited set of specifications. In using such a technique, greater scope could be give to the exploration of effects of other variables, possibly subjective in character, to allow for emotional behavior and other social phenomenon.

Apart from all the trappings of a utility theory of the incentive to commit murder, Ehrlich specifies a fairly common aggregative model, with no formal bridge between the microcosmic utility analysis and national supply function. The aspects of this function that resemble econometrics are:

1. Some of the variables are interdependent; the empirical estimates of probabilities of arrest, conviction given arrest, and execution given conviction are assumed to be mutually dependent.
2. Other variables are assumed to be exogenous, or independent.
3. The stochastic part of the murder supply function is assumed to be serially correlated, following a first-order autoregressive process.

Econometric models are generally designed so that they consist of some mutually dependent (endogenous) variables and some independent (exogenous) variables. The equations of such models are usually assumed to be linear in unknown parameters with additive stochastic parts that satisfy a first-order autoregressive process.

This is the substance of the econometrics of the model specification. The economic variables of the model are classified in the exogenous set and contribute nothing to the interdependence of the model that is usually characteristic of econometric systems. An interesting research challenge nowadays is to integrate economic and sociological systems with mutual feedback or interdependence between the sociological (or criminological) variables and the economic variables. Such an approach is lacking in the Ehrlich model; he assumes that economic factors affect criminal behavior but that criminal factors do not affect economic behavior through the economic variables that he has selected. This is certainly a drawback to the generality of his approach.

Given the specification of the single equation—some interdependent variables and autoregressive errors—Ehrlich followed the latest and best econometric practice in estimating the parameters of the equation. These generalized regression methods would be recommended whether the model were an econometric one or not, as long as it had the structure specified above by Ehrlich.

The two-stage least squares method used by Ehrlich takes account of the interdependence aspect, while the serial correlation adjustment takes account of the autoregressive aspect. None of the estimated autoregressive parameters is very large, and some are quite small. In such circumstances, the autore-gressive corrections are superfluous and may even lead to poorer estimates if used when they are not needed. This aspect of best econometric practice might well have been avoided in several cases, at least. The two-stage type of estimator is all right for the problem but probably contributes much less to the claimed superiority of Ehrlich's estimates than the reader may be brought to believe.

In fact, the real contribution to the strength of Ehrlich's statistical findings lies in the simple graph of the upsurge of the homicide rate after 1962, cou-pled with the fall in the execution rate in the same period. The whole statis-tical story lies in this simple pairing of these observations and not in the theoretical utility model, the econometric type specification, or the use of best econometric method. Everything else is relatively superficial and domi-nated by this simple statistical observation.

A. *Omitted Variables.* This leaves us with the question: Did the decline and eventual ending of executions during the 1960s cause some portion of the sharp increase in the homicide rate, or would the homicide rate have increased at least as much anyway?

To address this question, we can first acknowledge the obvious, that end-ing the practice of capital punishment in the 1960s does not constitute a con-trolled experiment from which one can safely draw conclusions about deter-rence by observing only homicides and executions. Factors other than the ending of capital punishment surely affected the homicide rate during this period. Ehrlich's use of explanatory factors other than the execution proba-bility in equation (1) is an explicit recognition of this fact. What may be less obvious is that the omission of factors other than those used by Ehrlich to "control" his analysis may have contributed to his finding a negative rela-tionship between the homicide rate and the execution probability.[7] Some of the factors omitted by Ehrlich have, in fact, been found previously to affect crime rates.

For example, Ehrlich himself found in an earlier (1973) study that long prison sentences, the conventional alternative to capital punishment, serve as an effective crime deterrent. This factor was omitted from Ehrlich's time-series analysis because of the unavailability of data. To the extent that his previous analysis is correct and to the extent that the length of prison sen-tences declined during the 1960s, Ehrlich's attributing the increase in homi-cides to the elimination of capital punishment could be erroneous.

We do find evidence that the actual time served in prison, both for homi-cides and for other offenses that often result in homicide, did indeed decline

---

7. We are grateful to Isaac Ehrlich and William Landes for reminding us that some of the omit-ted variables may have worked to understate the estimated deterrent effect of capital punish-ment. We refer here to the *net* effect of the omission of all other factors on the deterrence estimates.

in the 1960s. Based on *National Prisoner Statistics* figures for the 33 states that reported in both 1960 and 1970, we find that 46.8 percent of the prisoners released in 1960 who had been convicted of homicides had served at least 5 years; only 35.8 percent of those released in 1970, imprisoned for the same offenses, had served that long. The computer that printed out a significant negative regression coefficient for Ehrlich's execution variable might not have done so had it known that terms of incarceration for murders became more lenient during the 1960s.

Other factors omitted from Ehrlich's regression model also appear to have contributed to the increase in the homicide rate during this period. One of these is the availability of guns. The contribution of handguns to the murder upsurge of the 1960s has been indicated in a study by Newton and Zimring (1969). Phillips, in addition, has reported that from 1961 to 1970 the rate of murders with firearms increased from 2.5 to 6.1 per 100,000 persons (Phillips 1973). It is likely that increased gun possession may partly follow a relaxation in punishment, but gun possession is sure to have grown during the period for other reasons as well, such as the increased availability of inexpensive foreign models.

The importance of the omitted variables problem may be seen in another way. Crime increased generally during the 1960s. Some of the increase is no doubt due to factors measured by Ehrlich and some to yet other factors. It is sobering to note that while the FBI reported murders and non-negligent manslaughters to have increased by 74 percent from 1960 to 1970, burglaries increased by 142 percent, auto thefts by 183 percent, and larcenies ($50 and over) by 245 percent. Of these four crime categories, the only one potentially deterrable by capital punishment is the one that showed the most modest gain, even though executions came to a halt by 1967. This suggests to us that the strength of Ehrlich's statistical relationships between executions and homicides depends significantly on changes during this recent decade in variables omitted from the analysis, variables that would explain the increase in crime generally.[8]

B. Negative Bias in the Execution Measure. Ehrlich indicates in a footnote (1975a, p. 207) that he calculated his execution rate variable, $P_{e/c}$, as

$$P_{e/c} = \frac{E}{\hat{C}} = \frac{E}{Q \cdot P_a \cdot P_{c/a}} \tag{3}$$

where $\hat{C}$ is the estimated number of convictions, Q is the reported number

8. That Ehrlich's time series results depend upon the inclusion of the years since 1964 is clearly due to temporal heterogeneity, rather than to the loss of degrees of freedom in excluding the recent years. Ehrlich has reported results that indicate that his deterrence estimates are not weakened by the exclusion of the eight observations, 1933 through 1940 (Ehrlich 1975a, p. 410). He also indicated that the deterrent effect disappears when data from the six years 1964 through 1969 are excluded from the analysis (Ehrlich 1975b, p. 217).

of murders and non-negligent manslaughters, and P_a and $P_{c/a}$ are as defined in equation 1.

The use of Q both as the numerator of the homicide rate and as part of the denominator of the execution rate could have biased Ehrlich's estimate of the regression coefficient for $P_{e/c}$ toward the appearance of a deterrent effect. It is immediately apparent that any errors in the measurement of the true number of homicides could cause Q/N and $P_{e/c}$ to move in opposite directions. Sources of error in Ehrlich's measure of Q, based on FBI homicide statistics, have been thoroughly discussed by Hindelang (1974, pp. 2–5).[9]

What may not be so apparent is the magnitude of this bias, even for small errors in the measurement of homicides. If the homicide rate were in fact totally insensitive to changes in the execution rate, measurement errors even as small as those caused by Ehrlich's having used a homicide series rounded to the nearest 10 murders would have biased his estimate of this key relationship toward a negative unit elasticity.[10] That Ehrlich has estimated elasticities for $P_{e/c}$ considerably nearer to zero than to -1 could be regarded as evidence that the true elasticity is positive, indicating a counterdeterrent effect of capital punishment.

One might suspect that this bias would be diminished under constructions of $P_{e/c}$ that do not use current values of Q directly. In fact, not all of Ehrlich's constructions of $P_{e/c}$ use the immediate values of Q.[11] To test whether this bias is lessened when the current value of Q is not used directly to form the denominator of $P_{e/c}$, we have tested the effect of adding noise to Q in amounts that average 2 percent of Q, distributed normally, and use these values within the structure of Ehrlich's equation (6), from Table 3 (1975a, p. 410).[12] Equation 6 uses $P_{e/c}$ constructed as an endogenous variable, so that

9. For example, some murders and non-negligent manslaughters are never discovered, others are not reported to local authorities as such, local jurisdictions may define these terms differently, and some jurisdictions do not report to the FBI.

10. This can be seen by solving for values of E that force $P_{e/c}$ to be constant, such as the mean value Ehrlich computes for $P_{e/c}$ (which happens to be 0.0259, but any constant will do), and then adding a random disturbance term (distributed normally with mean zero) to Q in both the homicide rate and the execution rate. Under certain conditions worked out by Daniel Nagin (in this volume), the random disturbance terms will cause each k percent increase (or decrease) in $P_{e/c}$ to correspond with a k percent decrease (or increase) in Q/N, giving an elasticity of -1.

11. Ehrlich has informed us through correspondence that concern about this bias was a primary motivation for these alternative constructions.

12. This test consisted of using the basic data that produced a replication of equation (6), up to rounding errors; using the values of Q, P_a, and $P_{c/a}$ in this data and solving for values of E, for each observation, such that $P_{e/c}$ would equal its mean value, .0259; setting E equal to these solved values, a sufficient condition for producing artificially the circumstance of no effect of $P_{e/c}$ on Q/N; adding 2 percent mean noise to Q in both $P_{e/c}$ and Q/N to get new values of $P_{e/c}$ and Q/N; forming the endogenous counterpart to these revised values of $P_{e/c}$; and reestimating equation (6) with this counterpart and the original data for the other variables in the model.

current values of Q are not used directly in the estimate here. The result of this exercise is an estimated elasticity of -1.01 for the execution rate variable, which is consistent with our prediction of the previous paragraph.

This is by no means the only source of bias produced by Ehrlich's method of estimating values for $P_{e/c}$. We have found that another source of bias results from his having P_a and $P_{c/a}$ comprise part of the denominator of $P_{e/c}$ and having them serve also as separate explanatory variables. If these variables were all measured with perfect accuracy, they would be correlated with one another at least to the extent that they are substitute sanctions within the criminal justice system. They will surely be artificially correlated due to measurement errors, under Ehrlich's construction of $P_{e/c}$.[13]

We find that if P_a and $P_{c/a}$ were both measured with a mean random error as small as 2 percent, a deterrence elasticity of -0.05 would be produced even if, in fact, no relationship existed between the homicide rate and the conditional execution probability. If Ehrlich's estimates were accurate in every other respect, this bias alone would lead one to conclude that his estimates provide no support to the deterrence hypothesis. While it is often the case that measurement errors bias the regression coefficient toward zero, we have here a situation in which errors in three crucial variables—Q, P_a, and $P_{c/a}$—all appear to work in such a way as to bias the coefficient of $P_{e/c}$ negatively.[14]

C. Alternative Models. A more complete theoretical model specification ought to go in two directions:

1. Imbed the murder decision in a more general model of criminal behavior.
2. Integrate the economic and sociological or criminological variables into a more general model of behavior.

The criminal who commits murder may also have a propensity to commit other crimes. On the occasion of carrying out a criminal act, the final murder decision may be quite impulsive, but the criminal may weigh the penalty associated with a more serious crime against that associated with a less seri-

13. Errors are indeed evident. For example, Ehrlich created artificial values for $P_{c/a}$ for the years 1933, 1934, 1935, and 1961, for which data were missing. Errors are indicated also by visual inspection. It is not easy to explain, for instance, how factors other than measurement error could have caused the true probability of conviction given arrest for murder to have increased from 0.258 to 0.496 from 1936 to 1939. In addition, evidence has been presented by Bowers and Pierce (1975) that the FBI's estimates of arrests and convictions are based on nonrandom samples, with response rates that vary considerably over the period 1933 to 1969 (pp. 190–91).
14. Although we have not explicitly estimated the extent to which small errors in the measurement of P_a and $P_{c/a}$ also bias the elasticities Ehrlich estimates for these variables, due to multicollinearity with $P_{e/c}$, we are led by this analysis to question his estimates of these elasticities, too.

ous crime. A plausible mode of behavior may be one in which armed robbery will be carried out without murder if at all possible because the penalty, without murder, is less severe; therefore, murder will be committed only in an act of desperation. In such a situation, the murder decision depends not only on penalties associated with homicide but also with other lesser crimes. In this case, we write:

$$Q/N = f(P_a, P_{c/a}, P_{e/c}, \ldots q_a, q_{c/a}, \ldots)$$

where q_a and $q_{c/a}$ are probabilities of arrest and conviction given arrest associated with other crimes. There may be several such arguments in f.

The model is incomplete not only with respect to other variables affecting the murder decision but also with respect to the behavior of the law enforcement system. The whole point of casting the problem in a simultaneous equations mode is to consider jointly the actions of all the decision makers involved. If Q/N and $P_{e/c}$ are to be mutually dependent, the decision of the judicial system (subject to public opinion and many other factors) about the rules for the invocation of the death penalty must be simultaneously modeled. It is plausible to suggest that decisions about $P_{e/c}$ depend on the frequency of homicide and many other factors—notably society's ethical and moral values. We might write

$$P_{e/c} = g(Q/N, S, \ldots)$$

where S stands for societal values. Other variables, too, enter the g-function, but the whole process is not investigated by Ehrlich.

This means that the use of the two-stage least squares method as an estimation procedure might start from quite a different reduced form expression. Many exogenous variables in the system (S, for one) are candidates for inclusion. Without careful investigation, the problem is pretty much open at this stage. Ehrlich could argue, of course, that he has selected a subset of the relevant exogenous variables and consequently has obtained consistent estimates, but that is hardly an adequate stand in a small-sample situation such as the one at hand. There are, undoubtedly, significant small-sample biases associated with omission of relevant exogenous variables from the entire model.

In addition, variables representing other arrest/conviction rates could have been included as endogenous variables. These variables may not be readily measured with decent accuracy, but there is a way around this complication—namely, to introduce frequency of occurrence of other crimes in place of their penalty rates. In the theory of demand in economics, we may use the whole price vector as arguments or develop "mixed demand functions" with own penalties (prices) and other crime rates (quantities) as the arguments. In two-stage estimations for such an enlarged system, the reduced forms should include the specific exogenous variables from the behavioral equations associated with the other crimes.[15] It is quite evident that Ehrlich has only scratched the surface in serious model building and has a long way to go in order to establish his results as definitive.

Economic variables affect crime rates. It makes good sense to include labor force participation, income, and unemployment rate in the equation for Q/N. The same is true of police and other government expenditures. But do crime rates—the murder rate in particular—have an impact on the economy? Ehrlich assumes that they do not, but we think otherwise. For example, an increase in crime rates might cause a wave of business closures and could thereby increase unemployment rates. There is little doubt that police expenditures are influenced by Q/N. Although, in a purely formal sense, police expenditures for the previous year are used in Ehrlich's model, the exogeneity of such a variable cannot be established by a dating mechanism alone. At the macro level, there are many avenues for establishing relationships between crime rates and the unemployment rate. Crime of all sorts, including homicide, can impede the smooth functioning of the economy and thus affect unemployment or labor force participation.

Students of econometrics ought to learn very early that significant economic conclusions can rarely be drawn from estimates of single equations, much less from single parameters. Partial analysis is all right for giving empirical content to some piece of economic structure, but it is hardly ever adequate to the problem of policy formation. In the present case, where very serious national legal policy is being considered, it would be a travesty of model building to use only part of the necessary analysis to come to strong conclusions about a complete system problem. The problem being considered is serious enough that there is no compelling reason to try to draw a conclusion in a hurry from premature analysis.

In a separate paper critically examining Ehrlich's work, Passell and Taylor (1975) introduce the important distinction between a structural equation and the reduced form of a system. They also show that the relevant coefficient within the single equation is not simply the coefficient of execution given conviction, because the dependent variable, the number of murders, appears also in the denominator of another dependent explanatory variable—namely, the arrest rate. The partial variation of murders, Q, with respect to execution, E, can go either way, i.e., positive or negative—large or small—depending

15. There is an additional justification for including the rate or frequency of other crimes—doing so is likely to reduce the distortions produced by omitted variables. We have noted earlier that if the factors that caused crime generally to increase during the period on which Ehrlich's deterrence finding depends had been included, the estimated deterrent effect might have been quite different. The rate at which other crimes are committed might serve as a useful proxy for these factors.

on the joint variation of the arrest rate with the execution rate. That, however, is the whole point of simultaneous equation construction and estimation. It is extremely important to examine covariation between Q and E through the workings of complete system solutions and not through examination of isolated parameters or isolated equations. Ehrlich estimates an unrestricted reduced form regression to cope with this problem, but his reduced form is not derived from complete system construction and is not the appropriate equation through which to examine the total effect of E on Q.

III. An important issue in the debate over Ehrlich's findings has been the matter of replicability. The degree to which other investigators have been able to reproduce Ehrlich's results has been substantial, but not quite satisfying, in the sense that they have found approximately the same numerical estimates of coefficients, but not exactly the same. The discrepancies cannot be safely attributed to round-off error, the use of different computer programs (for the same estimators), or the use of different hardware. We are happy to report, however, that we can reproduce Ehrlich's main results up to round-off error, using his own data series, which he has kindly made available to one of the present authors. Other investigators have approximated some of his statistical series but have not used identical data, and results with fairly small samples (fewer than 35 observations in the present case) are often sensitive to small numerical changes in data.

For example, Ehrlich's equation 1 (Table 3) compares with our estimate as follows:

$\Delta^* Q / N =$

$$-3.176 - 1.553\Delta^* \hat{P}_a^o - 0.455\Delta^* \hat{P}_{c/a}^o - 0.039\Delta^* PXQ_1 - 1.336\Delta^* L$$

$$-3.238 - 1.537\Delta^* \hat{P}_a^o - 0.457\Delta^* \hat{P}_{c/a}^o - 0.039\Delta^* PXQ_1 - 1.341\Delta^* L$$

$$+0.630\Delta^* A + 1.481\Delta^* Y_p + 0.067\Delta^* U - 0.047\Delta^* T$$

$$+0.633\Delta^* A + 1.481\Delta^* Y_p + 0.067\Delta^* U - 0.047\Delta^* T$$

The top row of coefficients is taken from Ehrlich's Table 3, while the figures in the bottom row are taken from our computer sheets. The discrepancy in the constant term is associated with a slight difference in the origin for chronological time. The variables have the same meaning as in Ehrlich's article—namely, all are measured as natural logarithms except T and all are modified first differences, i.e., autoregressive transformations of the original variables, measured in logarithmic units. Similar results have been obtained for Ehrlich's equations 2 and 6 as well.

These coefficients are all the same, except for round-off error, as Ehrlich's, but his estimate of the residual variance is high. He reports the square root of this estimate as 0.052, while we calculate it as 0.047. The t-statistics associated with his estimated coefficients should have been correspondingly larger. His arguments about statistical significance—not magnitude of effect—are, therefore, weaker than they should be.

We cannot emphasize enough that the fact that we replicated his results in itself gives no support to his conclusions.[16] This replication serves only to ensure that our sensitivity tests are valid. If we did not perform these tests on an accurate replication of Ehrlich's data and methodology, we would have no assurance that the tests were really isolating the effects of specific model perturbations on the findings.

A. Temporal Heterogeneity. It was remarked earlier that the major statistical contribution to Ehrlich's results on the strength of the deterrent effect of capital punishment (i.e., execution by implementation of the death sentence) on the occurrence of homicides was the rise in the murder rate since 1962, coupled with the falling off in the implementation of capital punishment. It is possible to argue, in line with Ehrlich's findings, that the former was produced by the latter. But if the death penalty were really a basic deterrent, it should have acted as such in other periods as well, taking into account the whole range of variables being considered. The principal argument against changing the sample to investigate only the period up to 1962 is that valuable statistical observations are lost—not simply the observations that make the case, but observations that contribute in a general way to the overall number of degrees of freedom, which are precious and in short supply for analysis of the problem at hand.

Other investigators, particularly Passell and Taylor, have also made calculations dealing with the possibility that Ehrlich's results would not stand up in sample variations that dealt differently with the period after 1962. It is worthwhile reporting our own, however, since we are closer to a replication of Ehrlich's primary result, having the advantage of working with his own data set. We find that the truncated sample, 1935–62, leads to a slightly

---

16. Ehrlich has regarded previous replications as strong support of the deterrence hypothesis. He writes, for example (1975b, p. 210):

First and foremost, the Bowers and Pierce work, however inadvertently, has lent considerable strength to the case for the deterrent effect of capital punishment, because their application of the theory and econometric methods outlined in my paper over the entire period considered in my analysis produces results quite similar to my own.

This opinion assumes that Ehrlich's theory and empirical methods produce accurate estimates of the deterrence effect, which, of course, begs the basic issue addressed by those who have attempted to replicate his results.

smaller and statistically insignificant coefficient of the crucial execution variable. Our result is for the specification in Ehrlich's equation 6.

$$\Delta^*Q/N = -6.891 - 0.358\Delta^*\hat{P}_a^o - 0.304\Delta^*\hat{P}_{c/a}^o - 0.046\Delta^*P\hat{X}Q_1$$
$$ (2.089) \quad (0.424) \qquad (0.084) \qquad\qquad (0.048)$$

$$- 2.514\Delta^*L + 0.280\Delta^*A + 0.951\Delta^*Y_p$$
$$ (0.550) \qquad (0.160) \qquad (0.208)$$

$$+ 0.029\Delta^*U - 0.036\Delta^*T$$
$$ (0.017) \qquad (0.008)$$

$$R^2 = 0.967 \qquad SE = 0.027 \qquad \hat{\rho} = 0.015 \qquad D = 1.59$$

The corresponding estimates of the key coefficient $(\Delta^*P\hat{X}Q_1)$ in Ehrlich's equation (6) is -0.059 with a t-ratio of -1.73. It appears, therefore, that the deterrent effect does not show up as significantly in the period before 1962 as in the whole period that combines both pre- and post-1962 values for within-sample contrast.

It is not as though the combination of pre- and post-1962 data accounted for the significance of the coefficient of the execution variable at all, for it has had a sharp relationship after 1962. If we combine both parts of the sample together, into one overall equation specification with a "dummy" variable D to designate the period 1963–69 separately, we get

$$\Delta^*Q/N = -6.343 - 0.305D - 0.655\Delta^*\hat{P}_a^o - 0.317\Delta^*\hat{P}_{c/a}^o$$
$$ (3.483) \quad (0.073) \quad (0.679) \qquad (0.119)$$

$$- 0.059\Delta^*P\hat{X}Q_1 - 0.099D\Delta^*P\hat{X}Q_1 - 2.214\Delta^*L$$
$$ (0.055) \qquad\qquad (0.054) \qquad\qquad (0.903)$$

$$+ 0.412\Delta^*A + 1.141\Delta^*Y_p + 0.045\Delta^*U - 0.040\Delta^*T$$
$$ (0.234) \qquad (0.279) \qquad (0.026) \qquad (0.010)$$

$$R^2 = 0.909 \qquad SE = 0.045 \qquad \hat{\rho} = -0.148 \qquad D = 1.52$$

This equation suggests that the significance of the coefficient of the execution variable falls (from $t = -1.73$ to $t = -1.07$) if intercept and slope dummy variables are introduced to take account of differences in sample phases, but there are two difficulties with the interpretation of this result:

1. The coefficients of D are negative, indicating that in the later period there was a lower propensity to commit murder than in the earlier period. This appears to be counter-intuitive.
2. The serial correlation coefficient estimated to account for nonrandomness among residual variation is negative, while it is generally expected that it would be positive.

This experimental calculation, thus, is inconclusive because as an overall equation estimate it is not entirely plausible.

B. *Introduction of Other Crimes.* Equally important, in comparison with our investigation of robustness under changes in Ehrlich's sample period, is our consideration of alternative specifications, the most relevant being the joint consideration of other related crimes. We have introduced a measure of a crime index (excluding homicide). This index covers six crimes: rape, robbery, aggravated assault, burglary, larceny-theft, and auto theft. Data on frequency of such crimes are taken from the Uniform Crime Reporting Section of the FBI and are weighted in an average measure by using estimates of seriousness estimated by Wolfgang et al. (1972). The weights are, respectively, 0.390, 0.135, 0.227, 0.092, 0.060, and 0.095.

The basic equation, corresponding to Ehrlich's 1, with an index of other crime, CR, added as an endogenous variable, gives the result

$$\Delta^* Q/N = -6.243 - 0.468\Delta^* \hat{P}_a^o - 0.342\Delta^* \hat{P}_{c/a}^o - 0.025\Delta^* PXQ_1$$
$$(4.020) \quad (0.931) \qquad (0.151) \qquad\qquad (0.023)$$

$$+ 0.436\Delta^* \hat{CR} - 1.216\Delta^* L + 0.425\Delta^* A + 1.148\Delta^* Y_p$$
$$(0.298) \qquad\quad (0.860) \qquad\; (0.315) \qquad\;\; (0.375)$$

$$+ 0.038\Delta^* U - 0.056\Delta^* T$$
$$(0.035) \qquad\;\; (0.013)$$

$$R^2 = 0.901 \qquad SE = 0.045 \qquad \hat{\rho} = 0.341 \qquad D = 1.36$$

A number of coefficients change statistical status in this estimate, particularly in becoming insignificant, although many of the main features of Ehrlich's equation remain invariant. Nevertheless, the key estimate, for the coefficient of $\Delta^* PXQ_1$, becomes insignificant, as well as dropping in point value. The coefficient of CR, on the other hand, has a slightly lower associated t-ratio than the original estimate of the coefficient of PXQ_1. The result suggests a form of complementarity, not necessarily in the strict sense, between homicide and other criminal acts. For given values of the other variables being considered, the homicide rate is positively associated with a broad crime rate. We do not want to argue in any confident manner about the discovery or uncovering of an alternative effect, but we do argue very strongly that there is sufficient evidence in favor of alternative specifications and alternative judgments about the deterrent effect of the death penalty that one is not justified in drawing policy conclusions from Ehrlich's results.

It is possible to push the present line of investigation a bit further by attempting to distinguish between violent crime (other than homicide) and property crime. The violent category consists of rape, robbery, and aggravated assault among the six listed above. In this case, the effect is even more dramatic. The coefficient of violent crime is very strong and statistically significant, while the deterrent effect of the death penalty practically vanishes:

$$\Delta^* Q/N = -0.047 + 0.331\Delta^* \hat{P}_a^o - 0.096\Delta^* \hat{P}_{c/a}^o$$
$$(5.196) \quad (1.093) \qquad (0.233)$$

$$+ 0.005\Delta^* PXQ_1 + 1.099\Delta^* V\hat{C}R - 1.124\Delta^* L$$
$$(0.034) \qquad\qquad (0.424) \qquad\qquad (1.210)$$

$$- 0.008\Delta^* A - 0.405\Delta^* Y_p - 0.052\Delta^* U - 0.040\Delta^* T$$
$$(0.512) \qquad (0.788) \qquad (0.062) \qquad (0.016)$$

$$R^2 = 0.723 \qquad SE = 0.066 \qquad \hat{\rho} = 0.566 \qquad D = 1.85$$

The intercorrelation of violent crimes with homicide is so strong that it dominates the relationship to the extent of "crowding out" other effects. This result indicates that there is a complicated interrelationship among various types of crime and that a more detailed system of relationships, sorting out these associations, needs to be worked out before we can feel confident of having found the underlying structure of criminal behavior, particularly homicidal behavior.

In the case of property crime, the use of an index of its occurrence in the basic equation shows so little net effect that it has practically no influence on the estimated coefficients for Ehrlich's specification. It appears to be a case of strongly interrelated aspects of violent criminal behavior that is involved.

C. Linear Specification. Finally, in our examination of alternative specifications, we have looked (following Passell and Taylor as well as others) at a linear as opposed to a log-linear equation. It is worthwhile repeating this exercise here because we have been able to replicate Ehrlich's results, up to round-off error, with his data. As the others have found, the effect of the death penalty variable on the homicide rate is not significant in a linear form equation with the same variables that Ehrlich used. There is nothing in the statistical nature of our results to lead one to prefer a logarithmic specification, and there is certainly no *a priori* theoretical reason for using a log-linear instead of a straight linear regression. Using the same two-stage least squares estimator, with correction for autoregressive errors, we compute from a "search" algorithm for values of $\hat{\rho}$,

$$\Delta^* / N = 0.191 - 0.000579\Delta^* \hat{P}_a^o - 0.000517\Delta \hat{P}_{c/a}^o$$
$$(0.057) \quad (0.000412) \qquad (0.000197)$$

$$- 0.000439\Delta^* PXQ_1 - 0.256\Delta^* L + 0.184\Delta^* A$$
$$(0.01070) \qquad (0.076) \qquad (0.055)$$

$$+ 0.000116\Delta^* Y_p + 0.000325\Delta^* U - 0.00317\Delta^* T$$
$$(0.000019) \qquad (0.000178) \qquad (0.000511)$$

$$R^2 = 0.930 \qquad SE = 0.00225 \qquad \hat{\rho} = 0.245 \qquad D = 1.72$$

As Passell and Taylor emphasize, the principal change in this estimate in comparison with Ehrlich's equation 1 is that the coefficient of PXQ_1 has fallen to insignificance. Ehrlich (1975b, p. 219) reports a linear equation and reaches a different conclusion about the significance of the estimated coefficient of $\Delta^* PXQ_1$, but his estimated value of $\hat{\rho}$ apparently does not produce a (global) minimum sum of squared residuals.[17]

IV. The building and use of statistical models of structural relationships in the field of criminal behavior, human capital, and the broader interface between sociological and economic relationships is in its infancy. Many results look very promising, suggestive, and provocative. We might well classify this research effort as being at the stage that econometric modeling reached in the 1940s and 1950s. A great deal of further painstaking developmental work was necessary to build up econometrics to the point at which the numerical findings ceased to be just interesting from an academic viewpoint and became applicable in public policy analysis. We believe that current results must undergo the same kind of testing and scholarly scrutiny over a period of years before they are ready to be used in an application as serious as the one that is associated with the use of the death penalty.

In the first instance, application might be made to general questions of public policy in the field of criminology—such questions as budgetary allocations for police work, deployment of police personnel, or use of training programs. But it seems unthinkable to us to base decisions on the use of the death penalty on Ehrlich's findings, as the Solicitor General of the United States has urged (Bork et al. 1974, pp. 32–39). They simply are not sufficiently powerful, robust, or tested at this stage to warrant use in such an important case. They are as fragile as the most tentative of econometric estimates of parameters, and we know full well how uncertain such results are under extrapolation. It is not that Ehrlich's estimates are demonstrably wrong; it is merely that they are too uncertain and must, at best, be interpreted as tentative at this stage.

There is nothing wrong with Ehrlich's particular numerical findings. His arithmetic is correct; his formulation is imaginative; but application to the most serious of issues is premature. In short, we see too many plausible explanations for his finding a deterrent effect other than the theory that capital punishment deters murder.

Following is a list of reasons that Ehrlich's results cannot be used at this time to pass judgment on the use of the death penalty.

1. The conclusion is being drawn on the basis of the estimate of a single parameter in a single equation. It is standard econometric practice to make policy application judgment on the basis of complete system solutions (simulations). Ehrlich must specify and build his interrelated system

---

17. We searched over values of ρ between -0.6 and $+0.4$ in increments of 0.0005. The surface is quite flat over the interval. Double-precision computer calculations on our IBM 370/168 provided standard error estimates—for the second-stage regression equation—of 0.019422 and 0.0019401, with Ehrlich's $\hat{\rho}$ equal to -0.119 and our $\hat{\rho}$ equal to $+0.2445$, respectively.

before he can try to draw policy conclusions from his work. He may not
necessarily come to different conclusions, but there is no way of knowing
this in advance.

2. The estimate of the coefficient of the execution variable is not significantly negative if the sample is truncated at 1962, an index of other crimes
is introduced in the equation, or the equation is specified in linear form.

3. The absolute value of the estimate of the coefficient of the execution variable may be upwardly biased in an absolute sense, as a result of measurement error.

4. The partial effect of execution on homicides, if computed with allowance
for the fact that homicides are used to estimate the arrest rate, is not necessarily significantly negative.

5. Cross-sectional analyses have produced results that are not consistent with
the hypothesis that capital punishment deters homicide.

Sellin, Ehrlich, Passell, and others are to be congratulated on opening up
a fascinating area of research with much scholarly potential. It remains to
pursue this line of research to the point at which it can be used in the future
for making important contributions to legal policy. The deterrent effect of
capital punishment is definitely not a settled matter, and this is the strongest
social scientific conclusion that can be reached at the present time.

References

Baldus, D.C., and Cole, J.W.L. (1975) A comparison of the work of Thorsten Sellin
and Isaac Ehrlich on the deterrent effect of capital punishment. *Yale Law Journal* 85(2):170–86.

Becker, G.S. (1975) Crime and punishment: an economic approach. *Journal of Political Economy* 78(2):169–217.

Bork (Solicitor General) et al. (1974) *Fowler v. North Carolina*, U.S. Supreme Court
case no. 73-7031. Brief for U.S. as amicus curiae:32–39.

Bowers, W.J., and Pierce, G.L. (1975) The illusion of deterrence in Isaac Ehrlich's
research on capital punishment. *Yale Law Journal* 85(2):187–208.

Ehrlich, I. (1973) Participation in illegitimate activities: a theoretical and empirical
investigation. *Journal of Political Economy* 81(3):52–65.

Ehrlich, I. (1975a) The deterrent effect of capital punishment: a question of life and
death. *American Economic Review* 65(3):397–417.

Ehrlich, I. (1975b) Deterrence: evidence and inference. *Yale Law Journal* 85(2):209–
27.

Hindelang, M.J. (1974) The Uniform Crime Reports revisited. *Journal of Criminal
Justice* 2(1):1–17.

Newton, G.D., and Zimring, F.E. (1969) *Firearms and Violence in American Life.*
Staff report to the National Commission on the Causes and Prevention of
Violence. Washington, D.C.: U.S. Government Printing Office.

Passell, P. (1975) The deterrent effect of the death penalty: a statistical test. *Stanford
Law Review* 28(1):61–80.

Passell, P., and Taylor, J.B. (1975) The Deterrent Effect of Capital Punishment:

Another View. Discussion paper 74-7509. Columbia University Department of
Economics.

Peck, J.K. (1976) The deterrent effect of capital punishment: a comment. *Yale Law
Journal* 85(3):359–67.

Phillips, L. (1973) Crime control: the case for deterrence. Pages 65–84 in S. Rotten-
berg, ed., *The Economics of Crime and Punishment.* Washington, D.C.: American Enterprise Institute for Public Policy Research.

Sellin, T. (1959) *The Death Penalty.* Philadelphia: American Law Institute.

Wolfgang, M.E., Figlio, R.M., and Sellin, T. (1972) *Delinquency in a Birth Cohort.*
Chicago: University of Chicago Press.

§4.   The Deterrent Effect of the Death Penalty upon Prison Murder*

WENDY PHILLIPS WOLFSON

After the *Furman* decision in 1972, many states enacted new death penalty
legislation specially directed to the punishment of prisoners.[1] These statutes
applied the death penalty to one or combinations of two or more of the following: 1. murder of an on-duty correctional employee; 2. murder by a life-
term prisoner; 3. murder by any prisoner; 4. murder by a convicted capital
offender; and 5. murder by a convicted murderer. In particular, eight of these
states adopted in 1973 a mandatory death penalty for any homicide committed by an inmate serving a life sentence[2] or by an inmate convicted of a capital offense.[3]

The rationale behind this new legislation was characteristic of two arguments familiar to advocates of capital punishment. The first argument

---

1. See James R. Browning, "The New Death Penalty Statutes: Perpetuating a Costly Myth,"
   Gonzaga Law Review, 9, no. 3 (Spring 1974), 651–705, "The New Death Penalty Statutes,"
   Harvard Law Review, 87, no. 7 (1974), 1690–1719, at 1710–12, notes 145–46.
2. See Ind. Ann. Stat., Section 10-3401 (6) (iv) (Supp. 1973); La. Rev. Stat. Ann., Section 14:30(3)
   (Supp. 1974); Miss. ch. 576, Section 6 (1) (b), 1974 General Assembly (Apr. 23, 1974); Nev. Rev.
   Stat., Section 200.030 (1) (b) (1973); N.Y. ch. 367, Section 5, 1974 Legislative Assembly (May
   6, 1974); Okla. Stat. Ann. tit. 21, Section 701.1(8) (Supp. 1973); Wyo. Stat. Ann., Section 6-
   54(b)(x) (Supp. 1973). The effective dates of the above legislation were: Indiana, April 24, 1973;
   Louisiana, July 2, 1973; Mississippi, April 23, 1974; Nevada, July 1, 1973; New York, Septem-
   ber 1, 1974; Oklahoma, May 17, 1973; and Rhode Island, July 1, 1973.
3. See ch. 276 (1973) Idaho Laws 589; Ind. Ann. Stat., Section 10-3401(b)(6)(iii) (Supp. 1973); La.
   Rev. Stat. Ann., Section 14:30(3) (Supp. 1974); Wyo. Stat. Ann., Section 6-54(b)(iv) (Supp. 1973).
   The effective dates of the above legislation were: Idaho, July 1, 1973; Indiana, April 24, 1973;
   Louisiana, July 2, 1973, and Wyoming, May 1973.

stressed retribution and revenge, the "just deserts" philosophy that metes out a state-inflicted killing as the proper response to an offender-inflicted murder. Since a prison homicide indicates that "prison has failed to restrain the violence in these [convicts], . . . they deserve no more patience from the rest of us. Their lives are now, once and for all, forfeited to society."[4] Advanced on the grounds of a just punishment, the death penalty according to this argument both satisfies the public need for vengeance and appears to match the punishment to the crime. The other argument is based upon the notion of deterrence and implies that since dangerous conditions characterize prison life, both inmates and staff need the extra protection afforded by the threat of death to deter homicide. Essentially, the former argument is dogma and thus can only be rejected or accepted on the basis of faith and emotional belief. However, the rationale based upon deterrence can be further clarified by empirical testing.

One statistical measure of whether the deterrence argument is relevant to death penalty legislation is provided by a comprehensive study of reported prison homicides in state and federal prisons in 1973.[5] During that year, 124 persons—113 male inmates and 11 male staff—were murdered in prison.

Many of the findings from this study raise questions about assumptions traditionally associated with the deterrence argument. For example, those who defend capital punishment as a specific deterrent to prison homicide assume that prisoners and custodial guards require protection beyond that accorded to citizens outside. Yet, in 1973, the inmate's risk of being killed in prison did not exceed the victimization rate for criminal homicide in the general population outside.[6] Table 4-4-1 indicates that when adjustments[7] were made for the unusual age-race-sex distribution of the prisoner popula-

4. See Hugo Adam Bedau, *The Courts, the Constitution and Capital Punishment,* Lexington Books, 1977, p. 76, who discusses critically this attitude of vengeance.
5. See Sawyer Sylvester et al., *Prison Homicide,* Spectrum, 1977, and Wendy Phillips Wolfson, "The Patterns of Prison Homicide," unpub. Ph.D. dissertation, University of Pennsylvania, 1978. For other studies that relate to prison homicide and capital punishment, see Dogan Akman, "Homicides and Assaults in Canadian Penitentiaries," *Canadian Journal of Corrections,* 8 (1966): 284–299; Peter C. Buffum, "Prison Killings and Death Penalty Legislation," *The Prison Journal,* 53 (Spring–Summer 1973): 49–57; Peter C. Buffum, *Homosexuality in Prisons,* LEAA Report, Washington, D.C., Feb. 1972; Thorsten Sellin, "Homicides and Assaults in American Prisons: 1964," *Acta Criminologiae et Medicinae Legalis Japonica,* 13 (1965): 139–143 and "Homicides and Serious Assaults in Prisons: 1965," in Thorsten Sellin, *Capital Punishment,* New York: Harper & Row, 1967, pp. 154–160, and *The Penalty of Death,* Beverly Hills, Calif., Sage, 1980.
6. For a more detailed review of the relative risk of confinement, see Wolfson, op. cit., Chap. 3 and Sec. 4.3. In general, the murder rate in prison does not exceed the murder rate outside, although the young, white male has three times the victimization risk in prison that he does outside.
7. The adjustments utilize the technique of indirect standardization. In order to calculate the number of homicides expected from the prisoner population, the number of male inmates of differential age-race intervals are multiplied by the age-race-sex adjusted homicide rates from

tion, the number of observed inmate homicides did not exceed the number expected. In both the state and federal prison system, the total number of homicides in the expected and observed columns are nearly equivalent; that is, 105 homicides occurred in the state prison compared to the 102.35 expected, and in the federal system, the numbers are 10 and 9.65 respectively. This is not to say that the homicide risk for male prisoners approximates that of male citizens across all categories of age and race. For instance, the subtotals in the ratio column reveal that 3 to 4 times as many whites were killed as would have been predicted.[8] In general, though, this table documents that the male prisoner does not necessarily require more protection than his counterpart outside.

Likewise, for prison staff the hazards of prison life have probably been overestimated. The comparison of inmate risk to citizen risk can be paralleled by a comparison of murder rates of prison staff and of law enforcement officers.

Depending upon how the population-at-risk is defined, the calculation of the rate in each case differs. In most studies, the murder rate of the law enforcement officer has been based upon the resident population because the size of the police population was not known. Constructing a ratio of the number of male police murders to the resident male population results in an almost negligible police murder rate in 1973, namely, .01 per 10,000 male residents.[9] The substitution of the estimated male police population in the

---

the outside population and then the products are summed. Similar studies have also used the technique of indirect standardization. See the comparison of observed to expected number of assaults in the North Carolina prison system in Dan A. Fuller et al., "Violence and Victimization within the North Carolina Prison System," paper presented at the American Society of Criminology meetings, Tucson, Arizona, November 4–7, 1976. Also, a comparison of observed to expected number of homicides is discussed in Richard Block, "Homicide in Chicago: A Nine Year Study (1965–1973)," *The Journal of Criminal Law, Criminology and Police Science,* 66 (1975), pp. 496–510.

8. The comparison between the prisoner population and the male population fails to account for the difference in social class and the relation of race and class. Since mortality varies by social class, the homicide rate of the lower-class prisoner population should be compared to that of the population of lower socioeconomic males. Unfortunately, the risk of homicide by social class has not been computed. However, this type of comparison would explain why confinement appears to increase the risk of whites by a factor of between 3 and 4 while reducing the risk of blacks by two thirds. (Table 4-4-1) The prison selects lower class males from 1. the black population, which is disproportionately lower class, and 2. from the white population, which is more evenly distributed by class. If the homicide rate of white male prisoners was compared solely to that of lower-class white males (particularly in the South), the calculation of the homicide risk in prison would not favor blacks at the expense of whites.

9. This rate was constructed by dividing the 103 male police officers (county, local, and state) murdered in 1973 by the resident male population (1973) of 102,240,000. See Federal Bureau of Investigation, *Uniform Crime Reports: Law Enforcement Officers Killed,* Summary 1973, Washington, D.C., p. 1, and U.S. Bureau of Census, "Estimates of the Population of the United States, by Age, Sex and Race: 1970–1975," Current Population Reports, p. 25, No. 614, Washington, D.C., 1975, Table 2, p. 19.

Table 4-4-1. Comparison of Expected and Observed Number of Male Inmate Homicides, by Age and Race, 1973

The State Prison

Age	Male prisoner population[a]	Expected		Observed		Ratio of observed rate to expected rate
		U.S. homicide rate adjusted for age, race, and sex[b]	Expected number of homicides	Observed homicide rate in prison	Observed number of homicides	
White male[c]						
20–24	27,564	.000184	5.07	.000580	16	3.16
25–29	22,047	.000195	4.30	.000816	18	4.19
30–34	15,654	.000184	2.88	.000894	14	4.86
35–39	11,507	.000171	1.96	.000695	8	4.08
40–44	9,333	.000147	1.37	.000214	2	1.46
45–49	6,110	.000123	.75	.000327	2	2.66
50–54	3,656	.000098	.35	—	—	—
55–59	2,295	.000088	.20	—	—	—
60–64	1,325	.000069	.09	—	—	—
65–69	1,091	.000060	.07	—	—	—
Subtotal	100,582	.001319	17.04	.003526	60	2.67
Nonwhite male						
20–24	19,772	.001285	25.41	.000811	16	.63
25–29	14,823	.001594	23.62	.001011	15	.64
30–34	9,402	.001465	13.77	.000638	6	.44
35–39	7,349	.001290	9.48	.000544	4	.42
40–44	5,562	.001190	6.62	.000179	1	.15
45–49	3,406	.001043	3.55	—	—	—
50–54	1,936	.000797	1.54	.000516	1	.65
55–59	1,232	.000736	.91	.000811	1	1.09
60–64	520	.000493	.25	—	—	—
65–69	384	.000416	.16	.002604	1	6.25
Subtotal	64,386	.010309	85.31	.007114	45	.69
TOTAL	164,968		102.35		105[d]	.92

The Federal Prison

White male[c]						
20–24	4,012	.000184	.74	—	—	—
25–29	3,074	.000195	.60	.000975	3	5.00
30–34	2,335	.000184	.43	.000428	1	2.32
35–39	1,962	.000171	.34	.000509	1	2.94
40–44	1,582	.000147	.23	—	—	—
45–49	923	.000123	.11	—	—	—
50–54	661	.000098	.06	.003025	2	33.33
55–59	379	.000088	.03	—	—	—
60–64	238	.000069	.02	—	—	—
65–69	159	.000060	.01	—	—	—
Subtotal	15,325	.001319	2.57	.004937	7	3.76
Nonwhite male						
20–24	1,335	.001285	1.72	—	—	—
25–29	1,131	.001594	1.80	—	—	—
30–34	897	.001465	1.31	.003344	3	2.29
35–39	736	.001290	.94	—	—	—
40–44	599	.001190	.71	—	—	—
45–49	348	.001043	.36	—	—	—
50–54	157	.000797	.13	—	—	—
55–59	90	.000736	.06	—	—	—
60–64	68	.000493	.03	—	—	—
65–69	38	.000416	.02	—	—	—
Subtotal	5,399	.010309	7.08	.003344	3	.32
TOTAL	20,724		9.65	.003344	10	.71

[a] Michael Hindelang et al., *Sourcebook of Criminal Justice Statistics, 1974*, U.S. Department of Justice, Washington, D.C., 1975, Table 6.37, pp. 461–62.
[b] "Homicide Rates per 100,000 by Age, Color and Sex, United States, 1973," are unpublished data provided by special arrangement with the Mortality Statistics Branch, Division of Vital Statistics, Public Health Service, Rockville, Maryland.
[c] White male designation includes those of Spanish origin, e.g., Mexican-American and Puerto Rican.
[d] Includes the justifiable homicide of two inmate escapees.

denominator, though, increases the rate to 2.3 per 10,000 police employees.[10] Since the latter rate includes civilian employees as well as sworn police officers in the denominator, the comparison should use a staff murder rate based upon all correctional personnel in the population-at-risk. The male staff murder rate was 1 per 10,000 state correctional male employees.[11] Hence the police murder rate exceeded the staff murder rate by a factor greater than 2.

The limitation of this analysis is that it fails to take account of the uneven distribution of risk within the employee category. For example, among law enforcement personnel, the officer is at greater risk than the civilian employee, and the officer on patrol duty bears a greater risk than the officer performing clerical or administrative duties. That the police homicide was most likely to occur during patrol duty was less than coincidential: "the patrol officer is frequently in contact with suspicious individuals. Each of these situations constitutes a threat to the officer's personal safety. The patrol officer risks attack through frequent encounters with criminal offenders. . . ."[12]

Similarly, among prison staff the custodial guard was at greater risk than the administrative and rehabilitative employee and the guard patrolling the cellblock bore a greater risk than the guard assigned to tower duty. When the state prison personnel-at-risk were distributed by work assignment, the staff murder rate increased from 1 per 10,000 state prison male personnel to 3.5 per 10,000 surveyed state prison custodial staff. Unfortunately, whether the murder rate of the custodial guard was lower than the police patrol officer is impossible to test. The unavailability of statistics, by which the number of police employees could be cross-classified by function and work assignment, impedes the construction of the murder rate of the police officer on patrol.

However, the staff's risk of fatality can also be viewed against hazards of occupations other than law enforcement. In the industrial environment, fatal hazards to life (comparable to the probability of fatality assigned to prison staff) result from exposure to chemical agents, mechanical agents, infective agents, and physical agents (heat, noise, and radiation).[13]

10. The number of police murders, 103, was divided by the estimated male police population (1973) of 443,317. This population was first estimated as a ratio to resident population and then adjusted for sex. See, respectively, Federal Bureau of Investigation, *Uniform Crime Reports, 1973*, Table 52, p. 164 and Table 54, p. 166.
11. This rate was computed by dividing the 10 staff murder victims, employed by state correctional institutions, by the number of state correctional male personnel, 95,891. This population was estimated from the 1972 population and then adjusted for sex. See Michael Hindelang et al., *Sourcebook of Criminal Justice Statistics, 1974*, Table 1.77, p. 121, and Table 1.108, p. 157, respectively.
12. Federal Bureau of Investigation, *Uniform Crime Reports, 1973*, pp. 39, 42.
13. May R. Mayers, *Occupational Health*, Baltimore: Williams & Wilkins, 1969.

Among at least thirty-three broadly defined skilled and semi-skilled jobs,[14] the rate of fatality from work-related accidents far exceeded the fatality rate by homicide of the prison guard. Particularly dangerous were the work environments of the fireman, the miner, the construction worker,[15] and the timber feller,[16] who were more likely to die by violence than the correctional officer. Although no work environment is hazard free and occupational risk is relative, this is not to imply that the fatal work accident is as serious as the murder of a prison guard. However, in 1973, the risk of violent death incurred by the prison guard did not exceed that associated with several other positions. What most distinguishes the dangers of prison employment from other vocations is not the risk but the occurrence of staff murder in a setting designed to maintain order and effective control.

The question, though, is not whether those confined and those who supervise their confinement require more protection, but whether the threat of the death penalty affords extra protection by deterring murders in prison. Information of particular relevance to answering this question can be found in Table 4-4-2, which displays the distribution of reported prison homicides with respect to the jurisdiction's death penalty status, for the years 1964,[17] 1965[18] and 1973.[19] In 1973, with all jurisdictions reporting, over 90 percent of the inmate and staff murders occurred in retentionist jurisdictions, which suggests that the incidence of prison murder is not affected by the threat of the death penalty. Although fewer jurisdictions reported in 1964 and 1965, in the mid-1960s and the early 1970s the concentration of prison killings in retentionist jurisdictions has remained relatively constant. Since the death penalty was probably perceived as a greater threat in the mid-1960s than in the early 1970s, that is, before the de facto moratorium on executions (1967–73), evidently the degree of threat is also unrelated to the distribution of prison murders.

On the other hand, a review of prison homicide studies since the mid-1960s indicates that the composition of inmates who murder in prison has not remained constant. In 1973, 152 inmate offenders were identified for

14. U.S. Department of Health, Education, and Welfare, *Mortality by Occupation and Causes of Death Among Men 20–64 Years of Age,* Public Health Service, Vital Statistics, Special Report, Vol. 53, No. 3, Sept. 1963.

15. The probability of death by work-related injury of the construction worker was calculated from data presented in U.S. Department of Labor, *Occupational Injuries and Illnesses in the United States, by Industry, 1974,* Bureau of Labor Statistics, Washington, D.C. 1976, Table 1, p. 19, and Table 8, p. 22. The death of construction workers by injury happened to 2 of every 10,000 workers.

16. The death rate of the timber feller is 125 per 10,000 workers per year. See Stan Hager, "In the Logging Woods," *Harpers,* Oct. 1979, p. 35.

17. See Sellin, "Homicides and Assaults."

18. See Sellin, "Homicides and Serious Assaults."

19. See Wolfson, op. cit., pp. 219–22.

Table 4-4-2. Murders in U.S. Prisons by Status of Jurisdictions, 1973[a], 1965[b], 1964[c]

	1973					
	Death penalty retained		Death penalty abolished		Total	
Inmate Victims	95%	(107)	5%	(6)	100%	(113)
Staff Victims	91%	(10)	9%	(1)	100%	(11)
Total	94%	(117)	6%	(7)	100%	(124)

	1965					
	Death penalty retained		Death penalty abolished		Total	
Inmate Victims	85%	(45)	15%	(8)	100%	(53)
Staff Victims	100%	(8)		(0)	100%	(8)
Total	87%	(53)	13%	(8)	100%	(61)

	1964					
	Death penalty retained		Death penalty abolished		Total	
Inmate Victims	94%	(29)	6%	(2)	100%	(31)
Staff Victims		(0)		(0)		(0)
Total	94%	(29)	6%	(2)	100%	(31)

[a] Includes 52 jurisdictions: 50 states, District of Columbia, and federal prison system. Source: Wendy Phillips Wolfson, "The Patterns of Prison Homicide," unpub. Ph.D. Dissertation, University of Pennsylvania, 1978, p. 221, Table 52.

[b] Includes 47 jurisdictions: 45 states, District of Columbia, and federal prison system. Source: Thorsten Sellin, "Homicides and Serious Assaults in Prisons: 1965," in Thorsten Sellin, *Capital Punishment,* New York: Harper & Row, 1967, pp. 154–60.

[c] Includes 42 jurisdictions: 40 states, District of Columbia, and federal prison system. Source: Thorsten Sellin, "Homicides and Assaults in American Prisons: 1964," *Acta Criminologiae et Medicinae Legalis Japonica,* 13 (1965): 139–43.

approximately two thirds of the reported prison homicides. Of these assail-ants, over one quarter were serving time for murder. This proportion is two and one half times the percentage constituted by murderers in the general prison population, an overrepresentation that forces us to reconsider the low criminality level traditionally attributed to the incarcerated murderer by pre-vious investigators.[20] C. H. S. Jayewardene has claimed that "Homicide [in

20. Traditionally, the convicted murderer has a lower criminality level (fewer infractions, escapes, etc.) than other inmates, even when the analysis controls for age, race, and intelli-gence. G. Waldo, "The Criminality Level of Incarcerated Murderers and Non-Murderers," *Journal of Criminal Law, Criminology and Police Science,* 61 (1970), pp. 60–70.

prison] does not appear to be the prerogative of homicide convicts."[21] Sellin has asserted that "Generally speaking . . . murderous offenses [in prison] are committed by prisoners serving sentences for other crimes than murder. . . . Homicides do occur in prisons, but most of them are committed by people serving time for robbery, forgery or what have you."[22] Newer research does not contradict these generalizations, but it does suggest that the proportion of prison homicide committed by convicted murderers is higher than has hitherto been realized.

In fact, the proportion of imprisoned murderers who recidivate has steadily increased since the 1950s and 1960s. Of prison homicides committed between 1949 and 1958, Jayewardene[23] documented that only 18 percent were committed by murderers; of prison homicides committed in 1964, Sellin[24] reported that only 20 percent were committed by murderers. By 1973, 40 percent of the inmate homicides and 50 percent of the staff homicides were committed by those under sentence for murder. Whether this increase reflects the increasingly violent character of the persons incarcerated or other changes in the type of inmate under sentence for murder, for example, an increasing proportion of young, serious offense recidivists, is not clear.

With respect to death penalty legislation and deterrence, the growing role of the convicted murderer among prison homicides is worthy of further study. A flagrant weakness of the deterrence argument is that it assumes that imprisoned murderers will be deterred from killing by the same threat that, before prison, was insufficient to deter their homicidal behavior.[25] Statistically, the irrelevance of the death penalty threat to the imprisoned murderer is illustrated in Table 4-4-3. The percentage of imprisoned murderers who recidivate is approximately the same in abolitionist and retentionist jurisdictions. (The retentionist federal jurisdiction is excluded from this analysis because imprisoned murderers are generally confined to state correctional facilities.) The threat of the death penalty in the retentionist jurisdiction does not even exert an *incremental* deterrent effect over the threat of a lesser punishment in the abolitionist state.

Among the requirements for the death penalty to exert a deterrent effect, there are two of particular relevance to prison homicide. Prior to the commission of the crime, 1. the offender must reflect upon the cost of punishment and judge it intolerable, and 2. the offender must perceive the certainty of punishment as high. However, certain patterns of prison homicide,[26] partic-

21. C. H. S. Jayewardene, "Are Murderers Dangerous?" *Probation and Child Care Journal*, 2 (1962):33–35.
22. Sellin, *The Death Penalty*, Philadelphia: American Law Institute, 1959, p. 72; and *Capital Punishment*, p. 252.
23. See Jayewardene, op. cit.
24. See Sellin, "Homicides and Assaults."
25. See Sellin, "Homicides and Serious Assualts," pp. 154–60.
26. See Wolfson, op. cit., pp. 20–107.

Table 4-4-3. Imprisoned Murderers who Recidivate in Prison[a], by Status of Jurisdiction, 1973

	Death penalty retained		Death penalty abolished	
Imprisoned murderers who recidivate/Total imprisoned murderers	36/16,369	.21%	4/2120	.19%

[a] Includes all 50 state jurisdictions and the District of Columbia.

Source: U.S. Department of Justice, *Capital Punishment 1971–72,* National Prisoner Statistics Bulletin, Washington, D.C. December 1974, pp. 57–58, Table 16; *Census of Prisoners in State Correctional Facilities,* 1973, National Prisoners Statistics Special Report, Washington, D.C., December 1976 (corrected for sex).

ularly with respect to the number and type of assailant(s) committing the murder, suggest that both conditions are unlikely to operate in the prisoner's mind. For the typical single assailant, the prison homicide is spontaneous, altercation-provoked, and victim-precipitated. He is not likely to consider conditions 1 and 2 because, to him, "the risk of apprehension and threat of punishment were distant, abstract, irrelevant notions."[27] The typical multiple assailant, who relies upon the aid of co-participants, is more deliberate than impulsive; his modus operandi is characterized by planning, coordination, and unobserved action. He might well reflect upon the gain-risk ratio of the crime,[28] but he probably also knows that the risk of punishment for a contract killing is low: Less than one third of the multiple assailant prison homicides result in conviction. Even at that, a conviction merely means the imposition of a concurrent sentence upon one who already has a long term to serve. In short, for the multiple assailant—the perpetrator who is most likely to consider the cost of punishment—even the threat of execution is unlikely to deter him from murder.

That a conviction for a premeditated prison homicide never resulted in a punishment more severe than a concurrent sentence is surprising in light of the fact that 19 of the 124 prison homicides occurred in jurisdictions that had previously adopted mandatory death statutes.[29]

27. Marvin E. Wolfgang, "Criminal Homicide and the Subculture of Violence," Marvin E. Wolfgang, ed., *Studies in Homicide,* New York: Harper & Row, 1967, pp. 3–14.
28. For a fuller discussion of how the attractive gain-risk ratio acts to minimize the deterrent effect of the criminal justice system upon the criminal, see Benjamin Avi-Itzhak and Revel Shinnar, "Quantitative Models in Crime Control," *Journal of Criminal Justice,* 1 (1973), p. 189.
29. See notes 2 and 3. In 1973, the states in which prison homicides occurred after the adoption of a mandatory death provision, were: Indiana (2); Nevada (3); Rhode Island (2); Oklahoma (5); and Louisiana (7).

Table 4-4-4. Murders in U.S. Prisons by Status of Jurisdiction and Victim, 1973

	Mandatory death penalty adopted		Discretionary death penalty retained		Death penalty abolished		Total	
Inmate victims	95%	(18)	94%	(89)	86%	(6)	91%	(113)
Staff victims	5%	(1)	6%	(9)	14%	(1)	9%	(11)
Total	100%	(19)	100%	(98)	100%	(7)	100%	(124)

However, the background of most of the assailants who committed these 19 prison homicides did not meet either of the two statutory conditions necessary to impose a mandatory death penalty. Only four of these assailants were 1. serving life terms or 2. under sentence for a capital offense. Yet, despite the prosecution and conviction of all four, none received the mandatory death sentence. Why a less severe punishment was imposed is unclear. One explanation is that the mandatory death statute, legislated without regard to its enforceability and constitutionality, was never very likely to be applied.

It is difficult to ascertain whether the regular use of mandatory execution would have exerted an incremental deterrent effect over the threat of the death penalty upon prison homicide. Statistically, the threat of mandatory death exerted no more deterrent effect upon prison homicide than the discretionary death penalty. Table 4-4-4 compares the percentage of inmate murders to staff murders in each type of jurisdiction. Since the proportion of staff victims ranges between 5 percent and 6 percent in the mandatory as well as the discretionary jurisdictions, it is unpersuasive to argue that mandatory death will marginally increase the safeguards for prison staff.

Table 4-4-5 reveals whether the jurisdiction's status with respect to the death penalty affects the percentage of prison homicides that are deliberate gang killings. Murders are first classified by the variable, "suspected number

Table 4-4-5. Murders in U.S. Prisons by Status of Jurisdiction and Suspected Number of Assailants, 1973

Suspected number of assailants	Mandatory death penalty retained		Discretionary death penalty retained		Death penalty abolished		Total	
Single assailant	48%	(9)	41%	(40)	57%	(4)	43%	(53)
Multiple assailant	48%	(9)	46%	(45)	29%	(2)	45%	(56)
Unknown assailant	4%	(1)	13%	(13)	14%	(1)	12%	(15)
Total	100%	(19)	100%	(98)	100%	(7)	100%	(124)

of assailants." This variable is the number of assailants (one or more than one) recorded on the prison incident report for each prison homicide. By ignoring the category of murders with unknown assailants, Table 4-4-5 indicates that impulsive killings (single-assailant) and premeditated killings (multiple-assailant) are almost evenly divided between retentionist jurisdictions that adopted a mandatory death penalty and those that adopted a discretionary death penalty. The numbers in the abolitionist column are small but, consistent with the above findings, the premeditated, multiple-assailant prison killing does not predominate in jurisdictions that have eliminated the death penalty.

These findings contradict the assumptions of capital punishment advocates who have traditionally held that the threat of the death penalty, particularly the threat of mandatory death, will deter prison homicide and more specifically, the premeditated prison murder and the killing of the correctional employee. Death penalty advocates respond by arguing that during the early 1970s, prisoners—especially incarcerated murders—knew that the threat of execution was empty. However, Table 4-4-2 indicates that despite the use of executions in the mid-1960s, prison homicides still tended to occur in retentionist jurisdictions.

Although neither the threat nor use of execution is likely to deter the prison murder, execution can definitely insure a preventive effect. In fact, in 1973, if the state had executed rather than imprisoned all those capital murderers who recidivated, 32 lives would have been saved.[30] Before this alternative is embraced, however, two points should be noted. First, all the imprisoned murderers who recidivated were serving life terms by trial court sentences and not because of any commutations. Second, since no judge or jury can successfully predict which of the convicted and imprisoned murderers will recidivate,[31] in order to have saved the victims' lives, the state would have had to execute as well the 99.8 percent of imprisoned capital murderers who did not repeat their offenses. Not only would this policy have contradicted the principles of our criminal law, it would also have required society to sacrifice 577 persons for every victim spared.[32]

Just as executing all the imprisoned murderers to prevent a few from killing again is socially unacceptable, the study of prison homicide suggests that the threat of the death penalty is unlikely to deter them (or, for that matter, any prisoners under sentence for another crime) from murder in prison. The

---

30. Wolfson, op. cit., p. 224. Imprisoned murderers killed 32 inmates and staff; 12 imprisoned murderers were themselves killed; and imprisoned murderers killed an additional 8 inmates prior to 1973.
31. Sellin, *The Penalty of Death,* p. 110.
32. See Table 4-4-3. Total population of imprisoned murderers in 1973 was 18,489; 32 inmates and staff were murdered by imprisoned murderers. The ratio is 18,489 to 32 or 577 to 1.

low degree of certainty of any punishment for prison homicide and the doubtful constitutionality and infrequent use of the death penalty have weakened whatever deterrent effect it might otherwise have had.

Even in a society where the death penalty has been applied regularly, its power to deter prohibited behavior is low. In prison, an unofficial death penalty has frequently been meted out by inmates to each other to punish violations that are disruptive of the inmate organization. "[T]he convict code ... is an unwritten body of law used by the strong to enforce servitude on the weak. It *utilizes the death penalty,* and other physical abuse, as sanctions. ..."[33] Despite the high degree of certainty of such punishment, the violators have not been deterred; by disobedience to inmate leaders, other inmates continue to invite death by a contract killing.[34]

The threat of the death penalty fails to deter behavior prohibited by the inmate order just as it failed in 1973 to deter 94 percent of the prison homicides. The threat and use of less severe punishments also failed to deter both the crime for which the inmate assailant was under confinement and the murder in prison, a recidivist crime for one quarter of the assailants.

The conclusion that is suggested by these observations requires us to turn away from deterrence tactics in order to adopt measures designed to *reduce the risk* of prison murder. Effective measures to reduce this risk have been discussed elsewhere.[35] Briefly, it can be stated here that the most effective measure to reduce prison homicide, with the exception of an increase in "lock-down" time, would be to remove lethal weapons from the prisoners. The immense coordination and logistical problems of the prison inspection have tended to result in sporadic, incomplete, and short-lived confiscations of the prisoners' weapons. Nonetheless, the diversity and large number of weapons gathered have been remarkable. In order to restrict access to prison-fashioned weapons permanently, certain vocational/industrial programs should be eliminated.[36] For example, increasingly sophisticated weapons are easily manufactured[37] in the prison's sheet metal industry. Prison officials tend to reject this recommendation in the belief that the ingenuity of the inmate is sufficient to enable him to make dangerous weapons even from nonindustrial tools and equipment. The results of an experiment in a California prison, however, reveal that this belief is mistaken. When the sheet

33. See "Remarks on Inmate Self-Determination," by a prison superintendent, in *Prison Journal,* 57:2 (1977), p. 64.
34. See Wolfson, op. cit., Sec. 4.2.
35. See Ibid., pp. 225–27.
36. James B. Jacobs, "Prison Violence and Formal Organization," A. K. Cohen et al., *Prison Violence,* Lexington, Mass.: D.C. Heath, 1976, pp. 79–88.
37. Clair F. Rees, "Arsenals Behind Prison Walls," *Guns and Ammo,* 14 (January 1979), pp. 29–33.

metal industry was removed from the prison, metal daggers were reduced by 85 percent and fatal stabbings were reduced by 94 percent.[38]

Second, cells should be occupied by only one prisoner, whose key controls a pick-proof lock. A monitoring system should be undertaken to insure that the master key assigned to the staff cannot come into the possession of an inmate.[39]

Third, defects in the structural design of the prison require correction.[40] "Blind spots" need to be opened or permanently sealed and the high-rate assault locations (e.g., the shower and the yard) deserve constant and more concentrated staff supervision. Evidence indicates that as number of staff increases, the staff's sense of security increases and they are more likely to take swift action when they witness inmate assault.[41]

Fourth, the occurrence of a serious prison incident demands a review of the participant's security status. Repeatedly assaulted inmates require stricter security. Of course, high custody status does not necessarily result in increased safety. Almost 40 percent of the assailants and 30 percent of the victims had been classified in segregation and maximum custody.[42] Although this observation indicates that the security designation tends to be correctly assigned, it suggests that control in high custody areas is low and needs to be strengthened.

Fifth, since the highest homicide risk occurs during the first year served, the policy and safeguards associated with the introduction to the institution of new prisoners and custodial staff should be reviewed.[43]

Sixth, staff should be educated to recognize a potentially fatal injury. Medical advances have reduced the probability of fatality due to assault, but this is not characteristic of prison medical treatment. Therefore, more efficient hospitalization of the seriously injured is also needed.

Given that the deterrent effect of the death penalty for prison homicide is to be seriously doubted, it is clear that management and physical changes in the prison would do more than any legislated legal sanction to reduce the number of prison murders. This conclusion is not altogether new. It echoes

---

38. The test confirmed that fatal stabbings were reduced by 94% because dangerous metal daggers were reduced by 85%. Serious stabbings were reduced less (33 %) because weapons were still made from sharpened wood or plastic. See Howard Bidna, "Effects of Increased Security on Prison Violence," *Journal of Criminal Justice,* 3 (1975), pp. 33–45.

39. Carl Weiss and David James Friar, *Terror in the Prisons,* New York: Bobbs-Merrill, 1974, p. 3.

40. "Court Says Inmate Can Defend a Victim," *New York Times,* 8 February 1976.

41. Weiss and Friar, op. cit., p. 153.

42. See Wolfson, op cit., pp. 105–6. A review of the custody status and work assignment of assailants and victims indicated that those who had been classified maximum custody were not safe from attack and those who were repeatedly violent in prison had not been classified as a management problem.

43. See Wolfson, op. cit., p. 156.

an observation made by Sellin over fifteen years ago: "[T]he hazards of prison life . . . can be lessened only by institutional management."[44]

§ 5. Recidivism, Parole, and Deterrence

Beginning with God's judgment upon Cain, the first recorded murderer (Genesis 4:11–16), the traditional alternative to the death penalty has been banishment. During the past century in this country, banishment has taken the form of life imprisonment without possibility of release. At least since the past generation, however, most opponents of the death penalty have opposed this harsh alternative, and instead have favored imprisonment of indefinite duration, with eligibility for release upon favorable recommendation by the adult authority or parole board after a fixed minimum time. The result in all but a few cases is eventual release. For some time this has been the policy applied in all jurisdictions toward most offenders convicted of murder or other grave crimes against the person, property, or the state.

To some extent, the merits of abolishing the death penalty are tied to the adequacy of the alternative. How adequate, on moral and empirical grounds, is an alternative such as the one described above? Great publicity is given to the occasional convicted murderer who returns to crime, like Edgar Smith, who served 14 years on death row in New Jersey and finally was released in 1971, only to be returned to prison in California a few years later after he committed new crimes (see Chapter Five, §4). By way of mitigating any complaint against the policy of release raised by the Smith case, one might note that although Smith counts as a recidivist, at least he does not count as a recidivist murderer; his crimes after imprisonment for murder did not include a second murder. The problem is with some other released murderers.

On 21 April 1976, *The New York Times* reported that a parolee who had spent "more than five years" in prison for murder and who had been on parole since 1973 "pleaded guilty yesterday to the nearly identical slaying" of a young woman in 1975. A year or so earlier (18 February 1975), the *National Enquirer* carried a lurid story from death row in Georgia. There, Carl Isaacs, 21, was quoted as saying, "I believe in the death penalty to prevent people like me from killing . . . I started killing when I was 14 . . . I've killed 15 people. I can't help myself. If they let me out I'll kill more." A more recent story in the *Boston Globe* (30 July 1979) reported a staggering situa-

---

44. Sellin, "Homicides and Serious Assaults," p. 145.

tion confronting the Poughkeepsie (N.Y.) police. Joseph Fischer, 50, had been in prison half his life in New Jersey for murdering a teenage boy. In order "to get if off his chest," Fischer said, he told the police that in the year after he was released from prison, he had not only killed his elderly wife, but *twenty* other persons, from Arizona to Maine! Whether Isaac's and Fisher's confessions were true need not concern us; stories such as theirs fix in the public mind the image of the convicted murderer who, as soon as he is released, will kill again—and again, until he is stopped once and for all.

But are these cases representative? Do they show that it is wrong and dangerous to adopt a policy of complete abolition? Once a mandatory death penalty has been put aside by the legislatures or the courts—and *any* mandatory death penalty is now likely to be ruled unconstitutional (see Chapter Six)—incarceration of all convicted murderers becomes a theoretical possibility. It must be assumed that it is a manageable one as well. Every jurisdiction in the United States at present has adopted such a policy, so it cannot be argued that executions are necessary because some offenders cannot be incarcerated or released. (Besides, the discretionary death penalty already shows that the legislatures contemplate the possibility that trial courts will in fact sentence no one to death.)

Second, even if we believe that retribution is a legitimate goal of a system of punishment, we must concede that our legislatures and the constitution tacitly assume that long-term incarceration is retributive enough. (Of course if retribution is an irrelevent or immoral consideration in the present context, then we may ignore this point.)

Third, apart from statutes like the one sustained in *Jurek* v. *Texas* (1976), under which the sentencing court must make a judgment on the future dangerousness of the convicted murderer in order to recommend either a life or a death sentence (see Chapter Six), it has not been the practice to attempt to choose between life and death for a convicted felon on the basis of evidence concerning his likely *future* behavior. There is no reason to believe that the thousands of those sentenced to death by trial courts in this century have been so sentenced because the sentencing authority was shown evidence that these persons were more dangerous, more likely to assault and kill in prison or after release, than the many thousands of other convicts guilty of similar crimes but never sentenced to death. Nor is this true regarding those sentenced to death who have been executed. Denial of executive clemency is rarely based on a belief that the offender is and will remain an uncontrollable menace to society. Whether the tendency to take all of this into consideration, as encouraged by *Jurek*, is a desirable development in the law, must be doubted, given that accurate prediction of future dangerousness is virtually impossible, at least with our present knowledge and techniques.[1]

1. A decade ago, Morris and Hawkins noted that "all available prediction methods have relatively low predictive power ..." (1970:244). The chief problem, however, is not the

This brings us to "social defense"—prevention, incapacitation, and deterrence. One might expect that executions would prevent crime more effectively than imprisonment. This is not strictly correct, however. Executions *prevent crimes* only if the persons executed would have committed further crimes had they not been executed. Executions *incapacitate persons,* of course, whether or not they would have committed any further crimes, and they do this more effectively than prison can. Whether we may infer that executions prevent crimes through incapacitation depends upon what is to be inferred from the evidence regarding the crimes, especially the felonies—including criminal homicide—that are committed by capital offenders who were not (but might have been) executed and were instead imprisoned and subsequently released.

Such evidence as I have been able to collect on recidivism from various sources is indicative but far from conclusive. Table 4-5-1 shows that among 2646 murderers released in twelve states during the years 1900 through 1976, 88 were returned for conviction of a subsequent felony and 16 were returned for conviction of a subsequent criminal homicide. Table 4-5-2 is based on data supplied by the National Council on Crime and Delinquency (NCCD) in its Uniform Parole Reports (UPR). It shows that, nationwide, between the years 1965 and 1974, of 11,404 persons originally convicted of "willful homicide" and subsequently released from prison, 170 were returned during the first year for commission of a felony and 34 were returned during the first year for a subsequent criminal homicide. Tables 4-5-3 and 4-5-4 are also from the NCCD and cover each year of the first half-decade of the 1970s. They give us a fairly detailed breakdown of the parole outcome and subsequent offense record during the crucial first year after release of over 11,000 convicted murderers.[2] These data report 26 new offenses of "willful homicide" from a total group of released murderers.

While not complete, these data are encouraging. Although they prove that the popular belief is true, that murderers do sometimes kill again even after

---

underprediction of violence among those released (the false negatives); it is the *over*prediction (the false positives). For a review of the literature and statement of the political problems that sensible release policies confront, see Monahan 1978.

2. Although most recidivism is alleged to occur in the first year after release on parole, not all of it does. The Edgar Smith case may be more typical, as the study by Heilbrun et al. 1978 suggests. In their group of 164 male murderers whose parole from prison in Georgia ended between 1973 and 1976, 4% were recidivists during the first six months *after* parole termination, and by the time the study ended 56% had become postparole recidivists. National three-year follow-up data on recidivism *during* parole show a less extreme form of the same pattern. For all persons released from prison in 1972 and 1973 after conviction for willful homicide, the first-year recidivism totals were 7 new crimes of willful homicide and 34 other felonies (see text above, Table 4-5-4). After the next two years the recidivism totals for these cohorts increased by an additional 5 new crimes of willful homicide and an additional 52 other felonies (Gottfredson et al. 1978:698, 700, Tables 6.97 and 6.98; Parisi et al. 1979:671, Table 6.79).

Table 4-5-1. Recidivism of Convicted Murderers Released During Selected Years in Twelve States, 1900–76

	Murderers released	Subsequent conviction of criminal homicide	Subsequent other felony
California, 1945–54	342	1	1
Connecticut, 1947–60	60	0	7
Georgia			
1943–65	50	0	1
1973–76	164	8	21
Maryland, 1936–51	41	0	3
Massachusetts			
1941–50	47	0	4
1957–66	92	1	1
Michigan, 1938–72	432	0	1
New Jersey, 1907–60	31	0	1
New York			
1930–61	63	2	1
1945–61	514	3	15
Ohio, 1945–60	169	0	2
Oregon, 1939–64	15	0	1
Pennsylvania, 1932–69	607	1	29
Rhode Island, 1915–58	19	0	NI
Total	2646	16	88

NI = No information available.

Source: Information for individual states was taken from the following: California Assembly Report on the Death Penalty (1957), pp. 12–13; Connecticut Bar Journal, March 1961, pp. 50–51; Georgia Journal of Corrections, August 1974, p. 48, and (Georgia) Journal of Criminal Law & Criminology, 1978, pp. 110–13; Maryland Report on Capital Punishment (1962), p. 15; Massachusetts Report on the Death Penalty (1958), pp. 116–20, and Massachusetts Department of Corrections, Publication 5097 (1970); Ohio Report on Capital Punishment (1961), p. 82, and Michigan State University Office of Human Relations, occasional paper, June 26, 1973; (New Jersey) Rutgers Law Review, Fall 1964, pp. 47–48; (New York) Crime & Delinquency, January 1969, pp. 150–51 (first-degree murderers), and Crime and Delinquency, January 1969, pp. 150–51 (second-degree murderers); Ohio Report on Capital Punishment (1961), pp. 81–82; Oregon Law Review, December 1965, pp. 31–34; Pennsylvania Board of Probation and Parole, Report on Lifers Released (1969), and Bureau of Corrections, report on commuted lifers (1964); (Rhode Island) Massachusetts Report on the Death Penalty (1958), p. 32.

Table 4-5-2. Recidivism During First Year After Release, Convicted Murderers in the United States by Type of Subsequent Offense, 1965–75

Year of release	Number of murderers released	Subsequent conviction of willful homicide		Subsequent other major violation	
1965–67[a]	1,303	3	0.2%	15	1.2%
1967–69[b]	5,603	18	0.3%	86	1.5%
1974[c]	1,601	5	0.3%	22	1.4%
1975[d]	2,897	8	0.3%	47[e]	1.6%
Total	11,404	34	0.3%	170	1.5%

[a] UPR, December 1967.
[b] UPR, December 1972.
[c] UPR, September 1976; males only.
[d] UPR, level II, individual data, detailed study, 1978 forthcoming; males only.
[e] Calculated from a base of 2867 released murderers.

Source: Uniform Parole Reports (National Council on Crime and Delinquency).

Table 4-5-3. Parole Outcome in First Year After Release After Conviction of Willful Homicide, 1971–75

Year paroled		Total	Recommitted to prison with new major conviction	Continued on parole			Discharged	Returned to prison as a technical violator			Absconders
				A	B	C		A'	B'	C'	
1975		2,867	47	2,371	30	4	235	102	19	8	50
1974	M	1,601	27	1,456	8	2	NI	51	10	23	24
	F	184	1	173	1	1	NI	4	2	0	2
1973	M	1,786	19	1,648	16	1	NI	43	23	13	23
	F	212	1	203	2	1	NI	2	0	0	3
1972	M	2,165	24	1,950	22	4	NI	65	28	20	48
	F	275	1	251	1	0	NI	5	2	2	12
1971	M	2,143	18	1,914	7	3	NI	93	40	17	51
	F	269	1	250	0	0	NI	6	4	0	7
Total		11,502	139	10,216	87	16	NI	371	128	83	220

Note: **A** = No difficulty or a sentence of less than 60 days. **B** = New minor conviction(s). **C** = New major conviction(s). **A'** = No new conviction(s) and not in lieu of prosecution. **B'** = New minor or lesser conviction(s) or in lieu of prosecution. **C'** = in lieu of prosecution for new major offense(s). NI = No information available.

Source: Sourcebook of Criminal Justice Statistics 1978, Table 6.73, p. 666 (breakdown by sex not available); 1977, Tables 6.75 and 6.76, p. 678; 1976, Table 6.93, p. 736, and Table 6.94, p. 738; 1975, Table 6.47, p. 682, and Table 6.48, p. 683; 1974, Tables 6.62 and 6.63, pp. 492–93.

Table 4-5-4. New Offense in First Year After Release After Conviction for Willful Homicide, by Sex and Year, 1971–75

Year of release		Total	No offense	New offense						
				Willful homicide	Negligent manslaughter	Armed robbery	Unarmed robbery	Aggravated assault	Forcible rape	Other
1975[a]		2,897	2,824	8	3	18	6	6	1	31
1974	M	1,601	1,549	5	0	8	3	6	0	30
	F	184	182	0	0	0	0	1	0	1
1973	M	1,786	1,753	2	0	8	2	4	2	15
	F	212	210	0	0	1	0	0	0	1
1972	M	2,165	2,117	5	0	10	0	6	1	26
	F	275	271	1	0	0	0	0	0	3
1971	M	2,143	2,105	5	0	7	1	7	1	17
	F	269	268	0	0	1	0	0	1	0
Total		11,532	11,279	26	3	53	12	30	5	124

[a]Breakdown by sex not available

Source: Sourcebook of Criminal Justice Statistics 1978, p. 667; 1977, pp. 686, 688; 1976, pp. 745, 746; 1975, pp. 678, 680; 1974, pp. 489, 491.

years of imprisonment, the data also show that the number of such repeaters is very small. Both with regard to the commission of felonies generally and the crime of homicide, no other class of offender has such a low rate of recidivism.[3] So we are left to choose among clear alternatives. If we cannot improve release and parole procedures so as to turn loose *no one* who will commit a further murder or other felony, we have three choices. Either we can undertake to *execute every* convicted murderer; or we can undertake to *release none* of them; or we can reconcile ourselves to the fact that release procedures, like all other human institutions, are not infallible, and continue to try to improve rehabilitation and prediction during incarceration.

The moral cost of a policy of mandatory capital punishment is simply intolerable, and there is little evidence that anyone really favors this alternative. The moral and economic cost of abandoning parole release, or fixed terms short of natural life (say, ten years), is more than the public seems willing to pay. So the only alternative is the third, which in fact is already being practiced in all jurisdictions, with all prisoners except for the handful sentenced to death.

Is there any reason to believe that the failure of the vast majority of released murderers to commit another murder is owing to the postrelease effect on them of the death penalty as a deterrent? The record of such overwhelming nonrecidivism might, in theory, have precisely this explanation. From the data reported here, however, it looks at a glance as though such an explanation is quite implausible. Of the dozen jurisdictions reported in Table 4-5-1, two (Michigan and Rhode Island) are abolitionist. The other ten states authorized *and used* the death penalty in all the years during which the recidivism of their released murderers is reported. Yet the postrelease conduct of the murderers from the two abolition states was, if anything, better than the postrelease conduct of the murderers from the ten death penalty states. It appears, then, that the nonmurderous conduct of released murderers cannot be explained primarily by reference to the deterrent effects of the death penalty; it is even possible that deterrence plays no role whatever in explaining the nonmurderousness of most released murderers. More complete and uniform data (in more jurisdictions and for more years) and their scientifically valid analysis might alter this picture appreciably, but no such study has been done. Until it is, the interpretation above is about as far as our current knowledge can carry us.

---

3. "[P]aroled murderers actually present some of the best parole risks" (NCCD Newsletter, Uniform Parole Reports, December 1972, p. 2); "The percentage of Willful Homicide violators returned to prison on new commitments is, with one exception (Alcohol Laws Violated), the lowest in any offender group" (Neithercutt 1972:90); "[C]ompared with other groups, murderers are actually the best parole risks" (Stanton 1969:149).

§ 6.   Terrorism and the Death Penalty*

THOMAS PERRY THORNTON

A soberly argued discussion of ways and means of coping with terrorism was offered by C. L. Sulzberger in his *New York Times* column of July 7, just after the Entebbe operation [in 1976]. Mr. Sulzberger focused on practical steps rather than symbolic retribution, concluding his piece with a plea for executing "condemned" terrorists. Although he did not spell this idea out in detail and the idea is not novel, his article makes a good point of departure for discussing terrorism and the death penalty, because it raises the matter rationally and because Mr. Sulzberger is otherwise opposed to capital punishment.

The argumentation for executing terrorists runs as follows: when a person is apprehended and imprisoned for any kind of terrorist act, there is a substantial likelihood that other like-minded terrorists will seek to force his release by taking hostages and threatening to kill them unless their imprisoned comrade is set free. The nation holding the terrorist prisoner faces a dilemma: either acquiesce in the demand and release the prisoner, thus demonstrating once again that terrorism is a low-risk undertaking even for those who are caught; or refuse to yield to the demand and thereby endanger the lives of the innocent hostages. Indeed, even if the demands are met, the hostages will still have been subjected to the very considerable dangers routinely involved in such a situation. In Mr. Sulzberger's words, "every live convicted terrorist in prison increases the chance of dead innocents abroad."

If, however, convicted terrorists are executed, there will be no reason for their comrades to take hostages to force their release. At most there might be attempts to exact revenge. These, however, would probably be directed at police or judicial officials rather than innocent people who had no connection with the terrorist's execution and with whom the public does not readily identify.

Terrorism is, in fact, along with treason and murder committed by prisoners serving life terms, one of the prime tests of arguments against the death penalty. Terrorism is outrageous in the public view. The line of argumentation set forth by Mr. Sulzberger and others has a compelling rational content. But the death penalty is a gravely serious measure to invoke in any circum-

---

*Excerpted from Thomas Perry Thornton, "Terrorism and the Death Penalty," *America*, December 11, 1976, pp. 410–12. Reprinted with permission of America Press Inc. © 1976. All rights reserved.

stance, and in this case there are weighty legal and logical counterarguments in addition to the unavoidable moral considerations that weigh against any taking of life.

The initial problem is that of definition. What is, after all, "terrorism"? Its definition has been debated extensively in the scholarly literature for years. I am well satisfied with one I offered over a decade ago—"a symbolic act designed to influence political behavior by extranormal means, entailing the use or threat of violence"—but I have no illusions that this definition or any other could or should stand up before a court of law. Although we can define the phenomenon of terrorism broadly and certain acts are clearly terrorist by any reasonable definition, there are immense gray areas that would open the way to serious miscarriages of justice, for "terrorism" is a highly subjective concept. Attempts to develop international law concerning terrorism have foundered on the fact that one man's terrorist is the other man's freedom-fighter, whether he be a member of Black September or the Stern Gang.

This semantic ambiguity was illustrated during Daniel Patrick Moynihan's successful bid for the Democratic Senate nomination in New York this year. The former UN Ambassador suggested that his anti-terrorist record in the UN would in some way be relevant to stopping "terror" in the darkened streets of New York City, but in fact it is hard to see any connection between muggings and aircraft hijackings. In the present political and social context, we must live with the fact that "terrorism" is simply not a useful way of categorizing antisocial behavior, let alone a legally tenable definition of a capital crime.

The definitional problem cannot be avoided by defining hostage-taking, rather than terrorism, as the crime that triggers the death penalty. First, this would do little to meet the requirement of making terrorists harmless, since not all terrorist acts involve taking hostages or hijacking. (Very little IRA activity, for example, has involved hostage-taking.) Second, there are no doubt hundreds of hostage incidents in the United States every year, few of which have anything to do with terrorism and many of which are not very serious. Do we really want to extend the death penalty to all of these?

In a sense, terrorism is a description of a state of mind rather than a definition of specific criminal acts. A man may commit a political murder that can be defined reasonably as terrorism, and under many legal systems he would receive a death sentence. But a "terrorist" may also commit armed robbery that does not result in any deaths, and he would not be likely to receive more than a prison term. If, however, we define terrorism as the crime, irrespective of the content of the terrorist act, then both men would be executed in order to prevent like-minded comarades from seizing hostages to free either of them. In doing this, we would have moved onto novel legal terrain: we would be executing people, not for specific crimes that they have committed, but for what other people might do on their behalf. As illustrations of the logical dilemma let us take two hypothetical cases.

The first would be the semi-active accomplice of a fatal hijacking operation who provided shelter for the terrorist hijackers before the operation took place. Even if conspiracy to murder could be proved, the death penalty would be an extremely harsh sentence to impose. Yet this accomplice, if jailed, would be just as likely to trigger a subsequent hostage-taking operation to force his release as would terrorists who committed more serious crimes. The purpose of such operations is to generate publicity and get people out of jail. The specific grounds of imprisonment is a secondary consideration.

Closer to home, there is the Patricia Hearst case. Let us assume she had been captured during the bank robbery she participated in. Bank robbery is not a capital crime, but had there been legislation on the books in California that prescribed death for terrorists, Miss Hearst would certainly have had to be executed. The Symbionese Liberation Army was, if nothing else, a terrorist organization, and prevailing opinion at the time would have held that her SLA colleagues would likely have sought to force her release from prison by taking hostages. But would justice have been served?

A final dilemma is offered in two hypothetical hijacking cases. In one, an embezzler hijacks a plane and holds the passengers hostage in order to escape from the law. In the other, terrorists hold passengers hostage in pursuit of some political goal. Both fail and are captured, and the operations are bloodless. Hijacking that does not result in death is no capital crime under U.S. law, but the terrorists would be executed on the grounds that their sympathizers might try to force their release. The embezzler received only an additional jail term, because there is no reason to believe that anybody would mount a rescue operation on his behalf. Yet both have equally endangered lives by taking hostages. This would be a grossly unequal application of the law and would no doubt be unconstitutional in the United States.

We encounter still a further problem. In law-governed societies, at least, capital trials tend to take a considerable amount of time, and review and appeal processes can drag on even longer before a death sentence is carried out. Thus, would-be rescuers of captured terrorists still could have ample time to mount their rescue operation. Indeed, the chances of their doing so could be greatly increased if their imprisoned comrades face execution, for under present circumstances the only pressing motive to force a release is a political one. Making terrorism a capital crime could in this way raise the likelihood of hostage-taking operations, quite the opposite of what was originally intended. There is an obvious logical remedy: instruct law-enforcement officers to kill terrorists promptly upon capture, acting as apprehender, judge and executioner. The grotesqueness of this "logical conclusion" should be painfully obvious to all but the most hardened viewers of late-night Westerns.

Finally, although deterrence is not the issue at stake in this matter, it must be noted that there seems to be no correlation between deterrence and the death penalty. The threat of capital punishment is particularly unlikely to deter terrorists, given their total commitment to fighting a political or social order that they find abhorrent.

We cannot really divorce the question of capital punishment for terrorists from the broader question of the morality of the death penalty, as I have done thus far. It was a fitting coincidence that the Entebbe raid came within a few days of the Supreme Court's decision on *Gregg* v. *Georgia* that reopened the possibility of the death penalty in the United States, including, presumably, for terrorism if we choose to take that path. This is not the place to argue the pros and cons of the death penalty in general, but there is something to be learned by looking at the matter in the light of the terrorist problem.

If abhorrence of the perceived injustice of the political and social order is what drives men to terrorism and contempt for human life, the terrorist is only the child of his age. The criterion for capital punishment set forth in *Gregg* v. *Georgia* ("an expression of society's moral outrage at particularly offensive conduct") is simply the mirror image of the terrorist's outlook. It, too, decides that the price of outrage at this time in history is fairly set at human life. We must recognize that *Gregg* v. *Georgia* is not an arbitrary plunge backward in mankind's progress toward civilization and humaneness, decided in isolation by five misguided men. Rather, it is an accurate reflection of the attitudes of much of American society—a point that Justice Potter Stewart made abundantly clear in his decision. Many, perhaps most, Americans find the death penalty neither cruel nor unusual as an expression of their outrage. Taken together with widespread attitudes favoring liberal abortion laws, it is evident that a disturbingly large number of Americans do not place all that high a value on human life—at least not on the lives of inconvenient members of society. Terrorists, whether of the Black September or Hitler type, only take this attitude to its logical conclusion. Many of them are at least fully consistent in showing contempt for their own lives as well.

If this is the case, then the legal, moral and logical arguments about executing terrorists may not be relevant. Perhaps society does demand exemplary and symbolically satisfying retribution against terrorists as well as murderers—and, ultimately, rapists and muggers and others who commit "outrageous" crimes. After *Gregg* v. *Georgia,* the gates are open.

Increasingly throughout the civilized world, there is a widespread view that capital punishment is incompatible with humane society, and this growing consensus is one of the more substantial ethical accomplishments of recent years. Despite the court ruling, we still have hope to save it in the United States. There would be a spectacular irony, however, if terrorism were among the crimes that urge our society to restore the death penalty. The ultimate aim of the true terrorist is to undermine the values of the society that he detests. Mr. Sulzberger's abandonment of a long-held moral opposition to capital punishment shows that in one case, at least, the terrorists have been successful. Both individuals and societies at times take on the attributes of their tormentors as a means of self-protection. If we abandon our respect for life in order to cope with the terrorist, we will become an unwitting but sadly willing accomplice in his attempt to destroy us.

Stalin and Hitler, as well as contemporary dictators, have shown us that ruthless repression can root out the terrorism of political agitation. The price, however, has been the institution of another kind of terror. If twentieth-century history has taught us anything, it is that the terrorism of governments is vastly more destructive, both physically and morally, than the actions of a few dozen, or even hundreds of bomb-throwers, hijackers and assassins. Terrorism is real, and it is gruesome. It does not, however, pose the "clear and present danger" that, in the words of a much better Supreme Court opinion, is the sole justification for a society's violating its own values in the cause of self-preservation.

5

Criminal Justice and the Capital Offender

INTRODUCTION

Of all the traditional objections to the death penalty, none is more troubling than the fallibility of its administration and the risk this causes for the person wrongly accused of a capital crime. A criminal justice system without the death penalty may be no less prone to error, but release always remains a possibility after erroneous conviction and so does some kind of direct compensation for wrongful punishment. During the past generation, the chief complaints against the death penalty on moral and constitutional grounds have also stressed the fallibility of its administration, but mainly in two different directions.

First, it has been objected that the death penalty predictably falls on poor black offenders in particular and on members of the lowest social classes generally; for decades, white offenders and middle-class offenders have been virtually immune to its severities. Critics concede that there is nothing inherent in the death penalty as a mode of punishment, or in the laws under which it is administered, that makes such abuses unavoidable. But they also insist that the record of error is so strong and the causes of racial and class bias in our society so deeply rooted that little can be done in practice to remedy them in order to achieve a fair administration of the death penalty in the foreseeable future. The second objection is that capital punishment is capricious, random, and irrational in its application, in that it is visited on a handful of offenders (and by no means the handful that is the most dangerous) selected by no discernible principles or criteria from among the thousands of indicted and convicted murderers, rapists, and other felons. The death penalty, so this complaint goes, is wholly intolerable (and, since 1976, unconstitutional as well) if it is imposed in a mandatory way, whereas if it is left to courts to exercise their discretion in sentencing to life or to death, it will be freakish in its rarity—and so, either way, it must fail as a fair retributive punishment and as an even possibly effective deterrent. Thus opponents of the death penalty charge in effect a dilemma: Either the death penalty is freakishly and unpredictably rare, or it is all too predictably visited on the poor, black, and helpless; in either case, it is unfair and inefficient. It is crucial, therefore, to examine the central findings of empirical research where they are available to give an accurate picture of recent and current practice in the administration of the death penalty to determine which side has the better of the argument.

The problem is much larger than the familiar doubts about wrongful executions and racially biassed or capricious trial courts. Capital punishment, as astute critics have pointed out, casts its shadow across the workings of the criminal justice system wherever it enters as a relevant factor (see Black 1974). In almost any murder case, the death penalty can be used by the prosecutor as a threat, implicit or explicit, to secure a guilty plea on a lesser charge. It is always used by trial judges to determine who sits on the juries. It burdens the appellate courts, state and federal, which now review every death penalty case. It places a heavy responsibility on the chief executive in each death penalty jurisdiction, because in his hands lies the power to reprieve or commute a death sentence where appellate courts have refused to void it. These are but four of the major phases in the administration of criminal justice where the impact of the death penalty can be easily identified. Although there has been research on most of these (as well as some subsidiary) points of impact, there are no studies that present current and comprehensive national data on any of them. What is surveyed and reprinted in this chapter, therefore, can give only a sketchy picture, even if it is the best available, of a complex and inadequately studied process.

Social Class and Sex Bias. Data reprinted in Chapter Two show that the death penalty is rarely inflicted on women, even though women commit roughly one in five of all criminal homicides. The social-class bias of the death penalty has been shown by several studies in different jurisdictions; the unemployed and underemployed, the poorly educated, and the unskilled make up by far the largest group of persons under the death sentence at any given time (Bedau 1964b and 1965; Note 1969; Lewis 1979). These same factors, to be sure, tend to characterize all persons convicted of criminal homicide and sentenced to prison, yet cases of middle- and upper-class homicide in recent years are not unknown (Green & Wakefield 1979). Still, in the century and a third since Dr. John W. Webster, Professor of Medicine at Harvard, was hanged for murder, not many of his social standing, having been convicted as he was of criminal homicide, end up facing the executioner—

as the cases of Dr. Carl Coppolino in Florida[1] and Dr. Bernard Finch in California[2] dramatically illustrate. Whatever the explanation, few doctors, lawyers, professors, business executives, government officials—or law-enforcement officers—who kill someone ever face a death penalty for their crimes.

Racial Bias. For decades the complaint has been made that "sentences of death are disproportionately frequent in Southern states, and evidence of racial discrimination in capital sentencing is strong" (Amsterdam 1971a). White men were rarely indicted and sentenced to death for rape, and never for the rape of a black woman, whereas a black man convicted of raping a white woman was all but assured of a death sentence (many were instead lynched, a lawless form of capital punishment now a thing of the past but widely practiced within living memory).[3] This is the most dramatic type of case in which we can see how the racist heritage of our society made the death penalty fall with disproportionate and unfair frequency on nonwhite offenders. Not until the mid-1960s was careful research undertaken on this topic, but it fully vindicated the traditional complaint. In the excerpts reprinted below in §1, Marvin E. Wolfgang, Director of the Center for Criminal Justice and Criminology at the University of Pennsylvania, and his collaborator Marc Riedel provide a general review of the literature on race and the death penalty, followed by the data to support their judgment that the best explanation for the pattern of death sentences for rape in the South is the race of the (black) offender and of the (white) victim. Even the Office of the Solicitor General, which under the administration of President Nixon argued that the death penalty was not unconstitutional, nonetheless conceded that Wolfgang's research, based on data for the years 1945–65, "was careful and comprehensive, and we do not question its conclusion. . . ."[4]

What is the present situation? Is there evidence that race continues to be a factor unfairly influencing the outcome in death penalty cases, especially where murder is concerned? One major line of research on this question is being carried out at the Center for Applied Social Research, Northeastern University, under the direction of Dr. William J. Bowers, author of *Executions in America* (1974). An excerpt from his most recent findings is reprinted below as §2. Bowers has shown that in the important death penalty jurisdic-

1. See *The New York Times,* 27 September 1979, p. B18.
2. See Duffy 1962:235f, and Wolfe 1973:342, 365f.
3. See W. White 1969, and House Hearing 1978:126. Mr. Watt Espy, currently engaged in a long-term research project to record every legal execution in the history of the United States, recently testified that "In my research . . . in over 11,000 cases, I can recall only two where white men were hanged for murders of black men" (1980:195). He does not mention any in which white men were executed for the rape of black women.
4. Solicitor General 1975:5a, reprinted in Carrington 1978:210. For additional evidence from Wolfgang's research project on rape and the death penalty, see Wolfgang 1972, Wolfgang & Riedel 1975 and 1976. See also the evidence of racism reported by Bowers 1974:102.

tions of Florida, Georgia, and Texas, even under death penalty statutes designed to meet the objections that caused the Supreme Court to invalidate earlier death penalty laws in 1972, there is a measurable racial factor in convictions and sentences. Except that it is not so much the race of the offender that matters, or even the offender/victim racial combination (as in Wolfgang's research); it is the race of the victim. Whether white or black, the person who murders a white is far more likely to end up under a death sentence than is the person who murders a black. This suggests that trial courts in these jurisdictions evidently attach more gravity to the murder of a white than to the murder of a black. Earlier versions of this research, which showed essentially that same pattern, have been presented in evidence to trial courts in many death penalty cases in the South under the auspices of the Southern Poverty Law Center and Team Defense,[5] and also at Congressional hearings on pending federal death penalty legislation.[6] Whether the racial climate elsewhere in the South or in other states with large numbers under death sentence is much healthier may be doubted, as Bowers's data on Ohio show.

Availability and Competence of Counsel. The way that race affects the disposition of capital cases shows up not only in the sentencing studied by Wolfgang and Bowers. It can be seen throughout the trial process that begins with arrest and indictment. Prior to the landmark Scottsboro Boys case (*Powell v. Alabama*, 1932), it was not uncommon in the South, in cases involving black offenders and white victims, for indigent defendants to face trial on capital charges without any counsel until the onset of the trial. A more subtle abuse continues to plague indigent defendants of all races, and it is the unavailability of competent counsel. Modern defenders of the death penalty scoff at the idea of defendants (guilty or innocent) being "railroaded to the chair," and point to the widespread use of public defenders, dedicated trial counsel such as Team Defense, and the skillful advocacy at the appellate and postappellate levels such as the NAACP Legal Defense Fund attorneys provide. Overlooked are the many other death penalty cases where "ineffective assistance of trial counsel" is cited by the courts as so extensive and damaging to the defendant's chances before the jury as to warrant a new trial. The case of Jimmy Voyles, sentenced to death for murder in Lee County, Mississippi, in 1977 and reversed by order of the federal district court in 1980, is instructive and by no means unique.[7] Experienced criminal trial attorneys will say

5. See *The New York Times*, 6 March 1978, p. A11. Team Defense's most publicized death penalty case involved The Dawson Five in Georgia. See Pinsky 1977; and *The New York Times*, 2 August 1977, p. 12, and 20 December 1977, p. 20. See also Gettinger 1979:209f., 222f.

6. See *House Hearing* 1978:128ff., 142ff., and *Senate Hearings* 1978:41ff. For the latest research on racial aspects of the death penalty, see Radelet 1981.

7. *Voyles* v. *Watkins et al.* 489 F. Supp. 901 (D.D.C.: N.D., Miss.), decided 13 May 1980. See also *Frierson* v. *People*, 599 P.2d 587 (California Supreme Court, 1979).

that "no really capable defense lawyer should ever lose a capital case."[8] Perhaps; there is no doubt that inexperienced, overworked, and understaffed defense lawyers often do lose them.[9]

Plea Bargaining. For many years, most of the cases where the death penalty might be a factor have been settled well short of a death sentence because both sides agree to have the defendant plead guilty to a lesser charge—so called "plea bargaining." In New York City during the mid-1970s, for example, it has been reported that four out of five criminal homicide cases were settled in this way, including even a case where a nonwhite killed two white police officers.[10] The possibility of plea bargaining places the defendant who believes he is innocent, or at least innocent of first-degree murder, in an acute dilemma. If he pleads not guilty to all charges, as he has a right to do, then he runs the greatest risk of the death sentence; if he pleads guilty to a lesser charge, he guarantees himself a prison sentence whether he deserves it or not. The result can be more than ironic. As Julian Bond has pointed out, "On the date of his death, Spenkelink could have already been paroled if he had plea bargained and accepted the uncontested second-degree murder conviction offered him by the state."[11] The death penalty is thus a powerful weapon in the hands of any prosecutor who wants to convict the accused, even if the accused is never actually put on trial for his life.[12]

Capricious Sentences. Two recent studies (not reprinted here) show that there is likely to be no discernible justice in the pattern of indictments, convictions, and sentences for murder. In one (Bedau 1976) it was shown that in the Boston area, despite a law that provided a *mandatory* death penalty for anyone guilty of felony-murder-rape, *no one* was indicted, tried, convicted, or sentenced under this statute. Yet an analysis of all the murder cases over a period of twenty-five years (1946 through 1970) showed that in over a dozen cases (roughly one case in ten) this crime might well have been prosecuted. Evidently, the mandatory death penalty was used by prosecutors and courts to achieve discretionary sentencing results. The other study (Zimring et al. 1976) examined the outcome in the first two hundred homicide cases of 1970 that occurred in Philadelphia. That research showed the "going price" of

8. Interview with attorney Stanley J. Reibner, *Albany* (N.Y.) *Times Union*, 5 March 1978, p. A14.
9. For a general discussion, see Reed 1981.
10. *The New York Times*, 27 January 1975, p. 1, 26 October 1976, p. 38, and 23 November 1976, p. 1. In Massachusetts, between 1956 and 1965, 71% of all murder cases were settled by negotiated pleas (Carney & Fuller 1969).
11. *Savannah Morning News*, 28 July 1979, p. A4.
12. In Los Angeles, "the confessed 'trashbag killer' pleaded guilty . . . to 18 slayings for young boys and men in return for a prosecution promise that he would not get the death penalty." *The New York Times*, 22 February 1978, p. 14.

criminal homicide to be bimodal—either a brief two-year prison term or a very long twenty-year sentence. As for the death penalty, exactly three defendants received it; they were black and their victims white. In general, the extreme differences in sentencing severity seemed to depend not so much on the gravity of the offense as on irrelevant factors such as the race or social status of the offender and the victim.[13]

Scrupled Juries. Beginning in the early 1960s, several investigators argued that a capital trial jury from whom all persons with conscientious scruples against the death penalty had been excluded is more likely to convict a defendant on a given set of facts than is a jury more truly representative of community sentiment. If so, then the time-honored practice of excusing for cause the "scrupled juror" produces a conviction-prone jury (Oberer 1961; Jurow 1971). According to these investigations, the prosecutor in a death penalty case, whether he knows it or not, enters the court room with a definite edge over the defense on the issue of the defendant's guilt, no matter what the facts of the case turn out to be, merely because opponents of the death penalty will not sit in judgment of these facts. In *Witherspoon* v. *Illinois* (1968), the Supreme Court judged that the data and argument put before it on this issue were "too tentative and fragmentary" to overturn a death penalty conviction on this ground alone, although the Court did warn that the prosecution was not entitled to "stack the deck against" the defendant by constructing "a hanging jury."[14] However warranted this cautious judgment may have been more than a decade ago, the Court's warning was never more apt than now. The most recent investigations (not reprinted here) report the same conclusions as the earliest studies: Excluding jurors opposed to the death penalty not only produces a jury no longer representative of the whole community, it produces a jury "organized to convict" (Bronson 1980:33).[15]

Appellate Review. Since the 1940s, the Supreme Court of the United States has given increasingly close attention to the death penalty cases that come before it. Whether this is true of other appellate courts, state and federal, is not so clear; no one seems to have studied the records to show the quality and extent of review accorded to the hundreds of death penalty cases that crowd their dockets (recall Chapter One). In lieu of such studies, it is useful to examine the story told by Ramsey Clark, a former Attorney General of the United States, about his efforts as counsel for John Spenkelink during the

13. See the discussion in *The New York Times,* 4 April 1976, p. E15.
14. *Witherspoon* v. *Illinois,* 391 U.S. 510, at p. 523. For a discussion of the effect of the *Witherspoon* ruling on other death penalty cases, see Meltsner 1973 and Greenberg 1977:454ff.
15. See also Zeisel 1968, Bronson 1970, F. Goldberg 1970, Edison 1971, Stricker & Jurow 1974, Buckhout et al. 1977, and Haney 1980a and 1980b. For a discussion of the constitutional issues, see White 1973, Gillers 1980, and White 1980.

final hours before Spenkelink's execution in Florida (May 1979).[16] Reprinted below in §3, it illustrates, even if to an atypical degree, problems faced by every zealous attorney with a death row client, problems over which neither he nor his client but the appellate courts and the attorneys general of the states seeking to execute a prisoner have control.

Clemency. Since the mid-1960s, owing largely to the Supreme Court's continuing deliberations over the constitutionality of the death penalty, gubernatorial commutation of death sentences has been (save for Tennessee)[17] rare at best. Along with the legislatures, which refused to review current death penalty statutes pending their (in)validation by the Supreme Court, chief executives and pardon boards were unwilling to exercise their traditional clemency powers for much the same reasons. A conspicuous exception was Winthrop Rockefeller, Governor of Arkansas from 1967 to 1971. On 29 December 1970 he commuted all fifteen men on Arkansas's death row, perhaps a record number to be spared the death penalty in this way at any one time. Governor Rockefeller's thoughtful statement explaining his action deserves to be better known.[18] So do the arguments from former Supreme Court Justice Arthur L. Goldberg and Professor Charles L. Black, Jr., on behalf of the propriety (on both moral and constitutional grounds) of commuting death sentences despite the Supreme Court's decisions in 1976 that hold the death penalty to be not per se unconstitutional (see A. Goldberg 1976 and Black 1979). As for empirical studies on the actual exercise of clemency power in death penalty cases, and the criteria for its exercise, the only national study was completed some years ago (Abramowitz & Paget 1964).[19]

Errors of Justice. The arrest, prosecution, trial, conviction, sentence, and execution of the innocent is a large and important topic, but it is remarkably underresearched. Apart from the occasional paragraph or two buried in local newspapers, little has been written on the subject in the past decade (though see MacNamara 1969 and Lassers 1973). I have therefore undertaken to discuss it briefly, in §4 below, and have reprinted a newspaper account of one of the most dramatic cases of this sort in recent years—the Pitts and Lee case in Florida.

16. As Attorney General, Clark was the first to hold that office and testify in Congress for the Department of Justice against the death penalty. See Clark 1970, a revision of his Senate testimony of 2 July 1968; see *Senate Hearings* 1968:91–98.
17. In 1972, Governor Dunn announced his intention to commute the death sentences of all 21 persons on death row; in 1977 and 1979, Governor Blanton made headlines with his commutations. See *The New York Times*, 19 July 1972, p. 15; 21 September 1977, p. A14, and 17 January 1979, p. 14.
18. See Rockefeller 1971. Events surrounding Governor Rockefeller's decision to grant clemency have been discussed in Meltsner 1973.
19. A valuable study on clemency in Illinois is Lavinsky 1965.

There are, of course, many other topics that deserve not only mention but examination in a full discussion of the death penalty and the administration of criminal justice—such as the legal and empirical problems of determining the sanity of the condemned (Broderick 1979) and the effects on prisoners of long-term confinement on death row (Gallemore & Panton 1972, Johnson 1979). There is space here to consider in some detail only one in addition to those already identified. It concerns the actual costs of a system involving the death penalty in contrast to a system without it.

A Cost/Benefit Analysis. Nothing is more obvious than the fact that it is very inexpensive to execute a person; all one needs to pay for is a bit of rope, a jolt of electricity, or some cyanide acid, plus the executioner's fee and other incidental costs (transportation for official witnesses, etc.). However, it costs society several thousand dollars a year to keep a person behind bars (estimates of the cost vary considerably), and this mounts up into a five- or six-figure sum for a lifeterm prisoner. No complaint against abolition of the death penalty is more common than the one expressed in the rhetorical question, "Why should we pay to keep him behind bars for life when he has been convicted of horrible crimes, and might kill again if he gets the chance?" Those who argue this way may be surprised to learn that the 1970 commutation of fifteen Arkansas death sentences was reported to have saved the taxpayers an estimated $1.5 million by obviating the tremendous costs of appeals for indigent defendants;[20] and that in 1979 Georgia spent a reported $1 million for a new electric chair, death chamber, and barbed wire fences to keep away demonstrators who want to protest any resumption of executions.[21] Moralistic defenders (and critics as well) of the death penalty will view the whole issue with disdain from the start because, for them, the question is not how to save tax dollars at any price, but what justice requires by way of proper expenditures. Others, however, whose views on the death penalty are more eclectic or utilitarian cannot so easily ignore what might be called "the tax-payer's argument." One will look in vain, however, to current social science for an answer; there is no thoroughgoing dollars-and-cents cost/benefit analysis of the death penalty.[22] The best we have is the sketch of why the death penalty must be expected to raise the total costs of any criminal justice system of which it is a part; the argument is by Barry Nakell, a

20. *Time,* 11 January 1971, p. 50.
21. *Fellowship,* July/August 1980, p. 26. It has also been reported that it cost California half a million dollars to execute Caryl Chessman (T. Thomas 1970:21), and $1 million each to sentence Charles Manson and Sirhan Sirhan to death (Washington Research Project 1971:61).
22. See, however, the incisive note by Hans Zeisel, in *The New York Times,* 29 August 1977, p. 26. See also McKee & Sesnowitz 1976; and Browning 1974:654–77 ("The Costs and Benefits of Capital Punishment").

law professor at the University of North Carolina, and an edited version is reprinted in §5 below.

§1. Racial Discrimination, Rape, and the Death Penalty*

MARVIN E. WOLFGANG and MARC RIEDEL

I. Of the 3,859 persons executed for all crimes since 1930, 54.6 percent have been black or members of other racial minority groups. Of the 455 executed for rape alone, 89.5 percent have been nonwhite.[1] As census data clearly reveal, blacks in American society have consistently represented approximately 10 percent of the United States population.

These statistics alone, of course, do not reveal elements of judicial bias in the administration of criminal law. It is also well recognized that blacks in American society, with variations in time and place, have a criminal homicide rate that is between four and ten times greater than that of whites. Age, sex, and regional variations within the country are regularly taken into account when studies of homicide are made. There can be little argument about the fact that official police arrest and court adjudication records show a higher proportion of blacks than of whites arrested and convicted for criminal homicide. We are not here questioning the process of the differential arrest of blacks compared to whites nor the issue of varying degrees of evidentiary material for indictment of blacks compared with whites. What is at issue is whether, among persons who have been convicted of capital crimes, a statistically significantly higher proportion of blacks than of whites, all other things being relatively equal, are differentially sentenced to death. One of the important phrases in this statement is "relatively equal," for we need to know much more than is currently available about the circumstances of the crime, the previous record of the defendant, and the relationship between the victim and the offender before assertions of racial discrimination and bias can be made with utmost validity.

Many of the studies that have examined racial disparities in sentencing

1. Testimony of Marvin E. Wolfgang at hearings before the Subcommittee of the Committee on the Judiciary, March 16, 1972.

*Excerpted from "Race, Judicial Discretion, and the Death Penalty" by Marvin E. Wolfgang and Marc Riedel in volume no. 407 of *The Annals* of The American Academy of Political and Social Science, pp. 119–33. © 1973, by The American Academy of Political and Social Science. All rights reserved. Tables and footnotes have been renumbered and cross-references adjusted accordingly.

have attempted to control for one or more nonracial variables which might explain the differential imposition of the death penalty. The studies have been fragmentary and localized in particular states, but the findings have been in a consistent direction: blacks are disproportionately sentenced to death.[2]

As an example of research done to determine the effects of race while taking into account the effects of nonracial variables, Wolfgang, Kelly, and Nolde analyzed the records of 439 persons sentenced to death in Pennsylvania between 1914 and 1958 for first degree murder.[3] Of 147 blacks, only 11 percent had their sentences of death commuted to life imprisonment; whereas of 263 whites, 20 percent had their sentences commuted. The statistical association between being executed and being black was statistically significant ($\chi^2 = 4.33$; $p < 0.05$). As was asserted,

something more than chance has operated over the years to produce this racial difference . . . because the Negro/high-execution association is statistically pres-

2. Hugo Adam Bedau, "Capital Punishment in Oregon 1903–1964," *Oregon Law Review 45* (1965), p. 1, and "Death Sentences in New Jersey 1907–1960," *Rutgers Law Review 19* (1965), p. 1; William J. Bowers, *Discrimination in Capital Punishment: Characteristics of the Condemned* (unpublished transcript from the Russell B. Stearns Research Center, Northeastern University, 1972); Robert M. Carter and A. LaMont Smith, "The Death Penalty in California: A Statistical and Composite Portrait," *Crime and Delinquency 15* (1969), p. 62; George E. Danielson, *Facts and Figures Concerning Executions in California 1938–1962*, prepared with the assistance of the Assembly Legislative Reference Service, Sacramento, 1963; Harold Garfinkel, "Research Note on Inter- and Intra-Racial Homicides," *Social Forces 27* (1949), p. 369; Frank E. Hartung, "Trends in the Use of Capital Punishment," *The Annals 284* (1952), p. 8; Rupert C. Koeninger, "Capital Punishment in Texas 1924–1968," *Crime and Delinquency 15* (1969), p. 132; Charles S. Mangum, *The Legal Status of the Negro* (Chapel Hill: University of North Carolina Press, 1940); Maryland Legislative Council, Committee on Capital Punishment, *Report*, 1962; Donald H. Partington, "The Incidence of the Death Penalty for Rape in Virginia," *Washington and Lee Law Review 22* (1965), p. 43; James A. McCafferty, "The Death Sentence," in H. A. Bedau, ed., *The Death Penalty in America*, rev. ed. (New York: Doubleday, 1967); Ohio Legislative Service Commission, Staff Research Report no. 46, *Capital Punishment*, 1962; Pennsylvania Joint Legislative Committee on Capital Punishment, *Report*, 1961; Thorsten Sellin, "A Note on Capital Executions in the United States," *British Journal of Delinquency 1* (1960), p. 6; "A Study of the California Penalty Jury in First-Degree Murder Trials," *Stanford Law Review 21* (1969), p. 1297; Texas Department of Corrections, Division of Research, *A Synopsis of Offenders Receiving the Death Sentence in Texas*, Research Report no. 8, 1972; United Nations Economic and Social Council, Commission on Human Rights, *Capital Punishment in the Republic of South Africa*, unpublished working paper, 1964; Franklin H. Williams, "The Death Penalty and the Negro," *The Crisis 67* (1960), p. 501; Edwin D. Wolf, "Abstracts of Analysis of Jury Sentencing in Capital Cases," *Rutgers Law Review 19* (1964), p. 56.
3. Marvin E. Wolfgang, Arlene Kelly, and Hans C. Nolde, "Comparisons of the Executed and the Commuted among Admissions to Death Row," *Journal of Criminal Law, Criminology and Police Science 53* (September 1962), p. 301. The variables included in the study were type of murder, offender's age, race, occupation, marital status, whether native- or foreign-born, type of counsel, and reasons for commutations.

ent, some suspicion of racial discrimination can hardly be avoided. If such a relationship had not appeared, this kind of suspicion could have been allayed; the existence of the relationship, although not "proving" differential bias by the Pardon Boards over the years since 1914, strongly suggests that such bias has existed.

In this study there was no significant difference between race and the commission of felony murder. That is, the proportion of blacks and whites who had committed felony murder was not statistically different, yet 94 percent of black felony murderers were executed compared to 83 percent of white felony murderers. This latter was also a statistically significant difference, indicating that among offenders who had been sentenced to death and who had committed felony murder, blacks were executed more and commuted less than whites. Finally, it was noted in general that offenders with court-appointed counsel were more likely to be executed and offenders with private counsel more likely to be commuted to life imprisonment, but even among the court-appointed counsel, a statistically significantly higher proportion of blacks was executed than whites ($\chi^2 = p < 0.05$). The authors concluded:

> any empirical verification of previously assumed differences among persons who received society's ultimate sanction should be of value in understanding the operation of our legal principles. That race is one of these significant differences constitutes a social and political violation of the principle of equal justice. . . .[4]

In one of the early significant studies on race and capital punishment, Guy B. Johnson pointed out that the race of both the victim and the offender may be an important variable in understanding the penalties applied to homicides.[5] Using 220 homicide cases from Richmond, Virginia, from 1930 to 1939, and 330 homicides from five counties in North Carolina from 1930 to 1940, Johnson hypothesized that cases of black offenders whose victims were white would be viewed as the most serious homicides, followed by white offenders/white victims, black offenders/black victims, and white offenders/black victims.

Johnson found that of the 141 black/black cases, there were only 8 sentences of life imprisonment and no death sentences. Of the 22 cases of black offenders and white victims, 7 defendants received life imprisonment and 6 received the death penalty. Although the quality and quantity of data precluded further analysis, Johnson did conclude that "Negro versus Negro offenses are treated with undue leniency, while the Negro versus white offenses are treated with undue severity."[6]

The effects of the race of the offender, as well as racial combinations of offender and victim, on the imposition of the death penalty become more

4. Ibid., p. 311.
5. Guy B. Johnson, "The Negro and Crime," *The Annals 217* (September 1941), pp. 93–104.
6. Ibid., p. 98.

clear when studies on rape offenses are examined. Among persons sentenced to death for rape in North Carolina from 1909 to 1954, Elmer Johnson found that 56 percent of blacks compared to 43 percent of whites were executed.[7] A Florida study of sentences for rape between 1940 and 1964 noted that only six cases, or 5 percent, of white males who raped white females received the death penalty. But of the eighty-four black males who raped white women, forty-five, or 54 percent, received the death penalty, while none of the eight white offenders who raped black females received the death penalty.[8]

Data from the Federal Bureau of Prisons suggest that racial differentials are most clear among death sentences for rape. As we noted, 405 of the 455 persons executed for rape since 1930 were black; only 2 were from other racial minorities. All of the executions for rape were in southern or border states or the District of Columbia.[9] In Louisiana, Mississippi, Oklahoma, Virginia, West Virginia, and the District of Columbia not a single white man was executed for rape over the forty-two-year period from 1930 to 1972. Together, these jurisdictions executed 66 blacks. Arkansas, Delaware, Florida, Kentucky, and Missouri each executed 1 white man for rape since 1930, but together they have executed 71 blacks.

Findings of racial discrimination in previous studies, as well as suspicions of racial discrimination raised by the data from the Bureau of Prisons, have been reinforced recently by more conclusive findings based on refined and detailed analyses of rape convictions in several states where rape has been a statutory capital crime. Differential sentencing has required further examination to determine whether racial discrimination exists.

II. During the summer of 1965, research was initiated to examine in detail the relationship between race and sentencing for rape in eleven southern and border states in which rape was a capital offense. The study was sponsored by the NAACP Legal Defense Fund and conducted by the Center for Studies in Criminology and Criminal Law at the University of Pennsylvania by Professors Anthony Amsterdam and Marvin E. Wolfgang.

At each step in the development and implementation of the research design, from selection of the sample to analysis of the data, the emphasis was on the use of research criteria that would increase the reliability and objectivity of the data while minimizing sources of bias and subjectivity. Interfacing with scientific demands was the selection of dimensions of inquiry that would increase understanding of racial discrimination, if it existed, in a judicial system and that would also be of possible use in subsequent litigation.

7. Elmer H. Johnson, "Selective Factors in Capital Punishment," *Social Forces* 36 (December 1957), p. 165.
8. *Rape: Selective Electrocution Based on Race* (Miami: Florida Civil Liberties Union, 1964).
9. Bureau of Prisons, National Prisoner Statistics, *Capital Punishment* 1930–1968, Bulletin no. 45, August 1969.

The research findings were presented as evidence in six states to support petitioners' claims of racial discrimination in the administration of the death penalty. They were part of the brief in the *Maxwell* case argued before the U.S. Supreme Court[10] and part of the testimony offered before a subcommittee of the House of Representatives considering bills to suspend the death penalty for two years or to abolish it.[11]

Although eighteen American jurisdictions allowed the imposition of the death penalty for rape, substantial numbers of persons have been executed for this crime during the past thirty years in only twelve: Alabama, Arkansas, Florida, Georgia, Louisiana, Maryland, Mississippi, North Carolina, South Carolina, Tennessee, Texas, and Virginia. It was decided that the study could be profitably confined to these twelve states.

In order to form an empirical basis for conclusions about the effect of racial factors on capital sentencing for rape, it was necessary to gather data about a substantial number of rape cases in each state. Moreover, a sufficiently long period of time covered by the research was necessary in order to satisfy the notion of "custom," or of an institutionalized, systematic judicial norm of sentencing behavior; hence the twenty-year period used in this study.

To meet the demands of proper statistical analysis, cases could have been obtained by seeking every rape conviction in each state for a decade, or by selecting counties by standard statistical sampling techniques over a twenty-year period. This latter process was used. For each of the twelve states, a sample of counties was chosen to represent the urban-rural and black-white demographic distributions of each state. The counties chosen comprised more than 50 percent of the total population of the twelve states.[12] For the counties included in each state sample, every case of conviction for rape from January 1, 1945 to the summer of 1965 was recorded. Maryland was initially included in the survey, but time limitations precluded full data collection in that state. Therefore, data were gathered for a twenty-year period for over 3000 rape convictions in 230 counties in eleven states.[13]

The states included in the study were not only those that most often executed persons for rape; they also displayed an apparent racial disparity, for black offenders were more frequently executed than were white offenders. In seeking to explore the meaning of this apparent racial disparity in capital sentencing, only rape *convictions* were considered. It might be asserted that

---

10. *Maxwell* v. *Bishop*, 398 U.S. 262 (1970).
11. Wolfgang, Testimony, p. 165.
12. The sampling plan for each state in the study was developed with the assistance of John Monroe.
13. Deposition of written interrogatories to Marvin E. Wolfgang re *Willie Awkwright* v. *Asa D. Kelly, Jr. and Lamont Smith*, Case No. 5283 in the Superior Court of Tattnall County, Georgia.

blacks more frequently than whites commit rape, are more frequently arrested, or are more frequently charged with that offense. Whether these or any combination of these assertions were true was not questioned in this study. Instead, the focus was on the reliable and objectively ascertainable fact that defendants had been convicted for the crime of rape. Using this point of departure meant that the effect of racial factors on the criminal process prior to conviction could not be explored. There would be no way of knowing— if blacks were disproportionately sentenced to death for rape—whether the pattern could be accounted for by a disproportionate frequency in the commission of rapes by blacks or by a disproportionate frequency in the conviction of blacks for rape. However, *among convicted defendants,* it was possible to determine whether black defendants were disproportionately frequently sentenced to death and, if so, whether the disproportion could be explained by nonracial variables.

In order to explore the effect of racial as well as nonracial variables on the imposition of the death penalty, it was necessary to determine which variables could be obtained from the county records of rape convictions. In addition to collecting information on the race of the defendant and the victim and on the type of sentence, information was gathered about many nonracial variables that could be construed as mitigating or aggravating circumstances. If standards were sought for sentencing in capital cases, some of the nonracial variables listed below might be seriously considered. These were the variables included in the study reported here.

1. Offender characteristics
   a. age
   b. marital status
   c. prior criminal record
   d. previous imprisonment
   e. employment status
2. Victim characteristics
   a. age
   b. marital status
   c. dependent children
   d. prior criminal record
   e. reputation for chastity
3. Nature of relations between victim and offender
   a. offender known to victim
   b. prior sexual relations
4. Circumstances of offense
   a. contemporaneous offense
   b. type of entry—authorized or unauthorized
   c. location of offense—indoor or outdoor

    d. display of weapon
    e. carrying of weapon
    f. amount of injury to victim
    g. threatened victim
    h. degree of force employed
    i. victim made pregnant by offense
    j. one or multiple offenders
    k. date of offense
5. Circumstances of the trial
    a. plea
    b. defense of insanity
    c. appointed or retained counsel
    d. length of time of trial
    e. defense of consent
    f. whether defendant testified [. . .]

The method of analysis used to determine whether the death penalty is given disproportionately frequently to blacks employed the null hypothesis and the chi-square (χ^2) statistical test, for which $p < 0.05$ was chosen as the level of significance. One major null hypothesis stated that among all defendants convicted of rape there is no significant association between the race of the defendant and the type of sentence imposed. The second major null hypothesis stated that among all defendants convicted of rape there are no significant differences between the proportions of black defendants with white victims and all other classes of rape defendants sentenced to death. Both of these hypotheses were rejected in each state analyzed.

The data were compiled and analyzed in seven states—Alabama, Arkansas, Florida, Georgia, Louisiana, South Carolina, and Tennessee—for purposes of submitting testimony in litigation conducted by the Legal Defense Fund. Each state was separately reviewed with its own set of tables and conclusions. The findings were uniformly similar for each state and the conclusions the same. In future analyses planned by the Center for Studies in Criminology

Table 5-1-1. Race of Defendent, by Type of Sentence

	Death		Other		Total	
	Number	Percent	Number	Percent	Number	Percent
Black	110	13	713	87	823	100
White	9	2	433	98	442	100
Total	119		1146		1265	

Note: States included are Florida, Georgia, Louisiana, South Carolina, Tennessee. $\chi^2 = 41.9924$; $p < 0.001$.

Table 5-1-2. Racial Combinations of Defendant and Victim, by Type of Sentence

	Death		Other		Total	
	Number	Percent	Number	Percent	Number	Percent
Black defendant and white victim	113	36	204	64	317	100
All other racial combinations of defendant and victim	19	2	902	98	921	100
Total	132		1106		1238	

Note: States included are Arkansas, Florida, Georgia, Louisiana, South Carolina, Tennessee. $\chi^2 = 275.7192$; $p < 0.001$.

and Criminal Law, all states for which data are available will be comprehensively reviewed. In the present article, only a brief summary with an illustration of the procedure can be presented. In the tables that follow, the total number of cases varies by the particular factor analyzed because of differences in the availability of information over the twenty-year period in each of the states.

Among 1265 cases in which the race of the defendant and the sentence are known, nearly seven times as many blacks were sentenced to death as were whites. Among the 823 blacks convicted of rape, 110, or 13 percent, were sentenced to death; among the 442 whites convicted of rape, only 9, or 2 percent, were sentenced to death. The statistical probability that such a disproportionate number of blacks could be sentenced to death by chance alone is less than one out of a thousand. More particularly, a statistically significantly higher proportion of black defendants whose victims were white were sentenced to death. From a total of 1238 convicted rape defendants, 317 were black defendants with white victims, and 921 were all other racial combinations of defendant and victim—including black/black, white/white, and white/black. Of the 317 black defendants whose victims were white, 113, or approximately 36 percent, were sentenced to death. Of the 921 defendants involved in all other racial combinations of defendant and victim, only 19, or 2 percent, were sentenced to death. In short, black defendants whose victims were white were sentenced to death approximately eighteen times more frequently than defendants in any other racial combination of defendant and victim. Again, the probability of such a distribution, or such a relationship between the sentence of death and black defendants with white victims is, by chance alone, less than one out of a thousand.

But the obvious fact that there is differential sentencing by race as shown in Tables 5-1-1 and 5-1-2, does not alone permit a conclusion of racial discrimination in sentencing. We may hypothesize, for example, that, as a group, black rape defendants more often than white defendants commit another offense along with the commission of the rape offense. It could generally be asserted that the commission of a contemporaneous offense, like burglary or robbery, is an aggravating circumstance and could account for the disproportionate frequency with which black defendants receive the death penalty.

Because of these considerations, all the nonracial variables previously listed were introduced in a further examination of the associations between race and the imposition of the death penalty.

First, each nonracial variable was examined relative to type of sentence. If no significant relationship existed between the nonracial variable and type of sentence, further analysis of that variable was not undertaken for it could at that point be concluded that no significant difference in type of sentence occurred because of that variable. Table 5-1-3, however, illustrates that there is a significant association between offenses committed contemporaneously with the rape offense and type of sentence.

If there was a significant association between the nonracial variable and sentence, the nonracial variable was then cross-tabulated with the race of the defendant. If the resulting chi-square was not significant, no further analysis was performed. There could be, however, a significant association between the nonracial variable and race, as is shown in Table 5-1-4. This table indicates that among 572 black defendants, 150, or 26 percent, had committed contemporaneous offenses, while among white defendants 45, or 15 percent, had committed contemporaneous offenses.

Table 5-1-5 would seem to add one more piece of evidence that the nonracial variable of contemporaneous offenses is a contributory factor producing a more frequent imposition of the death penalty for blacks, particularly those with white victims. Data from this table indicate a significant association between the presence or absence of contemporaneous offenses and racial combinations of defendant and victim. Among the 146 black defendants with white victims, 40 percent had committed contemporaneous offenses, whereas only 14 percent of the 561 cases making up all other racial combinations involved contemporaneous offenses.

Table 5-1-3. Contemporaneous Offense, by Type of Sentence

	Death		Other		Total	
	Number	Percent	Number	Percent	Number	Percent
Contemporaneous offense	53	22	133	78	236	100
No contemporaneous offense	92	8	840	92	921	100
Total	125		1023		1148	

Note: States included are Arkansas, Florida, Georgia, Louisiana, South Carolina, Tennessee. $\chi^2 = 39.4915$; $p < 0.001$.

Table 5-1-4. Contemporaneous Offense, by Race of Defendant

| | Black | | White | | Total |
	Number	Percent	Number	Percent	Number
Contemporaneous offense	150	26	45	15	195
No contemporaneous offense	422	74	264	85	686
Total	572	100	309	100	881

Note: States included are Arkansas, Florida, Georgia, Louisiana, Tennessee. $\chi^2 = 15.1583$; $p < 0.001$.

Although it might appear that the presence or absence of contemporaneous offenses is a contributory factor, more refined procedure shows that it does not play a significant part in explaining the association between black defendants and the imposition of the death penalty. To perform this further analysis, the nonracial variable of contemporaneous offenses was split into two subgroups. The first subgroup included all cases in which the defendant had committed a contemporaneous offense—Table 5-1-6. Within this subgroup, chi-square analysis shows a significant association between racial combinations of defendant and victim and imposition of the death penalty. More specifically, among the fifty-eight black defendants with white victims, 39 percent received the death penalty, but among all other racial combinations of defendant and victim, only 3 percent of the eighty-one defendants received the death penalty.

For the other subgroup in which no contemporaneous offenses were committed, there is also a significant association between racial combinations of defendant and victim and the imposition of the death penalty. Table 5-1-7 indicates that among the 88 black defendants with white victims, 39 percent received the death penalty whereas among 480 cases of other racial combinations, only 2 percent received the death penalty.

Table 5-1-5. Contemporaneous Offense, by Racial Combinations of Defendant and Victim

| | Black defendant and white victim | | All other racial combinations of defendant/victim | | Total |
	Number	Percent	Number	Percent	Number
Contemporaneous offense	58	40	81	14	139
No contemporaneous offense	88	60	480	86	568
Total	146	100	561	100	707

Note: States included are Florida, Georgia, Tennessee. $\chi^2 = 45.3139$; $p < 0.001$.

Table 5-1-6. Racial Combinations of Defendant/Victim, by Type of Sentence Among All Cases in which Defendant Committed a Contemporaneous Offense

	Death		Other		Total	
	Number	Percent	Number	Percent	Number	Percent
Black defendant and white victim	22	39	36	61	58	100
All other racial combinations of defendant/victim	2	3	79	97	81	100
Total	24		115		139	

Note: States included are Florida, Georgia, Tennessee. χ^2 = 27.3231; $p < 0.001$.

It is important to repeat the final descriptive assertion derived from these data: It is not the presence of the nonracial factor of a contemporaneous offense that affects the decision to impose the death penalty more frequently on blacks. Rather, it is the racial factor of the relationship between the defendant and victim that results in the use of the death penalty. Whether or not a contemporaneous offense has been committed, if the defendant is black and the victim is white, the defendant is about eighteen times more likely to receive the death penalty than when the defendant is in any other racial combination of defendant and victim.

Over two dozen possibly aggravating nonracial variables that might have accounted for the higher proportion of blacks than whites sentenced to death upon conviction of rape have been analyzed. Not one of these nonracial factors has withstood the tests of statistical significance. That is, in none of the seven states carefully analyzed can it be said that any of the nonracial factors account for the statistically significant and disproportionate number of blacks sentenced to death for rape. This is a striking conclusion. It cannot be said that blacks are more frequently sentenced to death because they have a longer prior criminal record than whites, because they used more force on the victim, because they committed a robbery or burglary, because they entered premises without authorization, because they used a weapon or threatened the victim with a weapon, because they had an accomplice in the commission of the rape, because they impregnated the victim, because they more frequently attacked persons under age sixteen, and so forth. All the nonracial factors in each of the states analyzed "wash out," that is, they have no bearing on the imposition of the death penalty in disproportionate numbers upon blacks. The only variable of statistical significance that remains is race.

III. That blacks have been disproportionately sentenced to death and executed in the United States has long been noted. But general social differentials in sentencing may not alone denote racial discrimination, or failure of blacks to be given all due process in the administration of criminal justice. An elaborate research scheme, reported here, which collected data on capital rape convictions over a twenty-year period from 1945 to 1965, has now provided material on many nonracial variables to determine whether they, rather than race, could account for the disproportionately and significantly high frequency of blacks sentenced to death compared to whites.

Based upon a refined statistical analysis of rape convictions in states where rape has been a capital crime, this study shows that there has been a patterned, systematic, and customary imposition of the death penalty. Far from being "freakish" or capricious, sentences of death have been imposed on blacks, compared to whites, in a way that exceeds any statistical notion of chance or fortuity. Moreover, the systems of criminal justice in the jurisdictions studied have inflicted the death penalty on blacks in such disproportions without statutory or other legally acceptable bases. Thus, with the benefit of a carefully designed and objectively analyzed study of these conditions, it can be concluded that the significant racial differentials found in the imposition of the death penalty are indeed produced by racial discrimination.

The study has shown that racial discrimination has long existed and exists with currency above the conviction stage of the judicial process. That there may be more systematic features of racial differentials, from which discrimination may be inferred, remains for future and further research to determine. Discretion at earlier stages in the administration of justice could also carry elements of racial discrimination: arrest, hearing, plea bargaining, decisions to prosecute or drop charges, and many others, when death is a permissible penalty. Neither mandatory sanctions nor the reduction of racial discrimination at the sentencing stage would eliminate the untoward systemic effects of racial discrimination elsewhere in the processing of defendants. By declaring the death penalty unconstitutional, and reaffirming this declaration if necessary, the Supreme Court at least and at last removes the consequence of finality which differential justice has produced.

Table 5-1-7. Racial Combinations of Defendant/Victim, by Type of Sentence Among All Cases in Which Defendant Committed No Contemporaneous Offense

	Death		Other		Total	
	Number	Percent	Number	Percent	Number	Percent
Black defendant and white victim	34	39	54	61	88	100
All other racial combinations of defendant/victim	9	2	471	98	480	100
Total	43		525		568	

Note: States included are Florida, Georgia, Tennessee. $\chi^2 = 138.4186$; $p < 0.001$.

§2.   Racial Discrimination
and Criminal Homicide under
Post-*Furman* Capital Statutes*

WILLIAM J. BOWERS and GLENN L. PIERCE

In *Gregg* v. *Georgia* and companion cases, decided on July 2, 1976, the United States Supreme Court rejected the mandatory death penalty as provided for by the legislatures of Louisiana and North Carolina, but upheld guided discretion as formulated in the statutes of Florida, Georgia, and Texas. The Court reasoned that making the death penalty mandatory upon conviction removes sentencing discretion that should be exercised in the interest of "individualized" justice and that the total absence of discretion in sentencing may cause the trial of guilt to be colored by considerations of punishment (i.e., jury nullification). By contrast, it reasoned that providing specific sentencing guidelines to be followed in a separate postconviction phase of the trial would free the sentencing decision of arbitrariness and discrimination and, for that matter, free the guilt decision of sentencing considerations.

The Court accepted several different forms of guided discretion which vary in the limits they place on sentencing authorities. Least restrictive are "aggravating only" statutes, which enumerate aggravating circumstances and permit the jury to recommend death if it finds at least one such circumstance to be present. Intermediate in restrictions are "aggravating versus mitigating" statutes which list both aggravating and mitigating circumstances and give the jury discretion to recommend death, providing it finds that the aggravating "outweigh" the mitigating circumstances. Most restrictive are "structured discretion" statutes which make the death sentence strictly contingent upon the jury's findings of fact with respect to aggravation.

Georgia's post-*Furman* capital statute is an example of the "aggravating only" type. The statute lists ten aggravating and no mitigating circumstances. If the jury finds at least one aggravating circumstance it may, but need not, recommend death. The judge must sentence the defendant to death if the jury recommends it, and he must not do so if the jury recommends otherwise.

Florida's capital statute is of the "aggravating versus mitigating" type. The statute lists eight aggravating and seven mitigating circumstances. If an aggravating circumstance is found, death is presumed to be the proper sentence, unless one or more mitigating circumstances are also found and judged to "outweigh the aggravating circumstance(s)." The jury weighs the evidence

*Reprinted, with permission of the National Council on Crime and Delinquency, from William J. Bowers and Glenn L. Pierce, "Arbitrariness and Discrimination under Post-*Furman* Capital Statues," *Crime & Delinquency*, October 1980, pp. 563–635. The article has been excerpted; tables and footnotes have been renumbered and cross-references adjusted accordingly.

and advises the court as to the sentence. The judge need not follow the jury's advice: He can impose death even if the jury advises life, and he can impose life even if the jury advises death. He cannot, however, impose death unless the jury finds at least one aggravating circumstance.

Texas's capital statute is an example of the "structured discretion" type. For a murder to qualify as a capital offense, the jury must find the defendant guilty of at least one of five forms of aggravated murder defined in the statute. The jury then considers three further questions of aggravation in the determination of sentence. If it answers all three questions in the affirmative by unanimous vote, the judge must impose the death sentence; otherwise, the judge must not do so. Neither jury nor judge has sentencing discretion once findings are made with respect to these three issues of aggravation.

Each type of guided discretion statute upheld in the *Gregg* decision also provided for automatic appellate review of all death sentences. Most elaborate is Georgia's review process, which was explicitly formulated to determine

1. whether the sentence of death was imposed under the influence of passion, prejudice, or any other arbitrary factor, and
2. whether . . . the evidence supports the jury's or judge's finding of a statutory aggravating circumstance . . . and
3. whether the sentence of death is excessive or disproportionate to the penalty imposed in similar cases considering the crime and the defendant. . . .[1]

Justice White, in his *Gregg* opinion, observed that Georgia's statute

> gives the Georgia Supreme Court the power and the obligation to perform precisely the task . . . this Court . . . performed in *Furman;* namely, the task of deciding whether *in fact* the death penalty was being administered for any given class of crime in a discriminatory, standardless, or rare fashion.

Moreover, the Georgia statute makes special provisions for the application of this "similarity standard" in the appellate review of death sentences for excessiveness and disproportionality. To establish a baseline for comparison, it requires the state supreme court to compile the records of "all capital cases" in the state of Georgia in which sentences were imposed after January 1, 1970, and it provides the court with a special assistant and staff for this purpose. For the case under review, it requires the trial judge not only to transmit to the state supreme court a transcript and complete record of the trial, but also to complete a separate, standardized, questionnaire-type report about the defendant, the crime, and the circumstances of the trial. This too is submitted to the state supreme court for use in its review. After the court has made a proportionality review that upholds a death sentence, it is required by statute to cite in an appendix to its opinion all cases it has considered that are "similar" to the one reviewed.

1. Georgia Code Ann, sec. 27-2537.

The present study examines whether the new post-*Furman* capital statutes affirmed by the Supreme Court in the *Gregg* decision have, in fact, eliminated the arbitrariness and discrimination which rendered pre-*Furman* capital statutes unconstitutional. [. . .] The upcoming analysis deals with the first five years following the *Furman* decision. For Florida, Georgia, Texas, and Ohio, we examine criminal homicides committed between the effective dates (if occurring on the first of the month; if not, tabulations begin with the first of the following month) of their respective statutes (i.e., Florida: December 8, 1972; Georgia: March 28, 1973; Texas: January 1, 1974; Ohio: November 1, 1974) and the end of 1977, and the death sentences imposed under the post-*Furman* statutes for homicides occurring before 1978. The analysis of judicial processing in Florida is restricted to offenses that occurred before 1978 and reached the trial court dockets before the collection of data. Thus, December 31, 1977, is our cutoff date in the sense that offenses occurring after 1977, regardless of sentencing date, are excluded from this analysis.

The analysis proceeds in five sections: 1. arbitrariness by race, 2. arbitrariness by place, 3. arbitrariness by stages of the process, 4. arbitrariness and the review process, and 5. arbitrariness and the form of the law. In our analysis of racial differences all four states are examined, although we do not carry the Ohio data as far as we do the data for Florida, Georgia, and Texas. In our analysis of regional differences, we examine Florida and Georgia, excluding Texas because of ambiguities with respect to judicial circuits as a basis for grouping jurisdictions. Our analysis of judicial processing is based on information that was available only from Florida. Our analysis of appellate review incorporates data available only on Florida and Georgia. The final section of the empirical analysis, on the form of the law, draws a comparison between Florida and Georgia based on data available only from these two states. [. . .] [*Ed. note.* All of sections 2. and 4. are omitted, *infra.*]

By far the most substantial and consistent extralegal basis of differential treatment under pre-*Furman* statutes was race. All but a few studies found gross racial differences in the likelihood of a death sentence; race of both offender and victim was associated with differential treatment, and race of victim was a more prominent basis of differential treatment than race of offender. If the post-*Furman* statutes have remedied the previous ills, we should find no substantial or consistent differences by race in the likelihood of a death sentence for criminal homicide under the new statutes.

The likelihood of a death sentence by offender/victim racial categories in Florida, Georgia, Texas, and Ohio is shown in Table 5-2-1. It presents the estimated number of criminal offenders,[2] the number of persons sentenced to death, and the probability or likelihood of a death sentence given a homicide

---

2. The method of estimating the number of criminal homicides by offender/victim category is described in Appendix A [omitted], and the specific adjustment factors employed for each state are given in note a [also omitted] below Table 5-2-1.

Table 5-2-1. Probability of Receiving the Death Sentence in Florida, Georgia Texas, and Ohio for Criminal Homicide, by Race of Offender and Victim (from Effective Dates of Respective Post-*Furman* Capital Statutes Through 1977)

Offender/victim racial combinations	Estimated number of offenders[a]	Persons sentenced to death	Overall probability of death sentence
Florida			
Black kills white	240	53	.221
White kills white	1768	82	.046
Black kills black	1922	12	.006
White kills black	80	0	.000
Georgia			
Black kills white	258	43	.167
White kills white	1006	42	.042
Black kills black	2458	12	.005
White kills black	71	2	.028
Texas			
Black kills white	344	30	.087
White kills white	3616	56	.015
Black kills black	2597	2	.001
White kills black	143	1	.007
Ohio			
Black kills white	173	44	.254
White kills white	803	37	.046
Black kills black	1170	20	.017
White kills black	47	0	.000

[a]Based on information submitted by the police in the Supplementary Homicide Reports.

for each offender/victim racial combination in each state from the effective date of the post-*Furman* statute through 1977. The likelihood of a death sentence given a criminal homicide spans the criminal justice process from the initial investigation of the crime by the police through the sentencing of a convicted offender. That is, unlike studies that begin with a sample of indictments, these data will reflect the effects of differential law enforcement as well as differential court processing of criminal homicide cases. They incorporate the effects of discretion at arrest, charging, indictment, conviction, and sentencing in the handling of potentially capital crimes.

And what do these data show? Stark differences by race of both offender and victim in all four states are apparent in Table 5-2-1. The racial pattern is consistent across states and similar to the experience under pre-*Furman* statutes. Thus, black killers and the killers of whites are substantially more likely than others to receive a death sentence in all four states. And, as in the pre-*Furman* era, race of victim tends to overshadow race of offender as a basis for differential treatment (in fact, differences by race of offender would be altogether obscured if the data were tabulated without race of victim).[3] In Florida, the difference by race of victim is great. Among black offenders, those who kill whites are nearly forty times more likely to be sentenced to death than those who kill blacks. The difference by race of offender, although not as great, is also marked. Among the killers of whites, blacks are five times more likely than whites to be sentenced to death. To appreciate the magnitude of these differences, consider the following implications of these data: If all offenders in Florida were sentenced to death at the same rate as blacks who killed whites, there would be a total of 887 persons sentenced to death; 53 blacks who killed whites, 391 whites who killed whites, 425 blacks who killed blacks, and 18 whites who killed blacks—instead of the 147 death sentences actually imposed by the end of 1977.

In Georgia, the chances of a death sentence are slightly less in magnitude but remarkably similar in pattern to those in Florida. Overall, the likelihood of a death sentence is 30 percent lower in Georgia than in Florida (.026 for Georgia; .037 for Florida), but much of this difference is due to the greater proportion of black/black killings in Georgia. For the respective offender/victim racial categories, the differences are less: 24 percent lower for black offender/white victim killings, 9 percent lower for white/white killings, and 17 percent lower for black/black killings. Only the category of white offenders/black victims is noticeably different, as a result of two death sentences in Georgia and none in Florida. Hence, the difference in statutory form in these two states—"aggravating only" in Georgia and "aggravating versus mitigating" in Florida—appears to have only a slight and not an altogether consistent effect on the chances of a death sentence, and virtually no effect in controlling or correcting racial disparities.

In Texas, the chances that a murder will result in a death sentence are considerably less; indeed, the likelihood is only about one-third the chances in Florida and one-half the chances in Georgia.[4] But the pattern of racial

3. When race of victim is ignored, white offenders are more likely to receive a death sentence in three of these four states: Florida (white = .044, black = .030), Georgia (white = .040, black = .020), Texas (white = .015, black = .011). Without considering race of victim, black offenders exceed whites in the chances of a death sentence only in Ohio (white = .044, black = .048).

4. The latest statewide listing of death sentences available from the Texas Judicial Council was current as of May 1978, so it may not include some death sentences that were eventually imposed for murders committed in 1977 or earlier. Given a pace of about twelve death sentences per year in Texas, with an average elapsed time between offense and sentence of six to eight months, we estimate that roughly six to eight death sentences might have been missed. Our figures for Texas, therefore, may underrepresent death sentences by six to eight cases, not more than 10 percent of the total.

differences is still very much the same. In fact, despite the reduced chances of a death sentence in Texas, the racial differences, in relative terms, are generally greater.[5] Among black offenders, those with white victims are eighty-seven times more likely than those with black victims to receive the death penalty; and among the killers of whites, black offenders are six times more likely than white offenders to be sentenced to death. Perhaps the lower likelihood of a death sentence in Texas than in Florida and Georgia is a result of the more restrictive procedures of the "structured discretion" statute in Texas or of the more limited kinds of offenses which qualify for the death sentence in Texas. But it is clear that the Texas statute, despite its restrictiveness, has not eliminated differential treatment by race of offender and victim. On the contrary, race of offender and race of victim are responsible for more variation in the chances of a death sentence in Texas than in Florida or Georgia.

In Ohio, the pattern is the same; black killers and the killers of whites are more likely to receive the death sentence. Here the chances of a death sentence are greater overall than in the other three states. The relative differences by race of offender and victim are generally somewhat less than in Florida, Georgia, and Texas. Perhaps the greater likelihood of a death sentence in Ohio reflects the "quasi-mandatory" character of the Ohio statute, which was overturned in the *Lockett* decision for its failure to provide individualized treatment for convicted capital offenders. Since Ohio's statute has been invalidated by the Supreme Court, we have given the Ohio data less priority in our analysis and will not examine the operation of this statute further here.

In these four states, which accounted for approximately 70 percent of the nation's death sentences in the first five years after *Furman,* race of both offender and victim had a tremendous impact on the chances that a death sentence would be handed down. To understand to some extent the size of the effect of these racial differences, consider the following: The probability that a difference of this magnitude in the four states combined could have occurred by chance is so remote that it cannot be computed with available statistical programs. As computed, the probability is greater than 1 in 1 million for a chi square of 769.5 with 3 degrees of freedom. And this is a conservative estimate, since the overall pattern is not a composite of widely dif-

5. Furthermore, the Texas figures probably underestimate the extent to which blacks and whites, or members of minority groups versus the majority group, are treated differently. We know from the Texas Judicial Council reports that persons with Spanish surnames were overrepresented among those sentenced to death; eleven death sentences of such persons were imposed. But, because it was not possible to distinguish Hispanics from whites in the Supplementary Homicide Reports data, we could not tabulate the figures for blacks and whites excluding Hispanics or differentiate between blacks and Hispanics on the one hand and whites on the other.

ferent patterns from state to state, but rather is a reflection of the same essential pattern in states with differing mechanisms and procedures for guiding discretion.

The presence of differential treatment by race is unmistakable. But does it reflect the direct influence of race on the decisions made in the criminal justice process or could it be the result of legally relevant differences in the kinds of crimes committed by and against blacks and whites? A recent statement of this latter possibility can be found in the Fifth Circuit Court of Appeals opinion in *Spenkelink* v. *Wainwright*.[6] As recounted by the court, the Florida Attorney General argued

> that murders involving black victims have, in the past, generally been qualitatively different from murders involving white victims; as a general rule, . . . murders involving black victims have not presented facts and circumstances appropriate for the imposition of the death penalty.[7]

In a footnote, the court went on to quote Attorney General's Shevin's enumeration of these alleged differences: Murders involving black victims have in the past fallen into the categories of "family quarrels, lovers' quarrels, liquor quarrels, [and] barroom quarrels."[8]

In response to this argument, it would obviously be desirable to examine the chances of a death sentence by race of offender and victim separately for two categories of murder: those which by definition qualify for the death penalty and those which may or may not so qualify. In this connection, the statutes of Florida and Georgia make a felony circumstance—the fact that a homicide is committed in the course of another felony (e.g., rape, robbery)—an aggravating factor that qualifies the homicide for the death penalty. The Texas statute explicitly defines felony killing as one of the five categories of homicide that may lead to a death sentence. In effect, the distinction between felony and nonfelony homicides corresponds to the difference between crimes that definitely qualify for capital punishment and those that may or may not so qualify.

In the Supplementary Homicide Reports, the police indicate for each homicide whether it was committed in the course of another felony. The data we have obtained on death sentences imposed in the several states show for each crime whether it was accompanied by one or more felony circumstances. Notably, these data reveal that fewer than one out of five of the homicides in Florida, Georgia, and Texas were felony-type murders, but that more than four out of five of the death sentences in each of these states were imposed for felony-type murders. If, as the Florida Attorney General contended,

6. *Spenkelink* v. *Wainwright*, 578 F.2d 582 (CA5, 1978). (The spelling of the petitioner's name in the media reports and in the court briefs is often "Spinkellink" or "Spinkelink.")

7. Ibid., at 617.

8. Ibid., at 617, note 37.

Table 5-2-2. Probability of Receiving the Death Sentence in Florida, Georgia, and Texas for Felony and Nonfelony Murder, by Race of Offender and Victim (from Effective Dates of Respective Post-*Furman* Capital Statutes Through 1977)

Offender/victim racial combinations	Felony-type murder			Nonfelony-type murder		
	Estimated number of offenders[a]	Persons sentenced to death	Probability of death sentence	Estimated number of offenders[a]	Persons sentenced to death	Overall probability of death sentence
Florida						
Black kills white	143	46	.323	97	7	.072
White kills white	303	65	.215	1465	17	.012
Black kills black	160	7	.044	1762	5	.003
White kills black	11	0	.000	69	0	.000
Georgia						
Black kills white	134	39	.291	124	3	.024
White kills white	183	37	.202	823	6	.007
Black kills black	205	8	.039	2253	4	.002
White kills black	13	2	.154	58	0	.000
Texas						
Black kills white	173	28	.162	171	2	.012
White kills white	378	48	.127	3238	8	.002
Black kills black	121	2	.017	2476	0	.000
White kills black	30	1	.033	113	0	.000

[a] See Table 5-2-1.

Source: Supplementary Homicide Reports.

blacks are typically the victims of nonfelony-type murders, which do not present the "facts and circumstances appropriate for the imposition of the death penalty," the pattern of racial differences, at least with respect to race of victim, observed in Table 5-2-1 might possibly be attributable to this legally relevant difference in the types of homicide committed against blacks and whites.

The likelihood of a death sentence by offender/victim racial category is presented separately in Table 5-2-2 for felony and nonfelony-type murders in Florida, Georgia, and Texas. The importance of a felony circumstance as a determinant of the death sentence is immediately evident. For nearly every offender/victim racial category in each state, the death sentence is more likely for felony than for nonfelony murder—five to ten times more likely on the average within offender/victim racial categories.

But the table makes it equally clear that type of murder does not account for the racial differences in treatment observed in Table 5-2-1. For felony and for nonfelony homicides alike, the differences by race of both offender and victim shown in Table 5-2-1 are again evident. To be sure, as the Florida Attorney General argued in the *Spenkelink* case, black homicide victims are less likely than their white counterparts to be killed under the potentially capital, felony circumstances (evident from the base figures in the first and fourth columns of Table 5-2-2). But it is not true, as he alleged, that this difference in the kinds of murder perpetrated against blacks as compared with whites explains or accounts for the racial differences in treatment shown in Table 5-2-1.[9]

A closer examination of Table 5-2-2 reveals a slight but consistent specification of the pattern of racial differences in treatment by type of killing. For felony homicides, race of victim becomes more clearly the dominant factor. In each of the three states, by far the most substantial differences in the choice of a death sentence occur between those offenders who kill whites and those who kill blacks. In the case of nonfelony homicides, the overall pattern of differential treatment by race of offender and victim persists, but the greatest difference in both absolute and relative terms tends to be between the killings by blacks of white victims and all other racial combinations.

It appears, then, that among the kinds of killings least likely to be punished by death (i.e., nonfelony killings), the death sentence is used primarily in response to the most socially condemned form of boundary crossing—a crime against a majority group member by a minority group member. Among those offenders more commonly (but not usually or typically) punished by death (i.e., those committing a felony homicide), there is some suggestion that cases of boundary crossing in the opposite direction—with majority group offenders and minority group victims—are selected occasionally against the prevailing race of offender and victim influences for more severe treatment.[10] But this latter pattern is a minor variation on a major theme. The primary point is this: Among felony killings, for which the death penalty is more apt to be used, race of victim is the chief basis of differential treatment.

Table 5-2-2 also helps to clarify the effects of differences among the capital statutes of Florida, Georgia, and Texas. We noted in connection with Table

9. Ironically, the evidence of gross differences in the likelihood of a death sentence by race of victim presented in the *Spenkelink* appeal was restricted to cases of murder committed under felony circumstances (essentially the data for Florida in the first three columns of Table 5-2-2). With respect to these data, the argument that blacks were typically or disproportionately the victims of killings provoked by quarrels was essentially irrelevant. The data explicitly excluded the overwhelming majority of killings attributed to quarrels or similar passion-filled conflict. The failure to appreciate this point would appear to have been a fatal mistake even at the appellate level.

10. In each state the fewest homicides are reported for the white offender/black victim category. Hence, the likelihood estimates for this category are least stable, and comparisons between this category and the others are least reliable.

5-2-1 that the overall likelihood of a death sentence was somewhat greater in Florida than in Georgia, but that the differences were less for specific offender/victim racial categories. With the control for felony circumstances in Table 5-2-2, the differences between corresponding categories are still further reduced for killings under felony circumstances. Thus, compared with Florida, the likelihood of a death sentence in Georgia is 10 percent lower for black offender/white victim felony killings, 6 percent lower for white/white felony killings, and 11 percent lower for black/black felony killings. (The corresponding figures for all homicides in Table 5-2-1 are 24, 9, and 17 percent, respectively.) Among nonfelony killings, for which the death sentence is relatively unlikely, there are greater differences in some of the categories between the two states in relative terms. But by and large, the statutes of these two states yield similar levels and patterns in the use of the death penalty.

Moreover, Table 5-2-2 addresses a question raised earlier, about the manner in which the Texas "structured discretion" statute affects the likelihood of a death sentence. It is clear from Table 5-2-2 that the death sentence is less likely in Texas than in Florida or Georgia for felony as well as nonfelony killings. Obviously, the low likelihood of a death sentence in Texas is not simply the result of the statutory restrictions on the kinds of killings that qualify for the death penalty. It is evident that, for the kinds that qualify in all three states—namely, felony murders—Texas has relatively fewer death sentences. Apparently, the procedural questions of aggravation the Texas jury must answer have the effect of limiting the imposition of the death sentence in that state. These inferences are, of course, only as strong as the assumption that the killers are no more culpable and their crimes no more heinous in one state than another, or that the prosecutors, judges, and juries in the three states do not differ in their predilection for capital punishment.

The data in this section point to more than arbitrariness and discrimination in isolation. They reflect a twofold departure from even-handed justice which is consistent with a single underlying racist tenet: that white lives are worth more than black lives. From this tenet it follows that death as punishment is more appropriate for the killers of whites than for the killers of blacks and more appropriate for black than for white killers. Either discrimination by race of offender or disparities of treatment by race of victim of the magnitudes we have seen here are a direct challenge to the constitutionality of the post-*Furman* capital statutes. Together, these elements of arbitrariness and discrimination may represent a two-edged sword of racism in capital punishment which is beyond statutory control. [. . .]

We now know that there have been gross variations in the handlings of cases from offense through sentence by both race and location within the state, that these two extralegal factors have contributed independently to these variations in treatment, and that their effects are not attributable to the legally relevant difference between felony and nonfelony homicides. What we do not yet know is where in the criminal justice process the effects of race and place intrude and whether they are corrected by appellate review. In this section we examine discrete stages in the handling of potentially capital cases to find out whether the effects of such extralegal factors are concentrated at a particular point in the process or diffused and pervasive throughout the process. In the following section we will examine the appellate review process to see whether the differential treatment in presentencing and/or sentencing stages is corrected in the postsentencing stage of the process.

In the *Gregg* decision the Supreme Court held that mandatory capital statutes were unconstitutional and noted that they run the risk of having arbitrariness and discrimination displaced to earlier stages of the process—especially through "jury nullification" (the failure of a jury to convict an offender of a crime for which the death sentence is mandatory because, even though the jury may be convinced of the defendant's guilt, it is unwilling for other reasons to see the death sentence imposed). The Court reasoned that guided discretion statutes, on the other hand, would preserve individualized treatment in sentencing, eliminate arbitrariness and discrimination in sentencing, and, indeed, purge these ills from the exercise of discretion at earlier stages of the process.

In view of our findings thus far, the Court's assumption about the ability of guided discretion statutes to remove arbitrariness and discrimination from the overall processing of potentially capital cases appears to be mistaken. Whether the narrower assumption that such sentencing guidelines will eliminate these ills at the sentencing stage of the process remains uncertain at this point. This is particularly relevant since automatic appellate review of all death sentences is apt to become less effective as a tool for correcting such ills the further removed they are from the sentencing step of the process.

For this analysis we turn to the data on the processing of potentially capital cases in selected counties of Florida. Information was obtained on charges, indictments, convictions, and sentences in selected Florida counties. [...] These data can be used to examine discrete stages or decision points in the process: the decision to bring a first degree versus a lesser charge among all cases charged with criminal homicide; the decision to convict on a first degree murder charge versus acquit or convict on a lesser charge among all cases charged with first degree murder; and the decision to impose the death sentence versus a lesser sentence among all persons convicted of first degree murder.

Table 5-2-3 shows the likelihood of moving from one stage to the next in the judicial process for the various offender/victim racial categories. The pattern is clear and consistent. At each stage of the process, race of both offender and victim affects a defendant's chances of moving to the next stage.

Table 5-2-3. Charges, Indictments, Convictions, and Death Sentences in Florida for Criminal Homicide, by Race of Offender and Victim (from Effective Date of Post-*Furman* Statute Through 1977)

Offender/victim racial combinations	Numbers at each stage				Conditioned probability of moving between successive stages			
	All homicide charges at arraignment[a]	1st degree murder indictments	1st degree murder convictions	Death sentences	1st degree indictment given charge[a]	1st degree conviction given 1st degree indictment	Death sentence given 1st degree conviction	Overall probability of death sentence given charge[b]
Black kills white	67	193	83	39	.925	.430	.470	.187
White kills white	305	457	169	49	.666	.370	.290	.071
Black kills black	314	288	56	11	.366	.194	.196	.014
White kills black	21	20	3	0	.429	.150	.000	.000

[a]The figures in column 1 and the probabilities in column 5 are based on [a] subset of cases collected [. . .] of all homicide charges for offenses which occurred in 1976 or 1977.
[b]The probability of a death sentence given charges is calculated as the joint probability of columns 5, 6, and 7.

Race of victim differences are larger than race of offender differences at each stage, as they were from offense to death sentence in Florida, as shown in Table 5-2-1. As might be expected, the overall chances of a death sentence are greater in Table 5-2-3 than in Table 5-2-1; more of those charged with criminal homicide at arraignment (Table 5-2-3) than of those suspected and possibly arrested for criminal homicide (Table 5-2-1) will end up with a death sentence. [...]

The processing of felony- and nonfelony-type murder cases by race of offender and victim is shown in Table 5-2-4. For felony-related murders, racial differences are again present at each stage of the process (as in Table 5-2-3), and race of victim again predominates as the basis for differential treatment (as in tables 5-2-2 and 5-2-3). For the nonfelony murder cases, the pattern is different; for the most part, differential treatment occurs before sentencing. Differences by race of victim are evident at the conviction stage, and differences by race of both offender and victim are evident at the indictment stage. Thus, from charge through sentence (rightmost column of Table 5-2-4), the overall race of offender difference is due almost exclusively to the indictment stage, the overall difference by race of victim is due to the indictment and conviction stages, and very little of the overall difference is due to the sentencing stage of the process.

Two anomalies in Table 5-2-4 suggest further elements of differential treatment by race. The first is that the likelihoods of a death sentence for black offender/white victim and for white/white felony killings in Table 5-2-4 are less than the corresponding likelihoods in Table 5-2-2. This would seem unlikely. The felony-related cases in Table 5-2-4 have been charged with some level of criminal homicide in the courts, while those in Table 5-2-2 have only been reported as felony-type homicides by the police. We might reasonably expect more of those who reach the charging stage to receive a death sentence than of those who are reported and perhaps booked on a homicide charge by the police. Of course, this discrepancy could reflect a bias in the counties selected for the collection of court data.

A second anomaly may be the key to this paradox. The number of black felony killers of whites who were indicted for first degree murder is, according to Table 5-2-4, actually greater than the number committing such murders shown in Table 5-2-2. On the face of it, this appears impossible. Indeed, the larger number comes from a sample of selected counties while the smaller one represents the state as a whole. What this suggests is that a great many black offender/white victim homicides filed by the police as nonfelony killings are subsequently charged by the prosecutor as felony murders.

To a lesser extent, the same reclassification may be happening with white/white killings reported by the police as nonfelony homicides. Such upgrading of circumstances by prosecutors would certainly account for the lesser likelihood of a death sentence, using court data from indictment shown in Table

Table 5-2-4. Charges, Indictments, Convictions, and Death Sentences in Florida for Felony and Nonfelony Homicide, by Race of Offender and Victim (from Effective Date of Post-*Furman* Statute Through 1977)

Offender/victim racial combinations	Numbers at each stage				Conditional probability of moving between successive stages			
	All homicide charges at arraignment[a]	1st degree murder indictments	1st degree murder convictions	Death sentences	1st degree indictment given charge[a]	1st degree conviction given 1st degree indictment	Death sentence given 1st degree conviction	Overall probability of death sentence given charge[b]
Felony								
Black kills white	49	162	74	38	1.000	.456	.514	.234
White kills white	100	208	101	42	.970	.486	.416	.196
Black kills black	35	66	22	7	.800	.333	.318	.085
White kills black	1	10	2	0	—	.200	.000	—
Nonfelony								
Black kills white	18	31	9	1	.722	.290	.111	.023
White kills white	205	249	68	7	.522	.273	.103	.015
Black kills black	279	222	34	4	.312	.153	.118	.006
White kills black	20	10	1	0	.450	.100	.000	.000

[a]See Table 5-2-3
[b]See Table 5-2-3

5-2-4, than in Table 5-2-2, with the offense based on police data. And to the extent that other Florida prosecutors share the view expressed by the state's attorney general in the Spenkelink case, such upgrading of circumstances in white victim as opposed to black victim killings would be consistent with their perceptions and predispositions, if not prejudices. [...]

The differential treatment of these cases in terms of felony circumstances by race of offender and victim is unmistakable. When the cases reach the prosecutor's office, selective transformation occurs. Among blacks who kill whites, a majority of the cases in which police report no felony circumstance become felony-related cases in the court records. This occurs in every case the police report as a suspected felony. Among white/white killings this upgrading occurs for suspected felony cases, but it is less pronounced in the case of police-reported nonfelony killings. Among black/black killings there is little tendency for the courts to classify the circumstances of the cases as more severe than the police reports; indeed, there is a tendency for the courts to downgrade the court case records to reflect nonfelony circumstances when the police have reported a felony circumstance present. Either the police are peculiarly blind to the presence of a felony circumstance in the case of black killings of white victims, and overly sensitive to the hint of such a circumstance in black/black killings, or prosecutors are selectively transforming circumstances in police reports, not simply for advantage in any and all cases, but quite specifically in cases with white victims, especially if the offender is black. [...]

By way of summary at this point, suffice it to say that race is truly a pervasive influence on the criminal justice processing of potentially capital cases, one that is evident at every stage of the process we have been able to distinguish. It is an influence revealed not only in the movement from one stage to the next, but also in the decisions about circumstances, accompanying charges, and sentencing findings within the respective stages of the process. And it is an influence that persists despite separate sentencing hearings, explicitly articulated sentencing guidelines, and automatic appellate review of all death sentences. [...]

We have seen that the form of the law, as reflected in Ohio's quasi-mandatory statute and Texas's structured discretion statute, may affect the overall likelihood that a death sentence will be imposed, but without eliminating disparities of treatment by race of offender and victim. Furthermore, these racial disparities appear to be pervasive throughout the judicial process, as they were in the pre-*Furman* era, and they remain uncorrected by appellate review. Could it be that the laws themselves are the servants of extralegal purposes which "dictate where and when the death penalty will be most widely used ... and cause the legal functions of capital punishment to be displaced and compromised?"[11] Indeed, could it be that the form of the law,

11. Bowers, *Executions in America*, p. 166.

especially the nature of the sentencing guidelines, will be irrelevant except insofar as it establishes the legal framework through which extralegal purposes can be converted into legal actions?

If the death penalty's extralegal functions are the essential reason for its use, then we might expect to find that the laws under which it is imposed will be bent to accomplish these extralegal purposes. To illustrate the point, we offer the following hypothetical example. Suppose two states, A and B, have capital statutes with the very same list of aggravating circumstances. However, the statutes differ in that A's statute requires one aggravating circumstance and B's requires two such circumstances to be found for a death sentence to be imposed. Suppose, further, that the courts of states A and B are trying identical cases that vary among themselves in both legal and extralegal respects. Now, if the death sentence were strictly a function of legally relevant aggravating circumstances, we should expect to find more death sentences in state A, which requires fewer aggravating circumstances. If, on the other hand, the death sentence were a function of extralegal factors, such as race of offender and victim, we might expect to find the same number of death sentences in each state, but more aggravating circumstances cited by sentencing authorities in state B with the stricter requirement. Indeed, we might expect the aggravating circumstances found in state B to be disproportionately the less factual and more subjective of those circumstances enumerated in the statute.

Florida and Georgia have capital statutes that list very similar aggravating circumstances. Georgia's statute lists ten such circumstances [. . .] and Florida's lists eight [. . .]. In Georgia, a jury needs a finding of one and only one aggravating circumstance to recommend the death sentence. The trial judge is bound by the jury's recommendation. In Florida, on the other hand, aggravating must "outweigh" mitigating circumstances for the jury to recommend death as punishment, and the judge need not follow the jury's recommendation. It follows that sentencing authorities in Florida intent upon having the death penalty imposed can buttress this intention with each additional aggravating circumstance they find, whereas a Georgia jury can accomplish this purpose without risk by finding a single aggravating circumstance. If the death penalty is grounded in the extralegal functions it serves, we would expect Florida courts to find more aggravating circumstances than do courts in Georgia.

To examine this possibility, we have tabulated the aggravating circumstances found in Georgia and Florida for all cases on which reliable information could be obtained.[12] In Table 5-2-5 we list in abbreviated form the

12. In Georgia, the jury findings are reported by the trial judge in a questionnaire filed with the Georgia Supreme Court together with the transcript and other case materials as required by statute. The data on the jury findings with respect to aggravating circumstances were drawn from the published opinions of the Georgia Supreme Court, which routinely indicates the jury's findings of aggravation. In Florida, the jury makes a recommendation of life or death

Table 5-2-5. Aggravating Circumstances Found among Death
Sentences in Florida and Georgia (from Effective Dates of Respective
Post-*Furman* Capital Statutes)

Aggravating circumstances	Florida: % of total	Georgia: % of total
Accompanying felony	71	87
Vile, heinous, torturous, cruel	89	46
Pecuniary gain/Contracted murder	43	15
Prior felony conviction	35	6
Avoiding Arrest/Escaping conviction/In confinement	30	3
Risk to others	28	1
Murder officials/Disrupt government	20	4
Average number of circumstances found per case	3.16	1.63
(Total number of cases)	(92)	(99)

seven aggravating circumstances for which both Florida and Georgia have
close counterparts in wording and substance; and for each circumstance we
show the percentage of cases in which the circumstance was found. At the
bottom of the table we show the average number of aggravating circumstances found per case in each state.

To begin with, on the average there are twice as many aggravating circumstances reported for Florida compared with Georgia cases receiving the death
sentence—consistent with the argument that extralegal functions predominate. The findings of aggravation in the two states are most alike with respect
to the supposedly objective felony circumstance. In both states the large
majority of death sentences are handed down with felony circumstances
found by the sentencing authorities. In contrast, the findings of aggravation
most discrepant between the two states are those including the relatively
ambiguous terms, that is, the judgment that the crime was vile, heinous, torturous, cruel. In fact, there is a forty-three-point percentage spread between
the two states in this circumstance. Less than half Georgia's cases are judged
vile and heinous, compared with nine out of ten in Florida. For the remaining five aggravating circumstances, Florida exceeds Georgia in the proportion of cases found to have each of these circumstances. By every indication

without submitting a written statement of findings of aggravation. The trial judge files a
written sentencing memorandum with the Florida Supreme Court, which must report the
aggravating and mitigating circumstances present in the case and justify the finding that the
aggravating outweigh the mitigating circumstances. For Florida judges, memoranda available in sixty-three cases were consulted as the primary data source. Florida Supreme Court
opinions which provided statements of aggravating and mitigating circumstances quoting
or paraphrasing the trial judge's memorandum were also used as a data source.

here apart from the felony circumstance, it would appear that Florida's death sentences are handed down for much more aggravated murders than are Georgia's.

Are Florida's capital murders twice as heinous as Georgia's? In Table 5-2-6 we list seven objective indicators of aggravation, which can be expected to reflect the vile or heinous character of a killing. They include use of a gun as the murder weapon, which may reflect intent or premeditation; multiple offenders and multiple victims, both of which suggest an imbalance or excess in the circumstances leading to the killing; and youthful, elderly, and female victims, suggesting a relatively vulnerable victim whom the offender has attacked or exploited.

By most of these objective indicators, however, Georgia's capital murders would appear to be more heinous than Florida's. They are more often committed with a gun, by multiple offenders, and against female and elderly victims. Perhaps more important, the differences between the two states in any of the aggravating factors are not large, meaning that the crimes in these two states for which death sentences are imposed appear to be very much alike in objective indicators of aggravation.

These results are consistent with the proposition that the laws are bent to accomplish the extralegal functions of capital punishment. The crimes for which the death sentence is imposed in both states appear quite similar in objectively measured aggravating factors (Table 5-2-6); they are also quite similar in extralegal characteristics of offender and victim (Table 5-2-1). If the requirement that aggravating circumstances must outweigh mitigating

Table 5-2-6. Aggravating Factors Reported among Death Sentences in Florida and Georgia (from Effective Dates of Respective Post-*Furman* Capital Statutes)

Aggravating factors	Florida: % of total	Georgia: % of total
Gun as murder weapon	56[a]	65[c]
Multiple offenders	50	64
Female victim	36	36
Multiple victims	14	20
Victim 60 years or older	11[b]	23
Victim 16 years or younger	8[b]	10
Felony-related	82	87
(Total number of cases)	(92)	(99)

[a] Based on the 86 cases for which there is information on the murder weapon.

[b] Based on the 69 cases for which there is information on age of victim.

[c] Based on the 92 cases for which there is information on the murder weapon.

circumstances in Florida were actually guiding sentencing discretion, then we might expect the sentencing rate to be lower in Florida than in Georgia; but we know this is not the case. The likelihood of a death sentence is actually somewhat higher in Florida—.037 compared with .026 in Georgia.

These data suggest that sentencing authorities in Florida are finding aggravating circumstances in cases with respect to which Georgia sentencing authorities would not find aggravating factors. That the relatively ambiguous and subjective aggravating circumstance—namely, that the crime is vile and heinous—is the factor that most distinguishes the sentencing practices of Florida and Georgia provides support for this interpretation. In fact, this analysis suggests that the sentencing guidelines become the instruments of arbitrariness and discrimination, not their cure. [. . .]

§3.   Spenkelink's Last Appeal*

RAMSEY CLARK

The twelve-year unofficial moratorium on capital punishment in this country—a moratorium interrupted only by the death by firing squad of Gary Gilmore, who demanded to die—was ended by the electrocution of John Spenkelink on May 25. During the sixty-five hours prior to Spenkelink's death, a last-ditch appeal was mounted by two Georgia lawyers, Margie Pitts Hames and Millard Farmer, and former U.S. Attorney General Ramsey Clark, a longtime opponent of capital punishment. The following is Clark's account of that appeal, excerpted from a longer version. The issue Clark and his colleagues raised had not been previously considered in the six years of appeals in Spenkelink's case: Did he have adequate representation by his court-appointed counsel as required by the Sixth Amendment? The question was a grave one, but beyond that, Clark shows how the judicial system brushed it aside, brooking no further delays in the State of Florida's implacable drive to activate the death penalty.

The Editors [of *The Nation*]

John Spenkelink was scheduled to die at 7:00 A.M. Wednesday, May 23, at Raiford Prison in Florida. Tuesday morning I flew from my home in New York City to Jacksonville, where I was met by Henry Schwarzschild, director of the American Civil Liberties Union's Capital Punishment Project. We

*From Ramsey Clark, "Spenkelink's Last Appeal," *The Nation*, 27 October 1979, pp. 385, 400–404. Copyright 1979 The Nation Magazine.

drove to Starke, Florida, near Raiford Prison to protest the execution and to bear witness.

After a late-morning press conference outside the prison and another at mid-afternoon with Lois Spenkelink, John's mother, who brought what proved to be his last public statement, I had returned to town. I spent thirty minutes trying to place a telephone call and five reading the local paper. We ate a late lunch; then, to burn off energy while waiting for the all-night vigil, I took a walk through town and around the courthouse. As I crossed a filling-station apron on the main street, a young man ran up and said I had an emergency call at the motel. It was from Margie Pitts Hames, an Atlanta lawyer who is a friend and colleague in the A.C.L.U. It was 5:30 P.M.

Phones at the motel were tied up by the press. Circuits out of the small town of Starke were busy. After a few minutes we were able to place a call from the filling station and reached Margie in Tallahassee. She told me she had just talked to Millard Farmer, a Georgia lawyer who heads a compre-hensive litigation effort in death cases called Team Defense. Millard first studied the notes of a skilled appeals lawyer who had analyzed the trial tran-script carefully. This lawyer argued persuasively that the defense attorneys were ineffective. Reviewing the trial records himself, Millard was convinced that Spenkelink had been denied his Sixth Amendment right to the effective assistance of counsel. He had been formally authorized by John Spenkelink to enter his case earlier that day.

Margie had reviewed what Millard found, looked at parts of the trial record herself and agreed. She augmented Millard's work with her own find-ings and ideas and helped draft an original petition for a writ of *habeas cor-pus* raising the single question of effective counsel. Margie asked me to listen while she read the pleading; if I found it had merit, I was to fly to Atlanta and join them in presenting it to Judge Elbert P. Tuttle, a senior judge on the United States Court of Appeals for the Fifth Circuit.

She began a litany of allegations familiar to all who have followed capital trials in the United States these last years. John Spenkelink's trial attorneys were court-appointed. They lacked sufficient resources to prepare and con-duct the defense. One publicly stated that the case was beyond his compe-tence. One was absent during part of the jury selection to be with his wife in childbirth. He had not sought a delay in the proceeding or permission of the court to be absent.

Spenkelink's lawyers also failed to challenge the composition of the grand and petit juries. Both were later found to underrepresent blacks, women and young people—groups considered by most experienced attorneys to be favor-able to the defense in capital cases. The lawyers failed to ask that Spenkelink be tried separately from his co-defendant who was acquitted. Severance was authorized under Florida law and would seem strategically important. Coun-sel failed to challenge excessive security measures in the courtroom, which are generally thought to be prejudicial to a defendant. After reading the record, Millard Farmer believed the defense lawyers were too poorly informed on the rules of evidence and procedure in capital cases to conduct an effective defense. They had informed the jury in their closing argument that the judge could not impose a more severe sentence than the jury recommended. This may have encouraged the jury to ask for a maximum sentence, leaving the judge the full range of punishment alternatives. Counsel failed to obtain a transcript of questions asked prospective jurors, which was necessary in determining if they were constitutionally selected. The Florida Supreme Court ruled that all objections had been waived. With their client facing death, counsel did not request oral argument on appeal in the Supreme Court of Florida.

Next, Margie sketched in a background of John Spenkelink that convinced me he had not been adequately defended. With his strange foreign-sounding name, style, voice, appearance, a long criminal record, he had testified without any preparation or advice on how what he said might affect a jury. From years in prison, homosexuality and homosexual rape were something he could describe as naturally as jurors would a Sunday School picnic. A jury in Leon County, Florida, might find him guilty on his appearance and testimony alone.

Then came what was for me the clincher. Spenkelink's father was a paratrooper in World War II. He jumped with the 82nd Airborne Division. When it was nearly wiped out, he was transferred to the 101st. He fought in the Battle of the Bulge. The war weighed heavily on him. Life wasn't easy thereafter. To his son he was a hero.

One day, when John was 11, his father went into the garage, attached a hose to the car exhaust, started the motor, put the hose in his mouth and asphyxiated himself. John found his father dead on the garage floor with the hose in his mouth. The troubled youngster began a career of minor crime. Prison psychiatrists examining him over the years wrote that his criminal behavior was in large part due to the suicide of his father and that he was amenable to treatment. Incredibly, when the sentencing phase of the case was tried, these facts were not presented to mitigate the punishment. A jury would not give a death penalty in the face of such evidence. John Spenkelink was a second-generation casualty of World War II.

My own experience with capital cases, familiarity with the records of many other cases, and years spent working with the problems of obtaining lawyers to represent poor people accused of crime have taught me that the overwhelming majority of those on death row did not have effective assistance of counsel. Most were represented by court-appointed lawyers or public defenders. Few of these lawyers had much experience. All met with hatred from the community, the police and even the judiciary. They had no adequate resources to investigate and present a full defense. Their access to psychiatric and other professional services was severely limited. Many were afraid of their clients and unable to communicate meaningfully with them. Often they were so traumatized by the forces arrayed against them that they didn't press obvious points like fair jury selection, discovery of the prosecution case, insistence on public funds for investigation, or vigorously argue every issue.

Criminal defense counsel are usually young—conscientious and more courageous than the bar generally, but also less experienced, often overburdened with cases and usually underpaid and unable to finance the defense themselves. If the Sixth Amendment right to counsel is to have meaning, the question of effective assistance of counsel must be asked and answered constantly.

Lawyers hate to charge other lawyers with having failed to adequately represent a criminal defendant and rarely do. Where the defendant is indigent, it adds insult to injury. In death cases it is especially hard. Are you saying their indifference or incompetence cost a client his life?

Clark told Hames that he would leave immediately for Atlanta. On arriving, he hurried to Millard Farmer's office, where the petition for habeas corpus *was being typed up. By 11 P.M. Farmer, Hames and Clark were on the doorstep of Circuit Judge Elbert Tuttle. Tuttle, whom Clark has long regarded as "a genuine American hero," was for twenty years Chief Judge on the Court of Appeals for the Fifth Circuit during the stormy era of segregation cases, and consistently ruled to enforce constitutional principles in civil rights cases.*

Mrs. Tuttle answered the door, and graciously led us to her living room. As we settled down with Judge Tuttle, she retired. I had not seen him in a decade. Now in his early 80s, Judge Tuttle was as erect, dignified, alert and interested as ever. He knew of course why we were there. He stated at the outset that he was pleased to meet with us, that he would read our petition and hear our plea. But he cautioned us that he had not granted a writ of *habeas corpus* since assuming senior status a dozen years earlier and did not see how he could do so now. Then he asked why we had come from Florida to bring a Florida case to him. It was an important question. Forum shopping, as lawyers call it, offends the idea that courts dispense justice uniformly. It implies that judicial favoritism is being sought, an advantage gained by going outside the usual channels. The statute giving Judge Tuttle jurisdiction required an explanation of why the case was not taken to a Federal judge in Florida.

I gave him a hard, straight answer. This case had been in the courts for six years. The Federal district judges in Florida had reviewed it at length time and time again. It had been rejected on other grounds just the day before by the District Court in Florida. The Legal Defense Fund had made prodigious efforts at the District, Appellate and Supreme Courts levels.

Now we were eight hours away from an execution and a new and difficult question, never raised in the case, and one courts and lawyers alike abhor, was raised. Did Spenkelink's court-appointed Florida lawyers represent him effectively? There was little chance that judges with six years' involvement behind them would consider this new issue. And then it would be too late to go elsewhere. We needed a very courageous, very independent, open-minded and fair judge. That is why we chose Judge Tuttle. That is what I told him.

Millard Farmer described what he had found reviewing the trial record. Judge Tuttle was quick and to the point with questions. He knew the law and that he had jurisdiction and therefore the duty to decide. His first question was, why did a jury impose the death sentence?

Spenkelink's sentence cried out for explanation. This should not have been a capital case. Prosecutors pay little attention to murder among convicts. When blacks, convicts and other "despised poor" kill one another, our society has not cared so much as it does when "one of them kills one of us." Here there was a claim of self-defense, that the defendant had been homosexually raped and his money taken from him, that he had entered the motel room to recover his money and go his own way. The other man was older, bigger, stronger, had spent decades in prison and was in violation of parole at the time. He heard someone in his room. There was a struggle. He was killed. The death penalty is not normally asked for or given in such cases.

But Leon County, Florida, is special. More than half of all people on death rows in the nation are in three Southern states—Florida, Texas and Georgia. This unequal distribution only begins to suggest the severely limited number of jurisdictions prosecuting capital cases. Most of the more than 300 men in these three states were convicted in a handful of counties in each state. The prejudices of the prosecutors, political ambitions, local idiosyncracies, community attitudes in these counties were the determinants. Had these events occurred in nearly any of America's 3,000 other counties—or even in Leon County at another time—it is very unlikely the prosecutor would have asked for death.

Although I wasn't at the trial, only one explanation seemed an answer to Judge Tuttle's question: The jury hated John Spenkelink. His own testimony must have done it. An outsider with a strange name, a convict, a troublemaker, and finally a lifestyle that deeply offended the jury. A man describing his own rape, homosexual conduct, a life of crime, was scum, not to be believed, who ought to die.

The jury had heard no explanation of how Spenkelink came to be what he was. They didn't know that this man, as a child, had found his hero father dead, a suicide. Didn't know of the instability and pain in the family before the father's death. Didn't know how the child had been affected by finding the father he loved on the garage floor dead by his own hand.

When the story was told, Judge Tuttle did not hesitate. He said he would grant a stay of execution to permit consideration of the petition. He said it quietly, as simply as that. Did we have an order prepared? No, but Millard Farmer quickly wrote one out in longhand on a coffee table in Mrs. Tuttle's living room. While Millard wrote, the judge and I talked. He said he didn't favor abolition of the death penalty in all cases as he knew I did.

At 11:30 P.M. Judge Tuttle signed the order. We rushed to Millard's office in a state of euphoria. It was now after midnight. We encountered difficulty getting a phone call through to either the Governor in Tallahassee or the warden at Raiford. Millard found a pilot who would fly us to Florida, but before he could get the plane ready we had spoken with the authorities, who assured us that the stay would be honored without actual service of the papers. Millard arranged to have copies of our petition and Judge Tuttle's order available for the Attorney General that morning. We were confident that we would have full hearings on the issue of trial counsel's adequacy.

The stay of execution meant Judge Tuttle would either assign the matter to the appropriate district judge, or hear it himself. He wanted to meet with the parties to determine these issues Wednesday afternoon but the Attorney General's office declined. We outlined the issues and evidence for the hearing before I left. We could win this case, I felt. We could be ready for a hearing within weeks. I caught a flight to New York at 7 A.M.

Clark returned to New York, and the next day, Thursday, May 24, tried fruitlessly to reach Florida Attorney General Jim Smith, in order to learn if the State would seek an emergency review of Judge Tuttle's stay. Later, Clark learned that Smith had held a press conference at which he vowed that the execution would take place. Smith then flew to Washington and filed a motion in the U.S. Supreme Court to vacate Judge Tuttle's order. Clark and the other defense lawyers were given no chance to oppose this motion and Clark learned of it only after the results were announced. The Supreme Court, with only one dissent—Justice William Rehnquist—denied the State of Florida's appeal, and the stay held. Justice Rehnquist wrote that his "difficulty undoubtedly stems from six years of litigation." He said continuing appeals could "result in a situation where States are powerless to carry out a death sentence"; he was also critical of the defense's new contention that Spenkelink had not had effective counsel. Justice Rehnquist found it hard to believe that the defendant had suddenly determined this after six years of trial: "Either he does not believe the claim himself or he had held the claim in reserve, an insurance policy of sorts, to spring on a Federal judge of his choice if all else fails." Clark's response to this charge is: "To presume that a man whose life is at stake does not believe a claim made in his behalf with no evidence to support the presumption is a cavalier treatment of life and constitutional rights. To presume, as the exclusive alternative, that the claim was deliberately held in reserve as 'an insurance policy of sorts' is contrary to reason and the entire appellate history of the case which was vigorously

*presented. Mr. Justice Rehnquist decides issues of fact without the evidence
when a man's life is at stake."*

*The State had another card to play. At 7 P.M. on Thursday, as Clark was
about to go home, he received a call from the clerk of the U.S. Court of
Appeals in New Orleans, who told Clark that he was setting up a conference
call between three judges of the Court of Appeals—Judges James P. Coleman, Peter T. Fay and Alvin B. Rubin, who were to rule on a request from
the State of Florida that Judge Tuttle's stay of execution be set aside—Florida Attorney General Smith, and Millard Farmer, Margie Hames and Clark.
The call began (Judge Fay was unavailable), and the parties wrangled heat-
edly and inconclusively over technical questions of jurisdiction for an hour.*

The telephone conference was a nightmare. We were told at the beginning
not to record what was said. The court did not have our papers. We had not
seen the State's papers. Some factual statements in the State's papers were in
error, but we could not know this until we saw them some days later. We
were asked whether we had gone to Spenkelink and urged him to attack his
trial lawyers, to which we replied, if so, discipline us, do not kill him without
determining his rights. There was loose, unstudied, uninformed discussion
about whether Judge Tuttle had jurisdiction, whether he entered a final
order, whether the Court of Appeals had power to review his order.

It soon became clear that the bizarre late-night argument over long-dis-
tance phone among lawyers and judges who had not seen the papers in the
case nor been briefed on the issues was worse than meaningless; it was dangerous. I complained and Judge Coleman replied that he was not legally
required to give us the opportunity to discuss the matter over the telephone.
We asked for time to file affidavits and a response to the State's motion. The
merits of our petition for a writ of *habeas corpus* had been barely discussed.
A representative of the Attorney General's office, Margie, Millard and I made
some emotional conclusory statements and the call was over shortly after 8
P.M.

I returned home to wait. As the hour grew late, I became worried about
how I would get to Washington and the Supreme Court if the Court of
Appeals acted that evening. I phoned Judge Coleman, told him it was raining
in New York, there could be delays in transportation, the last flights and
trains were imminent, and that I must know whether I had to seek action by
the Supreme Court. He said he didn't know, they were having trouble agreeing, but he assured me I would have time to obtain review if it became necessary. I replied that Florida could march Spenkelink to the electric chair the
minute Judge Tuttle's stay was vacated. He said that as a former Attorney
General, he knew this and assured me any order his court might enter would
not be effective until I had time to seek review by the Supreme Court.

In view of the extraordinary procedure that had been followed, I had no
confidence what this meant. I called Attorney General Smith to urge him to

agree to time for briefing the issues before the Fifth Circuit. I told him we had done the court a disservice in the telephone discussion because no one had studied the issues or unusual procedures used. His public duty to fairness required study to be sure justice was done. He said he had been in the room in Tallahassee during the discussion, but decided not to speak. To my request, he answered only, "I couldn't do that."

About 11:50 P.M. the phone rang. It was the clerk of the Court of Appeals calling from New Orleans. He had an order to read. It was a page and a half. It cited four cases that had nothing to do with any issue before the Court of Appeals, and had not been mentioned before. It concluded, "We are convinced, for reasons which will hereafter be stated in a formal opinion, that the aforesaid stay should be vacated."

The order added, "The motion of Spenkelink for time in which to file supporting affidavits, etc., is denied. However, counsel on both sides have been given the benefit of an extensive discussion of the matter by conference telephone with a quorum of the court. Further ordered that this order vacating the stay of execution granted by Judge Tuttle shall become fully and formally effective at the hour of 9:30 o'clock Eastern daylight savings time, Friday, May 25, 1979. . . . Judge Rubin reserves the right to dissent for reasons to be assigned."

When I called Atlanta to tell Millard and Margie of the order, only nine and a half hours remained in which to present the matter to the Supreme Court. As a precaution, William M. Hames, Margie's husband and a senior partner in a distinguished Atlanta firm, had flown to Washington several hours earlier with a draft petition to the Supreme Court. We reworked it over the phone to conform to what we now knew of the actual order. Margie would call the changes to Bill in Washington. I would join him there. He would have the papers ready when I arrived.

The next commercial flight to Washington was at 7:00 A.M. Too late. The next train at 3:30 A.M. was due in Washington at 7:30. Too late. Joel Berger of the Legal Defense Fund helped me call charter flight companies but we could find nothing. So Jack Boger at the Legal Defense Fund picked me up shortly before 2 A.M. and we drove through heavy rain to Washington.

We could only seek a discretionary writ from the Supreme Court. It had denied such writs generally in death penalty cases since 1976. Indeed, although John Spenkelink had tried four times to obtain Supreme Court review, the Court had never considered his case on the merits. The Supreme Court had been battered by successive days of debate on a stay for him. On Thursday, it had denied two petitions in his case. It was hard to be optimistic now.

Bill Hames was already in the clerk's office when I arrived shortly after 6 A.M. I read the pleadings, we filed them and then waited for the clerk, Michael Rodak, to arrive.

Rodak came in about 7 A.M. He refused to see me. For more than an hour

Court officials would not say whether any Justice was in the building. We were to take it on faith that the Justices would actually see our pleading, a little painful when an execution is possible within hours. The procedure at that stage renders effective assistance of counsel meaningless. How can any lawyer be effective when he cannot know whether the judges receive his papers? The practice results from the Court's excessive desire for secrecy. Eventually, reporters told us who had been seen entering the building. Rodak continued to send word that he was "too busy" to see me. I could not find out whether the Court had notified the State of Florida that it was considering our petition.

Shortly after 10 A.M., I was handed an order. "The application for stay of execution, presented to Mr. Justice Powell and by him referred to the Court, is denied. Mr. Justice Brennan and Mr. Justice Marshall would grant the stay. Mr. Justice Blackmun took no part. . . ." At the bottom of the order were the initials W.E.B., apparently written by the Chief Justice of the United States. I wondered whether they were written larger, smaller, or the same as usual.

John Spenkelink was dead within half an hour. We are told he was denied the chance to make a last statement, verbally abused by the guards, fought removal from his cell, was gagged and forced to the chair. Three successive bolts of electricity were sent through his body. Parts of his body were burned. His fingers curled backward. An investigation of the methods of his execution has been made. There are still those who believe, like Dr. Guillotine, that there is a humane method.

As a lawyer I have no doubt that Judge James P. Coleman, joined by Judge Peter T. Fay, who did not see the papers we filed or hear arguments, violated John Spenkelink's constitutional right to due process of law. There can be only one explanation. Coleman wanted the man executed quickly, regardless of the law. Why the rush to execution? Why would he take the unprecedented action of reviewing the State's petition late at night without requiring it to be submitted first to Judge Tuttle? There is no greater expert on the very issues of jurisdiction the State raised than Elbert Tuttle. He is chairman of the Advisory committee on Civil Rules and vastly experienced in the subject matter.

The issues raised in the conference call were technical but very important.[1] Why did Coleman proceed after years of careful, painstaking litigation to compel exhausted lawyers and the court to discuss a life-and-death case late

---

1. Judge Coleman based jurisdiction on an appellate rule even though no appeal had been taken, so the case was not even properly before his court. He ignored the *habeas corpus* statute, which denies the Court of Appeals jurisdiction over original petitions for *habeas corpus*. He considered a stay order a "final order" in violation of a statute that required a certificate of probable cause—a stay order that was clearly made in order to preserve jurisdiction.

at night, over the phone, without exchanging papers, without giving time for review or study, without allowing time for supporting affidavits? Why did he not wait until Judge Fay could hear the argument? Why did he cite four irrelevant cases never mentioned in the papers or the discussion in an order written at home and dictated over the phone to a clerk?

How could he decide the matter without having facts to judge whether there had been effective assistance of counsel? Since Judge Fay did not hear argument and should not have voted, and because Judge Rubin ultimately dissented, how could he decide to vacate Judge Tuttle's order? And why had he not given his reasons? Judges deciding death cases ought to give reasons.

Having waited several weeks for the formal opinion he had promised, I called the clerk and inquired about it. I was called back and asked to send a letter. I did. No answer. I wrote again. Finally, on July 23, two months after John Spenkelink's execution, the clerk's office wrote "that in review of the action taken by the United States Supreme Court subsequent to that taken by the Court in the stay for Spenkelink, the majority of the panel does not intend to write anything further with reference to this case." Attached was a memo dated July 18 from Judge Rubin. "I reserved the right to dissent from the order issued by the panel in this case, and I now confirm that I do dissent, on procedural grounds, from that action." He too declined to give reasons.

I wrote the court on July 28, asked for reconsideration of the decision not to write an opinion and inquired: "Are we to believe a formal opinion has not been written because a formal opinion which justified the court's action which led immediately to Mr. Spenkelink's execution cannot be written?" There has been no reply. The courts must require a full review of the effectiveness of trial counsel and the adequacy of funds for investigation and expert witnesses in every capital case if Sixth Amendment rights are to be fulfilled. They should initiate procedures now to alleviate a pervasive problem.

Worse than Justice Rehnquist's hostility and Judge Coleman's abuse of power is the direction their petulance over delays takes. Courts may well resent the absurdity of years of appeals with hundreds on death row. It holds the judiciary up to ridicule. But that is no reason to kill a man.

The reason death cases drone on in our courts is that America no longer has the will for capital punishment. If we executed one person each working day it would be years before we would catch up with the backlog. We will not do it. And as the anguish increases it will become clear that equal protection of the laws is not possible with the death penalty. We will not even afford the accused, nearly always impoverished, the price of an adequate defense. It will be the capricious cases, Gary Gilmore with a desire to die, John Spenkelink denied due process, that result in death.

Eventually we will declare capital punishment unconstitutional. Someday we may even proclaim life the first human right.

§4. Miscarriages of Justice
and the Death Penalty

Some years ago, an experienced prosecutor and defender of the death penalty examined the issue of the "fallibility" of criminal justice in capital cases. He concluded: "I . . . feel that there is little chance for an innocent man to be sentenced to death" (Gerstein 1960:255). A few years earlier, however, a sociologically trained lawyer and opponent of the death penalty argued, after reviewing the history of judicial miscarriages, "it is highly probable that erroneous convictions for capital crimes are greatly underreported" (Pollack 1952:123). Superficially, it may look as if these are contradictory judgments. But "little chance" of a wrongful death sentence is not inconsistent with the occasional execution of an innocent man. There is also no inconsistency in a large but unknown number of erroneous capital *convictions,* and few if any erroneous death *sentences.* Courts can use discretionary powers to accept a plea bargain to a lesser offense or to sentence to prison rather than to death, thereby keeping "innocent men" from being "sentenced to death." In addition, it is possible to have an "erroneous conviction" of a person who is not truly innocent; the conviction may be of the correct person but secured on the basis of perjured testimony, a coerced confession, suppression of evidence favorable to the accused, or in a number of other ways that violate the rights of the guilty. Who is to count as "innocent," in any case? Only someone completely uninvolved in the crime? Or also someone involved, but quite peripherally? As long as questions of this sort can be controverted (if not by lawyers and judges, then by the ordinary man), it is extremely difficult to know what would suffice to show that an "innocent" person had been convicted, sentenced, or executed.

Yet even if the quotations above from Gerstein and Pollack can be read literally in ways to avoid contradiction, surely their spirit is incompatible. Where the one bolsters confidence in our relatively superior though not infallible judicial system, the other raises the haunting spectre of convict after convict unable to establish his innocence from the prison or the grave. Which view is more nearly correct?

Nearly twenty years ago I attempted to answer this question with the data then at my disposal. Putting aside the most notorious injustices (e.g., Mooney in California, the Scottsboro Boys in Alabama) as well as the highly controversial cases (e.g., Hauptmann in New Jersey, the Rosenbergs in New York) still left 74 cases between 1893 and 1962 involving criminal homicide, and thus the possibility of a death sentence, in which the evidence suggested that the following major errors had occurred: In each of the 74 cases, an innocent person was arrested and indicted; in 71, the innocent person was convicted and sentenced; in 30 (including 11 in states with no death penalty), there was a sentence to prison for life; in 31 cases, there was a sentence to death; in *eight an innocent person was executed* (Bedau 1964a:438).[1]

Newcomers to the death penalty controversy, along with many opponents of capital punishment, may have viewed these data as confirmation of their worst fears. Others were not so sure. First, it was pointed out, although some of these judicial miscarriages had occurred quite recently, the last execution of an allegedly innocent man was in the 1930s, and so was ancient history, a misleading guide to the administration of justice in capital cases for the 1960s and beyond. Second, defenders of the death penalty argued that with several thousand executions in the seventy years under review, the wrongful execution of only eight was evidence of the reliability and near infallibility of the system, not of the reverse. Surely, it could be argued, parole boards during those same seven decades had been far more fallible than the courts, since more than eight murderers released from prison had gone on to commit murder a second time (recall Chapter Four, §5). So what are we to make of the claims at present of an opponent of the death penalty who argues that capital punishment is "inevitably" prone to "mistake" in its administration (Black 1974)? Where is the evidence of all those mistakes?

It is impossible to give an adequate reply to these questions in no more than a few paragraphs (the same difficulty afflicts the even briefer remarks on these points in the essays by Amsterdam and Black in Chapter Eight). First, as the analysis above suggests, one needs to use the concepts of an "innocent man" and of a "mistake of justice" with some care and sophistication. Second, one needs to understand the incredibly deficient state of empirical research in this area and the problems faced in improving upon it. Finally, one needs to realize that despite these complexities and difficulties there is a cumulative record of error where the death penalty is or might be concerned, beginning with false confessions prior to arrest and ending with reprieves that came too late, a record that is bound to give any but the most callous reader serious pause. Each of these problems deserves closer examination; here there is space to consider only the first two.

What *should* count as a miscarriage of justice where the death penalty is or might be involved? In 1970, an Arkansas farmer was killed by one among a group of teenage youths. The boys were arrested and Joey Newton Kage-bien was the first to be tried; he was convicted of first-degree murder and sentenced to death. Joey was not tried for having shot the farmer, however; "all the testimony indicated that he was not the boy who fired the shot—and that he was asleep in the car during most of the arguing and scuffling. The

1. In an essay to be published elsewhere, I intend to report on fifty or more miscarriages of justice in capital cases, the results of once again having combed the sources at my disposal for the period 1930 through 1980; these fifty are all "new" cases and are to be added to the earlier list of 74 such cases published in the mid-1960s (see Bedau 1967b:434–452).

prosecution did not contend that Joey did the shooting. . . ." But he was present at the killing and he was found guilty of "aiding or abetting" the murder, a capital offense in most jurisdictions; there is little doubt that one of his pals did shoot and kill the farmer.[2] Was Joey "innocent" of first-degree murder? Was sentencing him to death at the discretion of the jury a "miscarriage of justice"? (Kagebien was one of the hundreds spared further risk of the electric chair by the *Furman* ruling in 1972.) In a very different sort of case, James Mullooly was convicted of manslaughter in 1963 in the shooting of an oil company executive in the New York Port Authority Terminal. There was no doubt that he killed the deceased, but nine years later (1972) the Manhattan Supreme Court agreed that Mullooly "lacked the mental capacity to stand trial" for the killing.[3] Was it, then, a "miscarriage of justice" to hold him responsible for the act, to convict him of a crime, and to punish him for it? If his excuse is legally and morally valid (and let us assume it is), should not his conviction for *any* degree of criminal homicide count as judicial error? Consider now a completely different kind of case. In 1973, a Tampa jury convicted Clifford Hallman of killing a woman, and sentenced him to death. While Hallman was on death row, it was established that the victim died because she "did not receive proper attention at the Tampa General Hospital emergency room." Hospital malpractice, not murder, was the cause of death, as the out-of-court settlement by the hospital with the deceased's estate indicated. The prosecuting attorney publicly conceded that Hallman deserved a new trial; although he did not get one, he did get his death sentence commuted.[4] The death sentence for Hallman, however reasonable it may have seemed to the jury in light of the facts presented at trial, could not in retrospect look appropriate. But does Hallman qualify as "innocent"? These three cases are the merest handful from a vast number that show it is not easy to decide what should count as a "miscarriage of justice," a "judicial error," or a "mistake," and that it ill-behooves anyone to be complacent about the reliability or infallibility of the criminal justice system under which we live.

Constructing a valid record of the worst cases—execution of the unquestionably innocent—entails solving some difficult problems. Most such cases remain in the limbo of uncertainty. *The New York Times* in 1978 reported a story originating in the *St. Petersburg Times* to the effect that the execution in 1964 of Sie Dawson, a black man, for the murder of a white woman and her child was not only unfair (he confessed only "after he was alone with white officials for several days"), it was far worse. He was, so the story went, innocent and known to be innocent ("the woman's husband had committed

2. *Boston Globe*, 6 September 1971, p. 57.
3. *The New York Times*, 16 December 1972, p. 35. Perhaps the most detailed discussion of a miscarriage of justice along these lines is to be found in Wright 1974.
4. *Tampa Tribune*, 25 July 1976, pp. 1A, 19; 26 July 1976, p. 1A; 27 July 1976, p. 1a; 28 July 1976, p. 1A; 29 July 1976, p. 1A; 27 July 1979, p. 1A. See also Gettinger 1979:166–182.

the crime").[5] The original news story merely reported allegations and was inconclusive; no subsequent inquiry known to me has established whether Dawson really was innocent. For every case thoroughly researched by experienced investigators, such as Edwin M. Borchard (1932), Earle Stanley Gardner (1952), Edward D. Radin (1964), and the most recent and perhaps the best, William J. Lassers (1973), there are several more like that of Sie Dawson where the question marks are never removed. The crucial difference is that, unlike those who survive a death sentence, receive exoneration, and have their full story told (e.g., Zimmerman 1973; Pitts and Lee, see below), Dawson is dead and all but forgotten.[6]

Once the convicted capital offender is dead, it becomes virtually impossible to set the record straight. Borchard, Gardner, and the rest confine themselves almost exclusively to erroneous death sentences that were *not* carried out. Herbert Ehrmann, in contrast, tried valiantly all his adult life to convince the world that Sacco and Vanzetti were wrongly executed in 1927 (Ehrmann 1960 and 1969). Walter and Miriam Schneir have made the execution of Julius and Ethel Rosenberg look like a scandalous miscarriage of justice (Schneir 1973). The latest effort of this sort is the reinvestigation by Anthony Scaduto in *Scapegoat* (1976) of the famous Lindbergh baby burglary-kidnapping-ransom-murder for which Bruno Richard Hauptmann was executed in 1936. If Scaduto is right, no far-reaching conspiracy railroaded Hauptmann to the electric chair, even though Hauptmann had nothing to do with the crimes for which he was put to death. The many who testified against him, as well as those who prosecuted and convicted him, did so convinced from the start of his guilt. Unconsciously and each for his or her own motives, they "bent the facts" in order to condemn him. Was Hauptmann (or were Sacco and Vanzetti, or the Rosenbergs) really innocent? How can we tell, fifty years later? More precisely, what forum exists in which to retry such cases? Who is entitled to render authoritative judgment on the work of posthumous investigators where the execution of an innocent man is alleged, argued, documented? It is doubtful whether anyone could ever "prove" that a ghastly error was committed when a famous convict, such as Hauptmann, let alone when an utterly obscure one, such as Dawson, was sent to his death.

5. *The New York Times,* 17 April 1978, p. A12.
6. Of the many cases currently under litigation in which wrongful conviction has been argued, none is more notorious than the case of Johnny Harris, who pled guilty in 1971 in Alabama to five capital charges, was imprisoned, and then convicted of killing a prison guard in 1974; he is currently under death sentence. See the statement by Bishop Paul Moore, Jr., on behalf of The Committee of 100 (NAACP Legal Defense and Educational Fund, Inc.), n.d. [1980]. In December 1980, another death penalty convict, Jerry Banks, was released from prison in Georgia after wrongful conviction of murder in 1975; see *The New York Times,* 26 December 1980, p. A31. In California, Aaron Lee Owens served eight years in prison, having been wrongfully convicted of a double murder in 1972; he was released in March 1981 by the same judge who had tried him. See *Boston Globe,* 7 March 1981, p. 3.

Then there are cases that are verified, but presented in such vague and sketchy detail that years later they are no more than a blur in the memory. Earle Stanley Gardner, famous for his Perry Mason detective thrillers and his "Court of Last Report," conducted in the pages of *Argosy* magazine in the 1950s, did much to expose and rectify wrongful convictions. He once reported how he averted an execution at the last moment in West Virginia, but he failed to name the year or the fortunate convict. All he said was that after his intervention, "I had the satisfaction of having a member of the Pardon Board . . . say, in effect, 'We have just finished running down all of the clues which you folks turned up in that case, and we have come to the conclusion that the defendant is absolutely innocent'" (Gardner 1970:539). If this is the case of someone who was scheduled to die but was spared and later exonerated and freed, it may well be one of the most dramatic instances in the past generation of judicial error averted at the last moment. As of now, it remains an anonymous and undatable event.

The full record must also include the cases of alleged judicial error that turn out not to have been so erroneous after all. Edgar Smith was brought to national attention while on New Jersey's death row thanks to the interest taken in his case during the 1960s by William F. Buckley, Jr., the well-known conservative columnist and host of the television show *Firing Line*. Sentenced to death for murder in 1957, Smith had always protested his innocence and struggled mightily to overturn his conviction. In his eleventh year on death row, one of New York's most prestigious publishing houses released his version of the crime, *Brief Against Death* (1968); it opens with a long and sympathetic introduction by Buckley. Three years later the federal courts at last awarded Smith the new trial he had sought for so long, on grounds of a coerced confession. New Jersey was given sixty days in which to retry him or set him free. After much deliberation, Smith chose to "confess" to the 1957 crime in open court; he was immediately sentenced to the time he had already served, and released. He promptly recanted his confession (Buckley described it as "court theater"), and explained it was designed to close the case by letting New Jersey salvage something from its fruitless efforts over fourteen years to execute him. Five years later, however, in San Diego, Smith was again in court, this time for kidnapping, assaulting, and attempting to murder a woman. He now admitted, theatrics behind him, that he had indeed committed the 1957 murder; he was convicted of his latest crimes and is now serving a life term in a California prison.[7] Thus the Smith case is not only the story of failed rehabilitation. It is also the story of a

7. *The New York Times,* 13 October 1971, p. 19; 7 December 1971, p. 1; 9 October 1976, p. 25; 14 November 1976, p. 37; 26 April 1977, p. 31; *New York Post,* 30 March 1977, p. 29; *Asbury Park Evening Press,* 12 December 1971, editorial page; *The National Observer,* 18 December 1971, p. 6; transcript of "The Edgar Smith Story—Part I," from *Firing Line,* program of 12 December 1971.

murderer who masqueraded as an innocent man for nearly twenty years. Perhaps Smith *was* the victim in 1957 of a coerced confession, so that a new trial was his due on that ground. But by 1976 his guilt was no longer in doubt. Perhaps some of the other cases that have been regarded as strong candidates for entry into the unofficial annals of judicial error also do not belong there.

Some miscarriages of justice, however, loom so large that no one can doubt them. One of the most dramatic recent cases of this sort is that of Freddie Pitts and Wilbert Lee, who spent 12 years in jail and prison in Florida, most of it on death row, for a crime they did not commit. A full version of their story is given in Gene Miller's book *Invitation to a Lynching* (1975). A briefer version, as told by *New York Times* correspondent James T. Wooton, is reprinted below.*

After 12 years in jail for someone else's crime, Freddie Pitts and Wilbert Lee walked out of prison here today, into the bright autumn sunshine and new lives as free men.

The state, which twice convicted them of murder and kept them on death row for nine years after another man confessed to the crime, gave them an executive pardon and $100 and sent them on their way.

They did not look back.

"Is it over, Freddie?" Mr. Lee asked softly as the gates of the Florida State Prison hummed and buzzed and then opened electronically in front of them.

"It's over, man," said Mr. Pitts as they strode through together. "It's really over."

So it was. What many have branded the saddest, most blatant miscarriage of justice in Florida's history was finally resolved—12 years, 1 month, 19 days after it all began. For some, it has embraced all that was notoriously and traditionally grievous in Southern society—the racism, the poverty, the bigotry given silent but forceful sanction by government and law. For others, it has been a painful laboratory for change—the indefatigable efforts of a Pulitzer Prize–winning journalist, two ill-paid lawyers, and a tiny cadre of black and white civil libertarians who were vindicated here today. But for Mr. Pitts and Mr. Lee, it was simply a nightmare.

On August 1, 1963, Mr. Pitts was a 28-year-old pulp cutter and Mr. Lee was a 20-year-old Army private on leave. That night, along with a woman and several other people, they pulled into a service station in Port St. Joe, a tiny town on the Gulf Coast, about 300 miles west of here. Because of a "whites only" restriction on the service station rest rooms, the two men, both black, argued with Jesse Burkett and Grover Floyd, Jr., the two white atten-

*James T. Wooton, "'It's Over' for Two Men Wrongly Imprisoned 12 Years," *The New York Times*, 20 September 1975, pp. 1, 13. ©1975 by The New York Times Company. Reprinted by permission.

dants. Three days later the bodies of the white men were found, shot to death. The woman who was with them accused Mr. Pitts and another soldier—not Mr. Lee—of the murders. When the Army provided a firm alibi for the second solder, she accused Mr. Lee instead, and the two men were arrested and charged with first-degree homicide.

They were beaten by policemen into a confession, they said, and pleaded guilty at their court-appointed lawyer's suggestion. "There is no other way," he was quoted as saying. They were sentenced to death on August 28, 1963, the same day the late Rev. Dr. Martin Luther King Jr. delivered his famous "I have a dream" speech in Washington. They were again convicted and again sentenced to death, but the Supreme Court's invalidation of capital punishment removed that burden. In the meantime, Willie Mae Lee, the woman who originally accused them, retracted her story and said she had been coerced into naming them as the killers—forced, she said, by the police "into naming somebody." While the prosecutors and other state officials knew of her retraction, they did not mention it. The case remained dormant until last year when Arthur Kennedy, an Alabama-born, Yale-educated lawyer who is Gov. Reubin Askew's legal adviser, read a draft-copy of Mr. Miller's soon-to-be published book about the case, *Invitation to a Lynching*.

Convinced of their innocence, Mr. Kennedy persuaded the Governor that there was at least a serious and substantial question of their guilt, and a long investigation was ordered. It culminated this week in the granting of an executive pardon, signed by Governor Askew and three members of his Cabinet. "The evidence which was not available at the trial and now [is] available is conclusive," the Governor said. "These men are not guilty."

Mr. Pitts and Mr. Lee were stoic when they heard the news. "I don't know how I feel," said Mr. Lee, now 32. "I don't think I will until I'm 300 or 400 miles away from this place."

Today, the two men appeared at a brief news conference wearing new, nonprison clothes. While both were taken back slightly by the herd of reporters and photographers, they seemed also to be very much in control of themselves. They were grim faced, and their tension was broken only once when both laughingly responded to a reporter's question about the single thing they did not have in prison that they most wanted now. "We'll just keep that to ourselves," said Mr. Pitts, now 40.

After two more hours of processing, shortly past noon they appeared at the gates with their attorneys. A guard inside touched a button and the gates slid open. From the windows of the three-story prison buildings, guarded by dozens of police dogs, 12-foot fences topped by barbed wire and obelisk gun towers, their former cell inmates shouted lusty farewells and words of encouragement—but Mr. Pitts and Mr. Lee did not look up or back. They just kept walking toward the cars that would take them first to Miami—and then to their new lives.

Their lawyer said they would go into seclusion for a while before making any firm decisions on future plans. They said it was possible that they might sue the state for compensation.

Watching their progress toward the cars, Mr. Miller, the 47-year-old reporter was characteristically muttering to himself. "God, that is a beautiful, beautiful sight," he said, and behind his glasses there were uncharacteristic tears.

§5. The Cost of the Death Penalty*

BARRY NAKELL

Many people mistakenly believe that it is less costly to execute a murderer than to keep him in prison for life. Although at one time capital punishment was cheap, we are no longer willing or able to march condemned prisoners expeditiously from the courthouse to waiting gallows. Today, considering all the costs—including the financial expense and the wear and tear on our courts and prisons—a system of capital punishment is considerably more expensive than a criminal justice system without capital punishment.

Do not misunderstand. The point is not that it is cheaper to keep a particular person in prison for life than it is to execute him. It is, rather, that the system—the judicial and correctional processes—will be less expensive if it is not burdened by a death penalty. [. . .]

The *trial process* is more expensive in a capital punishment system.

Ordinarily criminal cases, including murder cases, are resolved by guilty pleas and without the expense of a trial. Eight-five or 90 percent are determined that way.[1] All capital cases, by contrast, require jury trials—and the trials are longer, more complex, and more expensive than those in other cases, including other murder cases.

Although a defendant may be permitted to plead guilty to capital murder, few will do so. The reason is simple. Defendants plead guilty to win some measure of leniency, such as a reduction in the degree of the charges, the dismissal of other charges, or an expectation of favorable consideration in sentencing.[2] Their guilty pleas are the product of bargaining between their

---

1. See President's Commission on Law Enforcement and Administration of Justice, *Task Force Report: The Courts* 9 (1967).

2. Id.; see also *Santobello* v. *New York,* 404 U.S. 257, 260–61 (1971); *Brady* v. *United States,* 397 U.S. 742, 749–50 (1970).

*Excerpted from Barry Nakell, "The Cost of the Death Penalty." Reprinted by permission from the *Criminal Law Bulletin,* Volume 14, Number 1, January–February 1978, pp. 68–80. Copyright 1978, Warren, Gorham and Lamont Inc., 210 South Street, Boston, Mass. All Rights Reserved. Footnotes have been renumbered and cross-references adjusted accordingly.

lawyers and the prosecutors. Some defendants charged with capital murder will win concessions by the prosecutor in the form of a reduction of the degree of the crime to a lesser homicide, but then the case is no longer a capital one. No longer is it meaningful to talk about the death penalty in such a case. Here the existence of the death penalty only serves as bargaining leverage for the prosecutor.

When the death penalty is a real consideration in a case, the prosecutor has nothing to offer the defendant in exchange for a guilty plea. The natural result is that few defendants will plead guilty.

Even those who do plead guilty, however, will still have a jury trial on the issue of penalty. This means that every capital case will require a jury trial *(ten times as many jury trials as in noncapital cases)*—and that most will require at least two jury trials. But not only will there be more jury trials in capital cases, those trials will also be longer and more expensive.

Jury trials will be more protracted and more expensive in capital cases for several reasons. First, the jury selection process will be longer and involve more jurors. There is an inherently greater difficulty in selecting juries for capital cases because many prospective jurors are opposed to the death penalty. Opposition to the death penalty is not a ground for disqualifying a juror from service on a capital jury unless the juror is adamantly unwilling to vote for the death penalty in any case, regardless of the facts that are developed in the trial.[3] As a consequence, considerable time is spent in capital cases with the lawyers exploring with the jurors on voir dire their personal views regarding the death penalty. The upshot is still the disqualification of many jurors on this ground. In addition, each side is generally allotted a larger number of peremptory challenges in a capital case.

Capital cases naturally capture public attention and attendant publicity, and this fact further complicates their trials. Juries must be selected from among people whose views on the case have not been prejudiced by publicity.[4] This often means moving the trial of the case away from the publicity to a different county, subjecting the citizens there to the burdens of the trial of a capital case not involving their community. Or jurors may be summoned from another county to attend the trial in the county where the crime occurred. Either method increases the costs of the trial. Even then, the lawyers must take court time to discuss with the prospective jurors the effect, if any, that the publicity may have had on them, and this could result in the disqualification of more members of the panel.

Once the jury is selected, the trial is still more complex and longer than noncapital trials. Difficult issues such as the insanity defense are more likely

---

3. *Davis* v. *Georgia*, 97 S. Ct. 399 (1976); *Witherspoon* v. *Illinois*, 391 U.S. 510 (1968).
4. *Murphy* v. *Florida*, 421 U.S. 794 (1975); *Sheppard* v. *Maxwell*, 384 U.S. 333 (1966); *Rideau* v. *Louisiana*, 373 U.S. 723 (1963); *Irvin* v. *Dowd*, 366 U.S. 717 (1961).

to be raised,[5] and to be more expensive to litigate because of the necessary involvement of expert witnesses. When the trial reaches the second or penalty phase of the bifurcated process, the defendant's whole life is open for exploration. No longer is the trial confined by relevancy limitations to the circumstances surrounding a relatively narrow incident. Instead, any evidence that tends to shed light on the background, behavior, and beliefs of the defendant, or his personal, family, business, or social life, may be introduced, disputed, and debated.[6] Expert witnesses are likely to be called here, even if they were not called in the first trial, to evaluate these facts and explain their meaning to the jury.

The *appeals process* is more expensive in a capital punishment system.

When all that is over, there will be more appeals in these cases. If the judgment is death, the case will be appealed; indeed, most statutes provide for automatic appeal of death sentences.[7] The appeal will be more thorough, reflecting the same kinds of judicial concerns about assuring the reliability of the fact-finding and sentence-determining missions of the jury as prompted the more elaborate procedural machinery for death cases in the first place. Historical experience teaches that appellate courts are more likely to find errors in death than in noncapital cases, and that those errors are characteristically more likely to be found prejudicial. This applies to federal and state courts across the country. Much "bad law" has been written to accommodate the special concerns of courts in death cases. For examples: the United States Supreme Court decisions in *Witherspoon* v. *Illinois*[8] providing special rules against jury disqualification in capital cases,[9] in *United States* v. *Jackson*[10] providing special limitations on plea bargaining in capital cases, and in the 1976 death penalty cases themselves, providing special procedural requirements in capital cases.[11] This is not a new phenomenon. It is as old as the

---

5. See Goldstein, *The Insanity Defense* 143, 167–70 (1967); cf. *O'Connor* v. *Donaldson*, 422 U.S. 563 (1975); *Jackson* v. *Indiana*, 406 U.S. 715 (1972); *Humphrey* v. *Cady*, 405 U.S. 504 (1972); *Baxstrom* v. *Herold*, 383 U.S. 107 (1966).

6. See *Gregg* v. *Georgia*, 428 U.S. 153 (1976), at 203–204 (plurality opinion); *Proffitt* v. *Florida*, 428 U.S. 242 (1976), at 248 (plurality opinion); *Jurek* v. *Texas*, 428 U.S. 262 (1976), at 267, 276 (plurality opinion).

7. See, e.g., Fla. Stat. Ann. § 921.141(4) (Supp. 1976–1977); Ga. Code Ann. § 27-2537(a) (Supp. 1976); N.C. Gen. State. § 15-2000(d)(1) (Supp. 1977).

8. 391 U.S. 510 (1968).

9. Indeed, last term in *Davis* v. *Georgia*, 97 S. Ct. 399 (1976), the Court held that *Witherspoon* requires reversal of a capital sentence even if only one juror is excluded in violation of its principle.

10. 390 U.S. 570 (1968).

11. See also *Gardner* v. *Florida*, 97 S. Ct. 1197 (1977). In that case last term, the Supreme Court held that the Constitution forbids a trial judge to impose a death sentence on the basis of confidential information that is not disclosed to the defense. The judge may do so in noncapital cases. *Williams* v. *New York*, 337 U.S. 241 (1949). Indeed, the Court acknowledged in its plurality opinion in *Gardner* that five of the Justices "have now expressly recognized

death penalty in civilized countries. The broadening of the old "benefit of clergy" is a prominent historical example.[12] The reports of early state decisions provide other striking examples. One North Carolina decision voided a death sentence solely because the indictment contained the following misspelling in the description of the place of the fatal wound: "in and upon the aforesaid left *brest* of him."[13]

So, we will not only have more trials in capital cases, we will also have more *retrials*. The complex, expensive processes will be repeated more frequently than usual.

We must note further that the appellate review in capital cases will be by the state supreme courts. In ordinary cases in most states, intermediate courts of appeals relieve the state supreme courts of much of their workload. Not so with capital cases. They go directly to the state supreme courts.[14]

Furthermore, those courts will be required to perform a role new to most of them: they will have to review the *sentence* as well as the conviction. The new statutes provide for that procedure, and the 1976 death penalty cases probably require it. In order for appellate review of the sentence to fulfill its function in this scheme, the appellate court must have information about the actual practices of juries in deciding which cases deserve death and which do not, and probably also about the policies of prosecutors in selecting cases for capital consideration by juries.[15] This requires a new bureaucracy for data collection and evaluation to be available to the Supreme Court, an additional expense. The Georgia scheme upheld by the Supreme Court provides expressly for such bureaucratic assistance for its state supreme court,[16] but the Florida and Texas schemes, also upheld, do not. Although the bureau-

---

that death is a different kind of punishment than any other which may be imposed in this country." Id. at 1204.

12. 1 Stephen, *A History of the Criminal Law of England* 459–72 (1883).

13. *State* v. *Carter,* N.C. Court of Conf. Rep. 210 (1801).

14. See statutes cited at note 7 *supra.*

15. The statute upheld in *Gregg* v. *Georgia* requires the state supreme court to collect the records of all recent "capital felony cases." 428 U.S. 153, 167 n.10. The Supreme Court observed that the statute authorizes the state supreme court to consider not only cases in which a death sentence was actually meted out but also convictions for capital crimes that resulted in noncapital sentences, and that the Court "does consider appealed murder cases where a life sentence has been imposed." Id. at 204 n.56; see also id. at 233 n.11 (White J, concurring).

   Evidently, this comparative appellate review is acceptable to the Court even though it does not include a systematic method for the state court to canvass convictions for all capital crimes. Cf. id. at 225 (White, J., concurring). The Court said that it did not find "that the Georgia courts review process is ineffective." Id. at 204 n.56.

16. The statute upheld in *Gregg* v. *Georgia* specifically provides for the employment by the state supreme court of a staff to "accumulate the records of all capital felony cases" and "to compile such data as are deemed by the Chief Justice to be appropriate and relevant to the statutory questions concerning the validity of the sentence." Ga. Code Ann. § 27-2537(f), (g), (Supp. 1976); see *Gregg* v. *Georgia,* note 15 *supra,* at 167 n.10, 204 n.56.

cracy may not itself be constitutionally necessary or statutorily provided, it will develop if the state supreme courts take their role seriously in this regard, as they can certainly be expected to do. Thus, through the Administrative Office of the Courts, through a new agency established for this purpose, or by adding law clerks or administrative assistant to their present staffs to collect and analyze the necessary information, the state supreme courts will need additional expensive resources to carry out their responsibilities in death cases.

A state supreme court decision affirming a judgment of death does not finally settle the validity of the conviction and sentence. The exceptional example of Gary Gilmore notwithstanding, prisoners sentenced to death exhaust every imaginable avenue for relief. They seek review in the U.S. Supreme Court, file postconviction petitions in the state courts, file habeas corpus petitions in the federal courts, ask their governors for commutation, and then, if still unsuccessful, file more state and federal applications for review. Many other prisoners exhaust judicial resources in a similar manner, but all capital convicts do so. Moreover, the courts generally give all of their petitions conscientious scrutiny. The expenses involved in the compensation of the attorneys who represent them, the state attorney generals' officers who resist them, and the courts that review them need to be computed among the financial costs of the death penalty.

The *corrections process* suffers in a capital punishment system.

The death penalty imposes terrible strains on our prison system. Special security precautions require that a portion of state prisons be designated a "death row," a maximum security section warehousing condemned convicts during the years that their cases are processed through the appeals, habeas corpus, and clemency application stages. The expenses of "administering the unit add up to a cost substantially greater than the cost to retain them in prison for the rest of their lives."[17] The existence of such a cellblock has a deleterious effect on the prison of which it is a part and on the entire prison system. It increases tension by a geometric factor. It has a dehumanizing effect on inmates and staff alike—staff who serve only as custodians with no way to help or offer hope to its charges.

Without the sentence of death, the condemned would not necessarily be the most dangerous prison inmates demanding the limited single cells available for strict security. In consequence, the prison system is severely restricted in its ability to find secure space for its own troublemakers. This creates a maddening situation for corrections administrators.

The time surrounding an execution, shortly before and until some time after, is an extraordinarily difficult time in the prisons. The execution weighs

17. McGee, "Capital Punishment as Seen by a Correctional Administrator," 28 Fed. Probation 13–14 (June 1964).

heavily on all the inmates and guards, creating major and minor problems throughout the system.

An important observation that squares with commonsense expectations has been confirmed in empirical research:[18] The actual imposition of the death penalty under the new guided-discretion capital punishment systems has been similar to that under the former unguided discretion systems. Most of the defendants who go through the capital process of jury trial, possible appeal, penalty trial, possible retrial, appeal, possible postconviction challenges, possible commutation application, will ultimately avoid the death penalty and receive sentences of life imprisonment. The Supreme Court noted that juries with sentencing discretion in first-degree murder cases do not impose the death penalty "with any great frequency."[19] What this means is that after squandering the extraordinary resources, financial, judicial, and correctional, to make the life or death decision in these cases, these people will still be on our hands for life imprisonment—and all the expenses involved with that.

Thus, although it may cost less to execute a particular prisoner than to maintain him for life, it costs far more to finance a system by which we decide to execute some people and end up still maintaining for life many of the people processed through that system. Yet, the wear and tear of the process on our judicial and correctional systems and on the hearts and minds of our citizens and our government servants—and the exorbitant financial costs—have never been shown to serve a useful governmental purpose.

Some argue that the enormous cost is justified by the deterrence and retribution purposes of the death penalty.[20] But we have no reliable basis for believing that the death penalty serves either. [. . .]

Concern about costs seems petty when issues affecting life or death are at stake, and seems a pedestrian argument among the philosophical, moral, and religious positions against the death penalty. Those who are not convinced by the loftier arguments against the death penalty, however, should at least be persuaded by this cost-benefit analysis that capital punishment is a bad investment of public resources.

18. Riedel, "Discrimination in the Imposition of the Death Penalty: A Comparison of the Characteristics of Offenders Sentenced Pre-*Furman* and Post-*Furman*," 49 Temple L.Q. 261 (1976).

19. Woodson v. North Carolina, 428 U.S. 280, 295, 295–96 n.31.

20. The Supreme Court observed: "The death penalty is said to serve two principal social purposes: retribution and deterrence of capital crimes by prospective offenders." *Gregg* v. *Georgia*, note 15 *supra*, at 183 (plurality opinion). The Court observed that retribution is not "a forbidden objective nor one inconsistent with our respect for the dignity of men." Id. With regard to deterrence, the Court recognized that the results of the studies of the deterrent effect of capital punishment "simply have been inconclusive," id. at 185, but nevertheless surmised, without supporting data, id. at 186 n.34, that, for some murderers, "the death penalty undoubtedly is a significant deterrent." Id. at 185–186.

6

Is the Death Penalty
"Cruel and Unusual" Punishment?

INTRODUCTION

The continuing review that appellate courts seem willing to give to the constitutionality of the death penalty is actually a quite recent development (recall Chapter One). Underlying the essentially perfunctory review given in earlier decades to the now-familiar methods of execution (see M. Gardner 1978) was the assumption that the death penalty as such is without doubt consistent with the constitution. What other conclusion could be reached? Several passages of the federal constitution (adopted 1781) and the Bill of Rights (1789) take for granted that "life" may be forfeited in punishment, and the prohibition against "cruel and unusual punishment" (Eighth Amendment)—the most likely source of constitutional difficulty with capital punishment—was adopted at a time when hanging was the lawful punishment for many crimes (see Grannuci 1969). Two decades ago, however, change was in the wind. A pioneering law review article appeared (Gottlieb 1961), Justices Arthur J. Goldberg, William O. Douglas, and William J. Brennan wrote a novel dissent in a death-penalty-for-rape case, *Rudolph* v. *Alabama* (1963), and both the American Civil Liberties Union and the NAACP Legal Defense and Education Fund resolved to attack the death penalty head-on as unconstitutional (see Meltsner 1973). At the core of these developments was a challenge to the complacency with which the appellate courts had allowed the Eighth Amendment prohibition of "cruel and unusual punishment" to become dead-letter law. The result of these efforts transformed both the politics of the death penalty controversy (Bedau 1979) and the kinds of arguments that have come to dominate public debate.[1] It is the latter that specially concerns us here.

Arguments over the constitutionality of the death penalty can be divided into those that precede and those that begin with the watershed decision of *Furman* v. *Georgia* (1972). Pre-1972 decisions of the Supreme Court regarding the death penalty can usefully be grouped into three types. In one category were the decisions upholding a given mode of execution, however novel, on the unargued assumption that the death penalty itself was not "cruel and unusual punishment," e.g., *In re Kemmler* (1890), holding electrocution not to be unconstitutional. In a second category were those few but important decisions—notably, *Witherspoon* v. *Illinois* (1968) and *McGautha* v. *California* (1971)—holding in effect that if the death penalty was unconstitutional, it was not because it was in violation of the "due process" or "equal protection" clauses of the Fourteenth Amendment. In a third category were decisions in which the Court settled in favor of the defendant but in a manner that evaded addressing an important constitutional challenge to the death penalty laws themselves, e.g., *Boykin* v. *Alabama* (1969). Far more typical than these three kinds of cases, however, were the many involving a death sentence where the Court simply refused to intervene at all. In the vast majority of cases where there was appellate court intervention that averted an execution, it was not to nullify a death penalty *statute* nor even to invalidate a death *sentence* as such; it was only to order a new trial on the ground that the *conviction* of a capital crime was a violation of some fundamental constitutional protection, e.g., *Powell* v. *Alabama* (1932), holding that failure to provide counsel in a capital case violated "due process" as required under the Fourteenth Amendment.

Thus, the death penalty itself seemed immune to fundamental constitutional attack, and this invulnerability remained intact until a decade ago. The first break with tradition was *Ralph* v. *Warden,* a 1970 case in the federal Circuit Court of Appeals for Maryland. The court held that the death penalty for rape, where "the victim's life was neither taken nor endangered," was "disproportionate" to the gravity of the crime and so was an unconstitutionally "cruel and unusual punishment." The second was *People* v. *Anderson,* decided early in 1972 by the California Supreme Court at the very time the Burger Court was weighing its decision in *Furman.*[2] *Anderson* held that the

---

1. Wilson 1977:206ff. has claimed that recent arguments both for and against the death penalty have been largely "utilitarian" rather than based on appeals to "justice." This may be true of the public debate generated by advocates on both sides (see Chapters Seven and Eight, below); it is not true of the constitutional debate conducted and generated by the Supreme Court that began with *Furman.*

2. Mention should also be made of the variety of arguments against the death penalty on Eighth Amendment grounds that appeared after Gottlieb 1961 and that helped, however slightly, to pave the way for the decision in *Furman:* Bedau 1968; Greenberg & Himmelstein 1969; Rubin 1969; Goldberg & Dershowitz 1970; and Black 1971.

death penalty as such was "cruel or unusual punishment" in violation of California's state constitution. Against this background *Furman* v. *Georgia* was argued, decided, and announced on 29 June 1972.

In *Furman,* the Court ruled that the death penalty as then administered, with trial juries free to sentence to death or to life without any standards or guidelines to help (or force) them to make rational and uniform sentencing choices, was "cruel and unusual punishment in violation of the Eighth and Fourteenth Amendments." Because the Court majority was fractured five separate ways, however, it was no small exercise in interpretation to determine on precisely which issues the Justices agreed.[3] Undoubtedly uppermost in their minds was the belief that the evidence clearly showed the death penalty had been for some time inflicted in a "wanton" and "freakish" manner, except insofar as it was predictably reserved for "outcasts of society," "unpopular groups," the poor in general and the nonwhite poor in particular. From this they inferred that the death penalty as administered could not be serving effectively any legitimate social purposes (deterrence, retribution, denunciation) not better served by a less severe punishment free of these faults. So they were ready to infer as well that such a severe penalty as death cannot be consistent with the constitutional requirements specified in the Eighth and Fourteenth Amendments. In the excerpts printed below in §1, from four of the five members of the *Furman* majority, these and some subsidiary themes are plainly evident.

The dissenters, on the other hand, all Nixon-administration appointees and led by Chief Justice Warren E. Burger, were a solid bloc in defense of the death penalty. As individuals most of them indicated their opposition to executions as a matter of social policy. But as federal judges they were prepared to argue that this mode of punishment as currently administered was properly within the constitutional prerogatives of the several states to determine for themselves. Thus the posture of "judicial self-restraint" before the legislative branch and respect for the "federal compact" are themes recurrent in the opinions filed by the dissenters. They also challenged each of the central factual generalizations on which the majority relied: The death penalty has *not* been shown not to be a deterrent, or not to be a deterrent more effective than imprisonment; the practices of trial courts in sentencing to death or to life have *not* been shown to be arbitrary or racist; the evidence of general social repudiation of the death penalty is *not* conclusive or persuasive.[4]

Furman spawned controversy and criticism among legal and constitutional scholars.[5] More than that, it immediately provoked annoyance within

3. For a behind-the-scenes account of the Court's private deliberations in *Furman,* see Woodward & Armstrong 1979:204–20.
4. For a discussion of how the Supreme Court used (and misused) social science information in *Furman,* see White 1974; also Wolfgang 1978 and Daniels 1979.
5. See especially Polsby 1972; Wheeler 1972; A. Goldberg 1973; and Black 1974.

the Nixon administration,[6] and an angry backlash in several states, where legislatures promptly redrafted and re-enacted death penalty statutes that they believed would withstand the inevitable litigation over their constitutionality.[7] The legacy of *Furman* gave such legislatures only two options. The death penalty could be made *mandatory,* so that upon conviction there would be no question as to the sentence—a possible option (there were still in 1972 a few mandatory death statutes and *Furman* was understood not to have invalidated them) but not an attractive one, because it was so plainly a throwback to an earlier era (recall Chapter One). Or the death penalty could be made a consequence of *guided discretion.* For this purpose, the trial courts would have to adopt a "bifurcated" trial procedure, in the first part of which the issue of guilt would be settled in the usual way, and in the second or penalty phase the trial court's sentencing powers would be hedged with statutory criteria for deciding which convicted capital offenders would get death and which would be given life in prison. The Model Penal Code, developed by the American Law Institute during the 1950s and 1960s, had recommended this scheme (if the death penalty were not to be abolished) and so had the National Commission on Reform of Federal Criminal Laws in its 1971 report; but no legislature had seen fit to enact such requirements. Moreover, the Supreme Court itself had cast some doubt on the feasibility of this route in its 1971 ruling in *McGautha.*[8] Yet only this alternative offered tempting variations, at least some of which might pass constitutional muster. In 1976, after four years of silence during which thirty-five states enacted new death penalty laws and nearly 500 persons were again under death sentence, the Court ruled on both types of post-*Furman* capital statutes.[9]

In *Woodson* v. *North Carolina* and *Roberts* v. *Louisiana,* the Court argued that the mandatory alternative was inconsistent with the deeper meaning of *Furman.* But on the same day, in three other cases—*Gregg* v. *Georgia, Jurek* v. *Texas,* and *Proffitt* v. *Florida*—the Court ruled that the death penalty was not unconstitutional as such under the Eighth and Fourteenth Amendments, and at least these three statutory schemes were a rea-

6. A brief account is provided by Bedau 1973b; some conjectures on the significance of the Nixon administration's position will be found in Bedau 1979:63f.
7. The events in Florida are more or less typical, and have been better documented than elsewhere; see Ehrhardt et al. 1973, and Ehrhardt & Levinson 1973. On Texas, see Comment 1974.
8. Cf. the oft-quoted passage from the Court's opinion written by Justice John Marshall Harlan: "Those who have come to grips with the hard task of actually attempting to draft means of channeling capital sentencing discretion have confirmed the lesson taught by ... history.... To identify before the fact those characteristics of criminal homicides and their perpetrators which call for the death penalty, and to express these characteristics in language which can be fairly understood and applied by the sentencing authority, appear to be tasks which are beyond present human ability" (*McGautha* v. *California,* 402 U.S. 183, at 204).
9. For a digest and critique of these statutes, see Browning 1974 and Note 1974.

sonable response to the mandate of *Furman*.[10] As I have observed elsewhere, the common denominator that emerges from the Court's rulings in *Gregg, Jurek,* and *Proffitt* is that capital punishment is not unconstitutional as long as the statutes under which it is imposed provide, in one way or another, for 1. opportunity to put before the court information about the defendant to assist it in reaching the sentencing decision, 2. special emphasis on any mitigating factors that affect the defendant's blameworthiness, 3. common standards to guide trial courts in their sentencing decisions, and 4. review of every death sentence by a state appellate court (Bedau 1977a: 113). The Court's reasoning in these five cases filled more than a hundred pages, and three dozen separate opinions were filed. A representative fraction has been excerpted below, in §§2 and 3, from *Woodson* and *Gregg,* respectively, the two leading cases.

Since the Court's rulings in *Gregg, Jurek,* and *Proffitt,* it has generally been acknowledged that only a change in personnel on the Court itself and the passage of time are likely to produce any further major constitutional restrictions on the death penalty. *Furman* and *Woodson,* barring unfettered discretion and mandatory sentencing, respectively, are not likely to be modified, much less overturned, despite the narrow margins by which they were decided. Similarly, death penalties for crimes other than murder—notably, for rape—are likely to be judged excessively severe, disproportionate to the harm done in the crime, and therefore unconstitutional. But the death penalty for murder, especially in its aggravated forms and suitably defined by statutory sentencing criteria uniformly applied and scrutinized by mandatory review in state appellate courts, apparently will survive (see Donohue 1980).

These judgments have been confirmed in the several death penalty decisions by the Court since 1976. *Coker* v. *Georgia* (1977) effectively ended the possibility of a death penalty for rape where the victim is not killed (see White 1976).[11] *Eberheart* v. *Georgia* (1977) summarily dismissed the death penalty for kidnapping on the rationale (as in *Coker*) that the death penalty was "disproportionate" for this non-homicidal crime. *Harry Roberts* v. *Louisiana* (1977) nullified attempts to keep a mandatory death penalty as long as it was confined to a special category of victim, in this case, the killing of a police officer. *Lockett* v. *Ohio* and *Bell* v. *Ohio,* both decided in 1978, underlined the principle laid down in *Woodson* to the effect that trial courts must aim at "particularized" death sentences; to do so they must not be hampered by statutes that prevent them from considering "*any* aspect of a defendant's character or record" that the defendant's attorney proffers the court (empha-

10. The Court's private struggles over the decisions in these five cases has been recounted in Woodward & Armstrong 1979:430–42.

11. As recently as April 1981, however, a Tallahassee (Florida) judge sentenced to death, contrary to the jury's recommendation, a black male adult for the rape and sexual battery of his 8-year-old female cousin. *Gainesville* (Florida) *Sun*, 2 May 1981, p. 8B.

sis added). *Beck* v. *Alabama* (1980) struck down the part of the Alabama death statute that prohibited a conviction-minded jury from considering a verdict of guilt of a lesser included (noncapital) offense. Brief excerpts from the opinions in two of these cases have been included in §§4 and 5, below.

Perhaps the most interesting feature about the Court's rulings since *Gregg* is the degree to which the Court is willing to scrutinize the records of capital sentencing decisions to verify whether the post-*Furman* death statutes in actual day-by-day application yield results that are not in violation of the Eighth and Fourteenth Amendments. In *Gardner* v. *Florida* (1977), for example, the Court held that the Florida courts had failed to sentence Gardner and to review his death sentence in strict conformity with their own statutes. So egregious was the failure that Justice Thurgood Marshall was prompted to observe that "the blatant disregard exhibited by the courts below for the standards devised to regulate imposition of the death penalty calls into question the very basis for this Court's approval of that system in *Proffitt.*" Similarly, in *Godfrey* v. *Georgia* (1980), the Court held that the aggravating condition under which Godfrey had been sentenced to death (his offense, in the language of the statute, was "outrageously or wantonly vile, horrible or inhuman in that it involved torture, depravity of mind, or an aggravated battery to the person") had in practice been given such a broad and vague interpretation by the Georgia courts as to revive the worst features of the standardless death sentencing ruled against in *Furman.*

But it is the situation in Texas, under the statutes approved in *Jurek,* that has drawn the most fire from commentators. Texas requires as a necessary condition of every death sentence that the trial court find "a probability that the defendant would commit criminal acts of violence that would constitute a continuing threat to society" (*Texas Code of Criminal Procedure,* 37.071(b)(2)). Critics have had a field day, not only with the vagueness of this language, but with the irrelevance, as shown by the actual record in case after case, of what Texas prosecutors have put in evidence and juries accepted as proof of such a "probability."[12] It is hard to see how most Texas death sentences could survive close scrutiny by the Supreme Court, but the Court has yet to decide a case in which the content and patterns in these records become the focus of scrutiny.

Thus it appears that since 1976 the Court has moved cautiously and grudgingly, step-by-step, away from any wholehearted embrace of the very death statutes (and of the death sentences imposed under them) nominally inspired and validated by the Court's own rulings. The result leaves no one happy. Justice Marshall, who—with Justice Brennan—has been the staunchest opponent on the Court of the death penalty in any form, remarked recently that, in light of the actual death penalty cases reviewed and reversed since 1976, "the enterprise on which the Court embarked in *Gregg* v. *Georgia*

---

12. See Dix 1977 and 1978; P. Davis 1978b; and Black 1976. For a defense of the Texas statute, see Crump 1977.

... increasingly appears to be doomed to failure." Justice William Rehnquist, meanwhile, the only member of the Court who has not joined in even one decision against the death penalty, complained that "the Court has gone from pillar to post, with the result that the sort of reasonable predictability upon which legislatures, trial courts, and appellate courts must of necessity rely has been all but completely sacrificed." It seems highly unlikely that the near future will find the Court acting in a manner that will gratify either Justice Marshall or Justice Rehnquist.[13]

Although attacks on particular death sentences continue, and can be expected to do so in the future, the issues being raised on behalf of the convicted offender are unlike those that prompted the class-action suits of the 1960s that culminated in *Furman*. Instead, as the current digest of death penalty litigation summarized each month in the *Death Penalty Reporter*[14] shows, death sentences and the underlying capital convictions are under review in state and federal appellate courts on many grounds having nothing to do with the unconstitutionality of the death penalty per se. To this extent we have entered an era in which we can expect to see the development of largely non–Eighth Amendment criticisms of the death penalty and in this way something of a throwback to the period prior to the 1960s.[15]

§1.   Most Death Penalties Are Unconstitutional: *Furman* v. *Georgia* (1972)

[*Editor's note:* The decision in *Furman,* 408 U.S. 239 (1972), along with two related cases, *Jackson* v. *Georgia* and *Branch* v. *Texas,* was delivered on 29

13. Commentary on the constitutionality of death penalty statutes reviewed in or inspired by *Gregg, Jurek,* and *Proffitt* may be found in many sources, including: Bedau 1977a and 1977b; Black 1977 and 1978 (a portion of the latter is reprinted below, in Chapter Eight, §2); Radin 1978; R. Gardner 1978; Donnelly 1978; Palmer 1979; P. Davis 1978a; Richards 1977; and Adelstein 1979. Analysis of the constitutionality of the death penalty in particular states may also be consulted with profit: On Oregon, see Kanter 1979; on Texas, see note 12 above; on Wyoming, see McCall 1978. For views on the death penalty held by former Justices of the Supreme Court who did not participate in *Furman* or its progeny, see Fortas 1977; A. Goldberg & Dershowitz 1970; and A. Goldberg 1972, 1973, and 1976. For an unusually outspoken attack on the "arcane niceties" to which the Supreme Court has subjected all post-*Furman* death penalty cases, see the remarks of Justice Rehnquist in dissent in *Coleman* v. *Balkcom,* as reported in *The New York Times,* 28 April 1981, p. D23.

14. See note 4, Introduction to Chapter Two, for further information on this new serial.

15. Thus, double jeopardy has recently been extended to prevent a convicted murderer from being sentenced to death after conviction in a new trial, when at the first trial he was convicted and sentenced to imprisonment; see *Bullington* v. *Missouri,* as reported in *The New York Times,* 5 May 1981, p. B15. See, generally, Radin 1980.

June 1972. The Court divided 5 to 4, with the majority able to agree only on a brief *per curiam* judgment. Each of the five Justices in the majority wrote his own opinion, and none concurred in the opinion of any of the others—an unusually splintered majority. Justice Douglas's opinion, the last he was to write on the death penalty before illness forced his retirement from the Court, is reprinted here minus some footnote citations and text. The crucial "swing votes," provided by Justices Potter Stewart and Byron White, were explained in rather short opinions, reprinted here almost in their entirety (again, minus some references). Justice Brennan's opinion, one of the longest in this case and the most ambitious and sweeping in its attempt to present an articulated philosophy of Eighth Amendment penal jurisprudence, has been edited more severely, on grounds of space. Most of the content of Justice Marshall's lengthy opinion can be gleaned from the other four opinions and from other empirical and historical material elsewhere in this book, hence his opinion is not reprinted. Among the four dissenting Justices, each also filed an opinion. With the exception of Justice Harry A. Blackmun's, in which no other Justice concurred, the opinion each dissenter wrote was joined by all the other dissenters. Excerpts, however, have been reprinted here (with some footnotes omitted as well) only from the leading opinion in dissent by Chief Justice Burger. The full text of the decision and opinions in *Furman*, at 243 pages the longest in the history of the Supreme Court, is available only in the law reports. The best commentary on events surrounding the briefing, oral argument, and decision is to be found in Meltsner 1973:246–305. The fullest discussion of the *Furman* case, beginning with the crime itself, is to be found in Stevens 1978.]

Per Curiam. Petitioner in No. 69-5003 was convicted of murder in Georgia and was sentenced to death pursuant to Ga. Code Ann. § 26-1005 (Supp. 1971) (effective prior to July 1, 1969). 225 Ga. 253, 167 S.E.2d 628 (1969). Petitioner in No. 69-5030 was convicted of rape in Georgia and was sentenced to death pursuant to Ga. Code Ann. § 26-1302 (Supp. 1971) (effective prior to July 1, 1969). 225 Ga. 790, 171 S.E.2d 501 (1969). Petitioner in No. 69-5031 was convicted of rape in Texas and was sentenced to death pursuant to Tex. Penal Code, Art. 1189 (1961). 477 S.W.2d 932 (Tex. Ct. Crim. App. 1969). Certiorari was granted limited to the following question: "Does the imposition and carrying out of the death penalty in [these cases] constitute cruel and unusual punishment in violation of the Eighth and Fourteenth Amendments?" 403 U.S. 952 (1971). The Court holds that the imposition and carrying out of the death penalty in these cases constitutes cruel and unusual punishment in violation of the Eighth and Fourteenth Amendments. The judgment in each case is therefore reversed insofar as it leaves undisturbed the death sentence imposed, and the cases are remanded for further proceedings.

So ordered.

Mr. Justice Douglas, concurring. In these three cases the death penalty was imposed, one of them for murder, and two for rape. In each the determination of whether the penalty should be death or a lighter punishment was left by the State to the discretion of the judge or of the jury. In each of the three cases the trial was to a jury. They are here on petitions for certiorari which we granted limited to the question whether the imposition and execution of the death penalty constitutes "cruel and unusual punishment" within the meaning of the Eighth Amendment as applied to the States by the Fourteenth. I vote to vacate each judgment, believing that the exaction of the death penalty does violate the Eighth and Fourteenth Amendments. [. . .]

We cannot say from facts disclosed in these records that these defendants were sentenced to death because they were black. Yet our task is not restricted to an effort to divine what motives impelled these death penalties. Rather, we deal with a system of law and of justice that leaves to the uncontrolled discretion of judges or juries the determination whether defendants committing these crimes should die or be imprisoned. Under these laws no standards govern the selection of the penalty. People live or die, dependent on the whim of one man or of twelve. [. . .]

In a Nation committed to equal protection of the laws there is no permissible "caste" aspect of law enforcement. Yet we know that the discretion of judges and juries in imposing the death penalty enables the penalty to be selectively applied, feeding prejudices against the accused if he is poor and despised, lacking political clout, or if he is a member of a suspect or unpopular minority, and saving those who by social position may be in a more protected position. In ancient Hindu law a Brahman was exempt from capital punishment,[1] and in those days, "[g]enerally, in the law books, punishment increased in severity as social status diminished."[2] We have, I fear, taken in practice the same position, partially as a result of making the death penalty discretionary and partially as a result of the ability of the rich to purchase the services of the most respected and most resourceful legal talent in the Nation.

The high service rendered by the "cruel and unusual" punishment clause of the Eighth Amendment is to require legislatures to write penal laws that are evenhanded, nonselective, and nonarbitrary, and to require judges to see to it that general laws are not applied sparsely, selectively, and spottily to unpopular groups.

A law that stated that anyone making more than $50,000 would be exempt from the death penalty would plainly fall, as would a law that in terms said that blacks, those who never went beyond the fifth grade in school, those who made less than $3,000 a year, or those who were unpopular or unstable

1. See J. Spellman, Political Theory of Ancient India 112 (1964).
2. C. Drekmeier, Kingship and Community in Early India 233 (1962).

should be the only people executed. A law which in the overall view reaches that result in practice[3] has no more sanctity than a law which in terms provides the same.

Thus, these discretionary statutes are unconstitutional in their operation. They are pregnant with discrimination and discrimination is an ingredient not compatible with the idea of equal protection of the laws that is implicit in the ban on "cruel and unusual" punishments.

Any law which is nondiscriminatory on its face may be applied in such a way as to violate the Equal Protection Clause of the Fourteenth Amendment. *Yick Wo v. Hopkins,* 118 U.S. 356. Such conceivably might be the fate of a mandatory death penalty where equal or lesser sentences were imposed on the elite, a harsher one on the minorities or members of the lower castes. Whether a mandatory death penalty would otherwise be constitutional is a question I do not reach.

Mr. Justice Brennan, concurring. [. . .] We have very little evidence of the Framers' intent in including the Cruel and Unusual Punishments Clause among those restraints upon the new Government enumerated in the Bill of Rights. [. . .]

[T]he Framers were well aware that the reach of the Clause was not limited to the proscription of unspeakable atrocities. Nor did they intend simply to forbid punishments considered "cruel and unusual" at the time. The "import" of the Clause is, indeed, "indefinite," and for good reason. A constitutional provision "is enacted, it is true, from an experience of evils, but its general language should not, therefore, be necessarily confined to the

---

3. Cf. B. Prettyman, Jr., Death and The Supreme Court 296–297 (1961). "The disparity of representation in capital cases raises doubts about capital punishment itself, which has been abolished in only nine states. If a James Avery [345 U.S. 559] can be saved from electrocution because his attorney made timely objection to the selection of a jury by the use of yellow and white tickets, while an Aubry Williams [349 U.S. 375] can be sent to his death by a jury selected in precisely the same manner, we are imposing our most extreme penalty in an uneven fashion.

"The problem of proper representation is not a problem of money, as some have claimed, but of a lawyer's ability, and it is not true that only the rich have able lawyers. Both the rich and the poor usually are well-represented—the poor because more often than not the best attorneys are appointed to defend them. It is the middle-class defendant, who can afford to hire an attorney but not a very good one, who is at a disadvantage. Certainly William Fikes [352 U.S. 191], despite the anomalous position in which he finds himself today, received as effective and intelligent a defense from his court-appointed attorneys as he would have received from an attorney his family had scraped together enough money to hire.

"And it is not only a matter of ability. An attorney must be found who is prepared to spend precious hours—the basic commodity he has to sell—on a case that seldom fully compensates him and often brings him no fee at all. The public has no conception of the time and effort devoted by attorneys to indigent cases. And in a first-degree case, the added responsibility of having a man's life depend upon the outcome exacts a heavy toll."

form that evil had theretofore taken. Time works changes, brings into existence new conditions and purposes. Therefore a principle to be vital must be capable of wider application than the mischief which gave it birth." *Weems* v. *United States,* 217 U.S., at 373. [. . .]

There are, then, four principles by which we may determine whether a particular punishment is "cruel and unusual." The primary principle, which I believe supplies the essential predicate for the application of the others, is that a punishment must not by its severity be degrading to human dignity. The paradigm violation of this principle would be the infliction of a torturous punishment of the type that the Clause has always prohibited. Yet "[i]t is unlikely that any State at this moment in history," *Robinson* v. *California,* 370 U.S., at 666, would pass a law providing for the infliction of such a punishment. Indeed, no such punishment has ever been before this Court. The same may be said of the other principles. It is unlikely that this Court will confront a severe punishment that is obviously inflicted in wholly arbitrary fashion; no State would engage in a reign of blind terror. Nor is it likely that this Court will be called upon to review a severe punishment that is clearly and totally rejected throughout society; no legislature would be able even to authorize the infliction of such a punishment. Nor, finally, it is likely that this Court will have to consider a severe punishment that is patently unnecessary; no State today would inflict a severe punishment knowing that there was no reason whatever for doing so. In short, we are unlikely to have occasion to determine that a punishment is fatally offensive under any one principle.

Since the Bill of Rights was adopted, this Court has adjudged only three punishments to be within the prohibition of the Clause. See *Weems* v. *United States,* 217 U.S. 349 (1910) (12 years in chains at hard and painful labor); *Trop* v. *Dulles,* 356 U.S. 86 (1958) (expatriation); *Robinson* v. *California,* 370 U.S. 660 (1962) (imprisonment for narcotics addiction). Each punishment, of course, was degrading to human dignity, but of none could it be said conclusively that it was fatally offensive under one or the other of the principles. Rather, these "cruel and unusual punishments" seriously implicated several of the principles, and it was the application of the principles in combination that supported the judgment. That, indeed, is not surprising. The function of these principles, after all, is simply to provide means by which a court can determine whether a challenged punishment comports with human dignity. They are, therefore, interrelated, and in most cases it will be their convergence that will justify the conclusion that a punishment is "cruel and unusual." The test, then, will ordinarily be a cumulative one: If a punishment is unusually severe, if there is a strong probability that it is inflicted arbitrarily, if it is substantially rejected by contemporary society, and if there is no reason to believe that it serves any penal purpose more effectively than some less severe punishment, then the continued infliction of that punishment violates the command of the Clause that the State may not inflict inhuman and uncivilized punishments upon those convicted of crimes.

[...] I will analyze the punishment of death in terms of the principles set out above and the cumulative test to which they lead: It is a denial of human dignity for the State arbitrarily to subject a person to an unusually severe punishment that society has indicated it does not regard as acceptable, and that cannot be shown to serve any penal purpose more effectively than a significantly less drastic punishment. Under these principles and this test, death is today a "cruel and unusual" punishment.

I. Death is a unique punishment in the United States. In a society that so strongly affirms the sanctity of life, not surprisingly the common view is that death is the ultimate sanction. This natural human feeling appears all about us. There has been no national debate about punishment, in general or by imprisonment, comparable to the debate about the punishment of death. No other punishment has been so continuously restricted. [...] And those States that still inflict death reserve it for the most heinous crimes. Juries, of course, have always treated death cases differently, as have governors exercising their commutation powers. Criminal defendants are of the same view. [...] This Court, too, almost always treats death cases as a class apart. And the unfortunate effect of this punishment upon the functioning of the judicial process is well known; no other punishment has a similar effect.

The only explanation for the uniqueness of death is its extreme severity. Death is today an unusually severe punishment, unusual in its pain, it its finality, and in its enormity. No other existing punishment is comparable to death in terms of physical and mental suffering. [...]

The unusual severity of death is manifested most clearly in its finality and enormity. Death, in these respects, is in a class by itself. Expatriation, for example, is a punishment that "destroys for the individual the political existence that was centuries in the development," that "strips the citizen of his status in the national and international political community," and that puts "[h]is very existence" in jeopardy. Expatriation thus inherently entails "the total destruction of the individual's status in organized society." [*Trop* v. *Dulles*, 356 U.S., at 101.] "In short, the expatriate has lost the right to have rights." Id., at 102. Yet, demonstrably, expatriation is not "a fate worse than death." Id., at 125 [...]. Although death, like expatriation, destroys the individual's "political existence" and his "status in organized society," it does more, for, unlike expatriation, death also destroys "[h]is very existence." There is, too, at least the possibility that the expatriate will in the future regain "the right to have rights." Death forecloses even that possibility.

Death is truly an awesome punishment. The calculated killing of a human being by the State involves, by its very nature, a denial of the executed person's humanity. The contrast with the plight of a person punished by imprisonment is evident. An individual in prison does not lose "the right to have rights." A prisoner retains, for example, the constitutional rights to the free exercise of religion, to be free of cruel and unusual punishments, and to treatment as a "person" for purposes of due process of law and the equal protection of the laws. A prisoner remains a member of the human family. Moreover, he retains the right of access to the courts. His punishment is not irrevocable. Apart from the common charge, grounded upon the recognition of human fallibility, that the punishment of death must inevitably be inflicted upon innocent men, we know that death has been the lot of men whose convictions were unconstitutionally secured in view of later, retroactively applied, holdings of this Court. The punishment itself may have been unconstitutionally inflicted, see *Witherspoon* v. *Illinois,* 391 U.S. 510 (1968), yet the finality of death precludes relief. An executed person has indeed "lost the right to have rights." As one nineteenth century proponent of punishing criminals by death declared, "When a man is hung, there is an end of our relations with him. His execution is a way of saying, 'You are not fit for this world, take your chance elsewhere.'"[4]

In comparison to all other punishments today, then, the deliberate extinguishment of human life by the State is uniquely degrading to human dignity. I would not hesitate to hold, on that ground alone, that death is today a "cruel and unusual" punishment, were it not that death is a punishment of longstanding usage and acceptance in this country. I therefore turn to the second principle—that the State may not arbitrarily inflict an unusually severe punishment.

II. The outstanding characteristic of our present practice of punishing criminals by death is the infrequency with which we resort to it. The evidence is conclusive that death is not the ordinary punishment for any crime. [...]

When a country of over 200 million people inflicts an unusually severe punishment no more than 50 times a year, the inference is strong that the punishment is not being regularly and fairly applied. To dispel it would indeed require a clear showing of nonarbitrary infliction.

Although there are no exact figures available, we know that thousands of murders and rapes are committed annually in States where death is an authorized punishment for those crimes. However the rate of infliction is characterized—as "freakishly" or "spectacularly" rare, or simply as rare—it would take the purest sophistry to deny that death is inflicted in only a minute fraction of these cases. How much rarer, after all, could the infliction of death be?

When the punishment of death is inflicted in a trivial number of the cases in which it is legally available, the conclusion is virtually inescapable that it

4. Stephen, Capital Punishments, 69 Fraser's Magazine 753, 763 (1864).

is being inflicted arbitrarily. Indeed, it smacks of little more than a lottery system. The States claim, however, that this rarity is evidence not of arbitrariness, but of informed selectivity: Death is inflicted, they say, only in "extreme" cases.

Informed selectivity, of course, is a value not to be denigrated. Yet presumably the States could make precisely the same claim if there were ten executions per year, or five, or even if there were but one. That there may be as many as 50 per year does not strengthen the claim. When the rate of infliction is at this low level, it is highly implausible that only the worse criminals or the criminals who commit the worst crimes are selected for this punishment. No one has yet suggested a rational basis that could differentiate in those terms the few who die from the many who go to prison. Crimes and criminals simply do not admit of a distinction that can be drawn so finely as to explain, on that ground, the execution of such a tiny sample of those eligible. Certainly the laws that provide for this punishment do not attempt to draw that distinction; all cases to which the laws apply are necessarily "extreme." Nor is the distinction credible in fact. [. . .]

Furthermore, our procedures in death cases, rather than resulting in the selection of "extreme" cases for this punishment, actually sanction an arbitrary selection. For this Court has held that juries may, as they do, make the decision whether to impose a death sentence wholly unguided by standards governing that decision. *McGautha* v. *California,* 402 U.S. 183, 196–208 (1971). In other words, our procedures are not constructed to guard against the totally capricious selection of criminals for the punishment of death.

III. [. . .] From the beginning of our Nation, the punishment of death has stirred acute public controversy. Although pragmatic arguments for and against the punishment have been frequently advanced, this longstanding and heated controversy cannot be explained solely as the result of differences over the practical wisdom of a particular government policy. At bottom, the battle has been waged on moral grounds. The country has debated whether a society for which the dignity of the individual is the supreme value can, without a fundamental inconsistency, follow the practice of deliberately putting some of its members to death. In the United States, as in other nations of the western world, "the struggle about this punishment has been one between ancient and deeply rooted beliefs in retribution, atonement or vengeance on the one hand, and, on the other, beliefs in the personal value and dignity of the common man that were born of the democratic movement of the eighteenth century, as well as beliefs in the scientific approach to an understanding of the motive forces of human conduct, which are the result of the growth of the sciences of behavior during the nineteenth and twentieth centuries."[5] It is

5. T. Sellin, The Death Penalty, A Report for the Model Penal Code Project of the American Law Institute 15 (1959).

this essentially moral conflict that forms the backdrop for the past changes in and the present operation of our system of imposing death as a punishment for crime. [. . .]

The progressive decline in, and the current rarity of, the infliction of death demonstrate that our society seriously questions the appropriateness of this punishment today. The States point out that many legislatures authorize death as the punishment for certain crimes and that substantial segments of the public, as reflected in opinion polls and referendum votes, continue to support it. Yet the availability of this punishment through statutory authorization, as well as the polls and referenda, which amount simply to approval of that authorization, simply underscores the extent to which our society has in fact rejected this punishment. When an unusually severe punishment is authorized for wide-scale application but not, because of society's refusal, inflicted save in a few instances, the inference is compelling that there is a deepseated reluctance to inflict it. Indeed, the likelihood is great that the punishment is tolerated only because of its disuse. The objective indicator of society's view of an unusually severe punishment is what society does with it, and today society will inflict death upon only a small sample of the eligible criminals. Rejection could hardly be more complete without becoming absolute. At the very least, I must conclude that contemporary society views this punishment with substantial doubt.

IV. The final principle to be considered is that an unusually severe and degrading punishment may not be excessive in view of the purposes for which it is inflicted. This principle, too, is related to the others. When there is a strong probability that the State is arbitrarily inflicting an unusually severe punishment that is subject to grave societal doubts, it is likely also that the punishment cannot be shown to be serving any penal purpose that could not be served equally well by some less severe punishment.

The States' primary claim is that death is a necessary punishment because it prevents the commission of capital crimes more effectively than any less severe punishment. [. . .]

[. . .] We are not presented with the theoretical question whether under any imaginable circumstances the threat of death might be a greater deterrent to the commission of capital crimes than the threat of imprisonment. We are concerned with the practice of punishing criminals by death as it exists in the United States today. Proponents of this argument necessarily admit that its validity depends upon the existence of a system in which the punishment of death is invariably and swiftly imposed. Our system, of course, satisfies neither condition. A rational person contemplating a murder or rape is confronted, not with the certainty of a speedy death, but with the slightest possibility that he will be executed in the distant future. The risk of death is remote and improbable; in contrast, the risk of long-term imprisonment is near and great. In short, whatever the speculative validity of the assumption that the threat of death is a superior deterrent, there is no reason to believe that as currently administered the punishment of death is necessary to deter the commission of capital crimes. [. . .]

There is, however, another aspect to the argument that the punishment of death is necessary for the protection of society. The infliction of death, the States urge, serves to manifest the community's outrage at the commission of the crime. It is, they say, a concrete public expression of moral indignation that inculcates respect for the law and helps assure a more peaceful community. Moreover, we are told, not only does the punishment of death exert this widespread moralizing influence upon community values, it also satisfies the popular demand for grievous condemnation of abhorrent crimes and thus prevents disorder, lynching, and attempts by private citizens to take the law into their own hands.

The question, however, is not whether death serves these supposed purposes of punishment, but whether death serves them more effectively than imprisonment. There is no evidence whatever that utilization of imprisonment rather than death encourages private blood feuds and other disorders. Surely if there were such a danger, the execution of a handful of criminals each year would not prevent it. The assertion that death alone is a sufficiently emphatic denunciation for capital crimes suffers from the same defect. If capital crimes require the punishment of death in order to provide moral reinforcement for the basic values of the community, those values can only be undermined when death is so rarely inflicted upon the criminals who commit the crimes. Furthermore, it is certainly doubtful that the infliction of death by the State does in fact strengthen the community's moral code; if the deliberate extinguishment of human life has any effect at all, it more likely tends to lower our respect for life and brutalize our values. That, after all, is why we no longer carry out public executions. [. . .]

There is, then, no substantial reason to believe that the punishment of death, as currently administered, is necessary for the protection of society. The only other purpose suggested, one that is independent of protection for society, is retribution. [. . .]

Obviously, concepts of justice change; no immutable moral order requires death for murderers and rapists. The claim that death is a just punishment necessarily refers to the existence of certain public beliefs. The claim must be that for capital crimes death alone comports with society's notion of proper punishment. As administered today, however, the punishment of death cannot be justified as a necessary means of exacting retribution from criminals. When the overwhelming number of criminals who commit capital crimes go to prison, it cannot be concluded that death serves the purpose of retribution more effectively than imprisonment. The asserted public belief that murderers and rapists deserve to die is flatly inconsistent with the execution of a random few. As the history of the punishment of death in this country shows, our society wishes to prevent crime; we have no desire to kill criminals simply to get even with them.

In sum, the punishment of death is inconsistent with all four principles: Death is an unusually severe and degrading punishment; there is a strong probability that it is inflicted arbitrarily; its rejection by contemporary society is virtually total; and there is no reason to believe that it serves any penal purpose more effectively than the less severe punishment of imprisonment. The function of these principles is to enable a court to determine whether a punishment comports with human dignity. Death, quite simply, does not. [...]

Mr. Justice Stewart, concurring. The penalty of death differs from all other forms of criminal punishment, not in degree but in kind. It is unique in its total irrevocability. It is unique in its rejection of rehabilitation of the convict as a basic purpose of criminal justice. And it is unique, finally, in its absolute renunciation of all that is embodied in our concept of humanity.

For these and other reasons, at least two of my Brothers have concluded that the infliction of the death penalty is constitutionally impermissible in all circumstances under the Eighth and Fourteenth Amendments. Their case is a strong one. But I find it unnecessary to reach the ultimate question they would decide. [...]

The constitutionality of capital punishment in the abstract is not, however, before us in these cases. For the Georgia and Texas Legislatures have not provided that the death penalty shall be imposed upon all those who are found guilty of forcible rape. And the Georgia Legislature has not ordained that death shall be the automatic punishment for murder. In a word, neither State has made a legislative determination that forcible rape and murder can be deterred only by imposing the penalty of death upon all who perpetrate those offenses. [...]

Instead, the death sentences now before us are the product of a legal system that brings them, I believe, within the very core of the Eighth Amendment's guarantee against cruel and unusual punishments, a guarantee applicable against the States through the Fourteenth Amendment. *Robinson* v. *California,* 370 U.S. 660. In the first place, it is clear that these sentences are "cruel" in the sense that they excessively go beyond, not in degree but in kind, the punishments that the state legislatures have determined to be necessary. *Weems* v. *United States,* 217 U.S. 349. In the second place, it is equally clear that these sentences are "unusual" in the sense that the penalty of death is infrequently imposed for murder, and that its imposition for rape is extraordinarily rare. But I do not rest my conclusion upon these two propositions alone.

These death sentences are cruel and unusual in the same way that being struck by lightning is cruel and unusual. For, of all the people convicted of rapes and murders in 1967 and 1968, many just as reprehensible as these, the petitioners are among a capriciously selected random handful upon whom the sentence of death has in fact been imposed. My concurring Brothers have demonstrated that, if any basis can be discerned for the selection of these few to be sentenced to die, it is the constitutionally impermissible basis of race. See *McLaughlin* v. *Florida,* 379 U.S. 184. But racial discrimination has not been proved, and I put it to one side. I simply conclude that the Eighth and Fourteenth Amendments cannot tolerate the infliction of a sentence of death under legal systems that permit this unique penalty to be so wantonly and so freakishly imposed. [. . .]

Mr. Justice White, concurring. [. . .] The narrow question to which I address myself concerns the constitutionality of capital punishment statutes under which 1. the legislature authorizes the imposition of the death penalty for murder or rape; 2. the legislature does not itself mandate the penalty in any particular class or kind of case (that is, legislative will is not frustrated if the penalty is never imposed), but delegates to judges or juries the decisions as to those cases, if any, in which the penalty will be utilized; and 3. judges and juries have ordered the death penalty with such infrequency that the odds are now very much against imposition and execution of the penalty with respect to any convicted murderer or rapist. It is in this context that we must consider whether the execution of these petitioners would violate the Eighth Amendment.

I begin with what I consider a near truism: that the death penalty could so seldom be imposed that it would cease to be a credible deterrent or measurably to contribute to any other end of punishment in the criminal justice system. It is perhaps true that no matter how infrequently those convicted of rape or murder are executed, the penalty so imposed is not disproportionate to the crime and those executed may deserve exactly what they received. It would also be clear that executed defendants are finally and completely incapacitated from again committing rape or murder or any other crime. But when imposition of the penalty reaches a certain degree of infrequency, it would be very doubtful that any existing general need for retribution would be measurably satisfied. Nor could it be said with confidence that society's need for specific deterrence justifies death for so few when for so many in like circumstances life imprisonment or shorter prison terms are judged sufficient, or that community values are measurably reinforced by authorizing a penalty so rarely invoked.

Most important, a major goal of the criminal law—to deter others by punishing the convicted criminal—would not be substantially served where the penalty is so seldom invoked that it ceases to be the credible threat essential to influence the conduct of others. For present purposes I accept the morality and utility of punishing one person to influence another. I accept also the effectiveness of punishment generally and need not reject the death penalty as a more effective deterrent than a lesser punishment. But common sense and experience tell us that seldom-enforced laws become ineffective measures for controlling human conduct and that the death penalty, unless imposed with sufficient frequency, will make little contribution to deterring those crimes for which it may be exacted.

The imposition and execution of the death penalty are obviously cruel in the dictionary sense. But the penalty has not been considered cruel and unusual punishment in the constitutional sense because it was thought justified by the social ends it was deemed to serve. At the moment that it ceases realistically to further these purposes, however, the emerging question is whether its imposition in such circumstances would violate the Eighth Amendment. It is my view that it would, for its imposition would then be the pointless and needless extinction of life with only marginal contributions to any discernible social or public purposes. A penalty with such negligible returns to the State would be patently excessive and cruel and unusual punishment violative of the Eighth Amendment.

It is also my judgment that this point has been reached with respect to capital punishment as it is presently administered under the statutes involved in these cases. Concededly, it is difficult to prove as a general proposition that capital punishment, however administered, more effectively serves the ends of the criminal law than does imprisonment. But however that may be, I cannot avoid the conclusion that as the statutes before us are now administered, the penalty is so infrequently imposed that the threat of execution is too attenuated to be of substantial service to criminal justice. [. . .]

[P]ast and present legislative judgment with respect to the death penalty loses much of its force when viewed in light of the recurring practice of delegating sentencing authority to the jury and the fact that a jury, in its own discretion and without violating its trust or any statutory policy, may refuse to impose the death penalty no matter what the circumstances of the crime. Legislative "policy" is thus necessarily defined not by what is legislatively authorized but by what juries and judges do in exercising the discretion so regularly conferred upon them. In my judgment what was done in these cases violated the Eighth Amendment.

Mr. Chief Justice Burger, with whom Mr. Justice Blackmun, Mr. Justice Powell, and Mr. Justice Rehnquist join, dissenting. At the outset it is important to state that only two members of the Court, Mr. Justice Brennan and Mr. Justice Marshall, have concluded that the Eighth Amendment prohibits capital punishment for all crimes and under all circumstances. Mr. Justice Douglas has also determined that the death penalty contravenes the Eighth Amendment, although I do not read his opinion as necessarily requiring final abolition of the penalty. For the reasons set forth [elsewhere in] this opinion,

I conclude that the constitutional prohibition against "cruel and unusual punishments" cannot be construed to bar the imposition of the punishment of death.

Mr. Justice Stewart and Mr. Justice White have concluded that petitioners' death sentences must be set aside because prevailing sentencing practices do not comply with the Eighth Amendment. For the reasons set forth [elsewhere in] this opinion, I believe this approach fundamentally misconceives the nature of the Eighth Amendment guarantee and flies directly in the face of controlling authority of extremely recent vintage.

If we were possessed of legislative power, I would either join with Mr. Justice Brennan and Mr. Justice Marshall or, at the very least, restrict the use of capital punishment to a small category of the most heinous crimes. Our constitutional inquiry, however, must be divorced from personal feelings as to the morality and efficacy of the death penalty, and be confined to the meaning and applicability of the uncertain language of the Eighth Amendment. There is no novelty in being called upon to interpret a constitutional provision that is less than self-defining, but, of all our fundamental guarantees, the ban on "cruel and unusual punishments" is one of the most difficult to translate into judicially manageable terms. The widely divergent views of the Amendment expressed in today's opinions reveals the haze that surrounds this constitutional command. Yet it is essential to our role as a court that we not seize upon the enigmatic character of the guarantee as an invitation to enact our personal predilections into law. [. . .]

Counsel for petitioners properly concede that capital punishment was not impermissibly cruel at the time of the adoption of the Eighth Amendment. Not only do the records of the debates indicate that the Founding Fathers were limited in their concern to the prevention of torture, but it is also clear from the language of the Constitution itself that there was no thought whatever of the elimination of capital punishment. The opening sentence of the Fifth Amendment is a guarantee that the death penalty not be imposed "unless on a presentment or indictment of a Grand Jury." The Double Jeopardy Clause of the Fifth Amendment is a prohibition against being "twice put in jeopardy of life" for the same offense. Similarly, the Due Process Clause commands "due process of law" before an accused can be "deprived of life, liberty, or property." Thus the explicit language of the Constitution affirmatively acknowledges the legal power to impose capital punishment; it does not expressly or by implication acknowledge the legal power to impose any of the various punishments that have been banned as cruel since 1791. Since the Eighth Amendment was adopted on the same day in 1791 as the Fifth Amendment, it hardly needs more to establish that the death penalty was not "cruel" in the constitutional sense at that time.

In the 181 years since the enactment of the Eighth Amendment, not a single decision of this Court has cast the slightest shadow of a doubt on the constitutionality of capital punishment. [...] Nonetheless, the Court has now been asked to hold that a punishment clearly permissible under the Constitution at the time of its adoption and accepted as such by every member of the Court until today, is suddenly so cruel as to be incompatible with the Eighth Amendment. [...]

The Court's quiescence in this area can be attributed to the fact that in a democratic society legislatures, not courts, are constituted to respond to the will and consequently the moral values of the people [...] I do not suggest that the validity of legislatively authorized punishments presents no justiciable issue under the Eighth Amendment, but rather, that the primacy of the legislative role narrowly confines the scope of judicial inquiry. Whether or not provable, and whether or not true at all times, in a democracy the legislative judgment is presumed to embody the basic standards of decency prevailing in the society. This presumption can only be negated by unambiguous and compelling evidence of legislative default.

There are no obvious indications that capital punishment offends the conscience of society to such a degree that our traditional deference to the legislative judgment must be abandoned. It is not a punishment such as burning at the stake that everyone would ineffably find to be repugnant to all civilized standards. Nor is it a punishment so roundly condemned that only a few aberrant legislatures have retained it on the statute books. Capital punishment is authorized by statute in 40 States, the District of Columbia, and in the federal courts for the commission of certain crimes. On four occasions in the last 11 years Congress has added to the list of federal crimes punishable by death. In looking for reliable indicia of contemporary attitude, none more trustworthy has been advanced.

One conceivable source of evidence that legislatures have abdicated their essentially barometric role with respect to community values would be public opinion polls, of which there have been many in the past decade addressed to the question of capital punishment. Without assessing the reliability of such polls, or intimating that any judicial reliance could ever be placed on them, it need only be noted that the reported results have shown nothing approximating the universal condemnation of capital punishment that might lead us to suspect that the legislatures in general have lost touch with current social values.

Counsel for petitioners rely on a different body of empirical evidence. They argue, in effect, that the number of cases in which the death penalty is imposed, as compared with the number of cases in which it is statutorily available, reflects a general revulsion toward the penalty that would lead to its repeal if only it were more generally and widely enforced. It cannot be gainsaid that by the choice of juries—and sometimes judges—the death penalty is imposed in far fewer than half the cases in which it is available. To go further and characterize the rate of imposition as "freakishly rare," as petitioners insist, is unwarranted hyperbole. And regardless of its characterization, the rate of imposition does not impel the conclusion that capital punishment is now regarded as intolerably cruel or uncivilized.

It is argued that in those capital cases where juries have recommended mercy, they have given expression to civilized values and effectively renounced the legislative authorization for capital punishment. At the same time it is argued that where juries have made the awesome decision to send men to their deaths, they have acted arbitrarily and without sensitivity to prevailing standards of decency. This explanation for the infrequency of imposition of capital punishment is unsupported by known facts, and is inconsistent in principle with everything this Court has ever said about the functioning of juries in capital cases.

In *McGautha* v. *California,* decided only one year ago, the Court held that there was no mandate in the Due Process Clause of the Fourteenth Amendment that juries be given instructions as to when the death penalty should be imposed. After reviewing the autonomy that juries have traditionally exercised in capital cases and noting the practical difficulties of framing manageable instructions, this Court concluded that judicially articulated standards were not needed to insure a responsible decision as to penalty. Nothing in *McGautha* licenses capital juries to act arbitrarily or assumes that they have so acted in the past. On the contrary, the assumption underlying the *McGautha* ruling is that juries "will act with due regard for the consequences of their decision." 402 U.S. at 208. [. . .]

The responsibility of juries deciding capital cases in our system of justice was nowhere better described than in *Witherspoon* v. *Illinois* [. . .]

"[A] jury that must choose between life imprisonment and capital punishment can do little more—and must do nothing less—than express *the conscience of the community* on the ultimate question of life or death."

"And one of the most important functions any jury can perform in making such a selection is to maintain a link between contemporary community values and the penal system—a link without which the determination of punishment could hardly reflect 'the evolving standards of decency that mark the progress of a maturing society'" 391 U.S. at 519 and n.15 (emphasis added).

The selectivity of juries in imposing the punishment of death is properly viewed as a refinement on, rather than a repudiation of, the statutory authorization for that penalty. Legislatures prescribe the categories of crimes for which the death penalty should be available, and, acting as "the conscience of the community," juries are entrusted to determine in individual cases that the ultimate punishment is warranted. Juries are undoubtedly influenced in this judgment by myriad factors. The motive or lack of motive of the perpetrator, the degree of injury or suffering of the victim or victims, and the degree of brutality in the commission of the crime would seem to be prominent among these factors. Given the general awareness that death is no longer a routine punishment for the crimes for which it is made available, it is hardly surprising that juries have been increasingly meticulous in their imposition of the penalty. But to assume from the mere fact of relative infrequency that only a random assortment of pariahs are sentenced to death, is to cast grave doubt on the basic integrity of our jury system.

It would, of course, be unrealistic to assume that juries have been perfectly consistent in choosing the cases where the death penalty is to be imposed, for no human institution performs with perfect consistency. There are doubtless prisoners on death row who would not be there had they been tried before a different jury or in a different State. In this sense their fate has been controlled by a fortuitous circumstance. However, this element of fortuity does not stand as an indictment either of the general functioning of juries in capital cases or of the integrity of jury decisions in individual cases. There is no empirical basis for concluding that juries have generally failed to discharge in good faith the responsibility described in *Witherspoon*—that of choosing between life and death in individual cases according to the dictates of community values.[6]

[. . .] For, if selective imposition evidences a rejection of capital punishment in those cases where it is not imposed, it surely evidences a correlative affirmation of the penalty in those cases where it is imposed. Absent some

6. Counsel for petitioners make the conclusory statement that "[t]hose who are selected to die are the poor and powerless, personally ugly and socially unacceptable." Brief for Petitioner in No. 68-5027, p. 51. However, the sources cited contain no empirical findings to undermine the general premise that juries impose the death penalty in the most extreme cases. One study has discerned a statistically noticeable difference between the rate of imposition on blue collar and white collar defendants; the study otherwise concludes that juries do follow rational patterns in imposing the sentence of death. Note, A Study of the California Penalty Jury in First-Degree-Murder Cases, 21 Stan. L. Rev. 1297 (1969). See also H. Kalven & H. Zeisel, The American Jury 434–49 (1969).

Statistics are also cited to show that the death penalty has been imposed in a racially discriminatory manner. Such statistics suggest, at least as a historical matter, that Negroes have been sentenced to death with greater frequency than whites in several States, particularly for the crime of interracial rape. [. . .]

To establish that the statutory authorization for a particular penalty is inconsistent with the dictates of the Equal Protection Clause, it is not enough to show how it was applied in the distant past. The statistics that have been referred to us cover periods when Negroes were systematically excluded from jury service and when racial segregation was the official policy in many States. Data of more recent vintage are essential. See Maxwell v. Bishop, 398 F.2d 138, 148 (C.A. 8 1968), vacated, 398 U.S. 262 (1970). While no statistical survey could be expected to bring forth absolute and irrefutable proof of a discriminatory pattern of imposition, a strong showing would have to be made, taking all relevant factors into account.
[. . .]

clear indication that the continued imposition of the death penalty on a selective basis is violative of prevailing standards of civilized conduct, the Eighth Amendment cannot be said to interdict its use. [...]

While I would not undertake to make a definitive statement as to the parameters of the Court's ruling, it is clear that if state legislatures and the Congress wish to maintain the availability of capital punishment, significant statutory changes will have to be made. Since the two pivotal concurring opinions turn on the assumption that the punishment of death is now meted out in a random and unpredictable manner, legislative bodies may seek to bring their laws into compliance with the Court's ruling by providing standards for juries and judges to follow in determining the sentence in capital cases or by more narrowly defining the crimes for which the penalty is to be imposed. If such standards can be devised or the crimes more meticulously defined, the result cannot be detrimental. However, Mr. Justice Harlan's opinion for the Court in *McGautha* convincingly demonstrates that all past efforts "to identify before the fact" the cases in which the penalty is to be imposed have been "uniformly unsuccessful." 402 U.S. at 197. [...]

Real change could clearly be brought about if legislatures provided mandatory death sentences in such a way as to deny juries the opportunity to bring in a verdict on a lesser charge; under such a system, the death sentence could only be avoided by a verdict of acquittal. If this is the only alternative that the legislatures can safely pursue under today's ruling, I would have preferred that the Court opt for total abolition.

[...] I could more easily be persuaded that mandatory sentences of death, without the intervening and ameliorating impact of lay jurors, are so arbitrary and doctrinaire that they violate the Constitution. The very infrequency of death penalties imposed by jurors attests their cautious and discriminating reservation of that penalty for the most extreme cases. I had thought that nothing was clearer in history, as we noted in *McGautha* one year ago, than the American abhorrence of "the common-law rule imposing a mandatory death sentence on all convicted murderers." 402 U.S. at 198. [...]

Since there is no majority of the Court on the ultimate issue presented in these cases, the future of capital punishment in this country has been left in an uncertain limbo. Rather than providing a final and unambiguous answer on the basic constitutional question, the collective impact of the majority's ruling is to demand an undetermined measure of change from the various state legislatures and the Congress. While I cannot endorse the process of decisionmaking that has yielded today's result and the restraints that that result imposes on legislative action, I am not altogether displeased that legislative bodies have been given the opportunity, and indeed unavoidable responsibility, to make a thorough re-evaluation of the entire subject of capital punishment. [...]

§2. The Death Penalty Is Not
Per Se Unconstitutional:
Gregg v. *Georgia* (1976)

[*Editor's note:* The decision in *Gregg,* 428 U.S. 153–241 (1976), along with companion decisions upholding the capital statutes for murder in Texas *(Jurek* v. *Texas)* and in Florida *(Proffitt* v. *Florida),* was delivered on 2 July 1976. In these three cases, the Court was divided 7 to 2, Justices Brennan and Marshall dissenting, as they were to do in all the Court's subsequent pro-death penalty decisions. Portions of their opinions in dissent (with some foot-notes and citations excluded) are reprinted below. The Court majority split three ways. The plurality opinion and judgment of the Court, announced by Justice Stewart, was joined by Justices Lewis F. Powell, Jr., and John Paul Stevens; principal excerpts from this opinion (minus the opening section and some footnotes) are reproduced here. A second opinion, written by Justice White, was joined in part by the Chief Justice and Justice Rehnquist; it is also reprinted in part below. Justice Blackmun did not write an opinion of his own and did not join in the opinion of others in the majority, though he did concur in their judgment.]

Judgment of the Court, and opinion of Mr. Justice Stewart, Mr. Justice Pow-ell, and Mr. Justice Stevens, announced by Mr. Justice Stewart. [. . .] The Georgia statute, as amended after our decision in *Furman* v. *Georgia,* 408 U.S. 238 (1972), retains the death penalty for six categories of crime: murder, kidnaping for ransom or where the victim is harmed, armed robbery, rape, treason, and aircraft hijacking. Ga. Code Ann. §§26-1101, 26-1311, 26-1902, 26-2001, 26-2201, 26-3301 (1972). The capital defendant's guilt or innocence is determined in the traditional manner, either by a trial judge or a jury, in the first stage of a bifurcated trial.

If trial is by jury, the trial judge is required to charge lesser included offenses when they are supported by any view of the evidence. *Sims* v. *State,* 203 Ga. 668, 47 S.E. 2d 862 (1948). See *Linder* v. *State,* 132 Ga. App. 624, 625, 208 S.E. 2d 630, 631 (1974). After a verdict, finding, or plea of guilty to a capital crime, a presentence hearing is conducted before whoever made the determination of guilt. The sentencing procedures are essentially the same in both bench and jury trials. At the hearing:

[T]he judge [or jury] shall hear additional evidence in extenuation, mitigation, and aggravation of punishment, including the record of any prior criminal con-victions and pleas of guilty or pleas of nolo contendere of the defendant, or the absence of any prior conviction and pleas: Provided, however, that only such evidence in aggravation as the State has made known to the defendant prior to his trial shall be admissible. The judge [or jury] shall also hear argument by the defendant or his counsel and the prosecuting attorney ... regarding the punishment to be imposed. § 27-2503 (Supp. 1975)

The defendant is accorded substantial latitude as to the types of evidence that he may introduce. See *Brown* v. *State,* 235 Ga. 644, 647–650, 220 S.E. 2d 922, 925–926 (1975). Evidence considered during the guilt stage may be considered during the sentencing stage without being resubmitted. *Eberheart* v. *State,* 232 Ga. 247, 253, 206 S.E. 2d 12, 17 (1974).

In the assessment of the appropriate sentence to be imposed the judge is also required to consider or to include in his instructions to the jury "any mitigating circumstances or aggravating circumstances otherwise authorized by law and any of [10] statutory aggravating circumstances which may be supported by the evidence. ... " § 27-2534.1(b) (Supp. 1975). The scope of the nonstatutory aggravating or mitigating circumstances is not delineated in the statute. Before a convicted defendant may be sentenced to death, however, except in cases of treason or aircraft hijacking, the jury, or the trial judge in cases tried without a jury, must find beyond a reasonable doubt one of the 10 aggravating circumstances specified in the statute.[1] The sentence of death

---

1. The statute provides in part:

(a) The death penalty may be imposed for the offenses of aircraft hijacking or treason, in any case.

(b) In all cases of other offenses for which the death penalty may be authorized, the judge shall consider, or he shall include in his instructions to the jury for it to consider, any mitigating circumstances or aggravating circumstances otherwise authorized by law and any of the following statutory aggravating circumstances which may be supported by the evidence:

(1) The offense of murder, rape, armed robbery, or kidnapping was committed by a person with a prior record of conviction for a capital felony, or the offense of murder was committed by a person who has a substantial history of serious assaultive criminal convictions.

(2) The offense of murder, rape, armed robbery, or kidnapping was committed while the offender was engaged in the commission of another capital felony, or aggravated battery, or the offense of murder was committed while the offender was engaged in the commission of burglary or arson in the first degree.

(3) The offender by his act of murder, armed robbery, or kidnapping knowingly created a great risk of death to more than one person in a public place by means of a weapon or device which would normally be hazardous to the lives of more than one person.

(4) The offender committed the offense of murder for himself or another, for the purpose of receiving money or any other thing of monetary value.

(5) The murder of a judicial officer, former judicial officer, district attorney or solicitor or former district attorney or solicitor during or because of the exercise of his official duty.

(6) The offender caused or directed another to commit murder or committed murder as an agent or employee of another person.

(7) The offense of murder, rape, armed robbery, or kidnapping was outrageously or wantonly vile, horrible or inhuman in that it involved torture, depravity of mind, or an aggravated battery to the victim.

(8) The offense of murder was committed against any peace officer, corrections employee or fireman while engaged in the performance of his official duties.

may be imposed only if the jury (or judge) finds one of the statutory aggravating circumstances and then elects to impose that sentence. § 26-3102 (Supp. 1975). If the verdict is death the jury or judge must specify the aggravating circumstance(s) found. § 27-2534.1 (c) (Supp. 1975). In jury cases, the trial judge is bound by the jury's recommended sentence. §§ 26-3102, 27-2514 (Supp. 1975).

In addition to the conventional appellate process available in all criminal cases, provision is made for special expedited direct review by the Supreme Court of Georgia of the appropriateness of imposing the sentence of death in the particular case. The court is directed to consider "the punishment as well as any errors enumerated by way of appeal," and to determine:

1. Whether the sentence of death was imposed under the influence of passion, prejudice, or any other arbitrary factor, and
2. Whether, in cases other than treason or aircraft hijacking, the evidence supports the jury's or judge's finding of a statutory aggravating circumstance as enumerated in section 27.2534.1 (b), and
3. Whether the sentence of death is excessive or disproportionate to the penalty imposed in similar cases, considering both the crime and the defendant. § 27-2537 (Supp. 1975).

If the court affirms a death sentence, it is required to include in its decision reference to similar cases that it has taken into consideration. § 27-2537 (e) (Supp. 1975).[2]

A transcript and complete record of the trial, as well as a separate report

---

(9) The offense of murder was committed by a person in, or who has escaped from, the lawful custody of a peace officer or place of lawful confinement.

(10) The murder was committed for the purpose of avoiding, interfering with, or preventing a lawful arrest or custody in a place of lawful confinement, of himself or another.

(c) The statutory instructions as determined by the trial judge to be warranted by the evidence shall be given in charge and in writing to the jury for its deliberation. The jury, if its verdict be a recommendation of death, shall designate in writing, signed by the foreman of the jury, the aggravating circumstance or circumstances which it found beyond a reasonable doubt. In non-jury cases the judge shall make such designation. Except in cases of treason or aircraft hijacking, unless at least one of the statutory aggravating circumstances enumerated in section 27-2534.1(b) is so found, the death penalty shall not be imposed. § 27-2534.1 (Supp. 1975).

The Supreme Court of Georgia, in *Arnold v. State*, 236 Ga. 534, 540, 224 S.E.2d 386, 391 (1976), recently held unconstitutional the portion of the first circumstance encompassing persons who have a "substantial history of serious assaultive criminal convictions" because it did not set "sufficiently 'clear and objective standards.'"

2. The statute requires that the Supreme Court of Georgia obtain and preserve the records of all capital felony cases in which the death penalty was imposed after January 1, 1970, or such earlier date that the court considers appropriate. § 27-2537 (f) (Supp. 1975). To aid the court in its disposition of these cases the statute further provides for the appointment of a special assistant and authorizes the employment of additional staff members. §§ 27-2537 (f)–(h) (Supp. 1975).

by the trial judge, are transmitted to the court for its use in reviewing the sentence. § 27-2537 (a) (Supp. 1975). The report is in the form of a 6½-page questionnaire, designed to elicit information about the defendant, the crime, and the circumstances of the trial. It requires the trial judge to characterize the trial in several ways designed to test for arbitrariness and disproportionality of sentence. Included in the report are responses to detailed questions concerning the quality of the defendant's representation, whether race played a role in the trial, and, whether, in the trial court's judgment, there was any doubt about the defendant's guilt or the appropriateness of the sentence. A copy of the report is served upon defense counsel. Under its special review authority, the court may either affirm the death sentence or remand the case for resentencing. In cases in which the death sentence is affirmed there remains the possibility of executive clemency.

[. . .] We now consider specifically whether the sentence of death for the crime of murder is a *per se* violation of the Eighth and Fourteenth Amendments to the Constitution. We note first that history and precedent strongly support a negative answer to this question.

The imposition of the death penalty for the crime of murder has a long history of acceptance both in the United States and in England. The common-law rule imposed a mandatory death sentence on all convicted murderers. *McGautha* v. *California,* 402 U.S. 183, 197–198 (1971). And the penalty continued to be used into the twentieth century by most American States, although the breadth of the common-law rule was diminished, initially by narrowing the class or murders to be punished by death and subsequently by widespread adoption of laws expressly granting juries the discretion to recommend mercy. Id., at 199–200. See *Woodson* v. *North Carolina, post,* at 289–92.

It is apparent from the text of the Constitution itself that the existence of capital punishment was accepted by the Framers. At the time the Eighth Amendment was ratified, capital punishment was a common sanction in every State. Indeed, the First Congress of the United States enacted legislation providing death as the penalty for specified crimes. C. 9, 1 Stat. 112 (1790). The Fifth Amendment, adopted at the same time as the Eighth, contemplated the continued existence of the capital sanction by imposing certain limits on the prosecution of capital cases:

> No person shall be held to answer for a capital, or otherwise infamous crime, unless on a presentment or indictment of a Grand Jury . . . ; nor shall any person be subject for the same offense to be twice put in jeopardy of life or limb; . . . nor be deprived of life, liberty, or property, without due process of law. . . .

And the Fourteenth Amendment, adopted over three-quarters of a century later, similarly contemplates the existence of the capital sanction in providing that no State shall deprive any person of "life, liberty, or property" without due process of law.

For nearly two centuries, this Court, repeatedly and often expressly, has recognized that capital punishment is not invalid *per se*. [. . .]

[. . .] And in *Trop* v. *Dulles,* 356 U.S., at 99, Mr. Chief Justice Warren, for himself and three other Justices, wrote:

> Whatever the arguments may be against capital punishment, both on moral grounds and in terms of accomplishing the purposes of punishment. . . the death penalty has been employed throughout our history, and, in a day when it is still widely accepted, it cannot be said to violate the constitutional concept of cruelty.

Four years ago, the petitioners in *Furman* and its companion cases predicated their argument primarily upon the asserted proposition that standards of decency had evolved to the point where capital punishment no longer could be tolerated. The petitioners in those cases said, in effect, that the evolutionary process had come to an end, and that standards of decency required that the Eighth Amendment be construed finally as prohibiting capital punishment for any crime regardless of its depravity and impact on society. This view was accepted by two Justices. Three other Justices were unwilling to go so far; focusing on the procedures by which convicted defendants were selected for the death penalty rather than on the actual punishment inflicted, they joined in the conclusion that the statutes before the Court were constitutionally invalid.

The petitioners in the capital cases before the Court today renew the "standards of decency" argument, but developments during the four years since *Furman* have undercut substantially the assumptions upon which their argument rested. Despite the continuing debate, dating back to the nineteenth century, over the morality and utility of capital punishment, it is now evident that a large proportion of American society continues to regard it as an appropriate and necessary criminal sanction.

The most marked indication of society's endorsement of the death penalty for murder is the legislative response to *Furman.* The legislatures of at least 35 States have enacted new statutes that provide for the death penalty for at least some crimes that result in the death of another person. And the Congress of the United States, in 1974, enacted a statute providing the death penalty for aircraft piracy that results in death. These recently adopted statutes have attempted to address the concerns expressed by the Court in *Furman* primarily i. by specifying the factors to be weighed and the procedures to be followed in deciding when to impose a capital sentence, or ii. by making the death penalty mandatory for specified crimes. But all of the post-*Furman* statutes make clear that capital punishment itself has not been rejected by the elected representatives of the people.

In the only statewide referendum occurring since *Furman* and brought to our attention, the people of California adopted a constitutional amendment that authorized capital punishment, in effect negating a prior ruling by the Supreme Court of California in *People* v. *Anderson,* 6 Cal. 3d 628, 493 P. 2d

880, cert. denied, 406 U.S. 958 (1972), that the death penalty violated the California Constitution.

The jury also is a significant and reliable objective index of contemporary values because it is so directly involved. [. . .]

[. . .] The Court has said that "one of the most important functions any jury can perform in making . . . a selection [between life imprisonment and death for a defendant convicted in a capital case] is to maintain a link between contemporary community values and the penal system." *Witherspoon* v. *Illinois,* 391 U.S. 510, 519 n.15 (1968). It may be true that evolving standards have influenced juries in recent decades to be more discriminating in imposing the sentence of death. But the relative infrequency of jury verdicts imposing the death sentence does not indicate rejection of capital punishment *per se.* Rather, the reluctance of juries in many cases to impose the sentence may well reflect the humane feeling that this most irrevocable of sanctions should be reserved for a small number of extreme cases. See *Furman* v. *Georgia, supra,* at 338 (Burger, C.J., dissenting). Indeed, the actions of juries in many States since *Furman* is fully compatible with the legislative judgments, reflected in the new statutes, as to the continued utility and necessity of capital punishment in appropriate cases. At the close of 1974 at least 254 persons had been sentenced to death since *Furman,* and by the end of March 1976, more than 460 persons were subject to death sentences.

As we have seen, however, the Eighth Amendment demands more than that a challenged punishment be acceptable to contemporary society. The Court also must ask whether it comports with the basic concept of human dignity at the core of the Amendment. *Trop* v. *Dulles,* 356 U.S., at 100. Although we cannot "invalidate a category of penalties because we deem less severe penalties adequate to serve the ends of penology," *Furman* v. *Georgia, supra,* at 451 (Powell, J., dissenting), the sanction imposed cannot be so totally without penological justification that it results in the gratuitous infliction of suffering. Cf. *Wilkerson* v. *Utah,* 99 U.S., at 135–36; *In re Kemmler,* 136 U.S., at 447.

The death penalty is said to serve two principal social purposes; retribution and deterrence of capital crimes by prospective offenders.[3]

In part, capital punishment is an expression of society's moral outrage at particularly offensive conduct. This function may be unappealing to many, but it is essential in an ordered society that asks its citizens to rely on legal processes rather than self-help to vindicate their wrongs.

> The instinct for retribution is part of the nature of man, and channeling that instinct in the administration of criminal justice serves an important purpose in promoting the stability of a society governed by law. When people begin to believe that organized society is unwilling or unable to impose upon criminal

---

3. Another purpose that has been discussed is the incapacitation of dangerous criminals and the consequent prevention of crimes that they may otherwise commit in the future. [. . .]

offenders the punishment they "deserve," then there are sown the seeds of anarchy—of self-help, vigilante justice, and lynch law. *Furman* v. *Georgia, supra,* at 308 (Stewart, J., concurring).

"Retribution is no longer the dominant objective of the criminal law," *Williams* v. *New York,* 337 U.S. 241, 248 (1949), but neither is it a forbidden objective nor one inconsistent with our respect for the dignity of men. *Furman* v. *Georgia,* 408 U.S., at 394–95 (Burger, C.J., dissenting); id., at 452–54 (Powell, J., dissenting); *Powell* v. *Texas,* 392 U.S., at 531, 535–36. Indeed, the decision that capital punishment may be the appropriate sanction in extreme cases is an expression of the community's belief that certain crimes are themselves so grievous an affront to humanity that the only adequate response may be the penalty of death.[4]

Statistical attempts to evaluate the worth of the death penalty as a deterrent to crimes by potential offenders have occasioned a great deal of debate. The results simply have been inconclusive. As one opponent of capital punishment has said:

[A]fter all possible inquiry, including the probing of all possible methods of inquiry, we do not know, and for systematic and easily visible reasons cannot know, what the truth about this "deterrent" effect may be. . . .

The inescapable flaw is . . . that social conditions in any state are not constant through time, and that social conditions are not the same in any two states. If an effect were observed (and the observed effects, one way or another, are not large) then one could not at all tell whether any of this effect is attributable to the presence or absence of capital punishment. A "scientific"—that is to say, a soundly based—conclusion is simply impossible, and no methodological path out of this tangle suggests itself. C. Black, Capital Punishment: The Inevitability of Caprice and Mistake 25–26 (1974).

Although some of the studies suggest that the death penalty may not function as a significantly greater deterrent than lesser penalties, there is no convincing empirical evidence either supporting or refuting this view. We may

---

4. Lord Justice Denning, Master of the Rolls of the Court of Appeal in England, spoke to this effect before the British Royal Commission on Capital Punishment:

Punishment is the way in which society expresses its denunciation of wrong doing: and, in order to maintain respect for law, it is essential that the punishment inflicted for grave crimes should adequately reflect the revulsion felt by the great majority of citizens for them. It is a mistake to consider the objects of punishment as being deterrent or reformative or preventive and nothing else. . . . The truth is that some crimes are so outrageous that society insists on adequate punishment, because the wrong-doer deserves it, irrespective of whether it is a deterrent or not. Royal Commission on Capital Punishment, Minutes of Evidence, Dec. 1, 1949, p. 207 (1950)

A contemporary writer has noted more recently that opposition to capital punishment "has much more appeal when the discussion is merely academic than when the community is confronted with a crime, or a series of crimes, so gross, so heinous, so cold-blooded that anything short of death seems an inadequate response." Raspberry, Death Sentence, The Washington Post, Mar. 12, 1976, p. A27, cols. 5–6.

nevertheless assume safely that there are murderers, such as those who act in passion, for whom the threat of death has little or no deterrent effect. But for many others, the death penalty undoubtedly is a significant deterrent. There are carefully contemplated murders, such as murder for hire, where the possible penalty of death may well enter into the cold calculus that precedes the decision to act.[5] And there are some categories of murder, such as murder by a life prisoner, where other sanctions may not be adequate.

The value of capital punishment as a deterrent of crime is a complex factual issue the resolution of which properly rests with the legislatures, which can evaluate the results of statistical studies in terms of their own local conditions and with a flexibility of approach that is not available to the courts. *Furman* v. *Georgia, supra,* at 403–5 (Burger, C.J., dissenting). Indeed, many of the post-*Furman* statutes reflect just such a responsible effort to define those crimes and those criminals for which capital punishment is most probably an effective deterrent.

In sum, we cannot say that the judgment of the Georgia legislature that capital punishment may be necessary in some cases is clearly wrong. Considerations of federalism, as well as respect for the ability of a legislature to evaluate, in terms of its particular State, the moral consensus concerning the death penalty and its social utility as a sanction, require us to conclude, in the absence of more convincing evidence, that the infliction of death as a punishment for murder is not without justification and thus is not unconstitutionally severe.

Finally, we must consider whether the punishment of death is disproportionate in relation to the crime for which it is imposed. There is no question that death as a punishment is unique in its severity and irrevocability. *Furman* v. *Georgia,* 408 U.S., at 286–91 (Brennan, J., concurring); *id.,* at 306 (Stewart, J., concurring). When a defendant's life is at stake, the Court has been particularly sensitive to insure that every safeguard is observed. *Powell* v. *Alabama,* 287 U.S. 45, 71 (1932); *Reid* v. *Covert,* 354 U.S. 1, 77 (1957) (Harlan, J., concurring in result). But we are concerned here only with the imposition of capital punishment for the crime of murder, and when a life has been taken deliberately by the offender,[6] we cannot say that the punishment is invariably disproportionate to the crime. It is an extreme sanction, suitable to the most extreme of crimes.

We hold that the death penalty is not a form of punishment that may never be imposed, regardless of the circumstances of the offense, regardless of the

5. Other types of calculated murders, apparently occurring with increasing frequency, include the use of bombs or other means of indiscriminate killings, the extortion murder of hostages or kidnap victims, and the execution-style killing of witnesses to a crime.

6. We do not address here the question whether the taking of the criminal's life is a proportionate sanction where no victim has been deprived of life—for example, when capital punishment is imposed for rape, kidnaping, or armed robbery that does not result in the death of any human being.

character of the offender, and regardless of the procedure followed in reaching the decision to impose it. [. . .]

While *Furman* did not hold that the infliction of the death penalty *per se* violates the Constitution's ban on cruel and unusual punishments, it did recognize that the penalty of death is different in kind from any other punishment imposed under our system of criminal justice. Because of the uniqueness of the death penalty, *Furman* held that it could not be imposed under sentencing procedures that created a substantial risk that it would be inflicted in an arbitrary and capricious manner. [. . .]

Furman mandates that where discretion is afforded a sentencing body on a matter so grave as the determination of whether a human life should be taken or spared, that discretion must be suitably directed and limited so as to minimize the risk of wholly arbitrary and capricious action. [. . .]

While some have suggested that standards to guide a capital jury's sentencing deliberations are impossible to formulate, the fact is that such standards have been developed. When the drafters of the Model Penal Code faced this problem, they concluded "that it is within the realm of possibility to point to the main circumstances of aggravation and of mitigation that should be weighed *and weighed against each other* when they are presented in a concrete case." ALI, Model Penal Code § 201.6, Comment 3, p. 71 (Tent. Draft No. 9, 1959) (emphasis in original).[7] While such standards are by neces-

---

7. The Model Penal Code proposes the following standards:

(3) Aggravating Circumstances.

(a) The murder was committed by a convict under sentence of imprisonment.

(b) The defendant was previously convicted of another murder or of a felony involving the use or threat of violence to the person.

(c) At the time the murder was committed the defendant also committed another murder.

(d) The defendant knowingly created a great risk of death to many persons.

(e) The murder was committed while the defendant was engaged or was an accomplice in the commission of, or an attempt to commit, or flight after committing or attempting to commit robbery, rape or deviate sexual intercourse by force or threat of force, arson, burglary or kidnapping.

(f) The murder was committed for the purpose of avoiding or preventing a lawful arrest or effecting an escape from lawful custody.

(g) The murder was committed for pecuniary gain.

(h) The murder was especially heinous, atrocious or cruel, manifesting exceptional depravity.

(4) Mitigating Circumstances.

(a) The defendant has no significant history of prior criminal activity.

(b) The murder was committed while the defendant was under the influence of extreme mental or emotional disturbance.

(c) The victim was a participant in the defendant's homicidal conduct or consented to the homicidal act.

(d) The murder was committed under circumstances which the defendant believed to provide a moral justification or extenuation for his conduct.

(e) The defendant was an accomplice in a murder committed by another person and his participation in the homicidal act was relatively minor.

sity somewhat general, they do provide guidance to the sentencing authority and thereby reduce the likelihood that it will impose a sentence that fairly can be called capricious or arbitrary. Where the sentencing authority is required to specify the factors it relied upon in reaching its decision, the further safeguard of meaningful appellate review is available to ensure that death sentences are not imposed capriciously or in a freakish manner.

In summary, the concerns expressed in *Furman* that the penalty of death not be imposed in an arbitrary or capricious manner can be met by a carefully drafted statute that ensures that the sentencing authority is given adequate information and guidance. As a general proposition these concerns are best met by a system that provides for a bifurcated proceeding at which the sentencing authority is apprised of the information relevant to the imposition of sentence and provided with standards to guide its use of the information.

We do not intend to suggest that only the above-described procedures would be permissible under *Furman* or that any sentencing system constructed along these general lines would inevitably satisfy the concerns of *Furman*, for each distinct system must be examined on an individual basis. Rather, we have embarked upon this general exposition to make clear that it is possible to construct capital-sentencing systems capable of meeting *Furman*'s constitutional concerns. [. . .]

The basic concern of *Furman* centered on those defendants who were being condemned to death capriciously and arbitrarily. Under the procedures before the Court in that case, sentencing authorities were not directed to give attention to the nature or circumstances of the crime committed or to the character or record of the defendant. Left unguided, juries imposed the death sentence in a way that could only be called freakish. The new Georgia sentencing procedures, by contrast, focus the jury's attention on the particularized nature of the crime and the particularized characteristics of the individual defendant. While the jury is permitted to consider any aggravating or mitigating circumstances, it must find and identify at least one statutory aggravating factor before it may impose a penalty of death. In this way the jury's discretion is channeled. No longer can a jury wantonly and freakishly impose the death sentence; it is always circumscribed by the legislative guidelines. In addition, the review function of the Supreme Court of Georgia affords additional assurance that the concerns that prompted our decision in *Furman* are not present to any significant degree in the Georgia procedure applied here.

(f) The defendant acted under duress or under the domination of another person.

(g) At the time of the murder, the capacity of the defendant to appreciate the criminality [wrongfulness] of his conduct or to conform his conduct to the requirements of law was impaired as a result of mental disease or defect or intoxication.

(h) The youth of the defendant at the time of the crime. ALI Model Penal Code § 210.6 (Proposed Official Draft 1962)

For the reasons expressed in this opinion, we hold that the statutory system under which Gregg was sentenced to death does not violate the Constitution. Accordingly, the judgment of the Georgia Supreme Court is affirmed.

It is so ordered.

Mr. Justice White, with whom The Chief Justice and Mr. Justice Rehnquist join, concurring in the judgment. In *Furman* v. *Georgia,* 408 U.S. 238 (1972), this Court held the death penalty as then administered in Georgia to be unconstitutional. That same year the Georgia Legislature enacted a new statutory scheme under which the death penalty may be imposed for several offenses, including murder. The issue in this case is whether the death penalty imposed for murder on petitioner Gregg under the new Georgia statutory scheme may constitutionally be carried out. I agree that it may. [. . .]

The threshold question in this case is whether the death penalty may be carried out for murder under the Georgia legislative scheme consistent with the decision in *Furman* v. *Georgia, supra.* [. . .]

[. . .] The Georgia Legislature has made an effort to identify those aggravating factors which it considers necessary and relevant to the question whether a defendant convicted of capital murder should be sentenced to death. The jury which imposes sentence is instructed on all statutory aggravating factors which are supported by the evidence, and is told that it may not impose the death penalty unless it unanimously finds at least one of those factors to have been established beyond a reasonable doubt. The Georgia Legislature has plainly made an effort to guide the jury in the exercise of its discretion, while at the same time permitting the jury to dispense mercy on the basis of factors too intangible to write into a statute, and I cannot accept the naked assertion that the effort is bound to fail. As the types of murders for which the death penalty may be imposed become more narrowly defined and are limited to those which are particularly serious or for which the death penalty is peculiarly appropriate as they are in Georgia by reason of the aggravating-circumstance requirement, it becomes reasonable to expect that juries—even given discretion *not* to impose the death penalty—will impose the death penalty in a substantial portion of the cases so defined. If they do, it can no longer be said that the penalty is being imposed wantonly and freakishly or so infrequently that it loses its usefulness as a sentencing device. There is, therefore, reason to expect that Georgia's current system would escape the infirmities which invalidated it previous system under *Furman.* [. . .]

[I]f the Georgia Supreme Court properly performs the task assigned to it under the Georgia statutes, death sentences imposed for discriminatory reasons or wantonly or freakishly for any given category of crime will be set aside. Petitioner has wholly failed to establish, and has not even attempted to establish, that the Georgia Supreme Court failed properly to perform its task in this case or that it is incapable of performing its task adequately in all cases; and this Court should not assume that it did not do so. [. . .]

Petitioner's argument that prosecutors behave in a standardless fashion in deciding which cases to try as capital felonies is unsupported by any facts. Petitioner simply asserts that since prosecutors have the power not to charge capital felonies they will exercise that power in a standardless fashion. This is untenable. Absent facts to the contrary, it cannot be assumed that prosecutors will be motivated in their charging decision by factors other than the strength of their case and the likelihood that a jury would impose the death penalty if it convicts. Unless prosecutors are incompetent in their judgments, the standards by which they decide whether to charge a capital felony will be the same as those by which the jury will decide the questions of guilt and sentence. Thus defendants will escape the death penalty through prosecutorial charging decisions only because the offense is not sufficiently serious; or because the proof is insufficiently strong. This does not cause the system to be standardless any more than the jury's decision to impose life imprisonment on a defendant whose crime is deemed insufficiently serious or its decision to acquit someone who is probably guilty but whose guilt is not established beyond a reasonable doubt. Thus the prosecutor's charging decisions are unlikely to have removed from the sample of cases considered by the Georgia Supreme Court any which are truly "similar." If the cases really were "similar" in relevant respects, it is unlikely that prosecutors would fail to prosecute them as capital cases; and I am unwilling to assume the contrary.

Petitioner's argument that there is an unconstitutional amount of discretion in the system which separates those suspects who receive the death penalty from those who receive life imprisonment, a lesser penalty, or are acquitted or never charged, seems to be in final analysis an indictment of our entire system of justice. Petitioner has argued, in effect, that no matter how effective the death penalty may be as a punishment, government, created and run as it must be by humans, is inevitably incompetent to administer it. This cannot be accepted as a proposition of constitutional law. Imposition of the death penalty is surely an awesome responsibility for any system of justice and those who participate in it. Mistakes will be made and discriminations will occur which will be difficult to explain. However, one of society's most basic tasks is that of protecting the lives of its citizens and one of the most basic ways in which it achieves the task is through criminal laws against murder. I decline to interfere with the manner in which Georgia has chosen to enforce such laws on what is simply an assertion of lack of faith in the ability of the system of justice to operate in a fundamentally fair manner. [. . .]

Mr. Justice Brennan, dissenting. The Cruel and Unusual Punishments Clause "must draw its meaning from the evolving standards of decency that mark the progress of a maturing society." The opinions of Mr. Justice Stewart, Mr. Justice Powell, and Mr. Justice Stevens today hold that "evolving standards of decency" require focus not on the essence of the death penalty itself but primarily upon the procedures employed by the State to single out persons to suffer the penalty of death. Those opinions hold further that, so viewed, the Clause invalidates the mandatory infliction of the death penalty but not its infliction under sentencing procedures that Mr. Justice Stewart, Mr. Justice Powell, and Mr. Justice Stevens conclude adequately safeguard against the risk that the death penalty was imposed in an arbitrary and capricious manner.

In *Furman* v. *Georgia*, 408 U.S. 238, 257 (1972) (concurring), I read "evolving standards of decency" as requiring focus upon the essence of the death penalty itself and not primarily or solely upon the procedures under which the determination to inflict the penalty upon a particular person was made. [. . .] That continues to be my view. For the Clause forbidding cruel and unusual punishments under our constitutional system of government embodies in unique degree moral principles restraining the punishments that our civilized society may impose on those persons who transgress its laws. [. . .]

[. . .] I shall not again canvass the reasons that led to that conclusion. I emphasize only that foremost among the "moral concepts" recognized in our cases and inherent in the Clause is the primary moral principle that the State, even as it punishes, must treat its citizens in a manner consistent with their intrinsic worth as human beings—a punishment must not be so severe as to be degrading to human dignity. [. . .]

I do not understand that the Court disagrees that "[i]n comparison to all other punishments today . . . the deliberate extinguishment of human life by the State is uniquely degrading to human dignity." [408 U.S.,] at 291. For three of my Brethren hold today that mandatory infliction of the death penalty constitutes the penalty cruel and unusual punishment. I perceive no principled basis for this limitation. Death for whatever crime and under all circumstances "is truly an awesome punishment. The calculated killing of a human being by the State involves, by its very nature, a denial of the executed person's humanity. . . . An executed person has indeed 'lost the right to have rights.'" Id., at 290. Death is not only an unusually severe punishment, unusual in its pain, in its finality, and in its enormity, but it serves no penal purpose more effectively than a less severe punishment; therefore the principle inherent in the Clause that prohibits pointless infliction of excessive punishment when less severe punishment can adequately achieve the same purposes invalidates the punishment. Id., at 279. [. . .]

Mr. Justice Marshall, dissenting. In *Furman* v. *Georgia*, 408 U.S. 238, 314 (1972) (concurring), I set forth at some length my views on the basic issue presented to the Court in these cases. The death penalty, I concluded, is a cruel and unusual punishment prohibited by the Eighth and Fourteenth Amendments. That continues to be my view. [. . .]

Since the decision in *Furman*, the legislatures of 35 States have enacted new statutes authorizing the imposition of the death sentence for certain crimes, and Congress has enacted a law providing the death penalty for air piracy resulting in death. 49 U.S.C. §§ 1472 (i), (n) (1970 ed., Supp. IV). I would be less than candid if I did not acknowledge that these developments have a significant bearing on a realistic assessment of the moral acceptability of the death penalty to the American people. But if the constitutionality of the death penalty turns, as I have urged, on the opinion of an *informed* citizenry, then even the enactment of new death statutes cannot be viewed as conclusive. In *Furman,* I observed that the American people are largely unaware of the information critical to a judgment on the morality of the death penalty, and concluded that if they were better informed they would consider it shocking, unjust, and unacceptable. 408 U.S., at 360–69. A recent study, conducted after the enactment of the post-*Furman* statutes, has confirmed that the American people know little about the death penalty, and that the opinions of an informed public would differ significantly from those of a public unaware of the consequences and effects of the death penalty.[8]

Even assuming, however, that the post-*Furman* enactment of statutes authorizing the death penalty renders the prediction of the views of an informed citizenry an uncertain basis for a constitutional decision, the enactment of those statutes has no bearing whatsoever on the conclusion that the death penalty is unconstitutional because it is excessive. An excessive penalty is invalid under the Cruel and Unusual Punishments Clause "even though popular sentiment may favor" it. Id., at 331; *ante,* at 173, 182–83 (opinion of Stewart, Powell, and Stevens, JJ.); *Roberts* v. *Louisiana, post,* at 353–54 (White, J., dissenting). The inquiry here, then, is simply whether the death penalty is necessary to accomplish the legitimate legislative purposes in punishment, or whether a less severe penalty—life imprisonment—would do as well. *Furman, supra,* at 342 (Marshall, J., concurring).

The two purposes that sustain the death penalty as nonexcessive in the Court's view are general deterrence and retribution. [. . .]

The Solicitor General in his *amicus* brief in these cases relies heavily on a study by Isaac Ehrlich,[9] reported a year after *Furman,* to support the contention that the death penalty does deter murder. Since the Ehrlich study was not available at the time of *Furman* and since it is the first scientific study to suggest that the death penalty may have a deterrent effect, I will briefly consider its import.

The Ehrlich study focused on the relationship in the Nation as a whole

8. Sarat & Vidmar, Public Opinion, The Death Penalty, and the Eighth Amendment: Testing the Marshall Hypothesis, 1976 Wis. L. Rev. 171.
9. I. Ehrlich, The Deterrent Effect of Capital Punishment: A Question of Life and Death (Working Paper No. 18, National Bureau of Economic Research, Nov. 1973); Ehrlich, The Deterrent Effect of Capital Punishment: A Question of Life and Death, 65 Am. Econ. Rev. 397 (June 1975).

between the homicide rate and "execution risk"—the fraction of persons convicted of murder who were actually executed. Comparing the differences in homicide rate and execution risk for the years 1933 to 1969, Ehrlich found that increases in execution risk were associated with increases in the homicide rate. But when he employed the statistical technique of multiple regression analysis to control for the influence of other variables posited to have an impact on the homicide rate, Ehrlich found a negative correlation between changes in the homicide rate and changes in execution risk. His tentative conclusion was that for the period from 1933 to 1967 each additional execution in the United States might have saved eight lives. The methods and conclusions of the Ehrlich study have been severely criticized on a number of grounds.[10][. . .]

The most compelling criticism of the Ehrlich study is that its conclusions are extremely sensitive to the choice of the time period included in the regression analysis. Analysis of Ehrlich's data reveals that all empirical support for the deterrent effect of capital punishment disappears when the five most recent years are removed from his time series—that is to say, whether a decrease in the execution risk corresponds to an increase or a decrease in the murder rate depends on the ending point of the sample period.[11] This finding has cast severe doubts on the reliability of Ehrlich's tentative conclusions.[12] Indeed, a recent regression study, based on Ehrlich's theoretical model but using cross-section state data for the years 1950 and 1960, found no support for the conclusion that executions act as a deterrent.[13] [. . .]

The other principal purpose said to be served by the death penalty is retribution. The notion that retribution can serve as a moral justification for the sanction of death finds credence in the opinion of my Brothers Stewart, Powell, and Stevens, and that of my Brother White in *Roberts v. Louisiana, post,*

10. See Passell & Taylor, The Deterrent Effect of Capital Punishment: Another View (unpublished Columbia University Discussion Paper 74-7509, Mar. 1975), reproduced in Brief for Petitioner App. E in *Jurek v. Texas,* No. 75-5844, O. T. 1975; Passell, The Deterrent Effect of the Death Penalty: A Statistical Test, 28 Stan L. Rev. 61 (1975); Baldus & Cole, A Comparison of the Work of Thorsten Sellin & Isaac Ehrlich on the Deterrent Effect of Capital Punishment, 85 Yale L.J. 170 (1975); Bowers & Pierce, The Illusion of Deterrence in Isaac Ehrlich's Research on Capital Punishment, 85 Yale L.J. 187 (1975); Peck, The Deterrent Effect of Capital Punishment: Ehrlich and His Critics, 85 Yale L.J. 359 (1976). See also Ehrlich, Deterrence: Evidence and Inference, 85 Yale L.J. 209 (1975); Ehrlich, Rejoinder, 85 Yale L.J. 368 (1976). In addition to the items discussed in text, criticism has been directed at the quality of Ehrlich's data, his choice of explanatory variables, his failure to account for the interdependence of those variables, and his assumptions as to the mathematical form of the relationship between the homicide rate and the explanatory variables.

11. Bowers & Pierce, *supra,* n.10, at 197–98. See also Passell & Taylor, *supra,* n.10, at 2-66-2-68.

12. See Bowers & Pierce, *supra,* n.10, at 197–198; Baldus & Cole, *supra,* n.10, at 181, 183–85; Peck, *supra,* n.10, at 366–67.

13. Passell, *supra,* n.10.

p. 337. See also *Furman* v. *Georgia*, 408 U.S., at 394–95 (Burger, C.J., dissenting). It is this notion that I find to be the most disturbing aspect of today's unfortunate decisions.

The concept of retribution is a multifaceted one, and any discussion of its role in the criminal law must be undertaken with caution. On one level, it can be said that the notion of retribution or reprobation is the basis of our insistence that only those who have broken the law be punished, and in this sense the notion is quite obviously central to a just system of criminal sanctions. But our recognition that retribution plays a crucial role in determining who may be punished by no means requires approval of retribution as a general justification for punishment.[14] It is the question whether retribution can provide a moral justification for punishment—in particular, capital punishment—that we must consider.

My Brothers Stewart, Powell, and Stevens offer the following explanation of the retributive justification for capital punishment:

> The instinct for retribution is part of the nature of man, and channeling that instinct in the administration of criminal justice serves an important purpose in promoting the stability of a society governed by law. When people begin to believe that organized society is unwilling or unable to impose upon criminal offenders the punishment they "deserve," then there are sown the seeds of anarchy—of self-help, vigilante justice, and lynch law. *Ante,* at 183, quoting from *Furman* v. *Georgia, supra,* at 308 (Stewart, J., concurring).

This statement is wholly inadequate to justify the death penalty. As my Brother Brennan stated in *Furman,* "[t]here is no evidence whatever that utilization of imprisonment rather than death encourages private blood feuds and other disorders." 408 U.S., at 303 (concurring). It simply defies belief to suggest that the death penalty is necessary to prevent the American people from taking the law into their own hands.

In a related vein, it may be suggested that the expression of moral outrage through the imposition of the death penalty serves to reinforce basic moral values—that it marks some crimes as particularly offensive and therefore to be avoided. The argument is akin to a deterrence argument, but differs in that it contemplates the individual's shrinking from antisocial conduct, not because he fears punishment, but because he has been told in the strongest possible way that the conduct is wrong. This contention, like the previous one, provides no support for the death penalty. It is inconceivable that any individual concerned about conforming his conduct to what society says is "right" would fail to realize that murder is "wrong" if the penalty were simply life imprisonment.

The foregoing contentions—that society's expression of moral outrage

14. See e.g., H. Hart, Punishment and Responsibility 8–10, 71–83 (1968); H. Packer, Limits of the Criminal Sanction 38–39, 66 (1968).

through the imposition of the death penalty pre-empts the citizenry from taking the law into its own hands and reinforces moral values—are not retributive in the purest sense. They are essentially utilitarian in that they portray the death penalty as valuable because of its beneficial results. These justifications for the death penalty are inadequate because the penalty is, quite clearly I think, not necessary to the accomplishment of those results.

There remains for consideration, however, what might be termed the purely retributive justification for the death penalty—that the death penalty is appropriate, not because of its beneficial effect on society, but because the taking of the murderer's life is itself morally good. Some of the language of the opinion of my Brothers Stewart, Powell, and Stevens in [this case] appears positively to embrace this notion of retribution for its own sake as a justification for capital punishment.[15] They state:

> [T]he decision that capital punishment may be the appropriate sanction in extreme cases is an expression of the community's belief that certain crimes are themselves so grievous an affront to humanity that the only adequate response may be the penalty of death. *Ante,* at 184 (footnote omitted).

The plurality then quotes with approval from Lord Justice Denning's remarks before the British Royal Commission on Capital Punishment:

> "The truth is that some crimes are so outrageous that society insists on adequate punishment, because the wrong-doer deserves it, irrespective of whether it is a deterrent or not." *Ante,* at 184 n.30.

Of course, it may be that these statements are intended as no more than observations as to the popular demands that it is thought must be responded to in order to prevent anarchy. But the implication of the statements appears to me to be quite different—namely, that society's judgment that the murderer "deserves" death must be respected not simply because the preservation of order requires it, but because it is appropriate that society make the judgment and carry it out. It is this latter notion, in particular, that I consider to be fundamentally at odds with the Eighth Amendment. See *Furman v. Georgia,* 408 U.S., at 343–45 (Marshall, J., concurring). The mere fact that the community demands the murderer's life in return for the evil he has done cannot sustain the death penalty, for as the plurality reminds us, "the Eighth Amendment demands more than that a challenged punishment be acceptable

---

15. Mr. Justice White's view of retribution as a justification for the death penalty is not altogether clear. "The widespread reenactment of the death penalty," he states at one point, "answers any claims that life imprisonment is adequate punishment to satisfy the need for reprobation or retribution." *Roberts v. Louisiana, post,* at 354. (White, J., dissenting). But Mr. Justice White later states: "It will not do to denigrate these legislative judgments as some form of vestigial savagery or as purely retributive in motivation; for they are solemn judgments, reasonably based, that imposition of the death penalty will save the lives of innocent persons." *Post,* at 355.

to contemporary society." *Ante*, at 182. To be sustained under the Eighth Amendment, the death penalty must "[comport] with the basic concept of human dignity at the core of the Amendment," ibid.; the objective in imposing it must be "[consistent] with our respect for the dignity of [other] men." *Ante*, at 183. See *Trop* v. *Dulles*, 356 U.S. 86, 100 (1958) (plurality opinion). Under these standards, the taking of life "because the wrongdoer deserves it" surely must fall, for such a punishment has as its very basis the total denial of the wrongdoer's dignity and worth.

The death penalty, unnecessary to promote the goal of deterrence or to further any legitimate notion of retribution, is an excessive penalty forbidden by the Eighth and Fourteenth Amendments. I respectfully dissent from the Court's judgment upholding the sentences of death imposed upon the petitioners in these cases.

§3. Mandatory Death Penalties for Murder Are Unconstitutional: *Woodson* v. *North Carolina* (1976)

[*Editor's note:* The decision in *Woodson*, 428 U.S. 280–324 (1976), along with its companion case, *Roberts* v. *Louisiana*, was delivered on 2 July 1976, on the same day as the Court announced its decisions in *Gregg*, *Proffitt*, and *Jurek*. In *Woodson* and *Roberts*, the Court divided 5 to 4, as it had in *Furman*, with the judgment of the Court and plurality opinion presented by Justice Stewart. Joining him were Justices Powell and Stevens; excerpts from this opinion, minus some references and footnotes, are reprinted below. Justices Marshall and Brennan concurred with the majority judgment. The essence of their concurrences, here as in several of the Court's subsequent anti-death penalty decisions, was to reiterate their conclusion that the death penalty is per se unconstitutional. The members of the Court in dissent submitted two opinions. One, written by Justice White (and in part reprinted below), was joined by both the Chief Justice and Justice Rehnquist. The other was written by Justice Rehnquist; portions are reprinted below. Justice Blackmun, citing his dissenting opinion in *Furman*, also dissented.]

Judgment of the Court, and opinion of Mr. Justice Stewart, Mr. Justice Powell, and Mr. Justice Stevens, announced by Mr. Justice Stewart. [. . .] At the time of this Court's decision in *Furman* v. *Georgia*, 408 U.S. 238 (1972), North Carolina law provided that in cases of first-degree murder, the jury in its unbridled discretion could choose whether the convicted defendant should be sentenced to death or to life imprisonment.[1] After the *Furman* decision the Supreme Court of North Carolina in *State* v. *Waddell*, 282 N.C. 431, 194 S.E.2d 19 (1973), held unconstitutional the provision of the death penalty statute that gave the jury the option of returning a verdict of guilty without capital punishment, but held further that this provision was severable so that the statute survived as a mandatory death penalty law.

The North Carolina General Assembly in 1974 followed the court's lead and enacted a new statute that was essentially unchanged from the old one except that it made the death penalty mandatory. The statute now reads as follows:

> *Murder in the first and second degree defined; punishment.*—A murder which shall be perpetrated by means of poison, lying in wait, imprisonment, starving, torture, or by any other kind of willful, deliberate and premeditated killing, or which shall be committed in the perpetration or attempt to perpetrate any arson, rape, robbery, kidnapping, burglary or other felony, shall be deemed to be murder in the first degree and shall be punished with death. All other kinds of murder shall be deemed murder in the second degree, and shall be punished by imprisonment for a term of not less than two years nor more than life imprisonment in the State's prison. N.C. Gen. Stat. §14–17 (Cum. Supp. 1975).

It was under this statute that the petitioners, who committed their crime on June 3, 1974, were tried, convicted, and sentenced to death. [. . .]

The history of mandatory death penalty statutes in the United States [. . .] reveals that the practice of sentencing to death all persons convicted of a particular offense has been rejected as unduly harsh and unworkably rigid. The two crucial indicators of evolving standards of decency respecting the imposition of punishment in our society—jury determinations and legislative enactments—both point conclusively to the repudiation of automatic death sentences. At least since the Revolution, American jurors have, with some regularity, disregarded their oaths and refused to convict defendants where a death sentence was the automatic consequence of a guilty verdict. [. . .]

---

1. The murder statute in effect in North Carolina until April 1974 reads as follows:
   § 14–17. Murder in the first and second degree defined; punishment.—A murder which shall be perpetrated by means of poison, lying in wait, imprisonment, starving, torture, or by any other kind of willful, deliberate and premeditated killing, or which shall be committed in the perpetration or attempt to perpetrate any arson, rape, robbery, burglary or other felony, shall be deemed to be murder in the first degree and shall be punished with death: Provided, if at the time of rendering its verdict in open court, the jury shall so recommend, the punishment shall be imprisonment for life in the State's prison, and the court shall so instruct the jury. All other kinds of murder shall be deemed murder in the second degree, and shall be punished with imprisonment of not less than two nor more than thirty years in the State's prison. N.C. Gen. Stat. § 14–17 (1969).

[. . .] The consistent course charted by the state legislatures and by Congress since the middle of the past century demonstrates that the aversion of jurors to mandatory death penalty statutes is shared by society at large. [. . .]

Although the Court has never ruled on the constitutionality of mandatory death penalty statutes, on several occasions dating back to 1899 it has commented upon our society's aversion to automatic death sentences. In *Winston* v. *United States,* 172 U.S. 303 (1899), the Court noted that the "hardship of punishing with death every crime coming within the definition of murder at common law, and the reluctance of jurors to concur in a capital conviction, have induced American legislatures, in modern times, to allow some cases of murder to be punished by imprisonment, instead of by death." Id., at 310. Fifty years after *Winston,* the Court underscored the marked transformation in our attitudes towards mandatory sentences: "The belief no longer prevails that every offense in a like legal category calls for an identical punishment without regard to the past life and habits of a particular offender. This whole country has traveled far from the period in which the death sentence was an automatic and commonplace result of convictions. . . . " *Williams* v. *New York,* 337 U.S. 241, 247 (1949).

More recently, the Court in *McGautha* v. *California,* 402 U.S. 183 (1971), detailed the evolution of discretionary imposition of death sentences in this country, prompted by what it termed the American "rebellion against the common-law rule imposing a mandatory death sentence on all convicted murderers." Id., at 198. See id., at 198–202. Perhaps the one important factor about evolving social values regarding capital punishment upon which the Members of the *Furman* Court agreed was the accuracy of *McGautha*'s assessment of our Nation's rejection of mandatory death sentences. [. . .]

It is now well established that the Eighth Amendment draws much of its meaning from "the evolving standards of decency that mark the progress of a maturing society." *Trop* v. *Dulles,* 356 U.S., at 101 (plurality opinion). As the above discussion makes clear, one of the most significant developments in our society's treatment of capital punishment has been the rejection of the common-law practice of inexorably imposing a death sentence upon every person convicted of a specified offense. North Carolina's mandatory death penalty statute for first-degree murder departs markedly from contemporary standards respecting the imposition of the punishment of death and thus cannot be applied consistently with the Eighth and Fourteenth Amendments' requirement that the State's power to punish "be exercised within the limits of civilized standards." Id., at 100.[2]

---

2. Dissenting opinions in this case and in *Roberts* v. *Louisiana, post,* p. 325, argue that this conclusion is "simply mistaken" because the American rejection of mandatory death sentence statutes might possibly be ascribable to "some maverick juries or jurors." *Post,* at 309, 313, (Rehnquist, J., dissenting). See *Roberts* v. *Louisiana, post,* at 361 (White, J., dissenting). Since

A separate deficiency of North Carolina's mandatory death sentence statute is its failure to provide a constitutionally tolerable response to *Furman*'s rejection of unbridled jury discretion in the imposition of capital sentences. Central to the limited holding in *Furman* was the conviction that the vesting of standardless sentencing power in the jury violated the Eighth and Fourteenth Amendments. [. . .] It is argued that North Carolina has remedied the inadequacies of the death penalty statutes held unconstitutional in *Furman* by withdrawing all sentencing discretion from juries in capital cases. But when one considers the long and consistent American experience with the death penalty in first-degree murder cases, it becomes evident that mandatory statutes enacted in response to *Furman* have simply papered over the problem of unguided and unchecked jury discretion.

[. . .] North Carolina's mandatory death penalty statute provides no standards to guide the jury in its inevitable exercise of the power to determine which first-degree murderers shall live and which shall die. And there is no way under the North Carolina law for the judiciary to check arbitrary and capricious exercise of that power through a review of death sentences. Instead of rationalizing the sentencing process, a mandatory scheme may well exacerbate the problem identified in *Furman* by resting the penalty determination on the particular jury's willingness to act lawlessly. While a mandatory death penalty statute may reasonably be expected to increase the number of persons sentenced to death, it does not fulfill *Furman*'s basic requirement by replacing arbitrary and wanton jury discretion with objective standards to guide, regularize, and make rationally reviewable the process for imposing a sentence of death.

A third constitutional shortcoming of the North Carolina statute is its failure to allow the particularized consideration of relevant aspects of the character and record of each convicted defendant before the imposition upon him of a sentence of death. [. . .] A process that accords no significance to relevant facets of the character and record of the individual offender or the circum-

---

acquittals no less than convictions required unanimity and citizens with moral reservations concerning the death penalty were regularly excluded from capital juries, it seems hardly conceivable that the persistent refusal of American juries to convict palpably guilty defendants of capital offenses under mandatory death sentence statutes merely "represented the intransigence of only a small minority" of jurors. *Post*, at 312 (Rehnquist, Jr., dissenting). Moreover, the dissenting opinions simply ignore the experience under discretionary death sentence statutes indicating that juries reflecting contemporary community values, *Witherspoon* v. *Illinois*, 391 U.S., at 519, and n.15, found the death penalty appropriate for only a small minority of convicted first-degree murderers. [. . .] We think it evident that the uniform assessment of the historical record by Members of this Court beginning in 1899 in *Winston* v. *United States*, 172 U.S. 303 (1899), and continuing through the dissenting opinions of The Chief Justice and Mr. Justice Blackmun four years ago in *Furman*, see *supra*, at 296–98, and n.32, provides a far more cogent and persuasive explanation of the American rejection of mandatory death sentences than do the speculations in today's dissenting opinions.

stances of the particular offense excludes from consideration in fixing the ultimate punishment of death the possibility of compassionate or mitigating factors stemming from the diverse frailties of humankind. It treats all persons convicted of a designated offense not as uniquely individual human beings, but as members of a faceless, undifferentiated mass to be subjected to the blind infliction of the penalty of death.

[. . .] While the prevailing practice of individualizing sentencing determinations generally reflects simply enlightened policy rather than a constitutional imperative, we believe that in capital cases the fundamental respect for humanity underlying the Eighth Amendment, see *Trop* v. *Dulles*, 356 U.S., at 100 (plurality opinion), requires consideration of the character and record of the individual offender and the circumstances of the particular offense as a constitutionally indispensable part of the process of inflicting the penalty of death.

This conclusion rests squarely on the predicate that the penalty of death is qualitatively different from a sentence of imprisonment, however long. Death, in its finality, differs more from life imprisonment than a 100-year prison term differs from one of only a year or two. Because of that qualitative difference, there is a corresponding difference in the need for reliability in the determination that death is the appropriate punishment in a specific case.

It is so ordered.

Mr. Justice White, with whom The Chief Justice and Mr. Justice Rehnquist join, dissenting. [. . .] I reject petitioners' arguments that the death penalty in any circumstances is a violation of the Eighth Amendment and that the North Carolina statute, although making the imposition of the death penalty mandatory upon proof of guilt and a verdict of first-degree murder, will nevertheless result in the death penalty being imposed so seldom and arbitrarily that it is void under *Furman* v. *Georgia*. [. . .]

Mr. Justice Rehnquist, dissenting. [. . .] The plurality opinion's insistence [. . .] that if the death penalty is to be imposed there must be "particularized consideration of relevant aspects of the character and record of each convicted defendant" is buttressed by neither case authority nor reason. [. . .]

The plurality also relies upon the indisputable proposition that "death is different" for the result which it reaches [. . .]. But the respects in which death is "different" from other punishment which may be imposed upon convicted criminals do not seem to me to establish the proposition that the Constitution requires individualized sentencing.

One of the principal reasons why death is different is because it is irreversible; an executed defendant cannot be brought back to life. This aspect of the difference between death and other penalties would undoubtedly support statutory provisions for especially careful review of the fairness of the trial, the accuracy of the factfinding process, and the fairness of the sentencing procedure where the death penalty is imposed. But none of those aspects of the death sentence is at issue here. Petitioners were found guilty of the crime of first-degree murder in a trial the constitutional validity of which is unquestioned here. And since the punishment of death is conceded by the plurality not to be a cruel and unusual punishment for such a crime, the irreversible aspect of the death penalty has no connection whatever with any requirement for individualized consideration of the sentence.

The second aspect of the death penalty which makes it "different" from other penalties is the fact that it is indeed an ultimate penalty, which ends a human life rather than simply requiring that a living human being be confined for a given period of time in a penal institution. This aspect of the difference may enter into the decision of whether or not it is a "cruel and unusual" penalty for a given offense. But since in this case the offense was first-degree murder, that particular inquiry need proceed no further.

The plurality's insistence on individualized consideration of the sentencing, therefore, does not depend upon any traditional application of the prohibition against cruel and unusual punishment contained in the Eighth Amendment. The punishment here is concededly not cruel and unusual, and that determination has traditionally ended judicial inquiry in our cases construing the Cruel and Unusual Punishments Clause. *Trop* v. *Dulles*, 356 U.S. 86 (1958); *Robinson* v. *California*, 370 U.S. 660 (1962); *Louisiana ex rel. Francis* v. *Resweber*, 329 U.S. 459 (1947); *Wilkerson* v. *Utah*, 99 U.S. 130 (1879). What the plurality opinion has actually done is to import into the Due Process Clause of the Fourteenth Amendment what it conceives to be desirable procedural guarantees where the punishment of death, concededly not cruel and unusual for the crime of which the defendant was convicted, is to be imposed. This is squarely contrary to *McGautha*, and unsupported by any other decision of this Court. [. . .]

§4. The Mandatory Death Penalty for Killing a Police Officer: *Harry Roberts* v. *Louisiana* (1977)

[*Editor's note:* On 6 June 1977, the Court announced its decision in *Harry Roberts*, 431 U.S. 633 (1977), in a *per curiam* opinion in which five members of the Court—Justices Brennan, Stewart, Marshall, Powell, and Stevens—were joined. Portions of this opinion are reprinted below. The Chief Justice dissented, citing his dissent in the 1976 *Stanislaus Roberts* case and Justice White's dissent in *Woodson*. Justice Blackmun, joined by Justice Rehnquist, filed a dissenting opinion, and excerpts from it are reproduced below (minus some citations and footnotes). Justice Rehnquist, joined by Justice White, also wrote a dissenting opinion, portions of which (omitting some references and footnotes) are reprinted below.]

Per Curiam. Petitioner Harry Roberts was indicted, tried, and convicted of the first-degree murder of Police Officer Dennis McInerney, who at the time of his death was engaged in the performance of his lawful duties. As required by a Louisiana statute, petitioner was sentenced to death. La. Rev. Stat. Ann. § 14:30 (2) (1974).[1] On appeal, the Supreme Court of Louisiana affirmed his conviction and sentence. 331 So. 2d 11 (1976). Roberts then filed a petition for a writ of certiorari in this Court. The petition presented the question whether Louisiana's mandatory death penalty could be imposed pursuant to his conviction of first-degree murder as defined in subparagraph (2) of § 14:30.

Shortly before that petition was filed, we held in another case (involving a different petitioner named Roberts) that Louisiana could not enforce its mandatory death penalty for a conviction of first-degree murder as defined in subparagraph (1) of § 14:30 of La. Rev. Stat. Ann. (1974). *Roberts v. Louisiana,* 428 U.S. 325 (1976) (hereafter cited as *Stanislaus Roberts* for purposes of clarity). In the plurality opinion in that case, the precise question presented in this case was explicitly answered. [. . .]

In *Woodson v. North Carolina,* 428 U.S. 280, 304 (1976), this Court held

1. That section provides in part:

   First degree murder

   First degree murder is the killing of a human being:

   1. When the offender has a specific intent to kill or to inflict great bodily harm and is engaged in the perpetration or attempted perpetration of aggravated kidnapping, aggravated rape or armed robbery; or

   2. When the offender has a specific intent to kill, or to inflict great bodily harm upon, a fireman or a peace officer who was engaged in the performance of his lawful duties; or

   3. Where the offender has a specific intent to kill or to inflict great bodily harm and has previously been convicted of an unrelated murder or is serving a life sentence; or

   4. When the offender has a specific intent to kill or to inflict great bodily harm upon more than one person; [or]

   5. When the offender has specific intent to commit murder and has been offered or has received anything of value for committing the murder.

   For the purposes of Paragraph (2) herein, the term peace officer shall be defined [as] and include any constable, sheriff, deputy sheriff, local or state policeman, game warden, federal law enforcement officer, jail or prison guard, parole officer, probation officer, judge, district attorney, assistant district attorney or district attorneys' investigator.

   Whoever commits the crime of first degree murder shall be punished by death.

   In 1975, § 14:30 (1) was amended to add the crime of aggravated burglary as a predicate felony for first-degree murder. 1975 La. Acts, No. 327.

that "the fundamental respect for humanity underlying the Eighth Amendment . . . requires consideration of the character and record of the individual offender and the circumstances of the particular offense as a constitutionally indispensable part of the process of inflicting the penalty of death." In *Stanislaus Roberts, supra,* we made clear that this principle applies even where the crime of first-degree murder is narrowly defined. [. . .]

To be sure, the fact that the murder victim was a peace officer performing his regular duties may be regarded as an aggravating circumstance. There is a special interest in affording protection to these public servants who regularly must risk their lives in order to guard the safety of other persons and property.[2] But it is incorrect to suppose that no mitigating circumstances can exist when the victim is a police officer. Circumstances such as the youth of the offender, the absence of any prior conviction, the influence of drugs, alcohol, or extreme emotional disturbance, and even the existence of circumstances which the offender reasonably believed provided a moral justification for his conduct are all examples of mitigating facts which might attend the killing of a peace officer and which are considered relevant in other jurisdictions.

As we emphasized repeatedly in *Stanislaus Roberts* and its companion cases decided last Term, it is essential that the capital-sentencing decision allow for consideration of whatever mitigating circumstances may be relevant to either the particular offender or the particular offense.[3] Because the Louisiana statute does not allow for consideration of particularized mitigating factors, it is unconstitutional.

Accordingly, we hold that the death sentence imposed upon this petitioner violates the Eighth and Fourteenth Amendments and must be set aside. The judgment of the Supreme Court of Louisiana is reversed insofar as it upholds the death sentence upon petitioner. The case is remanded for further proceedings not inconsistent with this opinion.

It is so ordered.

Mr. Justice Blackmun, with whom Mr. Justice White and Mr. Justice Rehnquist join, dissenting. The Court, feeling itself bound by the plurality opinion in *Roberts* v. *Louisiana,* 428 U.S. 325 (1976) (hereafter *Stanislaus Roberts*), has painted itself into a corner. I did not join that plurality opinion, and I decline to be so confined. I therefore dissent from the Court's disposition of the present case and from its holding that the mandatory imposition of the death penalty for killing a peace officer, engaged in the performance of his lawful duties, constitutes cruel and unusual punishment in violation of the

2. We recognize that the life of a police officer is a dangerous one. [. . .]
3. We reserve again the question whether or in what circumstances mandatory death sentence statutes may be constitutionally applied to prisoners serving life sentences. [. . .]

Eighth and Fourteenth Amendments. I would uphold the State's power to impose such a punishment under La. Rev. Stat. Ann. § 14:30 (2) (1974), and I would reject any statements or intimations to the contrary in the Court's prior cases. [. . .]

Stanislaus Roberts was charged and convicted under a different subsection, that is, § 14:30 (1), of the Louisiana first-degree murder statute. See 428 U.S., at 327. [. . .] Subsection (1) provided a mandatory death penalty in the case where the killer had a specific intent to kill or to inflict great bodily harm and was engaged in the perpetration or attempted perpetration of aggravated kidnaping, aggravated rape, or armed robbery. [. . .] Subsection (2), in contrast, provides that first-degree murder is committed when the killer has a specific intent to kill, or to inflict great bodily harm upon, a fireman or a peace officer who is engaged in the performance of his lawful duties. *Ibid.* The two subsections obviously should involve quite different considerations with regard to the lawfulness of a mandatory death penalty, even accepting the analysis set forth in the joint opinions of last Term. Thus, to the extent that the plurality in *Stanislaus Roberts* alluded to subsections of the Louisiana law that were not before the Court, those statements are nonbinding dicta. It is indisputable that carefully focused consideration was not given to the special problem of a mandatory death sentence for one who has intentionally killed a police officer engaged in the performance of his lawful duties. I therefore approach this case as a new one, not predetermined and governed by the plurality in *Stanislaus Roberts*. [. . .]

I should note that I do not read the *per curiam* opinion today as one deciding the issue of the constitutionality of a mandatory death sentence for a killer of a peace officer for all cases and all times. Reference to the plurality opinion in *Stanislaus Roberts* reveals that the Louisiana statute contained what that opinion regarded as two fatal defects: lack of an opportunity to consider mitigating factors, and standardless jury discretion inherent in the Louisiana responsive verdict system. Without the latter, as here, a different case surely is presented. Furthermore, it is evident, despite the *per curiam's* general statement to the contrary, that mitigating factors need not be considered in every case; even the *per curiam* continues to reserve the issue of a mandatory death sentence for murder by a prisoner already serving a life sentence. [. . .] Finally, it is possible that a state statute that required the jury to consider, during the guilt phase of the trial, both the aggravating circumstance of killing a peace officer and relevant mitigating circumstances would pass the plurality's test. Cf. *Jurek* v. *Texas,* 428 U.S. 262, 270–71 (1976). For me, therefore, today's decision must be viewed in the context of the Court's previous criticism of the Louisiana system; it need not freeze the Court into a position that condemns every statute with a mandatory death penalty for the intentional killing of a peace officer.

Mr. Justice Rehnquist, with whom Mr. Justice White joins, dissenting. The Court today holds that the State of Louisiana is not entitled to vindicate its substantial interests in protecting the foot soldiers of an ordered society by mandatorily sentencing their murderers to death. This is so even though the State has demonstrated to a jury in a fair trial, beyond a reasonable doubt, that a particular defendant was the murderer, and that he committed the act while possessing "a specific intent to kill, or to inflict great bodily harm upon, . . . a peace officer who was engaged in the performance of his lawful duties. . . . " La. Rev. Stat. Ann. § 14:30 (2) (1974). That holding would have shocked those who drafted the Bill of Rights on which it purports to rest, and would commend itself only to the most imaginative observer as being required by today's "evolving standards of decency."

I am unable to agree that a mandatory death sentence under such circumstances violates the Eighth Amendment's proscription against "cruel and unusual punishments." I am equally unable to see how this limited application of the mandatory death statute violates even the scope of the Eighth Amendment as seen through the eyes of last Term's plurality in *Roberts* v. *Louisiana*, 428 U.S. 325 (1976) (hereafter *Stanislaus Roberts*). Nor does the brief *per curiam* opinion issued today demonstrate why the application of a mandatory death sentence to the criminal who intentionally murders a peace officer performing his official duties should be considered "cruel and unusual punishment" in light of either the view of society when the Eighth Amendment was passed, *Gregg* v. *Georgia*, 428 U.S. 153, 176–77 (1976); the "objective indicia that reflect the public attitude" today, id., at 173; or even the more generalized "basic concept of human dignity" test relied upon last Term in striking down several more general mandatory statutes.

While the arguments weighing in favor of individualized consideration for the convicted defendant are much the same here as they are for one accused of any homicide, the arguments weighing in favor of society's determination to impose a mandatory sentence for the murder of a police officer in the line of duty are far stronger than in the case of an ordinary homicide. [. . .]

Five Terms ago, in *Furman* v. *Georgia*, 408 U.S. 238 (1972), this Court invalidated the then-current system of capital punishments, condemning jury discretion as resulting in "freakish" punishment. The Louisiana Legislature has conscientiously determined, in an effort to respond to that holding, that the death sentence would be made mandatory upon the conviction of particular types of offenses, including, as in the case before us, the intentional killing of a peace officer while in the performance of his duties. For the reasons stated by Mr. Justice White for himself, The Chief Justice, Mr. Justice Blackmun, and me in his dissent in *Stanislaus Roberts, supra,* and by me in my dissent in *Woodson* v. *North Carolina*, 428 U.S. 280, 308 (1976), I am no more persuaded now than I was then that a mandatory death sentence for all, let alone for a limited class of, persons who commit premeditated murder constitutes "cruel and unusual punishment" under the Eighth and Fourteenth Amendments. [. . .]

Under the analysis of last Term's plurality opinion, a State, before it is constitutionally entitled to put a murderer to death, must consider aggravating and mitigating circumstances. It is possible to agree with the plurality in the general case without at all conceding that it follows that a mandatory death sentence is impermissible in the specific case we have before us: the deliberate killing of a peace officer. The opinion today is willing to concede that "the fact that the murder victim was a peace officer performing his regular duties may be regarded as an aggravating circumstance." *Ante,* at 636. But it seems to me that the factors which entitle a State to consider it as an aggravating circumstance also entitle the State to consider it so grave an aggravating circumstance that no permutation of mitigating factors exists which would disable it from constitutionally sentencing the murderer to death. If the State would be constitutionally entitled, due to the nature of the offense, to sentence the murderer to death *after* going through such a limited version of the plurality's "balancing" approach, I see no constitutional reason why the "Cruel and Unusual Punishments" Clause precludes the State from doing so without engaging in that process.

We are dealing here not merely with the State's determination as to whether particular conduct on the part of an individual should be punished, and in what manner, but also with what sanctions the State is entitled to bring into play to assure that there will be a police force to see that the criminal laws are enforced at all. It is no service to individual rights, or to individual liberty, to undermine what is surely the fundamental right and responsibility of any civilized government: the maintenance of order so that all may enjoy liberty and security. [. . .] Policemen are both symbols and outriders of our ordered society, and they literally risk their lives in an effort to preserve it. To a degree unequaled in the ordinary first-degree murder presented in the *Stanislaus Roberts* case, the State therefore has an interest in making unmistakably clear that those who are convicted of deliberately killing police officers acting in the line of duty be forewarned that punishment, in the form of death, will be inexorable. [. . .]

The historical and legal content of the "Cruel and Unusual Punishments" Clause was stretched to the breaking point by the plurality's opinion in the *Stanislaus Roberts* case last Term. Today this judicially created superstructure, designed and erected more than 180 years after the Bill of Rights was adopted, is tortured beyond permissible limits of judicial review. There is nothing in the Constitution's prohibition against cruel and unusual punishment which disables a legislature from imposing a mandatory death sentence on a defendant convicted after a fair trial of deliberately murdering a police officer.

§5. The Death Penalty for Rape: *Coker* v. *Georgia* (1977)

[*Editor's note:* The decision in *Coker*, 433 U.S. 485 (1977), was announced on 29 June 1977, the Court dividing 7 to 2. The plurality opinion and judgment of the Court, announced by Justice White, was joined by Justices Stewart, Blackmun, and Stevens. Excerpts from this opinion, omitting some citations and footnotes, are reprinted below. Justices Brennan and Marshall, citing their dissents in *Gregg*, joined in the judgment. Justice Powell, an excerpt of whose opinion is reprinted below, concurred in the judgment but not in the reasoning of the plurality. The Chief Justice and Justice Rehnquist joined in dissent, and a brief extract from their opinion is reprinted below.]

Mr. Justice White announced the judgment of the Court and filed an opinion in which Mr. Justice Stewart, Mr. Justice Blackmun, and Mr. Justice Stevens, joined. Georgia Code Ann. § 26-2001 (1972) provides that "[a] person convicted of rape shall be punished by death or by imprisonment for life, or by imprisonment for not less than 20 years. Punishment is determined by a jury in a separate sentencing proceeding in which at least one of the statutory aggravating circumstances must be found before the death penalty may be imposed. Petitioner Coker was convicted of rape and sentenced to death. Both conviction and sentence were affirmed by the Georgia Supreme Court. [...]

[...] In *Gregg*, after giving due regard to such sources, the Court's judgment was that the death penalty for deliberate murder was neither the purposeless imposition of severe punishment nor a punishment grossly disproportionate to the crime. But the Court reserved the question of the constitutionality of the death penalty when imposed for other crimes. 428 U.S., at 187 n.35.

That question, with respect to rape of an adult woman, is now before us. We have concluded that a sentence of death is grossly disproportionate and excessive punishment for the crime of rape and is therefore forbidden by the Eighth Amendment as cruel and unusual punishment.[1]

As advised by recent cases, we seek guidance in history and from the objective evidence of the country's present judgment concerning the acceptability of death as a penalty for rape of an adult woman. At no time in the last 50

---

1. Because the death sentence is a disproportionate punishment for rape, it is cruel and unusual punishment within the meaning of the Eighth Amendment even though it may measurably serve the legitimate ends of punishment and therefore is not invalid for its failure to do so. We observe that in the light of the legislative decisions in almost all of the States and in most of the countries around the world, it would be difficult to support a claim that the death penalty for rape is an indispensable part of the States' criminal justice system.

years has a majority of the States authorized death as a punishment for rape. In 1925, 18 States, the District of Columbia, and the Federal Government authorized capital punishment for the rape of an adult female. By 1971 just prior to the decision in *Furman* v. *Georgia,* that number had declined, but not substantially, to 16 States plus the Federal Government. *Furman* then invalidated most of the capital punishment statutes in this country, including the rape statutes, because, among other reasons, of the manner in which the death penalty was imposed and utilized under those laws.

[. . .] In reviving death penalty laws to satisfy *Furman*'s mandate, none of the States that had not previously authorized death for rape chose to include rape among capital felonies. Of the 16 States in which rape had been a capital offense, only three provided the death penalty for rape of an adult woman in their revised statutes—Georgia, North Carolina, and Louisiana. In the latter two States, the death penalty was mandatory for those found guilty, and those laws were invalidated by *Woodson* and *Roberts.* When Louisiana and North Carolina, responding to those decisions, again revised their capital punishment laws, they reenacted the death penalty for murder but not for rape; none of the seven other legislatures that to our knowledge have amended or replaced their death penalty statutes since July 2, 1976, including four States (in addition to Louisiana and North Carolina) that had authorized the death sentence for rape prior to 1972 and had reacted to *Furman* with mandatory statutes, included rape among the crimes for which death was an authorized punishment. [. . .]

The current judgment with respect to the death penalty for rape is not wholly unanimous among state legislatures, but it obviously weighs very heavily on the side of rejecting capital punishment as a suitable penalty for raping an adult woman.[2]

It was also observed in *Gregg* that "[t]he jury . . . is a significant and reliable index of contemporary values because it is so directly involved," 428 U.S., at 181, and that it is thus important to look to the sentencing decisions that juries have made in the course of assessing whether capital punishment is an appropriate penalty for the crime being tried. [. . .]

According to the factual submissions in this Court, out of all rape convictions in Georgia since 1973—and that total number has not been tendered—63 cases had been reviewed by the Georgia Supreme Court as of the time of oral argument; and of these, six involved a death sentence, one of which was set aside, leaving five convicted rapists now under sentence of death in the State of Georgia. Georgia juries have thus sentenced rapists to death six times since 1973. This obviously is not a negligible number; and the State argues

2. In *Trop* v. *Dulles,* 356 U.S. 86, 102 (1958), the Court took pains to note the climate of international opinion concerning the acceptability of a particular punishment. It is thus not irrelevant here that out of 60 major nations in the world surveyed in 1965, only 3 retained the death penalty for rape where death did not ensue. United Nations, Department of Economic and Social Affairs, Capital Punishment 40, 86 (1968).

that as a practical matter juries simply reserve the extreme sanction for extreme cases of rape and that recent experience surely does not prove that jurors consider the death penalty to be a disproportionate punishment for every conceivable instance of rape, no matter how aggravated. Nevertheless, it is true that in the vast majority of cases, at least 9 out of 10, juries have not imposed the death sentence.

These recent events evidencing the attitude of state legislatures and sentencing juries do not wholly determine this controversy, for the Constitution contemplates that in the end our own judgment will be brought to bear on the question of the acceptability of the death penalty under the Eighth Amendment. Nevertheless, the legislative rejection of capital punishment for rape strongly confirms our own judgment, which is that death is indeed a disproportionate penalty for the crime of raping an adult woman.

We do not discount the seriousness of rape as a crime. It is highly reprehensible, both in a moral sense and in its almost total contempt for the personal integrity and autonomy of the female victim and for the latter's privilege of choosing those with whom intimate relationships are to be established. Short of homicide, it is the "ultimate violation of self."[3] It is also a violent crime because it normally involves force, or the threat of force or intimidation, to overcome the will and the capacity of the victim to resist. Rape is very often accompanied by physical injury to the female and can also inflict mental and psychological damage.[4] Because it undermines the community's sense of security, there is public injury as well.

Rape is without doubt deserving of serious punishment; but in terms of moral depravity and of the injury to the person and to the public, it does not compare with murder, which does involve the unjustified taking of human life. Although it may be accompanied by another crime, rape by definition does not include the death or even the serious injury to another person.[5] The murderer kills; the rapist, if no more than that, does not. Life is over for the victim of the murderers; for the rape victim, life may not be nearly so happy as it was, but it is not over and normally is not beyond repair. We have the abiding conviction that the death penalty, which "is unique in its severity and revocability," 428 U.S. 187, is an excessive penalty for the rapist who, as such, does not take human life.

This does not end the matter; for under Georgia law, death may not be

3. Law Enforcement Assistance Administration Report, Rape and Its Victims: A Report for Citizens, Health Facilities, and Criminal Justice Agencies 1(1975), quoting Bard & Ellison, Crisis Intervention and Investigation of Forcible Rape, The Police Chief (May 1974), Reproduced as Appendix I-B to the Report.

4. See Note, The Victim In a Forcible Rape Case: A Feminist View, 11 Am. Crim. Law Rev. 335, 338 (1973); Comment, Rape and Rape Laws: Sexism in Society and Law, 61 Calif. L. Rev. 919, 922–23 (1973).

5. [Rape is "carnal knowledge of a female, forcibly and against her will. Carnal knowledge in rape occurs when there is any penetration of the female sex organ by the male sex organ." Ga. Code Ann. §26–2001 (1972)]

imposed for any capital offense, including rape, unless the jury or judge finds one of the statutory aggravating circumstances and then elects to impose that sentence. Section 26-3102 (Supp. 1975); *Gregg v. Georgia, supra,* at 165–66. For the rapist to be executed in Georgia, it must therefore be found not only that he committed rape but also that one or more of the following aggravating circumstances were present: 1. that the rape was committed by a person with a prior record of conviction for a capital felony; 2. that the rape was committed while the offender was engaged in the commission of another capital felony, or aggravated battery; or 3. the rape "was outrageously or wantonly vile, horrible or inhuman in that it involved torture, depravity of mind, or aggravated battery to the victim."[6] Here, the first two of these aggravating circumstances were alleged and found by the jury.

Neither of these circumstances, nor both of them together, change our conclusion that the death sentence imposed on Coker is a disproportionate punishment for rape. Coker had prior convictions for capital felonies—rape, murder and kidnapping—but these prior convictions do not change the fact that the instant crime being punished is a rape not involving the taking of life.

It is also true that the present rape occurred while Coker was committing armed robbery, a felony for which the Georgia statutes authorize the death penalty.[7] But Coker was tried for the robbery offense as well as for rape and received a separate life sentence for this crime; the jury did not deem the robbery itself deserving of the death penalty, even though accompanied by the aggravating circumstance, which was stipulated, that Coker had been convicted of a prior capital crime.[8]

We note finally that in Georgia a person commits murder when he unlawfully and with malice aforethought, either express or implied, causes the death of another human being. He also commits that crime when in the com-

---

6. There are other aggravating circumstances provided in the statute, [. . .] but they are not applicable to rape.
7. In *Gregg v. Georgia*, the Georgia Supreme Court refused to sustain a death sentence for armed robbery because, for one reason, death had been so seldom imposed for this crime in other cases that such a sentence was excessive and could not be sustained under the statute. As it did in this case, however, the Georgia Supreme Court apparently continues to recognize armed robbery as a capital offense for the purpose of applying the aggravating circumstances provisions of the Georgia Code.
8. Where the accompanying capital crime is murder, it is most likely that the defendant would be tried for murder, rather than rape; and it is perhaps academic to deal with the death sentence for rape in such a circumstance. It is likewise unnecessary to consider the rape-felony murder—a rape accompanied by the death of the victim which was unlawfully but nonmaliciously caused by the defendant.
   Where the third aggravating circumstance mentioned in the text is present—that the rape is particularly vile or involves torture or aggravated battery—it would seem that the defendant could very likely be convicted, tried and appropriately punished for this additional conduct.

mission of a felony he causes the death of another human being, irrespective of malice. But even where the killing is deliberate, it is not punishable by death absent proof of aggravating circumstances. It is difficult to accept the notion, and we do not, that the rape, with or without aggravating circumstances, should be punished more heavily than the deliberate killer as long as the rapist does not himself take the life of his victim. The judgment of the Georgia Supreme Court upholding the death sentence is reversed and the case is remanded to that court for further proceedings not inconsistent with this opinion.

So ordered.

Mr. Justice Powell, concurring in part and dissenting in part. I concur in the judgment of the Court on the facts of this case, and also in its reasoning supporting the view that ordinarily death is disproportionate punishment for the crime of raping an adult woman. Although rape invariably is a reprehensible crime, there is no indication that petitioner's offense was committed with excessive brutality or that the victim sustained serious or lasting injury. The plurality, however, does not limit its holding to the case before us or to similar cases. Rather, in an opinion that ranges well beyond what is necessary, it holds that capital punishment *always*—regardless of the circumstances—is a disproportionate penalty for the crime of rape. [. . .]

Today, in a case that does not require such an expansive pronouncement, the plurality draws a bright line between murder and all rapes—regardless of the degree of brutality of the rape or the effect upon the victim. I dissent because I am not persuaded that such a bright line is appropriate. As noted in *Snider* v. *Peyton*, 356 F. 2d 626, 627 (CA4 1966), "[t]here is extreme variation in the degree of culpability of rapists." The deliberate viciousness of the rapist may be greater than that of the murderer. Rape is never an act committed accidentally. Rarely can it be said to be unpremeditated. There also is wide variation in the effect on the victim. The plurality opinion says that "[l]ife is over for the victim of the murderer; for the rape victim, life may not be nearly so happy as it was, but it is not over and normally is not beyond repair." *Ante,* at 13. But there is indeed "extreme variation" in the crime of rape. Some victims are so grievously injured physically or psychologically that life *is* beyond repair.

Thus it may be that the death penalty is not disproportionate punishment for the crime of aggravated rape. [. . .]

Mr. Chief Justice Burger, with whom Mr. Justice Rehnquist joins, dissenting. In a case such as this, confusion often arises as to the Court's proper role in reaching a decision. Our task is not to give effect to our individual views on capital punishment; rather, we must determine what the Constitution permits a State to do under its reserved powers. In striking down the death penalty imposed upon the petitioner in this case, the Court has overstepped the bounds of proper constitutional adjudication by substituting its policy judgment for that of the state legislature. I accept that the Eighth Amendment's concept of disproportionality bars the death penalty for minor crimes. But rape is not a minor crime; hence the Cruel and Unusual Punishment Clause does not give the Members of this Court license to engraft their conceptions of proper public policy onto the considered legislative judgments of the States. Since I cannot agree that Georgia lacked the constitutional power to impose the penalty of death for rape, I dissent from the Court's judgment. [. . .]

7

For the Death Penalty

INTRODUCTION

Who argues today for the death penalty, and what is the distinctive flavor and emphasis of their arguments? What groups, if any, have spokesmen defending the death penalty? The five selections reprinted below serve as partial answers to these questions.

A century or more ago, when the social sciences were in their infancy and the death penalty a commonplace, the most vocal defenders of the death penalty in America were Christian clergymen (see Mackey 1974b). Even today, in fundamentalist, Bible-centered religious communities one can hear a case made for capital punishment that is largely, if not exclusively, presented in Biblical terms (see Vellenga 1959). But the role of this kind of argument elsewhere has been on the decline for years; it is simply not heard in serious journals of opinion, professional seminars, television debates and talk shows, or even in editorials or legislative hearings outside the Bible Belt.[1] Where once it would have been inexcusable to omit such views in a chapter such as this, it may now be done with less injustice. Besides, as the next chapter will note, organized religion in the United States (whether Catholic, Jewish, or Protestant), with a few notable exceptions,[2] has abandoned its traditional

1. Probably no argument for the death penalty on religious grounds is more perverse than the one that emerged in New York after the legislature enacted a new death penalty law in April 1978. In a letter to a church group, responding to their opposition to the new law, State Senator James Donovan is reported to have asked where Christianity would be today had "Jesus got 8 to 15 years with time off for good behavior." *The Washington Post*, 7 April 1978, p. B6.
2. In particular, Jehovah's Witnesses, Seventh Day Adventists, the Church of Jesus Christ of Latter Day Saints (Mormons), the American Baptist Convention, and certain conservative and orthodox Jewish groups.

305

support of (or silence on) the death penalty and instead openly favors its complete abolition.

The most sustained defense of the death penalty today comes from those whose official responsibilities are in law enforcement, ranging from those who must detect, arrest, and control persons charged with (or convicted of) capital crimes to those who draft death penalty legislation, argue for capital convictions in trial courts, or write the briefs to persuade appellate courts to uphold death sentences. It is thus members of police forces and district attorneys' offices, and spokesmen for their organizations, such as the International Association of Chiefs of Police (IACP) and the National District Attorneys Association (NDAA), who in recent years have most frequently spoken in favor of capital punishment. Of the many statements expressed from this position the testimony before the House Judiciary Committee in 1972 by Glen D. King on behalf of the IACP has been reprinted below as §1.[3] His statement is followed in §2 by a portion of the report of the Senate Committee on the Judiciary (1980) on behalf of S. 114, a bill designed to bring federal death penalty statutes into conformity with the recent Supreme Court rulings. Although the report did not have the endorsement of the Committee's chairman, Senator Edward M. Kennedy (along with Senators Culver and Leahy, he filed a dissenting report), it did include among its supporters the new (1981) Committee chairman and long-time advocate of capital punishment, Senator Strom Thurmond.[4]

This report was the culmination of a legislative process in the Senate covering several years and several different death penalty bills, among them S. 1382, on which hearings were held during 1978. Testifying on behalf of that bill for the Department of Justice was staff attorney Mary C. Lawton. Her remarks, reprinted in §3, present a government draftsman's view of a constitutionally unobjectionable death penalty statute. Her statement is interesting because it deals in part with the traditional capital crimes of treason and espionage, which tend to be ignored in most debates today. Abolitionists and retentionists alike are understandably preoccupied with the far more fre-

---

3. See Hoover 1959, 1960, and 1961; Allen 1960; Sendak 1971; McMahon 1973; also Carrington 1978. Mr. Carrington is the executive secretary of Americans for Effective Law Enforcement (AELE) and has testified in Congress on behalf of the death penalty; see, e.g., *House Hearing* 1972:222–241, reprinted in *Senate Hearing* 1973:228–35.

4. See especially his remarks as reported in *Congressional Record—Senate*, 26 April 1977, pp. S 6378– S 6382, along with the supporting remarks of Senators McClellan and Roth; also *Congressional Record—Senate*, 18 June 1980, pp. S 7373–S 7379, along with the supporting remarks of Senators Helms and Dole. Recent expression in Congress supporting a federal death penalty can be found in *House Report* 1980 from Representatives Lamar Gudger (pp. 698f.), Harold L. Volkmer (pp. 704f.), and James Sensenbrenner (pp. 717–20). During April and May 1981, further hearings were held in the Senate Judiciary Committee on S. 114, under the chairmanship of Senator Thurmond; see *Senate Hearings* 1981.

quent death sentences for murder, rape, and other crimes of personal violence. (Besides, espionage and treason are of relevance only where federal—
not state—death penalties are concerned.)

There are also scholars, essayists, moralists, and members of the learned
and academic professions generally who have come to the defence of the
death penalty in recent years. By their efforts they have in effect brought up
to date the long tradition of notable philosophers (Hobbes, Locke, Rousseau,
Kant, Hegel, Mill) who defended the death penalties of their day.[5] No doubt
the most durable academic apologist for capital punishment in the 1970s,
familiar as a lecturer to professional societies, often invited to appear before
legislative bodies, and prominent in debate before many audiences, is Ernest
van den Haag of New York University, whose *Punishing Criminals* (1975)
devotes two of its chapters to explaining and defending the death penalty.
Major portions of one of his recent essays are reprinted below in §4. But not
even he has devoted a whole book solely to arguing the case for executions.
That distinction belongs to Walter Berns, at the time Professor of Political
Science at the University of Toronto and now Resident Scholar at the American Enterprise Institute for Public Policy Research in Washington, D.C. His
book, *For Capital Punishment* (1979) showed him to be one of the nation's
most thoughtful proponents of the death penalty. Bern's book, taken as a
whole, mounts an argument that many readers will find persuasive.[6] The bulk
of one important chapter appeared in *Harper's Magazine* and in newspapers
just prior to the book's release, and that selection has been reprinted below
as §5. Both van den Haag and Berns make much of the desirability of capital
punishment from the moral point of view (though Berns's morality includes
little of the utilitarian thinking prominent in van den Haag's), and so their
arguments deserve the closest attention. Berns especially stresses the appropriateness of the moral indignation that grave criminal offenses provoke, and
implies that the death penalty alone adequately expresses this indignation.
These may not be novel views, but they are widely shared, even (as we have
seen in Chapter Six) on the bench of the Supreme Court.

A full and complete argument for the death penalty cannot be found, of
course, in any one of the short essays reprinted here. For that, each reader
must undertake to fit together the material in this chapter with other considerations quarried from writings scattered throughout this book. What the
essays below can provide is a succinct framework in terms of which a com-

---

5. See R. Gardner 1978 for a general review; see S. Goldberg 1974 and Leiser 1979 for recent
   defenses of the death penalty by philosophers. Apart from those few social scientists who
   defend the death penalty on deterrent grounds (see Chapter Four), most either oppose it or
   keep their views to themselves. A recent exception is Lehtinen 1977.
6. For reviews of this book, see G. Hughes 1979, Bedau 1980b, and van den Haag 1980.

prehensive and detailed defense might be fabricated and focussed, as the interests of each reader dictate, upon empirical, legal, or moral concerns.[7]

§1.   On Behalf of the Death Penalty*

GLEN D. KING

[. . .] I am sure that most persons who appear before this subcommittee urging legislation to abolish capital punishment do so because of a concern for human life. It is precisely for this reason that I urge the subcommittee to decide in favor of recommending a retention of this form of crime prevention.

The logic which urges an abolition of the death penalty in the interest of human life is more apparent than real. For I am convinced that ultimately abolition of capital punishment would result in a much greater loss of human life than would its retention.

It is admittedly tragic whenever the State in the most awesome exercise of its authority decides that capital punishment must be invoked, tragic because any loss of human life is a tragedy. But I submit to you that even in the tragedy of human death there are degrees, and that it is much more tragic for the innocent to lose his life than for the State to take the life of a criminal convicted of a capital offense.

My statement implies a belief that there is a direct relationship between the legal existence of capital punishment and the incidents of criminal homicide. Although statistics are generally unreliable in this area, I am convinced that such a relationship does exist. I am convinced that many potential murderers are deterred simply by their knowledge that capital punishment exists, and may be their fate if they commit the crime they contemplate.

I think it significant that during recent years we have seen a consistent

---

7. A partial list of writings in defense of the death penalty published prior to the mid-1960s may be found in Bedau 1967b:120ff. For more recent publications, in addition to those already cited above, see van den Haag 1968, 1969, and 1970 (replies in Bedau 1970a, 1971, and 1970b, respectively); Zoll 1971; M. Evans 1977; van den Haag 1977 (replying to Bedau 1977b); and Rice 1969:87–105. For a recent and highly qualified defense of the death penalty, on grounds that society does not have "a right but a *need* to express its outrage," see Mailer 1981. (Norman Mailer was awarded the Pulitzer Prize in 1980 for *The Executioner's Song*, his fictionalized account of the life of Gary Gilmore and his death in front of a Utah firing squad in 1977.)

*Excerpted from the testimony of Glen D. King, 10 May 1972, at the hearings before Subcommittee No. 3, Committee of the Judiciary, House of Representatives, 92nd Congress, 2nd Session, on H.R. 8414, etc., "Capital Punishment," U.S. Government Printing Office, Washington, D.C., 1972, pp. 391–400.

reduction in the number of incidents of capital punishment, and at the same time a very great increase in the number of criminal homicides.

As an example, in 1950, 82 convicted felons were executed, a very great percentage of whom were guilty of the crime of homicide. During the same year, 7020 criminal homicides were reported.

A decade later, the number of executions dropped to 56, and the number of criminal homicides rose to 9140.

Throughout the 1960s, we experienced a steady increase in the number of criminal homicides, with 14,590 recorded in 1969. During the same decade, we saw a practical end to the utilization of the death penalty. Since 1967, no executions have occurred in the United States, and there were only two that year. In 1966, there was only one instance in which this form of punishment was applied.

I realize that a very great number of factors are involved in this extremely complex question, and I do not suggest for a moment that the de facto end of the death penalty as a form of punishment is solely responsible for the burgeoning homicide rate in the United States. But I suggest it is equally unrealistic to assume that there is no relationship between the two.

The danger of resorting solely to statistics in attempting to determine the best course of action to follow in something as complex as the issue of the death penalty is illustrated by some of the statistics cited to support its abolition.

Opponents of capital punishment point to the criminal homicide rates in States which have legally banned the death penalty, and claim support for their beliefs in the fact that the statistics in these States are lower than in some in which capital punishment continues to be legally permissible.

The questionable nature of such statistics becomes immediately apparent when we realize that capital punishment as a practical matter has ceased to exist in all States. When 4 years pass without a single State exacting the death penalty, then statistics comparing States with capital punishment and those without become ridiculous.

We have in effect become a Nation in which capital punishment does not exist, and I am convinced that part of the results of this has been a very great increase in capital offenses.

It is equally as invalid to rely on emotional appeals, because there is an inherent element of emotion both in appeals to continue and to discontinue capital punishment.

Lurid descriptions of the death scene have painted a horrible picture of the execution. Of equal impact are descriptions of the savage atrocities visited upon innocent victims by those who commit murders and rapes. A description of the execution scene which revolts and repels is no more valid a basis upon which to make a decision than is the gore of the criminal homicide scene.

Our courts, with every justification, have refused to admit into evidence in the trial of an accused pictures and oral descriptions which repel human sensibilities and are revolting to human decency. The courts realize that reliance upon such methods cause conclusions to be reached on the basis of emotion rather than on the basis of logic.

Such an application can with equal validity be made to execution.

At one time in the history of man, 168 violations were capital offenses. It is to the credit of our forebears that they realized that the death penalty could not properly be applied in minor cases, but must be reserved to those cases of greatest magnitude.

I am convinced that an equal exercise of good judgment calls upon us to decide that conditions can exist in which this act of the utmost gravity is not only justified but is demanded, and that violations can be committed which are so reprehensible that no other form of punishment is suitable.

If we are to apply those methods which serve as the greatest deterrent, we are going to have to continue to suit the punishment to the offense.

The Nation's police officers are particularly concerned with this issue, not merely because they are called upon for direct involvement in the incidents which may result in the application of the death penalty, but because they themselves are so often the victims of offenses for which the death penalty may be assessed. We have in recent years seen a very great increase in the number of criminal assaults committed on the police officer, and in the number of injuries and fatalities resulting from those assaults.

Several of the five States which have partially abolished the death penalty have retained it for the killing of a police officer or a prison or jail guard who is in the performance of his duties. The States of New Mexico, New York, and Vermont have specifically cited such offenses as being justification for the exercise of the death penalty while prohibiting it in other criminal homicides.

Whether these States are correct in their partial abolition of the death penalty, they are unquestionably correct in their implication that the death of a police officer inflicted while that officer is acting in the line of duty is somewhat different and apart from other criminal homicides.

The policeman willingly subjects himself to a greater element of danger than most persons ever experience while protecting the citizens he serves. He is not, however, willing to be the victim of the criminal who uses violence as the method of obtaining that which he seeks. Nor is he willing to be the victim of felonious assault merely because his assailant knows that he can maim and kill without being subjected to meaningful and appropriate punishment.

Gentlemen, I am of the belief that capital punishment must be assessed only after every legal safeguard has been provided, and that it can be properly applied only with a full understanding of the very great gravity of its exercise.

But I am convinced, and I urge you to conclude, that capital punishment under carefully prescribed conditions and for highly selective offenses is a deterrent to certain kinds of crimes, and that the value of human life is not lessened but is rather protected by retention of the death penalty as a form of punishment. [...]

§2. Capital Punishment as a Matter of Legislative Policy*

COMMITTEE ON THE JUDICIARY, U.S. SENATE

[...] Despite the explicit approval by the Supreme Court for the death penalty as an appropriate sanction under the Eight Amendment of the Constitution, the basic issue of the use of the death penalty is so important that the Committee feels compelled to reiterate here the justifications for its use in the heinous crimes under the particular circumstances provided in S. 114.

The conclusion in favor of the retention of capital punishment for these crimes has its basis in the belief that the primary responsibility of society is the protection of its members so that they may live out their lives in peace and safety. Indeed, this is one of the main reasons why any society exists. Where the safety of its citizenry can no longer be guaranteed, society's basic reason for being disappears. In providing its members protection, society must do what is necessary to deter those who would break its laws and punish those who do so in an appropriate manner. It is the Committee's conclusion that capital punishment applied to the most serious offenses fulfills these functions.

The question of the deterrent effect of capital punishment has probably been the one point most debated by those favoring the abolition of the penalty and those desiring its retention. Several studies have been conducted purporting to show the absence of any correlation between the existence of the penalty and the number of capital crimes committed in a particular jurisdiction. The argument then follows that, since there exists no such relationship, the penalty serves no legitimate social purpose and should not be imposed.

If the absence of any correlation between the existence of the penalty and the frequency of capital crimes could actually be proved by these studies, the argument for abolition would be much stronger. Although entitled to con-

*Excerpted from "Establishing Constitutional Procedures for the Imposition of Capital Punishment," *Report of the Committee on the Judiciary, United States Senate . . . to accompany S. 114, 96th Congress, 1st Session*, Report No. 96-554, 17 January 1980, pp. 7–14. Some footnotes have been deleted and the others renumbered.

sideration, however, the value of these studies is seriously diminished by the unreliability of the statistical evidence used, the contrary experience of those in the field of law enforcement, and the inherent logic of the deterrent power of the threat of death.

With regard to the statistical evidence, the first and most obvious point is that those who are, in fact, deterred by the threat of the death penalty and do not commit murder are not included in the statistical data. There is no way to determine the number of such people. Secondly, even those favoring abolition agree that the available evidence on the subject of deterrence is, at best, inadequate. For example, Hugo Adam Bedau has described the difficulty in obtaining accurate data in this way:

> In a word, there is no exact information anywhere as to the volume of capital crimes in the United States. Difficult as it is to specify the capital laws for the nation as a whole, it is impossible with the present sort of criminal statistics to specify the exact amount of capital crimes for even one jurisdiction in even one year for even one crime.[1]

[...] In the absence of reliable statistical evidence, great weight must be placed on the experience of those who are most frequently called upon to deal with murderers and potential murderers and who are thus in the best position to judge the effectiveness of the remedy—our law enforcement officials. The vast majority of these officials continue to favor the retention of the death penalty as a deterrent to violent crime. As Sheriff Peter Pitchess of Los Angeles County testified before the California Senate Committee on the Judiciary:

> I can tell you that the overwhelming majority of people in law enforcement— the ones who are dealing with these criminals, the ones who are seeing them not as statistics but real live human beings, and who are studying their human behavior—are overwhelmingly convinced that capital punishment is a deterrent.[2]

The Honorable J. Edgar Hoover, the late Director of the Federal Bureau of Investigation, declared that:

> [t]he professional law enforcement officer is convinced from experience that the hardened criminal has been and is deterred from killing based on the prospect of the death penalty.[3]

1. "The Death Penalty in America, an Anthology," Hugo Adam Bedau, ed., p. 56, Doubleday (1964).
2. Hearings, report and testimony on Senate bill No. 1, Second Extraordinary Session, which proposed to abolish the death penalty in California and to substitute life imprisonment, without possibility of parole. California Legislature, Senate Committee on the Judiciary, p. 150 (1960).
3. "The Uniform Crime Reports of the United States," Federal Bureau of Investigation, p. 14 (1959).

In his testimony before the Subcommittee on Criminal Laws and Procedures on S. 1401, Mr. Edward J. Kiernan, President of the International Conference of Police Associations and a police officer with 30 years of service,
discussed the criminal's fear of the death penalty and declared that:

> sometimes the specter of that fear will stay a trigger finger at the critical
> moment.[4]

In his testimony on S. 1401, Mr. Arlen Specter, then district attorney of
Philadelphia, stated:

> I believe the death penalty is an effective deterrent against murder. I say that
> based upon more than 7 years as district attorney of Philadelphia, and dealing
> with a great many cases in that capacity. We have the frequent occurrence in
> the criminal courts of Philadelphia where professional burglars have expressed
> themselves on the point of not carrying a weapon on a burglary because of their
> concern there may be a scuffle, there may be a dispute, the weapon may be used
> and death may result, and prior to *Furman,* they may face the possibility of cap-
> ital punishment.[5]

The issue, for our purposes here, has been definitely resolved by the
Supreme Court in *Gregg* where it concluded that it is appropriate for a legislature to consider deterrence as a justification for the imposition of the
death penalty:

> Although some of the studies suggest that the death penalty may not function
> as a significantly greater deterrent than lesser penalties, there is no convincing
> empirical evidence either supporting or refuting this view. We may nevertheless
> assume safely that there are murderers, such as those who act in passion, for
> whom the threat of death has little or no deterrent effect. But for many others,
> the death penalty undoubtedly is a significant deterrent. There are carefully con-
> templated murders, such as murder for hire, where the possible penalty of death
> may well enter into the cold calculus that precedes the decision to act. And there
> are some categories of murder, such as murder by a life prisoner, where other
> sanctions may not be adequate.[6]

A frequently made argument in opposition to the idea of the death penalty
as a deterrent is that most homicides are crimes of passion against which no
penalty constitutes a true deterrent. Although it is true that many murders
are indeed the result of passion, it is equally true that a very large number are
the result of premeditation. Moreover, logic suggests that consequences can
influence conduct motivated by passion. As pointed out by the late Senator
John L. McClellan:

> It is sometimes said deterrence will not work with homicide, since murders
> are committed in the heat of passion, when the individual does not consider the

4. Senate Hearings (1973) at 157.
5. Id. at 70.
6. *Gregg* v. *Georgia,* at 185–86 (footnotes omitted).

consequences of his actions. This is true in some cases, but not all. As I have noted, of all murders committed in 1971, 27.5 percent were either known or suspected to have taken place during the commission of a felony. Premeditation, not passion, motivated these crimes. They were not situations of uncontrollable rage.

Where reason is present, the thought that one consequence of an individual's action is the forfeiture of his own life will, in most instances, serve as a deterrent.

Experience has proven this point. Recently, former criminal court Judge Samuel Leibowitz of New York, an eminent jurist who presided over many capital cases explained that, when he asked hardened criminals why they would not shoot their way out to escape capture, they would inevitably reply, "I was afraid of the hot seat, Judge."

Indeed, even in situations involving passion, the knowledge that murder will result in the swift termination of the murderer's own life must necessarily encourage restraint and self-control.[7]

Coupled with the great weight of experience is the inherent rationality of a deterrent effect. Senator DeConcini has observed that he doubts that deterrence can ever be empirically proven or disproven and "[u]ltimately, only the inherent logic that the threat of loss of one's life is a deterrent justifies capital punishment."[8] Clearly a person will be slow to undertake an action that will result in the loss of something which he values highly. Since life itself is the most highly prized possession an individual has, he will be most hesitant to engage in conduct which will result in its forfeiture. In the words of Mr. Richard E. Gerstein before the Section of Criminal Law of the American Bar Association:

> It is clear that for normal human beings no other punishment deters so effectively from committing murder as the punishment of death . . . [S]ince people fear death more than anything else, the death penalty is the most effective deterrent.[9]

But the death penalty ought not be thought of solely in terms of individual deterrence. It also has value in terms of social or general deterrence as well. By associating the penalty with the crimes for which it is inflicted, society is made more aware of the horror of those crimes, and there is instilled in its members the desire to avoid such conduct.

The incapacitating effect of capital punishment is clear. Obviously those who suffer this penalty are unable to commit similar crimes in the future. The question, then, becomes one of necessity. Is the death penalty necessary to adequately protect society in the future from the possible actions of those who have already committed capital crimes? The Committee is of the opinion that, in certain circumstances, it is.

7. See *supra* note 4 at 2–3.
8. See Senate Hearings (1977) at 51.
9. American Bar Association, Section of Criminal Law, 1959 proceedings, p. 16 (1960).

In some cases, imprisonment is simply not a sufficient safeguard against the future actions of criminals. Some criminals are incorrigibly anti-social and will remain potentially dangerous to society for the rest of their lives. Mere imprisonment offers these people the possibility of escape or, in some cases, release on parole through error or oversight. Even if they are successfully imprisoned for life, prison itself is an environment presenting dangers to guards, inmates and others. In each of these cases, society is the victim. Basically, there is no satisfactory alternative sentence for these individuals. Life imprisonment without parole, although at first appearing to be a reasonable answer, is in reality highly unsatisfactory. Such a sentence greatly increases the danger to guards and to other prisoners who come into contact with those who have been so sentenced. Mr. Wallace Reidt, former director of the Maryland Department of Parole and Probation, expressed it in this way:

> If capital punishment is abolished, there will be considerable pressure to prevent parole in life terms and there will be removed what I believe is a great deterrent in the handling of prisoners in institutions.
>
> Most persons connected with institutions feel that unless there is some fear of punishment or hope of reward that a good many lifetermers would cause a great deal of trouble in the institutions and make the work of prison officials much more dangerous than it now is.[10]

It cannot be overemphasized that it is not the Committee's desire to see capital punishment utilized as an alternative to efforts at rehabilitation. This simply is not the case. The members of the Committee recognize that still greater attempts must be made to enable our prison system to achieve its goal of restoring productive and useful individuals to society. We here discuss only a minute class of extremely dangerous persons.

The Committee finds also that capital punishment serves the legitimate function of retribution. This is distinct from the concept of revenge in the sense of the "eye for an eye" mentality; rather it is through retribution that society expresses its outrage, and sense of revulsion, toward those who undermine the foundations of civilized society by contravening its laws. It reflects the fact that criminals have not simply inflicted injury upon discrete individuals; they have also weakened the often tenuous bonds that hold communities together.

The retributive function of punishment in general, and capital punishment in particular, was discussed by Lord Justice Denning before the British Royal Commission on Capital Punishment:

> The punishment inflicted for grave crimes should adequately reflect the revulsion felt by the great majority of citizens for them. It is a mistake to consider the objects of punishment as being deterrent or reformative or preventive and noth-

10. Maryland Committee on Capital Punishment, Report, p. 23 (1962).

ing else. The ultimate justification of any punishment is not that it is a deterrent, but that it is the emphatic denunciation by the community of a crime; and from this point of view, there are some murders which, in the present state of public opinion, demand the most emphatic denunciation of all, namely the death penalty.[11]

Similarly, Justice Holmes wrote in "The Common Law":

> The first requirement of a sound body of law is that it should correspond with the actual feelings and demands of the community, whether right or wrong.

It is the view of the committee that these feelings rightly and justly warrant the imposition of capital punishment under some circumstances.

That men who take the lives of others in an unjustified manner may sometimes be subject to the extreme sanction of capital punishment reflects a social consensus that places great sanctity on the value of human life. It is a consensus that holds that individual offenders are responsible and accountable beings, having it within themselves to conduct themselves in a civilized manner. It is also a consensus that holds that there is no offense more repugnant and more heinous than the deprivation of an innocent person's life.

Murder does not simply differ in magnitude from extortion or burglary or property destruction offenses; it differs in kind. Its punishment ought to also differ in kind. It must acknowledge the inviolability and dignity of innocent human life. It must, in short, be proportionate. The Committee has concluded that, in the relatively narrow range of circumstances outlined in this bill, that the penalty of death satisfies that standard.

Apart from its legitimacy as one of the purposes of punishment, questions have arisen with respect to the constitutional validity of retribution as a basis for punishment, specifically capital punishment. This question was addressed by the Supreme Court in the *Gregg* case:

> In part, capital punishment is an expression of society's moral outrage at particularly offensive conduct. This function may be unappealing to many, but it is essential in an ordered society that asks its citizens to rely on legal processes rather than self-help to vindicate their wrongs.
>
> "The instinct for retribution is part of the nature of man, and channelling that instinct in the administration of criminal justice serves an important purpose in promoting the stability of a free society governed by law. When people begin to believe that organized society is unwilling or unable to impose upon

---

11. Quoted by Richard C. Donnelly, "Capital Punishment," inserted in 106 Cong. Rec. at p. A6284 (daily ed. Aug. 14, 1960). See also Walter Berns, "For Capital Punishment," Harper's Magazine, April 1979, p. 15; Ernest van den Haag, "The Collapse of the Case Against Capital Punishment," National Review, Mar. 31, 1978., p. 395; Sidney Hook. "The Death Sentence," The New Leader, Apr. 3, 1961, p. 18; Jacques Barzun, "In Favor of Capital Punishment," The American Scholar, Spring 1962, p. 181, reprinted in Hugo A. Bedau (ed.), "The Death Penalty in America," Anchor Books, 1967.

criminal offenders the punishment they 'deserve,' then there are sown the seeds of anarchy—of self-help, vigilante justice, and lynch law." *Furman* v. *Georgia, supra* at 308 (Stewart, J., concurring).

"Retribution is no longer the dominant objective of the criminal law," *Williams* v. *New York* 337 U.S. 241, 248 (1949), but neither is it a forbidden objective nor one inconsistent with our respect for the dignity of men. *Furman* v. *Georgia,* 408 U.S. at 394-5 (Burger, J., dissenting): *id.* at 452-4 (Powell, J., dissenting); *Powell* v. *Texas* 392 U.S. at 531, 535-6. Indeed, the decision that capital punishment may be the appropriate sanction in extreme cases is an expression of the community's belief that certain crimes are themselves so grievous an affront to humanity that the only adequate response may be the penalty of death.[12]

It is the conclusion of this Committee that it is not enough to proclaim the sanctity and import of innocent life. This must be, and can only be secured by, a society that is willing to impose its highest penalty upon those who threaten such life. As observed by Professor Walter Berns:

> We think that some criminals must be made to pay for their crimes with their lives, and we think that we, the survivors of the world they violated, may legitimately extract that payment because we, too, are their victims. By punishing them, we demonstrate that there are laws that bind men across generations as well as across (and within) nations, that we are not simply isolated individuals, each pursuing his selfish interests. . . .[13]

An argument that is often asserted in favor of abolition of capital punishment concerns the dangers of executing the innocent. It is pointed out that if such an error occurs, it is irremediable. The argument is then made that, since the cost of such a mistake is so great, the risk of permitting the death penalty to be imposed at all is unacceptable.

The Committee finds this argument to be without great weight, particularly in light of the procedural safeguards for ciminal defendants mandated by the Supreme Court in recent years. The Court's decision with respect to the rights of the individual, particularly those expanding the right to counsel, together with the precautions taken by any court in a capital case, have all but reduced the danger of error in these cases to that of a mere theoretical possibility. Indeed, the Committee is aware of no case where an innocent man has been put to death. Admittedly, however, due to the fallible nature of man, this possibility does continue to exist. Insofar as it does, it is the opinion of the Committee that this minimal risk is justified by the protection afforded to society by the death penalty. As stated in the minority report of the Massachusetts Special Commission:

> We do not feel, however, that the mere possibility of error, which can never be completely ruled out, can be urged as a reason why the right of the state to

12. *Gregg* v. *Georgia,* at 183–84 (footnotes omitted).
13. Walter Berns, "For Capital Punishment," Harper's Magazine, p. 15, April 1979.

inflict the death penalty can be questioned in principle. . . . All that can be expected of [human authorities] is that they take every reasonable precaution against the danger of error. When this is done by those who are charged with the application of the law, the likelihood that errors will be made descends to an irreducible minimum. If errors are then made, this is the necessary price that must be paid within a society which is made up of human beings and whose authority is exercised not by angels but by men themselves. It is not brutal or unfeeling to suggest that the danger of miscarriage of justice must be weighed against the far greater evils for which the death penalty aims to provide effective remedies. [. . .][14]

§3.   Statement on the Constitutionality of a Proposed Federal Death Penalty*

MARY C. LAWTON

[. . .] The bill provides a bifurcated trial in instances in which the death penalty may be imposed. A defendant who has pleaded guilty or been found guilty of a capital offense would be entitled to a second hearing before a jury or, upon his own motion and with approval of the court and the Government, before a court alone.

At that hearing, information would be considered concerning enumerated aggravating or mitigating factors surrounding the crime and the defendant. The burden of proving aggravating factors would be on the Government which would be limited to the introduction of admissible evidence and which would be required to prove the existence of such factors beyond a reasonable doubt. The burden of establishing the existence of mitigating factors would be on the defendant, but the rules of evidence would not limit the information which could be presented, and the burden of persuasion would be preponderance of the evidence.

No presentence report would be furnished in this proceeding.

The jury or the court, if there is no jury, would be required to return special findings setting forth the existence of aggravating or mitigating factors. The death penalty would be imposed only if aggravating factors are found to

14. McClellan, Grant S., ed., "Capital Punishment," p. 81 (1961).
*Excerpted from the statement of Mary C. Lawton, 27 April 1978, at the hearings before the Committee on the Judiciary, U.S. Senate, 95th Congress, 2nd Session, on S. 1382, "To Establish Rational Criteria for the Imposition of Capital Punishment," U.S. Government Printing Office, Washington, D.C., 1978, pp. 2–8.

exist, and then only if these factors are found sufficient to warrant the death penalty and are found to outweigh any mitigating factors that may exist. The various factors which may be considered are enumerated in the bill.

Imposition of the death penalty would be subject to appellate review, whether or not the underlying conviction is appealed.

The reviewing court would consider the trial evidence, the information adduced at the sentencing hearings, the procedures employed at the sentencing hearing, and the special findings of the court or jury. It would affirm the death penalty only if it found that it was not imposed under the influence of passion, prejudice, or any other arbitrary factor, was supported by the evidence as to the existence of aggravating and mitigating factors, and was not excessive considering both the defendant and the crime.

[...] S. 1382 closely tracks the provisions of the Georgia statute held constitutional in *Gregg* v. *Georgia,* 428 U.S. 153 (1976). The only major differences are in the uniquely Federal nature of some of the aggravating factors enumerated, such as the special factors to be considered in relation to treason or espionage and the direct reference to offenses such as Presidential assassination.

We are satisfied that the procedures set forth in S. 1382 overcome the constitutional deficiencies noted in *Furman* v. *Georgia,* 408 U.S. 238 (1972), and meet the requirements emphasized by the Court in *Gregg,* namely, that attention be focused on the particularized circumstances of the crime and on the defendant, that discretion be controlled by objective standards, that the sentencer be provided with all relevant evidence, and that there be appellate review of the death sentence.

The bill as reported by the subcommittee contains one significant change which may be important in satisfying the demands of due process. It specifically prohibits the furnishing of a presentence report to the court.

In *Gardner* v. *Florida,* 430 U.S. 349 (1977), the Supreme Court vacated a death penalty imposed under a Florida statute, which had been upheld in *Proffitt* v. *Florida,* 428 U.S. 242 (1976), because the sentencing court had reviewed a presentence report to which the defendant did not have complete access. The Court found this to be a denial of due process in the context of a sentencing hearing on the imposition of the death penalty.

While the *Gardner* case does not hold that the furnishing of a presentence report is in itself a denial of due process, it suggests that if a report is furnished to the court, all of it must be furnished to the defense in instances in which it may affect the imposition of the death penalty.

As introduced, S. 1382 would have permitted the withholding of portions of a presentence report for the protection of human life or for the protection of the national security. It is questionable whether this would have satisfied the standard announced in *Gardner.* Eliminating the report avoids this issue.

The primary issue you have requested us to address in this hearing is the constitutionality of S. 1382 in light of the Court's opinion in *Coker* v. *Georgia.*

In that case, the Court held that the Georgia death penalty statute, already found to be constitutional from a procedural standpoint, was unconstitutional insofar as it permitted the imposition of the death penalty for the rape of an adult woman, when death did not result. [. . .]

In two instances, [. . .] the bill would permit imposition of the death penalty for crimes not directly resulting in the death of another—treason, 18 U.S.C. 2381, and espionage, 18 U.S.C. 794. Thus, we must examine whether, under the rationale of *Coker,* the penalty may properly be imposed for those offenses.

The bill sets forth particular aggravating factors applicable to conviction of treason or espionage, and at least one of these factors would have to be present before the death penalty could be invoked.

The factors are: one, prior conviction of treason or espionage punishable by death or life imprisonment; two, knowingly creating a grave risk of substantial danger to national security; and, three, knowingly creating a grave risk of death to another.

In addition, the bill limits the instances in which the death penalty may be applied for espionage to those in which the information furnished involves nuclear weapons, spacecraft or satellite, early warning system of similar defense systems protecting against large-scale attack, or war plans, communications intelligence, cryptographic information or information on major weapons systems or defense strategy.

Under present law, to constitute espionage, such information must be supplied to a foreign government with intent to injure the United States or provide advantage to the foreign government.

To determine whether the imposition of the death penalty is constitutional with respect to these offenses, we must analyze whether it makes a measurable contribution to acceptable goals of punishment and whether or not it is excessive in proportion to the crime.

Among the goals of penology which may be examined in this connection are the incapacitation of the defendant from further crime, the deterrent effect of the death penalty on others who may be disposed to the crime, and the concept of retribution or the expression of moral outrage of the community (Cf. *Gregg* v. *Georgia,* supra.). Deference will be given to the legislative judgment on the effect of the penalty for particular offenses so long as it appears rational.

Clearly, the punishment of death, in all instances, incapacitates the defendant for the commission of further crime.

With respect to retribution, the Court in *Gregg* discussed the measure of appropriateness as whether the offense, in this case treason or espionage, is "so grievous an affront to humanity that the only adequate response may be the penalty of death" (428 U.S. at 184).

Treason is, of course, the ultimate offense against the Nation, and it has been viewed as warranting the death penalty since 1790 (Cf. 1 Stat. 112, 12 Stat. 589, R.S. §1873). Espionage has been punishable by the death penalty since 1917 (Cf. 40 Stat. 218). Limited as it would be by the aggravating factors and the particular subjects of espionage which would be subject to the penalty under S. 1382, it may be viewed as approaching the level of treason in terms of its detriment to the Nation and its people.

The deterrent effect of the death penalty on others who may be disposed to commit an offense is, of course, a subject of continuing debate and is difficult, if not impossible, to measure. Nevertheless, the Court in *Gregg* seemed willling to assume that deterrence is greater with respect to crimes which require planning and preparation, and treason and espionage certainly fall within this category (428 U.S. at 186).

On balance, it seems probable that a court would find that the punishment of death as applied to treason serves appropriate goals of penology. It is less certain whether a court would reach the same conclusion with respect to application of the death penalty to espionage but, limited as it is in S. 1382, it is our view that it too would be found to serve appropriate goals.

The second part of the test, whether the punishment is excessive with respect to the crime, is more difficult to assess. In *Coker*, the Court looked to the consensus among the States and the international community and the practice of juries in modern times, as well as to historic practice, to assess the relationship between the penalty and the offense. This is more difficult with respect to crimes as rare as treason and espionage of the magnitude covered in S. 1382.

Reference to the practice of the States is not particularly instructive in this instance. While some States may also include provisions relating to espionage or treason within their criminal codes, the crimes have generally been considered Federal in nature, affecting as they do the entire country. Thus, the judgment of State legislatures as to whether the death penalty is appropriate would seem to carry less weight with respect to these crimes than was the case with respect to rape.

As mentioned earlier, Federal law has permitted the death penalty for treason since 1790 and for espionage since 1917. However, of the 33 Federal executions carried out from 1930 to 1970, only 2 were for espionage—the Rosenbergs—and there was none for treason although the imposition of the death penalty for treason was specifically upheld in *Kawakita v. United States,* 343 U.S. 717 (1952).

There were also six executions for the related crime of sabotage in 1942.

The Federal experience, then, is limited in practice and provides little guidance apart from the consistency with which statutory law has authorized the penalty.

The attitude of the international community demonstrates some consistency in viewing the death penalty as appropriate for these particular crimes.

In a report on capital punishment to the United Nations, the Secretary General noted that many nations which have generally abolished capital punishment retain it for a few exceptional crimes such as those related to the security of the State ("Capital Punishment—Report of the Secretary General" par. 18, Feb. 23, 1973). More specifically the report notes, "The most common exceptional crimes punishable by death are treason and crimes relating to the security of the State." (Report par. 32.) Tables appended to the report show that the majority of member nations of the United Nations retain capital punishment—about 100 of them—and 15 other nations, while abolishing capital punishment for ordinary crimes, retain it for exceptional crimes.

A 1975 update of this report shows that the picture remains largely unchanged ("Capital Punishment" U.N. Doc. 5616, Feb 12, 1975).

While the practice in other nations is not conclusive in interpreting the requirements of our own Constitution, it does constitute a factor which courts may well consider in determining whether the penalty of death is excessive as applied to treason or espionage.

Approaching the question as the Court did in *Coker,* the consistent view of the Congress from the earliest days of the Nation and the agreement of most nations in the world today that treason warrants the death penalty in some cases strongly argues for the conclusion that the penalty is not grossly disproportionate to the defense.

This is particularly true in light of the aggravating factors which would be proved beyond a reasonable doubt before the penalty could be imposed. In our judgment, a court, applying these same criteria, would find the death penalty for treason to be constitutional if imposed in accordance with the procedures established in S. 1382.

The result is less clear with respect to the offense of espionage. The available information with respect to the law of other nations is less clear. The imposition of the penalty for this offense was first authorized in the United States only in 1917 and then only for acts committed during time of war. The last application of the penalty, in 1952, was for conduct occurring during time of war.

These factors might be given weight by a court in determining whether the death penalty is disproportionate to espionage in time of peace. On the other hand, S. 1382 narrowly circumscribes the situations in which the death penalty would be applicable to espionage, encompassing only the most serious and harmful breaches of security. Moreover, the current world situation is one in which massively destructive acts could occur without a formal declaration of war. Further, the bill would limit the circumstances in which the death penalty could be imposed to those involving a repeat offense, a very grave risk to the Nation, or a very grave risk to life.

We are inclined to believe that a court would sustain the death penalty for espionage in cases in which those elements were proved beyond a reasonable doubt, even if an actual state of war did not exist.

In summary, it is our view that S. 1382 satisfies both the substantive and procedural requirements of the Eighth Amendment, as it has been interpreted to date, and is, therefore, constitutional. [. . .]

§4. In Defense of the Death Penalty: A Practical and Moral Analysis*

ERNEST VAN DEN HAAG

Three questions about the death penalty so overlap that they must each be answered. I shall ask seriatim: Is the death penalty constitutional? Is it useful? Is the death penalty morally justifiable? [. . .]

Regardless of constitutional interpretation, the morality and legitimacy of the abolitionist argument regarding capriciousness, discretion, or discrimination, would be more persuasive if it were alleged that those selectively executed are not guilty. But the argument merely maintains that some guilty, but favored, persons or groups escape the death penalty. This is hardly sufficient for letting others escape it. On the contrary, that some guilty persons or groups elude it argues for *extending* the death penalty to them.[1]

Justice requires punishing the guilty—as many of the guilty as possible— even if only some can be punished, and sparing the innocent—as many of the innocent as possible, even if not all are spared. Morally, justice must always be preferred to equality. It would surely be wrong to treat everybody with equal injustice in preference to meting out justice to some. Justice cannot ever permit sparing some guilty persons, or punishing some innocent ones, for the sake of equality—because others have been unjustly spared or punished. In practice, penalties never could be applied if we insisted that they

1. Nor do I read the Constitution to command us to prefer equality to justice. Surely, "due process of law" is meant to do justice: and "the equal protection of the law" is meant to extend justice equally to all.

*Excerpted from Ernest van den Haag, "In Defense of the Death Penalty: A Legal—Practical— Moral Analysis." Reprinted by permission from the *Criminal Law Bulletin*, Vol. 14, No. 1, Jan.– Feb. 1978, pp. 51–68. Copyright 1978, Warren, Gorham and Lamont Inc., 210 South Street, Boston, Mass. All Rights Reserved. Footnotes have been renumbered.

cannot be inflicted on any guilty persons unless we are able to make sure that they are equally applied to all other guilty persons. Anyone familiar with law enforcement knows that punishments can be inflicted only on an unavoidably capricious selection of the guilty.

Although it does not warrant serious discussion, the argument from capriciousness looms large in briefs and decisions. For the last seventy years, courts have tried—lamentably and unproductively—to prevent errors of procedure, or of evidence collection, or of decision-making, by the paradoxical method of letting defendants go free as a punishment, or warning, to errant law enforcers. Yet the strategy admittedly never has prevented the errors it was designed to prevent—although it has released countless guilty persons.[2] There is no more merit in the attempt to persuade the courts to let all capital crime defendants go free of capital punishment because some have wrongly escaped it, than in attempting to persuade the courts to let all burglars go, because some have wrongly escaped detection or imprisonment.

Is the death penalty morally just and/or useful? This is the essential moral, as distinguished from the constitutional, question. Discrimination is irrelevant to this moral question. If the death penalty were distributed equally and uncapriciously and with superhuman perfection to all the guilty, but were morally unjust, it would be unjust in each case. Contrariwise, if the death penalty is morally just, however discriminatorily applied to only some of the guilty, it remains just in each case in which it is applied.

The utilitarian (political) effects of unequal justice may well be detrimental to the social fabric because they outrage our passion for equality before the law. Unequal justice also is morally repellent. Nonetheless unequal justice is still justice. The guilty do not become innocent or less deserving of punishment because others escaped it. Nor does any innocent deserve punishment because others suffer it. Justice remains just, however unequal, while injustice remains unjust, however equal. While both are desired, justice and equality are not identical. Equality before the law should be extended and enforced—but not at the expense of justice.

Capriciousness, at any rate, is used as a sham argument against capital punishment by abolitionists. They would oppose the death penalty if it could be meted out without any discretion. They would oppose the death penalty in a homogeneous country without racial discrimination. And they would oppose the death penalty if the incomes of those executed and of those spared were the same. Actually, abolitionists oppose the death penalty, not its possible maldistribution.

What about persons executed in error? The objection here is not that some of the guilty escape, but that some of the innocent do not—a matter far more

2. It seems odd that the courts, which have been willing to take a managerial role to remedy discrimination in schooling, should find no better remedy for discrimination or other errors in the distribution of penalties by the courts than to abolish the penalty distributed.

serious than discrimination among the guilty. Yet, when urged by abolitionists, this, along with all distributional arguments, is a sham. Why? Abolitionists are opposed to the death penalty for the guilty as much as for the innocent. Hence, the question of guilt, if at all relevant to their position, cannot be decisive for them. Guilt is decisive only to those who urge the death penalty for the guilty. They must worry about distribution—part of the justice they seek.

The execution of innocents believed guilty is a miscarriage of justice that must be opposed whenever detected. But such miscarriages of justice do not warrant abolition of the death penalty. Unless the moral drawbacks of an activity or practice, which include the possible death of innocent bystanders, outweigh the moral advantages, which include the innocent lives that might be saved by it, the activity is warranted. Most human activities—medicine, manufacturing, automobile and air traffic, sports, not to speak of wars and revolutions—cause the death of innocent bystanders. Nevertheless, if the advantages sufficiently outweigh the disadvantages, human activities, including those of the penal system with all its punishments, are morally justified.

Is there evidence supporting the usefulness of the death penalty in securing the life of the citizens? Researchers in the past found no statistical evidence for the effects sought, marginal deterrent effects, or deterrent effects over and above those of alternative sanctions. However, in the last few years new and more sophisticated studies have led Professor Isaac Ehrlich to conclude that over the period 1933–1969, "an additional execution per year ... may have resulted (on the average) in 7 or 8 fewer murders."[3] Other investigators have confirmed Ehrlich's tentative results. Not surprisingly, refutations have been attempted, and Professor Ehrlich has offered his rebuttals.[4] The matter will remain controversial for some time. However, two tentative conclusions can be drawn with some confidence. First, Ehrlich has shown that previous investigations, that did not find deterrent effects of the death penalty, suffered from fatal defects. Second, there is now some likelihood—much more than hitherto—of statistically demonstrating marginal deterrent effects.

Thus, with respect to deterrence, we must now choose:

1. To trade the certain shortening of the life of a convicted murderer against the survival of between seven and eight innocent victims whose future murder by others becomes more probable, unless the convicted murderer is executed;
2. To trade the certain survival of the convicted murderer against the loss of

3. Ehrlich, "The Deterrent Effect of Capital Punishment: A Question of Life and Death," *Amer. Econ. Rev.* (June 1975). In the period studied, capital punishment was already infrequent and uncertain. Its deterrent effect might be greater when more frequently imposed for capital crimes, so that a prospective offender would feel more certain of it.
4. See *Journal of Legal Studies* (Jan. 1977); *Journal of Political Economy* (June 1977); and *American Economic Review* (June 1977).

the lives of between seven and eight innocent victims, who are more likely to be murdered by others if the convicted murderer is allowed to survive.

Prudence as well as morality command us to choose the first alternative.[5]

If executions had a zero marginal effect, they could not be justified in deterrent terms. But even the pre-Ehrlich investigations did not demonstrate this. They merely found that an above-zero effect could not be demonstrated statistically. While we do not know at present the degree of confidence with which we can assign an above marginal deterrent effect to executions, we can be more confident than in the past. I should now regard it as irresponsible not to shorten the lives of convicted murderers simply because we cannot be altogether sure that their execution will lengthen the lives of innocent victims: It seems immoral to let convicted murderers survive at the probable—or even at the merely possible—expense of the lives of innocent victims who might have been spared had the murderers been executed.

In principle, one could experiment to test the hypothesis of zero marginal effect. The most direct way would be to legislate the death penalty for certain kinds of murder if committed, say, on weekdays, but never on Sunday. Or, on Monday, Wednesday, and Friday, and not on other days. (The days could be changed around every few years to avoid possible bias.) I am convinced there would be fewer murders on death-penalty than on life-imprisonment days. Unfortunately, the experiment faces formidable obstacles.[6]

Our penal system rests on the proposition that more severe penalties are more deterrent than less severe penalties. We assume, rightly, I believe, that a $5 fine deters rape less than a $500 fine, and that the threat of five years in prison will deter more than either fine.[7] This assumption of the penal system rests on the common experience that, once aware of them, people learn to avoid natural dangers the more likely these are to be injurious and the more severe the likely injuries. People endowed with ordinary common sense (a class which includes some sociologists) have found no reason why behavior with respect to legal dangers should differ from behavior with respect to natural dangers. Indeed, it does not. Hence, the legal system proportions threatened penalties to the gravity of crimes, both to do justice and to achieve deterrence in proportion to that gravity.

5. I thought so even when I believed that the probability of deterrent effects might remain unknown. (See van den Haag, "On Deterrence and the Death Penalty," *J. Crim. L.C. & P.S.* (June 1969).) That probability is now more likely to become known and to be greater than was apparent a few years ago.
6. It would, however, isolate deterrent effects of the punishment from incapacitating ones, and also from the effect of Durkheimian "normative validation" where it does not depend on threats.
7. As indicated before, demonstrations are not available for the exact addition to deterrence of each added degree of severity in various circumstances, and with respect to various acts. We have so far coasted on a sea of plausible assumptions.

Thus, if it is true that the more severe the penalty the greater the deterrent effect, then the most severe penalty—the death penalty—would have the greatest deterrent effect. Arguments to the contrary assume either that capital crimes never are deterrable (sometimes merely because not all capital crimes have been deterred), or that, beyond some point, the deterrent effect of added severity is necessarily zero. Perhaps. But the burden of proof must be borne by those who presume to have located the point of zero marginal returns before the death penalty.

As an additional commonsense observation, I should add that without the death penalty, we necessarily confer immunity on just those persons most likely to be in need of deterrent threats. Thus, prisoners serving life sentences can kill fellow prisoners or guards with impunity. Prison wardens are unlikely to prevent violence in prisons as long as they give humane treatment to inmates and have no threats of additional punishment available for the murderers among them who are already serving life sentences. I cannot see the moral or utilitarian reasons for giving permanent immunity to homicidal life prisoners, thereby endangering the other prisoners and the guards, and in effect preferring the life prisoners to their victims.

Outside the prison context, an offender who expects a life sentence for his offense may murder his victim, or witnesses, or the arresting officer, to improve his chances of escaping. He could not be threatened with an additional penalty for his additional crime—an open invitation. Only the death penalty could deter in such cases. If there is but a possibility—and I believe there is a probability—that it will, we should retain it.

However, deterrence requires that the threat of the ultimate penalty be reserved for the ultimate crime. It may be prevented by that threat. Hence, the extreme punishment should never be prescribed when the offender, because already threatened by it, might add to his crimes with impunity. Thus, rape, or kidnapping, should not incur the death penalty, while killing the victim of either crime should. This may not stop an Eichmann after his first murder, but it will stop most people before. The range of punishments is not infinite; it is necessarily more restricted than the range of crimes. Since death is the ultimate penalty, it must be reserved for the ultimate crime.

Consider now some popular arguments against capital punishment.

According to Beccaria, with the death penalty the "laws which punish homicide . . . themselves commit it," thus giving "an example of barbarity." Those who speak of "legalized murder" use an oxymoronic phrase to echo this allegation. Legally imposed punishments such as fines, incarcerations, or executions, although often physically identical to the crimes punished, are not crimes or their moral equivalent. The difference between crimes and lawful acts is not physical, but legal. Driving a stolen car is a crime, although not physically different from driving a car you own. Unlawful imprisonment and kidnapping need not differ physically from the lawful arrest and incarceration used to punish unlawful imprisonment and kidnapping. Finally, whether a lawful punishment gives an "example of barbarity" depends on how the moral difference between crime and punishment is preceived. To suggest that its physical quality, ipso facto, morally disqualifies the punishment, is to assume what is to be shown.

It is possible that all displays of violence, criminal or punitive, influence people to engage in unlawful imitations. This seems one good reason not to have public executions. But it does not argue against executions. Objections to displaying on television the process of violently subduing a resistant offender do not argue against actually engaging in the process.[8] Arguments against the public display of vivisections, or the painful medications, do not argue against either. Arguments against the public display of sexual activity do not argue against sexual activity. Arguments against public executions, then, do not argue against executions.[9] While the deterrent effect of punishments depends on their being known, the deterrent effect does not depend on punishments being carried out publicly. For example, the threat of imprisonment deters, but incarcerated persons are not on public display.

Abolitionists often maintain that most capital crimes are "acts of passion" that 1. could not be restrained by the threat of the death penalty, and 2. do not deserve it morally even if other crimes might. It is not clear to me why a crime motivated by, say, sexual passion, is morally less deserving of punishment than one motivated by passion for money. Is the sexual passion morally more respectable than others? More gripping? More popular? Generally, is violence in personal conflicts morally more excusable than violence among people who do not know each other? A precarious case might be made for such a view, but I shall not attempt to make it.

Perhaps it is true, however, that many murders are irrational "acts of passion" that cannot be deterred by the threat of the death penalty. Either for this reason or because "crimes of passion" are thought less blameworthy than other homicides, most "crimes of passion" are not punishable by death now.[10]

But if most murders are irrational acts, it would seem that the traditional threat of the death penalty has succeeded in deterring most rational people, or most people when rational, from committing the threatened act, and that

8. There is a good argument against unnecessary public displays of violence here. (See van den Haag, "What to Do About TV Violence," *The Alternative* (Aug./Sept. 1976).)

9. It may be noted that in Beccaria's time, executions were regarded as public entertainments. *Tempora mutantur et nos mutamur in illis.*

10. I have reservations on both these counts, being convinced that many crimes among relatives and friends are as blameworthy and as deterrable as crimes among strangers. Thus, major heroin dealers in New York are treatened with life imprisonment. In the absence of the death penalty, they find it advantageous to have witnesses killed. Such murders surely are not acts of passion in the classical sense, although they occur among associates. They are in practice encouraged by the penal law.

the fear of the penalty continues to deter all but those who cannot be deterred by any penalty. Hardly a reason for abolishing the death penalty. Indeed, that capital crimes are committed mostly by irrational persons and only by some rational ones would suggest that more might commit these crimes if the penalty were lower. This hardly argues against capital punishment. Else, we would have to abolish penalties whenever they succeed in deterring people. Yet, abolitionists urge that capital punishment be abolished because capital crimes are often committed by the irrational—as though deterring the rational is not quite enough.

Finally, some observations on an anecdote reported by Boswell and repeated ad nauseam. Dr. Johnson found pickpockets active in a crowd assembled to see one of their number hanged. He concluded that executions do not deter. His conclusion does not follow from his observation.

1. Since the penalty Johnson witnessed was what pickpockets had expected all along, they had no reason to reduce their activities. Deterrence is expected to increase only when penalties do.

2. At most, a public execution could have had the deterrent effect Dr. Johnson expected because of its visibility. But it may have had a contrary effect: The spectacle of execution was probably more fascinating to the crowd than other spectacles; public executions thus might distract attention from the activities of pickpockets and thereby increase their opportunities more than other spectacles would. Hence, an execution crowd might have been more inviting to pickpockets than other crowds. (As mentioned before, deterrence depends on knowledge, but does not require visibility.)

3. Even when the penalty is greatly increased, let alone when it is unchanged, the deterrent effect of penalties is usually slight with respect to those already committed to criminal activities.[11] Deterrence is effective by restraining people as yet not committed to criminal occupation from entering it.

The risk of a penalty is the cost of crime offenders must expect. When this cost is high enough, relative to the expected benefit, it will deter a considerable number of people who would have entered an occupation—criminal or otherwise—had the cost been lower. In this respect, the effects of the costs of crime are not different from the effects of the cost of automobiles or movie tickets, or from the effects of the cost of any occupation relative to its benefits. When (comparative) net benefits decrease because of cost increases, the flow of new entrants does. But those already in the occupation usually continue.

4. Finally, Dr. Johnson did not actually address the question of the deterrent effect of execution in any respect whatever. To do so, he would have had to compare the number of pocket-picking episodes in the crowd assem-

11. The high degree of uncertainty and arbitrariness of penalization in Johnson's time may also have weakened deterrent effects. Witnessing an execution cannot correct this defect.

bled to witness the execution with the number of such episodes in a similar crowd assembled for some other purpose. He did not do so, probably because he thought that a deterrent effect occurs only if the crime is altogether eliminated. That is a common misunderstanding. Crime can only be reduced, not eliminated. However harsh the penalties, there are always nondeterrables. Thus, most people can be deterred, but never all.

One popular moral objection to capital punishment is that it gratifies the desire for revenge, regarded as unworthy. The Bible quotes the Lord declaring: "Vengeance is mine" (Romans 12: 19). He thus legitimized vengeance and reserved it to Himself. However, the Bible also enjoins, "the murderer shall surely be put to death" (Numbers 35: 16–18), recognizing that the death penalty can be warranted—whatever the motive. Religious tradition certainly suggests no less.[12]

The motives for the death penalty may indeed include vengeance. Vengeance as a compensatory and psychological reparatory satisfaction for an injured party, group, or society, may be a legitimate human motive—despite the biblical injunction. I do not see wherein that motive is morally blameworthy. When regulated and directed by law, vengeance also is socially useful: Legal vengeance solidifies social solidarity against lawbreakers and is the alternative to the private revenge of those who feel harmed.

However, vengeance is irrelevant to the death penalty, which must be justified by its purpose, whatever the motive. An action, or rule, or penalty, is neither justified nor discredited by the motive for it. No rule should be discarded or regarded as morally wrong because of the motive of those who support it. Actions, or rules, or penalties, are justified by their intent and by their effectiveness in achieving it, not by the motives of supporters.[13] Capital punishment is warranted if it achieves its purpose: doing justice and deterring crime, regardless of whether it gratifies vengeful feelings.

We must examine now the specific characteristics of capital punishment before turning to its purely moral aspects. Capital punishment is feared above all punishments because 1. it is not merely irreversible as most other penalties are, but also irrevocable; 2. it hastens an event, which unlike pain, deprivation, or injury, is unique in every life and never has been reported on by anyone. Death is an experience that cannot actually be experienced and ends

12. Since religion expects both justice and vengeance in the world to come, the faithful may dispense with either in this world, and with any particular penalties, although they seldom have. But a secular state must do justice here and now, it cannot assume that another power, elsewhere, will do justice where its courts did not.

   For that matter, Romans 12:19 barely precedes Romans 13:4, which tells us [the ruler] "beareth not the sword in vain for he is the minister of God, a revenger to execute wrath upon him that doeth evil." It is not unreasonable to interpret Romans 12:19 to mean that revenge is to be delegated by the injured to the authorities.

13. Different motives (the reasons why something is done) may generate the same action (what is done), purpose, or intent, just as the same motive may lead to different actions.

all experience.[14] Because it is as unknown as it is certain, death is universally feared. The fear of death is often attached to the penalty that hastens it—as though, without the penalty, death would not come. 3. When death is imposed as a deliberate punishment by one's fellow men, it signifies a complete severing of human solidarity. The convict is rejected by human society, found unworthy of sharing life with it. This total rejection exacerbates the natural separation anxiety and fear of annihilation. The marginal deterrent effect of executions depends on these characteristics, and the moral justification of the death penalty, above and beyond the deterrent effect, does no less.

Hitherto I have relied on logic and fact. Without relinquishing either, I must appeal to plausibility as well, as I turn to questions of morality unalloyed to other issues. For, whatever ancillary service facts and logic can render, what one is persuaded to accept as morally right or wrong ultimately depends on what seems to be plausible.

If there is nothing for the sake of which one may be put to death, can there be anything worth dying for? If there is nothing worth dying for, is there any moral value worth living for? Is a life that cannot be transcended by anything beyond itself more valuable than one that can be transcended? Is existence, life, itself a moral value never to be given up for the sake of anything? Does a value system in which any life, however it is lived, becomes the highest of goods, enhance the value of human life or cheapen it? I shall content myself here with raising the questions.[15]

"The life of each man should be sacred to each other man," the ancients tell us. They unflinchingly executed murderers.[16] They realized it is not enough to proclaim the sacredness and inviolability of human life. It must be secured as well, by threatening with the loss of their own life those who violate what has been proclaimed as inviolable—the right of innocents to live. Else, the inviolability of human life is neither credibly proclaimed nor actually protected. No society can profess that the lives of its members are secure if those who did not allow innocent others to continue living are themselves allowed to continue living—at the expense of the community. Does it not cheapen human life to punish the murderer by incarcerating him as one does a pickpocket? Murder differs in quality from other crimes and deserves, therefore, a punishment that differs in quality from other punishments.

14. Actually, being dead is no different from not being born, a (non)experience we all had before being born. But death is not so perceived. The process of dying, a quite different matter, is confused with it. In turn, dying is feared mainly because death is anticipated, even though death is feared because it is confused with dying.

15. Insofar as these questions are psychological, empirical evidence would not be irrelevant. But it is likely to be evaluated in terms depending on moral views.

16. Not always. On the disastrous consequences of periodic failure to do so, Sir Henry Maine waxes with eloquent sorrow in his *Ancient Law* 408–09.

If it were shown that no punishment is more deterrent than a trivial fine, capital punishment for murder would remain just, even if not useful. For murder is not a trifling offense. Punishment must be proportioned to the gravity of the crime, if only to denounce it and to vindicate the importance of the norm violated. Thus, all penal systems proportion punishments to crimes. The worse the crime the higher the penalty deserved. Why not the highest penalty—death—for the worst crime—wanton murder? Those rejecting the death penalty have the burden of showing that no crime deserves capital punishment[17]—a burden which they have not so far been willing to bear.

Abolitionists are wrong when they insist that we all have an equally inalienable right to live to our natural term—that if the victim deserved to live, so does the murderer. That takes egalitarianism too far for my taste: The crime sets victim and murderer apart; if the victim died, the murderer does not deserve to live. The thought that there are some who think that murderers have as much right to live as their victims oppresses me. So does the thought that a Stalin or a Hitler should have the right to go on living.

Never to execute a wrongdoer, regardless of how depraved his acts, is to proclaim that no act can be so irredeemably vicious as to deserve death—that no human being can be wicked enough to be deprived of life. Who actually believes that? I find it easier to believe that those who affect such a view do so because of a failure of nerve. They do not think themselves—and therefore anyone else—competent to decide questions of life and death. Aware of human frailty they shudder at the gravity of the decision and refuse to make it. The irrevocability of a verdict of death is contrary to the modern spirit that likes to pretend that nothing ever is definitive, that everything is open-ended, that doubts must always be entertained and revisions made. Such an attitude may be proper for inquiring philosophers and scientists. But not for courts. They can evade decisions on life and death only by giving up their paramount duties: to do justice, to secure the lives of the citizens, and to vindicate the norms society holds inviolable.

One may object that the death penalty either cannot actually achieve the vindication of violated norms, or is not needed for it. If so, failure to inflict death does not belittle the crime, nor imply that the life of the criminal is of greater importance than the moral value he violated, or the harm he did to his victim. But it is not so. In all societies, the degree of social disapproval of wicked acts is expressed in the degree of punishment threatened.[18] Thus, pun-

17. One may argue that some crimes deserve more than execution, and that on the above reasoning, torture may be justified. But penalties have already been reduced to a few kinds—fines, confinement, and execution—so the issue is academic. Unlike the death penalty, torture also has become repulsive to us. (Some reasons for this public revulsion are listed in Chapter X [of] van den Haag, *Punishing Criminals: Concerning a Very Old and Painful Question* (1975).)
18. Social approval is usually less unanimous, and the system of rewards reflects it less.

ishments both proclaim and enforce social values according to the importance given to them. There is no other way for society to affirm its values. To refuse to punish any crime with death, then, is to avow that the negative weight of a crime can never exceed the positive value of the life of the person who committed it. I find that proposition implausible.

§5.   The Morality of Anger*

WALTER BERNS

Until recently, my business did not require me to think about the punishment of criminals in general or the legitimacy and efficacy of capital punishment in particular. In a vague way, I was aware of the disagreement among professionals concerning the purpose of punishment—whether it was intended to deter others, to rehabilitate the criminal, or to pay him back—but like most laymen I had no particular reason to decide which purpose was right or to what extent they may all have been right. I did know that retribution was held in ill repute among criminologists and jurists—to them, retribution was a fancy name for revenge, and revenge was barbaric—and, of course, I knew that capital punishment had the support only of policemen, prison guards, and some local politicians, the sort of people Arthur Koestler calls "hanghards" (Philadelphia's Mayor Rizzo comes to mind). The intellectual community denounced it as both unnecessary and immoral. It was the phenomenon of Simon Wiesenthal that allowed me to understand why the intellectuals were wrong and why the police, the politicians, and the majority of the voters were right: We punish criminals principally in order to pay them back, and we execute the worst of them out of moral necessity. Anyone who respects Wiesenthal's mission will be driven to the same conclusion.

Of course, not everyone will respect that mission. It will strike the busy man—I mean the sort of man who sees things only in the light cast by a concern for his own interests—as somewhat bizarre. Why should anyone devote his life—more than thirty years of it!—exclusively to the task of hunting down the Nazi war criminals who survived World War II and escaped punishment? Wiesenthal says his conscience forces him "to bring the guilty ones to trial." But why punish them? What do we hope to accomplish now by punishing SS Obersturmbannführer Adolf Eichmann or SS Obersturmbannführer. Franz Stangl or someday—who knows?—Reichsleiter Martin Bormann? We surely don't expect to rehabilitate them, and it would be fool-

*Excerpted from For Capital Punishment by Walter Berns. © 1979 by Walter Berns. Published by Basic Books, Inc., New York. Reprinted by permission.

ish to think that by punishing them we might thereby deter others. The answer, I think, is clear: We want to punish them in order *to pay them back*. We think they must be made to pay for their crimes with their lives, and we think that we, the survivors of the world they violated, may legitimately exact that payment because we, too, are their victims. By punishing them, we demonstrate that there are laws that bind men across generations as well as across (and within) nations, that we are not simply isolated individuals, each pursuing his selfish interests and connected with others by a mere contract to live and let live. To state it simply, Wiesenthal allows us to see that it is right, morally right, to be angry with criminals and to express that anger publicly, officially, and in an appropriate manner, which may require the worst of them to be executed.

Modern civil-libertarian opponents of capital punishment do not understand this. They say that to execute a criminal is to deny his human dignity; they also say that the death penalty is not useful, that nothing useful is accomplished by executing anyone. Being utilitarians, they are essentially selfish men, distrustful of passion, who do not understand the connection between anger and justice, and between anger and human dignity.

Anger is expressed or manifested on those occasions when someone has acted in a manner that is thought to be unjust, and one of its origins is the opinion that men are responsible, and should be held responsible, for what they do. Thus, as Aristotle teaches us, anger is accompanied not only by the pain caused by the one who is the object of anger, but by the pleasure arising from the expectation of inflicting revenge on someone who is thought to deserve it. We can become angry with an inanimate object (the door we run into and then kick in return) only by foolishly attributing responsibility to it, and we cannot do that for long, which is why we do not think of returning later to revenge ourselves on the door. For the same reason, we cannot be more than momentarily angry with any one creature other than man; only a fool and worse would dream of taking revenge on a dog. And, finally, we tend to pity rather than to be angry with men who—because they are insane, for example—are not responsible for their acts. Anger, then, is a very human passion not only because only a human being can be angry, but also because anger acknowledges the humanity of its objects: it holds them accountable for what they do. And in holding particular men responsible, it pays them the respect that is due them as men. Anger recognizes that only men have the capacity to be moral beings and, in so doing, acknowledges the dignity of human beings. Anger is somehow connected with justice, and it is this that modern penology has not understood; it tends, on the whole, to regard anger as a selfish indulgence.

Anger can, of course, be that; and if someone does not become angry with an insult or an injury suffered unjustly, we tend to think he does not think much of himself. But it need not be selfish, not in the sense of being provoked only by an injury suffered by oneself. There were many angry men in America when President Kennedy was killed; one of them—Jack Ruby—took it upon himself to exact the punishment that, if indeed deserved, ought to have been exacted by the law. There were perhaps even angrier men when Martin Luther King, Jr., was killed, for King, more than anyone else at the time, embodied a people's quest for justice; the anger—more, the "black rage"—expressed on that occasion was simply a manifestation of the great change that had occurred among black men in America, a change wrought in large part by King and his associates in the civil-rights movement: the servility and fear of the past had been replaced by pride and anger, and the treatment that had formerly been accepted as a matter of course or as if it were deserved was now seen for what it was, unjust and unacceptable. King preached love, but the movement he led depended on anger as well as love, and that anger was not despicable, being neither selfish nor unjustified. On the contrary, it was a reflection of what was called solidarity and may more accurately be called a profound caring for others, black for other blacks, white for blacks, and, in the world King was trying to build, American for other Americans. If men are not saddened when someone else suffers, or angry when someone else suffers unjustly, the implication is that they do not care for anyone other than themselves or that they lack some quality that befits a man. When we criticize them for this, we acknowledge that they ought to care for others. If men are not angry when a neighbor suffers at the hands of a criminal, the implication is that their moral faculties have been corrupted, that they are not good citizens.

Criminals are properly the objects of anger, and the perpetrators of terrible crimes—for example, Lee Harvey Oswald and James Earl Ray— are properly the objects of great anger. They have done more than inflict an injury on an isolated individual; they have violated the foundations of trust and friendship, the necessary elements of a moral community, the only community worth living in. A moral community, unlike a hive of bees or a hill of ants, is one whose members are expected freely to obey the laws and, unlike those in a tyranny, are trusted to obey the laws. The criminal has violated that trust, and in so doing has injured not merely his immediate victim but the community as such. He has called into question the very possibility of that community by suggesting that men cannot be trusted to respect freely the property, the person, and the dignity of those with whom they are associated. If, then, men are not angry when someone else is robbed, raped, or murdered, the implication is that no moral community exists, because those men do not care for anyone other than themselves. Anger is an expression of that caring, and society needs men who care for one another, who share their pleasures and their pains, and do so for the sake of the others. It is the passion that can cause us to act for reasons having nothing to do with selfish or mean calculation; indeed, when educated, it can become a generous passion, the passion

that protects the community or country by demanding punishment for its
enemies. It is the stuff from which heroes are made.

A moral community is not possible without anger and the moral indignation that accompanies it. Thus the most powerful attack on capital punishment was written by a man, Albert Camus, who denied the legitimacy of
anger and moral indignation by denying the very possibility of a moral community in our time. The anger expressed in our world, he said, is nothing
but hypocrisy. His novel *L'Etranger* (variously translated as *The Stranger* or
The Outsider) is a brilliant portrayal of what Camus insisted is our world, a
world deprived of God, as he put it. It is a world we would not choose to live
in and one that Camus, the hero of the French Resistance, disdained. Nevertheless, the novel is a modern masterpiece, and Meursault, its antihero (for
a world without anger can have no heroes), is a murderer.

He is a murderer whose crime is excused, even as his lack of hypocrisy is
praised, because the universe, we are told, is "benignly indifferent" to how
we live or what we do. Of course, the law is not indifferent; the law punished
Meursault and it threatens to punish us if we do as he did. But Camus the
novelist teaches us that the law is simply a collection of arbitrary conceits.
The people around Meursault apparently were not indifferent; they expressed
dismay at his lack of attachment to his mother and disapprobation of his
crime. But Camus the novelist teaches us that other people are hypocrites.
They pretend not to know what Camus the opponent of capital punishment
tells: namely, that "our civilization has lost the only values that, in a certain
way, can justify that penalty . . . [the existence of] a truth or a principle that
is superior to man." There is no basis for friendship and no moral law; therefore, no one, not even a murderer, can violate the terms of friendship or
break that law; and there is no basis for the anger that we express when
someone breaks that law. The only thing we share as men, the only thing
that connects us one to another, is a "solidarity against death," and a judgment of capital punishment "upsets" that solidarity. The purpose of human
life is to stay alive.

Like Meursault, Macbeth was a murderer, and like *L'Etranger,* Shakespeare's *Macbeth* is the story of a murder; but there the similarity ends. As
Lincoln said, "Nothing equals *Macbeth.*" He was comparing it with the
other Shakespearean plays he knew, the plays he had "gone over perhaps as
frequently as any unprofessional reader ... *Lear, Richard Third, Henry
Eighth, Hamlet*"; but I think he meant to say more than that none of these
equals *Macbeth.* I think he meant that no other literary work equals it. "It
is wonderful," he said. *Macbeth* is wonderful because, to say nothing more
here, it teaches us the awesomeness of the commandment "Thou shalt not
kill."

What can a dramatic poet tell us about murder? More, probably, than anyone else, if he is a poet worthy of consideration, and yet nothing that does

not inhere in the act itself. In *Macbeth,* Shakespeare shows us murders committed in a political world by a man so driven by ambition to rule that world that he becomes a tyrant. He shows us also the consequences, which were terrible, worse even than Macbeth feared. The cosmos rebelled, turned into chaos by his deeds. He shows a world that was not "benignly indifferent" to what we call crimes and especially to murder, a world constituted by laws divine as well as human, and Macbeth violated the most awful of those laws. Because the world was so constituted, Macbeth suffered the torments of the great and the damned, torments far beyond the "practice" of any physician. He had known glory and had deserved the respect and affection of king, countrymen, army, friends, and wife; and he lost it all. At the end he was reduced to saying that life "is a tale told by an idiot, full of sound and fury, signifying nothing;" yet, in spite of the horrors provoked in us by his acts, he excites no anger in us. We pity him; even so, we understand the anger of his countrymen and the dramatic necessity of his death. *Macbeth* is a play about ambition, murder, tyranny; about horror, anger, vengeance, and, perhaps more than any other of Shakespeare's plays, justice. Because of justice, Macbeth has to die, not by his own hand—he will not "play the Roman fool, and die on [his] sword"—but at the hand of the avenging Macduff. The dramatic necessity of his death would appear to rest on its *moral* necessity. Is that right? Does this play conform to our sense of what a murder means? Lincoln thought it was "wonderful."

Surely Shakespeare's is a truer account of murder than the one provided by Camus, and by truer I mean truer to our moral sense of what a murder is and what the consequences that attend it must be. Shakespeare shows us vengeful men because there is something in the souls of men—then and now—that requires such crimes to be revenged. Can we imagine a world that does not take its revenge on the man who kills Macduff's wife and children? (Can we imagine the play in which Macbeth does not die?) Can we imagine a people that does not hate murderers? (Can we imagine a world where Meursault is an outsider only because he does not *pretend* to be outraged by murder?) Shakespeare's poetry could not have been written out of the moral sense that the death penalty's opponents insist we ought to have. Indeed, the issue of capital punishment can be said to turn on whether Shakespeare's or Camus' is the more telling account of murder.

There is a sense in which punishment may be likened to dramatic poetry. Dramatic poetry depicts men's actions because men are revealed in, or make themselves known through, their actions; and the essence of a human action, according to Aristotle, consists in its being virtuous or vicious. Only a ruler or a contender for rule can act with the freedom and on a scale that allows the virtuousness or viciousness of human deeds to be fully displayed. Macbeth was such a man, and in his fall, brought about by his own acts, and in the consequent suffering he endured, is revealed the meaning of morality. In

Macbeth the majesty of the moral law is demonstrated to us; as I said, it teaches us the awesomeness of the commandment Thou shalt not kill. In a similar fashion, the punishments imposed by the legal order remind us of the reign of the moral order; not only do they remind us of it, but by enforcing its prescriptions, they enhance the dignity of the legal order in the eyes of moral men, in the eyes of those decent citizens who cry out "for gods who will avenge injustice." That is especially important in a self-governing community, a community that gives laws to itself.

If the laws were understood to be divinely inspired or, in the extreme case, divinely given, they would enjoy all the dignity that the opinions of men can grant and all the dignity they require to ensure their being obeyed by most of the men living under them. Like Duncan in the opinion of Macduff, the laws would be "the Lord's anointed," and would be obeyed even as Macduff obeyed the laws of the Scottish kingdom. Only a Macbeth would challenge them, and only a Meursault would ignore them. But the laws of the United States are not of this description; in fact, among the proposed amendments that became the Bill of Rights was one declaring, not that all power comes from God, but rather "that all power is originally vested in, and consequently derives from the people;" and this proposal was dropped only because it was thought to be redundant: the Constitution's preamble said essentially the same thing, and what we know as the Tenth Amendment reiterated it. So Madison proposed to make the Constitution venerable in the minds of the people, and Lincoln, in an early speech, went so far as to say that a "political religion" should be made of it. They did not doubt that the Constitution and the laws made pursuant to it would be supported by "enlightened reason," but fearing that enlightened reason would be in short supply, they sought to augment it. The laws of the United States would be obeyed by some men because they could hear and understand "the voice of enlightened reason," and by other men because they would regard the laws with that "veneration which time bestows on everything."

Supreme Court Justices have occasionally complained of our habit of making "constitutionality synonymous with wisdom." But the extent to which the Constitution is venerated and its authority accepted depends on the compatibility of its rules with our moral sensibilities; despite its venerable character, the Constitution is not the only source of these moral sensibilities. There was even a period, before slavery was abolished by the Thirteenth Amendment, when the Constitution was regarded by some very moral men as an abomination: Garrison called it "a covenant with death and an agreement with Hell," and there were honorable men holding important political offices and judicial appointments who refused to enforce the Fugitive Slave Law even though its constitutionality had been affirmed. In time this opinion spread far beyond the ranks of the original abolitionists until those who held it composed a constitutional majority of the people, and slavery was abolished.

But Lincoln knew that more than amendments were required to make the Constitution once more worthy of the veneration of moral men. That is why, in the Gettysburg Address, he made the principle of the Constitution an inheritance from "our fathers." That it should be so esteemed is especially important in a self-governing nation that gives laws to itself, because it is only a short step from the principle that the laws are merely a product of one's own will to the opinion that the only consideration that informs the law is self-interest; and this opinion is only one remove from lawlessness. A nation of simple self-interested men will soon enough perish from the earth.

It was not an accident that Lincoln spoke as he did at Gettysburg or that he chose as the occasion for his words the dedication of a cemetery built on a portion of the most significant battlefield of the Civil War. Two-and-a-half years earlier, in his First Inaugural Address, he had said that Americans, north and south, were not and must not be enemies, but friends. Passion had strained but must not be allowed to break the bonds of affection that tied them one to another. He closed by saying this: "The mystic chords of memory, stretching from every battlefield, and patriot grave, to every living heart and hearthstone, all over this broad land, will yet swell the chorus of the Union, when again touched, as surely they will be, by the better angels of our nature." The chords of memory that would swell the chorus of the Union could be touched, even by a man of Lincoln's stature, only on the most solemn occasions, and in the life of a nation no occasion is more solemn that the burial of the patriots who have died defending it on the field of battle. War is surely an evil, but as Hegel said, it is not an "absolute evil." It exacts the supreme sacrifice, but precisely because of that it can call forth such sublime rhetoric as Lincoln's. His words at Gettysburg serve to remind Americans in particular of what Hegel said people in general needed to know, and could be made to know by means of war and the sacrifices demanded of them in wars: namely, that their country is something more than a "civil society" the purpose of which is simply the protection of individual and selfish interests.

Capital punishment, like Shakespeare's dramatic and Lincoln's political poetry (and it is surely that, and was understood by him to be that), serves to remind us of the majesty of the moral order that is embodied in our law, and of the terrible consequences of its breach. The law must not be understood to be merely a statute that we enact or repeal at our will, and obey or disobey at our convenience—especially not the criminal law. Wherever law is regarded as merely statutory, men will soon enough disobey it, and will learn how to do so without any inconvenience to themselves. The criminal law must possess a dignity far beyond that possessed by mere statutory enactment or utilitarian and self-interested calculations. The most powerful means we have to give it that dignity is to authorize it to impose the ultimate penalty. The criminal law must be made awful, by which I mean inspiring, or commanding "profound respect or reverential fear." It must remind us of the moral order by which alone we can live as *human* beings, and in America, now that the Supreme Court has outlawed banishment, the only punishment that can do this is capital punishment.

The founder of modern criminology, the eighteenth-century Italian Cesare Beccaria, opposed both banishment and capital punishment because he understood that both were inconsistent with the principle of self-interest, and self-interest was the basis of the political order he favored. If a man's first or only duty is to himself, of course he will prefer his money to his country; he will also prefer his money to his brother. In fact, he will prefer his brother's money to his brother, and a people of this description, or a country that understands itself in this Beccarian manner, can put the mark of Cain on no one. For the same reason, such a country can have no legitimate reason to execute its criminals, or, indeed, to punish them in any manner. What would be accomplished by punishment in such a place? Punishment arises out of the demand for justice, and justice is demanded by angry, morally indignant men; its purpose is to satisfy that moral indignation and thereby promote the law-abidingness that, it is assumed, accompanies it. But the principle of self-interest denies the moral basis of that indignation.

Not only will a country based solely on self-interest have no legitimate reason to punish; it may have no need to punish. It may be able to solve what we call the crime problem by substituting a law of contracts for a law of crimes. According to Beccaria's social contract, men agree to yield their natural freedom to the "sovereign" in exchange for his promise to keep the peace. As it becomes more difficult for the sovereign to fulfill his part of the contract, there is a demand that he be made to pay for his nonperformance. From this comes compensation or insurance schemes embodied in statutes whereby the sovereign (or state), being unable to keep the peace by punishing criminals, agrees to compensate its contractual partners for injuries suffered at the hands of criminals, injuries the police are unable to prevent. The insurance policy takes the place of law enforcement and the *posse comitatus,* and John Wayne and Gary Cooper give way to Mutual of Omaha. There is no anger in this kind of law, and none (or no reason for any) in the society. The principle can be carried further still. If we ignore the victim (and nothing we do can restore his life anyway), there would appear to be no reason why— the worth of a man being his price, as Beccaria's teacher, Thomas Hobbes, put it—coverage should not be extended to the losses incurred in a murder. If we ignore the victim's sensibilities (and what are they but absurd vanities?), there would appear to be no reason why—the worth of a woman being *her* price—coverage should not be extended to the losses incurred in a rape. Other examples will no doubt suggest themselves.

This might appear to be an almost perfect solution to what we persist in calling the crime problem, achieved without risking the terrible things sometimes done by an angry people. A people that is not angry with criminals will not be able to deter crime, but a people fully covered by insurance has no need to deter crime: they will be insured against all the losses they can, in principle, suffer. What is now called crime can be expected to increase in volume, of course, and this will cause an increase in the premiums paid, directly or in the form of taxes. But it will no longer be necessary to apprehend, try, and punish criminals, which now costs Americans more than $1.5 billion a month (and is increasing at an annual rate of about 15 percent), and one can buy a lot of insurance for $1.5 billion. There is this difficulty, as Rousseau put it: To exclude anger from the human community is to concentrate all the passions in a "self-interest of the meanest sort," and such a place would not be fit for human habitation.

When, in 1976, the Supreme Court declared death to be a constitutional penalty, it decided that the United States was not that sort of country; most of us, I think, can appreciate that judgment. We want to live among people who do not value their possessions more than their citizenship, who do not think exclusively or even primarily of their own rights, people whom we can depend on even as they exercise their rights, and whom we can trust, which is to say, people who, even in the absence of a policeman, will not assault our bodies or steal our possessions, and might even come to our assistance when we need it, and who stand ready, when the occasion demands it, to risk their lives in defense of their country. If we are of the opinion that the United States may rightly ask of its citizens this awful sacrifice, then we are also of the opinion that it may rightly impose the most awful penalty; if it may rightly honor its heroes, it may rightly execute the worst of its criminals. By doing so, it will remind its citizens that it is a country worthy of heroes.

8

Against the Death Penalty

INTRODUCTION

Argument against the death penalty in the United States has a history of two hundred years,[1] and several themes have remained relatively constant. Abolitionists have always claimed that capital punishment is not an effective deterrent, or anyway not a better deterrent than long-term imprisonment; that it imposed unreasonable risks in the possibility of executing the wrong persons; that a willingness to use it tends to brutalize society; that it has never been administered in a morally unobjectionable manner; and that it is used mainly against relatively defenseless members of minority groups. During the past generation, opposition to the death penalty has been put into the context of a larger struggle to wipe out the worst vestiges of our long heritage of racism. This in turn has helped bring the death penalty under challenge from the Bill of Rights in a manner virtually inconceivable in the 1950s, a development reviewed in Chapter Six. It is also true that during recent decades the attack on the death penalty has been less frequently buttressed than it once was with abstract moralistic or religious principles—for example, the individual's right to life, or the sanctity of human life. Instead, abolitionists have stressed practical tendencies and characteristics of the way criminal justice is actually administered for crimes of homicide, rape, and other grave offenses. (This emphasis is true even of organizations such as Amnesty International, whose campaign against the international use of the death penalty is firmly rooted in its defense of human rights; see below, §5.) At present, therefore, the typical arguments against the death penalty not only retain

1. For an excellent anthology tracing this full history, see Mackey 1976, and the sources cited and reprinted therein.

those features that earlier abolitionists, such as Benjamin Rush (1745–1813) or Robert Rantoul (1805–52), would recognize, they also introduce newer considerations appropriate to the current social perceptions and moral tone of our society. The five selections that follow in this chapter are intended to represent the arguments of this sort that are currently being read or heard wherever serious debate and reflection on the death penalty occurs.

One of the most dedicated and influential opponents of the death penalty in the United States, who since the mid-1960s has spoken, written, and done more on behalf of this cause than anyone else, is Anthony G. Amsterdam, a law professor (at the time, at Stanford University; he is now at New York University) and the chief architect of the NAACP Legal Defense and Educational Fund's litigation campaign against the death penalty.[2] Although Amsterdam is well known in legal circles and especially in the nation's highest appellate courts—his name has appeared on countless briefs in death penalty cases from Florida to California—he rarely writes on this topic for other audiences.[3] His essay reprinted below as §1 is an exception; it was given originally as a lecture in 1977 on the anniversary of the Supreme Court's rulings in *Woodson* and *Gregg,* a major victory and defeat (respectively) for the litigation campaign Amsterdam had directed and inspired with his leadership. His lecture was not aimed at reopening the constitutional question. Instead, he presented the case for abolition on moral and empirical grounds, colored by considerations arising out of his unparalleled experience and phrased to provide an argument that is comprehensive yet remarkably concise.

No doubt the legal writer against the death penalty in recent years who has been most widely read and discussed is Charles L. Black, Jr., Sterling Professor of Law at Yale Law School and author of *Capital Punishment: The Inevitability of Caprice and Mistake* (1974). In that book, and in a series of subsequent essays, he has detailed a stream of criticism of the "new" death penalty statutes.[4] As he explained in the preface to his lecture reprinted in part as §2 below, "For about five years now, I have been going up and down the land, in print sometimes but mostly not in print, trying to persuade my fellow citizens that the penalty of death ought to be abolished." His theme in these writings and lectures has been the one implied by the subtitle of his book: The death penalty as it actually exists, not as it might possibly be imagined to be administered by angels or wholly rational and infallible human beings, is too clumsy, final, brutal to be tolerated; and those who defend it must reckon with these realities. The same theme, of course, is to be found

2. For an account of Amsterdam's work in the LDF campaign, see Meltsner 1973.
3. The text of the major LDF brief against the death penalty, of which Amsterdam was the chief author, was filed in *Aikens* v. *California* (1971), and has been reprinted (minus documentary appendices) in Mackey 1976:265–88. See also Amsterdam 1971a and 1971b.
4. See Black 1976, 1977, and 1978. His views as presented in his 1974 book have been criticized by Walter Berns (1979:179ff).

in other essays in this chapter, but Black has given it an unusually sustained development.

Since the mid-1960s, the brunt of public argument and education against the death penalty nationwide has been borne by the American Civil Liberties Union. In policy statements, pamphlets, news releases, memoranda, and above all in public debates and in legislative and clemency hearings, representatives of the ACLU have attempted to persuade their audiences to repeal, or not reintroduce, death penalty laws and to suspend or forego executions. Since 1976, the director of ACLU's Capital Punishment Project has been Henry Schwarzschild. After the Supreme Court in that year upheld the capital statutes of Florida, Georgia, and Texas, Schwarzschild also organized the National Coalition Against the Death Penalty, which (in his words, taken from the preface to his testimony excerpted below in §3) is "a coordinating agency for over fifty major national and regional organizations in the fields of religion, public-interest law, the minority communities, professional, community, and political concerns, all come together in their commitment to the abolition of capital punishment generally and to the prevention of executions in particular."[5] This is a far cry from earlier decades, when the national voices against the death penalty were few and faint—chiefly the Women's International League for Peace and Freedom, a few religious organizations, and the now-departed American League to Abolish Capital Punishment.[6] The statement reprinted below is one of many that Schwarzschild has prepared for public hearings; this one was given to the House Committee on the Judiciary in 1978 on the portion of the proposed revision of the Federal Rules of Criminal Procedure that deals with imposing the death penalty.[7] Schwarzschild's testimony is not confined to procedural questions, however; he concentrates instead on examining the public's apparent support for the death penalty (recall Chapter Three) and how this can be understood in a manner that does not require Congress or state legislatures to bow to it.

Although it was once true that organized religion in America took no official view on the death penalty, and that clergymen of all faiths were to be found among its defenders, most of the major religious denominations in the

5. A list of the member organizations of the National Coalition, as of 1978, may be found in *Senate Hearing* 1978:402–7 and in *House Hearing* 1978:30–31. The latest organization to join the National Coalition is Law Enforcement Against Death (LEAD), currently chaired by John Buckley, formerly Sheriff of Middlesex County (Mass.). See *Boston Sunday Globe,* 4 January 1981, p. A7.

6. See, for example, the testimony submitted by these groups in *House Hearing* 1960.

7. Other statements and testimony by Schwarzschild appear in *Senate Hearing* 1977:35–43 and *Senate Hearing* 1978:72–94. Opposition to the death penalty has also been expressed, of course, by members of the Senate itself. See especially *Senate Report* 1980:31–33, for the views of Senators Kennedy, Culver, and Leahy. The late Senator Philip A. Hart, long an articulate opponent of capital punishment, argued persuasively against S. 1401 (the predecessor to S. 114 in the most recent Congress) in *Senate Report* 1974:31–52.

country have for some years been in opposition to capital punishment. Their views have been conveniently set forth in the pamphlet *Capital Punishment: What the Religious Community Says* (1978), published by the National Interreligious Task Force on Criminal Justice.[8] Important as these position statements by the churches are, their brevity and somewhat doctrinaire quality limit their persuasive effect; and some might complain that these statements rest too heavily on sociological considerations and not enough on the actual teachings of the Bible. More subtle in this respect, and provocative, is the essay reprinted as §4 below, by theologian John Howard Yoder now teaching at the University of Notre Dame and The Associated Mennonite Biblical Seminaries in Indiana. Two decades ago, under the auspices of the Mennonites, Professor Yoder published a pamphlet, *The Christian and Capital Punishment* (1961), unfortunately not very widely known. In his more recent essay reprinted here, he presents what surely must be one of the most succinct and Biblically rooted criticisms of capital punishment from a Christian perspective ever written. Roman Catholics [9] and non-Christians may find unwelcome and inconclusive much of his argument. Nor will it probably persuade the fundamentalist Christian defenders of the death penalty, though it should prove a challenge to their skill and integrity at Biblical exegesis and interpretation.[10] What it does do is add a different—and welcome—dimension to the overwhelmingly secular (constitutional, legal, historical, empirical, rational) discussions in this chapter that criticize and reject the death penalty.[11]

To conclude this chapter and the book, I have chosen to reprint the 1980 proposal by Amnesty International (AI), the London-based international human-rights organization, to have a Presidential Commission appointed in the United States to investigate the death penalty. Since its founding in 1961, and as part of its worldwide program in defense of human rights, AI has opposed the death penalty. Its views on this subject gained international publicity when, concurrent with its receipt in Oslo of the Nobel Peace Prize in 1977, AI held an international conference in Stockholm to protest the death

8. The pamphlet has been reprinted in *Senate Hearing* 1978:362–99 and also in *House Hearing* 1978:32–69.
9. For a careful review of Roman Catholic thinking on the death penalty, see Compagnoni 1979 and Dailey 1979. See also Castelli 1973, Beristain 1977, and the testimony of Bishop Ernest L. Unterkolfer in *House Hearing* 1978:94–103. The text of the 1980 statement by the Conference of Catholic Bishops opposing the death penalty is reprinted in *Death Penalty Reporter*, December 1980.
10. Mormons will find interesting the careful discussion of their church's doctrinal position on blood atonement in M. Gardner 1979a. Those with an interest in historical Jewish law will want to study Cohn 1970.
11. See also the criticism of the death penalty by the anthropologists Colin Turnbull (1978) and Margaret Mead (1978), the sociologist Jack P. Gibbs (1978b), and the philosophers Thomas W. Satre (1975) and David Hoekema (1979). I have criticized the death penalty in several publications; see especially Bedau 1959, 1967a, 1973a, 1977b, and 1980a.

penalty. Two years later it published *The Death Penalty* (1979), an indispensable survey of the status of the death penalty around the world. AI's proposal for a Presidential Commission is not, therefore, tendered in a spirit of moral neutrality or scientific curiosity. It arises out of the settled conviction that the death penalty is a violation of human rights, and that anyone who undertakes an impartial and thorough investigation will reach the same conclusion. Despite a certain tendentiousness in AI's proposal, its argument sets the death penalty controversy in the United States within a wider international legal and moral perspective.

§1.   Capital Punishment*

ANTHONY G. AMSTERDAM

My discussion of capital punishment will proceed in three stages.

First, I would like to set forth certain basic factual realities about capital punishment, like the fact that capital punishment is a fancy phrase for legally killing people. Please forgive me for beginning with such obvious and ugly facts. Much of our political and philosophical debate about the death penalty is carried on in language calculated to conceal these realities and their implications. The implications, I will suggest, are that capital punishment is a great evil—surely the greatest evil except for war that our society can intentionally choose to commit.

This does not mean that we should do away with capital punishment. Some evils, like war, are occasionally necessary, and perhaps capital punishment is one of them. But the fact that it is a great evil means that we should not choose to do it without some very good and solid reason of which we are satisfactorily convinced upon sufficient evidence. The conclusion of my first point simply is that the burden of proof upon the question of capital punishment rightly rests on those who are asking us to use our laws to kill people with, and that this is a very heavy burden.

Second, I want to review the justifications that have been advanced to support capital punishment. I want to explore with you concepts such as retribution and deterrence, and some of the assumptions and evidence about them. The conclusion of my second point will be that none of these reasons which we like to give ourselves for executing criminals can begin to sustain the burden of proof that rightfully rests upon them.

Third, I would like to say a word about history—about the slow but abso-

*From Anthony G. Amsterdam "Capital Punishment." © The Stanford Magazine, Fall/Winter 1977, pp. 42–47. Reprinted with permission of the Stanford Alumni Association.

lutely certain progress of maturing civilization that will bring an inevitable end to punishment by death. That history does not give us the choice between perpetuating and abolishing capital punishment, because we could not perpetuate it if we wanted to. A generation or two within a single nation can retard but not reverse a long-term, worldwide evolution of this magnitude. Our choice is narrower although it is not unimportant: whether we shall be numbered among the last generations to put legal killing aside. I will end by asking you to cast your choice for life instead of death. But, first, let me begin with some basic facts about the death penalty .

I. The most basic fact, of course, is that capital punishment means taking, living, breathing men and women, stuffing them into a chair, strapping them down, pulling a lever, and exterminating them. We have almost forgotten this fact because there have been no executions in this country for more than ten years, except for Gary Gilmore whose combined suicide and circus were so wildly extravagant as to seem unreal. For many people, capital punishment has become a sanitized and symbolic issue: Do you or do you not support you local police? Do you or do you not care enough about crime to get tough with criminals? These abstractions were never what capital punishment was about, although it was possible to think so during the ten-year moratorium on executions caused by constitutional challenges to the death penalty in the courts. That is no longer possible. The courts have now said that we can start up executions again, if we want to. Today, a vote for capital punishment is a vote to kill real, live people.

What this means is, first, that we bring men or women into court and put them through a trial for their lives. They are expected to sit back quietly and observe decent courtroom decorum throughout a proceeding whose purpose is systematically and deliberately to decide whether they should be killed. The jury hears evidence and votes; and you can always tell when a jury has voted for death because they come back into court and they will not look the defendant or defense counsel in the eyes. The judge pronounces sentence and the defendant is taken away to be held in a cell for two to six years, hoping that his appeals will succeed, not really knowing what they are all about, but knowing that if they fail, he will be taken out and cinched down and put to death. Most of the people in prison are reasonably nice to him, and even a little apologetic; but he realizes every day for that 700 or 2,100 days that they are holding him there helpless for the approaching slaughter; and that, once the final order is given, they will truss him up and kill him, and that nobody in that vast surrounding machinery of public officials and servants of the law will raise a finger to save him. This is why Camus once wrote that an execution

> is not simply death. It is just as different . . . from the privation of life as a concentration camp is from prison. . . . It adds to death a rule, a public premeditation known to the future victim, an organization . . . which is itself a source of

moral sufferings more terrible than death ... [Capital punishment] is ... the
most premeditated of murders, to which no criminal's deed, however calculated
... can be compared .... For there to be an equivalency, the death penalty
would have to punish a criminal who had warned his victim of the date at which
he would inflict a horrible death on him and who, from that moment onward,
had confined him at his mercy for months. Such a monster is not encountered
in private life.

I will spare you descriptions of the execution itself. Apologists for capital
punishment commonly excite their readers with descriptions of extremely
gruesome, gory murders. All murders are horrible things, and executions are
usually a lot cleaner physically—although, like Camus, I have never heard of
a murderer who held his victim captive for two or more years waiting as the
minutes and hours ticked away toward his preannounced death. The clinical
details of an execution are as unimaginable to me as they are to most of you.
We have not permitted public executions in this country for over 40 years.
The law in every state forbids more than a few people to watch the deed
done behind prison walls. In January of 1977, a federal judge in Texas ruled
that executions could be photographed for television, but the attorneys general of 25 states asked the federal Court of Appeals to set aside that ruling,
and it did. I can only leave to your imagination what they are trying so very
hard to hide from us. Oh, of course, executions are too hideous to put on
television; we all know that. But let us not forget that it is the same hideous
thing, done in secret, which we are discussing under abstract labels like "capital punishment" that permit us to talk about the subject in after-dinner con-
versation instead of spitting up.

In any event, the advocates of capital punishment can and do accentuate
their arguments with descriptions of the awful physical details of such hideous murders as that of poor Sharon Tate. All of us naturally and rightly
respond to these atrocities with shock and horror. You can read descriptions
of executions that would also horrify you (for example, in Byron Eshelman's
1962 book, *Death Row Chaplain*, particularly pages 160-61), but I prefer not
to insult your intelligence by playing "can you top this" with issues of life
and death. I ask you only to remember two things, if and when you are
exposed to descriptions of terrifying murders.

First, the murders being described are not murders that are being done by
us, or in our name, or with our approval; and our power to stop them is
exceedingly limited even under the most exaggerated suppositions of deterrence, which I shall shortly return to question. Every execution, on the other
hand, is done by our paid servants, in our collective name, and we can stop
them all. Please do not be bamboozled into thinking that people who are
against executions are in favor of murders. If we had the individual or the
collective power to stop murders, we would stop them all—and for the same
basic reason that we want to stop executions. Murders and executions are

both ugly, vicious things, because they destroy the same sacred and mysterious gift of life which we do not understand and can never restore.

Second, please remember therefore that descriptions of murders are relevant to the subject of capital punishment only on the theory that two wrongs make a right, or that killing murderers can assuage their victims' sufferings or bring them back to life, or that capital punishment is the best deterrent to murder. The first two propositions are absurd, and the third is debatable—although, as I shall later show, the evidence is overwhelmingly against it. My present point is only that deterrence *is* debatable, whereas we *know* that persons whom we execute are dead beyond recall, no matter how the debate about deterrence comes out. That is a sufficient reason, I believe, why the burden of proof on the issue of deterrence should be placed squarely upon the executioners.

There are other reasons too. Let me try to state them briefly.

Capital punishment not merely kills people, it also kills some of them in error, and these are errors which we can never correct. When I speak about legal error, I do not mean only the question whether "they got the right man" or killed somebody who "didn't do it." Errors of that sort do occur: Timothy Evans, for example, an innocent man whose execution was among the reasons for the abolition of the death penalty in Great Britain. If you read Anthony Scaduto's recent book, *Scapegoat,* you will come away with unanswerable doubts whether Bruno Richard Hauptmann was really guilty of the kidnaping of the Lindbergh infant for which he was executed, or whether we killed Hauptmann, too, for a crime he did not commit.

In 1975, the Florida Cabinet pardoned two black men, Freddie Lee Pitts and Wilbert Lee, who were twice tried and sentenced to death and spent 12 years apiece on death row for a murder committed by somebody else. This one, I am usually glibly told, "does not count," because Pitts and Lee were never actually put to death. Take comfort if you will but I cannot, for I know that only the general constitutional attack which we were then mounting upon the death penalty in Florida kept Pitts and Lee alive long enough to permit discovery of the evidence of their innocence. Our constitutional attack is now dead, and so would Pitts and Lee be if they were tried tomorrow. Sure, we catch some errors. But we often catch them by extremely lucky breaks that could as easily not have happened. I represented a young man in North Carolina who came within a hair's breadth of being the Gary Gilmore of his day. Like Gilmore, he became so depressed under a death sentence that he tried to dismiss his appeal. He was barely talked out of it, his conviction was reversed, and on retrial a jury acquitted him in 11 minutes.

We do not know how many "wrong men" have been executed. We think and pray that they are rare—although we can't be sure because, after a man is dead, people seldom continue to investigate the possibility that he was innocent. But that is not the biggest source of error anyway.

)

What about *legal* error? In 1968, the Supreme Court of the United States held that it was unconstitutional to exclude citizens from capital trial juries simply because they had general conscientious or religious objections to the death penalty. That decision was held retroactive; and I represented 60 or 70 men whose death sentences were subsequently set aside for constitutional errors in jury selection. While researching their cases, I found the cases of at least as many more men who had already been executed on the basis of trials infected with identical errors. On June 29, 1977, we finally won a decision from the Supreme Court of the United States that the death penalty is excessively harsh and therefore unconstitutional for the crime of rape. Fine, but it comes too late for the 455 men executed for rape in this country since 1930—405 of them black.

In 1975, the Supreme Court held that the constitutional presumption of innocence forbids a trial judge to tell the jury that the burden of proof is on a homicide defendant to show provocation which reduces murder to manslaughter. On June 17, 1977, the Court held that this decision was also retroactive. Jury charges of precisely that kind were standard forms for more than a century in many American states that punished murder with death. Can we even begin to guess how many people were unconstitutionally executed under this so-called retroactive decision?

Now what about errors of fact that go to the degree of culpability of a crime? In almost every state, the difference between first- and second-degree murder—or between capital and noncapital murder—depends on whether the defendant acted with something called "premeditation" as distinguished from intent to kill. Premeditation means intent formed beforehand, but no particular amount of time is required. Courts tell juries that premeditation "may be as instantaneous as successive thoughts in the mind." Mr. Justice Cardozo wrote that *he* did not understand the concept of premeditation after several decades of studying and trying to apply it as a judge. Yet this is the kind of question to which a jury's answer spells out life or death in a capital trial—this, and the questions whether the defendant had "malice aforethought," or "provocation and passion," or "insanity," or the "reasonableness" necessary for killing in self-defense.

I think of another black client, Johnny Coleman, whose conviction and death sentence for killing a white truck driver named "Screwdriver" Johnson we twice got reversed by the Supreme Court of the United States. On retrial a jury acquitted him on the grounds of self-defense upon exactly the same evidence that an earlier jury had had when it sentenced him to die. When ungraspable legal standards are thus applied to intangible mental states, there is not merely the possibility but the actuarial certainty that juries deciding substantial volumes of cases are going to be wrong in an absolutely large number of them. If you accept capital punishment, you must accept the reality—not the risk, but the reality—that we shall kill people whom the law says that it is not proper to kill. No other outcome is possible when we presume to administer an infallible punishment through a fallible system.

You will notice that I have taken examples of black defendants as some of my cases of legal error. There is every reason to believe that discrimination on grounds of race and poverty fatally infect the administration of capital justice in this country. Since 1930, an almost equal number of white and black defendants has been executed for the crime of murder, although blacks constituted only about a tenth of the nation's population during this period. No sufficiently careful studies have been done of these cases, controlling variables other than race, so as to determine exactly what part race played in the outcome. But when that kind of systematic study *was* done in rape cases, it showed beyond the statistical possibility of a doubt that black men who raped white women were disproportionately sentenced to die on the basis of race alone. Are you prepared to believe that juries which succumbed to conscious or unconscious racial prejudices in rape cases were or are able to put those prejudices wholly aside where the crime charged is murder? Is it not much more plausible to believe that even the most conscientious juror—or judge, or prosecuting attorney—will be slower to want to inflict the death penalty on a defendant with whom he can identify as a human being; and that the process of identification in our society is going to be very seriously affected by racial identity?

I should mention that there have been a couple of studies—one by the *Stanford Law Review* and the other by the Texas Judicial Council —which found no racial discrimination in capital sentencing in certain murder cases. But both of these studies had methodological problems and limitations; and both of them also found death-sentencing discrimination against the economically poor, who come disproportionately from racial minorities. The sum of the evidence still stands where the National Crime Commission found it ten years ago, when it described the following discriminatory patterns. "The death sentence," said the Commission, "is disproportionately imposed and carried out on the poor, the Negro, and members of unpopular groups."

Apart from discrimination, there is a haphazard, crazy-quilt character about the administration of capital punishment that every knowledgeable lawyer or observer can describe but none can rationally explain. Some juries are hanging juries, some counties are hanging counties, some years are hanging years; and men live or die depending on these flukes.

However atrocious the crime may have been for which a particular defendant is sentenced to die, "[e]xperienced wardens know many prisoners serving life or less whose crimes were equally, or more atrocious." That is a quotation, by the way, from former Attorney General Ramsey Clark's statement to a congressional subcommittee; and wardens Lewis Lawes, Clinton Duffy, and others have said the same thing.

With it I come to the end of my first point. I submit that the deliberate judicial extinction of human life is intrinsically so final and so terrible an act as to cast the burden of proof for its justification upon those who want us to do it. But certainly when the act is executed through a fallible system which assures that we kill some people wrongly, others because they are black or poor or personally unattractive or socially unacceptable, and all of them quite freakishly in the sense that whether a man lives or dies for any particular crime is a matter of luck and happenstance, *then,* at the least, the burden of justifying capital punishment lies fully and heavily on its proponents.

II. Let us consider those justifications. The first and the oldest is the concept of *retribution:* an eye for an eye, a life for a life. You may or may not believe in this kind of retribution, but I will not waste your time debating it because it cannot honestly be used to justify the only form of capital punishment that this country has accepted for the past half-century. Even before the judicial moratorium, executions in the United States had dwindled to an average of about 30 a year. Only a rare, sparse handful of convicted murderers was being sentenced to die or executed for the selfsame crimes for which many, many times as many murderers were sent away to prison. Obviously, as Professor Herbert Wechsler said a generation ago, the issue of capital punishment is no longer "whether it is fair or just that one who takes another person's life should lose his own. . . . [W]e do not and cannot act upon. . . [that proposition] generally in the administration of the penal law. The problem rather is whether a small and highly random sample of people who commit murder. . . . ought to be despatched, while most of those convicted of . . . [identical] crimes are dealt with by imprisonment."

Sometimes the concept of retribution is modernized a little with a notion called *moral reinforcement*—the ideal that we should punish very serious crimes very severely in order to demonstrate how much we abhor them. The trouble with *this* justification for capital punishment, of course, is that it completely begs the question, which is *how severely* we ought to punish any particular crime to show appropriate abhorrence for it. The answer can hardly be found in a literal application of the eye-for-an-eye formula. We do not burn down arsonists' houses or cheat back at bunco artists. But if we ought not punish all crimes exactly according to their kind, then what is the fit moral reinforcement for murder? You might as well say burning at the stake or boiling in oil as simple gassing or electrocution.

Or is it not more plausible—if what we really want to say is that the killing of a human being is wrong and ought to be condemned as clearly as we can— that we should choose the punishment of prison as the fitting means to make this point? So far as moral reinforcement goes, the difference between life imprisonment and capital punishment is precisely that imprisonment continues to respect the value of human life. The plain message of capital punishment, on the other hand, is that life ceases to be sacred whenever someone with the power to take it away decides that there is a sufficiently compelling pragmatic reason to do so.

But there is still another theory of a retributive sort which is often advanced to support the death penalty, particularly in recent years. This is the argument that *we*—that is, the person making the argument—we no longer believe in the outworn concept of retribution, but the *public*—they believe in retribution, and so we must let them have their prey or they will lose respect for law. Watch for this argument because it is the surest sign of demagogic depravity. It is disgusting in its patronizing attribution to "the public" of a primitive, uneducable bloodthirstiness which the speaker is unprepared to defend but is prepared to exploit as a means of sidestepping the rational and moral limitations of a *just* theory of retribution. It out-judases Judas in its abnegation of governmental responsibility to respond to popular misinformation with enlightenment, instead of seizing on it as a pretext for atrocity. This argument asserts that the proper way to deal with a lynch mob is to string its victim up before the mob does.

I don't think "the public" is a lynch mob or should be treated as one. People today are troubled and frightened by crime, and legitimately so. Much of the apparent increase of violent crime in our times is the product of intensified statistics keeping, massive and instantaneous and graphic news reporting, and manipulation of figures by law enforcement agencies which must compete with other sectors of the public economy for budget allocations. But part of the increase is also real, and very disturbing. Murders ought to disturb us all, whether or not they are increasing. Each and every murder is a terrible human tragedy. Nevertheless, it is irresponsible for public officials—particularly law enforcement officials whom the public views as experts—first to exacerbate and channel legitimate public concern about crime into public support for capital punishment by advertising unsupportable claims that capital punishment is an answer to the crime problem, and then to turn around and cite public support for capital punishment as justification when all other justifications are shown to be unsupportable. Politicians do this all the time, for excellent political reasons. It is much easier to advocate simplistic and illusory solutions to the crime problem than to find real and effective solutions. Most politicians are understandably afraid to admit that our society knows frighteningly little about the causes or cure of crime, and will have to spend large amounts of taxpayers' money even to begin to find out. The facile politics of crime do much to explain our national acceptance of capital punishment, but nothing to justify it.

Another supposed justification for capital punishment that deserves equally brief treatment is the notion of *isolation* or *specific deterrence*—the idea that we must kill a murderer to prevent him from murdering ever again. The usual forms that this argument takes are that a life sentence does not mean a life sentence—it means parole after 7, or 12, or 25 years; and that, within prisons themselves, guards and other prisoners are in constant jeopardy of death at the hands of convicted but unexecuted murderers.

It amazes me that these arguments can be made or taken seriously. Are we really going to kill a human being because we do not trust other people—the people whom we have chosen to serve on our own parole boards—to make a proper judgment in his case at some future time? We trust this same parole board to make far more numerous, difficult, and dangerous decisions: hardly a week passes when they do not consider the cases of armed robbers, for example, although armed robbers are much, much more likely statistically to commit future murders than any murderer is to repeat his crime. But if we really do distrust the public agencies of law—if we fear that they may make mistakes—then surely that is a powerful argument *against* capital punishment. Courts which hand out death sentences because they predict that a man will still be criminally dangerous 7 or 25 years in the future cannot conceivably make fewer mistakes than parole boards who release a prisoner after 7 or 25 years of close observation in prison have convinced them that he is reformed and no longer dangerous.

But pass this point. If we refuse to trust the parole system, then let us provide by law that the murderers whose release we fear shall be given sentences of life imprisonment without parole which *do* mean life imprisonment without parole. I myself would be against that, but it is far more humane than capital punishment, and equally safe.

As for killings inside prisons, if you examine them you will find that they are very rarely done by convicted murderers, but are almost always done by people imprisoned for crimes that no one would think of making punishable by death. Warden Lawes of Sing Sing and Governor Wallace of Alabama, among others, regularly employed murder convicts as house servants because they were among the very safest of prisoners. There are exceptions, of course; but these can be handled by adequate prison security. You cannot tell me or believe that a society which is capable of putting a man on the moon is incapable of putting a man in prison, keeping him there, and keeping him from killing while he is there. And if anyone says that this is costly, and that we should kill people in order to reduce government expenditures, I can only reply that the cost of housing a man for life in the most physically secure conditions imaginable is considerably less than the cost of putting the same man through all of the extraordinary legal proceedings necessary to kill him.

That brings me to the last supposed justification for the death penalty: *deterrence*. This is the subject that you most frequently hear debated, and many people who talk about capital punishment talk about nothing else. I have done otherwise here, partly for completeness, partly because it is vital to approach the subject of deterrence knowing precisely what question you want to ask and have answered. I have suggested that the proper question is *whether there is sufficiently convincing evidence that the death penalty deters murder better than does life imprisonment so that you are willing to accept responsibility for doing the known evil act of killing human beings— with all of the attending ugliness that I have described—on the faith of your conviction in the superior deterrent efficacy of capital punishment.*

If this is the question, then I submit that there is only one fair and reasonable answer. When the Supreme Court of the United States reviewed the evidence in 1976, it described that evidence as "inconclusive." Do not let anybody tell you—as death-penalty advocates are fond of doing—that the Supreme Court held the death penalty justifiable as a deterrent. What the Court's plurality opinion said, exactly, was that "there is no convincing evidence *either supporting or refuting* . . . [the] view" that "the death penalty may not function as a significantly greater deterrent than lesser penalties." *Because* the evidence was inconclusive, the Court held that the Constitution did not forbid judgment either way. But if the evidence is inconclusive, is it *your* judgment that we should conclusively kill people on a factual theory that the evidence does not conclusively sustain?

I hope not. But let us examine the evidence more carefully because —even though it is not conclusive—it is very, very substantial; and the overwhelming weight of it refutes the claims of those who say that capital punishment is a better deterrent than life imprisonment for murder.

For more than 40 years, criminologists have studied this question by a variety of means. They have compared homicide rates in countries and states that did and did not have capital punishment, or that actually executed people more and less frequently. Some of these studies compared large aggregates of abolitionist and retentionist states; others compared geographically adjacent pairs or triads of states, or states that were chosen because they were comparable in other socioeconomic factors that might affect homicide. Other studies compared homicide rates in the same country or state before and after the abolition or reinstatement of capital punishment, or they compared homicide rates for the same geographic area during periods preceding and following well publicized executions. Special comparative studies were done relating to police killings and prison killings. All in all, there were dozens of studies. Without a single exception, *none* of them found that the death penalty had any statistically significant effect upon the rate of homicide or murder. Often I have heard advocates of capital punishment explain away its failures by likening it to a great lighthouse: "We count the ships that crash," they say, "but we never know how many saw the light and were saved." What these studies show, however, is that coastlines of the same shape and depth and tidal structure, with and without lighthouses, invariably have the same number of shipwrecks per year. On that evidence, would you invest your money in a lighthouse, or would you buy a sonar if you really wanted to save lives?

In 1975, the first purportedly scientific study ever to find that capital punishment *did* deter homicides was published. This was done by Isaac Ehrlich of Chicago, who is not a criminologist but an economist. Using regression analysis involving an elaborate mathematical model, Ehrlich reported that every execution deterred something like eight murders. Naturally, supporters of capital punishment hurriedly clambered on the Ehrlich bandwagon.

Unhappily, for them, the wagon was a factory reject. Several distinguished econometricians—including a team headed by Lawrence Klein, president of the American Economic Association—reviewed Ehrlich's work and found it fatally flawed with numerous methodological errors. Some of these were technical: it appeared, for example, that Ehrlich had produced his results by the unjustified and unexplained use of a logarithmic form of regression equation instead of the more conventional linear form—which made his findings of deterrence vanish. Equally important, it was shown that Ehrlich's findings depended entirely on data from the post-1962 period, when executions declined and the homicide rate rose *as a part of a general rise, in the overall crime rate that Ehrlich incredibly failed to consider.*

Incidentally, the nonscientific proponents of capital punishment are also fond of suggesting that the rise in homicide rates in the 1960s and the 1970s, when executions were halted, proves that executions used to deter homicides. This is ridiculous when you consider that crime as a whole has increased during this period; that homicide rates have increased about *half* as much as the rates for all other FBI Index crimes; and that whatever factors are affecting the rise of most noncapital crimes (which *cannot* include cessation of executions) almost certainly affect the homicide-rate rise also.

In any event, Ehrlich's study was discredited and a second, methodologically inferior study by a fellow named Yunker is not even worth criticizing here. These are the only two scientific studies in 40 years, I repeat, which have ever purported to find deterrence. On the other hand, several recent studies have been completed by researchers who adopted Ehrlich's basic regression-analysis approach but corrected its defects. Peter Passell did such a study finding no deterrence. Kenneth Avio did such a study finding no deterrence. Brian Forst did such a study finding no deterrence. If you want to review all of these studies yourselves, you may find them discussed and cited in an excellent article in the 1976 *Supreme Court Review* by Hans Zeisel, at page 317. The conclusion you will have to draw is that—during 40 years and today—the scientific community has looked and looked and looked for any reliable evidence that capital punishment deters homicide better than does life imprisonment, and it has found no such evidence at all.

Proponents of capital punishment frequently cite a different kind of study, one that was done by the Los Angeles Police Department. Police officers asked arrested robbers who did not carry guns, or did not use them, *why* they did not; and the answers, supposedly, were frequently that the robber "did not want to get the death penalty." It is noteworthy that the Los Angeles Police Department has consistently refused to furnish copies of this study and its underlying data to professional scholars, apparently for fear of criticism. I finally obtained a copy of the study from a legislative source, and I can tell you that it shows two things. First, an arrested person will tell a police officer anything that he thinks the officer wants to hear. Second, police officers, like all other human beings, hear what they want to hear. When a robber tries to say that he did not carry or use a gun because he did not wish to risk the penalties for homicide, he will describe those penalties in terms of whatever the law happens to be at the time and place. In Minnesota, which has no death penalty, he will say, "I didn't want to get life imprisonment." In Los Angeles, he will say, "I didn't want to get the death penalty." Both responses mean the same thing; neither tells you that death is a superior deterrent to life imprisonment.

The real mainstay of the deterrence thesis, however, is not evidence but intuition. You and I ask ourselves: Are we not afraid to die? Of course! Would the threat of death, then, not intimidate us to forbear from a criminal act? Certainly! *Therefore,* capital punishment must be a deterrent. The trouble with this intuition is that the people who are doing the reasoning and the people who are doing the murdering are not the same people. You and I do not commit murder for a lot of reasons other than the death penalty. The death penalty might perhaps also deter us from murdering—but altogether needlessly, since we would not murder with it or without it. Those who are sufficiently dissocialized to murder and are not responding to the world in the way that we are, and we simply cannot "intuit" their thinking processes from ours.

Consider, for example, the well-documented cases of persons who kill *because* there is a death penalty. One of these was Pamela Watkins, a baby-sitter in San Jose who had made several unsuccessful suicide attempts and was frightened to try again. She finally strangled two children so that the state of California would execute her. In various bizarre forms, this "suicide-murder" syndrome is reported by psychiatrists again and again. (Parenthetically, Gary Gilmore was probably such a case.) If you intuit that somewhere, sometime, the death penalty *does* deter some potential murders, are you also prepared to intuit that their numbers mathematically exceed the numbers of these wretched people who are actually induced to murder by the existence of capital punishment?

Here, I suggest, our intuition does—or should—fail, just as the evidence certainly does fail, to establish a deterrent justification for the death penalty.

There is simply no credible evidence, and there is no rational way of reasoning about the real facts once you know them, which can sustain this or any other justification with the degree of confidence that should be demanded before a civilized society deliberately extinguishes human life.

III. I have only a little space for my final point, but it is sufficient because the point is perfectly plain. Capital punishment is a dying institution in this last quarter of the twentieth century. It has already been abandoned in law or in fact throughout most of the civilized world. England, Canada, the Scandinavian countries, virtually all of Western Europe except for France and Spain have abolished the death penalty. The vast majority of countries in the Western Hemisphere have abolished it. Its last strongholds in the world—apart from the United States—are in Asia and Africa, particularly South Africa. Even the countries which maintain capital punishment on the books have almost totally ceased to use it in fact. In the United States, considering only the last half century, executions have plummeted from 199 in 1935 to approximately 29 a year during the decade before 1967, when the ten-year judicial moratorium began.

Do you doubt that this development will continue? Do you doubt that it will continue because it is the path of civilization—the path up out of fear and terror and the barbarism that terror breeds, into self-confidence and decency in the administration of justice? The road, like any other built by men, has its detours, but over many generations it has run true, and will run true. And there will therefore come a time—perhaps in 20 years, perhaps in 50 or 100, but very surely and very shortly as the lifetime of nations is measured—when our children will look back at us in horror and unbelief because of what we did in their names and for their supposed safety, just as we look back in horror and unbelief at the thousands of crucifixions and beheadings and live disembowelments that our ancestors practiced for the supposed purpose of making our world safe from murderers and robbers, thieves, shoplifters, and pickpockets.

All of these kinds of criminals are still with us, and will be with our children—although we can certainly decrease their numbers and their damage, and protect ourselves from them a lot better, if we insist that our politicians stop pounding on the whipping boy of capital punishment and start coming up with some real solutions to the real problems of crime. Our children will cease to execute murderers for the same reason that we have ceased to string up pickpockets and shoplifters at the public crossroads, although there are still plenty of them around. Our children will cease to execute murderers because executions are a self-deluding, self-defeating, self-degrading, futile, and entirely stupid means of dealing with the crime of murder, and because our children will prefer to be something better than murderers themselves. Should we not—can we not—make the same choice now?

§2.   Death Sentences and
Our Criminal Justice System*

CHARLES L. BLACK, JR.

[...] Whatever may have been the case in the past, the death penalty for a long time has been and definitely promises to continue being administered by a system that is characterized by a large amount of arbitrariness and mistake-proneness. Those who are to die have been chosen by a process which, at every critical stage, proceeds on no clearly articulated or understandable criteria. This starts with the stage of charging and pleading; the decision of the prosecutor as to what to charge and as to whether to offer a plea-bargain is not only unfettered and unreviewable but also without any clear and authoritative standards for the exercise of discretion. The luck of the draw in the jury is what I have called it, the luck of the draw. In a great majority of cases, the jury is instructed upon and may find "guilty" upon a lesser included offense, rather than on the charge that makes the defendant eligible for death; there is no review of this decision, and even instruction from the bench upon the difference between first and second degree murder, on premeditation, on the provocation that justifies or compels a manslaughter finding, and so on, is necessarily vague, for the law itself is vague. The "insanity defense," allowed in every state but in no state given a really intelligible definition, is a wild joker in the deck. At the separate sentencing stage, the state statutes, most of them recently put in place, contain other wild jokers which make unfaultable and unreviewable a decision for death or against death at this point. The decision for or against clemency is designedly standardless. The net effect is that virtually full discretion exists, taking the system as a whole, to select or not to select the particular defendant, out of the very many who might have been eligible, for suffering the supreme agony. Such a system, it seems to me, is not good enough for making this choice.

Now I am going to do what might seem a most arrogant thing, though I believe that on reflection you will not find it so. I am going to ask that tentatively, and for this short time only, we assume that the foregoing is a correct description of the system by which eligibility for death is established and acted upon. I make this quite temporary draft upon your patience and kindness because my aim in this talk is not to reargue this thesis but rather to place it in relation to other thoughts and questions about the penalty of death. [...]

On that theme, then: The question [...] whether it is right to kill such

---

*Excerpted from Charles L. Black, Jr., "Reflections on Opposing the Penalty of Death," 10 *St. Mary's L.J.* (1978), pp. 1–12. Reprinted with permission of the author and the publisher. Copyright reserved by St. Mary's Law Journal.

people as are chosen by our system as it stands—is not a peripheral or side-question. It is not a needless complication of a simple question, or a needlessly confusing combination of two separate questions. It is the *only* question that actually confronts us. We are not presently confronted, as a political society, with the question whether something called "the state" has some abstract right to kill "those who deserve to die." We are confronted by the single unitary question posed by reality: "Shall we kill those who are chosen to be killed by our legal process as it stands?" My own work has been principally devoted to trying to throw more light on one aspect of that single unitary question—that part of it which invites inquiry as to the nature of the system as it stands. Strictly, for this purpose, it doesn't really make any difference at all what I think about the abstract rightness of capital punishment. There exists no abstract capital punishment.

Of course, it might be said that the single unitary question that now confronts us might change its aspect very quickly, by drastic improvements in the systems for choosing those who are to die. But the present systems, out in the states, are the best the states have been able to come up with in the years since the *Furman* case against a far longer background of thought and experience. Their defects, in process and in concepts that work themselves out only in process, are deeply rooted in the law of decades and even of centuries past. There is not, realistically, the smallest chance of major improvement, *transforming* improvement, in any time soon to come. And even if there were, we are confronted right now with the question of sending to death row or not sending to death row, killing or not killing, persons already chosen or in the process of being chosen by the systems as they stand. Not even the most optimistic looker-forward can avoid or evade this question.

Yet I am now myself in what I might loosely call a philosophic vein, and I cannot restrain myself from talking to you about the deepest of the thoughts that have come to me from being asked, perhaps five hundred times, "Would you favor the death penalty if it were administered by a perfect system?" My own philosophic depths, which are, I am afraid, rather shallow as philosophic depths go, have finally been stirred to produce the counter-question, "What can this person mean by a 'perfect system'?" And here, again, the dominant theme must be the *processual* theme. It is impossible to stress this too strongly, or too often.

I can sketch imaginatively, though in the pale tones of utter political impossibility, some aspects of the system which could be brought to something that might be called perfection, as human perfection goes. For example—and I know what a ludicrous example it is, in the world we actually live in—it is imaginable that every capital defendant might be furnished by the state, at every stage, with the best counsel money can buy, and with completely adequate funds for investigation, for expert witnesses, and for everything else that you or I would hock our souls to get if we had anyone dear to us standing accused of a capital offense. Since we would all do this, presumably we consider it advantageous to have and to use these resources. By clearest consequence, we must consider it disadvantageous not to have them. When I got off the plane recently in a Western state, some people were falling all over me to let me know that there were three men currently in the death house there without any lawyers at all to prepare their federal appeal papers—and time was running. Thinking of that situation, and many others like it, I almost laugh at what I am about to say. But I can at least imagine that a civilized state might decide that, before leading a person into a small room to be killed, it should afford the best, and not the grudgingly conceded bedrock minimum, of resources for making a defense. If that were to be done, the system would be, in that one aspect alone, perfected.

Even as to this kind of perfectibility, I wonder why anybody wants to raise the question now. I have always been patient on these occasions, but I find it difficult to treat this question as anything but diversionary. You raise the terrible question, "Shall we kill poor people who have been furnished minimal legal representation and next to no other resources for preparing a defense?" and the reply is "What would you say if the state furnished each capital defendant with means actually sufficient for putting up the best possible defense?" Is it possible that the questioner is not seeking, consciously or unconsciously, to direct the attention—his own attention, perhaps—away from one aspect of the terrible, and terribly real, issue that actually confronts him, and me, and all of us?

On many other questions of perfectibility, or even of susceptibility of improvement, I am not so sure I can even imagine what the questioner means, or supply a meaning for him. Here, again, attention to processual issues brings some clarity.

Let us take the simplest plane—that of fact. What does it mean to speak of a "perfect" system in this regard? That predication has no operational meaning unless a better, more reliable system is used to check factual determinations, but what is the guarantee that this system itself possesses infallibility, or any given degree of rightness? (Of course such a system is merely imaginary.)

But this is rather abstract. Let's take a middling-complicated question of mixed physical and psychological fact, coupled with a normative judgment: "Did the defendant kill the victim because of a reasonable belief that his own life was threatened?" Now no improvement in the legal system is ever going to enable the fact-finding tribunal to witness personally even the external events under examination. Whether the deceased pulled a knife, or looked as if he were going to pull a knife, is all a matter of inference from testimony, very often the testimony of the defendant, and in other cases almost always the testimony, given much later, of witnesses to a rapidly moving, exciting course of events. Whether the defendant believed the victim had a knife is a question of psychological fact, but of great difficulty of investigation. Whether the belief was "reasonable" is a matter of *ad hoc* evaluation by a jury. How can all this be changed?

A level deeper, we come to the pure question of mental state, and its evaluation. I put the matter in that general way because I am aware that some now favor the doing away with the so-called "insanity defense." But I cannot imagine that any moral society could look on mental state as totally irrelevant to the question whether death was deserved as a penalty. Yet I cannot imagine, either, how the techniques for dealing with this, with which our legal culture has without success struggled for so long, could be refined so as to eliminate arbitrariness and mistake from judgment.

In Brooklyn recently, a white policeman shot and killed, apparently without provocation, a black youth of 15. The defense, supported by medical testimony, was that the policeman had suffered a sudden psychological seizure or episode. The jury acquitted. I do not impugn their judgment; it may well have been right. But what I ask you to consider is what the chances would be of a black youth, who without provocation shot and killed a policeman, and proferred the same defense. Wherever the verbal line is drawn, and under whatever name, between those states of mind which qualify for death and those which do not, arbitrariness and mistake will continue to rule.

Sometimes I think the question, "What would you do if the death-choice system were perfected?" is like the question, "What would you do if 40% of the people in the United States learned to speak pretty good Japanese by next New Year's Day?" —a question that states an hypothesis not physically impossible, not even psychologically impossible case by case, but absolutely impossible from the social and political point of view. But sometimes I think the question is more like, "What would you do if an amoeba were taught to play the piano?" I dare say the question concerns a mixture of both these things—the politically and socially impossible, and the rigorously impossible even to the imagination.

Let me turn to the very closely connected question—the question of the actual existence of mistake in death cases. It must be conceded, that there are very few instances of established mistake in cases where execution has occurred. But I think, that on reflection you may agree with me that this is, literally, quite meaningless—and I choose that word carefully. Such reflection must, again, attend to *processual* issues.

First, and perhaps most important, there are in our legal system no procedures or tribunals or jurisdictions for "establishing" that someone should not, under law, have suffered death. When one says that there are few "established" cases of this wrong, what is he talking about? Many people think a mistake was made in the famous *Rosenberg* case. But where do they file the papers, for an official declaration? The mere publication of new evidence, or of new views about the evidence, "establishes" nothing. This is to be strongly contrasted with the situation as to imprisonment, where there is always a real party in interest to move for a new trial; there are exceedingly weighty difficulties about such a motion, but it is at least a possibility.

Secondly, there is a lack of the energizing effect of there being something tangible that can be accomplished by demonstrating mistake. A person in prison wants out. His family and friends want him out. How many resources can be devoted to mere name-clearing, by the relatives and friends of those men whom I just mentioned, who could hardly get lawyers to prepare their federal papers, while they were still alive?

But the difficulty is vastly deeper. For our society is totally committed to executing, not all who have committed homicide, but only some, selected in accordance with certain procedures and certain criteria. If these procedures err, if these criteria are incorrectly applied, then "mistake" *as to execution* has occurred. And the trouble is that, through virtually their entire range, these subsidiary criteria, the ones actually set up for the death choice, are either exceedingly difficult of establishment, so that a jury's verdict, even if based on a guess, can hardly be definitely faulted, or are too lacking in meaning for the concept of "mistake" to apply.

Let me go back to the defense of "reasonable belief that one's life is endangered." Only a belief in direct divine guidance of the jury could lead anyone to think that the verdict on this is always right. But try to imagine how one would, after execution, go about faulting that verdict.

Or, to revert to a deeper level, all states, including Texas, are committed to not executing persons as to whom there exists some mitigating mental or psychic condition, usually referred to as the "insanity defense." Let's go back to the case of the policeman who shot the 15-year-old boy. His insanity defense was submitted to the jury, and they bought it. But if they hadn't, and if he had been executed—as would be possible in some states—how would one go about *establishing* that this was a mistake? Of course there is no way; this is so clear that your first reaction might be to think the question silly. If that is what you think, I think it is because the "insanity defense" typically poses a question, which is not in fact understood by either the judge or the jury. Of course one cannot at a later time establish "mistake" as to the answer to this question, when that answer has resulted in the killing by law of the defendant. Neither can one establish the correctness of the answer.

Some states are committed to refraining from executing people convicted under the felony-murder doctrine, where the defendant's participation in the felony was "relatively minor." Some states are committed to considering the defendant's "age" or "youth." These questions are typical of the question so vague that no answer can be established as wrong, or right Of course "mistake" cannot be established as to the answers to such questions, and could not be established even if a tribunal existed charged with that responsibility. But what does that tell us as to the nature of the question?

Or take, for a final example, your famous Texas "Question 2," asked of the jury at the punishment hearing. The jury must determine, "beyond a reasonable doubt" that "there is a probability that the defendant would commit criminal acts of violence that would constitute a continuing threat to society...."

I have examined this question from many sides in previous writings. What I am saying now is that, if there is any seriousness in law or life, Texas has quite seriously committed herself *not* to kill persons as to whom this question ought to be answered "no." An execution in such a case is a mistaken execution. But try to imagine how one would go about establishing, after the execution, that a mistake had been made—or had not been made.

I think the upshot of all this is that, in greatest part, the concept of "establishment of mistaken execution" simply evaporates. No tribunals, no procedures, no tangible energizing motivation, and no sufficient concepts exist for performing this act of "establishment." This again is a point at which abstraction from process is fatal to understanding, or to meaningful conclusions.

I have spoken at length, and only touched a few points of interest to me—and I hope to you. The room is endless for reflection on this penalty. Those who, like me, oppose it can ask no more than that you reflect upon it; this reflection on your part is in the end our only chance of victory.[...]

§3.   In Opposition to Death Penalty Legislation*

HENRY SCHWARZSCHILD

[...] You know the classic arguments about the merits of the death penalty:

> Its dubious and unproved value as a deterrent to violent crime;
> The arbitrariness and mistakes inevitable in any system of justice instituted and administered by fallible human beings;
> The persistent and ineradicable discrimination on grounds of race, class, and sex in its administration in our country's history (including the present time);
> The degrading and hurtful impulse toward retribution and revenge that it expresses;

*Excerpted from the statement submitted by Henry Schwarzschild, 19 July 1978, at the hearing before the Subcommittee on Criminal Justice of the Committee on the Judiciary, House of Representatives, 95th Congress, 2nd Session, on H.R. 13360, "Sentencing in Capital Cases," U.S. Government Printing Office, Washington, D.C., 1978, pp. 23–31.

The barbarousness of its process (whether by burning at the stake, by hanging from the gallows, by frying in the electric chair, by suffocating in the gas chamber, by shooting at the hands of a firing squad, or by lethal injection with a technology designed to heal and save lives);

Even the deeply distorting and costly effect the death penalty has upon the administration of the courts, upon law enforcement, and upon the penal institutions of the country.

Let me therefore concentrate my remarks upon a few selected issues about which much unclarity exists in the public mind, in the media, and even in many legislative chambers.

I want to discuss these issues in the context of the evident support of public opinion for the reintroduction of capital punishment in the country. Let me be candid: For the past few years, public opinion polls, whether national or regional, have tended to reflect a substantial majority of the American people affirming their support for the death penalty, to the level of between 65 percent and 75 percent—enough to make many an elected official surrender his or her religious or moral principles against capital punishment. As little as twenty years ago, the polls reflected almost precisely the opposite distribution of views in the country. It is not hard to infer what has turned the American people back toward support of so atavistic and demonstrably useless a criminal sanction. The causes are (a) the rising rate of violent crime in the past two decades, (b) the increasing panic about the rising crime rate, together with a justified (as well as exaggerated) fear for the safety of lives and property, (c) the understandable reaction to a terrible series of assassinations and attempted assassinations of our national leaders and other prominent personalities (President John Kennedy, Senator Robert Kennedy, the Rev. Dr. Martin Luther King Jr., Governor George Wallace, Malcolm X, Medger Evers, and others), (d) the rise of international terrorism, including aircraft hijackings and the murder of prominent political and business leaders as well as the random political killings of innocent victims, (e) many years of the effective discontinuation of capital punishment and the remoteness from actual experience of its horrors, and finally (f) a largely subliminal but sometimes almost articulated racism that attributes most violent criminality to the minority community, that knows quite well that the poor and the black are most often the subjects of the death penalty, and that thinks that's just the way it ought to be.

What, then, are the rational answers to this series of partly understandable and partly impermissible misconceptions in the American public?

True, violent crime has risen sharply in the past two decades, but to begin with it has been abundantly demonstrated by social research that the availability of the death penalty has no effect whatsoever upon the rate of violent crime; to the contrary, there is some scientific evidence that death sentences imposed and carried out may, for peculiar reasons of social and psychic pathology, be an incentive to further acts of violence in the society. Furthermore, while the rates of most major, violent felonies have been rising—most probably by reason of increased urbanization, social mobility, economic distress, and the like—the rate of non-negligent homicide has been rising at a rate *slower* than the other major felonies, and non-negligent homicide is, of course, the only crime for which the death penalty has been declared constitutionally permissible by the Supreme Court. The crisis in violent crime, such as it is, has therefore been least acute in the area of homicide. Indeed, in the past three years, the murder rate in this country has actually been declining. Thirdly, there is an appalling number of about 20,000 non-negligent homicides in this country per year. But we would have to return to the condition of the mid-1950s to execute as many as one hundred persons per year, and even that would constitute only one in every two hundred murderers. In other words, we have always picked quite arbitrarily a tiny handful of people among those convicted of murder to be executed, not those who have committed the most heinous, the most revolting, the most destructive murders, but always the poor, the black, the friendless, the life's losers, those without competent, private attorneys, the illiterate, those despised or ignored by the community for reasons having nothing to do with their crime. Ninety-nine and one-half percent of all murderers were never executed—and the deterrent value (which very likely does not exist at all in any case) is reduced to invisibility by the overwhelming likelihood that one will not be caught, or not be prosecuted, or not be tried on a capital charge, or not be convicted, or not be sentenced to death, or have the conviction or sentence reversed on appeal, or have one's sentence commuted.

And if we took the other course and eliminated those high chances of not being executed, but rather carried out the death penalty for every murder, then we should be executing 400 persons per week, every week of the month, every month of the year—and that, Mr. Chairman, should strike even the most ardent supporters of the death penalty as a bloodbath, not as a civilized system of criminal justice.

Assassinations and terrorism are well known to be undeterrable by the threat of the death penalty. They are acts of political desperation or political insanity, always committed by people who are at least willing, if not eager, to be martyrs to their cause. Nor would executing terrorists be a preventive against the subsequent taking of hostages for the purpose of setting political assassins or terrorists free. There would of course be a considerable interval of time between arrest and execution, at least for the purpose of trial and the accompanying processes of law, and during that time their fellow activists would have a far more urgent incentive for taking hostages, since not only the freedom but the very lives of their arrested and sentenced colleagues would be at stake. Let me only respectfully add that distinguished fellow citzens of ours such as Senator Edward Kennedy and Ms. Coretta King, who have suffered terrible sadness in their lives at the hands of assassins, are committed opponents of the death penalty.

There has been only one execution in the United States since 1967, that of Gary Mark Gilmore, by a volunteer firing squad in Utah on January 17, 1977. Gilmore's execution troubled the public conscience less than it might have otherwise because of his own determination to die. The public and perhaps the legislators of our states and in the Congress have forgotten in a decade that was virtually without executions what sort of demoralizing and brutalizing spectacle executions are. There are now enough people on death row in the country to stage one execution each and every single day for more than a year, to say nothing of the other people who are liable to be sentenced to death during that time. We will again know the details of men crazed with fear, screaming like wounded animals, being dragged from the cell, against their desperate resistance, strapped into the electric chair, voiding their bowels and bladder, being burned alive, almost breaking the restraints from the impact of the high voltage, with their eyeballs popping out of their sockets, the smell of their burning flesh in the nostrils of the witnesses. The ghastly experience of men being hanged, their heads half torn off their bodies, or of the slow strangulation in the gas chamber, or of the press sticking their fingers into the bloody bullet holes of the chair in which Gilmore sat to be executed by rifles, or the use of forcible injection by a paralyzing agent— these reports will not ennoble the image of the United States of America that wants to be the defender of human rights and decency in a world that has largely given up the death penalty as archaic.

No one in this Committee surely is guilty of that shoddiest of all impulses toward capital punishment, namely the sense that white, middle-class people, irrespective of their crime, in fact hardly ever get sentenced to death and in such an extremely rare case are virtually never executed. You, Mr. Chairman and Members, and I and probably everyone in this hearing room are in fact absolutely immune, no matter what ghastly crime we might commit, from the likelihood of being executed for it. The penalty of death is imposed almost entirely upon members of what the distinguished social psychologist Kenneth B. Clark has referred to as "the lower status elements of American society."

Blacks have always constituted a dramatically disproportionate number of persons executed in the United States, far beyond their share of capital crimes, and even as we sit here today they represent half of the more than 500 persons on the death rows of our state prisons. Indeed, not only the race of the criminal is directly proportional to the likelihood of his being sentenced to death and executed but the race of the victim of the crime as well. The large majority of criminal homicides are still disasters between people who have some previous connection with each other (as husband and wife, parent and child, lovers, business associates, and the like), and murder is therefore still largely an intra-racial event, i.e. black on black or white on white. Yet while half the people under sentence of death right now are black (showing egregious discrimination on the grounds of the race of the murderer), about 85 percent of their victims were white.

In other words, it is far more likely to get the murderer into the electric chair or the gas chamber if he has killed a white person than if he had killed a black person, quite irrespective of his own race. (I say "he" in this context for good reason: the death penalty is also highly discriminatory on grounds of sex. Of the 380 death-row inmates in the country today, only two are women, and even they are far more likely objects of executive commutation of their death sentences than their male counterparts.)

Let me add here that, to the extent to which fear of crime and greater exposure to it, combined with inadequate police protection and more callous jurisprudence, has made the minority communities also voice increasing support for the death penalty, they have not yet fully realized that the death penalty will not protect them from what they (and all of us) rightly fear but that their support of capital punishment will only put their brothers and husbands and sons in jeopardy of being killed by the same state that has been unable properly to protect their lives, their rights, or their property to begin with.

In sum: The public is deeply uninformed about the real social facts of the death penalty and is responding to the seemingly insoluble problem of crime by a retreat to the hope that an even more severe criminal penalty will stem the tide of violence. But it will not. We do not know what will. Judges and lawyers do not know, philosophers and criminologists don't, not even civil libertarians or legislators know the answer—if any of us did, we would have long since accomplished our purpose of reducing crime to the irreducible minimum. But legislators are not therefore entitled to suborn illusory solutions merely because they would garner widespread though uninformed public approval, in order to signal to the electorate that they are "tough on crime." Capital punishment does not deal with crime in any useful fashion and in fact deludes the public into an entirely false sense of greater security about that complex social problem. The death penalty is a legislative way of avoiding rather than dealing with the problem of crime, and the American public will come to learn this very dramatically and tragically if the Congress should unwisely enact the bill before you today.

Two final words about public support for the death penalty.

There are strong indications that the public in great numbers answers in the affirmative when asked whether they support capital punishment because they want a death penalty law on the books in the hope that this threat will deter criminals from committing violent crimes. Many, perhaps most, of the people who support the enactment of the death penalty do not want executions and would be horrified at being asked to sentence a living human being to a premediated, ceremonial, legally sanctioned killing. They want deterrence, not electrocutions; prevention, not lethal injections; safety, not firing squads. But a re-enactment by this Congress of a federal death penalty statute will give them at best only electrocutions or lethal injections or firing squads, but neither deterrence nor crime prevention nor safety from violence.

The last stand of supporters for the death penalty, when all the other arguments have been rebutted or met, is that of retribution or revenge, the proposition that a murderer has forfeited his life and that we should kill him as an act of abstract equity, irrespective of whether executions serve any social purpose whatsoever. We do not need to preach to each other here this morning, but it is important to have it said once more that civilized societies have instituted systems of justice precisely in order to overcome private acts of retribution and revenge and that they have done so with the understanding that social necessity and social usefulness will be the guideposts of their punishments. Since there has never been and cannot be a showing of social usefulness or social necessity for capital punishment, the virtually unanimous voices of the religious community of our land, our leading thinkers and social analysts, in unison with enlightened opinion for hundreds, perhaps thousands, of years should guide your actions on this matter. Whatever the understandable, bitter, vengeful impulses might be of any of us who suffer the disastrous tragedy of having someone we love or respect murdered by pathological or cruel killers, the society's laws are written not to gratify those impulses but to channel them into helpful, healing, and life-sustaining directions. Gratifying the impulse for revenge is not the business of a government that espouses the humane and liberating ideas expressed in our Declaration of Independence and Constitution. It would be rather a return to the darkest instincts of mankind. It would be arrogating unto the state, unto government, either the god-like wisdom to judge who shall live and who shall die or else the totalitarian arrogance to make that judgment. We, as a nation, have foresworn that idolatry of the state that would justify either of these grounds for the legally sanctioned killing of our fellow citizens, of any human being, except perhaps in personal or national self-defense.

Mr. Chairman: The question before the country and before the Congress ultimately is whether it is the right of the state, with premeditation, with the long foreknowledge of the victim, under color of law, in the name of all of us, with great ceremony, and to the approval of many angry people in our land, to kill a fellow citizen, a fellow human being, to do that which we utterly condemn, which we utterly abhor in him for having done. What does the death penalty, after all, say to the American people and to our children? That killing is all right if the right people do it and think they have a good enough reason for doing it! That is the rationale of every pathological murderer walking the street: he thinks he is the right person to do it and has a good reason for doing his destructive deed. How can a thoughtful and sensible person justify killing people who kill people to teach that killing is wrong? How can you avert your eyes from the obvious: that the death penalty and that executions in all their bloody and terrible reality only aggravate the deplorable atmosphere of violence, the disrespect for life, and brutalization of ourselves that we need to overcome?

If the death penalty were shown, or even could be shown, to be socially necessary or even useful, I would personally still have a deep objection to it. But those who argue for its re-enactment have not and cannot meet the burden of proving its necessity or usefulness. At the very least, before you kill a human being under law, do you not have to be absolutely certain that you are doing the right thing? But how can you be sure that the criminal justice system has worked with absolute accuracy in designating this single person to be the guilty one, that this single person is the one that should be killed, that killing him is the absolutely right thing to do? You cannot be sure, because human judgment and human institutions are demonstrably fallible. And you cannot kill a man when you are not absolutely sure. You can (indeed sometimes you must) make sure that he is incapacitated from repeating his crime, and we obviously accomplish that by ways other than killing him. And while there is fallibility there also, death is different: it is final, irreversible, barbarous, brutalizing to all who come into contact with it. That is a very hurtful model for the United States to play in the world, it is a very hurtful model for a democratic and free government to play for its people. [...]

§4.   A Christian Perspective*

JOHN HOWARD YODER

It should not be necessary to argue that Christ's teaching and his work lead Christians to challenge the rightness of taking life under any circumstances, even when secular justice seems to sanction killing. When Jesus was asked to rule on an offense which at that time meant the death penalty, his answer was clearly to abolish the punishment. Jesus declared it wrong indirectly by demanding that first the judges and executioners must be sinless (John 8). This is in line with Jesus' teachings about the worth of every life before God

*From John Howard Yoder, "The Death Penalty: A Christian Perspective." Reprinted with permission from the January 1979 issue of *The Interpreter*, a publication of the United Methodist Church. Copyright 1979.

(Matthew 6), and our responsibility to see Christ in the needy neighbor (Matthew 25).

This respect for life is not a literal interpretation of the sixth commandment, but a deep spiritual principle. Life (the soul or the personality) is sacred because "God made man in his own image" (Genesis 9:6). If we love God whom "No man has seen. . . ." (1 John 4:12), we must show it in our love for others, including a concern for bodily welfare.

Christian faith is "this-worldly," in a sense more materialistic than any other religion; it knows of no way to love a person without caring for bodily life. If there were no Ten Commandments and no Sermon on the Mount, what we know about Christ's life, death and Resurrection still would suffice to sanctify human life. To sanctify means to set apart as belonging to God alone, and that is just what the Bible says about human life: it is not ours to take.

What does it mean to be made in God's image? Why is life sacred? To be made in God's image means to be capable of fellowship; the sole reason for our fellowship with others and with God is our bodily existence. Our destiny beyond death is dependent on the deeds and choices "done in the body" (2 Corinthians 5:10).

In The Old Testament, life was sacred—except for that of the murderer and the enemy. By trading places with the guilty and with his enemies, by dying in a murderer's stead (Barabbas), and by teaching us that there is no moral difference between friend and enemy as far as their claim on our love is concerned, Jesus closed the loophole. The lifeblood of each person belongs to God alone. Life is sacred because in the fallen world, Christ is our chance for repentance.

To take a life is to deprive that person of a future and thereby of all possibility of being reconciled with God and humankind. Only in this life can we repent; only in life can our brothers and sisters benefit by our love.

The Christian concern is redemptive; Christ's giving himself for his enemies is redemption. God's attitude toward the unworthy is our guide to a redemptive view of humankind.

This is all very well for Christians, but can we ask the unbelieving to share this respect for life? Did not God ordain the state to restrain evil and to punish evildoers? We must turn our attention to some serious arguments at this point. We must begin with the certainty that death is not God's highest will for any person. If lives must be taken, the advocates, not the opponents, of capital punishment have the burden of proof.

One set of arguments favoring the death penalty states that it is God's will or the demand for moral order that life should be paid for with life. The Genesis story serves as an excellent case in point. "Whoever sheds the blood of man, by man shall his blood be shed. . . ." (Genesis 9:6), speaks of some kind of death penalty.

A closer study of these earliest chapters of the Bible indicates that the death penalty is not so much a requirement as a limitation. The background of the story is corruption (Genesis 4–6); vengeance was the general pattern. Cain slew his brother Abel for a paltry offense. We read also Lamech's vicious boast: "I have slain a man for wounding me, a young man for striking me. If Cain is avenged sevenfold, truly Lamech seventy-sevenfold" (Genesis 4:23–24). Vengeance, this example shows, was out of proportion to the offense.

Therefore, begin realistically as the Bible does. Vengeance does not need to be commanded; it happens. It is a normal response of fallen humanity to a situation that calls forth hostility. Primitive peoples show the same pattern as Lamech: the inter-tribal wars of Borneo, the gang justice of the Sicilian hills and the American underworld, the proverbial "feudin' hillbillies." Vengeance and countervengeance raise the toll of suffering any one offense causes far beyond proportion to the original damage done.

If we ask what end was served by the institution of civil order, either in primitive societies or as Genesis 9 reports, it is an error to think vengeance is necessary or emphasized. Vengeance is happening; it must be controlled. The significance of civil order, therefore, is that it attempts to limit vengeance to a level equivalent to the offense. It is one way God's grace works against sin.

The first murder recorded in Genesis was followed by an act of God protecting the murderer from those who would threaten him (Genesis 4:15). The rules: "Eye for eye, tooth for tooth, hand for hand, foot for foot, burn for burn, wound for wound, stripe for stripe" (Exodus 21:24–25), are supplemented by rules defining acceptable substitutions. By Jesus' time most of these penalties had evolved to the point that they could be absolved through payments of money.

Just as the law of Moses in Deuteronomy 24 does not approve divorce, but concedes (to "your hardness of heart . . ." Matthew 19:8) to regulate the separations that were already taking place, so the law of talion (legal retaliation) does not command, but limits vengeance as a concession. The provision for cities of refuge added another limitation of vengeance. For certain kinds of killing (e.g., unintentional manslaughter) there should be opportunity to escape the avenger.

In the Sermon on the Mount and in Romans 12:19–21 vengeance is declared illegitimate; Jesus' death is a proclamation of forgiveness. Both are steps in the direction already taken by Genesis 9 and Exodus 21. Vengeance is not God's highest intent for our relations with one another; permitting it within the limits of justice (i.e., equivalent injury) was never his purpose.

What God always wanted to do with evil, and what he wants us today to do with it is to swallow it up, to drown it in the bottomless sea of his love. A divine moral order demanding that one evil be paid for by another evil does not exist. True enough, in a sinful world this does happen. The sinner brings vengeance upon himself or herself, and God uses it within his providential purpose.

The New Testament, especially the Epistle to the Hebrews, shows that Old Testament ceremonial requirements are fulfilled and ended in the sacrifice of Christ. "Once for all" is the triumphant proclamation of the Epistle. Henceforth no more blood, no more sacrifices are needed to testify to the sacredness of life. The cross has wiped away the moral and ceremonial basis of capital punishment.

The only direct New Testament reference to capital punishment is in John 8. Romans 13 deals with the principle that Christians should submit to the established civil authorities. It affirms that even they are instituted to serve the good (Romans 13:4). This text alone, however, does not spell out what the good is. The sword of which Paul writes, the *machaira*, is the symbol of judicial authority; it is not the instrument the Romans used for executing criminals. Even if it were, the passage would say nothing of the tempering effect that Christian witness should have on society's institutions. Neither the passage in Romans nor comparable ones in the Epistles of Timothy or Peter speak to this issue of the state taking life. The incident from the life of Jesus remains our first orientation point.

The striking thing about Jesus' attitude toward the woman patently guilty of a capital offense is not what he says about capital punishment but the context into which he places the problem. He does not deny that such prescriptions were part of the Mosaic code, but he raises two other considerations that profoundly modify the significance of that code for his day and ours.

First, he raises the issue of the moral authority of judge and executioner: "He that is without sin among you, let him first cast a stone at her" (John 8:7 King James Version). Second, he applies to this woman's offense, which is a civil offense, his authority to forgive sin. There is no differentiation between the religious and the civil which says that God may forgive the sinner, but justice still must be done.

Once again we see the expiation wrought by Christ is politically relevant. Like divorce (Matthew 19:8), like the distortions of the law that Jesus corrects in Matthew 5, and like war and the institution of slavery, capital punishment is one of those infringements on the divine will that take place in society.

The new level of brotherhood on which the redeemed community is to live cannot be directly enforced on the larger society. If the new level be of the Gospel, it must work as a ferment, as salt and as light. This is true especially if, as in the case of the Anglo-Saxon world, the larger society claims some kind of Christian sanction for its existence and its social pattern. If Christ is not only prophet and priest but also king, the border between the Church and the world cannot be impermeable to moral truth. Something of the crossbearing, forgiving ethics of the Kingdom cannot but become relevant to the civil order.

Can we claim that something only Christians affirm to believe in, namely the work of Christ, should really have given us new light on the nature of secular society, even for non-Christians? Does not the claim that the cross has something to do with the death penalty confuse two completely unrelated matters?

This question must be faced seriously, but the answer of the Bible seems clear. Christians call Jesus not only priest, prophet and teacher, but lord and king; these are political names. The unfaithfulness of Christians begins when they admit in certain realms of their life it would be confusing to bring Christ and the meaning of his teaching and life to bear on their problems. Certainly, non-Christians will insist that our religion and our politics should not be mixed. But their reason for this insistence is not that Jesus has nothing to do with civil society, but rather that they are not Christian.

If we confess it is the Lamb that was slain who is "Worthy . . . to receive power and wealth and wisdom and might and honor and glory and blessing!" (Revelation 5:12), we are relating the cross to politics. Whatever we believe about Christ we must apply to all our behavior, no matter how many of our neighbors remain unconvinced.

Of course, the fact of people's belief will mean their society will not fully keep the law of God. When it falls short of righteousness, God will nonetheless know how to use that disobedience to his glory. However, this is no reason for Christians to justify and defend the lower level of behavior that results from unbelief, whether it be in the political realm or elsewhere.

Christians, especially Christians who at other times and places have testified to their high respect for the sacredness of human life, are letting their silence speak for them. Their indifference testifies that as far as they are concerned this matter is one about which the Lord they profess to represent has no opinion.

Is this silent testimony of conformity the one we want to give? It is my conviction that such a testimony is one which we cannot conscientiously take the responsibility before our Lord. If we confess his lordship over every knee and tongue, we must believe. If we believe it we must proclaim that killing criminals is not God's will even for a sub-Christian society. We must make this testimony real to the men who make and who execute the laws, not leaving it to an occasional request for mercy.

What should Christians do? First, we should become informed. Our convictions on this matter should be as well thought through as those concerning military service. We should contribute to awakening public opinion by speaking to our neighbors and writing to newspapers. We should witness to legislators, especially if and when abolition legislation is being considered. We should assure our church leadership, locally, and on a statewide and denomination wide level of our support in any approaches they might make to legislative committees, through conference resolutions, or through other channels of testimony.

Underlying all this effort, justifying it, and enabling it, we should remind ourselves that when we are instructed to "pray for kings and all who are in high places" it is concrete measures like this that we are to have in mind. "That we may lead a quiet and peaceable life" does not mean that Christians are to be interested primarily in their own tranquility. It means that the purpose of government is to keep all violence within society at a minimum. In our land and in our day one of the best ways to testify to this divine imperative is to proclaim to the state the inviolability of human life.

§5. Proposal for a Presidential Commission on the Death Penalty in the United States of America*

AMNESTY INTERNATIONAL

1. As a worldwide human rights organization, Amnesty International is deeply concerned about the reintroduction of the death penalty in the United States of America and the resumption of executions. In September 1979 Amnesty International published a country-by-country survey of death penalty laws and practices throughout the world, together with an analysis of the international legal norms which favor the progressive abolition of capital punishment. From 3 to 11 December 1979, Martin Ennals, Secretary General of Amnesty International, carried out a human rights mission to the United States, visiting California, Ohio, Georgia and Washington, D.C., for discussions about the death penalty with state and federal officials, legislators, community organizations, the media and others.

2. On the basis of the Secretary General's visit and other material gathered at its International Secretariat in London, Amnesty International recommends the establishment of a Presidential Commission to study the death penalty in the United States. Amnesty International's principal reason for this recommendation is that the death penalty is not merely an issue of penal sanction for criminal conduct but is itself a matter of internationally recognized human rights.

3. In the view of Amnesty International, the death penalty violates the

*This is a reprint of the complete text of the proposal, released for publication by Amnesty International in April 1980. Copyright © 1980 Amnesty International Publications.

right to life and the right not to be subjected to cruel, inhuman or degrading treatment or punishment as guaranteed in the Universal Declaration of Human Rights, a document which the United States is pledged to uphold. The reintroduction of the death penalty, whether on the state or federal level, also contravenes both spirit and letter of recent United Nations resolutions for which the United States has voted and of international agreements which the United States has signed and whose ratification the President strongly supports.

4. The United Nations General Assembly in Resolution 32/61 of 8 December 1977 reaffirmed that "the main objective to be pursued in the field of capital punishment is that of progressively restricting the number of offences for which the death penalty may be imposed with a view to the desirability of abolishing this punishment."

5. Article 6 of the International Covenant on Civil and Political Rights imposes restrictions on the use of the death penalty "in countries which have not abolished [it]" and states: "Nothing in this article shall be invoked to delay or to prevent the abolition of capital punishment by any State Party to the present Covenant."

6. Article 4 of the American Convention on Human Rights prohibits the reintroduction of the death penalty in countries that have abolished it. Recent moves to reintroduce the death penalty in federal and state legislation contravene these international agreements.

7. Although the United States has not yet ratified the International Covenant on Civil and Political Rights and the American Convention on Human Rights, it has expressed its moral obligation to abide by them by signing them. The Vienna Convention on the Law of Treaties provides that a signatory nation has an obligation to do nothing that would defeat the object and purpose of any signed treaties.

8. In Principle VII of the Final Act (1975) of the Conference on Security and Cooperation in Europe (the Helsinki Final Act), the participating states declare their intention to act in conformity with the Universal Declaration of Human Rights and to fulfil their obligations under other international declarations and agreements in the field of human rights, specific mention being made of the International Covenants.

9. Amnesty International's concern also stems from the growing number of men and women who are being sentenced to death in the United States. As of February 1980, there were more than 600 people under sentence of death in the United States, one of the largest such populations known in the world. Over the last six months, prisoners have been sentenced to death at the rate of approximately 10 a month. Should executions of even a small number of those currently under sentence of death actually occur, the government's position on human rights would be undermined and the tendency of other governments to respond to political or social unrest with executions would to that extent be reinforced.

10. Since the 1972 United States Supreme Court decision in *Furman* v. *Georgia,* which overturned existing death penalty laws, 36 states have introduced new death penalty legislation to comply with Supreme Court guidelines, and similar attempts are being made in other states. There is also a move to introduce new federal death penalty legislation.

11. International human rights treaties also make reference to the continuing validity of national human rights standards. Article 5, paragraph 2, of the International Covenant on Civil and Political Rights provides: "There shall be no restriction upon or derogation from any of the fundamental human rights recognized or existing in any State Party to the present Covenant pursuant to law, conventions, regulations or custom on the pretext that the present Covenant does not recognize such rights or that it recognizes them to a lesser extent."

12. At the national level, the imposition of the death penalty by the states of the United States arguably violates a number of federal constitutional guarantees. Although the United States Supreme Court has not declared the death penalty to be *per se* unconstitutional, the manner in which the death penalty is carried out, the pattern of its infliction and the fairness of state statutory procedures are all matters of federal concern. Although the federal government does not have a direct role in state law enforcement, it is charged with the enforcement of several guarantees of rights in the United States Constitution. The states must, for example, afford all citizens the right to due process of law and the equal protection of the laws. Both the Executive and the Congress have constitutionally mandated roles in enforcing federal constitutional requirements in the several states. Under Article II of the United States Constitution the President is required to "preserve, protect, and defend the Constitution of the United States," he is charged with the duty to enforce federal laws, and he is empowered to recommend legislation "as he shall judge necessary and expedient" to the Congress. Under Section 5 of the Fourteenth Amendment, the Congress is given explicit authority "to enforce, by appropriate legislation" the right of all citizens not to be deprived by the states of equal protection of laws, due process of law, or the "privileges or immunities of citizens of the United States."

13. A Presidential Commission on the death penalty would be particularly timely now because of the world attention focused on the death penalty this year. The United Nations Economic and Social Council will have the question of capital punishment on its agenda this spring in preparation for the Sixth United Nations Congress on the Prevention of Crime and the Treatment of Offenders which meets in August–September 1980 in Caracas, Venezuela. The death penalty is one of the main items on the agenda of the Caracas Congress. It will be recalled that the Fifth United Nations Congress in 1975 was responsible for drafting the United Nations Declaration on Torture which played an important role in establishing the world consensus against torture and cruel, inhuman and degrading treatment or punishment.

The death penalty will be on the agenda of the United Nations General Assembly in autumn 1980 as a follow-up to the Congress, just as torture was in 1975.

14. The establishment of a Presidential Commission on the death penalty to study all aspects of the issue would enable the United States to play a positive role in these deliberations. Establishment of such a Commission would reaffirm the commitment of the United States to international human rights standards and would demonstrate that the United States recognizes the human rights dimensions of the questions of the death penalty. Establishment of a Presidential Commission would further demonstrate the commitment at the highest level of government to a full and objective study of this question, a study which could serve as an example both for the states within the United States and for other members of the United Nations.

15. Since the Second World War, several study commissions on the death penalty have been established in other countries. Among them were the Royal Commission on Capital Punishment in Great Britain, whose report was published in 1953; the Canadian Joint Committee of the Senate and House of Commons on Capital and Corporal Punishment and Lotteries, whose report was published in 1956; and the Ceylon Commission of Inquiry on Capital Punishment, whose report was published in 1959. Most recently, the Minister of Justice of Jamaica in June 1979 appointed a committee to "consider and report within a period of 18 months whether liability under the criminal law in Jamaica to suffer death as a penalty for murder should be abolished, limited or modified and if so to what extent, by what means and for how long, and under what conditions persons who would otherwise have been made to suffer capital punishment should be detained and what changes in the existing law and the penal system would be required."

16. The three previous Commissions—those in Great Britain, Canada and Ceylon—succeeded in collecting and publishing new information on the administration of the death penalty in their respective countries. Each report constituted an unimpeachable and authoritative record of the national experience of capital punishment and was used in subsequent deliberations on death penalty legislation.

17. In a similar way a Presidential Commission in the United States would serve to remove the issue of capital punishment from the political and emotional climate which presently surrounds it. The Commission's report and recommendations could provide federal and state officials, legislators and the public with an objective body of information to guide decisions on this issue.

18. Specifically, the Commission should be empowered to gather and examine information on the following aspects of the death penalty:

    i. The Death Penalty and International Human Rights

        In view of the growing international consensus that the death penalty is incompatible with internationally recognized human rights standards, the Commission should examine the conflict between the retention of the death penalty and the United States' formal pledges and commitments to international human rights standards. The Commission should also examine the impact of the resumption of executions on the United States' position on human rights, and the undermining of the United States' moral authority to question executions in other countries.

ii. The Death Penalty and United States Constitutional Rights and Guarantees

a. *The cruelty of death row.* 1. It has long been the practice in the United States for prisoners under sentence of death to be segregated from other prisoners on what has come to be known as "death row." They are placed there not because they are dangerous but because they have been convicted of capital murder. Prisoners under sentence of death wait there, often in isolation and under special deprivations and restraints, until the hour of their execution. For many prisoners, and for their families, this has been a living death, lasting for months and years. Yet apart from testimony introduced in the courts in some recent cases, there has been little examination of death row conditions, or of the justification for its existence. The Commission should consider whether the psychological and physical conditions of death row constitute cruel and unusual punishment as prohibited by the United States Constitution and violate the prisoners' right to equal treatment under the law.

2. By common law and under certain state statutes, execution of the insane is prohibited. Because of the stresses of death row, it is possible that a number of prisoners become insane while awaiting execution. Recent reports suggest that psychiatric treatment is absent or inadequate in most prisons and that procedures for determining legal insanity are unreliable and arbitrary. The Commission should examine the question of the determination of the mental condition of prisoners at the time of execution. It should also consider whether prevailing conditions in death row contravene the United Nations Standard Minimum Rules for the Treatment of Prisoners, in particular Rule 8, which sets forth criteria for the separation of prisoners (the nature of a prisoner's sentence is not among them); Rule 22, which stipulates that every institution should have a medical officer with knowledge of psychiatry and a psychiatric service "for the diagnosis and, in proper cases, the treatment of states of mental abnormality," and that sick prisoners who require specialized treatment should be transferred to specialized institutions or civil hospitals; and Rule 57, which states that "the prison system shall not, except as incidental to justifiable segregation or the maintenance of discipline, aggravate the suffering inherent in [imprisonment]."

b. *Discrimination in the imposition of capital punishment.* The President's Commission on Law Enforcement and Administration of Justice, appointed by President Lyndon B. Johnson, stated in its 1967 report that in the United States "the death penalty is disproportionately imposed and carried out on the poor, the Negro, and the members of unpopular groups." The proposed Presidential Commission should investigate whether this remains the case, and if so, attempt to determine the reasons for it. The Commission should also examine recent data showing that the death penalty is imposed disproportionately on those who kill whites, whether or not the killers themselves are white (that is, that the administration of the death penalty may be seen to place a higher value on the life of a white victim that on the life of a non-white victim).

c. *Arbitrariness of indictments and prosecutions.* The Commission should examine studies of felony indictments in death penalty jurisdictions which suggest that, apart from racial and economic factors, there is no clear pattern in determining whether a person accused of homicide is indicted and prosecuted for capital murder or instead for second-degree murder or manslaughter. This apparent arbitrariness would seem to result from discretion on whether or not to prosecute, from plea-bargaining policies and from other factors. Jurisdictions vary in the degree of randomness and arbitrariness in prosecutors' practice, but there is some evidence that virtually every jurisdiction lacks legal standards to indicate which offenders will face a death sentence and which will not.

d. *Possibility of error.* There have been a number of cases in the United States and other countries in which innocent people have been sentenced to death and executed. The Commission should examine the adequacy of current legal safeguards to prevent such errors. In deciding whether to sentence a person to death, a judge or jury must determine not only whether the defendant committed a homicide but also whether it was first or second degree, whether the defendant was sane or insane, and whether other "aggravating" or "mitigating" circumstances applied. It is important to know whether there are or could ever be adequate guidelines for making such judgments where the penalty is irreversible.

e. *Adequacy of legal representation of the poor.* It is a recognized fact that most prisoners under sentence of death are poor. In consequence, they cannot afford counsel of their choice and have been represented by state-appointed lawyers. The Commission needs to consider whether such counsel is adequate. Equally needed is a study of legal representation in capital cases in state and federal proceedings beyond the direct appeal. Most states make no provision for state-financed legal representation in such "post-conviction proceedings."

f. *Fairness of state clemency procedures.* The procedures for determining which prisoners shall have their death sentences commuted to life imprisonment vary widely from state to state. Some research indicates that these highly informal and discretionary procedures are affected by racial and economic factors. A systematic examination of the clemency process throughout the country would provide important clarification in this area.

g. *Fairness of jury selection in death penalty cases.* It is still common practice in capital cases to exclude potential jurors who express opposition to the death penalty. The Commission should examine evidence that this practice produces juries who are biased against defendants both in the determination of guilt or innocence and in sentencing.

iii. Social Consequences of the Death Penalty

a. *Impact of the death penalty on crime.* The Commission should review recent econometric studies and comparisons of crime statistics in states and countries where the death penalty has been practiced and then abandoned to determine whether there is any evidence that the death penalty has a special deterrent effect.

b. *Impact on the criminal justice system.* The Commission should gather information on the impact of the death penalty on the administration of justice with regard to rate of disposition of cases, special due process requirements, notoriety of cases, and the determination of innocence or guilt. Because costs are sometimes cited as an argument for retention of the death penalty, the Commission may also wish to examine this aspect of the problem.

c. *Impact on the correctional system.* The Commission should study the impact of executions on the correctional system with regard to security, morale, guard and prisoner brutality, the effect on the surrounding community, and the reputation of the correctional system.

d. *Impact on families of the victims of crime.* The Commission could usefully examine the needs of the families of victims and whether, on ethical and psychological grounds, executions constitute an appropriate response to their grief.

e. *Impact on family members of the condemned prisoner.* Any punishment of an offender can affect his or her family as well, but the death penalty is a qualitatively different punishment. The Commission should examine the degree of suffering and psychological damage which the death penalty imposes on the relatives of those who are to be (or have been) executed.

f. *Impact on public respect for life and for law.* The Commission should consider the atmosphere created by an execution; what message it communicates to different sectors of the population; whether it tends to enhance or devalue life and the public's sense of justice.

iv. Alternatives to the Death Penalty

a. *Basis of public support.* The Commission should try to discover the reasons for public support for the death penalty, what the public wants to see accomplished, and what factors lead to demands for execution in particular cases. Such information could be vital for any discussion of alternatives to the death penalty.

b. *Alternative penalties.* Various countries and various states of the United States have abolished the death penalty at one time or another without experiencing a consequent increase in the rate of homicide. It would be useful to study what alternative penalties they have used and what their experiences have been. The Commission in this connection could examine recent proposals from criminologists and law enforcement personnel on how to deal most constructively with those who commit murder and other violent crimes.

19. There can be no more serious act of government than the deliberate killing of a human being. Yet more than 600 men and women are currently under sentence of death in the United States and several more are sentenced to death each week. Before the United States proceeds on a path that could lead to widespread executions, it should examine at the highest level all the information available on the social impact, constitutionality and desirability of such a policy.

20. Amnesty International expresses its strong hope that a Presidential Commission on the death penalty will be established and that there will be a moratorium on all executions until the Commission reports its findings. Amnesty International hopes that the Commission will provide evidence leading to the total abolition of the death penalty in the United States of America.

References

I *Bibliographies*

Materials published prior to 1970 relevant to the death penalty in America are given the fullest listing in Bowers 1974:403–52. See also Bedau 1964a:565–74, somewhat revised in Bedau 1967b:565–74. Mackey 1976:333–43 includes references of historical interest that stretch back to the eighteenth century. A very useful bibliography, organized by subtopic, is Douglas B. Lyons, "Capital Punishment—A Selected Bibliography," *Criminal Law Bulletin* 8:783–802 (1972). Recent magazine and other semi-popular literature are cited in Isenberg 1977:155–60. By far the most elaborate bibliographical effort is to be found in Charles W. Triche III, *The Capital Punishment Dilemma 1950–1977: A Subject Bibliography,* Troy, N.Y.: The Whitston Publishing Co. Valuable as this bibliography is for the years covered, it cites virtually none of the scholarly, scientific, or legal literature published during the period and is largely confined to newspaper and magazine articles.

II *U.S. Government Documents and Serials*

Department of Justice. Bureau of Justice Statistics. *National Prisoner Statistics—Capital Punishment.* Washington, D.C.: U.S. Government Printing Office, annually under various titles and by different agencies since 1950.

Federal Bureau of Investigation, Department of Justice. *Crime in the United States—Uniform Crime Reports.* Washington, D.C.: U.S. Government Printing Office, annually since 1930.

House Hearings
    1960   "Abolition of Capital Punishment." Subcommittee No. 2, Committee on the Judiciary, 86th Congress, 2nd Session, on H.R. 870. May. Washington, D.C.: U.S. Government Printing Office.

1972   "Capital Punishment." Subcommittee No. 3, Committee on the Judiciary, 92nd Congress, 2nd Session, on H.R. 8414, etc. March–May. Washington, D.C.: U.S. Government Printing Office.

1978   "Sentencing in Capital Cases." Subcommittee on Criminal Justice, Committee on the Judiciary, 95th Congress, 2nd Session, on H.R. 13360. July. Washington, D.C.: U.S. Government Printing Office.

House Report

1980   "Criminal Code Revision Act of 1980." Committee on the Judiciary, 96th Congress, 2nd Session, No. 96-1396. Washington, D.C.: U.S. Government Printing Office.

National Advisory Committee on Criminal Justice Standards and Goals.

1976   *Disorders and Terrorism: Report of the Task Force on Disorders and Terrorism.* Washington, D.C.: U.S. Government Printing Office.

Senate Hearings

1968   "To Abolish the Death Penalty." Subcommittee on Criminal Laws and Procedures, Committee on the Judiciary, 90th Congress, 2nd Session, on S. 1760. March–July. Washington, D.C.: U.S. Government Printing Office.

1971   "Reform of the Federal Criminal Laws." Subcommittee on Criminal Laws and Procedures, Committee on the Judiciary, 92nd Congress, 1st Session. February. Washington, D.C.: U.S. Government Printing Office.

1973   "Imposition of Capital Punishment." Subcommittee on Criminal Laws and Procedures, Committee on the Judiciary, 93rd Congress, 1st Session, on S. 1, etc. February–July. Washington, D.C.: U.S. Government Printing Office.

1977   "To Establish Constitutional Procedures for the Imposition of Capital Punishment." Subcommittee on Criminal Laws and Procedures, Committee on the Judiciary, 95th Congress, 1st Session, on S. 1382. May. Washington, D.C.: U.S. Government Printing Office.

1978   "To Establish Rational Criteria for the Imposition of Capital Punishment." Committee on the Judiciary, 95th Congress, 2nd Session, on S. 1382. April–May. Washington, D.C.: U.S. Government Printing Office.

1981   "Capital Punishment." Committee on the Judiciary, 97th Congress, 1st Session, on S. 114. April-May. Washington, D. C.: U. S. Government Printing Office.

Senate Reports

1974   "To Establish Rational Criteria for the Imposition of Capital Punishment." Committee on the Judiciary, 93rd Congress, 1st Session, No. 93-721. March. Washington, D.C.: U.S. Government Printing Office.

1980   "Establishing Constitutional Procedures for the Imposition of Capital Punishment." Committee on the Judiciary, 96th Congress, 1st Session, No. 96-554. January. Washington, D.C.: U.S. Government Printing Office.

Solicitor General

1974   Brief for the United States as Amicus Curiae, Fowler v. North Carolina. Supreme Court, October Term 1974, Robert H. Bork, Solicitor General.

1975 Brief for the United States as Amicus Curiae, Gregg v. Georgia, etc. Supreme Court, October Term 1975, Robert H. Bork, Solicitor General.

III General

Abrahamsen, D.
1973 *The Murdering Mind.* New York: Harper & Row.

Abramowitz, E., and D. Paget
1964 "Executive Clemency in Capital Cases." *New York University Law Review* 39:136–92.

Adelstein, R.P.
1979 "Informational Paradox and the Pricing of Crime: Capital Sentencing Standards in Economic Perspective." *Journal of Criminal Law & Criminology* 70:281–98.

Alix, E.K.
1978 *Ransom Kidnapping in America, 1874–1974.* Carbondale and Edwardsville, Ill.: Southern Illinois University Press.

Allen, E.J.
1960 "Capital Punishment: Your Protection and Mine." *Police Chief* 27:22ff.

Amnesty International
1979 *The Death Penalty.* London: Amnesty International Publications.

Amsterdam, A.G.
1971a "Comments—Racism in Capital Punishment." *Black Law Journal* 1:185.
1971b "Guest Opinion: The Case against the Death Penalty." *Juris Doctor* 2(2):11–12.

Andenaes, J.
1970 "The Morality of Deterrence." *University of Chicago Law Review* 37:649–64.
1974 *Punishment and Deterrence.* Ann Arbor, Mich.: University of Michigan Press.

Archer, D., and R. Gartner
1976 "Violent Acts and Violent Times: A Comparative Approach to Postwar Homicide Rates." *American Sociological Review* 41:937–63.
1978 "Legal Homicide and Its Consequences." Pp. 219–34 in Kutash et al. 1978.

Archer, D., R. Gartner, R.A. Kent, and T. Lockwood
1978 "Cities and Homicide: A New Look at an Old Paradox." *Comparative Studies in Sociology* 1:73–95.

Auerbach, S.
1974 "Common Myths about Capital Criminals and Their Victims." *Georgia Journal of Corrections* 3(2):41–54.

Bailey, W.C.
1974 "Murder and the Death Penalty." *Journal of Criminal Law & Criminology* 65:416–23.
1975 "Murder and Capital Punishment: Some Further Evidence." *American Journal of Orthopsychiatry* 45:669–88.

1976a "Rape and the Death Penalty: A Neglected Area of Deterrence Research." Pp. 336–58 in Bedau and Pierce 1976.

1976b "Use of the Death Penalty vs. Outrage at Murder: Some Additional Evidence." *Crime & Delinquency* 22:31–9.

1977a "Imprisonment v. the Death Penalty as a Deterrent to Murder." *Law and Human Behavior* 1:239–60.

1977b "Deterrence and the Violent Sex Offender: Imprisonment vs. the Death Penalty." *Journal of Behavioral Economics* 6:107–44.

1978   "Deterrence and the Death Penalty for Murder in Utah: A Time-Series Analysis." *Journal of Contemporary Law* 5:1–20.

1979a "The Deterrent Effect of the Death Penalty for Murder in California." *Southern California Law Review* 52:743–64.

1979b "The Deterrent Effect of the Death Penalty for Murder in Ohio: A Time-Series Analysis." *Cleveland State Law Review* 28:51–81.

1979c "Deterrence and the Death Penalty for Murder in Oregon." *Willamette Law Review* 16:67–85.

1979d "An Analysis of the Deterrent Effect of the Death Penalty in North Carolina." *North Carolina Central Law Journal* 10:29–52.

1980a "Deterrence and the Celerity of the Death Penalty: A Neglected Question in Deterrence Research." *Social Forces* 58:1308–33.

1980b "Capital Punishment and Lethal Assaults against Police." Unpublished ms.

1980c "A Multivariate Cross-Sectional Analysis of the Deterrent Effect of the Death Penalty." *Sociology and Social Research* 64:183–207.

Bailey, W.C., and R.P. Lott
1977   "An Empirical Examination of the Inutility of Mandatory Capital Punishment." *Journal of Behavioral Economics* 6:153–88.

Bailey, W.C., and R.D. Peterson
1980   "A Longitudinal Analysis of the Deterrent Effect of the Death Penalty for Murder in New York." Unpublished ms.

Baldus, D.C., and J.W.L. Cole
1975   "A Comparison of the Work of Thorsten Sellin and Isaac Ehrlich on the Deterrent Effect of Capital Punishment." *Yale Law Journal* 85:170–86.

Barnett, A.
1978   "Crime and Capital Punishment: Some Recent Studies." *Journal of Criminal Justice* 6:291–303.

1979   "The Deterrent Effect of Capital Punishment: A Test of Some Recent Studies." Unpublished ms.

Barnett, A., D.J. Kleitman, and R. C. Larson
1975   "On Urban Homicide: A Statistical Analysis." *Journal of Criminal Justice* 3:85–110.

Barnett, A., E. Essenfeld, and D.J. Kleitmann
1979   "Urban Homicide: Some Recent Developments." Unpublished ms.

Beccaria, C.
1764   *On Crimes and Punishments.* H. Paolucci (tr.). Indianapolis, Ind.: Bobbs-Merrill (1963).

Bechdolt, B.V., Jr.
    1977   "Capital Punishment and Homicide and Rape Rates in the United States: Time Series and Cross Sectional Regression Analyses." *Journal of Behavioral Economics* 6:33–66.

Bedau, H.A.
    1959   "The Case against the Death Penalty." *New Leader* 42:19–21.
    1964a   *The Death Penalty in America: An Anthology.* New York: Doubleday.
    1964b   "Death Sentences in New Jersey: 1907–1960." *Rutgers Law Review* 19:1–64.
    1965   "Capital Punishment in Oregon, 1903–64." *Oregon Law Review* 45:1–39.
    1967a   "A Social Philosopher Looks at the Death Penalty." *American Journal of Psychiatry* 123:1361–70.
    1967b   *The Death Penalty in America: An Anthology,* rev. ed. New York: Doubleday.
    1968   "The Courts, the Constitution, and Capital Punishment." *Utah Law Review* 1968:201–39. Reprinted in Bedau 1977a.
    1970a   "The Death Penalty as a Deterrent: Argument and Evidence." *Ethics* 80:205–17. Reprinted in Bedau 1977a.
    1970b   "A Concluding Note." *Ethics* 81:76.
    1971   "Deterrence and the Death Penalty: A Reconsideration." *Journal of Criminal Law, Criminology and Police Science* 61:539–48. Reprinted in Bedau 1977a.
    1973a   *The Case against the Death Penalty.* New York: American Civil Liberties Union.
    1973b   "The Nixon Administration and the Deterrent Effect of the Death Penalty." *University of Pittsburgh Law Review* 34:557–66.
    1976   "Felony Murder Rape and the Mandatory Death Penalty: A Study in Discretionary Justice." *Suffolk University Law Review* 10: 493–520.
    1977a   *The Courts, the Constitution, and Capital Punishment.* Lexington, Mass.: Heath.
    1977b   "The Death Penalty: Social Policy and Social Justice." *Arizona State Law Journal 1977* (Number 4):769–95.
    1977c   *The Case against the Death Penalty.* New York: American Civil Liberties Union.
    1978   "Rough Justice: The Limits of Novel Defenses." *Hastings Center Report,* December: 8–11.
    1979   "The Death Penalty in the United States: Imposed Law and the Role of Moral Elites." Pp. 45–68 in S.B. Burman and B.E. Harrell-Bond (eds.), *The Imposition of Law.* New York: Academic Press.
    1980a   "Capital Punishment." Pp. 148–82 in T. Regan (ed.), *Matters of Life and Death.* New York: Random House.
    1980b   Book review of W. Berns, *For Capital Punishment: Crime and the Morality of the Death Penalty. Ethics* 90:450–52.
    1980c   "The 1964 Death Penalty Referendum in Oregon." *Crime & Delinquency* 26:528–36.

Bedau, H.A., and C.M. Pierce (eds.)
    1976   *Capital Punishment in the United States.* New York: AMS Press.
Bedau, H.A., and M. Zeik
    1979   "A Condemned Man's Last Wish: Organ Donation & A 'Meaningful'
            Death." *Hastings Center Report,* February:16–17.
Bell, J.B.
    1978   *A Time of Terror: How Democratic Societies Respond to Revolutionary
            Violence.* New York: Basic Books.
Beristain, A.
    1977   "Capital Punishment and Catholicism." *International Journal of Crim-
            inology and Penology* 5:321–35.
Berkson, L.C.
    1975   *The Concept of Cruel and Unusual Punishment.* Lexington, Mass.:
            Heath.
Berns, W.
    1979   *For Capital Punishment: Crime and the Morality of the Death Penalty.*
            New York: Basic Books.
Bernstein, T.
    1975   "Theories of the Causes of Death from Electricity in the Late Nineteenth
            Century." *Medical Instrumentation* 9:267–73.
Beyleveld, D.
    1979   "Identifying, Explaining and Predicting Deterrence." *British Journal of
            Criminology* 19:205–24.
    1980   *A Bibliography on General Deterrence Research.* Westmead, Farnbor-
            ough, Hampshire, England: Saxon House.
Black, C.L., Jr.
    1971   "The Crisis in Capital Punishment." *Maryland Law Review* 31:289–311.
    1974   *Capital Punishment: The Inevitability of Caprice and Mistake.* New
            York: Norton.
    1976   "Due Process for Death: *Jurek* v. *Texas* and Companion Cases." *Catholic
            University Law Review* 26:1–16.
    1977   "The Death Penalty Now." *Tulane Law Review* 51:429–45.
    1978   "Reflections on Opposing the Penalty of Death." *St. Mary's Law Journal*
            10:1–12.
    1979   "Governor's Dilemma." *New Republic,* 28 Apr.:12–13.
Black, T., and T. Orsagh
    1978   "New Evidence on the Efficiency of Sanctions as a Deterrent to Homi-
            cide," *Social Science Quarterly* 58 (Number 4):616–31.
Blackstone, W.
    1769   *Commentaries on the Laws of England.* Vol. 4. Oxford: Clarendon
            Press.
Bluestone, H., and C.L. McGahee
    1962   "Reaction to Extreme Stress: Impending Death by Execution." *Ameri-
            can Journal of Psychiatry* 119:393–96.
Blumstein, A., J. Cohen, and D. Nagin (eds.)
    1978   *Deterrence and Incapacitation: Estimating the Effects of Criminal Sanc-
            tions on Crime Rates.* Washington, D.C.: National Academy of Sciences.

Böckle, F., and J. Pohier (eds.)
  1979   *The Death Penalty and Torture*. New York: Seabury Press.
Borchard, E.M.
  1932   *Convicting the Innocent: Errors of Criminal Justice*. New Haven,
          Conn.: Yale University Press.
Bowers, W.J.
  1974   *Executions in America*. Lexington, Mass.: Heath.
Bowers, W.J., and G.L. Pierce
  1975   "The Illusion of Deterrence in Isaac Ehrlich's Research on Capital Pun-
          ishment." *Yale Law Journal* 85:187–208.
  1980a   "Deterrence or Brutalization: What Is the Effect of Executions?" *Crime
          & Delinquency* 26:453–84.
  1980b   "Arbitrariness and Discrimination under Post-*Furman* Capital Statutes."
          Crime & Delinquency 26:563–635.
Boyes, W.J., and L.R. McPheters
  1977   "Capital Punishment as a Deterrent to Violent Crime: Cross Section
          Evidence." *Journal of Behavioral Economics* 6:67–86.
Broderick, D.J.
  1979   "Insanity of the Condemned." *Yale Law Journal* 88:533–64.
Bronson, E.J.
  1970   "On the Conviction Proneness and Representativeness of the Death-
          Qualified Jury: A Study of Colorado Veniremen." *University of Colo-
          rado Law Review* 42:1–32.
  1980   "The Exclusion of Scrupled Jurors in Capital Cases: The California
          Evidence on Conviction Proneness and Representativeness." Unpub-
          lished ms.
Browning, J.R.
  1974   "The New Death Penalty Statutes: Perpetuating a Costly Myth." *Gon-
          zaga Law Review* 9:651–705.
Buckhout, R., E. Baker, M. Perlman, and R. Spiegel
  1977   "Jury Attitudes & the Death Penalty." *Social Action and the Law* 3:80–
          81.
Bye, R.T.
  1919   *Capital Punishment in the United States*. Philadelphia: Committee of
          Philanthropic Labor of Philadelphia Yearly Meeting of Friends.
Campion, Donald R., S.J.
  1955   "The State Police and the Death Penalty," Appendix F, Part II, *Min-
          utes of Proceedings and Evidence*, no. 20, Joint Committee of the Sen-
          ate and the House of Commons on Capital Punishment, Corporal
          Punishment and Lotteries, pp. 735–8. Reprinted in Bedau 1964a and
          1967b.
Cardarelli, A.P.
  1968   "An Analysis of Police Killed by Criminal Action: 1961–1963." *Journal
          of Criminal Law, Criminology and Police Science* 59:447–53.
Cardozo, B.N.
  1931   *Law and Literature and Other Essays and Addresses*. New York: Har-
          court, Brace.

Carney, F.J., and A.L. Fuller
    1969   "A Study of Plea Bargaining in Murder Cases in Massachusetts." *Suffolk University Law Review* 3:291–307.
Carrington, F.G.
    1978   *Neither Cruel nor Unusual.* New Rochelle, N.Y.: Arlington House.
Castelli, J.
    1973   "Theology Shifting on Death Penalty." *National Catholic Reporter,* 6 Apr.:1ff.
Cederblom, J.B. and W.L. Blizek (eds.)
    1977   *Justice and Punishment.* Cambridge, Mass.: Ballinger.
Chandler, D.B., and D.M. Andrus
    1979   "Changing Opinions on the Death Penalty: The Effects of Information and Advocacy on Law Students' Attitudes." Unpublished ms.
Clark, R.
    1970   *Crime in America.* New York: Simon and Schuster.
Cloninger, D.O.
    1977   "Death and the Death Penalty: A Cross-Sectional Analysis." *Journal of Behavioral Economics* 6:87–106.
Clutterbuck, R.
    1975   *Living With Terrorism.* London: Faber & Faber.
Cobin, H.L.
    1964   "Abolition and Restoration of the Death Penalty in Delaware." Pp. 359–73 in Bedau 1964a and 1967b.
Cohn, H.H.
    1970   "The Penology of the Talmud." *Israeli Law Review* 5:53–74.
Comment
    1974   "House Bill 200: The Legislative Attempt to Reinstate Capital Punishment in Texas." *Houston Law Review* 11:410–23.
Comment
    1978   "Capital Punishment: Death for Murder Only." *Journal of Criminal Law & Criminology* 69:179–95.
Comment
    1978   "The Constitutionality of Imposing the Death Penalty for Felony Murder." *Houston Law Review* 15:356–87.
Comment
    1979   "Deterrence and the Death Penalty: A Temporal Cross-Sectional Approach." *Journal of Criminal Law & Criminology* 70:235–54.
Compagnoni, F.
    1979   "Capital Punishment and Torture in the Tradition of the Catholic Church." Pp. 39–53 in Böckle and Pohier 1979.
Conway, D.A.
    1974   "Capital Punishment and Deterrence: Some Considerations in Dialogue Form." *Philosophy & Public Affairs* 3 (Number 4):431–43.
Cooper, D.D.
    1974   *The Lesson of the Scaffold: The Public Execution Controversy in Victorian England.* Athens, Ohio: Ohio University Press.

Crump, D.
    1977   "Capital Murder: The Issues in Texas." *Houston Law Review* 14:531–81.

Curran, W.J., and W. Casscells
    1980   "The Ethics of Medical Participation in Capital Punishment by Intravenous Drug Injection." *New England Journal of Medicine* 302:226–30.

Cutler, J.E.
    1907   "Capital Punishment and Lynching." *Annals of the American Academy of Political and Social Science* 29:622–25.

Dailey, T.G.
    1979   "The Church's Position on the Death Penalty in Canada and the United States." Pp. 121–25 in Böckle and Pohier 1979.

Dalzell, G.W.
    1955   *Benefit of Clergy in America and Related Matters.* Winston-Salem, N.C.: J.F. Blair.

Daniels, S.
    1979   "Social Science and Death Penalty Cases." *Law and Policy Quarterly,* July:336–72.

Dann, R.H.
    1935   "The Deterrent Effect of Capital Punishment." Friends' Social Service Series No. 29:1–20.
    1952   "Capital Punishment in Oregon." *Annals of the American Academy of Political and Social Science* 284:110–14.

Davis, C.
    1980   *Waiting For It.* New York: Harper & Row.

Davis, P.C.
    1978a   "The Death Penalty and the Current State of the Law." *Criminal Law Bulletin* 14:7–17.
    1978b   "Texas Capital Sentencing Procedures: The Role of the Jury and the Restraining Hand of the Expert." *Journal of Criminal Law & Criminology* 69:300–10.

Diamond, B.L.
    1975   "Murder and the Death Penalty: A Case Report." *American Journal of Orthopsychiatry* 45:712–22.

Dinnerstein, L.
    1968   *The Leo Frank Case.* New York: Columbia University Press.

Dix, G.E.
    1977   "Administration of the Texas Death Penalty Statutes: Constitutional Infirmities Related to the Prediction of Dangerousness." *Texas Law Review* 55:1343–1414.
    1978   "Participation by Mental Health Professionals in Capital Murder Sentencing." *International Journal of Law and Psychiatry* 1:283–308.

Donnelly, S.J.M.
    1978   "A Theory of Justice, Judicial Methodology and the Constitutionality of Capital Punishment: Rawls, Dworkin, and a Theory of Criminal Responsibility." *Syracuse Law Review* 29:1109–1174.

Donahue, J.J.
   1980   "*Godfrey v. Georgia:* Creative Federalism, the Eighth Amendment, and
           the Evolving Law of Death." *Catholic University Law Review* 30:13–
           64.
Duffy, C.T.
   1962   *88 Men and 2 Women.* Garden City, N.Y.: Doubleday.
Edison, M., with comments by R.H. Kuh and F. Cohen
   1971   "The Empirical Assault on Capital Punishment." *Journal of Legal Edu-
           cation* 23:2–24.
Ehrhardt, C.W., and L.H. Levinson
   1973   "Florida's Legislative Response to *Furman:* An Exercise in Futility?"
           Journal of Criminal Law & Criminology 64:10–21.
Ehrhardt, C.W., P.A. Hubbart, L.H. Levinson, W.McK. Smiley, Jr., and T.A. Wills
   1973   "The Future of Capital Punishment in Florida: An Analysis and Rec-
           ommendations." *Journal of Criminal Law & Criminology* 64:2–10.
Ehrlich, I.
   1975a   "The Deterrent Effect of Capital Punishment: A Question of Life and
           Death." *American Economic Review* 65:397–417.
   1975b   "Deterrence: Evidence and Inference." *Yale Law Journal* 85:209–27.
   1977a   "The Deterrent Effect of Capital Punishment: Reply." *American Eco-
           nomic Review* 67:452–58.
   1977b   "Capital Punishment and Deterrence: Some Further Thoughts and
           Additional Evidence." *Journal of Political Economy* 85:741–88.
Ehrlich, I., and J.C. Gibbons
   1977   "On the Measurement of the Deterrent Effect of Capital Punishment and
           the Theory of Deterrence." *Journal of Legal Studies* 6:35–50.
Ehrlich, I., and R. Mark
   1977   "Fear of Deterrence: A Critical Evaluation of the 'Report of the Panel
           on Research on Deterrent and Incapacitative Effects.'" *Journal of Legal
           Studies* 6:293–316.
Ehrmann, H.B.
   1960   *The Untried Case: The Sacco-Vanzetti Case and the Morelli Gang.* New
           York: Vanguard Press.
   1969   *The Case That Will Not Die: Commonwealth vs. Sacco and Vanzetti.*
           Boston: Little, Brown.
Elliott, R.G.
   1940   *Agent of Death: The Memoirs of an Executioner.* New York: Dutton.
Ellsworth, P.C., and L. Ross
   1976   "Public Opinion and Judicial Decision Making: An Example from
           Research on Capital Punishment." Pp. 152–71 in Bedau and Pierce 1976.
   1980   "Public Opinion and Capital Punishment: A Close Examination of the
           Views of Abolitionists and Retentionists." Unpublished ms.
Erskine, H.
   1970   "The Polls: Capital Punishment." *Public Opinion Quarterly* 34:290–307.
Espy, W.
   1980   "The Death Penalty in America: What the Record Shows." *Christianity
           and Crisis,* 23 June:191–95.

Evans, A.E.
  1973   "Aircraft Hijacking: What Is Being Done?" *American Journal of International Law* 67:641–71.

Evans, M.S.
  1977   "The Case for Capital Punishment." *Human Events,* Feb. 12:8ff.

Finkel, R.H.
  1967   "A Survey of Capital Offenses." Pp. 22–31 in Sellin 1967.

Farrer, C.
  1958   Book review of Arthur Koestler, *Reflections on Hanging. American Journal of Psychiatry* 115: 566–67.

Fisher, J.C.
  1976   "Homicide in Detroit: The Role of Firearms." *Criminology* 14:387–400.

Fletcher, G.P.
  1978   *Rethinking Criminal Law.* Boston: Little, Brown.

Forst, B.E.
  1977   "The Deterrent Effect of Capital Punishment: A Cross-State Analysis of the 1960's." *Minnesota Law Review* 61:743–67.

Fortas, A.
  1977   "The Case against Capital Punishment." *New York Times Magazine,* 23 Jan.:9ff.

Fox, J.A.
  1977   "The Identification and Estimation of Deterrence: An Evaluation of Yunker's Model." *Journal of Behavioral Economics* 6:225–42.

Friedman, L.S.
  1979   "The Use of Multiple Regression Analysis to Test for a Deterrent Effect of Capital Punishment: Prospects and Problems." Pp. 61–87 in S. Messinger and E. Bittner (eds.), *Criminology Review Yearbook.* Beverly Hills, Calif.: Sage.

Gallemore, J.L., Jr., and J.H. Panton
  1972   "Inmate Responses to Lengthy Death Row Confinement." *American Journal of Psychiatry* 129:167–72.

Gardner, E.S.
  1952   *The Court of Last Resort.* New York: W. Sloane Associates.
  1970   "Helping the Innocent." *U.C.L.A. Law Review* 17:535–41.

Gardner, M.R.
  1978   "Executions and Indignities—An Eighth Amendment Assessment of Methods of Inflicting Capital Punishment." *Ohio State Law Journal* 39:96–130.
  1979a   "Mormonism and Capital Punishment: A Doctrinal Perspective, Past and Present." *Dialogue—A Journal of Mormon Thought* 12:9–26.
  1979b   "Illicit Legislative Motivation as a Sufficient Condition for Unconstitutionality under the Establishment Clause—A Case for Consideration: The Utah Firing Squad." *Washington University Law Quarterly* 1979:435–99.

Gardner, R.L.
  1978   "Capital Punishment: The Philosophers and the Court." *Syracuse Law Review* 29:1175–1216.

Garfinkel, H.
    1949   "Inter- and Intra-racial Homicides." *Social Forces* 27:370–381.
Gerstein, R.M.
    1960   "A Prosecutor Looks at Capital Punishment." *Journal of Criminal Law,
            Criminology, and Police Science* 51:252–56.
Gertz, E.
    1968   "They Won't Be Hanging Danny Deever: Some Random Reflections on
            the Death Penalty." *Tri Quarterly,* Winter:219–30.
Gettinger, S.
    1979   *Sentenced to Die: The People, the Crimes, and the Controversy.* New
            York: Macmillan.
Gibbs, J.P.
    1975   *Crime, Punishment, and Deterrence.* New York: Elsevier.
    1977   "A Critique of the Scientific Literature on Capital Punishment and
            Deterrence." *Journal of Behavioral Economics* 6:279–310.
    1978a   "Deterrence, Penal Policy, and the Sociology of Law." *Research in Law
            and Sociology* 1:101–14.
    1978b   "The Death Penalty, Retribution and Penal Policy." *Journal of Criminal
            Law & Criminology* 69:291–99.
    1978c   "Preventive Effects of Capital Punishment Other Than Deterrence."
            Criminal Law Bulletin 14:34–50.
    1978   "Assessing the Deterrence Doctrine: A Challenge for the Social and
            Behavioral Sciences." *American Behavioral Scientist* 22:653–77.
Gillers, S.
    1980   "Deciding Who Dies." *University of Pennsylvania Law Review* 129:1–
            124.
Glaser, D.
    1976   "A Response to Bailey." *Crime & Delinquency* 22:40–43.
    1977   "The Realities of Homicide versus the Assumptions of Economists in
            Assessing Capital Punishment." *Journal of Behavioral Economics* 6:243–
            68.
    1979   "Capital Punishment—Deterrent or Stimulus to Murder? Our Unexam-
            ined Deaths and Penalties." *University of Toledo Law Review* 10:317–
            33.
Glaser, D., and M.S. Zeigler
    1974   "Use of the Death Penalty v. Outrage at Murder." *Crime and Delin-
            quency* 20:333–38.
Godwin, J.
    1978   *Murder U.S.A.: The Ways We Kill Each Other.* New York: Ballantine.
Goldberg, A.J.
    1972   "Forward—the Burger Court 1971 Term: One Step Forward, Two Steps
            Backward?" *Journal of Criminal Law, Criminology and Police Science*
            63:463–65.
    1973   "The Death Penalty and the Supreme Court." *Arizona Law Review*
            15:355–68.
    1976   "States Can Say 'No' to the Death Penalty Despite Court Ruling." *Bos-
            ton Globe,* 16 Aug.:17.

Goldberg, A.J., and A.M. Dershowitz
  1970   "Declaring the Death Penalty Unconstitutional." *Harvard Law Review* 83:1773–1819.
Goldberg, F.
  1970   "Toward Expansion of *Witherspoon:* Capital Scruples, Jury Bias, and Use of Psychological Data to Raise Presumptions in the Law." *Harvard Civil Rights—Civil Liberties Law Review* 5:53–69.
Goldberg, S.
  1974   "On Capital Punishment." *Ethics* 85:67–74.
Gottfredson, M. R., M.J., Hindelang, and T. J. Flanagan (eds.)
  1978   *Sourcebook of Criminal Justice Statistics—1977.* Washington, D.C.: U.S. Department of Justice.
Gottlieb, G.H.
  1961   "Testing the Death Penalty." *Southern California Law Review* 34:268–81.
Grannuci, A.F.
  1969   "'Nor Cruel and Unusual Punishments Inflicted:' The Original Meaning." *California Law Review* 57:839–65.
Graves, W.F.
  1956   "A Doctor Looks at Capital Punishment," *Medical Arts and Sciences* 10:137–41. Reprinted in Bedau 1964a and 1967b.
Green, E., and R.P. Wakefield
  1979   "Patterns of Middle and Upper Class Homicide." *Journal of Criminal Law & Criminology* 70:172–81.
Greenberg, J.
  1977   *Cases and Materials on Judicial Process and Social Change: Constitutional Litigation.* St. Paul, Minn.: West.
Greenberg, J., and J. Himmelstein
  1969   "Varieties of Attack on the Death Penalty." *Crime and Delinquency* 15:112–20.
Gross, H.
  1979   *A Theory of Criminal Justice.* New York: Oxford University Press.
Guillot, E.E.
  1952   "Abolition and Restoration of the Death Penalty in Missouri." *Annals of the American Academy of Political and Social Science* 284:105–9.
Guttmacher, M.S.
  1960   *The Mind of the Murderer.* New York: Farrar, Straus.
Hamilton, V.L., and L. Rotkin
  1979   "The Capital Punishment Debate: Public Perceptions of Crime and Punishment." *Journal of Applied Social Psychology* 9:350–76.
Hardman, C.D.
  1977   "Notes at an Unfinished Lunch." *Crime & Delinquency* 23:365–71.
Haney, C.
  1980a   "Juries and the Death Penalty: Readdressing the *Witherspoon* Question." *Crime & Delinquency* 26:512–27.
  1980b   "On the Selection of Capital Juries: The Biasing Effects of the Death Qualification Process." Unpublished ms.

Hartung, F.E.
    1952   "Trends in the Use of Capital Punishment." *Annals of the American Academy of Political and Social Science* 284:8–19.
Hayner, N.S., and J.R. Cranor
    1952   "The Death Penalty in Washington State." *Annals of the American Academy of Political and Social Science* 284:101–4.
Heilbrun, A.B., Jr., L.C. Heilbrun, and K.L. Heilbrun
    1978   "Impulsive and Premeditated Homicide: An Analysis of Subsequent Parole Risk of the Murderer." *Journal of Criminal Law and Criminology* 69:108–14.
Hindelang, M.J., C.S. Dunn, L.P. Sutton, and A.L. Aumick (eds.)
    1974   *Sourcebook of Criminal Justice Statistics—1973.* Washington, D.C.: U.S. Department of Justice.
    1975   *Sourcebook of Criminal Justice Statistics—1974.* Washington, D.C.: U.S. Department of Justice.
    1976   *Sourcebook of Criminal Justice Statistics—1975.* Washington, D.C.: U.S. Department of Justice.
Hindelang, M.J., M.R. Gottfredson, C.S. Dunn, and N. Parisi (eds.)
    1977   *Sourcebook of Criminal Justice Statistics—1976.* Washington, D.C.: U.S. Department of Justice.
Hoekema, D.
    1979   "Capital Punishment: The Question of Justification." *Christian Century,* 28 Mar.:338–42.
Hoenack, S.A., and W.C. Weiler
    1980   "A Structural Model of Murder Behavior and the Criminal Justice System." *American Economic Review* 70:327–41.
Hoenack, S.A., R.T. Kudrle, and D.L. Sjoquist
    1978   "The Deterrent Effect of Capital Punishment: A Question of Identification." *Policy Analysis,* Fall:491–527.
Hoover, J.E.
    1959   *Uniform Crime Reports 1959.* Washington, D.C.: Department of Justice.
    1960   *F.B.I. Law Enforcement Bulletin* 29 (Number 6, June 1960):1–2.
    1961   *F.B.I. Law Enforcement Bulletin* 30 (Number 6, June 1961):1–2.
Hughes, G.
    1979   "License to Kill." *New York Review of Books,* 28 June:22–25.
Hughes, T.P.
    1965   "Harold P. Brown and the Executioner's Current: An Incident in the AC-DC Controversy." Publications in the Humanities Number 70. Cambridge, Mass.: Massachusetts Institute of Technology, Department of Humanities.
Isenberg, I. (ed.)
    1977   *The Death Penalty.* New York: H.W. Wilson.
Jackson, B., and D. Christian
    1980   *Death Row.* Boston: Beacon Press.
Johnson, R.
    1979   "Under Sentence of Death: The Psychology of Death Row Confinement." *Law and Psychology Review* 5:141–92.
    1980   "Warehousing for Death." *Crime & Delinquency* 26:545–62.

Junker, J.M.
  1962   "The Death Penalty Cases: A Preliminary Comment." *Washington Law Review* 48:95–109.

Jurow, G.L.
  1971   "New Data on the Effect of a 'Death Qualified' Jury on the Guilt Determination Process." *Harvard Law Review* 84:567–611.

Kanter, S.
  1979   "Dealing with Death: The Constitutionality of Capital Punishment in Oregon." *Willamette Law Review* 16:1–65.

Kaye, J.M.
  1967   "The Early History of Murder and Manslaughter." *Law Quarterly Review* 83:365–95, 569–601.

Keedy, E.R.
  1949   "History of the Pennsylvania Statute Creating Degrees of Murder." *University of Pennsylvania Law Review* 97:759–77.

Kevorkian, J.
  1959   "Capital Punishment or Capital Gain?" *Journal of Criminal Law, Criminology and Police Science* 50:50–51.
  1960   *Medical Research and the Death Penalty.* New York: Vantage.

King, D.R.
  1978   "The Brutalization Effect: Execution Publicity and the Incidence of Homicide in South Carolina." *Social Forces* 57:683–87.

King, R.
  1961   "Some Reflections on Do-It-Yourself Capital Punishment." *American Bar Association Journal* 47:668–70.

Klebba, A.J.
  1975   "Homicide Trends in the United States, 1900–74." *Public Health Reports* 90:195–204.

Kleck, G.
  1979   "Capital Punishment, Gun Ownership, and Homicide." *American Journal of Sociology* 84 (Number 4):882–910.

Knowlton, R.E.
  1953   "Problems of Jury Discretion in Capital Cases." *University of Pennsylvania Law Review* 101:1099–1136.

Kringel, A.J.
  1974   "The Death Penalty as an Inciter of Criminal and Self-Directed Violence, on Execution Eve and Execution Day." *Georgia Journal of Corrections* 3(2):85.

Kutash, I.L., S.B. Kutash, and L.B. Schlesinger (eds.)
  1978   *Violence: Perspectives on Murder and Aggression.* San Francisco: Jossey-Bass.

Lassers, W.J.
  1973   *Scapegoat Justice: Lloyd Miller and the Failure of the American Legal System.* Indianapolis, Ind.: Indiana University Press.

Lavinsky, M.B.
  1965   "Executive Clemency: Study of a Decisional Problem Arising in the Terminal Stages of the Criminal Process." *Chicago-Kent Law Review* 42:13–51.

Lawes, L.E.
    1924   *Man's Judgment of Death*. New York: Putnam.
Lehtinen, M.W.
    1977   "The Value of Life—An Argument for the Death Penalty." *Crime &
            Delinquency* 23:237–52.
Leiser, B.M.
    1979   *Liberty, Justice, and Morals*, 2d ed. New York: Macmillan.
Lewis, P.W.
    1979   "Killing the Killers: A Post-*Furman* Profile of Florida's Condemned."
            Crime & Delinquency 25:200–218.
Lofland, J.
    1977   "The Dramaturgy of State Executions." Pp. 273–325 in *State Executions
            Viewed Historically and Sociologically*. Montclair, N.J.: Patterson
            Smith.
López-Rey, M.
    1980   "General Overview of Capital Punishment as a Legal Sanction." *Federal
            Probation* 44:18–23 (March).
Lord, C.G., L. Ross, and M.R. Lepper
    1979   "Biased Assimilation and Attitude Polarization: The Effects of Prior The-
            ories on Subsequently Considered Evidence." *Journal of Personality and
            Social Psychology* 37:2098–2109.
Lundsgaarde, H.P.
    1977   *Murder in Space City*. New York: Oxford University Press.
Machlin, M., and W.R. Woodfield
    1961   *Ninth Life*. New York: Putnam.
Mackey, P.E.
    1974a   "The Inutility of Mandatory Capital Punishment: An Historical Note."
            Boston University Law Review 54:32–35.
    1974b   "An All-Star Debate on Capital Punishment, Boston, 1854." *Essex Insti-
            tute Historical Collections* 110:181–99.
    1976   *Voices Against Death: American Opposition to Capital Punishment,
            1787–1975*. New York: Burt Franklin.
MacNamara, D.E.J.
    1969   "Convicting the Innocent." *Crime and Delinquency* 15:57–61.
Magee, D.
    1980   *Slow Coming Dark: Interviews on Death Row*. New York: Pilgrim
            Press.
Mailer, N.
    1981   "Until Dead: Thoughts on Capital Punishment." *Parade: The Sunday
            Newspaper Magazine*, 8 February: 6–9, 11.
Malone, P. A.
    1979   "Death Row and the Medical Model." *Hastings Center Report*, Octo-
            ber: 5–6.
Massachusetts
    1958   *Report and Recommendations of the Special Commission Established
            for the Purpose of Investigating and Studying the Abolition of the Death
            Penalty in Capital Cases*. Boston: Wright and Patten.

McAninch, W.S.
    1981   "Legal Status of the Death Penalty in South Carolina." Pp. 60–101 in
           B.L. Pearson (ed.), *The Death Penalty in South Carolina.* Columbia, S.C.:
           Aclusc Press.

McCall, D.J.
    1978   "The Evolution of Capital Punishment in Wyoming: A Reconciliation
           of Social Retribution and Humane Concern?" *Land and Water Review*
           13:865–907.

McGehee, E.G., and W.H. Hildebrand (eds.)
    1964   *The Death Penalty: A Literary and Historical Approach.* Boston: Heath.

McKee, D.L., and M.L. Sesnowitz
    1976   "Welfare Economic Aspects of Capital Punishment." *American Journal
           of Economics and Sociology* 35:41–47.

McMahon, D.F.
    1973   "Capital Punishment." *FBI Law Enforcement Bulletin* 42 (Number 2,
           February):20–21.

Mead, M.
    1978   "A Life for a Life: What That Means Today." *Redbook,* June:56–
           60.

Meltsner, M.
    1973   *Cruel and Unusual: The Supreme Court and Capital Punishment.* New
           York: Random House.

Mill, J.S.
    1868   "Parliamentary Debate on Capital Punishment within Prisons Bill."
           Hansard's Parliamentary Debate (3d Series). 21 Apr. Pp. 271–78 in G.
           Ezorsky (ed.), *Philosophical Perspectives on Punishment.* Albany, N.Y.:
           State University of New York Press, 1972.

Monahan, J.
    1978   "The Prediction of Violent Criminal Behavior: A Methodological Cri-
           tique and Prospectus." Pp. 244–69 in A. Blumstein, J. Cohen, and D.
           Nagin (eds.), *Deterrence and Incapacitation: Estimating the Effects of
           Criminal Sanctions on Crime Rates.* Washington, D.C.: National Acad-
           emy of Sciences.

Morris, N.
    1956   "The Felon's Responsibility for the Lethal Acts of Others." *University
           of Pennsylvania Law Review* 105:50–81.

Morris, N. and G. Hawkins
    1970   *The Honest Politician's Guide to Crime Control.* Chicago: University of
           Chicago Press.
    1977   *Letter to the President on Crime Control.* Chicago: University of Chi-
           cago Press.

Nakell, B.
    1978   "The Cost of the Death Penalty." *Criminal Law Bulletin* 14:69–80.

National Interreligious Task Force on Criminal Justice, Work Group on the Death
           Penalty.
    1978   *Capital Punishment: What the Religious Community Says.* New York:
           National Interreligious Task Force on Criminal Justice.

Neithercutt, M.G.
    1972   "Parole Violation Patterns and Commitment Offense." *Journal of Research in Crime and Delinquency* 9:87–98.
New York Legislative Commision on Capital Punishment
    1888   *Report.*
Note
    1957   "Felony Murder as a First Degree Offense." *Yale Law Journal* 66:427–35.
Note
    1958   "Post-Conviction Remedies in California Death Penalty Cases." *Stanford Law Review* 11:94–135.
Note
    1969   "A Study of the California Penalty Jury in First-Degree-Murder Cases." *Stanford Law Review* 21:1326–65.
Note
    1972   "Capital Punishment in Virginia." *Virginia Law Review* 58:97–142.
Note
    1974   "Discretion and the Constitutionality of the New Death Penalty Statutes." *Harvard Law Review* 87:1690–1719.
Oberer, W.E.
    1961   "Does Disqualification of Jurors for Scruples against Capital Punishment Constitute Denial of Fair Trial on Issue of Guilt?" *Texas Law Review* 39:545–67.
Palmer, L.I.
    1979   "Two Perspectives on Structuring Discretion: Justices Stewart and White on the Death Penalty." *Journal of Criminal Law & Criminology* 70:194–213.
Parisi, N., M.R. Gottfredson, M.J. Hindelang, and T.J. Flannagan (eds.)
    1979   *Sourcebook of Criminal Justice Statistics—1978.* Washington, D.C.: U.S. Government Printing Office.
Partington, D.H.
    1965   "The Incidence of the Death Penalty for Rape in Virginia." *Washington and Lee Law Review* 22:43–75.
Passell, P.
    1975   "The Deterrent Effect of the Death Penalty: A Statistical Test." *Stanford Law Review* 28:61–80.
Passell, P., and J.B. Taylor
    1976   "The Deterrence Controversy: A Reconsideration of the Time Series Evidence." Pp. 359–71 in Bedau and Pierce 1976.
Phillips, D.P.
    1980   "The Deterrent Effect of Capital Punishment: New Evidence on an Old Controversy." *American Journal of Sociology* 86:139–48.
Pinsky, M.
    1977   "Legal Aid in the 'Death Belt.'" *The Nation,* 26 Mar.:367–68.
Plucknett, T.F.T.
    1956   *A Concise History of the Common Law,* 5th ed. London: Butterworth.

Pollack, O.
1952 "The Errors of Justice." *Annals of the American Academy of Political and Social Science* 284:115–23.

Polsby, D.
1972 "Death of Capital Punishment? *Furman* v. *Georgia*." Pp. 1–40 in P. Kurland (ed.), *Supreme Court Review*. Chicago: University of Chicago Press.

Powers, E.
1966 *Crime and Punishment in Early Massachusetts 1620–1692: A Documentary History*. Boston: Beacon Press.

Prettyman, B., Jr.
1961 *Death and the Supreme Court*. New York: Harcourt, Brace.

Radelet, M.I.
1981 "Racial Characteristics and the Imposition of the Death Penalty." Unpublished ms.

Radin, E.D.
1964 *The Innocents*. New York: Morrow.

Radin, M.J.
1978 "The Jurisprudence of Death: Evolving Standards for the Cruel and Unusual Punishments Clause." *University of Pennsylvania Law Review* 126:989–1064.
1980 "Cruel Punishment and Respect for Persons: Super Due Process for Death." *Southern California Law Review* 53:1143–85.

Radzinowicz, L.
1948 *A History of English Criminal Law and Its Administration from 1750*. Vol. 1. London: Stevens.

Rankin, J.H.
1979 "Changing Attitudes toward Capital Punishment." *Social Forces* 58:194–211.

Reed, J.W.
1981 "Ineffective Assistance of Counsel in Capital Cases: Toward a Higher Standard." *Death Penalty Reporter* 1:1–6 (January).

Rice, C.E.
1969 *The Vanishing Right to Life*. Garden City, N.Y.: Doubleday.

Richards, D.A.J.
1977 *The Moral Criticism of Law*. Encino and Belmont, Calif.: Dickenson.

Riddell, W.R.
1929 "Judicial Execution by Burning at the Stake in New York." *American Bar Association Journal* 15:373–76.

Riedel, M.
1976 "Discrimination in the Imposition of the Death Penalty: A Comparison of the Characteristics of Offenders Sentenced Pre-*Furman* and Post-*Furman*." *Temple Law Quarterly* 49:261–87.

Robin, G.D.
1963 "Justifiable Homicide by Police Officers." Pp. 88–100 in Wolfgang 1967.

Rockefeller, W.
1971 "Executive Clemency and the Death Penalty." *Catholic University Law Review* 21:94–102.

Royal Commission on Capital Punishment
    1953   *Report.* London: Her Majesty's Stationery Office.
Rubin, S.
    1969   "The Supreme Court, Cruel and Unusual Punishment, and the Death
            Penalty." *Crime and Delinquency 15*:121–31.
Samuelson, G.W.
    1969   "Why Was Capital Punishment Restored in Delaware?" *Journal of
            Criminal Law, Criminology and Police Science* 60:148–51.
Sarat, A.
    1977   "Deterrence and the Constitution: On the Limits of Capital Punish-
            ment." *Journal of Behavioral Economics* 6:311–60.
Sarat, A., and N. Vidmar
    1976   "Public Opinion, the Death Penalty, and the Eighth Amendment:
            Testing the Marshall Hypothesis." *Wisconsin Law Review* 1976:171–
            206.
Satre, T.W.
    1975   "The Irrationality of Capital Punishment." *Southwestern Journal of Phi-
            losophy* 6:75–87.
Savitz, L.D.
    1958   "A Study of Capital Punishment." *Journal of Criminal Law, Criminol-
            ogy, and Police Science* 49:338–41.
Scaduto, A.
    1976   *Scapegoat: The Lonesome Death of Bruno Richard Hauptmann.* New
            York: Putnam.
Schedler, G.
    1976   "Capital Punishment and Its Deterrent Effect." *Social Theory and Prac-
            tice* 4:47–56.
Schneir, W. and M.
    1973   *Invitation to an Inquest.* Baltimore: Penguin.
Schuessler, K.R.
    1952   "The Deterrent Influence of the Death Penalty." *The Annals of
            the American Academy of Political and Social Science* 284:54–
            62.
Sellin, T.
    1955   "The Death Penalty and Police Safety," Appendix F, Part I, *Minutes of
            Proceedings and Evidence,* No.20, Joint Committee of the Senate and
            House of Commons on Capital Punishment and Corporal Punishment
            and Lotteries, pp. 718–28.
    1959   *The Death Penalty.* Philadelphia: The American Law Institute.
    1967   *Capital Punishment.* New York: Harper & Row.
    1980   *The Penalty of Death.* Beverly Hills, Calif.: Sage.
Sendak, T.L.
    1971   "Criminal Violence: How about the Victim?" *Vital Speeches of the Day*
            37:574–76.
Sesnowitz, M., and D. McKee
    1977   "On the Deterrent Effect of Capital Punishment." *Journal of Behavioral
            Economics* 6:217–24.

Sherman, L. W.
    1980   "Execution Without Trial: Police Homicide and the Constitution." *Vanderbilt Law Review 33:* 71–100.

Sherman, L., and R.H. Langworthy
    1979   "Measuring Homicide by Police Officers." *Journal of Criminal Law & Criminology 70:*546–60.

Shipley, M.
    1909   "Does Capital Punishment Prevent Convictions?" *American Law Review 43:*321–34.

Sickler, J.S. (ed.)
    1948   *Rex et Regina v. Lutherland* (facsimile of *Blood Will Out . . .* 1691). Woodstown, N.J.: Seven Stars Press.

Smith, E.
    1968   *Brief Against Death.* New York: Knopf.

Smith, G.W.
    1977   "The Value of Life—Arguments against the Death Penalty: A Reply to Professor Lehtinen." *Crime & Delinquency 23:*253–59.

Smith, T.W.
    1975   "A Trend Analysis of Attitudes toward Capital Punishment, 1936–1974." Pp. 257–318 in J.A. Davis, *Studies of Social Change since 1948,* vol. II. Chicago: University of Chicago, National Opinion Research Center, 1976.

Solomon, G.F.
    1975   "Capital Punishment as Suicide and as Murder." *American Journal of Orthopsychiatry 45:*701–11.

Spear, C.
    1844   *Essays on the Punishment of Death,* 7th ed. Boston: Charles Spear.

Stanton, J.M.
    1969   "Murderers on Parole." *Crime and Delinquency 15:* 149–55.

Stevens, L.A.
    1978   *Death Penalty: The Case of Life vs. Death in the United States.* New York: Coward, McCann & Geoghegan.

Stotsky, I.P.
    1977   "Capital Punishment." *University of Miami Law Review 31:*841–67.

Stricker, G., and G.L. Jurow
    1974   "The Relationship between Attitudes toward Capital Punishment and Assignment of the Death Penalty." *Journal of Psychiatry and Law* 2:415–22.

Teeters, N.K.
    1960   "Public Executions in Pennsylvania, 1682 to 1834." *Journal of the Lancaster County Historical Society 64:*85–164.

Thackeray, W.M.
    1840   "Going to See a Man Hanged." Pp. 58–64 in McGehee and Hildebrand 1964.

Thomas, C.W.
    1977   "Eighth Amendment Challenges to the Death Penalty: The Relevance of Informed Public Opinion." *Vanderbilt Law Review 30:*1005–30.

1980   "The Eighth Amendment and the Death Penalty: A Century of Indeci-
        sion." Unpublished ms.
Thomas, C.W., and S.C. Foster
    1975   "A Sociological Perspective on Public Support for Capital Punishment."
            American Journal of Orthopsychiatry 45:641–57.
Thomas, C.W., and R.G. Howard
    1977   "Public Attitudes toward Capital Punishment: A Comparative Analysis."
            Journal of Behavioral Economics 6:189–216.
Thomas, C.W., and D.T. Mason
    1980   "Public Opinion on Capital Punishment." Unpublished ms.
Thomas, T.
    1970   *This Life We Take: A Case against the Death Penalty,* 4th rev. San Fran-
            cisco: Friends Committee on Legislation.
Thornton, T.P.
    1976   "Terrorism and the Death Penalty." *America,* 11 Dec.: 410–12.
Tullock, G.
    1974   "Does Punishment Deter Crime?" *The Public Interest,* Summer: 103–11.
Turnbull, C.
    1978   "Death by Decree: An Anthropological Approach to Capital Punish-
            ment." *Natural History* 87:51–67.
van den Haag, E.
    1968   "On Deterrence and the Death Penalty." *Ethics* 78:280–88.
    1969   "On Deterrence and the Death Penalty." *Journal of Criminal Law,
            Criminology and Police Science* 60:141–47.
    1970   "Deterrence and the Death Penalty: A Rejoinder." *Ethics* 81:74–75.
    1975   *Punishing Criminals: Concerning a Very Old and Painful Question.*
            New York: Basic Books.
    1977   "A Response to Bedau." *Arizona State Law Journal* 1977 (Number
            4):797–802.
    1978   "In Defense of the Death Penalty: A Legal-Practical-Moral Analysis."
            Criminal Law Bulletin 14:51–68.
    1980   Book review of W. Berns, *For Capital Punishment: Crime and the
            Morality of the Death Penalty. American Political Science Review*
            74:470–71.
Vellenga, J.J.
    1959   "Is Capital Punishment Wrong?" *Christianity Today* 4(1):7–9.
Vidmar, N.
    1974   "Retributive and Utilitarian Motives and Other Correlates of Canadian
            Attitudes Toward the Death Penalty." *Canadian Psychologist* 15:337–
            56.
Vidmar, N., and T. Dittenhoffer
    1981   "Informed Public Opinion and Death Penalty Attitudes." *Canadian
            Journal of Criminology* 23:43–56.
Vidmar, N., and P. Ellsworth
    1974   "Public Opinion and the Death Penalty." *Stanford Law Review* 26:1245–
            70.

von Hirsch, A.
    1976   *Doing Justice: The Choice of Punishments.* New York: Hill and Wang.

Washington Research Project
    1971   *The Case Against Capital Punishment.* Washington D.C.: Washington Research Project.

West, L.J.
    1975   "Psychiatric Reflections on the Death Penalty." *American Journal of Orthopsychiatry* 45:689–700.

Wheeler, M.E.
    1972   "Toward a Theory of Limited Punishment II: The Eighth Amendment after *Furman* v. *Georgia.*" *Stanford Law Review* 25:62–83.

White, W.
    1969   *Rope and Faggot: A Biography of Judge Lynch.* New York: Arno Press and The New York Times.

White, W.S.
    1973   "The Constitutional Invalidity of Convictions Imposed by Death-Qualified Juries." *Cornell Law Review* 58:1176–1220.
    1974   "The Role of the Social Sciences in Determining the Constitutionality of Capital Punishment." *Duquesne Law Review* 13:279–301.
    1976   "Disproportionality and the Death Penalty: Death as a Punishment for Rape." *University of Pittsburgh Law Review* 38:145–84.
    1980   "Death-Qualified Juries: The Prosecution-Proneness Argument Reexamined." *University of Pittsburgh Law Review* 41:353–406.

Wilson, J.Q.
    1977   *Thinking about Crime.* New York: Vintage.

Wolfe, B.H.
    1973   *Pileup on Death Row.* Garden City, N.Y.: Doubleday.

Wolfgang, M.E.
    1958   *Patterns in Criminal Homicide.* Philadelphia: University of Pennsylvania Press.
    1967   *Studies in Homicide.* New York: Harper & Row.
    1972   "Racial Discrimination in the Death Sentence for Rape." Pp. 109–20 in Bowers 1974.
    1978   "The Death Penalty: Social Philosophy and Social Science Research." *Criminal Law Bulletin* 14:18–33.

Wolfgang, M.E., and M. Riedel
    1973   "Race, Judicial Discretion, and the Death Penalty." *Annals of the American Academy of Political and Social Science* 407:119–33.
    1975   "Rape, Race, and the Death Penalty in Georgia" *American Journal of Orthopsychiatry* 45:658–68.
    1976   "Rape, Racial Discrimination and the Death Penalty." Pp. 99–121 in Bedau and Pierce 1976.
    1979   "Race, Discretion and the Death Penalty." Final Report submitted to the National Institute of Law Enforcement and Criminal Justice and to the Ford Foundation.

Woodward, B., and S. Armstrong
   1979   *The Brethren: Inside the Supreme Court.* New York: Simon and Schuster.
Wright, D.D.
   1974   *To Die Is Not Enough: A True Account of Murder and Retribution.* Boston: Houghton Mifflin.
Yoder, J.H.
   1961   *The Christian and Capital Punishment.* Institute of Mennonite Studies Series Number 1. Newton, Kan.: Faith and Life Press.
Yunker, J.A.
   1976   "Is the Death Penalty a Deterrent to Homicide? Some Time Series Evidence." *Journal of Behavioral Economics* 5:45–81.
   1977   "An Old Controversy Renewed: Introduction to the *JBE* Capital Punishment Symposium." *Journal of Behavioral Economics* 6:1–32.
Zeisel, H.
   1968   *Some Data on Juror Attitudes towards Capital Punishment.* Chicago: University of Chicago Law School, Center for Studies in Criminal Justice.
   1976   "The Deterrent Effects of the Death Penalty: Facts v. Faith." Pp. 317–43 in P.E. Kurland (ed.), *The Supreme Court Review.* Chicago: University of Chicago Press.
Zimmerman, I.
   1973   *Punishment Without Crime.* New York: Manor Books.
Zimring, F.E., J. Eigen, and S. O'Malley
   1976   "Punishing Homicide in Philadelphia: Perspectives on the Death Penalty." *University of Chicago Law Review* 43:227–52.
Zoll, D.A.
   1971   "A Wistful Goodbye to Capital Punishment." *National Review,* 3 Dec.:1351–54.

Table of Cases

Roberts, Harry v. Louisiana, 431 U.S. 633 (1977)
Roberts, Stanislaus v. Louisiana, 428 U.S. 325 (1976)
Rudolph v. Alabama, 375 U.S. 889 (1963)
Spenkelink v. Wainwright, 578 F.2d 582 (C.C.A. 5th Cir. 1978)
Stein v. New York, 346 U.S. 156 (1953)
United States v. Jackson, 390 U. S. 570 (1968)
United States v. Weedell, 567 F.2d 767 (C.C.A. 8th Cir. 1977)
Voyles v. Watkins, 489 F. Supp. 901 (1980)
Witherspoon v. Illinois, 391 U.S. 510 (1968)
Woodson et al. v. North Carolina, 428 U.S. 280 (1976)

Index